Lecture Notes in Computer Science   11699

More information about this series at http://www.springer.com/series/7408

Alexander Romanovsky ·
Elena Troubitsyna · Ilir Gashi ·
Erwin Schoitsch · Friedemann Bitsch (Eds.)

Computer Safety, Reliability, and Security

SAFECOMP 2019 Workshops
ASSURE, DECSoS, SASSUR, STRIVE, and WAISE
Turku, Finland, September 10, 2019
Proceedings

 Springer

Editors
Alexander Romanovsky (ORCID)
Newcastle University
Newcastle-upon-Tyne, UK

Elena Troubitsyna
Åbo Akademi University
Turku, Finland

Ilir Gashi
City, University of London
London, UK

Erwin Schoitsch (ORCID)
AIT Austrian Institute of Technology
Vienna, Austria

Friedemann Bitsch (ORCID)
Thales Deutschland GmbH
Berlin, Germany

ISSN 0302-9743   ISSN 1611-3349 (electronic)
Lecture Notes in Computer Science
ISBN 978-3-030-26249-5   ISBN 978-3-030-26250-1 (eBook)
https://doi.org/10.1007/978-3-030-26250-1

LNCS Sublibrary: SL2 – Programming and Software Engineering

This Springer imprint is published by the registered company Springer Nature Switzerland AG
The registered company address is: Gewerbestrasse 11, 6330 Cham, Switzerland

Preface

The SAFECOMP Workshop Day has for many years preceded the SAFECOMP Conference, attracting additional participants. The SAFECOMP Workshops have become more attractive since they started generating their own proceedings in the Springer LNCS series (Springer LNCS vol. 11699, the book in your hands; the main conference proceedings are LNCS 11698). This meant adhering to Springer's guidelines, i.e., the respective international Program Committee of each workshop had to make sure that at least three independent reviewers reviewed the papers carefully. The selection criteria were different from those for the main conference since authors were encouraged to submit workshop papers, i.e., on work in progress and potentially controversial topics. In total, 32 regular papers (out of 43) were accepted. Two invited papers were added (one in the DECSOS Workshop and one in the STRIVE Workshop), and all workshops included an Introduction written by the chairs.

All five workshops are sequels to earlier workshops, two of them last year for the first time, which shows continuity of their relevance to the scientific and industrial community:

- ASSURE 2019 – 7th International Workshop on Assurance Cases for Software-Intensive Systems, chaired by Ewen Denney, Ganesh Pai, Ibrahim Habli, and Irfan Sljivo
- DECSoS 2019 – 14th ERCIM/EWICS/ARTEMIS Workshop on Dependable Smart Embedded and Cyber-Physical Systems and Systems-of-Systems, chaired by Erwin Schoitsch and Amund Skavhaug
- SASSUR 2019 – 8th International Workshop on Next Generation of System Assurance Approaches for Safety-Critical Systems, chaired by Alejandra Ruiz, Jose Luis de la Vara, John Favaro, and Fabien Belmonte
- STRIVE 2019 – Second International Workshop on Safety, securiTy, and pRivacy In automotiVe systEms, chaired by Gianpiero Costantino and Ilaria Matteucci
- WAISE 2019 – Second International Workshop on Artificial Intelligence Safety Engineering, chaired by Zakaria Chihani, Simos Gerasimou, Andreas Theodorou, and Guillaume Charpiat

The workshops provide a truly international platform for academia and industry.

It has been a pleasure to work with the SAFECOMP chairs, Elena Troubitsyna and Alexander Romanovsky, and with the Publication Chair, Friedemann Bitsch, the Workshop Chairs, Program Committees, and the authors. Thank you to all for your good cooperation and excellent work!

September 2019   Erwin Schoitsch

Organization

Committees

EWICS TC7 Chair

Francesca Saglietti   University of Erlangen-Nuremberg, Germany

General Chairs and Program Co-chairs

Alexander Romanovsky   Newcastle University, UK
Elena Troubitsyna   KTH Royal Institute of Technology, Sweden
                                              and Åbo Akademi, Finland

General Workshop Chairs

Ilir Gashi   CSR, City University London, UK
Erwin Schoitsch   AIT Austrian Institute of Technology, Austria

Publication Chair

Friedemann Bitsch   Thales Deutschland GmbH, Germany

Local Organizing Committee

Elena Troubitsyna   Åbo Akademi, Finland
Minna Carla   Åbo Akademi, Finland
Christel Engblom   Åbo Akademi, Finland
Inna Vistbackka   Åbo Akademi, Finland

Workshop Chairs

ASSURE 2019

Ewen Denney   SGT/NASA Ames Research Center, USA
Ibrahim Habli   University of York, UK
Ganesh Pai   SGT/NASA Ames Research Center, USA
Irfan Sljivo   Mälardalen University, Sweden

DECSoS 2019

Erwin Schoitsch   AIT Austrian Institute of Technology, Austria
Amund Skavhaug   NTNU, Norway

SASSUR 2019

Alejandra Ruiz Lopez   Tecnalia, Spain
Jose Luis de La Vara   Carlos III University of Madrid, Spain
John Favaro   Intecs, Italy
Fabien Belmonte   Alstom, France

STRIVE 2019

Gianpiero Costantino   IIT-CNR, Italy
Ilaria Matteucci   IIT-CNR, Italy

WAISE 2019

Zakaria Chihani   CEA LIST, France
Simos Gerasimou   University of York, UK
Andreas Theodorou   Umeå University, Sweden
Guillaume Charpiat   Inria, France

Supporting Institutions

European Workshop on
Industrial Computer Systems –
Reliability, Safety and Security

Kungliga Tekniska högskolan –
Royal Institute of Technology

Newcastle University

Åbo Akademi

Austrian Institute of Technology

City University London

Thales Deutschland GmbH

Intel

Lecture Notes
in Computer Science (LNCS),
Springer Science + Business Media

Austrian Computer Society

ARTEMIS Industry Association

Electronic Components and Systems
for European Leadership - Austria

Verband österreichischer
Software Industrie

European Research
Consortium for Informatics
and Mathematics

Contents

**2nd International Workshop on Artificial Intelligence
Safety Engineering (WAISE 2019)**

7th International Workshop on Assurance Cases for Software-Intensive Systems (ASSURE 2019)

7th International Workshop on Assurance Cases for Software-Intensive Systems (ASSURE 2019)

Ewen Denney[1], Ibrahim Habli[2], Ganesh Pai[1], and Irfan Sljivo[3]

[1] SGT/NASA Ames Research Center, Moffett Field, CA 94035, USA
{ewen.denney,ganesh.pai}@nasa.gov
[2] University of York, York YO10 5DD, UK
ibrahim.habli@york.ac.uk
[3] Mälardalen University, 721 23 Västerås, Sweden
irfan.sljivo@mdh.se

1 Summary

This volume contains the papers presented at the 7th International Workshop on Assurance Cases for Software-intensive Systems (ASSURE 2019), collocated this year with the 38th International Conference on Computer Safety, Reliability, and Security (SAFECOMP 2019), in Turku, Finland. As with the previous six editions of ASSURE, this year's workshop aims to provide an international forum for presenting emerging research, novel contributions, tool development efforts, and position papers on the foundations and applications of assurance case principles and techniques. The workshop goals are to: (i) explore techniques to create and assess assurance cases for software-intensive systems; (ii) examine the role of assurance cases in the engineering lifecycle of critical systems; (iii) identify the dimensions of effective practice in the development/evaluation of assurance cases; (iv) investigate the relationship between dependability techniques and assurance cases; and, (v) identify critical research challenges towards defining a roadmap for future development.

This year's program, which commenced with a keynote talk by Ivica Crnkovic, contains a diverse selection of assurance case research: the combination of argument notation and alternative hazard analysis techniques such as systems theoretic process analysis (STPA), life cycle assurance, modular safety cases, and incremental certification.

2 Acknowledgements

We thank all those who submitted papers to ASSURE 2019 and congratulate those authors whose papers were selected for inclusion into the workshop program and proceedings. We especially thank our distinguished Program Committee members:

- Simon Burton, Bosch Research, Germany
- Martin Feather, NASA Jet Propulsion Laboratory, USA

- Barbara Gallina, Mälardalen University, Sweden
- Alwyn Goodloe, NASA Langley Research Center, USA
- Jérémie Guiochet, LAAS-CNRS, France
- Yoshiki Kinoshita, Kanagawa University, Japan
- John Rushby, SRI, USA
- Philippa Ryan Conmy, Adelard, UK
- Daniel Schneider, Fraunhofer IESE, Germany
- Mark-Alexander Sujan, University of Warwick, UK
- Kenji Taguchi, CAV Technologies Co. Ltd., Japan
- Sean White, NHS Digital, UK

who provided useful feedback to the authors. Their efforts have resulted in a successful seventh edition of the ASSURE workshop series. Finally, we thank the organizers of SAFECOMP 2019 for their support of ASSURE 2019.

Combining GSN and STPA for Safety Arguments

Celso Hirata[1]([✉]) [iD] and Simin Nadjm-Tehrani[2] [iD]

[1] Instituto Tecnológico de Aeronáutica, São José dos Campos, SP, Brazil
hirata@ita.br
[2] Linköping University, 581 83 Linköping, Sweden
simin.nadjm-tehrani@liu.se

Abstract. Dependability case, assurance case, or safety case is employed to explain why all critical hazards have been eliminated or adequately mitigated in mission-critical and safety-critical systems. Goal Structuring Notation (GSN) is the most employed graphical notation for documenting dependability cases. System Theoretic Process Analysis (STPA) is a technique, based on System Theoretic Accidents Model and Process (STAMP), to identify hazardous control actions, scenarios, and causal factors. STPA is considered a rather complex technique, but there is a growing interest in using STPA in certifications of safety-critical systems development. We investigate how STAMP and STPA can be related to use of assurance cases. This is done in a generic way by representing the STPA steps as part of the evidence and claim documentations within GSN.

Keywords: GSN · Assurance case · STAMP · STPA

1 Introduction

Assurance case or safety case has been employed in many safety-critical systems such as avionics, nuclear, and railway control systems. It is used to explain why all critical hazards that create unacceptable risks have been eliminated or adequately mitigated in mission-critical and safety-critical systems.

Goal Structuring Notation (GSN) [1, 2] is a graphical notation that is used in assurance cases, well-represented in both academia and industry. In general, it is used with other hazard analysis techniques.

Systems-Theoretic Accident Model and Processes (STAMP) is an accident causality model, based on system theory [3]. System-Theoretic Process Analysis (STPA) [4] is a technique, based on STAMP, to identify hazardous control actions, scenarios, and causal factors. STPA is considered a rather complex technique to be used since it requires a different analysis perspective compared to other hazard analysis techniques, such as fault tree analyses, failure modes and effects analyses. STPA derives the analysis in terms of control actions, feedbacks, and other interactions.

There is growing interest in using STAMP and STPA in certifications and definitions of standards of safety-critical systems development because it is claimed that STPA is able to identify more loss scenarios due to hazards in the concept stage of

---

The original version of this chapter was revised: The presentation of figure 2 has been corrected. The correction to this chapter is available at https://doi.org/10.1007/978-3-030-26250-1_35

© Springer Nature Switzerland AG 2019
A. Romanovsky et al. (Eds.): SAFECOMP 2019 Workshops, LNCS 11699, pp. 5–15, 2019.
https://doi.org/10.1007/978-3-030-26250-1_1

development life cycle [5]. There is also growing interest in adopting GSN as part of OMG standards and other practical guidelines [6].

In the best practice, an engineering organization starts a dependability case early in the development life cycle, using the case's structure to influence assurance-centred actions throughout the life cycle. In this paper, we pose the question: how does a systems engineer leverage the benefits of STPA when analysing safety at the concept stage, and weave the argumentation structure into an assurance case with GSN?

Building an assurance case based on STPA can aid determining what claims can be made, what assumptions, contexts and justifications are employed by STPA, and how evidence, potentially created by alternative techniques, can be used to support such claims.

We investigate how STAMP/STPA can be combined with GSN so that one contributes with the safety analysis and the other with safety case construction. We use a simple example to illustrate the joint approach, and then go ahead with making a generic pattern that will aid applying the technique to other examples.

Using this preliminary investigation, we find it feasible to use GSN for supporting certification decisions, improving communication among safety engineers, and importing the argumentation structure from a (favourite) safety analysis approach, in this case STPA. This is useful for those engineers who are familiar with GSN but may have resorted to other hazard analysis techniques earlier. Conversely, we create a pattern for employing STPA analyses when creating evidence in assurance cases, in particular using GSN.

The rest of paper is organized as follows. The next section provides the background and related work. Section 3 presents the assurance case building on STPA using GSN. In Sect. 4, we discuss the case and conclude our work.

2 Background and Related Work

We begin by providing a brief overview of the used approaches and then compare with the related works.

2.1 GSN, STAMP and STPA

Assurance case is a reasoned and compelling argument, supported by a body of evidence, that a system, service or organization operates as intended for a defined application in a defined environment. Assurance cases have particular foci or contexts. The contexts can vary depending on concerns, for instance, safety and security, or within phases or activities of development process, such as design and implementation.

Goal Structuring Notation (GSN) [1, 2, 7] is a graphical notation for creating assurance cases that can be used to explicitly document the elements and structure of an argument and the argument's relationship to evidence.

An argument is defined as a connected series of claims intended to establish an overall claim. Claims can be structured as a hierarchy of claims and sub-claims that are supported by evidences. Claims and sub-claims are *goals* and are represented by rectangles. Evidence is asserted to support the truth of the claim and it is also known as *solution*. Evidence is represented as a circle. *Strategy*, which is represented by a parallelogram, is the reasoning or the nature of the argument that links the claim to its sub-claims. *Context*, which is represented by rectangles with round corners, helps documenting the operational usage environment for the objective to be relevant or the strategy. It helps describing how a claim or strategy should be interpreted.

Most claims and argumentation strategies are expressed in the context of assumptions. The assumptions must be valid for the claim or the strategy to be valid. *Assumptions* are represented by ellipses. Claims and argumentation strategies need justifications to be acceptable. Justifications are also represented by ellipses. A diamond attached to an element, indicates that a line of argument has not been developed yet.

Two types of linkages between GSN elements are *SupportedBy* and *InContextOf*. SupportedBy relationships – represented by lines with solid arrowheads – indicate inferential or evidential relationships between elements. InContextOf relationships – represented as lines with hollow arrowheads – declare contextual relationships.

Systems-Theoretic Accident Model and Processes (STAMP) [3] is based on three concepts: (i) a Safety Control Structure (SCS) – which is a hierarchical representation of the system under analysis on which upper level components impose constraints on lower level components; (ii) a Process Model - a model of the process being controlled; and (iii) Safety Constraints – restrictions that the system components must satisfy to assure safety.

System-Theoretic Process Analysis (STPA) [4] is a technique based on STAMP for accident analysis. STPA has four main steps. *Define the Purpose of the Analysis* aims to identify losses, hazards, and the system boundary. *Model the Control Structure* captures functional relationships and interactions using STAMP. The third step - *Identify Unsafe Control Actions* - identifies the potentially Unsafe Control Actions (UCA) and associated safety constraints. For each Control Action (CA) – a command usually issued towards the controlled process – the analyst must identify cases where a CA can be hazardous. The fourth step – *Identify Loss Scenarios* - reveals potential causes of issuing UCAs. For each UCA identified earlier, the goal is to discover scenarios and associated causal factors that can lead the system to a hazardous state, and to generate safety requirements.

In general, each unsafe control action can be inverted to define a constraint. In this work, we opt to employ unsafe control actions instead of constraints in the argumentations because unsafe control actions are also required in the fourth step of STPA *Identify Loss Scenarios*. Safety constraints and requirements assist designers in eliminating or mitigating the potential causes of unsafe control and the occurrence of hazards. The fourth step demands safety analysts' expertise, time, and effort for elaboration and verification. It is common to miss cases (e.g. scenarios, causal factors, requirements) when performing this step. So all other existing methods that can strengthen elaboration and verification can be useful, for instance formal model-based analysis – but this is outside the scope of this paper.

2.2   Related Work

Rinehart et al. [8] provide an extensive report on assurance case practices and their effectiveness. They link the success of assurance cases to evidences, and show that goal-orientation and explicit argumentation are core strengths of assurance case methods. They posit that the assurance methods are more comprehensive than conventional methods such as fault tree analysis, failure modes and effects analysis, and are typically employed in conjunction with them. However, the report lacks references to STAMP/STPA. Rinehart et al. also observed that many academic research papers involve small toy example cases. On the other hand, practitioner reports tend to focus on lessons learned and experience, without presenting to the reader how the complexity of large systems is handled. This is a considerable concern in their view. We will come back to this later in our discussion.

Dependability cases are being recommended as a good way to explain why all critical software hazards have been eliminated or adequately mitigated in mission-critical and safety-critical systems. Goodenough and Barry [9] present an example of a software-related hazard to show the value that a dependability case adds to a traditional hazard analysis. The example shows the power of the claims-arguments-evidence structure to clarify the hazards and show why the selected mitigations are effective.

Complementarily, STPA includes software and human operators in the analysis, ensuring that the hazard analysis captures potential causal factors of losses. In one study, STPA not only found all the causal scenarios found by the more traditional analyses but also identified more scenarios compared to those [4].

Model-based analysis of architectural decisions that inevitably impact safety analyses spans over another category of work. These lead to provision of concrete evidence and support for safety arguments. An example is the methods and tools proposed by Hugues and Delange [10]. For a broader view of how modelling, verification, hazard analysis, and safety assurance argument documentation can interact, we refer the reader to Denney and Pai [11] but we will not focus on model-driven verification for generation of evidence in this paper. Rather, we focus on the combination of the high-level arguments captured in GSN and hazard analysis through STPA respectively.

3   Using GSN to Document Application of STPA

In this section, we first apply the basic idea of the paper using a running example that clarifies the different roles for each approach. Then we go on to create a general pattern that is based on an abstraction of this example and hopefully a good basis for further work.

3.1   The Train Door Controller as Running Example

We use a simple system - Train Door Controller (TDC) - as an example which was earlier described in Thomas' work [12], and as a well-known example helps to ease the understanding of argumentations. We assume that the STPA analysis is already made. The results of the analysis include identification of accidents, hazards, safety control structure (controller, door actuator, door system, sensors of person and door position, control actions, feedbacks, input and output of the controlled process, external communications, process model, and algorithm), unsafe control actions, scenarios and causal factors, and safety requirements. Figure 1 shows the safety control structure of the TDC.

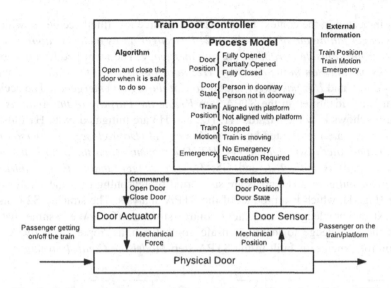

Fig. 1. Safety control structure of train door controller (adapted from [12]).

Figure 2 shows the GSN notation for goal *G1: Train Door Controller is free from unacceptable risks leading to identified accidents.*

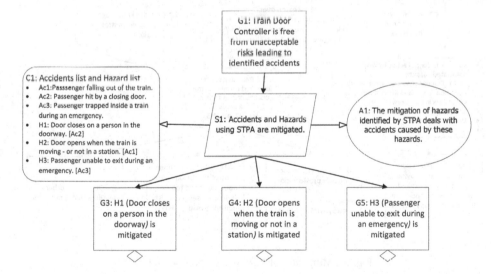

Fig. 2. Goal: *Train door controller is free from the identified accidents.*

The aim is to show that this goal is achieved by identifying hazards through STPA and showing that they are mitigated. The goal G1 is addressed by arguing about accidents and hazards using the strategy S1. This strategy can only be executed in the context of knowledge of identified accidents and hazards (C1). S1 assumes that *the mitigation of hazards identified by STPA deals with accidents caused by these hazards.*

(A1). As indicated in the context for S1, TDC has three identified accidents, which are *Ac1: Passenger falling out of the train, Ac2: Passenger hit by a closing door*, and *Ac3: passenger trapped inside a train during an emergency*. The identified hazards are *H1: door closes on a person in the doorway, H2: door opens when the train is moving or not in a station*, and *H3: passenger unable to exit during an emergency*. The accidents and hazards are identified in the STPA step *Define the Purpose of the Analysis*.

Figure 3 shows how the hazards H1, H2, and H3 are mitigated (with H1 illustrated in detail). These are represented by the goals G3: *H1 (Door closes on a person in the doorway) is mitigated, G4: H2 (Door opens when the train is moving or not in a station) is mitigated*, and *G5: H3 (Passenger unable to exit during an emergency) is mitigated*. The goals are supported by reasoning over the safety control structure (Fig. 1), which is a product of the STPA analysis. The strategy S2 considers the context of knowledge of the safety control structure (C2). We assume that SCS provides the knowledge to identify unsafe control actions, represented by A3. The safety control structure is built in the STPA step *Model the Control Structure*.

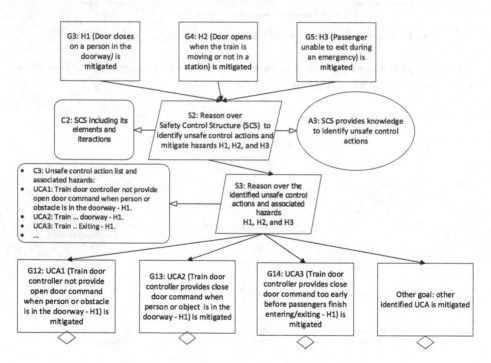

Fig. 3. Mitigation of hazards: goals 3, 4, and 5.

G3, G4, and G5 are supported by the goal G12, G13, and G14 using the strategy S3 in the context of knowledge of the list of unsafe control actions (C3), which is result of the STPA step *Identify unsafe control actions*. The strategy S3 considers the list of unsafe control actions and their associated hazards. For instance, the UCA1 (Train door controller not provide open door command when person or obstacle is in the doorway) is associated to hazard H1.

Figure 4 shows how the goal G12: *UCA1 (Train door controller not provide open door command when person or obstacle is in the doorway) is mitigated.* G12 must be supported by the identified scenarios and causal factors of the unsafe control action UCA1 being addressed.

As an example, Fig. 4 shows two scenarios and causal factors of UCA1: CF1 and CF2. The two scenarios and causal factors are addressed by the goals G16 and G17. G16 refers to CF1 *(Process model inconsistent: the process model does not consider that the controller must open the door when person or obstacle is in the doorway)* being addressed while G17 refers to CF2 *(Sensor with inadequate operation: the sensor is not operating reliably; it does not sense that a person or obstacle is in the doorway)* being addressed. Both scenarios and causal factors are addressed through the strategy S5 in the context of knowledge of the list of scenarios and causal factors (C5). This list is the result of the STPA Step *Identify Loss Scenarios.*

Figure 5 shows how the goal G16: *CF1 (Process model inconsistent: the process model does not consider that the controller must open the door when person or obstacle is in the doorway) is addressed.* G16 is supported by one undeveloped goal G20 *(Req1 is correctly and completely implemented and verified).* Req1 is the requirement *When Door state is "person in doorway" and Door position is "Partially open" then "Open door" control action shall be issued.* As the goal is not part of STPA, it will not be analysed further. The goal is justified through the strategy S6 in the

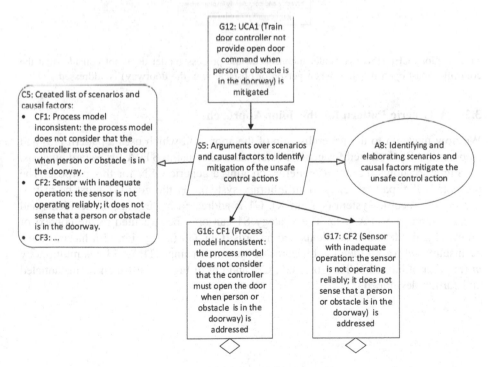

Fig. 4. Goal: UCA1 (Train door controller not provide open door command when person or obstacle is in the doorway) is mitigated.

context of knowledge of the list of requirements (C7). This list is also the result of the STPA Step Identify Loss Scenarios.

Other requirements can be produced. For the causal factor CF2 of Fig. 4, the following requirements can be generated: *Probability of sensor failure per year shall be less than 0.01* (Req 2) and *Sensor continuous correct operation shall be monitored* (Req 3). The implementation and verification of these requirements shall be developed.

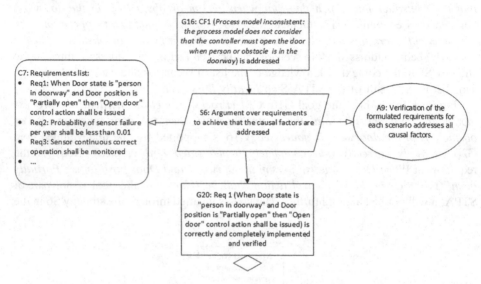

Fig. 5. Goal: CF1 (Process model inconsistent: the process model does not consider that the controller must open the door when person or obstacle is in the doorway) is addressed.

3.2   A Generic Pattern for the Joint Approach

We now move on to the generalisation of the approach, which uses a pattern [13] and elaborates a GSN created for generic safety assurance using STPA for hazard analysis.

Figure 6 shows the use of patterns, creating a generic GSN for this purpose. The presented GSN pattern refers to an arbitrary system, i.e. the goal G1 must be instantiated for a specific system (system X). G1 is addressed by arguing on accidents and hazards through STPA (S1). The strategy S1 can only be executed in the context of knowledge of identified accidents and hazards (C1). G3 (mitigation of a hazard) must be instantiated for all identified hazards of system X using STPA. G3 has multiplicity m (number of hazards). The goals G5, G7, and G9 in Fig. 6 must then be instantiated and further developed.

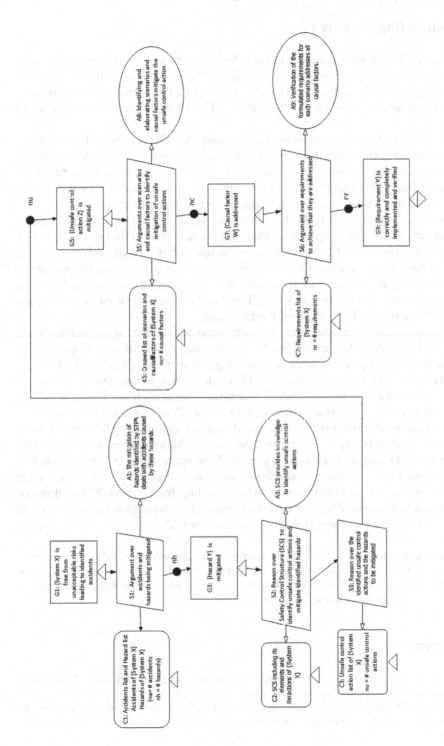

Fig. 6. GSN pattern for system X is free from unacceptable risks leading to accidents.

4   Concluding Remarks

In this paper, we presented the use of GSN for safety assurance in combination with STPA for hazard analysis, and illustrated it using a Train Door Controller System. The presented generic GSN pattern will aid documenting that a system is free from unacceptable risks leading to accidents identified by STPA through mitigating the identified hazards.

The GSN safety case documentation complements STPA, which is a complex hazard analysis technique employed in the concept stage of development. STPA involves many steps, which are not easy to follow and understand. Embedding the outcomes of the STPA analysis in GSN hopefully helps understanding how the steps of STPA can support the ultimate safety claim in later certification stages.

Conversely, through the GSN documentation we are able to identify the contexts that make the STPA claims justifiable. They include *Accident list and hazard list (C1)*, *Safety control structure (C2)*, *Unsafe control action list (C3)*, *List of Scenarios and causal factors (C5)*, and *List of requirements (C7)*. These contexts are the product of the STPA analysis and are critical to make the claim that "the system is free from unacceptable risks leading to accidents". These contexts may be used as certification goals to be verified in later stages of the life cycle.

Patterns provide a suitable means to foster systematic artefact reuse and aid in the development of new safety cases. We believe that the elaborated generic pattern can help the documentation of assurances cases of any system using GSN and STPA.

In the TDC STPA analysis, there are 13 unsafe control actions and 3 safe control actions that if not followed are unsafe. These unsafe situations result in dozens of scenarios and causal factors, which result in dozens of GSNs. This is obviously a consequence of the system complexity which would lead to a multiplicity of documents to be reviewed or analysed using supporting tools, no matter which pattern would be deployed.

Future works include applying the presented pattern to more examples, including more realistic cases. A different and clearly interesting direction of work that we are currently pursuing is to combine with meta-modelling from the model-based development approaches, and also use the relevant verification results as evidence that would enrich the overall safety case when documented with GSN.

Acknowledgements. The work of the first author was supported by CNPq (grant numbers 403921/2016-3 and 306186/2018-7). The work of the second author was supported by the national projects on aeronautics (NFFP7-04890) and the research centre on Resilient Information and Control Systems (www.rics.se).

References

1. Kelly, T.: Arguing safety – a systematic approach to managing safety cases. Ph.D. thesis, Department of Computer Science, University of York (1998)
2. Kelly, T., Weaver, R.: The goal structuring notation - a safety argument notation. In: Proceedings of the Dependable Systems and Networks Workshop on Assurance Cases (2004)

3. Leveson, N.: Engineering a Safer World: Systems Thinking Applied to Safety. MIT Press, Cambridge (2011)
4. Leveson, N., Thomas, J.: STPA Handbook (2018). https://psas.scripts.mit.edu/home/. Accessed 5 June 2019
5. Thomas, J.: STPA in Industry Standards (2019). https://psas.scripts.mit.edu/home/2019-stamp-workshop-presentations/. Accessed 5 June 2019
6. Rinehart, D., Knight, J., Rowanhill, J.: Current practices in constructing and evaluating assurance cases with applications to aviation. NASA/CR– 2015-218678 (2015)
7. The Assurance Case Working Group: Goal Structuring Notation Community Standard (Version 2) (2018). https://scsc.uk/scsc-141B. Accessed 5 May 2019
8. Rinehart, D., Knight, J., Rowanhill, J.: Understanding what it means for assurance cases to 'work'. NASA/CR–2017-219582 (2017)
9. Goodenough, J., Barry, M.: Evaluating Hazard Mitigations with Dependability Cases, AIAA 2009-1943, AIAA Infotech@Aerospace Conference. Seattle, Washington (2009)
10. Hugues, J., Delange, J.: Model-based design and automated validation of ARINC653 architectures using the AADL. In: Cyber-Physical System Design from an Architecture Analysis Viewpoint. Springer, Singapore (2017)
11. Denney, E., Pai, G.: Tool support for assurance case development. Autom. Softw. Eng. **25** (3), 435–499 (2018)
12. Thomas, J.: Extending and automating a systems-theoretic hazard analysis for requirements generation and analysis (Doctoral dissertation, MIT) (2013)
13. Kelly, J., McDermid, J.: Safety case construction and reuse using patterns. In: Proceedings of 16th International Conference on Computer Safety, Reliability and Security (SAFECOMP) (1997)

A Modelling Approach for System Life Cycles Assurance

Shuji Kinoshita, Yoshiki Kinoshita, and Makoto Takeyama[✉]

Kanagawa University, 2946 Tsuchiya, Hiratsuka, Kanagawa 259-1293, Japan
{ shuji, yoshiki, makoto-takeyama }@progsci.info.kanagawa-u.ac.jp

Abstract. System assurance involves assuring properties of both a target system itself and the system life cycle acting on it. Assurance of the latter seems less understood than the former, due partly to the lack of consensus on what a 'life cycle model' is. This paper proposes a formulation of life cycle models that aims to clarify what it means to assure that a life cycle so modelled achieves expected outcomes. Dependent Petri Net life cycle model is a variant of coloured Petri nets with inputs and outputs that interacts and controls the real life cycle being modelled. Tokens held at a place are data representing *artefacts together with assurance* that they satisfy conditions associated with the place. The 'propositions as types' notion is used to represent evidence(proofs) for assurance as data included in tokens. The intended application is a formulation of the DEOS life cycle model with assurance that it achieves open systems dependability, which is standardised as IEC 62853.

Keywords: System assurance · Dependent Petri Nets · IEC 62853

1 Introduction

A system life cycle model provides stakeholders with a basis for understanding the state of the life cycle and communicating how the goals of the life cycle are being achieved. It organizes activities into stages and is depicted traditionally as interlinked boxes of stages and decision gates [1,2]. How it may be used or what the picture means is often underspecified, making its rigorous modelling difficult. The picture may be taken as a depiction of a state machine. However, having a single stage as the current state of the life cycle model is too restrictive since in reality several stages can be active at the same time on several parts of a system. This results in confusing caveats about life cycle models: stages are interdependent and overlapping, stages do not necessarily occur one after another, iteration and recursion are possible on all paths, and so forth [2].

Towards rigorous modelling, (1) we regard a life cycle model as a controller that tries to bring the life cycle into the intended state with assurance that the goals are being achieved, (2) we consider the system as a collection of issues on services that need not be in the same stage or acted on at the same time, and

© Springer Nature Switzerland AG 2019
A. Romanovsky et al. (Eds.): SAFECOMP 2019 Workshops, LNCS 11699, pp. 16–27, 2019.
https://doi.org/10.1007/978-3-030-26250-1_2

(3) we formulate life cycle models in terms of a variant of coloured Petri nets [3], which we call Dependent Petri Nets (DPN). Tokens of DPN represent issues that progress through stages independently or in a defined coordination with each other. Issues may be further split to sub-issues or merged.

The intended application is a formulation of the DEOS life cycle model [4] with assurance that it achieves open systems dependability [5]. The Petri net formulation of DEOS life cycle model allows natural modelling of situations where parts or versions of a system progress through different life cycle stages concurrently.

The rest of the paper is organised as follows: Sect. 2 gives relevant background information. Section 3 introduces a definition of DPN. Section 4 presents DEOSLCM, our formulation of DEOS life cycle model using DPN. Section 5 discusses how DEOSLCM can be used to assure dependability of system life cycle and Sect. 6 concludes the paper.

Related Work. Modelling of system life cycles, or more generally that of business processes, has been intensely studied particularly in the context of compliance checking [6]. The Regorous approach [7,8] models business processes using the BPMN notation with its Petri net-like semantics, and checks the models' compliance against regulatory requirements that are formalized in Formal Contract Logic. It is applied to compliance checking of safety processes against requirements of ISO 26262 in the automotive sector [9]. The main difference between our approach and the Regorous approach is that our model incorporates evidence (proofs) of requirements satisfaction as concrete data. Another difference is that in our approach those pieces of evidence are about actual life cycle activities and gathered throughout the run of a life cycle, whereas the Regorous approach seems to focus on veryifing its business process models at the design time of those models.

Simon and Stoffel [10] employs Petri nets to formulate software life cycle processes in the sense of ISO/IEC 12207:1995 *Software life cycle processes*, to estabish a mathematical methodology for software development. Hull et al. [11] introduces the Guard-Stage-Milestone (GSM) meta-model that is intended to be a basis for formal verification and reasoning on business entity life cycles.

2   Background: DEOS Life Cycle Model

DEOS Life Cycle Model. DEOS life cycle model (Fig. 1) has iterative nature implemented by the "double loop" structure. Each box represents a life cycle stage [2] implemented by life cycle processes provided in [1]. The inner loop addresses short term, emergency responses to failures. The outer loop addresses longer term activities to adopt the system to accommodate changes in the environment, system purpose, etc. Together, they aim to achieve service continuity over extended periods of time notwithstanding unanticipated changes and failures.

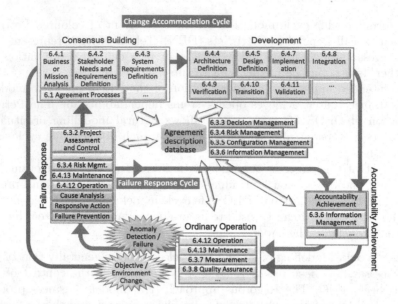

Fig. 1. DEOS life cycle model ([4] and [5] Annex A)

Picture Is Not a State Machine. Figure 1 lacks much details necessary for building a model that enables assurance arguments. Figure 1 indicates a transition system, but its states and transitions are not explicitly specified. A straightforward interpretation where the boxes are states and arrows are transition fails because a life cycle model must be able to represent the situation where several stages are active on different parts of a system. For example, after the failure response to an unanticipated failure of the system, both the operation stage (for prompt resumption) and the consensus building stage (for planning a next version of the system) must be activated.

3   Dependent Petri Nets (DPN)

Petri net [12] is a formal model of concurrent activities as a transition system. Coloured Petri nets (CPN) [3] extends the notion of tokens at a place from indistinguishable representation of resources to individual data whose data type (*colour set*) is specified by the place. DPN extends CPN further with I/O and with dependent transitions that can choose target places depending on consumed token data and inputs.

A dependent Petri net (*Place*, *Tran*, *Colour*, *Input*, *Output*, *source*, *Guard*, *target*, *action*) consists of the following data.

– *Place* is a set of *places*.
– *Tran* is a set of *transitions*.

- *Colour*(*p*) for place *p* is a set of *tokens* that can be placed at *p*. *Colour*(−) defines the set *Binding*(*ps*) = {[$x_0, x_1, \cdots, x_{n-1}$] | $x_i \in$ *Colour*(p_i)} of lists of tokens for list *ps* = [$p_0, p_1, \cdots, p_{n-1}$] of places.
- *Input* is a set of *inputs*.
- *Output* is a set of *outputs*.
- *source*(*t*) for transition *t* is a list of *source* places.
- *Guard*(*t*)(*i*)(*xs*), for transition *t*, input *i* and binding *xs* ∈ *Binding*(*source*(*t*)), is a decidable proposition.
- *target*(*t*) for transition *t* is a function sending input *i*, binding *xs* ∈ *Binding*(*source*(*t*)) and proof *g* ∈ *Guard*(*t*)(*i*)(*xs*) to a list *target*(*t*)(*i*)(*xs*)(*g*) of *target* places.
- *action*(*t*) is a function sending input *i*, binding *xs* ∈ *Binding*(*source*(*t*)) and proof *g* ∈ *Guard*(*t*)(*i*)(*xs*) to a pair (*o*, *ys*) ∈ *Output* × *Binding*(*target* (*t*)(*i*)(*xs*)(*g*)).

A *marking* *m* of the dependent Petri net is an assignment, to each place *p*, of a list *m*(*p*) of tokens in *Colour*(*p*). We write *Marking* for the set of markings.

Given a list *ps* = [$p_0, p_1, \cdots, p_{n-1}$] and marking *m*, the list *bindings*(*ps*)(*m*) ∈ (*Binding*(*ps*) × *Marking*)* is the list of all the pairs ([$x_0, x_1, \cdots, x_{n-1}$], *m*′) such that x_i is selected from *m*(p_i) and that *m*′ is the result of removing x_i's from *m*, i.e., *m*′ assigns to place *p* the sublist of *m*(*p*) that excludes those x_i's with $p_i = p$.

A transition *t* is *enabled* for an input *i* and marking *m* if there is a pair (*xs*, *m*′) in *bindings*(*source*(*t*))(*m*) such that *Guard*(*t*)(*i*)(*xs*) has a proof. A transition *t* enabled for input *i* and marking *m* may *fire*. When *t* fires, a pair (*xs*, *m*′) enabling *t* is selected from *bindings*(*source*(*t*))(*m*), tokens *xs* is consumed, *action*(*t*)(*i*)(*xs*)(*g*) is computed with a proof *g* ∈ *Guard*(*t*)(*i*)(*xs*) producing an output *o* and new tokens *ys* ∈ *Binding*(*target*(*t*)(*i*)(*xs*)(*g*)), and the net is marked with the new marking *m*″ assigning to place *p* the list *ys*++*m*′(*p*).

A dependent Petri net defines a labelled transition system. Its states are markings and the labelled transition relation is {*m* $\xrightarrow{(t,i,o)}$ *m*″| ⋯ } using letters in the previous paragraph.

It is crucial for *action*(*t*) to perform input/output with the environment in order to use a dependent Petri net as a model of a controller. That its target places may depend on consumed tokens and inputs data is in a sense for convenience, as the same effect can be obtained by multiple variants $t^0, t^1, \cdots$ of *t* with different *Guard*(t^i). However, data dependent transitions allow a more natural formulation of decision gates.

4   DPN Life Cycle Model

4.1   Running Examples

As a running example, Fig. 2 depicts DEOSLCM, a DPN formulation of the DEOS life cycle model. Circles are places. Boxes are transitions. Incoming arcs to a transition *t* shows that the arcs' source places constitute the list *source*(*t*).

Dots attached to t represent different values taken by $target(t)$. The targets of arcs outgoing from one dot shows the list $target(t)(i)(xs)(g)$ for some input i, binding xs and proof g. Other DPN data is not depicted.

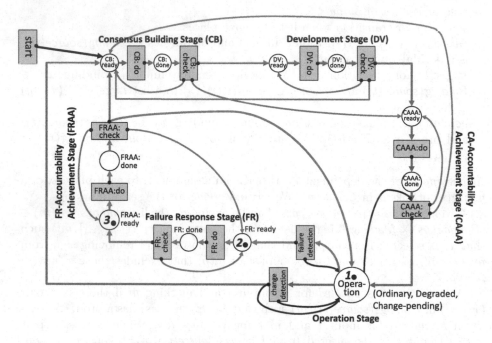

Fig. 2. DEOSLCM: formulation of DEOS life cycle model

The network structure of DEOSLCM provides a framework of 'issue driven development' where issues are represented by tokens. The system is comprising issues, each of which is about a service $s \in Svc = \{s_0, s_1, ...\}$. A possible progression of an issue shown in Fig. 2 is: (1) operating service s must be monitored (the green dot 1); (2) detected failure of s must be responded (dot 1 becoming dot 2); (3) the failure response must be accounted (dot 2 becoming dot 3).

Generally, multitudes of issues are worked on at the same time and are represented by that many tokens placed at various places. The so-called RUP 'hump' diagram [13] corresponds to a plotting of the number of tokens at each place along the progression of the life cycle.

4.2   Issue = Token = Bundle of Artefacts with Assurance

A token represents an issue on a service to be worked on in the system life cycle. The place where the token is placed represents the status of the issue, e.g., the next transition that works on the issue and the condition that the issue must satisfy for the next work to begin. The token models a bundle of artefacts associated with the issue at the place *together with assurance that the artefacts satisfies the condition.* Assurance is modelled as a piece of data that is a formal proof in the propositions as types paradigm [14, 15].

Generally, for each place p and service s, we require definitions of (1) a set $A_{p,s}$ whose element represents a bundle of artefacts associated with s when s is at p and (2) a predicate $R_{p,s}(-)$ representing requirements on $a \in A_{p,s}$ such that evidence $e \in R_{p,s}(a)$ assures that a shows that s is achieving outcomes expected at p. We then define *Colour*(p) to be $\{(s, a, e)|s \in Svc, a \in A_{p,s}, e \in R_{p,s}(b)\}$.

Example: Token at Place Operation. Consider a situation where a service s of the system is operating normally. With the DPN model (Fig. 2), we represent such a situation by a marking that contains a token $t \in$ *Colour*(Operation) at place Operation. Each element of the set $A_{Op,s}$ represents a bundle of artefacts associated with a service s when s is in operation. The predicate $R_{Op,s}(-)$ represents requirements on $a \in A_{Op,s}$ such that evidence $e \in R_{Op,s}(a)$ assures that a shows s is operating normally. *Colour*(Operation) is then defined to be $\{(s, a, e)|s \in Svc, a \in A_{Op,s}, e \in R_{Op,s}(a)\}$.

Artefacts in bundle $a \in A_{Op,s}$ include, for example, system specification of s, stakeholder agreement on operation of s and on accountability, monitoring reports and operation logs on s. Requirements on a may include that a shows that s is operating according to the specification and agreement, and that a shows that s is being monitored for potential failures. Having a token $t = (s, a, e) \in$ *Colour*(Operation) at place Operation in the current marking of Fig. 2 thus represents that s is currently operating normally.

Distinction Between Artefacts and Evidence. Distinction between artefacts $a \in A_{p,s}$ and evidence $e \in R_{p,s}(a)$ is made to force explicit formulation of the conditions for artefacts to have proper contents. For example, a requirement "stakeholders shall be identified" may have a list of names called "stakeholder list" as the corresponding artefact. However, having this list is far from satisfying the requirement. The list must satisfy various consistency and completeness conditions in relation to other available data. $R_{p,s}(-)$ specifies these conditions and data that counts as evidence of their satisfaction. Evidence data is to be machine-checked in the paradigm of propositions as types.

4.3   Transitions Modelling Life Cycle Stages

For a transition $t \in$ *Tran*, the function *action*(t) models how a life cycle stage consumes and produces artefacts with assurance modelled by tokens. The function's type and the intended meaning of each argument and result are as follows.

$$action(t) \in (inp \in Input)(xs \in Bindings(source(t)))(g \in Guard(t)(inp)(xs)) \rightarrow$$
$$Output \times Bindings(target(t)(inp)(xs)(g))$$

– *inp* is input data taken from the real world outside the model (e.g., artefacts newly created or modified, a stakeholder's signature for approval, field test results). It reflects the situation of the real world at the time when the transition t fires.

- xs is the list of tokens consumed by firing t. Writing $[p_0, ..., p_{n-1}]$ for the source place list *source*(t), $xs = [x_0 \in Colour(p_0), ..., x_{n-1} \in Colour(p_{n-1})]$.
- g is a proof that t is enabled given *inp* and xs. g is automatically constructed when and only when *Guard*$(t)(inp)(xs)$ holds, by a decision algorithm. Presence of g guarantees that computation of *action*$(t)(inp)(xs)(g)$ in the model succeeds without exceptions or infinite looping.
- For the result $(out \in Output, ys \in Bindings(target(t)(inp)(xs)(g))$, *out* is output data to the real world outside the model and ys is the list of tokens produced by firing t. For example, *out* may be work-requests to human participants of the real life cycle or error-reports about *inp*. *out* may also be outputs to external systems supporting the life cycle. Writing $[q_0, ..., q_{m-1}]$ for the target place list *target*$(t)(inp)(xs)(g)$, tokens $ys = [y_0 \in Colour(q_0), ..., y_{m-1} \in Colour(q_{m-1})]$ are computed from *inp* and xs and model artefacts with assurance produced by the life cycle stage.

Do-Check Loops: Interactions Between the Model and the Real World.
In Fig. 2, most stages have the pattern of (ready)-[do]-(done)-[check]. Motivation for this is to express interactions between computing of *action*(t) in the model and performance of life cycle processes in the real world without conflating the two. For example, Development stage of Fig. 2 is intended to model the following interactions (Fig. 3, the label of a part refers to the so-labelled list item below).

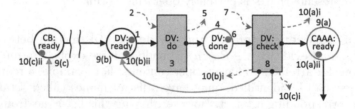

Fig. 3. Do-check loops in the development stage

1. A token x at DV:ready typically includes data for system specification (of various maturity), unsatisfactory system validation results from previous iterations, and estimation on required development resources.
2. $inp \in Input$ taken by *action*(DV:do) may include an information on development resources currently available, review results on the artefacts developed in the last iteration, and authorization to start development.
3. A decision algorithm on *Guard*(DV:do)$(inp)([x])$ transforms information on estimated and required resources and priority given in review result into either a proof g of that *action*(DV:do)$(inp)([x])(-)$ can be computed meaningfully or a proof that it cannot. Here we assume the case where g is produced.

4. *target*(DV:do)(*inp*)([*x*])(*g*) is [DV:done] (the singleton list of DV:done).

Let us write (*out* ∈ *Output*, [*y*] ∈ [*Colour*(DV:done)]) for the value of *action*(DV:do)(*inp*)([*x*])(*g*).

5. *out* may include: revised system specifications reflecting the review results in *inp*, work requests to developers that triggers actual development processes, information on resources to be used.
6. Token *y* may include: success criteria to judge artefacts to be produced by the actual development processes that is invoked by *out*, record of the work being done together with rationale for it.
7. *inp'* ∈ *Input* taken by *action*(DV:check) may include: artefacts produced by the actual development processes, signatures from stakeholders accountable for the processes, reports on problems encountered during the processes.
8. *Guard*(DV:check)(*inp'*)([*y*]) typically amounts to trivially true proposition with proof triv.
9. *target*(DV:check)(*inp'*)([*y*])(triv) computes to one of the following depending on *inp'* and *y*: (a) [CAAA:ready] if artefacts in *inp'* pass the success criteria given in *y* and if no problem is reported in *inp'*; (b) [DV:ready] if the artefacts do not pass the criteria and if the problem reports indicate that stakeholder requirements need not be revised; (c) [CB:ready] otherwise, i.e., if agreements on stakeholder requirements and other arrangements need to be revised.

Let us write (*out'*, [*z*]) for the value of *action*(DV:check)(*inp'*)([*y*])(triv).

10. Its intended meaning differs depending on the value of *tgt* = *target* (DV:check)(*inp'*)([*y*])(triv).
    (a) If *tgt* = [CAAA:ready], **i.** *out'* typically contains little significant information and **ii.** token *z* at CAAA:ready may include information on the aspects of development work done that needs to be accounted for to relevant stakeholders, such as rationale for the development, reasoning why artefacts produced is judged acceptable.
    (b) If *tgt* = [DV:ready], **i.** *out'* may include work-requests to review system specifications etc., and to produce recommended actions for the next iteration of development and **ii.** token *z* at DV:ready is as explained for *x*, including reasons why the artefacts did not pass the success criteria.
    (c) If *tgt* = [CB:ready], **i.** *out'* may include work-requests to review agreements on stakeholder requirements etc., and to produce recommended actions for rebuilding consensus and **ii.** token *z* at CB:ready may include the reasons why the artefacts did not pass the success criteria and why rebuilding consensus is deemed necessary.

The function *action*(*t*) is meant to be computed in the model without human intervention. This is not to expect some sophisticated automation for processing and decision making, but to require sufficiently precise identification and characterisation of artefacts and other necessary information in real world (including expert judgements and approvals of accountable stakeholders), so that explicit, formal rules for processing and decision making can be developed and agreed upon by all relevant stakeholders. Transitions can be subdivided as necessary to refine the timing when the model takes in such information from the real world.

Issue Splitting and Merging. The main reason to adopt Petri nets for life cycle modelling is that real life cycles necessarily contain concurrent, related activities in a life cycle. For example, after activities to achieve accountability for a service failure, the issue regarding this service failure splits into two issues: (1) promptly resume the service possibly at a degraded level and (2) revise the service for prevention of failure recurrence and a longer-term improvement. While the degraded service is operating, the revision of service is agreed upon by affected stakeholders, is developed, and is accounted for to obtain agreement for deployment. At this time, two issues are merged into one issue that is to operate the revised service normally, retiring the previous version of the service.

This situation can be represented by issue splitting and merging in our model. In Fig. 2, $action$(FRAA:check)$(inp)([x])(g)$ consumes one token $x = (s, \cdots)$ at FRAA:done representing the issue of accountability achievement for a failure of service s, takes inputs inp from real world on the reaction of affected stakeholders, and, if they are determined to be satisfactory, produces two tokens y_1 at Operation (degraded operation of s) and y_2 at CB:ready (consensus building for the revision of s). y_2 goes through transformation by succeeding stages and becomes a token y_3 at CAAA:done (achieving accountability for revision). y_1 and y_3 are then consumed by $action$(CAAA:check)$(inp)([y_1, y_3])$, producing one token y_4 at Operation. This models the merging of the two issues y_1 and y_3. $Guard$(CAAA:check)$(inp)[-, -]$ enables CAAA:check only when two tokens are related, preventing CAAA:check from merging two unrelated issues.

5   Assurance of System Life Cycle Using DPN Models

System assurance involves assuring properties of not only a target system itself but also the system life cycle acting on it. The informal claim to be assured is *"At any time, each required outcome for each issue (service) is achieved or being achieved."*

For our example, we consider conformance to the international standard IEC 62853 [5], which provides 4 process views a system life cycle must realise to achieve open systems dependability. Conformance to IEC 62853 requires an assurance case demonstrating that all outcomes of the 4 process views are achieved.

Assurance of the system life cycle includes assurance of the ability to produce a 'current' assurance case whenever demanded, where the current assurance case assures that each outcome is either achieved or, if not, will be achieved by current plans for actions (under appropriately justified assumptions on future behaviours of the real life cycle).

We formulate the top-level claim statement for assurance of the system life cycle as the property of its DPN model in the following form.

For any reachable marking $m \in$ *Marking*, for each outcome O, for each place $p \in$ *Place*, for each token $x \in m(p)$ at p, $[\![O]\!](m, p, x)$ holds.

$[\![O]\!](m,p,x)$ is a proposition representing the aspects of outcome O relevant to x at p in m. The current assurance case for the life cycle is produced when demanded by generating and integrating arguments that $[\![O]\!](m,p,x)$ holds for all tokens xs in m from the assurance data carried by xs.

The above formulation with $[\![O]\!](m,p,x)$ expresses the idea that assurance of·an outcome O is not a one-shot activity done and finished in one life cycle stage. How O should be continually assured at every life cycle stage depends on the nature of O intended in the life cycle being modelled. For example:

- O = "Stakeholders of the system are identified." ([5], (6.2.2 a)1))
  An agreed list of stakeholders is produced in a token at CB:done and evidence of its appropriateness is attached at DV:ready. However, actual stakeholders may change, e.g., new stakeholders may be discovered while performing CAAA:check. Every stage X's X:check transition should check the validity of the current list of stakeholders and should send the relevant token back to CB:ready if the list is found invalid. More generally, effects of changes in the real world should be considered even if achievement of outcomes is thought to be stable in traditional views.
- O = "When a breach of an agreement occurs, the stakeholders accountable for it provide in a timely manner the remedies for the non-accountable stakeholders and society in general." ([5], (6.3.2 h))
  While O is phrased for a service in Operation, evidence for O needs to be produced at DV:ready, CAAA:ready, etc., as agreements on remedies, as plans to realise them, as their validation results, as performance of remedies provided, etc., together with evidence of their appropriateness. More generally, for every outcome that appears to concern only a particular life cycle stage, two kinds of derived outcomes should be considered: preparations necessary at preceding stages and desired consequences at following stages.
- O ="The system life cycle is improved continually." ([5], (6.5.2 e))
  Outcomes concerned with the life cycle as a whole need to be decomposed to sub-outcomes for each life cycle stage together with the argument that integrates achievement of per-stage sub-outcomes when the 'current' assurance argument for the whole life cycle is demanded.

6 Conclusion and Future Work

A formulation of life cycle models is proposed that aims to clarify what it means to assure that a life cycle so modelled achieves expected outcomes. Future work includes the following.

- Details on token data and transition functions needs to be developed. For identification of relevant artefacts ($A_{p,s}$ in Sect. 4.2), we plan to adopt ISO/IEC/IEEE 15289 [16], which identifies information items used in the life cycle processes of [1], which in turn implement the process views of [5]. Requirements on artefacts ($R_{p,s}$ in Sect. 4.2) and outcomes ($[\![O]\!](m,p,x)$ in Sect. 5) will be formulated together so that proofs of the former can be automatically integrated to proofs of the latter. We plan to define transition functions (*action*(t) in Sect. 4.3) in a formal language Agda [17] that guarantees correctness of functions/proofs with respect to given specifications.

- The formulation of DPN needs to be refined to construct complex life cycle models with understandability and sufficient faithfulness to the reality. The ability to form composite transtions/places from constituent ones as hierarchical modules is crucial. Timing behaviours of transitions should be specifiable in order to formulate and assure outcomes containing generic wording such as "in a timely manner" and "promptly". Global constraints among issues, such as those arising from resource competition and overall priorities, should be formulated and taken into account when controlling progression of issues.
- Effectiveness of the approach need to be evaluated against proper assessment criteira together with a more extensive review of related work along the line of [6]. Case studies using prototype implementations of the approach in the form of workflow management tools/workflow engines are necessary.

Acknowledgments. This work is supported by the project TIGARS (Towards Identifying and closing Gaps in Assurance of autonomous Road vehicleS), a partnership between Adelard LLP, City University in London, the University of Nagoya, Kanagawa University, and WITZ Corporation. TIGARS is a part of the Assuring Autonomy International Programme (AAIP) at the University of York, UK, an initiative funded by Lloyd's Register Foundation and the University of York. The authors thank anonymous reviewers for helpful comments including pointers to related work, and members of the DEOS consortium for discussions on how to realise conceptual requirements in IEC 62853 in more concrete terms.

References

1. ISO, IEC and IEEE: ISO/IEC/IEEE 15288:2015 Systems and software engineering - System life cycle processes (2015)
2. ISO, IEC and IEEE: ISO/IEC/IEEE 24748–1:2018 Systems and software engineering - Life cycle management - Part 1: Guidelines for life cycle management (2018)
3. Jensen, K.: Coloured Petri Nets: Basic Concepts, Analysis Methods and Practical Use, vol. 1. Springer, Heidelberg (2013)
4. Tokoro, M. (ed.): Open Systems dependability—Dependability Engineering for Ever-Changing Systems, 2nd edn. CRC Press, Boca Raton (2015)
5. IEC: IEC 62853 Open systems dependability (2018)
6. Ly, L.T., et al.: Compliance monitoring in business processes: functionalities, application, and tool-support. Inform. Syst. **54**, 209–234 (2015)
7. Governatori, G.: The regorous approach to process compliance. In: 2015 IEEE 19th International Enterprise Distributed Object Computing Workshop. IEEE (2015)
8. Hashmi, M., Governatori, G., Wynn, M.T.: Normative requirements for regulatory compliance: an abstract formal framework. Inform. Syst. Front. **18**(3), 429–455 (2016)
9. Casterallnos Ardila, J.P., Gallina, B.: Formal contract logic based patterns for facilitating compliance checking against ISO 26262. In: 1st Workshop on Technologies for Regulatory Compliance, pp. 65–722 (2017)

10. Simon, E., Stoffel, K.: State machines and petri nets as a formal representation for systems life cycle management. In: Proceedings of IADIS International Conference Information Systems, pp. 275–272. IADIS Press, Barcelona (2009)
11. Hull, R., et al.: Introducing the guard-stage-milestone approach for specifying business entity lifecycles. In: Bravetti, M., Bultan, T. (eds.) WS-FM 2010. LNCS, vol. 6551, pp. 1–24. Springer, Heidelberg (2011). https://doi.org/10.1007/978-3-642-19589-1_1
12. Petri, C.A.: Kommunikation mit Automaten. Schriften des Institut für Instrumentelle Mathematik. Universität Bonn (1962)
13. Heijstek, W., Chaudron, M.: Evaluating rup software development processes through visualization of effort distribution. In: 2008 34th Euromicro Conference Software Engineering and Advanced Applications. IEEE (2008)
14. Kinoshita, Y., Takeyama, M.: Assurance case as a proof in a theory—towards formulation of rebuttals. In: Dale, C., Anderson, T. (eds.) Assuring the Safety of Systems, pp. 205–230. SCSC, Greenville (2013)
15. Martin-Löf, P.: Intuitionistic Type Theory. Studies in Proof Theory, vol. 1. Bibliopolis, Naple (1984). Notes by Giovanni Sambin
16. ISO, IEC and IEEE: ISO/IEC/IEEE 15289:2017 Systems and software engineering - content of life-cycle information items (documentation) (2017)
17. Agda Team: The Agda Wiki. https://wiki.portal.chalmers.se/agda/pmwiki.php. Accessed 10 June 2019

Modular Safety Cases for Product Lines Based on Assume-Guarantee Contracts

Damir Nešić[✉] and Mattias Nyberg

KTH Royal Institute of Technology, 100 44 Stockholm, Sweden
{damirn,matny}@kth.se

Abstract. Safety cases are recommended, and in some cases required, by a number of standards. In the *product line* context, unlike for single systems, safety cases are inherently complex because they must argue about the safety of a *family of products* that share various types of engineering assets. Safety case *modularization* has been proposed to reduce safety case complexity by separating concerns, modularizing tightly coupled arguments, and localizing effects of changes to particular modules. Existing modular safety-case approaches for product lines propose a feature-based modularization, which is too coarse to modularize the claims of different types, at different levels of abstraction. To overcome these limitation, a novel, modular safety-case architecture is presented. The modularization is based on a *contract-based specification* product-line model, which jointly captures the component-based architecture of systems and corresponding safety requirements as *assume-guarantee* contracts. The proposed safety-case architecture is analyzed against possible product-line changes and it is shown that it is robust both with respect to fine and coarse-grained, and also product and implementation-level changes. The proposed modular safety case is exemplified on a simplified, but real automotive system.

Keywords: Modular safety case · Assume-guarantee contract · Product line

1 Introduction

An increasing number of domains is regulated by safety standards [6,18] that recommend, and in some cases mandate, the construction of a *safety case* [18] as an explicit argument for system safety. In such domains, e.g. automotive, aerospace, or defense, companies often develop *families of products* typically implemented as *product lines* [1,9,21]. *Product lines* [15] are popular because of their economic benefits, although their adoption requires significant technical and organizational changes. More specifically, by *systematically reusing* existing engineering assets, e.g. requirements or software, the product line approach enables quick and efficient development of new product configurations, thus leading to a portfolio of products that satisfy the needs of various customers [17].

© Springer Nature Switzerland AG 2019
A. Romanovsky et al. (Eds.): SAFECOMP 2019 Workshops, LNCS 11699, pp. 28–40, 2019.
https://doi.org/10.1007/978-3-030-26250-1_3

For example, in automotive domain, one vehicle model can have millions of distinct configurations [21]. Because of their extensibility, and costly adoption, product lines are maintained over a period of years. Product configurations are continuously introduced or deprecated and in such context, a safety case will change often. Therefore, it is desirable to *incrementally certify* new configurations, *reuse* existing safety case arguments, and ensure that safety case changes are proportional to the number of changed engineering assets, and not to the number of configurations that use these assets.

In the context of single systems, previous literature has investigated the principles for *safety-case modularization* [3,4,7] in order to achieve incremental certification. The idea of *modular safety-cases* is that tightly-coupled safety claims can be developed as independent *safety-case modules* which can then be *composed* into the overall safety case. The only approach to present a specific modular safety-case architecture for a product-line safety case is Oliveira [13]. This approach, modularizes the safety case according to *features* and their structure, where a feature is an abstract, user-visible characteristics of the product. An implementation of a feature typically includes multiple types of components, e.g. sensors, control units, mechanical parts, and typically spans across several control units connected via a communication buss. Consequently, creating a single safety module to argue about the safety of a whole feature will result in a large module, containing diverse claims, all of which contradicts the idea of smaller, tightly-coupled claims within modules. On the other hand, because product lines encourage the reuse of components for the implementation of multiple features, the content of safety case modules in [13] will overlap and result in an increased number of inter-module dependencies. Also, the work in [13] does not show that the composition of arguments in feature-based modules, leads to sound argumentation about the safety of each product configuration.

To overcome these limitations, the present paper proposes a *modular safety-case architecture* for a product-line safety case, based on the safety-case construction method from Nešić et al. [12]. The approach in [12] relies on a formal *Contract-Based Specification* (CBS) model of a product line to construct a product-line safety case. More specifically, a CBS model captures both the product-level and implementation-level structure of a configurable *component-based* architecture, and a modular *assume-guarantee contract* specification of the corresponding safety requirements. The proposed safety-case architecture is structured according to the components, from product down to the implementation-level, and the assume-guarantee contracts that they should satisfy. The arguments within safety-case modules correspond to four specific types of conditions defined by the CBS framework. Showing that a CBS model of a product line, and its corresponding implementation satisfy these conditions, is sufficient to claim that each product configuration satisfies a specific top-level safety property. The proposed safety-case architecture is analyzed against possible product-line changes, and it is shown that unlike [13] the safety-case architecture is unaffected, and that different types of changes, at different levels of abstraction, are localized to specific modules. To exemplify the approach, we use a simplified, but real, system from the heavy vehicle manufacturer Scania.

Paper Structure. Sect. 2 presents the background and Sect. 3 describes the modular safety-case architecture. Section 4 analyzes the impact of possible product-line change scenarios. Section 5 discusses the safety case architecture and is followed by related work in Sect. 6 and conclusions in Sect. 7.

2   Background

This section summarizes the approach in Nešić et al. [12]. This approach describes a formal, assume-guarantee contract-framework for the modeling of arbitrary product lines, based on which primarily product-based claims can be generated in GSN format. The approach allows reasoning about various types of functional properties, e.g. safety or security, and although amenable to automation, this section provides only the necessary intuition about the approach.

2.1   A Model of the Product Line

Conceptually, a product line is partitioned into the *problem space, solution space,* and a *mapping* between them. The problem space contains an implementation-independent representation of all possible configurations of the product. Typically, the possible configurations are captured by a *feature model* [15], which is essentially a set of Boolean constraints over the set of *features*. Features are the functional and non-functional properties of the product that are of interest to the customer. By selecting *features* from the feature model, subject to the Boolean constraints, a particular *product configuration* is selected.

The *solution space* contains the artifacts that implement the product configurations from the problem space, i.e. each product configuration can be mapped to a particular set of artifacts. In [12], a *Contract-Based Specification* (CBS) framework is used as the solution space representation.

CBS Framework. Various CBS frameworks have been proposed, e.g. [19,20], all with the purpose to formally capture the essence of common systems engineering activities, irregardless of the domain, development process, or type of system. To this end, the basic concepts in CBS frameworks are: (i) *component C* which models any type of a physical or logical component, (ii) *specification S* which models a requirement that a component should implement, (iii) *implementation relation,* which models the fact that a real-world component implements a specification, (iv) *fulfills relation* which models the fact that one requirement *logically entails* another requirement, and (v) *component composition* which models the component integration operation. The components that are composed of other components are referred to as *composite,* otherwise they are referred to as *atomic.* Some CBS frameworks consider the concept of a *component port* to manage component interfaces. Work in [12] assumes that specifications are expressed in terms of component ports, but does not consider ports explicitly. Note that the CBS framework does not make assumptions about the format of specifications or components. Specifications can be in natural language or mathematical expressions, while components can be expressed in SysML, Simulink, C-code etc. The goal of the CBS framework is to establish sufficient conditions under which it can be claimed that specifications of heterogeneous systems are consistent, and possible to verify against an implementation.

To aid comprehension, Fig. 1a visualizes a CBS model of a simplified, vehicle-level function from Scania vehicles, the *Fuel Level Display* (FLD), modeled by the composite component C_{FLD}. From the safety perspective, the FLD must ensure that the indicated fuel volume corresponds to the actual volume in the fuel tank. Otherwise, if a higher fuel volume is indicated, the vehicle might run out of fuel mid-drive, thus leading to engine shutdown and loss of power steering which is essential for heavy vehicles. The vehicle-level function implemented by component C_{FLD}, closely corresponds to the concept of an *item* in ISO 26262 and to the concept of a feature from product line engineering.

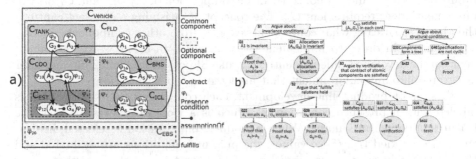

Fig. 1. CBS model of FLD and corresponding safety case fragment.

As can be seen from Fig. 1a, C_{FLD} is composed of C_{TANK}, C_{COO}, C_{BMS}, and C_{ICL}, where C_{ICL} models the vehicle *Instrumentation Cluster* which indicates the fuel level, C_{COO} and C_{BMS} model *control units* that estimate the fuel volume in different configurations, and C_{TANK} models the fuel tank with the corresponding fuel sensor. Furthermore, the control unit C_{COO} is composed of C_{EST} which models the C-code SW module that implements the fuel volume estimation. Note that in Fig. 1a, C_{BMS} and C_{EST} are both atomic components although they are different in nature. In other words, it is a design decision how detailed the components will be, depending on the granularity of the specifications that they should implement. For example, C_{BMS} and C_{ICL} might be procured from suppliers and there is no need to further refine their structure.

To enable modular component development, the CBS framework defines *assume-guarantee contracts* to express component requirements. A contract is a pair of specifications, denoted $K = (A, G)$, where the first one is called the *assumption* and the second one the *guarantee*. Safety requirements are typically modeled as guarantees within contracts. For example, G_1 is the top-level safety requirement of FLD stating that *"the indicated fuel volume should correspond to the actual fuel volume"*. G_1 is fulfilled by G_6 stating that *"the fuel volume indicated by C_{ICL} corresponds to the actual fuel volume"* but because C_{ICL} does not estimate the fuel volume, G_6 can hold only under the assumption A_7, modeled by relation *assumptionOf*, stating that *"estimated fuel volume corresponds to the actual volume"*. In the context of ISO 26262, guarantee G_1 corresponds closely to a *safety goal*, G_6 to a *functional safety requirement*, C_{ICL} to a *system* etc.

Contracts can be *allocated to* components, e.g. (A_1, G_1) is allocated to C_{FLD} in Fig. 1a, to express the intention that a component should *satisfy* the contract. A component satisfies a contract, if whenever C is composed with some component C_e called the *environment*, where C_e implements A, *then the composition of C_e and C implements the guarantee G*. To exemplify, component C_{COO} from Fig. 1a can be developed in isolation to satisfy contract (A_3, G_3). To claim that safety requirement G_3 is implemented, the environment must implement A_3. The *fulfills* relation between G_2 and A_3 declares the intention that if G_2 is implemented then also A_3 is. Consequently, if C_{TANK} satisfies (A_2, G_2), and the fulfills between G_2 and A_3 holds, then the composition of C_{TANK} and C_{COO} will implement safety requirement G_3. The concept of satisfying a contract captures the idea of separating what components expects from other components, i.e. the environment, in order to implement the guarantee. In other words, a component can be developed independently, e.g. like SEooC in ISO26262 [6], and later integrated into any environment that implements the assumption.

To support product line development, each component and specification is labeled with a presence condition φ_i which is a Boolean expression over the features in the feature model. When a product configuration is selected, i.e. features are assigned true/false values, the presence conditions are evaluated and the artifacts whose presence conditions evaluate to *true* are the ones that correspond to the selected product configuration. For example, presence conditions φ_4 and φ_6 in Fig. 1a define that in some configurations C_{FLD} contains C_{COO} with C_{EST}, while in others it contains C_{BMS} where both components perform the fuel volume estimation. As intuition suggests, absence of configuration mismatches must be ensured, i.e. either C_{EST} or C_{BMS} are selected but never both.

Given the presented framework, the work in [12] *proves* that the contract allocated to the top level component is satisfied in each product configuration if the CBS model of a product line, i.e. the product line design, and its implementation satisfy the following four types of conditions: **(i)** a set of structural constraints on the CBS model that represent common architectural guidelines, e.g. *high-cohesion low-coupling* or *separation of concerns*, **(ii)** a set of constraints called *invariance conditions* which mitigate the mentioned configuration mismatches, **(iii)** *logical entailment* holds between specifications related by the fulfills relation, i.e. the requirement breakdown is complete, and **(iv)** implementation of each atomic component satisfies the contract allocated to it, e.g. verified through testing.

Showing that a CBS model and the corresponding implementation satisfy the four types of conditions, corresponds to constructing a product-based argument that all product configurations satisfy a top-level safety requirement. The soundness of such argument follows from the described proof. Figure 1b shows the argument developed from the CBS model of FLD according to the approach in [12]. As shown, the constructed safety case fragment is monolithic, i.e. claims and evidence are structured according to the four types of conditions without considering the FLD structure. As the next section shows, the safety case fragment in Fig. 1b is amenable to modularization because the four types of conditions can be verified separately for any contract, allocated to any component while preserving the overall claim soundness.

3   Modular Safety-Case Architecture for Product Lines

In this section, we show how CBS models can be leveraged to obtain a *modular* safety case for a complete product line expressed using the GSN format.

Several concerns should be considered for the modularization strategy. Firstly, it is necessary to argue about the problem space, e.g. it is impossible to select a vehicle without brakes, the solution space, e.g. the braking system is safe, and the problem-solution space mapping, e.g. if brakes are selected, the corresponding electro-mechanical brake components are selected. Secondly, safety standards for multiple domains, e.g. in automotive or railway, are derived from IEC 61508 [5] where the safety activities start with *hazard* identification, and continue with the definition and refinement of safety requirements that *mitigate* the hazards. Similar process is proposed in the aerospace guideline ARP4754 [16], thus, a majority of safety cases must argue about the completeness of the identified hazards, and their mitigation by defined safety requirement. Thirdly, and as noted in [4,7], the modularization of the safety case should closely resemble the modularization of the system so that an isolated change in the product line results in an isolated change of the safety case. Finally, *high cohesion* within and *low coupling* between the modules [4,7] should be achieved in order to truly enable division of work, i.e. detailed domain knowledge within an engineering group should be sufficient to create and maintain a particular module.

3.1   The Structure of a Modular Safety Case

According to the GSN format guidelines, the claim structure *"progresses downwards, from the most abstract claim"* [14]. Based on the previous discussion, in a decreasing level of abstraction, the hierarchy of the proposed modular safety case contains three types of modules: (i) product-line related, (ii) hazard related, and (iii) contract, i.e. system structure related.

Product-Line Related Modules. Because the overall goal is to show that a *"Product line is safe"*, this is the most abstract claim captured by the root goal. Guided by the conceptual division of product line into three parts, immediately less abstract claims are: **(i)** the implementation of each valid product configuration is safe, **(ii)** only valid product configurations can be selected in the problem space, and **(iii)** the mapping from the problem space to the solution space is correct. Because each of these claims may require extensive support, and because they are mutually independent, each of them should belong to a separate module.

Applying these principles to the CBS model from Fig. 1a results in the claims contained by module M1, shown in Fig. 3, where M1 is the top module of the FLD modular safety-case architecture shown in Fig. 2. For now we assume that product-level functions are independent and decompose the claim that the implementation of each product configuration is safe into sub-claims that each product-level function *that can comprise* a product configuration is safe, e.g. C_{FLD}, C_{EBS} etc. While the claims that all product-level functions are safe can be developed from their CBS models, the two other types of claims are not further elaborated due to space limitations. However, evidence supporting the claims about the solutions space and problem-to-solution space mapping can be produced automatically by using the method in [11].

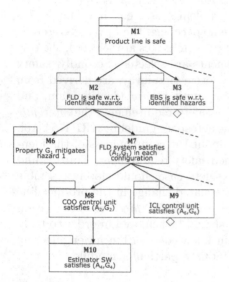

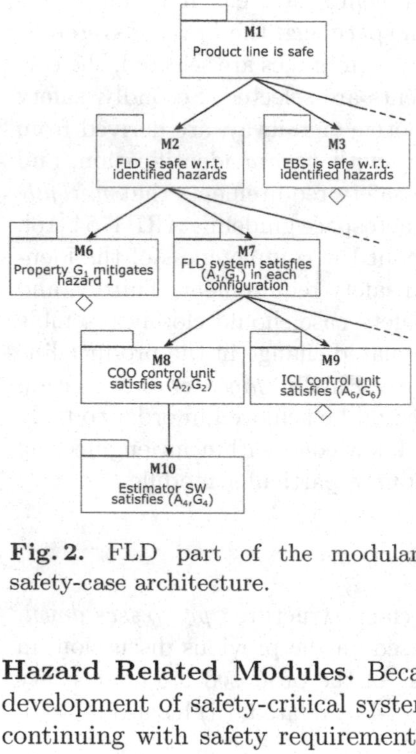

Fig. 2. FLD part of the modular safety-case architecture.

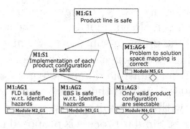

Fig. 3. Content of module M1

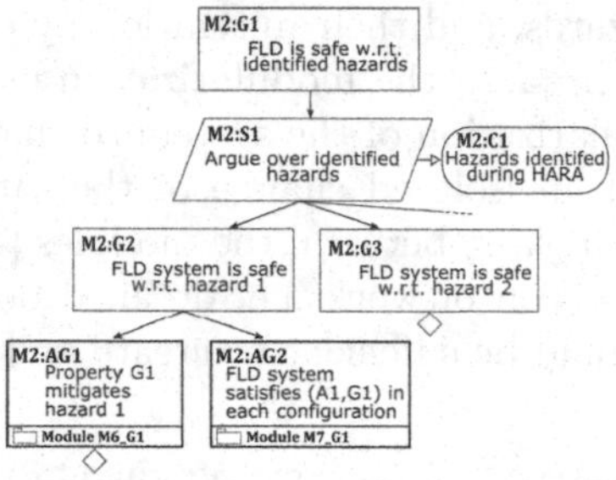

Fig. 4. Content of module M2

Hazard Related Modules. Because various standards recommend to start development of safety-critical systems by identifying product-level hazards and continuing with safety requirements that *mitigate* these hazards, the modular safety-case structure reflect this process. To capture such argumentation, Denney et al. [2] propose and combine the *Extended Hazard-Directed Breakdown* and the *Requirement Breakdown* pattern. Here, we follow similar reasoning and the most abstract product-based claims about the safety of a product-level function has two-legs where the first leg argues that each identified hazard is *mitigated* by a top-level safety requirement, and the second leg argues that the product-level functions *implements* this safety requirement. Unlike [2], the CBS framework supports product lines, and precisely defines the four types of conditions under which it can be claimed that a system satisfies a top-level safety requirement.

Applying this reasoning to FLD yields the argumentation in Fig. 4 which is contained by module M2. Because the CBS framework captures safety requirements as guarantees of contracts, the first leg argues that the guarantee G_1 of a contract allocated to the C_{FLD} mitigates a product-level hazard, and the second leg argues that the contract to which G_1 belongs, is satisfied by C_{FLD}. Developing the argumentation that a component satisfies a contract allocated to it, corresponds to verifying that the CBS model and its the real-world implementation satisfy the previously described four types of conditions. The argumentation that a specification mitigates a hazard is not elaborated due to space limitations but the interested reader is referred to the *hazard-avoidance* and *ALARP* pattern [8].

Contract Related Modules. As discussed in Sect. 2, arguing that a product-level function satisfies the contract allocated to it, corresponds to showing that a CBS model, and its implementation, satisfy the four types of conditions. To construct the modules, we use the fact that arguing about the conditions per-component preserves the soundness of the overall claim. Specifically, for each contract $K = (A, G)$, allocated to a composite component C, composed of direct subcomponents C_i, the corresponding module M contains the following claims:

(i) Claims and evidence that the CBS model for C satisfies structural constraints. These claims and evidence are local to M. If C is an atomic component without further structure, then these claims are omitted. The evidence can be produced automatically by using the approach in [10].
(ii) Claims and evidence that the invariance constraints are satisfied. This argumentation is also local to module M. If C is not composed of further components, i.e. it is *atomic*, then the clams about the *composition invariance* are omitted. The evidence can be produced by encoding the invariance constraints as the *Boolean satisfiability* problem.
(iii) Claims and evidence that fulfills relations hold. If there exists a specification S_i that fulfills A or G, it must be shown that S_i logically entails A or G. This argumentation is local to M and depending on the integrity level and formalism used to write the specifications, e.g. free text or logical formulas, the supporting evidence might be produced manually, or by formal verification.
(iv) Claims that subcomponents C_i satisfy own contracts. These claims relate to components $C_i \neq C$ and contracts $K_i \neq K$, thus this argumentation belongs to modules $M_i \neq M$ and the claims from this step are captured as *away goals*. If C is an atomic component, then instead of an away goal a solution node should be created with a reference to verification results showing that C satisfies the allocated contract.

Irregardless of the level of abstraction, i.e. product-level functions or SW component, claims (i)–(iv) should be established. As an example, Fig. 5 shows the content of module M8. Besides standard GSN elements, dashed lines and dashed circles indicate that some goals are omitted but these argumentations legs end in solution nodes. Note that if a component, e.g. C_{COO}, is developed

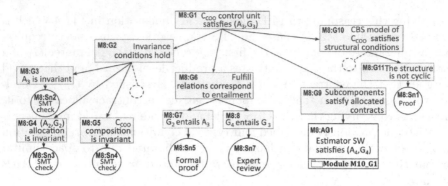

Fig. 5. Contents of module M8

by a supplier and sold to different OEMs, then goals M8:G7 and M8:G8 cannot be instantiated because the supplier does know which specification from the environment will fulfill A_3. Developing a safety module for C where such goals are uninstantiated, and instantiating them once C is integrated into the final product, directly supports the ISO 26262 SEooC concept, and in general *argumentation reuse*. In contrast, if the product including C_{COO} is developed by a single organization, then the developer of C_{COO} must ensure that irregardless of its allocation, there exists a specification, such as G_2, that fulfills A_3. In this way, the developer of C_{COO} ensures that A_3 assumes only as much as the environment can offer.

4   Maintenance of the Obtained Modular Safety Case

Given the concepts of the underlying CBS framework, there are various types of product-line changes that can impact the modules in the proposed safety-case architecture. In this section we list the possible change scenarios and analyze some of them in order to compare the presented modular safety-case to the one presented in [13].

The possible change scenarios are: (S1) valid product configurations are added or removed; (S2) a safety requirement, i.e. a contract (A, G), changes; (S3) a safety requirement, i.e. a contract (A, G), is added or removed; (S4) a component is changed or removed; (S5) a contract (A, G) is re-allocated from one component to another; and (S6) a specification that fulfills an assumption or a guarantee is changed. Due to space limitations, we consider only the details of two scenarios.

(S1): *Valid product configurations are added or removed.* The set of valid product configurations can be changed either by adding new features, or by changing the allowed combinations of existing features, which are specified by a feature model. Because the safety-case architecture in [13] has the same structure as the feature model, a change of the set of valid product configurations will lead to a change in the safety-case architecture, even if the product-line implementation does not change. For example, it is undesirable to change the structure of the safety case if the currently *mandatory* FLD becomes *optional* for autonomous vehicles. When a feature-model change implies a change in the implementation of a feature, irregardless of the type of implementation-change, a single safety-case module will be affected in the safety case from [13]. For example, if the top-level safety requirement of FLD changes, or if the fuel-level sensor changes, the same module will be affected. This contradicts the idea that modular safety-cases should localize the effects of different types of changes to dedicated modules.

Being independent of the feature model, the proposed modular safety-case architecture will change only if the product line implementation changes. Although a change in the feature model will not affect the safety-case architecture, new safety case evidence will be required; namely the evidence about the problem space, e.g. M1:AG3, problem-to-solution space mapping, e.g. M1:AG4, and about invariance conditions, e.g. M8:Sn2. Because the proposed safety-case is modularized according to components and safety requirements at different abstraction levels, any change in the implementation, i.e. in components or requirements, will be confined to the corresponding safety-case modules.

(S2): *A safety requirement, i.e. a contract* (A, G) *changes.* Assume that the FLD top-level safety requirement changes so that G_1 in Fig. 1a allows a $\pm 10\%$ deviation of the indicated compared to the actual fuel volume. Neither the approach in [13], nor the approaches presenting the principles of safety case modularization [3, 4, 7], consider the scenario where a safety requirement changes. From [13] it can be only be concluded that the affected safety-case module will be the one corresponding to the feature which should implement the requirement.

In the proposed modular safety-case architecture, a change of a single requirement will result in a change in a single safety-case module that argues exactly about that requirement being satisfied. Unlike in [13], and due to the underlying CBS framework, a change in a requirement will invalidate the evidence that the requirement breakdown is complete, and that the designated component implements the new requirement. In other words, a change of a requirement will result in a clear set of *verification obligations* that must be discharged in order to make overall safety-case claim sound. Note that the number of impacted safety-case modules will be equal to the number of changed safety requirements and not the number of product configurations that should satisfy these requirements.

5   Discussion

The purpose of this work, in conjunction with [12], is to provide a framework for the specification of arbitrary product lines, and the creation of corresponding modular safety cases. For example, if an organization develops all components used in a product line, the corresponding CBS model will be detailed and the safety-case claims will be fine-grained. If an organization primarily buys components, the corresponding CBS model and safety case will be coarser. In either case, the size of the proposed modular safety case will scale linearly with the number of safety requirements and components that implement them, and not with the number of product configurations, which can reach millions.

Because organizational structures of companies are typically aligned with the structure of systems they develop, the presented modularization according to components, and requirements that these components satisfy, allows clear distribution of work during the safety-case creation and maintenance. Vertically, the safety-case architecture structures the modules from more to less abstract claims about product-level functions, which are similar to features. In this way, groups developing a specific function could be responsible for the corresponding set of modules, e.g. all modules related to C_{FLD} and its components. Horizontally, the modular safety-case structures the modules according to contracts, i.e. safety requirements, that particular components satisfy. Therefore, a group developing a specific component, e.g. C_{COO}, could be responsible for all modules related to that component. Because the claims within modules relate to a single requirement, and a single component, they are closely related according to *high cohesion* principle.

Many of the benefits of the presented approach stem from the underlying, formal CBS framework. Although formal methods are known to be difficult to adopt, safety standards such as ISO 26262 or IEC 61508 highly recommend semi-formal and recommend formal methods for requirements specification, software-architecture specification, and software verification of high integrity systems. Because the CBS framework allows natural language requirements, it can be used both as a semi-formal, or fully formal framework with formal requirements.

Besides the benefits, the proposed modular safety-case has few limitations. Currently, the approach does not consider the production and post-production part of the safety lifecycle. Also primarily due to lack of space, the proposed modularization does not consider claims about component independence although CBS frameworks can reason about such concepts [20].

6   Related Work

As mentioned in Sect. 1, [13] is the only approach that presents a particular modular, feature-based, safety-case architecture for product lines. Several other works focus on principles of safety case modularization [3,4,7] for single systems. Each of these papers emphasize that in order to achieve the benefits of a modular safety-case, its structure should resemble the technical structure of the system.

The work in [7] views modular safety case through the lens of safety case maintenance. The work defines high-level principles for the development of modular safety-cases, whose structure is optimized by considering component-based system changes. More specifically, the work provides a process to analyze the most probable system changes and use them to optimize the modular safety-case architecture so that it is robust exactly with respect to those changes. Work in [4] applies the method from [7] on an avionics software system, and reports about the benefits and limitations. The modularization is guided by two graphs referred to as DGRs and DGCs, which captures the dependencies between software components. The dependencies in DGRs and DGCs resemble assume-guarantee relations but the exact syntax and semantics of DGRs and DGCs is not discussed. The work in [3] reports the experience after using the modular extension of the GSN format, e.g. away goals, away context, modules, and *safety-case contracts*, for a modular safety case in a real industrial project. The main contribution is a list of suggestions for improvements of several GSN constructs that were perceived as challenging to use. Unlike the assume-guarantee contracts in the CBS framework, *safety-case contracts* are GSN elements used to decouple explicitly connected GSN goals in order to isolate one goal from the impact of a change in another goal.

7   Conclusion

Safety cases for complex safety-critical systems, and especially for a *product line* of such systems, are inherently complex. For single systems, safety case *modularization* has been proposed as the *divide and conquer* approach to facilitate easier creation and maintenance of complex safety cases. In the product-line context, the modularization principles [3,4,7] have been used to propose a specific, modular safety-case architecture [13], but the feature-based modules are too coarse to modularize the claims of different types, at different abstraction levels. The present paper proposes a general, modular safety-case architecture where the safety modules capture both fine and coarse-grained, and both product and implementation-level claims. The proposed modular safety-case argues that all product configurations, possibly millions in some domains, satisfy a particular safety requirement. In terms of size, the number of safety case modules scales with the number of product-line safety requirements and components, and not the number of product configurations. Because the approach is based on a product-line model expressed in a formally sound *assume-guarantee* contracts-based framework, the proposed modular safety case argumentation is also sound.

As future work, we plan to extend the presented approach with process-based arguments, and CBS-based reasoning about component independence.

Acknowledgments. This work has been funded by Vinnova under the ECSEL PRYS-TINE project, ref. number 2018-01764. The authors thank the reviewers for constructive comments.

References

1. Andersson, H., Herzog, E., ölvander, J.: Experience from model and software reuse in aircraft simulator product line engineering. IET **55**, 595–606 (2013)
2. Denney, E., Pai, G.: Safety case patterns: theory and applications. Technial report, NASA Ames Research Center, February 2015
3. Fenn, J., Hawkins, R., Williams, P., Kelly, T.: Safety case composition using contracts - refinements based on feedback from an industrial case study. In: Redmill, F., Anderson, T. (eds.) The Safety of Systems. Springer, London (2007)

4. Fenn, L., Hawkins, R.D., Williams, P.J., Kelly, T.P., Banner, M.G., Oakshott, Y.: The who, where, how, why and when of modular and incremental certification. In: Proceedings of the 2nd ICSS, pp. 135–140. IET, October 2007
5. IEC: IEC 61508 - functional safety of electrical/electronic/programmable electronic safety-related systems (2010)
6. ISO 26262: Road vehicles - Functional safety, November 2011
7. Kelly, T.: Using software architecture techniques to support the modular certification of safety-critical systems. In: Proceedings of the 11th Australian SCS Workshop, pp. 53–65. SCS (2006)
8. Kelly, T.P.: Arguing safety - a systematic approach to managing safety cases (1998)
9. Mukelabai, M., Nešić, D., Maro, S., Berger, T., Steghöfer, J.P.: Tackling combinatorial explosion: a study of industrial needs and practices for analyzing highly configurable systems. In: Proceedings of the 33rd ACM/IEEE ASE. ACM (2018)
10. Nešić, D., Nyberg, M.: Verifying contract-based specifications of product lines using description logic. In: Proceedings 31st International DL Workshop, p. 13 (2018)
11. Nešić, D., Nyberg, M.: Multi-view modeling and automated analysis of product line variability in systems engineering. In: Proceedings of the 20th SPLC. ACM (2016)
12. Nešić, D., Nyberg, M., Gallina, B.: Constructing product-line safety cases from contract-based specifications. In: Proceedings of the 34th ACM/SIGAPP SAC, New York, USA, pp. 2022–2031 (2019)
13. de Oliveira, A.L., Braga, R.T.V., Masiero, P.C., Papadopoulos, Y., Habli, I., Kelly, T.: Supporting the automated generation of modular product line safety cases. In: Zamojski, W., Mazurkiewicz, J., Sugier, J., Walkowiak, T., Kacprzyk, J. (eds.) Theory and Engineering of Complex Systems and Dependability. AISC, vol. 365, pp. 319–330. Springer, Cham (2015). https://doi.org/10.1007/978-3-319-19216-1_30
14. Origin Consulting (York) Limited: GSN community standard version 2, January 2018
15. Pohl, K., Böckle, G., van Der Linden, F.J.: Software Product Line Engineering: Foundations, Principles and Techniques. Springer, Heidelberg (2005). https://doi.org/10.1007/3-540-28901-1
16. SAE International: Guidelines for development of civil aircraft and systems (2010)
17. Schmid, K., Verlage, M.: The economic impact of product line adoption and evolution. IEEE Softw. 19(4), 50–57 (2002)
18. UK MoD: 00–56: Safety management requirements for defence systems (1996)
19. Vincentelli, A.S., Damm, W., Passerone, R.: Taming Dr. Frankenstein: contract-based design for cyber-physical systems. Eur. J. Control 18(3), 217–238 (2012)
20. Westman, J., Nyberg, M.: Preserving contract satisfiability under non-monotonic composition. In: Baier, C., Caires, L. (eds.) FORTE 2018. LNCS, vol. 10854, pp. 181–195. Springer, Cham (2018). https://doi.org/10.1007/978-3-319-92612-4_10
21. Wozniak, L., Clements, P.: How automotive engineering is taking product line engineering to the extreme. In: Proceedings of the 19th SPLC. ACM (2015)

14th International ERCIM/EWICS/ARTEMIS Workshop on Dependable Smart Embedded Cyber-Physical Systems and Systems-of-Systems (DECSoS 2019)

14th International ERCIM/EWICS/ARTEMIS Workshop on Dependable Smart Cyber-Physical Systems and Systems-of-Systems (DECSoS 2019)

European Research and Innovation Projects in the Field of Dependable Cyber-Physical Systems and Systems-of-Systems

Erwin Schoitsch[1] and Amund Skavhaug[2]

[1] Center for Digital Safety & Security, AIT Austrian Institute of Technology GmbH, Vienna, Austria
Erwin.Schoitsch@ait.ac.at
[2] Department of Mechanical and Industrial Engineering, NTNU (The Norwegian University of Science and Technology), Trondheim, Norway
Amund.Skavhaug@ntnu.no

1 Introduction

The DECSoS workshop at SAFECOMP follows already its own tradition since 2006. In the past, it focussed on the conventional type of "dependable embedded systems", covering all dependability aspects as defined by Avizienis, Lapries, Kopetz, Voges and others in IFIP WG 10.4. To put more emphasis on the relationship to physics, mechatronics and the notion of interaction with an unpredictable environment, massive deployment and highly interconnected systems of different type, the terminology changed to "cyber-physical systems" (CPS) and "Systems-of-Systems" (SoS). The new megatrend (and hype?) IoT ("Internet of Things") as a super-infrastructure for CPS as things added a new dimension with enormous challenges. Collaboration and co-operation of these systems with each other and humans, and the interplay of safety, cybersecurity, privacy (as new aspect of interest because of massive deployment in public use and "Big Data" issues), and reliability are leading to new challenges in verification, validation and certification/qualification, as these systems operate in an unpredictable environment and are themselves open, adaptive and highly automated or even (partly) autonomous. Examples are e.g. the smart power grid (power plants and power distribution and control), smart transport systems (rail, traffic management with V2V and V2I facilities, air traffic control systems), advanced manufacturing systems ("Industry 4.0"), mobile co-operating autonomous vehicles and robotic systems, smart health care, smart buildings up to smart cities and the like.

Society as a whole strongly depends on CPS and SoS - thus it is important to consider dependability (safety, reliability, availability, security, privacy, maintainability, etc.), resilience, robustness and sustainability in a holistic manner. CPS and SoS are a targeted research area in Horizon 2020 and public-private partnerships such as the ECSEL JU (Joint Undertaking) (Electronic Components and Systems for European Leadership), which integrated the former ARTEMIS (Advanced Research and Technology for Embedded Intelligence and Systems), ENIAC and EPoSS efforts. Industry and research ("private") are represented by the industrial associations ARTEMIS-IA, AENEAS (for ENIAC, semiconductor industry) and EPoSS ("Smart Systems Integration"), the public part are the EC and the national public authorities of the member states. Funding comes from the EC and the national public authorities ("tri-partite funding": EC, member states, project partners). Besides ECSEL, other JTIs (Joint Technology Initiatives), who organize their own research & innovation agenda and manage their work programs and calls as separate legal entities according to Article 187 of the Lisbon Treaty, are: Innovative Medicines Initiative (IMI), Fuel Cells and Hydrogen (FCH), Clean Sky, Bio-Based Industries, Shift2Rail and Single European Sky Air Traffic Management Research (SESAR).

Besides these Joint Undertakings there are many other so-called contractual PPPs, where funding is completely from the EC (now Horizon 2020 program only), but the work program and strategy are developed together with a private partner association, e.g. Robotics cPPP SPARC with euRobotics as private partner. Others are Factories of the Future (FoF), Energy-efficient Buildings (EeB), Sustainable Process Industry (SPIRE), European Green Vehicles Initiative (EGVI), Photonics, High Performance Computing (HPC), Advanced 5G Networks for the Future Internet (5G), the Big Data Value PPP and the cPPP for Cybersecurity Industrial Research and Innovation, and some others. These PPPs cover highly prioritized areas of European research and innovation.

2 ARTEMIS/ECSEL: The European Cyber-Physical Systems Initiative (Electronic Components and Systems)

Some ECSEL Projects which have "co-hosted" the Workshop, at least by providing Posters at a booth of the DECSOS chair from AIT, have been finished this year before Summer (see reports in last year's Springer Safecomp 2018 Workshop Proceedings, LNCS 11094). This year, mainly H2020/ECSEL projects and a few nationally funded projects are "co-hosting" the DECSOS Workshop by contributions from partners:

- AQUAS ("Aggregated Quality Assurance for Systems", (https://aquas-project.eu/),
- SECREDAS ("Product Security for Cross Domain Reliable Dependable Automated Systems"), (https://www.ecsel.eu/projects/secredas), contributing to the ECSEL Lighthouse Cluster "Mobility.E").
- Productive 4.0 ("Electronics and ICT as enabler for digital industry and optimized supply chain management covering the entire product lifecycle"), (https://productive40.eu/), (leading the ECSEL Lighthouse Projects Cluster "Industry4.E").

- iDev40 ("Integrated Development 4.0", https://www.ecsel.eu/projects/idev40), contributing to ECSEL Lighthouse Cluster "Industry4.E".
- Safe-DEED ("Safe Data-Enabled Economic Development"), a HORIZON 2020 project (https://safe-deed.eu/)
- GeniusTex (funded by German Federal Ministry for Economic Affairs and Energy (BMWi))
- SMARTEST (funded by German Federal Ministry for Economic Affairs and Energy (BMWi))

which means, that results of these projects are partially reported in presentations at the DECSoS-Workshop. Some presentations refer to work done within companies or institutes, not referring to particular public project funding.

Other important ECSEL projects in the context of DECSOS are the two large ECSEL "Lighthouse" projects for Mobility.E and for Industry4.E, which aim at providing synergies by cooperation with a group of related European projects in their area of interest, for which each of them has already in the first year organized joint project conferences:

- AutoDrive ("Advancing fail-aware, fail-safe, and fail-operational electronic components, systems, and architectures for fully automated driving to make future mobility safer, affordable, and end-user acceptable"), (https://autodrive-project.eu/), (leading project of the ECSEL Lighthouse Cluster "Mobility.E").
- Productive 4.0 ("Electronics and ICT as enabler for digital industry and optimized supply chain management covering the entire product lifecycle"), (https://productive40.eu/), (Leading project of the ECSEL Lighthouse Cluster "Industry4.E"), which was already mentioned above.

New H2020/ECSEL projects which started this or second half of last year, and may be reported about next year at this workshop or SAFECOMP 2020, are

- AfarCloud (Aggregated Farming in the Cloud, https://www.ecsel.eu/projects/afarcloud, started Sept. 2018), the only "Smart Farming" project in ECSEL context.
- ARROWHEAD Tools (European investment in digitalisation and automation solutions for the European industry, which will close the gaps that hinder the IT/OT integration by introducing new technologies in an open source platform for the design and run-time engineering of IoT and System of Systems; https://arrowhead.eu/arrowheadtools)
- Comp4Drones (Framework of key enabling technologies for safe and autonomous drones' applications, https://artemis-ia.eu/project/180-COMP4DRONES.html; starting Sept. 2019).

Short descriptions of the projects, partners, structure and technical goals and objectives are described on the project websites and the ECSEL project website (https://www.ecsel.eu/projects). See also the Acknowledgement at the end of this introduction.

3   This Year's Workshop

The workshop DECSoS'19 provides some insight into an interesting set of topics to enable fruitful discussions during the meeting and afterwards. The mixture of topics is hopefully well balanced, with a certain focus on multi-concern assurance issues (cybersecurity & safety, plus privacy, co-engineering), on safety and security analysis, and on IoT applications. Presentations are mainly based on ECSEL, Horizon 2020, and nationally funded projects mentioned above, and on industrial developments of part-ners' companies and universities. In the following explanations, the projects which at least partially funded the work presented, are mentioned.

The session starts with an introduction and overview to the ERCIM/EWICS/ARTEMIS DECSOS Workshop, setting the European Research and Innovation scene. The first session on **Safety & Security Analysis** comprises two presentations:

(1) Comparative Evaluation of Security Fuzzing Approaches *by Loui Al Sardy, Andreas Neubaum, Francesca Saglietti and Daniel Rudrich.*

This presentation compares security fuzzing approaches with respect to different characteristics commenting on their pro and cons concerning both their potential for exposing vulnerabilities and the expected effort required to do so. These pre-liminary considerations based on abstract reasoning and engineering judgement are subsequently confronted with experimental evaluations based on the application of three different fuzzing tools. Finally, an example inspired by a real-world appli cation illustrates the importance of combining different fuzzing concepts. This work was funded by BMWi (Germany) under the project SMARTEST.

(2) Assuring compliance with protection profiles with ThreatGet, *by Magdy El Sadany, Christoph Schmittner and Wolfgang Kastner.*

ThreatGet is a new tool for security analysis, based on threat modelling. The tool is integrated into a model-based engineering platform, supporting an iterative and model-based risk management process. The modelling and operation of Threat-Get, and how it can be used for security by design, is explained. As a specific use case, it is demonstrated how ThreatGet can assess compliance with a protection profile. This work was funded by the H2020/ECSEL Project AQUAS.

The second session covers **Safety/Security/Privacy Systems Co-Engineering** by three papers:

(1) A Survey on the Applicability of Safety, Security and Privacy Standards in Developing Dependable Systems, *by Lijun Shan, Behrooz Sangchoolie, Peter Folkesson, Jonny Vinter, Erwin Schoitsch, Claire Loiseaux (invited paper).*

This is an invited paper and reports on a survey on Safety, Security and Privacy standardization, conducted in context of the ECSEL project SECREDAS, and addressing the involvement of partners in standardization, use of standards, use of tools for V&V and qualification/certification, and the requirements for certification/qualification in context of their work and products.

(2) Combined Approach for Safety and Security, *by Siddhartha Verma, Thomas Gruber and Christoph Schmittner.*

The dependence and conflicts among dependability attributes (safety, security, reliability, availability etc) have become increasingly complex and are critical. They cannot be considered in isolation, therefore, combined approaches for safety, security and other attributes are required. This presentation provides a matrix based approach (inspired from ANP (Analytical Network Process)) for combined risk assessment for safety and security. This work was funded by the H2020/ECSEL Project AQUAS.

(3) Towards Integrated Quantitative Security and Safety Risk Assessment *by Jürgen Dobaj, Christoph Schmittner, Michael Krisper and Georg Macher.*

There are still existing gaps in integrated safety and security risk assessment. This presentation proposes a solution to achieve coordinated risk management by applying a quantitative security risk assessment methodology. This methodology extends established safety and security risk analysis methods with an integrated model, denoting the relationship between adversary and victim, including the used capabilities and infrastructure. This model is used to estimate the resistance strength and threat capabilities, to determine attack probabilities and security risks.

The third and last session is dedicated to **IoT Applications**, a general and diverse topic nowadays for all areas of CPS and IoT in a connected (smart) world:

(1) The session starts with a safety analysis in context of a Smart City Environment as application domain: "Potential use of safety analysis for risk assessments in Smart City Sensor network applications", *by Torge Hinrichs and Bettina Buth.*

Smart City applications strongly rely on sensor networks for the collection of data and their subsequent analysis. This presentation discusses whether methods from dependability engineering could be used to identify potential risk relating to safety and security of such applications. The use case is a sensor network for *air quality analysis* and dynamic traffic control based on these data.

(2) The second presentation covers the Health Domain: "Increasing Safety of Neural Networks in Medical Devices", *by Uwe Becker.*

In the medical devices domain neural networks are used to detect certain medical/decease indications. Although, currently medical devices mostly use neural networks to provide some guidance information or to propose some treatment or change of settings, safety and reliability of the neural network are paramount. Internal errors or influences from the environment can cause wrong inferences. This presentation will describe the experiences made and the ways used in order to both increase safety and reliability of a neural network in a medical device.

(3) The last presentation is more on a rather not safety critical, but may be in future important, issue, and is a typical IoT mass deployment application: voting by a large crowd without individual counting, but via a smart wrist band.

"Smart Wristband for Voting", *by Martin Pfatrisch, Linda Grefen and Hans Ehm.* The work was partially funded by the H2020/ECSEL projects Productive4.0, iDev40, Safe-DEED and the German BMWi project GeniusTec.

As chairpersons of the workshop, we want to thank all authors and contributors who submitted their work, Friedemann Bitsch, the SAFECOMP Publication Chair, and the members of the International Program Committee who enabled a fair evaluation through reviews and considerable improvements in many cases. We want to express our thanks to the SAFECOMP organizers, who provided us the opportunity to organize the workshop at SAFECOMP 2019 in Turku (Åbo). Particularly we want to thank the EC and national public funding authorities who made the work in the research projects possible. We do not want to forget the continued support of our companies and organizations, of ERCIM, the European Research Consortium for Informatics and Mathematics with its Working Group on Dependable Embedded Software-intensive Systems, and EWICS, the creator and main sponsor of SAFECOMP, with its working groups, who always helped us to learn from their networks.

We hope that all participants will benefit from the workshop, enjoy the conference and accompanying programs, and will join us again in the future!

Erwin Schoitsch
AIT Austrian Institute of Technology
Center for Digital Safety & Security
Vienna, Austria

Amund Skavhaug
NTNU, Norwegian University of S&T
Department of Mechanical and Industrial Engineering
Trondheim, Norway

Acknowledgements. Part of the work presented in the workshop received funding from the EC (H2020/ECSEL Joint Undertaking) and the partners National Funding Authorities ("tri-partite") through the projects AQUAS (737475), Productive4.0 (737459), AutoDrive (737469), SECREDAS (783119), iDev40 (783163) and AfarCloud (783221). Other EC funded projects are e.g. in Horizon 2020 Safe-DEED (825225). Some projects received national funding, e.g. SMARTEST and GeniusTex (Germany, BMWi), see individual acknowledgements in papers.

4   International Program Committee

Friedemann Bitsch	Thales Transportation Systems GmbH, Germany
Peter Daniel	EWICS TC7, UK
Francesco Flammini	Ansaldo; University "Federico II" of Naples, Italy
Maritta Heisel	University of Duisburg-Essen, Germany
Willibald Krenn	AIT Austrian Institute of Technology, Austria
Georg Macher	Graz University of Technology, Austria
Dejan Nickovic	AIT Austrian Institute of Technology, Austria
Frank Ortmeier	Otto-von-Guericke-University Magdeburg, Germany
Thomas Pfeiffenberger	Salzburg Research, Austria
Francesca Saglietti	University of Erlangen-Nuremberg, Germany
Christoph Schmittner	AIT Austrian Institute of Technology, Austria
Christoph Schmitz	Zühlke Engineering AG, Switzerland

Daniel Schneider   Fraunhofer IESE, Kaiserslautern, Germany
Erwin Schoitsch   AIT Austrian Institute of Technology, Austria
Amund Skavhaug   NTNU Trondheim, Norway
Mark-Alexander Sujan   University of Warwick, UK

Comparative Evaluation of Security Fuzzing Approaches

Loui Al Sardy[(⊠)], Andreas Neubaum[(⊠)], Francesca Saglietti[(⊠)],
and Daniel Rudrich

Software Engineering (Informatik 11), University of Erlangen-Nuremberg,
Martensstr. 3, 91058 Erlangen, Germany
{loui.alsardy, andreas.neubaum, francesca.saglietti,
daniel.rudrich}@fau.de

Abstract. This article compares security fuzzing approaches with respect to different characteristics commenting on their pro and cons concerning both their potential for exposing vulnerabilities and the expected effort required to do so. These preliminary considerations based on abstract reasoning and engineering judgement are subsequently confronted with experimental evaluations based on the application of three different fuzzing tools characterized by diverse data generation strategies on examples known to contain exploitable buffer overflows. Finally, an example inspired by a real-world application illustrates the importance of combining different fuzzing concepts in order to generate data in case fuzzing requires the generation of a plausible sequence of meaningful messages to be sent over a network to a software based controller as well as the exploitation of a hidden vulnerability by its execution.

Keywords: Security fuzzing · Software vulnerability · Buffer overflow ·
Integer constraint analysis · Random testing · Structural coverage

1 Introduction

Especially in case of safety-relevant applications the need for ensuring the secure behaviour of software is evident, as are the complexity and inherent limitations of such a crucial task. Several different approaches have been and are being designed, developed and applied in modern security engineering for the purpose of maximizing the chances of early detecting unsecure anomalies during a pre-operational testing phase. Such approaches suffer, however, from severe limitations.

On the one hand, in general the problem of systematically excluding the presence of security flaws may involve undecidable problems such that a definitive answer cannot be guaranteed to be derivable within affordable time via analytical reasoning. On the other hand, non-deterministic approaches as being provided by an increasing number of security fuzzers clearly have to rely on random search processes whose success depends on both the underlying data generation strategy and the significance of pre-defined stopping rules.

These crucial limitations of the current state-of-the-art in security and safety engineering build the motivation for the considerations presented in the rest of this

A. Romanovsky et al. (Eds.): SAFECOMP 2019 Workshops, LNCS 11699, pp. 49–61, 2019.
https://doi.org/10.1007/978-3-030-26250-1_4

article; it is intended to compare different existing and recently arising fuzzing concepts and approaches in terms of their expected reliability and effort and to illustrate the theoretical conclusions by concrete case studies.

2 Related Work

Security fuzzing consists of extensive testing of security-critical programs based on the repeated, automatic variation of parameter values with the purpose of exposing hidden vulnerabilities such that they can be removed before they may be exploited by users with malicious intents.

Different automatic test case generation tools denoted as fuzzers are offered on the commercial market and in the public domain sector; further testing approaches were developed within research projects. Their design may differ with respect to several properties such as the following ones.

- **The target** may be focused to the identification of predefined vulnerability classes (e.g. buffer overflows, s. [1]), or rather including the search for any kind of behavioural anomalies [5, 12, 17, 18]; obviously, a generic search allowing for the accurate detection of any weakness would be preferable, but it is likely to suffer from lower sharpness and thus lower probability of success than a process dedicated to the recognition of selected behavioural patterns.
- **Structural constraints** on data generation may be missing (e.g. [17, 18]) such as to allow for any random instantiation within a given domain, or rather define a detailed data structure [5, 12] involving syntactical constraints induced by grammar rules, or logical constraints induced by the semantics of individual elements and their relations; evidently, in the latter case generation is likely to involve a more time-consuming generation process which may be worth doing or even become necessary in order to focus the search process on meaningful data, e.g. in case they include physical properties of a power plant to be sent via message passing to a controller by plant sensors resp. by the controller to plant actuators.
- **The evolution of the generation process** may be blind in case of memory-less data mutation cycles [12], or targeted in case data generation is based on feedback provided by preceding cycles [1], typically by evaluating the degree of fulfilment of guidance conditions, as addressed below. For example, in case of genetic algorithms, evolution proceeds by measuring the *fitness* of current test data to decide which data to discharge from further consideration and which to maintain (either unchanged or modified by genetic operators like mutation or recombination), hereby aiming at learning from the past by saving genetic material considered as valuable.
- **The constraints guiding test progress** may be exhaustive in capturing necessary and sufficient logical requirements for the exposal of exploitable vulnerabilities [1], or rather simply refer to behaviour-unspecific properties reflecting the search width so far achieved [e.g. 2, 5, 12, 16–18]; in the former case guidance aims at maximizing the search depth by favouring the generation of data more likely to expose the vulnerabilities targeted, while anomaly-unspecific guidance may be limited to

the maximization of the search width so far achieved, e.g. in terms of code coverage measures achieved [2, 16–18]. Evidently, search width does not necessarily grow with the chances of success in exposing a security weakness, while search depth does in case it is correctly guided by necessary and sufficient constraints.

- **The monitoring criteria** applied to identify anomalous behaviour may be extremely generic, e.g. limited to the recognition of a crash or a hang [17, 18], or rather involve a check of finer granularity, e.g. by monitoring the movement of the instruction pointer and its effects on memory space by buffer overflowing; evidently, it is easier to implement generic monitors, but they may reveal as too superficial to unhide the effects of sophisticated attacks enabling the execution of malicious code.
- **The stopping rules** governing the termination of the search process may require the fulfilment of vulnerability-specific guidance constraints (such as those derived by integer constraint analysis (ICA), s. [1, 6, 14] and below), or just the achievement of generic search width measures determined by code coverage or time [2, 16–18]; evidently, in the former case the search stops only with the successful exposal of at least one vulnerability (but may never terminate in case of fully secure software), while in the latter case the search may stop as soon as a minimum code coverage, data amount or test time is achieved (which evidently does not necessarily coincide with a demonstration of flawlessness).

The variety of these aspects and the trade-offs between them show how complex it is to decide on which approach to rely and how much to do so. Such questions build the motivation for the conceptual comparison and for the experimental evaluation presented in the following sections.

3 Comparison of Three Fuzzing Approaches

3.1 Conceptual Comparison

In order to better illustrate the differences between fuzzing approaches and to support decision-making concerning their choice, in the following three different approaches are considered, among them, two fuzzing tools available in the public domain and an approach recently developed by part of the authors within the research project SMARTEST (s. [1]).

- **AFL** (American Fuzzy Lop [18]) is a public domain tool not specifically targeting particular vulnerability classes. Its evolution is very cursorily guided by a maximization of code coverage; in order to do so, however, the tool does not explicitly exploit knowledge derivable from the control flow structure of the application; it just favors the mutation of new data in case they contribute to increase code coverage. The tool monitors the external behavior for evident failures like crashes or hangs, it does not explicitly support the detection of internal errors induced by illegal internal memory overwriting effects.
- **Radamsa** [12] is also a mutation-based, public domain tool targeting the exposal of any kind of vulnerability. It mainly differs from AFL by the fact that data generation

evolves by mutation without any systematic guidance. In other words, the data generated is not evaluated nor favoured on the basis of a presumed fitness to evolve to better data. In particular, it does not require coverage metrics nor predicate satisfaction degrees to evaluate evolution progress. However, generation does not proceed fully randomly, it rather takes into account the input structure as well as the frequency of occurrence of input elements. Furthermore, it does not support any behavioural monitoring nor does it provide any error report; internal or external anomalous program behaviour must be made observable by additional user-defined scripts.

- **CGE** (Constraint-Guided Evolution [1]) denotes an evolutionary approach developed and implemented within the research project SMARTEST. It is dedicated to the exposal of a specific vulnerability class, namely buffer overflowing. In spite of being meanwhile well-known, the latter is still the major cause of malicious attacks, as confirmed by statistical surveys [3, 4] as well as recent accident reports [8, 14]. In order to trigger a buffer overflow, test data generation is preceded by a static code inspection based on integer constraints analysis (ICA [6, 15]). For any code instruction involving a writing access to buffer variables, two predicates can be derived: a predicate ensured to be fulfilled upon reaching, but before executing the instruction considered and a predicate reflecting the occurrence of buffer overflowing. In order to expose the potential buffer overflow during testing the conjunction of both predicates must be satisfied by appropriate test data; these are generated via genetic algorithms guided by the degree of fulfilment of the underlying constraint. For details concerning constraint-guided evolution of test data generation the reader is kindly referred to [1]. Evidently, this approach aims at maximizing search depth. In case of no finding, further values, a. o. test time, test amount or code coverage may be used as quality indicators related to search width.

The rest of this article focuses on a comparison of these three testing techniques, as each one of them represents a fundamentally different approach, namely:

- testing aimed at code coverage (AFL),
- testing based on the structure of given inputs (Radamsa),
- testing guided by genetic algorithms and aimed at the fulfilment of logical constraints (CGE).

The comparative evaluation presented in the following concerns the identification of exploitable buffer overflows; in general, the static analysis of such vulnerabilities is known to involve undecidable problems in case of loops whose number of iterations cannot be statically predetermined. For this reason, further testing approaches based on symbolic execution (s. [2, 16]) and relying on the use of classical SAT solvers are not included in the following evaluation.

Table 1 summarizes the main differences between the three approaches presented.

3.2   Experimental Evaluation

In the following, the theoretical considerations presented in the previous section will be complemented by practical experiences gained by applying the techniques mentioned

Table 1. Summary of conceptual differences between fuzzing approaches

Property / Fuzzing approach	AFL	Radamsa	CGE
Target	Generic target, exposal of any vulnerability	Generic target, exposal of any vulnerability	Specific target (buffer overflow), may be re-instantiated to allow for further targets
Input model	Generation does not use an input model	Generation takes into account input structure	Not explicitly addressed, could be included
Mutation/evolution	Evolution based on guided data mutation	Memoryless evolution by mutation based on initial data	Evolution based on genetic operators and fitness function
Guidance	Data generation guided towards maximization of code coverage	Data generation based on input structure and frequency of elements, not systematically guided	Data generation guided towards maximization of the degree of fulfilment of ICA conditions
Monitoring	Only monitoring of evident failures (such as crashes and hangs)	No tool support, user-defined by additional script	No explicit monitoring of anomalous behaviour
Stopping rule	User abortion or predefined time limit	No tool support, user-defined	Fulfilment of guiding condition or exhaustion of test time
View on SUT	Grey-box (only control flow visible)	Black-box (no code visible)	White-box (control flow and data values used)
Search strategy	Maximize search width	Random search based on initial input	Maximize search depth

on five examples provided by the following codes containing exploitable buffer overflows and requiring increasing levels of logical complexity in order to expose them:

- example 1 (Skey_Challenge [9]), example 2 (Socket_Printf [10]) and example 3 (fb_realpath [11]) were taken from the Common Vulnerabilities and Exposures Database and relate to the open source project wu-ftpd at Washington University. All of them are classified as critical, potentially enabling an attacker to gain root privileges on the system;
- example 4 (read and write [1]) and example 5 (Turing machine, s. Appendix) were designed at FAU-SWE such as to hide buffer overflow vulnerabilities posing particular difficulties in being exposed.

For each of the 5 target programs (example 1 to example 5) 5 independent initial data was randomly generated according to the constraints shown in Table 2. Each input was successively run by each tool resulting in 5 test runs for each fuzzing approach, where a test run was executed until an overflow was exposed or at the latest after 5 test hours.

Table 2. Initial data generation

Example	Input string length generation	Input string element generation
Skey_Challenge Socket_Printf fb_realpath	String length randomly generated from integer set {0,…, 1500}	Each string element randomly selected from set {a,…,z, A,…Z, 0,…9, /}
Read and write Turing machine		Each string element randomly selected from integer set {1,…, 99999}

In order to determine whether and when a buffer overflow occurred, a hardware watch point is placed after the last element of the buffer via a Linux system call *ptrace*. As soon as a buffer overflow is exposed, the control is transferred to a trap handler where a timestamp is recorded and the application is crashed. Therefore, this technique ensures the identification of arbitrary buffer overflow occurrences, even if they do not directly involve application crashes, hangs or other malicious behaviour.

The average results observed are shown in Table 3, while the details concerning the testing environment as well as the outcome of the individual test runs are reported in the Appendix, Tables A.1, A.2, A.3, A.4, A.5 and A.6. The table entries refer to execution time, in particular they do not include the preliminary static analysis required by the approach CGE.

Table 3. Summary of fuzzing results (number of successful runs, average execution time in case of detection)

Example / Fuzzer	AFL		Radamsa		CGE	
Example 1	5/5	<4 s	5/5	<1 s	5/5	<1 s
Example 2	5/5	10 m 29 s	5/5	39 s	5/5	<1 s
Example 3	0/5	n.a.	1/5	1 h 11 m 12 s	5/5	<1 s
Example 4	0/5	n.a.	0/5	n.a.	5/5	<8 s
Example 5	0/5	n.a.	0/5	n.a.	5/5	1 h 27 m 10 s

3.3 Interpretation of Experimental Results Based on Conceptual Comparison

On the whole, the results gained by experimental evaluation confirm some of the conceptual differences already highlighted, namely:

- target-generic fuzzers had less chances of exposing buffer overflow effects within the predefined time limit than the dedicated approach, especially in case of complex buffering logic;
- except for the particularly simple case Skey_Challenge, target-generic fuzzers – when successful – took longer to expose buffer overflow effects than the dedicated approach.

The superiority of the dedicated approach CGE in both success rate and execution time is explainable by the theoretical background provided by ICA which enables the search to target exactly those input data with maximal chances to expose the vulnerability. On the other hand, this approach requires additional effort in order to derive manually the constraints guiding test data generation. In addition, the scope of this approach is currently limited to the detection of buffer overflow effects, although its search pattern could be re-instantiated such as to cope with further vulnerabilities.

Focusing on the two general purpose tools it can be noticed that for the non-obvious examples Radamsa performed better and faster than AFL. Considering in more detail example-specific differences leads to the following insight:

- in case of example 1 resp. example 2, coverage maximization can be achieved very fast (by 1 or 2 run(s)) and the buffer overflow is triggered by sufficiently large data. These requirements are easily fulfilled by AFL and Radamsa;
- example 3 requires an input path with the exact length MAXPATHLEN + 1 (any further increase in path length results in a regular program termination). By its capability to introduce minor changes (also in length) to the original input structure, the tool Radamsa has better chances than AFL of triggering the buffer overflow. In addition, AFL is likely to waste search effort by targeting the coverage of branches which are not traversable during regular operation (e.g. due to exception handling);
- example 4 is characterized by increasing the number of elements in the buffer only in case of alternatingly increasing and decreasing input values; on the other hand, example 5 requires a. o. to assign a very specific value to at least one array element. In both cases the selection of data triggering the buffer overflow should address conceptual levels going beyond mere control flow and input structure, i.e. trespassing the limitations posed by AFL and Radamsa.

4 Combination of Different Fuzzing Approaches

4.1 Networked Applications

The experimental evaluation endorsed by the theoretical considerations illustrated above may lead to the conclusion that the CGE testing approach alone may be sufficient to cope with arbitrary buffer over- resp. underflowing vulnerabilities. In spite of the promising results gained so far, such a conclusion would be misleading when considering a wider user-machine context than done so far.

In fact, in case of networked applications (e.g. automatically controlled power plants) the inputs capturing current physical plant properties as measured by appropriate sensors reach the controlling software by consecutive messages sent over a network; similarly, the responses of the controller are sent to corresponding actuators.

Such networks might be misused for the purpose of triggering unsafe plant behaviour by manipulation, deletion or replacement of messages.

In order to test for the potential of such attacks, the search for data must be much more sophisticated than before, as messages must comply to several types of constraints (e.g. protocol-specific input format, physical properties referring to trends and plausibility, consistency among redundant sensors, s. [13]) in order to avoid being discharged by the communication medium or by the controller before the vulnerability is triggered. Therefore, an analysis of exploitable flaws within a networked application has to extend a well-founded code-based search by a meaningful model of valid messages. An example is shortly summarized in the next sub-section.

4.2   Example

The peculiarities of networked, automatically controlled applications will be illustrated via a simplified model of a distillation plant inspired by [7], where the model behaviour is restricted to a kernel functionality excluding the following (in general relevant) aspects from further consideration:

- the automatic control of the coolant flow;
- the measurement of the distillate temperature used to control the coolant flow;
- the automatic control of the filling level in the boiling vessel, assuming the filling might be done manually, if required;
- the final bottling of the resulting distillate.

Based on these simplifications, the inputs cyclically reaching the control software by message passing consist of the following data:

- the pressure P in the boiling vessel;
- the temperature T in the boiling vessel;
- the filling level F of the distillate collecting tank.

Based on this information, the software-based controller monitors successive pressure values and supervises their fluctuation by continuously checking their trends. In particular, it checks for the plausibility of the messages received by evaluating the fulfilment of the following physical constraints:

- constraints on the absolute value of each cyclic measurement of P, T and F which must be bounded by predefined critical pressure and temperature limits as well as by the maximum filling level of the collecting tank;
- constraints on the change of rate of individual parameters, e.g. by requiring an increase of temperature per second lower than 2 °C;
- constraints on the quantitative relation between parameters, e.g. by requiring the level increase ΔF in the distillate collecting tank to correspond to the volume of water evaporated in the boiling vessel under given temperature T and pressure P.

In addition to these physical constraints, message generation must also comply to

- protocol-based constraints enabling the communication of the messages over the network, e.g. concerning message number, sender, receiver, read/write operations, sensor values, sensor status, checksum, etc.

In order to exclude critical insider attacks during operation, their potential has to be evaluated by a sound security-targeted testing phase. This demands in particular for an accurate input model enriched by an appropriate constraint language. Based on such a model, constrained data generation may be used to yield plausible test message sequences, at the same time enforcing the fluctuation of at least one of the process parameters, hereby supporting the early identification of exploitable vulnerabilities.

5 Summary and Conclusions

This article illustrated the differences between some existing fuzzing approaches by particularly highlighting their major properties, a.o.

- the target they pursue,
- whether or not they rely upon an initial input structure,
- whether successively generated data evolves on the basis of experience gained with previously generated data or rather in a memory-less way,
- which guidance, if any, systematically supports evolution,
- which indicator(s), if any, provide(s) orientation to evolution,
- which instruments monitor behaviour such as to ensure observability of malicious behaviour;
- which criteria are used to stop the search process.

The approaches may differ in particular w.r.t. their view on the subject under test which may be black-, grey- or white-box as well as in the strategy driving search which may be random-, width- or depth-based.

Such differences were illustrated by means of three existing approaches successively applied to 5 examples. The quantitative results were subsequently commented upon in the light of the theoretical differences previously illustrated. They highlight the complementarity of dedicated test approaches focused on particular vulnerability classes and of generic test approaches targeting the exposal of arbitrary vulnerabilities.

Finally, the user-machine context so far considered was extended to include software executing input messages sent over a network. Malicious attacks based on the generation and circulation of forged messages exposing software vulnerabilities while maintaining message trustworthiness captured by syntactic and semantic constraints were considered. It was argued that in such cases the fuzzing approach should combine mutation-based search techniques with a sound input model enriched by an appropriate constraint language.

Acknowledgment. The authors gratefully acknowledge that part of the work presented was supported by the German Federal Ministry for Economic Affairs and Energy (BMWi), project SMARTEST.

Appendix

Table A.1. System environment

Host	OS: Windows 7 Enterprise 64 bit
	CPU: Intel (R) Core (TM) i5-4590 CPU, 3.30 GHz, 4 cores, RAM: 16 GB
Guest	OS: Ubuntu 18.04.1 LTS 64 bit, Kernel: 4.18.20, RAM: 2 GB

Table A.2. Execution time for overflow detection for example 1

Run / Tool	AFL	Radamsa	CGE
Run 1	<1 s	<1 s	<1 s
Run 2	<1 s	<1 s	<1 s
Run 3	<1 s	<1 s	<1 s
Run 4	<1 s	<1 s	<1 s
Run 5	12 s	<1 s	<1 s
Average time	<4 s	<1 s	<1 s

Table A.3. Execution time to overflow detection for example 2

Run / Tool	AFL	Radamsa	CGE
Run 1	10 m 10 s	7 s	<1 s
Run 2	10 m 16 s	1 s	<1 s
Run 3	10 m 33 s	2 m 52 s	<1 s
Run 4	10 m 15 s	9 s	<1 s
Run 5	11 m 11 s	6 s	<1 s
Average time	10 m 29 s	39 s	<1 s

Table A.4.   Execution time to overflow detection for example 3

Run / Tool	AFL	Radamsa	CGE
Run 1	No detection	No detection	<1 s
Run 2	No detection	1 h 11 m 12 s	<1 s
Run 3	No detection	No detection	<1 s
Run 4	No detection	No detection	<1 s
Run 5	No detection	No detection	<1 s

Table A.5.   Execution time to overflow detection for example 4:

Run / Tool	AFL	Radamsa	CGE
Run 1	No detection	No detection	<3 s
Run 2	No detection	No detection	<2 s
Run 3	No detection	No detection	<3 s
Run 4	No detection	No detection	<7 s
Run 5	No detection	No detection	<23 s
Average time in case of success	n.a.	n.a.	<8 s

Table A.6.   Execution time to overflow detection for example 5:

Run / Tool	AFL	Radamsa	CGE
Run 1	No detection	No detection	49 m 59 s
Run 2	No detection	No detection	39 m 38 s
Run 3	No detection	No detection	2 h 55 m 35 s
Run 4	No detection	No detection	1 h 58 m 56 s
Run 5	No detection	No detection	51 m 42 s
Average time in case of success	n.a.	n.a.	1 h 27 m 10 s

```c
#define MEML 50000
#define PARL 256

int mem[MEML];
int list[128];
int listFillLevel = 0;

void process2(unsigned int next) {
        if (next != 500) {
                list[listFillLevel] = next;
                if (listFillLevel < 127)
                        listFillLevel++;

                return;
        }

        for (int i = 0; i < MEML; i++)
                mem[i] = 0;

        int p = 0;
        while (list[p] != 0) {
                int c = list[p] % 10;

                switch (c) {
                  case 1: {
                        int r = list[++p] % PARL;
                        int a = list[++p] % PARL;
                        int c = list[++p] % PARL;
                        printf("%3i: ADD %i, %i, %i\n", p - 3, r, a, c);
                        mem[r] = mem[a] + c;
                        ++p;
                        break;
                  } case 2: {
                        int r = list[++p] % PARL;
                        printf("%3i: DEC %i\n", p - 1, r);
                        mem[r] = mem[r] - 1;
                        ++p;
                        break;
                  } case 3: {
                        int v = list[++p] % PARL;
                        int t = list[++p] % PARL;
                        int f = list[++p] % PARL;
                        printf("%3i: JMP %i, %i, %i\n", p - 3, v, t, f);
                        if (mem[v] == 0) {
                                int i = mem[t];
                                mem[i] = 1;
                                ++p;
                        }
                        else p = f;
                        break;
                  } default: p = (p + 1);
                }
        }
}
```

Code of example 5 (Turing machine)

References

1. Al Sardy, L., Saglietti, F., Tang, T., Sonnenberg, H.: Constraint-based testing for buffer overflows. In: Gallina, B., Skavhaug, A., Schoitsch, E., Bitsch, F. (eds.) SAFECOMP 2018. LNCS, vol. 11094, pp. 99–111. Springer, Cham (2018). https://doi.org/10.1007/978-3-319-99229-7_10
2. Cadar, C., Dunbar, D., Engler, D.: KLEE: unassisted and automatic generation of high-coverage tests for complex systems programs. In: USENIX Symposium on Operating Systems Design and Implementation (OSDI 2008). USENIX Association (2008)
3. Cisco: Most Common CWE Vulnerabilities, annual cybersecurity report (2018)
4. Cisco: CWE threat category activity, midyear security report (2015)
5. Eddington, M.: Peach Fuzzer (2019). http://peachfuzzer.com/
6. Evans, D., Larochelle, D.: Improving security using extensible lightweight static analysis. IEEE Softw. 19, 42–51 (2002). https://doi.org/10.1109/52.976940
7. Makarov, A., Billowie, O.: Steuerung einer Destillationsanlage, interner Bericht. Hochschule Magdeburg-Stendal, Fachbereich IWID, Institut für Elektrotechnik (2008)
8. MITRE Corporation: A buffer overflow vulnerability in WhatsApp VOIP stack allowed remote code execution via specially crafted series of SRTCP packets sent to a target phone number, Common Vulnerabilities and Exposures Database (CVE), CVE-2019-3568 (2019)
9. MITRE Corporation: Buffer overflow in the skey_challenge function in ftpd.c for wu-ftp daemon (wu-ftpd) 2.6.2, Common Vulnerabilities and Exposures Database (CVE), CVE-2004-0185 (2004)
10. MITRE Corporation: Buffer overflow in the SockPrintf function in wu-ftpd 2.6.2, Common Vulnerabilities and Exposures Database (CVE), CVE-2003-1327 (2003)
11. MITRE Corporation: Off-by-one Error in fb_realpath(), Common Vulnerabilities and Exposures Database (CVE), CVE-2003-0466 (2003)
12. Oulu University Secure Programming Group (OUSPG): Radamsa (2010). https://www.ee.oulu.fi/roles/ouspg/Radamsa
13. Saglietti, F., Meitner, M., von Wardenburg, L., Richthammer, V.: Analysis of informed attacks and appropriate countermeasures for cyber-physical systems. In: Skavhaug, A., Guiochet, J., Schoitsch, E., Bitsch, F. (eds.) SAFECOMP 2016. LNCS, vol. 9923, pp. 222–233. Springer, Cham (2016). https://doi.org/10.1007/978-3-319-45480-1_18
14. Schneider Electric Software Security Response Center: InduSoft Web Studio and InTouch Machine Edition – Remote Code Execution Vulnerability, Security Bulletin LFSEC00000125 (2018)
15. Shahriar, H., Zulkernine, M.: Classification of static analysis-based buffer overflow detectors. In: 4th International Conference on Secure Software Integration and Reliability Improvement Companion (SSIRI-C). IEEE (2010). https://doi.org/10.1109/ssiri-c.2010.28
16. Shoshitaishvili, Y., Wang, R., et al.: (State of) the art of war: offensive techniques in binary analysis. In: IEEE Symposium on Security and Privacy. IEEE (2016)
17. Swiecki, R.: Hongfuzz (2018). www.github.com/google/hongfuzz
18. Zalewski, M.: American Fuzzy Lop (AFL) (2017). http://lcamtuf.coredump.cx/afl/

Assuring Compliance with Protection Profiles with ThreatGet

Magdy El Sadany[1,2], Christoph Schmittner[1(✉)], and Wolfgang Kastner[2]

[1] Austrian Institute of Technology, Giefinggasse 4, 1210 Vienna, Austria
christoph.schmittner@ait.ac.at
[2] Automation Systems Group, TU Wien, Vienna, Austria

Abstract. We present ThreatGet a new tool for security analysis, based on threat modeling. The tool is integrated into a model-based engineering platform, supporting an iterative and model-based risk management process. We explain the modeling and operation of ThreatGet and how it can be used for security by design. As a specific use case, we demonstrate how ThreatGet can assess compliance with a protection profile.

Keywords: ThreatGet · Protection profiles · Threat analysis

1 Introduction

In recent years, we have experienced a rapid development of technology. More and more application areas are moving towards an Internet-like architecture. The basic building blocks are shifting from humans towards measuring devices, sensors, controllers and actuators, interconnected by a diverse set of communication technologies. Platforms aggregate data and optimize control strategies. The behavior is changing from "Internet of People" to "Internet of Things (IoT)". These developments are one of the core causes behind ongoing developments towards smart production, smart mobility, smart cities and smart communities. Due to the potential impact on all areas of live, we need to ensure that we can trust and rely on these systems and their interactions [1].

As an example, IoT is one of the building blocks for future projects in smart transportation such as cooperative and automated vehicles. Vehicles are already composed of interconnected sensors, control units and actuators. In the future, vehicles and the transportation infrastructure will form a network on their own, ending up in an intelligent transportation system (ITS). Platforms in the ITS will collect information from road users and the environment, extend the perception horizon to avoid accidents and optimize traffic flow. Such a system, the nature of control over traffic behavior and the collected personal data require a systematic consideration of security. Due to the complexity and interconnectivity of these systems, security needs to be integrated into the engineering workflow from the very beginning by following the principle of "security by design". Supporting "security by design" is a consistent and iterative approach towards risk management.

© Springer Nature Switzerland AG 2019
A. Romanovsky et al. (Eds.): SAFECOMP 2019 Workshops, LNCS 11699, pp. 62–73, 2019.
https://doi.org/10.1007/978-3-030-26250-1_5

A generic approach to managing any type of risk is defined in ISO3100:2018. Here, an iterative process is proposed, consisting of the following steps [7]:

- Defining the scope
- Assessing the risk
  1. Risk identification
  2. Risk analysis
  3. Risk evaluation
- Risk treatment

This guidance is refined by ISO27005:2018 for security risk management, following the same basic process. For the identification of risks, a process of identifying the assets, followed by identifying the threats is proposed. One suggested approach towards threat identification is the usage of threat catalogues [8].

This paper presents an automated and model-based threat identification, based on formally specified threat catalogues. We demonstrate a potential application for assuring the compliance with protection profiles, demonstrating how threat modeling can be used iteratively through the engineering process.

2   State-of-the-Art

In addition to ISO 31000 which defines the generic risk management framework, ISO31010:2009 presents an overview about techniques for risk management. Due to the generic nature, not all recommended methods are usable for security risks. Recommended and suitable methods include brainstorming, check-lists or scenario-based methods. Most of them are rather unsystematic and handled in a subjective manner [9].

Threat modeling addresses these issues by defining an abstract model of threats, which is applied to a system to identify potential threats for this system. It was integrated into the Microsoft Secure Development Lifecycle. Microsoft published a Threat Modeling Tool as a plug-in for "Visio" [2].

There are a number of software tools available to support the threat modeling process. Table 1 gives an overview about the available solutions.

While the implementation and approach differ between the tools, none of them was developed for embedded/IoT and none of the solutions is easily integrated into model-based engineering. Overall, these issues led to the development of a prototype threat model in Enterprise Architect (EA) by the Austrian Institute of Technology (AIT). The tool was optimized as part of a bachelor thesis at Vienna University of Technology [10].

3   ThreatGet

ThreatGet is a tool that recognizes, understands and identifies the potential negative actions. It is based on Enterprise Architect developed and maintained by Sparx System [3]. EA is a widely used platform for model-based

Table 1. Overview about available threat modeling solutions

Name	License	Platform	System model	Threat model	Domain
Threat modeling tool [11]	Free	Plugin for visio	Data flow diagram (visio)	extendable STRIDE	Web, cloud
IriusRisk [12]	Free community, commercial	Stand alone	Questionnaires	Risk pattern libraries	Software
ThreatModeler [13]	Commercial	Stand alone	Data flow diagram	Vast	Enterprise systems, app
PyTM [14]	Open source	Stand alone	Data flow diagram, sequence diagram	extendable Threat model	Web, cloud
SecuriCAD [15]	Free community, commercial	Stand alone	System architecture	Attack simulations	Enterprise
SD elements [16]	Commercial	Stand alone	Requirements, questionnaire	Threat model	Software
Tutamantic [17]	Commercial	Web-based as a service	Data flow diagram (visio)	Threat model	Software
OWASP threat dragon project [18]	Open source	Web-based	System diagram	Threat model	Web, cloud
Mozilla SeaSponge [19]	Open source	Web-based	System diagram	Threat model	Web, cloud

systems engineering. This integration allows ThreatGet to be used through the engineering workflow and applied iteratively. ThreatGet examines the models, charts, objects, and connections in the system for subsequent threat analysis and risk analysis. The available system elements in ThreatGet are divided into these basic categories:

- Actor,
- Sensor,
- Vehicle Unit,
- Data Store,
- Communication Interface,
- Communication Flow

Both the objects and the connections already have the corresponding properties (called tagged values in EA) when they are created. Tagged values are used to describe security and analysis relevant properties for elements. Predefined elements have a set of proposed tagged values. However, the extension of these properties is possible and thus it is feasible that the user customizes the properties. In addition to the properties, there is a database in the background that contains the objects. This allows the list of elements to be extendable by the user.

The further functionality and the sequence of the ThreatGet operation will be explained on the basis of an example of a generic interaction in a vehicle.

3.1 Application Example

As shown in Fig. 1, the connections in ThreatGet are directed connections.

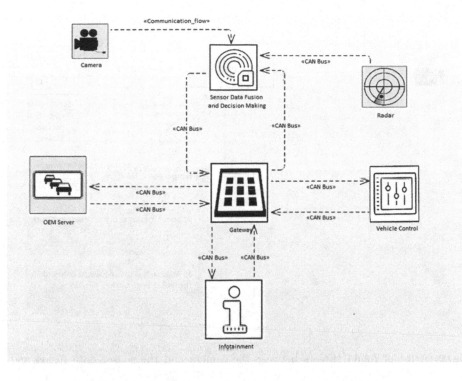

Fig. 1. A generic interaction in an autonomous vehicle

The example involves a data flow between the objects transmitted through directed communications. The camera and the radar pick up the data from an external environment and pass it on to the "Sensor Data Fusion and Desicion Making" unit. The data is transmitted to the gateway. The gateway unit then collects the data from different locations and then forwards it to "Vehicle Unit". The VU then uses the data to control and then responds with a result that is sent to the remaining units.

Through the use of directed connections, it is also possible to define information source and sinks. Thus, it is possible to check whether a message can be attacked or not. In the first step of the analysis, a separate diagram with the corresponding possible threats is created for all pairs of objects which are connected. In our example, ten diagrams are generated. Figure 2 shows one of them.

Once all diagrams have been created, an overview of all threats is automatically derived. Here the diagram of the selected connection is displayed on the left side. All threats are presented in the form of a table on the right side of the overview. The displayed diagram on the left side is a dynamic representation, thus the diagram will change, depending on which threat is selected. The table is also dynamic, and the evaluation of each threat can be adapted. Below the table is a summary of the risk assessment. In ThreatGet, we differentiate between

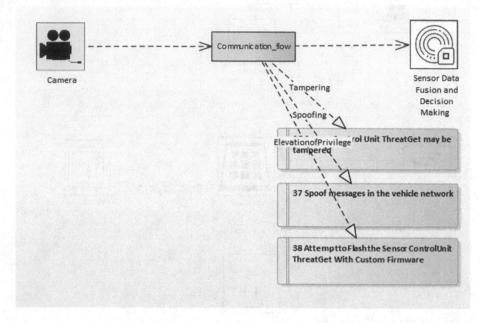

Fig. 2. A list of found threats between the camera and the sensor data fusion and decision making.

automatic and manual risk evaluation. The automatic risk evaluation includes values suggested by ThreatGet. These values can be adapted by the user in a manual risk evaluation.

For rating impact we use the following levels:

- Trivial,
- Minor,
- Moderate,
- Major,
- Critical.

And the likelihood is divided into:

- Remote,
- Unlikely,
- Possible,
- Likely,
- Certain.

ThreatGet allows to export the results as a report. When creating a report, the user is free to include the complete analysis or a specific selection in the report. This has the advantage that only relevant information is displayed in the report. The format of the report can be in different filetypes, such as rtf,

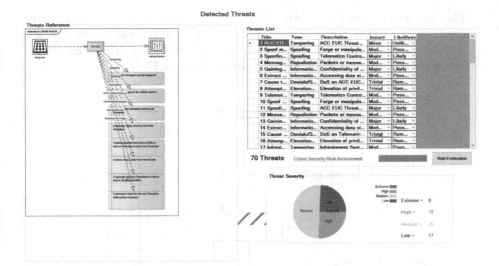

Fig. 3. Overview of the found threats with the diagram on the left side, the table on the right side, and the risk analysis below

docx or pdf. The documentation also describes the connection, its description, the identified threats and the risk level (Fig. 3).

The dynamic extension of ThreatGet makes it possible to check a system for different security standards and threat databases without much effort. This allows a parallel refinement of the system during development and the applied threat database. As an example, we demonstrate applying ThreatGet to show compliance with a set of security requirements.

4   Case Study: Protetction Profile for a Digital Tachograph

In the case study, we will demonstrate how ThreatGet can be used to show compliance with the protetction profile for a Digital Tachograph – Vehicle Unit (VU PP) of 2016 [5].

4.1   Common Criteria

The Common Criteria (CC) aims at defining a structured way to (a) describe security needs and (b) evaluate if this security needs are addressed. CC is aimed at three groups of users.

- Developers
- Reviewers
- Consumers

The protection profiles set the minimum dimensions to an agreed and required minimum. The protection profiles contain certain security requirements for a specific system and define it as a Target of Evaluation (ToE). Examples and overview of such protection profiles can be found in Fig. 4.

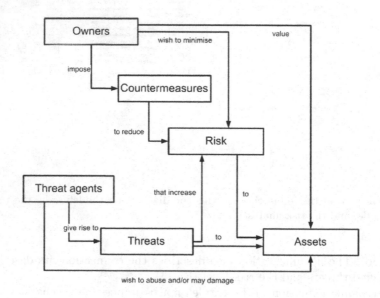

Fig. 4. Structure of a CC model

A system possesses certain assets which are of value for the system owner. These assets are endangered by threat agents. Threat agents cause threats to the system which is aimed at the assets and posses a certain risk which the system owner would like to mitigate. This is done by certain countermeasures. A protection profile describes the system/application under consideration with its assets as target of evaluation (ToE). For this system and its assets the considered threat agents and, based on the threat agents and assets, the threats are described. Based on this, a security concept and security requirements are defined. This is done based on a set of security functional requirements (SFR). In order to assure that this level of security is also achieved. Security assurance requirements (SAR) are also available.

4.2 Protection Profiles for a Digital Tachograph – Vehicle Unit (VU PP)

A protection profiles defines a generic security concept, based on a high-level description of threats. Threat modeling allows to a) model the describes security problems (threats) but also the proposed security functional requirements. We present here the transformation of two SFR into rules in ThreatGet (Fig. 5).

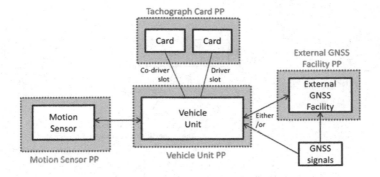

Fig. 5. Protection profiles context [5]

FDP_ACF.1.2(5:IS)

"The TSF shall enforce the following rules to determine if an operation among controlled subjects and controlled objects is allowed:" [5]

- "the vehicle unit shall ensure that data related to vehicle motion, the real-time clock, recording equipment calibration parameters, tachograph cards and human user's inputs may only be processed from the right input sources" [5]

FDP ACF.1.2(5:IS) requires as technical measures that communication between the mentioned elements and to the mentioned elements is authenticated and validated. In our example, we show the communication between the vehicle unit and the real-time clock. The system is shown in Fig. 6. The undirected connection is replaced by two directional connections. In Fig. 7, the result of the operation is visible. ThreatGet points to the missing security properties for the system and identifies missing measures in the security concept.

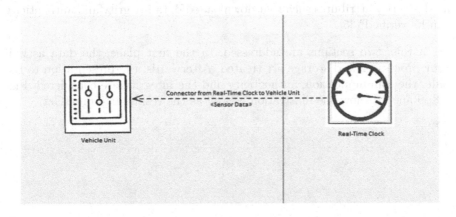

Fig. 6. Communication between the real-time clock and a VU

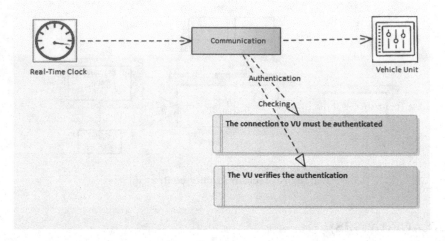

Fig. 7. Result of ThreatGet operation

FDP_ETC.2.4

"The TSF shall enforce the following rules when user data is exported from the TOE [5]":

- "tachograph cards data update shall be such that, when needed and taking into account card actual storage capacity, most recent data replace oldest data" [5],
- "the vehicle unit shall export data to tachograph cards with associated security attributes such that the card will be able to verify its integrity and authenticity" [5],
- "the vehicle unit shall download data to external storage media with associated security attributes such that downloaded data integrity and authenticity can be verified" [5].

As a rule, two sections are addressed. In the first place, the data as well as your processing and storage are treated. Afterwards, the presentation to the outside, the communication, authenticity and the integrity are considered. Figures 8, 9 and 10 show the illustration as well as the results in ThreatGet.

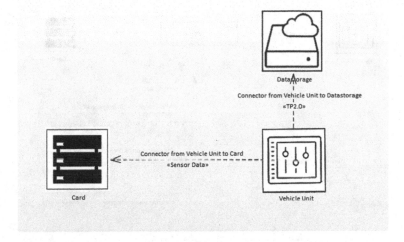

Fig. 8. Communication between the VU, card and the data storage

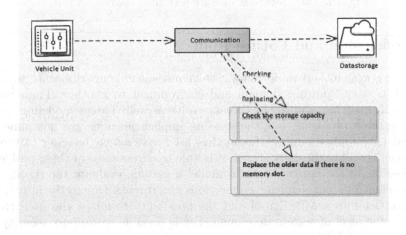

Fig. 9. ThreatGet operation illustrates the first rule

4.3 Evaluation

The tool helps to safe cost and time, that make analyzing for a huge number of vehicular units in a short time to define the common security weaknesses in the vehicle. That helps to identify a massive amount of potential threats which are threaten the security mechanism of a vehicle in the early stages of the development life-cycle process to conclude the security-by-design.

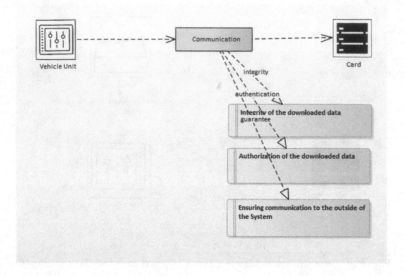

Fig. 10. The ThreatGet operation clarifies the second rule

5   Conclusion and Future Plan

Modeling a system and performing risk management is an elaborate topic as the threats vary from one domain and environment to another. The systems are steadily evolving, and so the threats evolve as well. Threat modeling is able to tackle these problems, but the existing implementations are not aimed at IoT and have limited support for model-based systems engineering. Although ThreatGet is still in the early stages, it is able to adress some of these problems. It is possible in the current state to model a system, evaluate the results and also to define different elements, connections and threats. Due to the integration of ThreatGet into a MBSE tool and the possibility to adapt the used threat model to the level of system development it is possible to support security-by-design in a model-driven development process in different application domains. We demonstrated here one way to do this by showing how ThreatGet can be used to check security functional requirements from the Common Criteria.

Acknowledgments. The work published here has received funding from the AQUAS project, under grant agreement No. 737475. The project is co-funded by grants from Austria, the Czech republic, Germany, Italy, France, Spain, The UK, and ECSEL JU.

References

1. Checkoway, S. et al.: Comprehensive experimental analyses of automotive attack surfaces. In: USENIX Security Symposium (2011)
2. Swiderski, Frank, Snyder, Window: Threat Modeling (Microsoft Professional), vol. 7. Microsoft Press, Sebastopol (2014)

3. parxSystems. http://sparxsystems.com/products/ea/. Accessed 30 Oct 2018
4. Shaaban, A.M., Schmittner, C.: Security chain tool for IoT secure applications. Austrian Institute of Technology – Digital Safety and Security (2019)
5. Bundesamtfür Sicherheit in der Informationstechnik. Digital tachograph - vehicle unit (VU PP). https://www.bsi.bund.de. Accessed 01 May 2019
6. Shaaban, A.M., Schmittner, C., Latzenhofer, M., Hofer, M.: Contribution title. A proposal for a comprehensive automotive cybersecurity reference architecture. In: The Seventh International Conference on Advances in Vehicular Systems, Technologies and Applications (2018)
7. ISO: ISO 31000 - Risk management - guidelines (2018)
8. ISO/IEC: Information technology – Security techniques – Information security risk management (2018)
9. IEC 31010: Risk management – Risk assessment techniques. Pub. L. No. IEC 31010 (2009)
10. Ramos, A.L., Ferreira, J.V., Barcelo, J.: Model-based systems engineering: an emerging approach for modern systems. IEEE Trans. Syst. Man Cybern. Part C (Appl. Rev.) **42**(1), 101–111 (2012). https://doi.org/10.1109/TSMCC.2011.2106495. Accessed 01 May 2019
11. Microsoft Threat Modeling Tool 2016. https://www.microsoft.com/en-us/download/details.aspx?id=49168. Accessed 01 May 2019
12. Threat Modeling at the speed of DevOps. https://continuumsecurity.net/. Accessed 01 May 2019
13. threatmodeler https://threatmodeler.com/. Accessed 01 May 2019
14. A Pythonic framework for threat modeling. https://github.com/izar/pytm. Accessed 01 May 2019
15. Automated Threat Modeling and Attack Simulations. https://www.foreseeti.com/. Accessed 01 May 2019
16. Security Compass - SDElements. https://www.securitycompass.com/sdelements/. Accessed 01 May 2019
17. Tutamantic. http://www.tutamantic.com/. Accessed 01 May 2019
18. OWASP Threat Dragon. https://www.owasp.org. Accessed 01 May 2019
19. Threat modelling tool from Mozilla. https://github.com/mozilla/seasponge. Accessed 01 May 2019

A Survey on the Applicability of Safety, Security and Privacy Standards in Developing Dependable Systems

Lijun Shan[1], Behrooz Sangchoolie[2(✉)], Peter Folkesson[2],
Jonny Vinter[2], Erwin Schoitsch[3], and Claire Loiseaux[1]

[1] Internet of Trust, Paris, France
{lijun.shan,claire.loiseaux}@internetoftrust.com
[2] RISE Research Institutes of Sweden, Borås, Sweden
{behrooz.sangchoolie,peter.folkesson,
jonny.vinter}@ri.se
[3] Austrian Institute of Technology, Vienna, Austria
Erwin.schoitsch@ait.ac.at

Abstract. Safety-critical systems are required to comply with safety standards. These systems are increasingly digitized and networked to an extent where they need to also comply with security and privacy standards. This paper aims to provide insights into how practitioners apply the standards on safety, security or privacy (Sa/Se/Pr), as well as how they employ Sa/Se/Pr analysis methodologies and software tools to meet such criteria. To this end, we conducted a questionnaire-based survey within the participants of an EU project SECREDAS and obtained 21 responses. The results of our survey indicate that safety standards are widely applied by product and service providers, driven by the requirements from clients or regulators/authorities. When it comes to security standards, practitioners face a wider range of standards while few target specific industrial sectors. Some standards linking safety and security engineering are not widely used at the moment, or practitioners are not aware of this feature. For privacy engineering, the availability and usage of standards, analysis methodologies and software tools are relatively weaker than for safety and security, reflecting the fact that privacy engineering is an emerging concern for practitioners.

Keywords: Safety · Security · Privacy · Standards · Dependable systems

1 Introduction

In safety-critical industrial sectors such as automotive, rail and health, automated systems need to conform to safety criteria which are usually specified in the form of safety standards. For example, IEC 61508, titled Functional Safety of Electrical/Electronic/Programmable Electronic Safety-related Systems [1], is the basic functional safety standard applicable to many kinds of industry. As products in such domains are increasingly computerized, networked and personalized, they need to meet criteria on information security and user privacy which are specified by security and privacy standards.

© Springer Nature Switzerland AG 2019
A. Romanovsky et al. (Eds.): SAFECOMP 2019 Workshops, LNCS 11699, pp. 74–86, 2019.
https://doi.org/10.1007/978-3-030-26250-1_6

Compared to safety standards, the practice of security and privacy standards in the industrial sectors is more recent. The practitioners, i.e. organizations who apply the standards in developing products or services, face a wide scope of security/privacy standards originally targeted at IT systems. Meanwhile, new security/privacy standards for specific industrial sectors are emerging. Given various standards with different origins published by diverse standardization organizations, for the practitioners it is not obvious which standards are available or under development, which ones they should comply with, and what are the benefits of conforming to the standards. For the developers of the standards, it is also not evident how well the standards are accepted by the practitioners and other stakeholders.

The main objective of this paper is to provide new insights into practitioners' usage and perspectives regarding the standards on safety or security or privacy (Sa/Se/Pr). For this purpose, an empirical study has been conducted in the form of a questionnaire-based survey during the course of an EU ECSEL Joint Undertaking project called SECREDAS [2]. The project deals with product security and safety for dependable automated systems in the domains of automotive, railway and health. The consortium consists of 69 academic or industrial partners from 15 countries. Our questionnaire solicited their feedback on how they apply relevant standards, and how they employ analysis methodologies or tools in their daily work to meet Sa/Se/Pr criteria. With 21 valid responses, we conducted an analysis to answer a set of intended research questions.

The results of the survey, both qualitatively and quantitatively, can help practitioners, researchers, standardization bodies and other stakeholders to view the overall status of Sa/Se/Pr engineering of dependable automated systems. The qualitative result of our study is a wide spectrum of applicable standards, assessment methodologies and software tools. This result may help practitioners to perceive the state-of-the-art of both the Sa/Se/Pr criteria and the available engineering methods/tools to meet the criteria. The quantitative analysis reveals the practices of various standards, methodologies and software tools, which helps potential users of the standards/methods/tools to focus on the most influential ones. For the developers of the standards/methodologies/tools, the results indicate the effects of their work and the interests of the practitioners.

2 Research Method

This section presents the research questions, survey design, data collection and analysis, as well as the threats to validity of our survey.

2.1 Research Questions

The survey covers three inter-related themes on Sa/Se/Pr engineering: technical standards, analysis methodologies, and COTS (Commercial Off-The-Shelf) software tools. There are some overlaps between standards and methodologies, as certain standards refer to existing methodologies as guidance for performing specific activities. For example, SAE J3061 [3], titled Cybersecurity Guidebook for Cyber-Physical Vehicle Systems, specifies a security engineering process for automotive systems. For security risk analysis, which is an iterative activity during the security engineering process, SAE

J3061 recommends a number of applicable methodologies e.g. EVITA [4], TVRA [5], OCTAVE [6] and HEAVENS [7]. Nevertheless, such methodologies can be applied independent of the standard, and vice versa.

Within the scope of this paper, we formulated the following research questions (RQs).

- *RQ1*. What standards are applicable for Sa/Se/Pr engineering of dependable systems and what are the differences (if any) between the availability of safety, security and privacy standards?
- *RQ2*. How are the Sa/Se/Pr standards practiced?
- *RQ3*. How do the practitioners follow the Sa/Se/Pr analysis methodologies?
- *RQ4*. How do the practitioners employ Sa/Se/Pr engineering tools?

2.2 Survey Design

Our questionnaire consists of an introduction to the purpose of the study and 5 sections with 17 questions in total[1]. The standards under study are grouped into 8 categories according to the targeted industrial sectors and their subjects in terms of Sa/Se/Pr, as shown in Fig. 1, where "cross-domain" refers to the standards applicable to various industrial sectors. We excluded security boxes from the Rail and Health domains as security is only partially addressed in these domains.

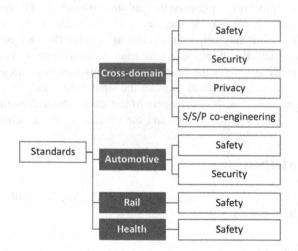

Fig. 1. Categories of the standards under study

---

[1] The questionnaire could be found at:
  http://www.internetoftrust.com/wp-content/uploads/2019/06/Secredas_Questionnaire_Standards_public.pdf.

2.3   Data Collection

The target population of the survey are SECREDAS participants, who conduct activities related to Sa/Se/Pr of automated systems in either or both of the following aspects:

a. Developing automated systems. For example, automotive OEM/Tier 1/Tier 2 companies and IT companies produce technologies, products or services for vehicles which need to meet Sa/Se/Pr requirements.
b. Providing supporting technologies, products or services. For example, research institutes conduct research on Sa/Se/Pr engineering methods or testing tools.

Figure 2 shows the composition of the SECREDAS consortium and that of the respondents to our questionnaire. As shown in the figure, the major participants of SECREDAS are from academia, IT industry and automotive industry, so as the respondents to our questionnaire.

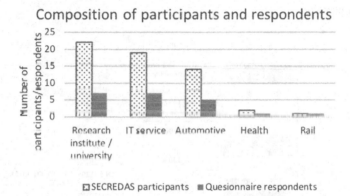

Fig. 2. SECREDAS consortium and respondents

The questionnaire was published and advertised in several plenary or group meetings of the SECREDAS project. To improve the readability of the questions, we conducted a pilot survey within five SECREDAS participants and revised the presentation of the questions following their feedback, before disseminating the questionnaire to the SECREDAS consortium. The survey data was collected from 05 Nov 2018 until 10 Feb 2019.

2.4   Threats to Validity

Construct Validity. Construct validity refers to the question: does the test measure what it was meant to measure? Validity threats to our survey involve (i) the range of standards/methodologies/tools under study, and (ii) the provision of options in some questions. Concerning the range of the study, we enumerated typical standards/methodologies/tools which may be interesting to practitioners. The threat of providing incomplete lists was mitigated by allowing respondents to complement them with whatever they consider as relevant. Note that a respondent could not see the input from any other individual respondent. Typical options of answers were suggested to certain questions for helping respondents to understand the questions. The threat of providing an incomplete list of options was mitigated by allowing respondents to give any answer instead of restricting them to the given options.

External Validity. External validity refers to the generalizability of the outcomes. The study is not meant to generalize its conclusion beyond its context. Seeing that the SECREDAS participants are not equally distributed in the 4 industrial sectors, we do not seek to compare the practices of the standards between different domains.

3   Qualitative Analysis

To answer *RQ1*, this section presents the qualitative results, including a collection of applicable standards and a comparison between the availability of standards on safety, security and privacy.

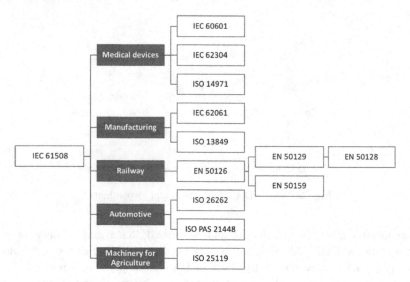

Fig. 3. Functional safety standards: given and complemented

A set of functional safety standards have been published as variants of IEC 61508 [1] for specific industrial sectors. Figure 3 shows those listed in the questionnaire plus ISO 25119 [8] which was supplemented by respondents.

Table 1 summarizes the security and privacy standards given in the questionnaire and those complemented by respondents. The table shows that compared to safety standards, security standards are less inter-related to one another and are published by more diverse standardization associations. A few security standards target specific industrial sectors, notably SAE J3061 [3] and ISO/SAE CD 21434 [9] for automotive. We observed that compared to the given standards which are on a higher level, some of the complemented standards are on a detailed specialized level. The table also shows that compared to safety and security standards, privacy standards are less numerous.

Table 1. Security/privacy standards: given and complemented

	Given	Complemented
Cross-domain (security)	• IEC 62443 [13] • ISO 2700X [15] • ISO 15408 [17] • NIST 800 [19]	• GlobalPlatform specifications [10] • ETSI TS 101 733 [11] 903 [12] • ETSI TS 102 204 [14] • eIDAS Security Regulation [16] • RFC cryptographic [18] • TISAX VDA ISA [20] • ETSI TS 103 532 Data Access Control [21] • BSI Grundschutz [22]
Cross-domain (privacy)	• ISO 29100 [24] • ISO 27550 [26]	• GlobalPlatform Privacy framework [23] • ISO/IEC 19286 [25] • GDPR [27] • Standard Data Protection Model [28]
Automotive (security)	• SAE J3061 [3] • ISO/SAE CD 21434 [9]	–

In the category of Sa/Se/Pr co-engineering, the questionnaire lists only one standard IEC TR 63069 [29] while no standard was supplemented by the respondents.

> *RQ1-Answer*: Safety standards for specific industrial sectors are available, as specializations of one basic standard i.e. IEC 61508 [1]. A wider range of security standards from different origins are applicable, while few target specific industrial sectors. Privacy standards are less numerous than safety or security standards, and there is no privacy standard targeting specific sectors.

4 Quantitative Analysis

To answer *RQ2 - RQ4*, this section presents the results of our quantitative analysis on the received responses. The analysis focuses on the standards, analysis methodologies and tools enumerated in the questionnaire. We chose to leave the respondent-supplemented ones out of the quantitative analysis, because the information we obtained is too little to draw representative conclusions.

4.1 Practices of Standards

In the questionnaire, over each standard we posed the following three questions as the refinement of *RQ2*:

- *RQ2.1*. Is the standard applied in the daily work? If YES:
- *RQ2.2*. What is the motivation of applying the standard? Suggested options include:

a. Required by regulation;
b. Required by customer;
c. As guidelines of product/service development.

• **RQ2.3**. How is the conformance with the standard evaluated? Suggested options include:

a. 3rd-party evaluation, e.g. qualification or certification;
b. Self-evaluation.

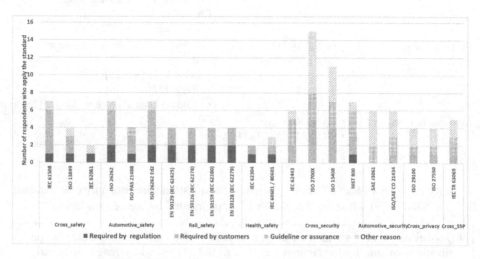

Fig. 4. Application of standards and the motivations

(1) **Application of standards and motivations.** Figure 4 presents our analysis result concerning questions *RQ2.1* and *RQ2.2*. The figure shows that cross-domain security standards ISO 2700X [15] and ISO 15408 [17] are the most applied ones.

In order to answer *RQ2.2*, we harmonized the answers so that each of them falls into one and only one of four disjoint groups, i.e. the three given options plus "other reason". As the questionnaire allows a respondent to give any answer to a question, within the responses who claim applying a certain standard, some select more than one motivation, while some select none of the suggested options. Note that the three suggested options reflect three levels of obligation, where "Required by regulation" is the most obligatory one and "As guidelines" is the least. We harmonized the answers to focus on the most obliging motivation for applying each standard, so as to reveal the role of each standard in Sa/Se/Pr engineering perceived by the practitioners. For example, Fig. 4 shows that 7 respondents apply IEC 61508 [1], where one is required at least by regulations, and five are by customers but not by regulations. It is worth noting that the basic safety standard IEC 61508 [1] and the automotive safety standard ISO 26262 [30] are not mandatory in a legal sense, but relevant in case of court rulings considering "Best Practices" and "State of the Art" as basis. Therefor they are de facto mandatory and required by customers on all tier x levels.

Figure 4 reveals a difference between the motivation of conforming to the safety standards and that of the security/privacy standards. The two leading reasons for applying safety standards are firstly "Required by customers" and secondly "Required by regulation". Each of the safety standards is utilized by at least one respondent for complying with regulations. For security/privacy standards, in contrast, "Required by regulation" is rarely a reason, with only one exception of NIST 800 [19].

(2) **Evaluation of conformance to standards.** Once an organization applies a standard, it may perform some activity to determine whether it complies with the requirements of the standard. Such activity can be either self-evaluation or 3rd-party evaluation, where the latter includes, but is not limited to, qualification and certification. Figure 5 shows the result of *RQ2.3* on how the practitioners evaluate the conformance to the standards, where "No evaluation" represents the case where a respondent claimed applying a standard but did not choose any conformance evaluation. Here, similar to the analysis on *RQ2.2*, we harmonized the answers to *RQ2.3* by taking the strictest conformance evaluation within each answer. Hence each response who claims to apply a specific standard is placed into one and only one of the three groups in descending order of rigorousness: 3rd-party evaluation, Self-evaluation and No evaluation. Figure 5 shows little difference on the employed conformance evaluation between the individual standards. However, "No evaluation" takes a significant proportion on security/privacy standards, which is not the case for safety standards.

(3) **Safety standards vs. security/privacy standards.** The above analysis reveals that the practices of security/privacy standards are less mature than that of safety standards in terms of conformance evaluation. Also, the customers and authorities require less application of security/privacy standards than safety standards, possibly because they just started to perceive the importance of industrial products' conformance to security/privacy standards. These two observations reflect the fact that security/privacy are relatively new concerns to safety-critical industries.

Regarding Sa/Se/Pr co-engineering, IEC TR 63069 [10], the only standard positioned in this category in the questionnaire, is rarely practiced, probably because it is under publication first half of 2019 and hence less known to the practitioners. The result of this survey indicates that the multi-concern co-engineering challenge needs more consideration. Besides, standards are evolving with more concerns over Sa/Se/Pr co-engineering. The latest edition of safety standard IEC 61508 and that of ISO 26262 include requirements to think of cybersecurity if it impacts safety. These two standards are complemented by latest security standards IEC 62443 [13] and ISO/SAE CD 21434 [9], respectively. ISO/SAE CD 21434 [9] is already referenced in the draft regulation of UNECE for vehicle cybersecurity [31].

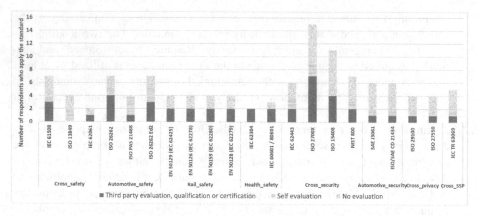

Fig. 5. Conformance evaluation with respect to the standards.

RQ2-Answer: On the application of standards, no significant difference is observed between individual Sa/Se/Pr standards. The conformance to safety standards is significantly more often imposed by customers and regulators than that of security/privacy standards. The conformance of safety standards is slightly more rigorously evaluated than that of security/privacy standards.

4.2   Practices of Analysis Methodologies

To evaluate the Sa/Se/Pr posture of a product/service or an organization, systematic assessment needs to be performed as an integrated and iterative activity throughout Sa/Se/Pr engineering. Our questionnaire investigates the practices of the methodologies which support such Sa/Se/Pr analysis. Figure 6 shows the number of responses which claim using each methodology. For example, 8 respondents apply FMEA [32]. The figure shows that on safety, all the three methodologies listed in the questionnaire are almost equally used. The usage of different security analysis methods varies significantly. The usage of privacy analysis methodologies is minor, so as the combined Sa/Se/Pr analysis methodologies.

RQ3-Answer: Concerning safety analysis methodologies, FMEA [32], FTA [33] and HARA (Hazard Analysis and Risk Assessment) [30] are commonly used. Concerning security analysis methodologies, the STRIDE model [34] and the Common Criteria [35] are the most commonly used. The usage of security analysis methodologies is less convergent than of safety ones.

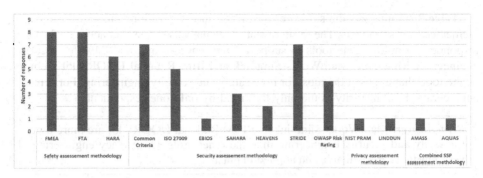

Fig. 6. Usage of safety, security or privacy analysis methods.

4.3 Usage of Commercial Off-The-Shelf (COTS) Tools

The survey investigates the practitioners' employment of COTS (Commercial Off-The-Shelf) tools for meeting Sa/Se/Pr requirements, and which properties each tool serves. Note that the questionnaire posed questions on two categories of tools: COTS tools and in-house tools, while only COTS tools are discussed in this paper for the sake of anonymizing the respondents.

Table 2. Tools: given and complemented

Given	• Ansys SCADE code generators • Cadence Automotive Functional Safety IBM Rational DOORS kit • Mentor Graphics • Veloce • IBM Rational DOORS kit • Parasoft C/C++ test • LDRA tool suite • MathWorks Simulink
Complemented	• Enterprise Architect • Axivion Suite • Code Composer MISRA 2004 Coverity (static code analysis) • BugSeng ECLAIR • Git versioning system • HP Fortify Static code analyzer • ITEM Toolkit • Jenkins (unit testing) • Jira • Lauterbach Trace32 Debugger and Tracer • Medini • Microsoft Threat Modeling • Nexus IQ • PTC Integrity • Rational Clearquest (Defect tracking) • Tenable Nessus • Webinspect

Table 2 summarizes the software tools listed in the questionnaire and those complemented by respondents. The result of statistical analysis shows that about 38% of the respondents employ some tools to support safety engineering, and 24% for security engineering. Moreover, MathWorks Simulink and IBM Rational DOORS kit seem to be the tools that are used the most for both safety and security engineering. For privacy engineering, PTC integrity is the only tool used by only one respondent.

> *RQ4-Answer*: MathWorks Simulink and IBM Rational DOORS kit are more used for safety and security engineering than the other tools. On privacy engineering, very few tools are available and applied in practices.

5 Conclusion

To the best of our knowledge, there is little empirical study on the industrial sectors' practices of Sa/Se/Pr standards. The survey in this paper fills this gap by gathering feedback from the practitioners in real-world settings. Given that the sampling is not sufficient enough to be generalized, the observations we made from the responses are suggestive rather than definitive.

The analysis reveals that security/privacy standards are gaining popularity in safety-critical industrial sectors, though both their development and their practices are less mature than that of safety standards. Practitioners have more diverse options on the selection of security analysis methodologies, compared to that of safety analysis. Some COTS tools are applicable on Sa/Se/Pr engineering, where the availability and employment of tools for privacy engineering are still weak. Some standards linking safety and security engineering are not widely used, indicating that a multi-concern point of view for Sa/Se/Pr co-engineering is not yet widely adopted.

Note that this paper presents our observations over the responses without investigating their underlying reasons, because the limited number of responses does not facilitate a well-grounded further analysis. Some questions, for example, whether the age of a standard or the adoption by regulatory bodies can explain why some standards are more popular than others, remain interesting analysis angles for future work.

The survey described in this paper is part of a larger research effort aimed at devising an integrated Sa/Se/Pr evaluation framework for safety-critical systems. Another line of future research is to motivate practitioners to become more involved in standardization.

Acknowledgements. This work was partly supported by the SECREDAS project with the JU Grant Agreement number 783119, and the partners national funding authorities.

References

1. IEC61508:2010 Functional safety of electrical/electronic/programmable electronic safety-related systems. Standard, International Electrotechnical Commission (IEC) (2010)
2. SECREDAS project. http://secredas.eu. Accessed 03 Apr 2019
3. SAE J3061-2016 Cybersecurity Guidebook for Cyber-Physical Vehicle Systems. Standard, Society of Automotive Engineers (SAE) (2016)
4. Henniger, O., Ruddle, A., Seudié, H., Weyl, B., Wolf, M., Wollinger, T.: Securing vehicular on-board IT systems: the EVITA project. In: VDI/VW Automotive Security Conference, p. 41 (2009)
5. ETSI TS 102 165-1 V5.2.3 (2017-10) CYBER; Methods and protocols; Part 1: Method and proforma for Threat, Vulnerability, Risk Analysis (TVRA). Standard, European Telecommunications Standards Institute (ETSI) (2017)
6. Alberts, C.J., Dorofee, A.: Managing Information Security Risks: The OCTAVE Approach. Addison-Wesley Longman Publishing Co., Inc., Boston (2002)
7. HEAling Vulnerabilities to ENhance Software Security and Safety (HEAVENS) project. https://research.chalmers.se/en/project/5809. Accessed 03 Apr 2019
8. ISO 25119:2018 Tractors and machinery for agriculture and forestry – Safety-related parts of control systems. Standard, International Organization for Standardization (ISO) (2018)
9. ISO/SAE CD 21434 Road Vehicles – Cybersecurity engineering. Standard, International Organization for Standardization (ISO), under development
10. GlobalPlatform Specifications. https://globalplatform.org/specs-library/. Accessed 03 Apr 2019
11. ETSI TS 101 733 V2.2.1 (2013-04) Electronic Signatures and Infrastructures (ESI); CMS Advanced Electronic Signatures (CAdES). Standard, European Telecommunications Standards Institute (ETSI) (2013)
12. ETSI TS 101 903 V1.4.1 (2009-06) XML Advanced Electronic Sig- natures (XAdES). Standard, European Telecommunications Standards Institute (ETSI) (2009)
13. IEC 62443:2018 Security for industrial automation and control systems. Standard, International Electrotechnical Commission (IEC) (2018)
14. ETSI TS 102 204 V1.1.4 (2003-08) XML Advanced Mobile Commerce (M-COMM); Mobile Signature Service; Web Service Interface. Standard, European Telecommunications Standards Institute (ETSI) (2003)
15. ISO/IEC 27000 family - Information security management systems. Standard, International Organization for Standardization (ISO) (2018)
16. eIDAS: Regulation (EU) No 910/2014 of the European Parliament and of the Council of 23 July 2014 on electronic identification and trust services for electronic transactions in the internal market and repealing Directive 1999/93/EC. Regulation, The European Parliament and the Council of the European Union (2014)
17. ISO/IEC 15408:2009 Information technology – Security techniques – Evaluation criteria for IT security. Standard, International Organization for Standardization (ISO) (2015)
18. RFCs Internet cryptographic standards. Standard, Federal Information Processing Standards (FIPS)
19. NIST Special Publication 800-series. Standard, National Institute of Standards and Technology (NIST) (2018)
20. Trusted Information Security Assessment Exchange (TISAX). Standard, German Association of the Automotive Industry (VDA) (2017)
21. ETSI TS 103 532 V1.1.1(2018-03) CYBER; Attribute Based Encryption for Attribute Based Access Control. Standard, European Telecommunications Standards Institute (ETSI) (2018)

22. BSI IT-Grundschutz. Standard, German Federal Office for Information Security (BSI) (2015)

23. GlobalPlatform Privacy Framework v1.0. Standard, GlobalPlatform (2017)

24. ISO/IEC 29100:2011 Information technology – Security techniques – Privacy framework. Standard, International Organization for Standardization (ISO) (2011)

25. ISO/IEC 19286:2018 Identification cards – Integrated circuit cards – Privacy-enhancing protocols and services. Standard, International Organization for Standardization (ISO) (2018)

26. ISO/IEC PDTR 27550: Information technology – Security techniques – Privacy engineering. Standard, International Organization for Standardization (ISO), under development

27. General Data Protection Regulation (GDPR): Regulation, European Parliament and Council of the European Union (2018)

28. Standard Data Protection Model (SDP Model): Standard, German Federal and State Commissioners (2017)

29. IEC TR 63069 ED1: Industrial-process measurement, control and automation - Framework for functional safety and security. Standard, International Electrotechnical Commission (IEC), under development

30. ISO 26262:2018 Road vehicles – Functional safety. Standard, International Organization for Standardization (ISO) (2018)

31. Draft Recommendation on Cyber Security of the Task Force on Cyber Security and Over-the-air issues of UNECE WP.29 GRVA. Standard, United Nations Economic Commission for Europe (UNECE) (2018)

32. Stamatis, D.H.: Failure Mode and Effect Analysis: FMEA from Theory to Execution. ASQ Quality Press, Milwaukee (2003)

33. Ericson, C.A.: Fault tree analysis. In: System Safety Conference, Orlando, Florida, vol. 1, pp. 1–9 (1999)

34. Shostack, A.: Threat Modeling: Designing for Security. Wiley, Hoboken (2014)

35. Common Criteria. https://www.commoncriteriaportal.org. Accessed 03 Apr 2019

Combined Approach for Safety and Security

Siddhartha Verma[1], Thomas Gruber[1(✉)], Christoph Schmittner[1(✉)], and P. Puschner[2(✉)]

[1] Austrian Institute of Technology, Giefinggasse 4, 1210 Vienna, Austria
{Siddhartha.Verma,thomas.gruber,christoph.schmittner}@ait.ac.at
[2] Vienna University of Technology, Institute of Computer Engineering,
1040 Vienna, Austria
peter@vmars.tuwien.ac.at

Abstract. With evolution in Cyber-Physical Systems, the dependence and conflicts among dependability attributes (safety, security, reliability, availability etc) have become increasingly complex. We can not consider these dependability attributes in isolation, therefore, combined approaches for safety, security and other attributes are required. In this document, we provide a matrix based approach (inspired from ANP (Analytical Network Process)) for combined risk assessment for safety and security. This approach allows combined risk assessment considering dependence and conflict among attributes. The assessment results for different dependability attributes (such as safety, security etc.) are provided in the ANP matrix. We will discuss approaches such as Fault Tree Analysis (FTA), Stochastic Colored Petri Net (SCPN) Analysis, Attack Tree Analysis (ATA), Failure Mode Vulnerability and Effect Analysis (FMVEA) for evaluation of concerned attributes and achieving our goal of combined assessment.

Keywords: FTA · FTDMP · SCPN · ATA · FMVEA · ANP ·
Safety · Security · Combined risk assessment

1 Introduction

System design, development and operation are subject to high dependability constraints, including Safety, Reliability, Availability, Security. The classical Security goal consists of the attributes Confidentiality, Integrity, Availability (CIA). STRIDE [1] (Spoofing identity, Tampering with data, Repudiation, Information disclosure, Denial of service and Elevation of privilege) indicates the mode by which security can be compromised. With evolution in cyber-physical systems, the dependence and conflicts among the competing attributes have become increasingly complex. Therefore, it is not possible to satisfy system's requirement w.r.t. all the competing attributes by classical isolated attribute analysis (analysing all attributes in isolation), without considering inter-dependence and conflicts in an integral manner throughout the design iterations.

© Springer Nature Switzerland AG 2019
A. Romanovsky et al. (Eds.): SAFECOMP 2019 Workshops, LNCS 11699, pp. 87–101, 2019.
https://doi.org/10.1007/978-3-030-26250-1_7

System Design is an iterative process, System Architecture is designed with the use of security patterns, expert tactics and other dependability patterns until the requirements w.r.t all the competing attributes are satisfied. For example, Architectural Analysis For Security (AAFS) [2] proposes a combination of three approaches to design security, namely Tactic-oriented Architectural Analysis (ToAA), Pattern-oriented Architectural Analysis (PoAA) and Vulnerability-oriented Architectural Analysis. System design starts with the safety and security analysis (identifying the hazards and security threats) and risk assessment of the system. For example Hazard Analysis and Risk Assessment (HARA) [3] and Threat Analysis and Risk Assessment [4]. The state of the art practiced good approaches for safety-security co-analysis and co-assessment are Security-aware Hazard Analysis and Risk Assessment (SAHARA) [5] and FMVEA (Failure Mode Vulnerability and Effect Analysis) [6].

These approaches (SAHARA and FMVEA), however, have some limitations, this is also mentioned in the paper "Security Application of Failure Mode and Effect Analysis" [6]. The FMVEA approach analyzes only single causes of an effect, i.e it does not consider multiple concurrent attacks and multi-stage attacks, i.e. it does not consider logical combination of attacks. Similarly in safety, reliability and availability evaluation, it considers only single point failures and no concurrent multiple failures, i.e. it does not allow logical combination of failures.

In the next sections of this document we will discuss in detail how we can eliminate these limitations by introduction of FTA and SCPN, and by introduction of ATA (using propositional and multiset semantics) with the semiquantitative threat risk assessment approach proposed in FMVEA for security analysis. For co-analysis and co-assessment we need to consider complex inter-connections between FTA and ATA, these inter-connections may represent dependence or conflicts among attributes. This complex inter-connected tree structure makes the co-assessment and co-engineering complicated; with every design strategy choosen for a particular or a set of attribute requirement (as a result of co-assessment), it is necessary to consider the impact on other attributes due to dependence and conflicts. In next sections we propose a matrix based approach inspired from ANP [7–10] which makes it easy and efficient to take into consideration the dependence and conflicts among attributes for co-assessment. This approach helps in taking design decisions smartly to help reduce the number of design iterations.

2   Safety, Reliability and Availability Analysis

Many domain-specific standards have been elaborated by IEC, ISO and CEN-ELEC, most of them are based on the generic concepts of IEC 61508, which relies on process quality for coping with systematic faults and on probabilistic concepts for stochastic hardware faults. In this work we will consider stochastic hardware faults for quantitative evaluation, systematic faults are irrelevant for such evaluation, systematic faults are handled through rigorous verification, formal methods play an important role in examining the system behaviour exhaustively to assure certainty of correctness. However, systematic faults exploited by security attacks will be considered and corresponding security risk will be evaluated in Sect. 4 of this work. The Safety requirements are determined by Safety Integrity Level (SIL) which can be determined by matrix of three other factors - Severity (Scale of Impact), Exposure (to hazardous zone) and controllability (possibility to avoid). SIL is related to Maximum Tolerable Hazard Rate (THR-Dangerous failures per hour which lead to hazard).

FMEA and FTA are among the most commonly used safety and reliability analysis methodologies. FMEA [11,12] is a bottom-up approach, it examines all the potential failure modes within a system in order to determine their effects on the system. FMEA analysis typically involves a diverse team of people to increase the probability that all failures will be identified. FMEA has a limitation, it is more suited to analysing systems which have no redundancy and no multiple failures. FTA [13] is a top-down approach, it analyzes the relationships between a top event and the causes of the event (component failures). FTA allows logical combination of events/failures using logical gates to analyze systems with multiple initiating faults and high levels of redundancy. Therefore, FMEA and FTA can be combined in a failure analysis to gain the individual benefits of both approaches [14].

FTA experiences certain limitations such as classical fault trees do not consider repairing events, therefore availability evaluation and modeling fault tolerant systems with repairable events is not possible. Other limitation could be modeling failure/repair dependencies or dynamic behaviour of the system such as Standby Systems. To overcome the limitations of the fault tree, it was combined with a Markov process and named FTDMP (Fault Tree Driven Markov Process) [16] or DFTA (Dynamic Fault Tree Analysis) [17]. However, modeling a complex system will lead to a state explosion problem, which may be possible to avoid by breaking the tree into independent subtrees. A large amount of work is available for analysing the reliability and availability of the system using a Markov process e.g. [15,18,19]. Markov models experience a state explosion problem in modeling complex systems with dynamic behavior.

Generalized Stochastic Petri Nets (GSPN) model dynamic and concurrent behavior of the complex systems more efficiently than Markov models. The dynamic behavior in such models is represented by movement of tokens. GSPN is an extension of Petri Nets (PN) [20,21] and Stochastic Petri Nets (SPN) [22,23]. GSPN [24] introduces two additional dynamic modeling notations, inhibitor arcs (the absence of tokens enables transition) and immediate transition (no delay required for firing the transition).

3   SCPN for Dependability Analysis

SCPN [26] (Stochastic Colored Petri Nets) combines the strength of GSPN with a high level programming language, making them very powerful in modeling large, complex, dynamic systems in a very compact way. SCPN has colored tokens, which means the attribute of each token can be uniquely defined unlike GSPN and also the movement of tokens is uniquely defined by conditions and constraints in the transition object; this allows modeling complex dynamic behavior in a very efficient and compact way. Therefore, we will use SCPN for RAMS analysis with the TimeNET [27] tool. Among all the benefits of SCPN, one more advantage of SCPN is, that, it is an easy graphical model based analysis which allows the user to model complex dynamic systems very conveniently.

4   Attack Tree Analysis and Security Risk Analysis

Attack Tree Analysis (ATA) is a prominent graphical model technique used for modeling attack scenarios (occurrence of threats, vulnerability w.r.t threat) for security analysis, introduced as a security analogue for fault trees. Several works exist regarding the quantitative evaluation of attack-trees for security risk assessment [28,29]. Work in [30] consists of predicting cyber attack rates based on data driven analytics. In [29] the author uses attack duration and probability of success of attack for quantitative evaluation of attack trees by translating attack trees to stochastic timed automata. However, in most of the modern systems such information is not available, also the factors involved in determining these values are very dynamic because of the presence of an intelligent adversary. Therefore, we will focus on semi-quantitative approaches for evaluation of attack trees and security risk analysis. For the probability of occurrence of a threat, we will use the semi-quantitative vulnerability scoring system proposed by FMVEA (Failure Mode Vulnerability and Effect Analysis) [6], as it comprehensively considers parameters responsible for exploitation of vulnerabilities. FMVEA consists of four parameters, Reachability, Availability of Information (AOI), Capability of the attacker (COA) and Equipment Required (ER). The scores corresponding to these parameters are listed in Fig. 1. Finally, the sum of all four parameters gives the semi-quantitative value for the attack probability.

Parameter	Values			
COA	Amateur (3)	Working in the domain (2)	Hacker, domain expert (1)	Expert team from multiple domains (0)
AOI	Information publicly available (3)	Information available for maintenance for customer / operator (2)	Information available for production, OEM system integrator (1)	Information available in company of supplier (0)
Reachability	Always accessible via untrusted networks (3)	accessible via private networks or part time accessible via untrusted networks (2)	part time accessible via private networks or easily accessible via physical (1)	Only accessible via physical (0)
ER	Publicly available standard IT devices / SW (3)	Publicly available specialized IT devices / SW (2)	Tailor-made proprietary IT devices / SW (1)	Multiple Tailor-made proprietary IT devices / SW (0)

Fig. 1. Vulnerability scoring proposed by FMVEA

Classically, an attack tree model consists of a top level goal which is recursively refined into sub-goals using AND (conjunction) and OR (disjunction) logical gates to describe how attack propagates through the system. For the security

analysis we will use propositional logic and multiset attack tree semantics which
have been proposed in literature [31,32], combined with the FMVEA based vulnerability scoring scheme. For the attack tree evaluation we need to define how
attacks are propagating through the logical AND and OR gates to the top goals
i.e. to evaluate the impact of basic attack steps (BAS) which are on the bottom of the attack tree, to the top goals. We can define the attack tree as set of
bundles by using multiset semantics, so we get possible alternates for reaching
the attack goals of the attack tree (Disjunctive Normal Form - DNF). Since we
will do the risk analysis of all these alternates individually, the OR relationship
among the child nodes is already taken care of. For the AND relationship the
combined attack probability is taken to be the lowest of the attack probabilities among the child nodes, as is used in the SAFURE project [33]. Although
combined probability might be lower than the lowest attack probability, but we
will always be on safer-side with this assumption, also considering the scenario
of co-ordinated attacks this assumption will be more closer to reality.

To demonstrate the above approach for the evaluation of an attack tree,
we will construct an attack tree as shown in Fig. 2 from the threats described
in [34,35], classified based on different network layers. The attack steps which
are involved in more than one attack scenario are represented with a numerical
suffix. for ex. basic attack step blackholeattack.1 and blackholeattack.2 means
that blackhole attack is involved in two scenarios.

We will mention the attack steps (pas - parent attack state, cas - child attack
states) involved in the attack tree, pas- network layer attack (cas - black hole
attack, wormhole attack), pas- physical layer attack (cas - jamming and interfering, interception), pas - security threats in transport layer (cas- synchronization
flooding attack, Session hijacking, acknowledgement flooding attack), pas - session hijacking (cas - obtaining IP address, address resolution protocol poisoning),
pas - obtaining IP address (cas - sniffing the traffic, routing attacks such as blackhole and wormhole attacks), pas - application layer attack (cas - breaking the
network firewall, exploit data transmission application), pas - vehicle application attacks (cas - breaking the network firewall, exploit software application
weakness to escalate privilege to get access to in-vehicle system), pas - breaking
the network firewall (cas - exploiting authentication mechanism of the network
firewall, routing attacks such as blackhole and wormhole attacks).

For every higher attack state, we will evaluate the multiset (DNF) as shown in
Figs. 3 and 4 (we have not mentioned some higher attack states here such as G1,
Goal, S2 etc. becuase of space constraint). Each multiset consist of bundles or
sets which are related with disjunction and each bundle or set consists of basic
attack steps which are related with conjunction, i.e. each set is an alternate
attack path to that attack state where all the basic attack steps of the set must
be executed successfully. The second row of the table in Figs. 3 and 4 represents
the severity of impact on that state.

The vulnerability score for attack steps will be provided based on FMVEA
parameters. Please consider work [36] to have a detailed overview of FMVEA
based vulnerability scoring, the discussion regarding the vulnerability scoring of

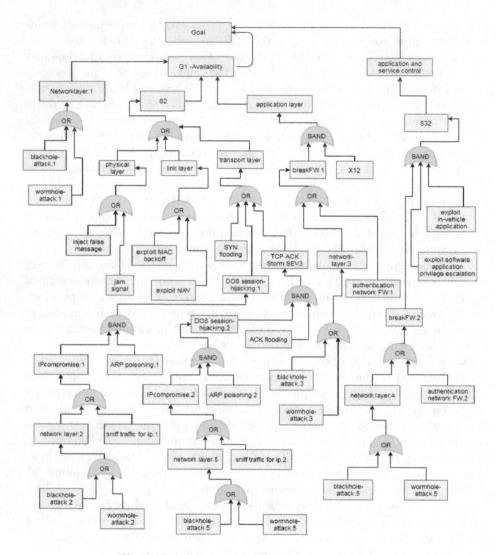

Fig. 2. Attack tree for VANET (source [34,35])

Severity Classification			
2	2	2	3
link layer	DOS-sessionhijacking.2	DOS-sessionhijacking.1	TCP ACK Storm-SEV3
exploit MAC backoff	SAND(black hole attack.5, ARP Poisoning.2)	SAND(black hole attack.2, ARP Poisoning.1)	SAND(black hole attack.5, ARP Poisoning.2,ACK flooding)
exploit NAV	SAND(worm hole attack.5, ARP Poisoning.2)	SAND(worm hole attack.2, ARP Poisoning.1)	SAND(worm hole attack.5, ARP Poisoning.2,ACK flooding)
	SAND(sniff traffic for ip.2, ARP Poisoning.2)	SAND(sniff traffic for ip.1, ARP Poisoning.1)	SAND(sniff traffic for ip.2, ARP Poisoning.2,ACK flooding)

Fig. 3. Multi-sets (DNF) for each higher attack state

Severity Classification

	3		4	
transport layer	application layer		S32	Application and service control
SYN flooding SAND(black hole attack.2, ARP Poisoning.1) SAND(worm hole attack.2, ARP Poisoning.1)	SAND(black hole attack.3, X12)		SAND(black hole attack.4, exploit software application privilege escalation, exploit in vehicle application)	SAND(black hole attack.4, exploit software application privilege escalation, exploit in vehicle application)
SAND(sniff traffic for ip.1, ARP Poisoning.1) SAND(black hole attack.5, ARP Poisoning.2,ACK flooding)	SAND(worm hole attack.3, X12)		SAND(worm hole attack.4, exploit software application privilege escalation, exploit in vehicle application)	SAND(worm hole attack.4, exploit software application privilege escalation, exploit in vehicle application)
SAND(worm hole attack.5, ARP Poisoning.2,ACK flooding) SAND(sniff traffic for ip.2,ARP Poisoning.2, ACK flooding)	SAND(authentication network firewall.1, X12)		SAND(authentication network firewall.2, exploit software application privilege escalation, exploit in vehicle application)	SAND(authentication network firewall.2, exploit software application privilege escalation, exploit in vehicle application)

Fig. 4. Multi-sets (DNF) for each higher attack state

the attack steps is out of scope because of space constraint. The FMVEA scores corresponding to all the basic attack steps are provided in Fig. 6. Reachability scores for some basic attack steps is left blank, this is the case where this attack is in sequential conjunction with some preceding attack, so the reachability score for this attack will be same as preceding attack. The classification of severity separates different aspects of consequences of security threats: operational, safety related, privacy and financial, these components have rating from 0 to 4, as mentioned in the SAFURE project [33] for the automotive domain as shown in Fig. 5. For every attack set or bundle we will consider the critical basic attack step as the one which has lowest vulnerability score, as the state can not be reached until this basic attack step is successful. Therefore, as a final result we will get all the critical basic attack steps and secuity risk scores corresponding to higher attack states as shown in Fig. 7. In Fig. 7 the shaded cells provide risk scores for the corresponding higher attack state (on x axis) and associated basic attack step (on y axis). Some basic attack steps such as "snif trafic for ip" may be involved in more than one attack scenario. The unshaded entries are likelihood (vulnerability scores). The security risk is defined as the product of attack probability and severity of impact. For different application domains the severity class can be described by the domain experts with appropriate adaptation. Based on the risk score, appropriate Secuity Level Target is assigned (SL-T). Based on the SL-T rating appropriate security control strategy or set of control strategies can be implemented to secure the system. FMVEA Risk Scores can be mapped to Standard Risk Scores (if defined by standard organisation) for assignment of security levels, e.g. IEC 62443-3-2 standard document assigns SL-T ranging 0–4 based on risk scores ranging 0–25.

Severity	Aspect of security threats			
	Safety (S)	Privacy (P)	Financial (F)	Operational (O)
0	-No injuries	-No unauthorize access to data	- No financial loss	- No impact on operational performance
1	- Light or moderate injuries	-Anonymous data only (no specific driver or vehicle data)	- low level loss	- Impact not discernible to driver
2	-Severe injuries (survival probable) -Light / moderate injuies for multiple vehicles	-Identification of vehicle or driver -Anonymous data for multiple vehicles	- Moderate loss	-Driver aware of performance degradation -Indiscernible impacts for multiple vehicles
3	-Life threatning (survival uncertain) or fatal injuies -Severe injuries for multiple vehicles	-Driver or vehicle tracking - Identification of driver or vehicle for multiple vehicles	-Heavy loss - Moderate losses for multiple vehicles	-Significant impact on performance - Noticeable impact for multiple vehicles
4	Life threatning or fatal injuries for multiple vehicles	Driver or vehicle tracking for multiple vehicles	Heavy losses for multiple vehicles	Significant impact for multiple vehicles

Fig. 5. Severity classification scheme : automotive domain

BASIC ATTACK STEPS	R, C, A, ER	BASIC ATTACK STEPS	R, C, A, ER	BASIC ATTACK STEPS	R, C, A, ER
black hole attack	3, 2, 3, 3	ACK flooding	3, 1, 2, 1	SYN flooding	3, 2, 2, 2
worm hole attack	3, 3, 3, 3	inject false message	1, 3, 2, 2	authentication network firewall	2, 1, 2, 2
sniff traffic for ip	1, 2, 2, 1	jam signal	1, 2, 2, 1	X12	_, 1, 1, 2
ARP Poisoning	3, 2, 2, 2	exploit MAC backoff	2, 2, 2, 2	exploit software application privilege escalation	_, 2, 2, 3
		exploit NAV	2, 2, 2, 2	exploit in vehicle application	_, 1, 1, 1
C- Capability of attacker, A- Availability of information, R- Reachability, ER- Equipment required					

Fig. 6. Vulnerability scores for basic attack steps

5 Matrix Based Combined Risk Assessment for Co-engineering

With increasing functionality and complexity in cyber-physical systems, we must also consider the increasing dependence and conflicts among these attributes. Here we provide a matrix based approach inspired from ANP where in a single matrix different attributes can be tracked along with their interdependences. In the matrix, hierarchical failure propagation and threat propagation structure is defined with inter-connections between them, to consider dependence, which gives it a network structure. The network structure is due to consideration of dependence among all the elements of the hierarchical structure which is why all the elements are on the row as well as on the column.

To demonstrate this matrix we will take same example ' Security assessment in vehicular networks '. In addition, for failure analysis part we will analyse the system with SCPN simulation in TimeNET tool as shown in Fig. 8.

	DOS-session hijacking	TCP ACK Storm - SEV3	physical layer	link layer	transport layer	network layer	S2	application layer	S32	G1-Availability	Application and service control	GOAL-SYSTEM
sniff traffic for ip	12	18			6	6				6		6
ARP Poisoning	18				9	9				9		9
ACK flooding		21			7	7				7		7
inject false message			16			8				8		8
jam signal			12			6				6		6
exploit MAC backoff				16		8				8		8
exploit NAV				16		8				8		8
SYN flooding					9	9				9		9
black hole attack						22				11		11
worm hole attack						24				12		12
X12								21		7		7
exploit in vehicle application									24		6	6

Fig. 7. Security risk for all the higher attack states

The simulation result is shown in Fig. 9, it also represents the hierarchical structure of the system. For example the subsystem ECUBA consist of two child subsystem BAFA and STAFA with failure rate 0.145 and .313 failure/year. The subsystem DAFA consist of two child components BA2O and BA1O with conjunction relation, the BA2O is considered as critical component for BAFA subsystem as BA2O has higher MTTF (mean time to failure), therefore BA1O is reduced to 0, however it should be noticed that the impact of BA1O has been already considered during simulation for evaluation of failure rate of BAFA.

The matrix represented in Fig. 10 is the final supermatrix, the entries in row 1 is not visually clear because of the space constraint, but they are exactly similar to column 1 entries. (Row2..29, col1) and (row1, col 2..29) represents the baisc attack steps and higher attack states. The rectangular matrix entries (row2..29, col 2..29) represents the hierarchical attack tree structure, which represents the impact of basic attack steps on the bottom of the attack tree to all the higher attack states. Similarly, (Row30..47, col1) and (row1, col 30..47) represents the baisc failure causes and higher failed states.The rectangular matrix entries (row30..47, col 30..47) in Fig. 10 represents the hierarchical failure tree structure, which represents the impact of basic failure causes on the bottom of the fault tree to all the higher failed states. The supermatrix is evaluated in three steps, due to space constraint we are not able to show the first two matrices, but we can discuss, the results of hierarchical fault tree analysis and attack tree analysis is put into the matrix (named unweighted matrix), the cells corresponding to these entries are shown as shaded cells in Fig. 10. All the shaded cells in unweighted matrix are non-zero, and all other entries are zero, the entries in bold are zero, after this, all the vulnerability scores and failure rate values are normalized to one, this is called weighted matrix. Higher power of a weighted supermatrix becomes constant and is called supermatrix, this matrix is then

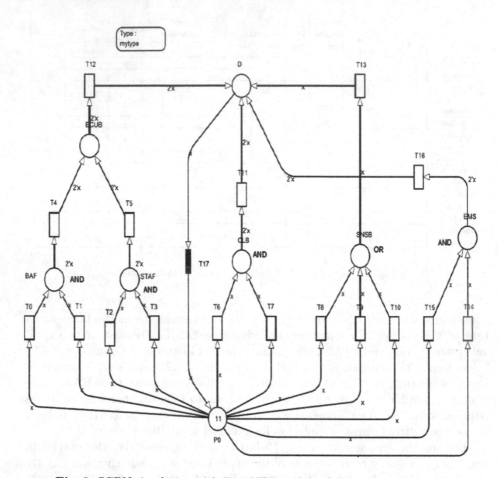

Fig. 8. SCPN simulation with TimeNET tool for failure rate evaluation

	BA2O	BA1O	STA1O	STA2O	CLB1O	CLB2O	SNSB1O	SNSB2O	SNSB3O	EMS2O	EMS1O	AND BAFA	AND STAFA	AND CLBA	OR SNSBA	AND EMSA	OR ECUBA	OR D
BA2O	0.145	0	0	0	0	0	0	0	0	0	0	0.145	0	0	0	0	0	0
BA1O	0	0	0	0	0	0	0	0	0	0	0	0	0	0	0	0	0	0
STA1O	0	0	0.313	0	0	0	0	0	0	0	0	0	0.313	0	0	0	0	0
STA2O	0	0	0	0	0	0	0	0	0	0	0	0	0	0	0	0	0	0
CLB1O	0	0	0	0	0.322	0	0	0	0	0	0	0	0	0.322	0	0	0	0
CLB2O	0	0	0	0	0	0	0	0	0	0	0	0	0	0	0	0	0	0
SNSB1O	0	0	0	0	0	0	0.524	0	0	0	0	0	0	0	0.524	0	0	0
SNSB2O	0	0	0	0	0	0	0	0.216	0	0	0	0	0	0	0.216	0	0	0
SNSB3O	0	0	0	0	0	0	0	0	0.524	0	0	0	0	0	0.524	0	0	0
EMS2O	0	0	0	0	0	0	0	0	0	0.197	0	0	0	0	0	0.197	0	0
EMS1O	0	0	0	0	0	0	0	0	0	0	0	0	0	0	0	0	0	0
BAFA	0	0	0	0	0	0	0	0	0	0	0	0	0	0	0	0	0.145	0
STAFA	0	0	0	0	0	0	0	0	0	0	0	0	0	0	0	0	0.313	0
CLBA	0	0	0	0	0	0	0	0	0	0	0	0	0	0	0	0	0	0.322
SNSBA	0	0	0	0	0	0	0	0	0	0	0	0	0	0	0	0	0	1.263
EMSA	0	0	0	0	0	0	0	0	0	0	0	0	0	0	0	0	0	0.197
ECUBA	0	0	0	0	0	0	0	0	0	0	0	0	0	0	0	0	0	0.457
D	0	0	0	0	0	0	0	0	0	0	0	0	0	0	0	0	0	0

Fig. 9. SCPN simulation results for failure rate evaluation - hierarchical

	sf	sf	A	A	in	ja	e	e	S	bl	a	wo	X	e	IP	IP	D	DC	TC	p	lii	tr	a	ne	S2	a	S	G1	A	Ap	GOA	BA2O	B	STA1O	S	CLB1O	CI	SNSB	SNSB	SNSB	EMS2	E	BAFA	STAFA	CLBA	SNSB	EMSA	ECUBA	D
sniff traffic for ip.2	6	0	0	0	0	0	0	0	0	0	0	0	0	0	6	0	6	0	0	6	0	6	0	0	**6**	0	**6**	0	0	0	**6**	0	0	0	0	0	0	0	0	0	0	0	0	0	0	0	0	0	0
sniff traffic for ip.1	0	6	0	0	0	0	0	0	0	0	0	0	0	0	0	6	0	6	0	0	6	0	6	0	**6**	0	**6**	0	0	0	**6**	0	0	0	0	0	0	0	0	0	0	0	0	0	0	0	0	0	0
ARP Poisoning.1	0	0	9	0	0	0	0	0	0	0	0	0	0	0	0	0	0	0	9	0	0	0	9	0	**9**	0	**9**	0	0	0	**9**	0	0	0	0	0	0	0	0	0	0	0	0	0	0	0	0	0	0
ACK flooding	0	0	0	7	0	0	0	0	0	0	0	0	0	0	0	0	0	0	0	7	0	0	7	0	**7**	0	**7**	0	0	0	**7**	0	0	0	0	0	0	0	0	0	0	0	0	0	0	0	0	0	0
inject false message	0	0	0	0	8	0	0	0	0	0	0	0	0	0	0	0	0	0	0	8	0	0	0	8	**8**	0	**8**	0	0	0	**8**	0	0	0	0	0	0	0	0	0	0	0	0	0	0	0	0	0	0
jam signal	0	0	0	0	0	6	0	0	0	0	0	0	0	0	0	0	0	0	0	6	0	0	0	6	**6**	0	**6**	0	0	0	**6**	0	0	0	0	0	0	0	0	0	0	0	0	0	0	0	0	0	0
exploit MAC backoff	0	0	0	0	0	0	8	0	0	0	0	0	0	0	0	0	0	0	0	8	0	0	0	8	**8**	0	**8**	0	0	0	**8**	0	0	0	0	0	0	0	0	0	0	0	0	0	0	0	0	0	0
exploit NAV	0	0	0	0	0	0	0	8	0	0	0	0	0	0	0	0	0	0	0	8	0	0	0	8	**8**	0	**8**	0	0	0	**8**	0	0	0	0	0	0	0	0	0	0	0	0	0	0	0	0	0	0
SYN flooding	0	0	0	0	0	0	0	0	9	0	0	0	0	0	0	0	0	0	0	0	9	0	9	0	**9**	0	**9**	0	0	0	**9**	0	0	0	0	0	0	0	0	0	0	0	0	0	0	0	0	0	0
black hole attack.1	0	0	0	0	0	0	0	0	0	11	0	0	0	0	0	0	0	0	0	0	0	0	11	0	**11**	0	**11**	0	0	0	**11**	0	0	0	0	0	0	0	0	0	0	0	0	0	0	0	0	0	0
worm hole attack.1	0	0	0	0	0	0	0	0	0	0	12	0	0	0	0	0	0	0	0	0	0	0	12	0	**12**	0	**12**	0	0	0	**12**	0	0	0	0	0	0	0	0	0	0	0	0	0	0	0	0	0	0
X12	0	0	0	0	0	0	0	0	0	0	0	7	0	0	0	0	0	0	0	0	0	0	0	7	**7**	0	**7**	0	0	0	**7**	0	0	0	0	0	0	0	0	0	0	0	0	0	0	0	0	0	0
exploit in vehicle application	0	0	0	0	0	0	0	0	0	0	0	0	6	0	0	0	0	0	0	0	0	0	0	6	0	0	**6**	0	0	0	**6**	0	0	0	0	0	0	0	0	0	0	0	0	0	0	0	0	0	0
IPCompromise.2	0	0	0	0	0	0	0	0	0	0	0	0	0	0	6	0	0	0	0	0	0	0	0	0	0	0	0	0	0	0	0	0	0	0	0	0	0	0	0	0	0	0	0	0	0	0	0	0	0
IPCompromise.1	0	0	0	0	0	0	0	0	0	0	0	0	0	0	0	0	0	0	0	0	0	0	0	0	0	0	0	0	0	0	0	0	0	0	0	0	0	0	0	0	0	0	0	0	0	0	0	0	0
DOS-sessionhijacking	0	0	0	0	0	0	0	0	0	0	0	0	0	0	0	0	0	0	0	0	0	0	0	0	0	0	0	0	0	0	0	0	0	0	0	0	0	0	0	0	0	0	0	0	0	0	0	0	0
DOS-sessionhijacking	0	0	0	0	0	0	0	0	0	0	0	0	0	0	0	0	0	0	0	0	0	0	0	0	0	0	0	0	0	0	0	0	0	0	0	0	0	0	0	0	0	0	0	0	0	0	0	0	0
TCP ACK Storm-SEV3	0	0	0	0	0	0	0	0	0	0	0	0	0	0	0	0	0	0	0	0	0	0	0	0	0	0	0	0	0	0	0	0	0	0	0	0	0	0	0	0	0	0	0	0	0	0	0	0	0
physical layer	0	0	0	0	0	0	0	0	0	0	0	0	0	0	0	0	0	0	0	0	0	0	0	0	0	0	0	0	0	0	0	0	0	0	0	0	0	0	0	0	0	0	0	0	0	0	0	0	0
link layer	0	0	0	0	0	0	0	0	0	0	0	0	0	0	0	0	0	0	0	0	0	0	0	0	0	0	0	0	0	0	0	0	0	0	0	0	0	0	0	0	0	0	0	0	0	0	0	0	0
transport layer	0	0	0	0	0	0	0	0	0	0	0	0	0	0	0	0	0	0	0	0	0	0	0	0	0	0	0	0	0	0	0	0	0	0	0	0	0	0	0	0	0	0	0	0	0	0	0	0	0
network layer.1	0	0	0	0	0	0	0	0	0	0	0	0	0	0	0	0	0	0	0	0	0	0	0	0	0	0	0	0	0	0	0	0	0	0	0	0	0	0	0	0	0	0	0	0	0	0	0	0	0
S2	0	0	0	0	0	0	0	0	0	0	0	0	0	0	0	0	0	0	0	0	0	0	0	0	0	0	0	0	0	0	0	0	0	0	0	0	0	0	0	0	0	0	0	0	0	0	0	0	0
application layer	0	0	0	0	0	0	0	0	0	0	0	0	0	0	0	0	0	0	0	0	0	0	0	0	0	0	0	0	0	0	0	0	0	0	0	0	0	0	0	0	0	0	0	0	0	0	0	0	0
S32	0	0	0	0	0	0	0	0	0	0	0	0	0	0	0	0	0	0	0	0	0	0	0	0	0	0	0	0	0	0	0	0	0	0	0	0	0	0	0	0	0	0	0	0	0	0	0	0	0
G1-Availability	0	0	0	0	0	0	0	0	0	0	0	0	0	0	0	0	0	0	0	0	0	0	0	0	0	0	0	0	0	0	0	0	0	0	0	0	0	0	0	0	0	0	0	0	0	0	0	0	0
Application and servi...	0	0	0	0	0	0	0	0	0	0	0	0	0	0	0	0	0	0	0	0	0	0	0	0	0	0	0	0	0	0	0	0	0	0	0	0	0	0	0	0	0	0	0	0	0	0	0	0	0
GOAL-SYSTEM	0	0	0	0	0	0	0	0	0	0	0	0	0	0	0	0	0	0	0	0	0	0	0	0	0	0	0	0	0	0	0	0	0	0	0	0	0	0	0	0	0	0	0	0	0	0	0	0	0
BA2O	0	0	0	0	0	0	0	0	0	0	0	0	0	0	0	0	0	0	0	0	0	0	0	0	0	0	0	0	0	0	0	0.145	0	0	0	0	0	0	0	0	0	0.145	0	0	0	0	0	**0.145**	**0.145**
BA1O	0	0	0	0	0	0	0	0	0	0	0	0	0	0	0	0	0	0	0	0	0	0	0	0	0	0	0	0	0	0	0	0	0	0	0	0	0	0	0	0	0	0	0	0	0	0	0	0	0
STA1O	0	0	0	0	0	0	0	0	0	0	0	0	0	0	0	0	0	0	0	0	0	0	0	0	0	0	0	0	0	0	0	0	0	0.313	0	0	0	0	0	0	0	0.313	0	0	0	0	0	**0.313**	**0.313**
STA2O	0	0	0	0	0	0	0	0	0	0	0	0	0	0	0	0	0	0	0	0	0	0	0	0	0	0	0	0	0	0	0	0	0	0	0	0	0	0	0	0	0	0	0	0	0	0	0	0	0
CLB1O	0	0	0	0	0	0	0	0	0	0	0	0	0	0	0	0	0	0	0	0	0	0	0	0	0	0	0	0	0	0	0	0	0	0	0	0.322	0	0	0	0	0	0.322	0	0	0	0	0	0	**0.322**
CLB2O	0	0	0	0	0	0	0	0	0	0	0	0	0	0	0	0	0	0	0	0	0	0	0	0	0	0	0	0	0	0	0	0	0	0	0	0	0	0	0	0	0	0	0	0	0	0	0	0	0
SNSB1O	0	0	0	0	0	0	0	0	0	0	0	0	0	0	0	0	0	0	0	0	0	0	0	0	0	0	0	0	0	0	0	0	0	0	0	0	0	0.524	0	0	0	0.524	0	0	0	0	0	0	**0.524**
SNSB2O	0	0	0	0	0	0	0	0	0	0	0	0	0	0	0	0	0	0	0	0	0	0	0	0	0	0	0	0	0	0	0	0	0	0	0	0	0	0	0.216	0	0	0.216	0	0	0	0	0	0	**0.216**
SNSB3O	0	0	0	0	0	0	0	0	0	0	0	0	0	0	0	0	0	0	0	0	0	0	0	0	0	0	0	0	0	0	0	0	0	0	0	0	0	0	0	0.524	0	0.524	0	0	0	0	0	0	**0.524**
EMS2O	0	0	0	0	0	0	0	0	0	0	0	0	0	0	0	0	0	0	0	0	0	0	0	0	0	0	0	0	0	0	0	0	0	0	0	0	0	0	0	0.197	0	0.197	0	0	0	0	0	0	**0.197**
EMS1O	0	0	0	0	0	0	0	0	0	0	0	0	0	0	0	0	0	0	0	0	0	0	0	0	0	0	0	0	0	0	0	0	0	0	0	0	0	0	0	0	0	0	0	0	0	0	0	0	0
BAFA	0	0	0	0	0	0	0	0	0	0	0	0	0	0	0	0	0	0	0	0	0	0	0	0	0	0	0	0	0	0	0	0	0	0	0	0	0	0	0	0	0	0	0	0	0	0	0	0	0
STAFA	0	0	0	0	0	0	0	0	0	0	0	0	0	0	0	0	0	0	0	0	0	0	0	0	0	0	0	0	0	0	0	0	0	0	0	0	0	0	0	0	0	0	0	0	0	0	0	0	0
CLBA	0	0	0	0	0	0	0	0	0	0	0	0	0	0	0	0	0	0	0	0	0	0	0	0	0	0	0	0	0	0	0	0	0	0	0	0	0	0	0	0	0	0	0	0	0	0	0	0	0
SNSBA	0	0	0	0	0	0	0	0	0	0	0	0	0	0	0	0	0	0	0	0	0	0	0	0	0	0	0	0	0	0	0	0	0	0	0	0	0	0	0	0	0	0	0	0	0	0	0	0	0
EMSA	0	0	0	0	0	0	0	0	0	0	0	0	0	0	0	0	0	0	0	0	0	0	0	0	0	0	0	0	0	0	0	0	0	0	0	0	0	0	0	0	0	0	0	0	0	0	0	0	0
ECUBA	0	0	0	0	0	0	0	0	0	0	0	0	0	0	0	0	0	0	0	0	0	0	0	0	0	0	0	0	0	0	0	0	0	0	0	0	0	0	0	0	0	0	0	0	0	0	0	0	0
D	0	0	0	0	0	0	0	0	0	0	0	0	0	0	0	0	0	0	0	0	0	0	0	0	0	0	0	0	0	0	0	0	0	0	0	0	0	0	0	0	0	0	0	0	0	0	0	0	0

Fig. 10. Unnormalized supermatrix with separate domain specific analysis

unnormalized to get the failure rate and vulnerability scores. The entries in bold appear as a result of the supermatrix evaluation, because now the impact of basic failure/attacks is represented on all the higher hierarchical levels while in unweighted matrix just on immediate next hierarchical level.

Fig. 11. Unnormalized supermatrix with cross domain interaction

(Row2..29, col 30..47) represents the impact of security attacks on safety and (row30..47, col 2..29) represents the impact of failures on security. After supermatrix evaluation using the domain specific analysis results of failure analysis and attack tree analysis, now we consider the interaction, cross domain impact.

To demonstrate this we assume that the basic attack step inject false message and exploit MAC backoff has impact on subsystem BAFA failure and STAFA failure. Considering this cross domain impact, now the final supermatrix will be reduced to supermatrix as shown in Fig. 11. We can observe that the impact of basic attack step inject false message and exploit MAC backoff has no impact on higher attack state, but it has impact on higher failed states (represented in bold font). The supermatrix structure generated in Fig. 10 allows us to generate this cross domain interaction structure. This supermatrix provides a state based fault tree-attack tree structure and analysis for co-engineering design decisions and trade-offs. Since, the supermatrix tracks each part of the system in a hierarchical manner, it is easy to assess if a safety or a security requirement corresponding to any particular part of system is satisfied or not, as different sub-systems of a system may have different safety and/or security requirements.

6 Conclusion and Further Work

We used SCPN to analyse large, complex and dynamic systems compactly. We also discussed, how we can analyse security, combining attack tree semantics with FMVEA based scoring and the mentioned threat propagation scheme (for the AND gate). Finally, we presented a matrix based approach which tracks all concerned dependability attributes in hierarchical manner, in a single matrix, with consideration of dependences among them. The final supermatrix evaluates the impact of failures and attacks on top dependability goals, which will help us in taking design decisions in a guided way, to reduce the number of design iterations, in achieving the desired set of dependability attributes. In future work, we would like to use this approach in some use cases. We will further work on how to rank alternatives, where each alternative is a set of possible design strategies or decisions which can be implemented for a given system.

Acknowledgments. The work published here has received funding from the AQUAS project, under grant agreement No. 737475. The project is co-funded by grants from Austria, the Czech republic, Germany, Italy, France, Spain, The UK, and ECSEL JU.

References

1. Shostack, A.: Threat Modeling: Designing for Security. Wiley, Hoboken (2014)
2. Ryoo, J., Kazman, R., Anand, P.: Architectural analysis for security (2015)
3. Stolte, T., Bagschik, G., Reschka, A., Maurer, M.: Hazard analysis and risk assessment for an automated unmanned protective vehicle (2017)
4. Ma, Z., Schmittner, C.: Threat modeling for automotive security analysis
5. Macher, G., Sporer, H., Armengaud, E., Kreiner, C.: SAHARA: a security-aware hazard and risk analysis method (2015)
6. Schmittner, C., Gruber, T., Puschner, P., Schoitsch, E.: Security application of failure mode and effect analysis (FMEA). In: Bondavalli, A., Di Giandomenico, F. (eds.) SAFECOMP 2014. LNCS, vol. 8666, pp. 310–325. Springer, Cham (2014). https://doi.org/10.1007/978-3-319-10506-2_21

7. Satty, T.L.: The AHP and ANP: applications to decisions under risk (2008)
8. Kadoic, N., Redep, N., Divjak, B.: Decision Making with the Analytic Network Process
9. Satty, T.L.: How to make a decision: the analytic hierarchy process (1990)
10. Satty, T.L.: The Analytic Network Process
11. Pentti, H., Helminen, A.: FMEA of software-based automation systems (2002)
12. Reifer, D.J.: Software failure modes and effects analysis (1979)
13. Kabir, S.: An overview of FTA and its application in model based dependability analysis (2017)
14. Peeters, J.F.W., Basten, R.J.I., Tinga, T: Improving failure analysis efficiency by combining FTA and FMEA in a recursive manner (2018)
15. Rausand, M., Hoyland, A.: System Reliability Theory (2004)
16. Talebberrouane, M., Khan, F., Lounis, Z.: Availability analysis of safety critical systems using advanced fault tree and stochastic Petri net formalisms (2016)
17. Squair, M.: System Safety: M9 FTA V1.1: UNSW Canberra (2015)
18. Morant, A., Gustafson, A., Söderholm, P., Kraik, P., Kumar, U.: Safety and availability evaluation of railway operation based on the state of signaling systems
19. Alizadeh, S., Sriramula, S.: Unavailability assessment of redundant safety instrumented systems subject to process demand. University of Aberdeen, UK (2017)
20. Bobbio, A.: System modelling with petri nets. Istituto Elettrotecnico Nazionale Galileo Ferraris Strada delle Cacce 91, 10135 Torino, Italy (1990)
21. Wang, J.: Petri nets for dynamic event-driven system modeling. Department of Software Engineering, Monmouth University
22. Marsan, M.A.: Stochastic petri nets: an elementary introduction. Dipartimento di Scienze dell' Informazione, Universita di Milano, Italy
23. Hillston, J.: Performance modelling: lecture 7 stochastic petri nets. School of Informatics. The University of Edinburgh, Scotland (2017)
24. Balbo, G.: Introduction to GSPN. In: 7-th International School on Formal Methods for the Design of Computer, Communication and Software Systems (2007)
25. Liu, Z., et al.: RAMS analysis of hybrid redundancy system of subsea blowout preventer based on SPN (2013)
26. Gehlot, V., Nigro, C.: An introduction to systems modeling and simulation with colored petri nets. In: Proceedings of the 2010 Winter Simulation Conference (2010)
27. TimeNET: Tool for the performability evaluation, stochastic colored petri nets
28. Flammini, F., Marrone, S., Vittorini, V.: PN modelling of physical vulnerability
29. Kumar, R., Stoelinga, M.: Quantitative security and safety analysis with attack-fault trees. University of Twente, The Netherlands (2010)
30. Zhan, Z., Xu, M., Xu, S.: Predicting cyber attack rates with extreme values
31. Mauw, S., Oostdijk, M.: Foundations of attack trees. In: Won, D.H., Kim, S. (eds.) ICISC 2005. LNCS, vol. 3935, pp. 186–198. Springer, Heidelberg (2006). https://doi.org/10.1007/11734727_17
32. Kumar, R.: Truth or dare: quantitative security risk analysis using attack trees. Ph.D. Thesis, University of Twente (2018)
33. Petschnigg, C., et al.: SAFURE - architecture models and patterns for safety and security (2016)
34. Mokhtara, B., Azab, M.: Survey on security issues in vehicular ad hoc networks. Alexandria Eng. J. **54**, 1115–1126 (2015)

35. Du, S., Zhu, H.: Security assessment via attack tree model. In: Du, S., Zhu, H. (eds.) Security Assessment in Vehicular Networks. Springer, New York, NY (2013). https://doi.org/10.1007/978-1-4614-9357-0_2
36. Schmittner, C., Ma, Z., Reyes, C., Dillinger, O., Puschner, P.: Using SAE J3061 for automotive security requirement engineering. In: Skavhaug, A., Guiochet, J., Schoitsch, E., Bitsch, F. (eds.) SAFECOMP 2016. LNCS, vol. 9923, pp. 157–170. Springer, Cham (2016). https://doi.org/10.1007/978-3-319-45480-1_13

Towards Integrated Quantitative Security and Safety Risk Assessment

Jürgen Dobaj[1]([✉])[iD], Christoph Schmittner[2][iD], Michael Krisper[1][iD], and Georg Macher[1][iD]

[1] Graz University of Technology, 8010 Graz, Austria
{juergen.dobaj,michael.krisper,georg.macher}@tugraz.at
[2] AIT Austrian Institute of Technology, 1020 Vienna, Austria
christoph.schmittner@ait.ac.at

Abstract. Although multiple approaches for the combination of safety and security analysis exist, there are still some major gaps to overcome before they can be used for combined risk management. This paper presents the existing gaps, based on an overview of available methods, which is followed by the proposal towards a solution to achieve coordinated risk management by applying a quantitative security risk assessment methodology. This methodology extends established safety and security risk analysis methods with an integrated model, denoting the relationship between adversary and victim, including the used capabilities and infrastructure. This model is used to estimate the resistance strength and threat capabilities, to determine attack probabilities and security risks.

Keywords: Security analysis · Safety analysis · Risk assessment · Threat analysis · Threat modeling · SAHARA · FMVEA · Diamond · FAIR

1 Introduction

Formerly, security played only a secondary role in safety- and mission-critical systems, since these systems were not connected to the Internet or the outer world. However, with the introduction of Internet-of-Things (IoT) and cyber-physical system (CPS) concepts into multiple industrial domains, the industry is undergoing enormous change towards highly interconnected and globally distributed automation and control systems, ranging from intelligent transportation systems [5] and industrial systems [27], to smart homes and smart cities [4]. Security mechanisms are responsible for protecting these systems from unwanted access or malicious attacks. Therefore, system security becomes an essential factor affecting the safety of mission-critical systems. Consequently, this requires an holistic dependability engineering approach integrating both, security and safety.

© Springer Nature Switzerland AG 2019
A. Romanovsky et al. (Eds.): SAFECOMP 2019 Workshops, LNCS 11699, pp. 102–116, 2019.
https://doi.org/10.1007/978-3-030-26250-1_8

In particular, dependability is defined by multiple attributes (availability, reliability, safety, confidentiality, integrity, maintainability) that must be maintained and assured at a sufficient level. This is commonly achieved by considering the risk of potential threats (faults, errors, failures), followed by applying adequate risk reduction mechanisms (fault prevention, fault tolerance, fault removal, fault forecasting). It should be noted, that the term fault is quite generic, ranging from systematic weaknesses in software to insufficiently designed hardware.

Risk reduction denotes the effort to deliberately reduce risks to a tolerable level, instead of fantasizing about reducing all risks to zero, which makes it inevitable to prioritize risks and risk treatments. Risk treatment is defined as a cyclic process [10] of: (1) assessing existing risk treatments; (2) deciding if the residual risks are tolerable; (3) generating new risk treatments, if not tolerable; and again (4) assessing the new risk treatments. There are multiple risk treatments available, however, in dependable systems it is often required to implement specific measures for achieving a tolerable risk level. Therefore, decisions about risk treatments directly influence system engineering, requiring an evaluation of where engineering resources should be dedicated. Risk is generally defined by the likelihood and impact of a loss event classified according to only partially comparable categories (e.g. safety, financial, operational, privacy/confidentiality, ...). For example, functional safety considers safety impacts based on faults, errors, and failures of electric/electronic/programmable electronic (E/E/PE) elements. As long as risks compare similar categories, a similar likelihood scale can be used, which enables decisions on the required risk reduction mechanisms. However, different categories should not be mixed up, like financial loss and harm to human lives should be considered separately.

In the context of connected systems, it is essential to not only consider safety risks, but also security risks originating from malicious manipulations by e.g., internal or external actors. Such manipulations might have an impact on the same dependability attribute, but the resulting failure may be differently categorized, making it difficult to prioritize the risk treatments accordingly. Hence, there is and will be an ever increasing need to coordinate between the engineering processes that focus on different dependability attributes in system engineering [18]. This coordination requires combined methods as well as a common language for communicating and comparing risks. Whoever decides on the treatment of risks, should therefore, be provided with risk ratings in comparable scales.

In contrast to the statistical failure probability concept known from the safety domain, system security does not exclusively depend on statistical information about vulnerabilities and weaknesses, instead it is mainly driven by the interaction of an (human or machine) attacker against the resistance of a system. Integrating such human aspirations and motivations for mischief or selfish advantage into a likelihood system for risk is difficult, therefore imposing significant restricts to both, the coordination of security with safety risks, as well as with all other dependability attributes. While there are methods for combined considerations [16], they are still lacking some of the properties needed for a full risk analysis, meaning identification and evaluation, which was a major finding of this paper and gives us open challenges to resolve, for protecting safety critical systems against malicious attacks [14].

In the course of this document, a discussion of related work and state-of-the-art analysis methods is provided in Sect. 2, which we expand by a brief discussion of the methods actual limitations to enable combined security and safety risk assessment. In Sect. 3, we introduce a new model for assessing the probability of security attacks in dependable CPSs. Therefore, we propose an approach that is based on established methods for combined considerations of safety and security features, which is accomplished by an established method for security incident analysis. This model is then used in Sect. 3.2 as qualified information framework to quantitatively classify the probability of cybersecurity attacks, by adapting and extending an established method for IT-security risk assessment. Section 3.3 presents an illustrative example, followed by an outlook and a closing discussion in Sect. 4.

2   Background

In this section an overview of relevant standards and context of related work is given. To that aim, also the differences of cyber-security and safety, as well as the applied integrated methods are briefly described. Additionally, as first contribution of this work, a comparison between established integrated risk assessment methods is given in Sect. 2.3.

2.1   Safety vs. Security

The idea of safety and security co-design has become a major trend of recent publications and is expected to appear more often in the future, also due to the upcoming security standards for safety critical domains, and the requirements on communication and coordination between safety and security. However, one of the main challenges of this merging of safety and security disciplines is the different level of maturity in the standards and the available knowledge in the domains. Safety, as well as security engineering focus on system-wide features and need to be integrated adequately into the existing process landscape; both having a major impact on product development and product release, as well as for company brand.

Therefore, a tight integration and cooperation between these two domains seems obvious and essential. The difference between safety and security, and one of the major show stoppers, is the very different point-of-view and the fundamentally different engineering approaches and nomenclatures. This issue has already been partially described and tackled in [18].

Beside this, functional safety engineering approaches focus on defects, failures, and errors, which can be foreseen (with reservations) at design-time, as well as on mathematical models based on failure probabilities and system models. Therefore, functional safety standards are defining domain specific processes and methods for the development of safety-critical embedded systems. They target the minimization of systematic failures during development (e.g., requirement not implemented in the development phase) as well as the control of random failures during operation (e.g., component break-down). These standards rely on efficient quality management in project, and systematic hazard identification and management along the entire development life-cycle. Sound technical concept and validation planning, as well as trace management between these different items is a central aspect for safety augmentations.

On the contrary, security standards often just provide a set of high-level guiding principles for the life-cycle process framework, some basic guiding principles on cyber-security, or focus on a subset of the complete engineering process; but there are no common base practices or methodologies which are shared. Common Criteria [13], for example, is a detailed standard for security evaluation, but not applicable to security engineering.

Safety and security features have mutual impacts, sometimes similarities, and interdisciplinary values in common. However, these different attributes might lead to different targets, and mutual impact between safety and security exist. This even goes as far, that safety and security features frequently appear to be in total contradiction to the overall system features. A straight forward example of this contradiction can be shown by an electrical steering column lock system. In the security context, the system locks the steering column when in doubt, because this doubt area might result from an attack. From the safety perspective, however, it is highly undesirable to lock the steering column. Since, the issue involved might well be an occurrence directly before a high speed corner turn and would leave the driver without control over the steering wheel.

In addition to that, using non-integrated methods to manage these different attributes might lead to inconsistencies, which are identified in late development phases. Therefore, a solid information handover and a cooperative dependability engineering by cross-domain expert teams are required [16].

2.2 Qualitative vs. Quantitative Methods

Many established methods use qualitative assessments based on ordinal scales e.g. rating the severity of a safety hazard on a scale between 0 and 3, or rating the threat level of a security threat on a scale from "no security impact" to "moderate relevance" and "high security and possible safety relevance". Typically these ratings consist of 2 to 3 ordinal scales which get combined either by addition or multiplication to obtain a final risk rating based on thresholds. Such qualitative assessments methods based on ordinal scales and so called "risk matrices" have several shortcomings including e.g., range compression/poor resolution, risk inversion, ambiguity, and neglecting correlations, which is shown in several publications by Hubbard et al. [7,8], and Cox et al. [2,3].

To avoid such pitfalls, we propose to apply a fully quantitative assessment method like factor analysis of information risk (FAIR), which is based upon the estimation of event frequencies, system vulnerabilities, and event impacts using probability distributions that enable to also take the respective uncertainty (or confidence - as it is called in the diamond model) of an estimation into account.

2.3 Comparison of Established Integrated Risk Assessment Methods

As already mentioned, risk management is an essential step in the development of critical systems. On a domain-independent level, risk management is defined by ISO 31000 [10]. For ISO and IEC standards the ISO/IEC Directives, Part 1 [12] requires all product or industry/economic sector specific risk management standards to reference or reproduce ISO 31000. ISO 31000 mentions quantitative and qualitative risk analysis and states that specific results should be consistent and comparable for effective risk management, e.g., all risks in comparable scales. Outside of ISO and IEC standards, there is also work on risk management. National institute of standards and technology (NIST), for example, published in 2012 *NIST Special Publication 800-30 (SP800-30) "Guide for Conducting Risk Assessments"* [15], for guidance in conducting risk assessments on federal information systems and organizations. SP800-30 also refers to the ISO 31000 risk management standards. In its main part, quantitative, qualitative and semi-quantitative approaches are discussed. In its annex a potential approach similar to (FAIR) is presented, where the likelihood of an event is divided into (a) a likelihood, that an adversary is initiating a threat event; and (b) a likelihood, that the threat event results in an adverse impact (i.e., a successful attack). Semi-quantitative values are given, and NIST SP800-30 warns that it can be challenging to assign a likelihood to a particular "bin" (e.g., 0–15, 16–35, 36–70), especially if it is between two levels.

In recent work [17], Macher et al., focused on enhancing the development lifecycle for automotive CPS by analyzing state-of-the-art methods for integrated security, safety, and reliability engineering. Their finally proposed framework is based on security-aware hazard and risk analysis (SAHARA), failure mode, vulnerabilities and effects analysis (FMVEA), and attack tree analysis (ATA), representing a promising approach for the integrated design of safe and secure systems in the automotive domain, which is the reason why we use them in our approach too. A comprehensive overview and comparison of related methods can be found in [16].

While SAHARA and FMVEA have its origin in the automotive sector, our proposed integrated risk management approach is not restricted to a specific domain. Instead, it supports the general level of ISO 31000 and allows to manage uncertainty and missing information in a risk management process.

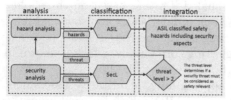

(a) Illustration of the SAHARA method.

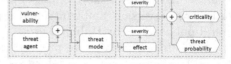

(b) Illustration of the FMVEA method.

Fig. 1. Overview of the approaches for integrated risk assessment methods.

The SAHARA method, illustrated in Fig. 1(a), depicts a systematic approach to quantify the security impact on dependable safety-related systems on system level [19]. Therefore, the method combines the automotive hazard analysis and risk assessment (HARA) [11] approach with STRIDE [21] threat modelling.

The FMVEA method, illustrated in Fig. 1(b), is based on the failure mode and effects analysis (FMEA) as described in IEC 60812 [9] with additional support for security analysis, also based on the STRIDE threat modelling approach [22] . FMVEA uses a threat&failure-mode-effect model for its safety and security risk analysis targeted towards the item level.

Integrated Risk Assessment. Both methods, SAHARA and FMVEA, describe integrated approaches that extend established safety risk analysis methods to not only classify the risk of system failures, but also the risk of security threats. For this cybersecurity risk classification the methods define schemes similar to those known from safety engineering. However, instead of finding and rating potential system failures and failure causes, cybersecurity risk assessment is targeted towards identifying and rating potential vulnerabilities and threats and the interplay of both with assumed attackers. Therefore, the methods provide rating schemes to assess (i) the attacker strength, denoted by the attacker capabilities, intention, and know-how; (ii) the system resistance, partially denoted by static security measures classified by the system reachability, structure, and required attack tools; and (iii) the impact of a successful attack, denoted by the effects on the system and its environment.

The attacker strength and the system resistance are combined to estimate the probability of a potentially successful attack. The attack probability and impact determine the criticality level of a security threat, which is also used to indicate the safety relevance of a security threat. Beside the criticality level, the SAHARA method also specifies a so called security level (SecL) to provide guidance in selecting the appropriate number of countermeasures that should be considered [19]. The FMVEA, on the other hand, uses the resulting risk priority number (RPN) as a comparable indicator to focus the development efforts on the most critical issues and system areas [22].

For determining the SecL and RPN, both methods rely on qualitative measures. However, qualitative measures are not suitable for mathematical models to calculate the overall vulnerability of the system. Moreover, the measures lack calibration with the failure probability to enable a integrated combined safety and security risk management [22]. Another, general limitation of both methods is the restriction to analyze only single causes of an effect [22]. Hence, multi-stage attacks could be overlooked, which, however, would be of particular relevance for analyzing security attacks.

2.4   The Diamond Model of Intrusion Analysis

The *diamond model of intrusion analysis* [1] is an established formal method to analyze cyber-incidents after their occurrence. Figure 2(a) illustrates a diamond that represents a basic atomic element of any intrusion activity, also denoted as (security) event. The key assumption of the diamond model is that *"for every intrusion event there exists an* **adversary** *taking a step towards an intended goal by using a* **capability** *over* **infrastructure** *against a* **victim** *to produce a result"* [1]. Hence, an event is composed of four core-features (described later in Sect. 3.1): adversary, capability, infrastructure, and victim. These features are arranged in the shape of a diamond, where the edges represent the underlying relationships between the features. The diamond further defines meta-features to support higher-level constructs, which includes linking multiple events to form activity threads and attack graphs. These threads and graphs are illustrated in Fig. 2(b). Activity threads and attack graphs are comparable to attack trees [23]. An **activity thread** consists of a set of diamonds representing an attack path through the graph. An **attack graph** enumerates multiple paths an adversary could have taken in the attack, while an activity thread represents an already identified attack path.

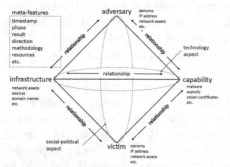

(a) Illustration of he diamond model of in-   (b) Illustration of activity threats and at-
trusion analysis (adapted from [1]).   tack graphs (adapted from [1]).

Fig. 2. Excerpt of the diamond modelling capabilities.

After the detection of an incident, there is generally limited information about the attack sequence and exploited vulnerabilities available. Thus, the major idea of the diamond model is that the events, threads, and graphs form a documentation and information framework that facilitates the structured analysis of such incidents. This helps analysts to ask the right questions to uncover missing links, vulnerabilities, and the actual adversary. By assigning confidence values to both, core- and meta-features, the confidence into the actual analysis is documented.

2.5 The FAIR Method for Risk Analysis

The FAIR method is a way of determining the risk of an attack event [25]. It is based on splitting risk into several sub-factors to more easily evaluate IT-security and operational risk [6,25,26], as shown in Fig. 3(a). These sub-factors are rated in the form of expert judgements by describing the minimum, maximum, and most likely value including a confidence rating. The judgements, as shown in Fig. 3(b) and (c), are modelled as program evaluation and review technique (PERT) probability distributions, which originates in project management and was first used by the US Navy to estimate time plans for missions [20].

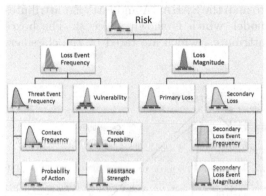

(a) The FAIR taxonomy showing the sub-factor decomposition, each heaving a probability assigned (adapted from [26]).

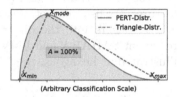

(b) The PERT distribution.

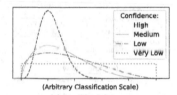

(c) The same judgement with different confidence levels.

Fig. 3. Overview of the FAIR taxonomy and the PERT distribution.

3 Contribution: Towards a Quantitative Integrated Risk Assessment Method

In the preceding sections we compared the SAHARA [19] and FMVEA [22] methods for integrated risk assessment in CPS. Subsequently, the diamond model [1] and the FAIR method [25] are introduced to now propose an integrated quantitative risk assessment model that maps features, described by SAHARA and FMVEA, into the diamond model. We propose a methodology for quantitative security risk assessment by combining all these methods, which enables the analysis of security and failure event chains, as well as a coordinated risk management. Therefore, we are using a combined terminology from both, Diamond and FAIR.

3.1   Combining SAHARA, FMVEA, and Diamond into One Model

As already discussed in the previous sections, there exists potential for improving the established integrated risk analysis methods. Since, the diamond model describes a structured model and process for cyber incidents analysis, we propose that the model is capable to complement the integrated methods enabling a more comprehensive risk analysis.

The key assumption of the diamond model is that *"for every intrusion event there exists an adversary taking a step towards an intended goal by using a capability over infrastructure against a victim to produce a result"* [1]. Such an event is modeled by four core-features: (i) the adversary, (ii) the capability, (iii) the infrastructure, and (iv) the victim; as well as arbitrary definable meta-features. We use this meta-features to map the SAHARA and FMVEA attributes and classifiers into the diamond model, which is shown in Fig. 4. The boxes represent SAHARA and FMVEA attributes, which are rated by the classifiers illustrated as hexagons.

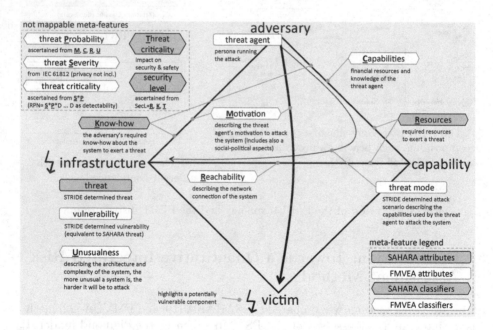

Fig. 4. Illustration of the diamond model including the mapping of the security attributes and their classifiers described by SAHARA and FMVEA.

(i) The adversary feature describes a set of adversaries (e.g., in/outsiders, individuals, groups, and organizations) which seek to compromise a system to satisfy their intent and needs. An adversary could be described by (a) an adversary operator, the person conducting the intrusion activity; and (b) an adversary customer, the entity that benefits form the conducted activity and generally acts as the funding entity, but might be the same person as the operator [1].

The SAHARA method does not explicitly describe or classify an adversary, however, the adversary is implicitly describes by its KNOW-HOW and the RESOURCE classifiers. The KNOW-HOW classifier determines the knowledge and insight an adversary requires to attack the infrastructure, distinguishing between black-, grey-, and white-box views. The method further names adversary examples (e.g., average driver, electrician, mechanic, ...) for each of the views imposing capabilities on the adversary. Hence, KNOW-HOW is mapped onto two edges describing both, the $adversary - infrastructure$ and the $adversary - capability$ relationship. The RESOURCE classifier determines the required resources an adversary must possess to attack the infrastructure, ranging from no tool support to advanced tool support. The RESOURCE classifiers is mapped onto the $adversary - capability$ relationship describing the tools required to deliver an attack over infrastructure, described by the $capability - infrastructure$ relationship.

In contrast, the FMVEA method explicitly states the adversary as threat agent classified according to ISO 27005 [24] making the mapping obvious. The ISO 27005 classification also characterizes the adversaries CAPABILITIES described by its financial resources and knowledge. FMVEA refines this by its MOTIVATION classifier, which takes both, technical and social-political aspects into account, described by the $adversary - infrastructure$ and $adversary - victim$ relationships.

(ii) The capability feature captures the tools and techniques an adversary used within a diamond event. This can be divided into (a) the capability capacity, all vulnerabilities and exposures of the target system that could potentially be utilized by the adversary; and (b) the capability arsenal, the actual set of the adversary's capability. The capacity is used to also document non-exploited vulnerabilities providing input for potential system improvements [1].

(iii) The infrastructure feature describes physical and/or logical communication structures that are used by the adversary to deliver a capability, maintain control of capabilities, and effect results on the victim. The infrastructure feature is divided into three types: (a) type 1 infrastructure, is fully controlled or owned by the adversary or which they may be in physical proximity; (b) type 2 infrastructure, is controlled by an (witting or unwitting) intermediary, which is typically the infrastructure an adversary uses to obfuscate its actions; (c) service providers, are organizations that (witting or unwitting) provide services critical for availability of type 1 and type 2 infrastructure [1].

Both, SAHARA and FMVEA, are based on the STRIDE [21] threat modelling approach to identify and categorize potential THREATS and VULNERABILITIES of the infrastructure. The FMVEA method uses this categorization to describe and identify potential THREAT MODES specifying the manner in which security fails, which is similar to the failure modes of safety. In terms of the diamond model a THREAT MODE can be described as the resources and infrastructure used by the adversary to deliver its capabilities, represented as the $adversary - capability - infrastructure$ relationship.

(iv) The victim feature describes the target of the adversary and against whom vulnerabilities and exposures are exploited and capabilities used. It is useful to divide the victim assets into (a) victim persona, the people and organizations targeted whose assets are exploited and attacked; and into (b) victim assets, the attack surface consisting of networks, systems, hosts, etc. against which the adversary directs their capabilities. It should be considered that in multi-stage attacks a victim asset, can be the end target in one event and then leveraged as the infrastructure in further events. Thus, one must always be aware that the target of an activity may not necessarily be the victim. Further, the victim assets often exist both, inside and outside a persona's control or visibility. However, still available for targeting by an adversary, which commonly includes cloud-based data storage and applications [1].

3.2   Extending FAIR for Risk Analysis Based on Diamond Events

After mapping the attributes from SAHARA and FMVEA to the diamond model, we have a qualified information basis for estimating the actual probability, severity and risk of a diamond event. For this estimation we apply and extend the FAIR method to give consolidated and refined expert judgements of the resulting risk within a diamond event. We implemented this in a mathematical framework to combine and propagate probabilities for quantitative security and safety risk analysis, providing the basis for future applications.

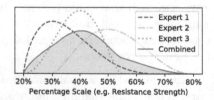 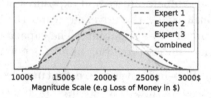

(a) Multiple expert judgements of probability values for resistance strength are combined into a mixture distribution.

(b) Multiple expert judgements for magnitude of impact (in this case: the loss of money) are combined.

Fig. 5. Combination of multiple expert judgements shown for different scales of value ranges. The area under the distribution is always normalized to 100%.

Combining Multiple Expert Judgements. We refined the FAIR method by combining multiple expert judgements to obtain a more realistic probability space for the respective value distribution. The resulting mixture probability distribution supports multiple centers of mass, better reflecting the given judgements, and also supporting differing confidence levels between single judgements. Figure 5(a) and (b) show examples of such mixture distributions from multiple experts. It is possible to mix different distribution types within the mixture model, so we are not limited to PERT distributions only.

3.3   Discussion of Enhancements and Open Issues

This section provides an illustrative example, shown in Fig. 6, that summarizes
and critically discusses the proposed approach. Like most integrated methods, as
outlined in Sect. 2, SAHARA and FMVEA are based on threat modelling to identify potential security risks. Both, SAHARA and FMVEA, use the STRIDE threat
modelling approach [21] as starting point for their security analysis, as indicated
on the top-left corner in Fig. 6. Our approach utilizes the diamond attack graphs
to model and document the identified threats and attack scenarios recognized by
applying the STRIDE approach. The obtained attack graphs have the advantage,
that the analysis of attack event chains is supported, similar to attack trees [23].
Moreover, their meta-feature concept makes attack graphs more generic, allowing to easily extend the model with additional information, including trace links
to requirements, and implementations, as well as capturing and classifying other
dependability attributes, like safety. Furthermore, the diamonds emphasize the
technical and social-political relationships between adversary and victim, which
supports analysts and designers in identifying otherwise not found vulnerabilities
and threats, as well as missing information. This observation is illustrated by the
SAHARA and FMVEA classifier mapping, which mainly describe the upper diamond half characterizing the system **threat capability** for the FAIR judgement.
The lower diamond half, reflecting the victim and its defense capability, is only partially described by the reachability and unusualness classifiers, representing static

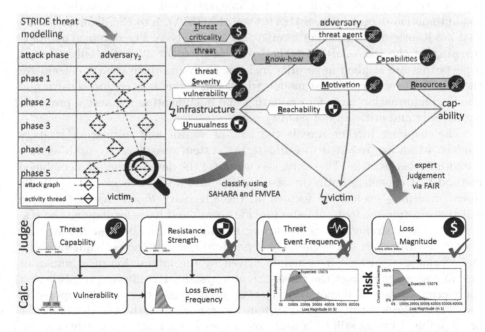

Fig. 6. Illustrative example showing the transition from FMVEA and SAHARA to
the Diamond model and evaluating the risk with FAIR. The check-marks indicate, if
additional classifiers or information is required to obtain profound expert judgements.

security measures only. To better estimate the system **resistance strength**, the proposed model needs to be extended to provide additional classifiers, also covering active security measures that deter, detect, report, and react against threats.

Actually, none of the methods (i.e., SAHARA, FMVEA, FAIR) supports estimating the **threat event frequency**, since only the probability of the single first attack is rated, and no potentially subsequent attacks (by different adversaries) are considered. While this is aligned with the idea of "failure" in the sense of safety, it is insufficient for analyzing security risks, due to fact that an attack could occur multiple times by multiple attackers without necessarily resulting in faults or failures.

The threat criticality ensures that safety relevant threats are handed over to safety management, and together with the threat severity, they already provide a good basis for estimating the **loss magnitude** of a diamond event.

In short, the proposed method provides the basic premises to integrate/combine security and safety risk assessment by providing means for an integrated quantification approach and a holistic model supporting both, threat and mitigation modelling.

4   Conclusion and Future Work

The primary contribution of this paper is the the definition of a method for integrating security into a combined risk assessment model. To obtain this model we mapped the classifiers described by two integrated risk analysis methods from the automotive domain (i.e., SAHARA and FMVEA), into the diamond model that has its origin in the field of security incident analysis. The obtained mapping reveals that the risk analysis methods do not consider all potentially relevant aspects that are studied in security incident analysis, which clearly encourages the usefulness of a combined model, which can serve as a comprehensive and qualified information basis for evaluating and documenting the actual probability, severity and criticality of security risks.

The mapping further reveals the lack of victim and mitigation strategy models, which are required to estimate the system resistance strength against potential cyber-attacks. Therefore, we encourage the development of a combined method that considers both, threat modelling and mitigation modelling. While *threat modelling* exclusively focuses on the adversary *threat capabilities*, a so called *mitigation model* would also provide a profound basis for judging the system *resistance strength*. Another strong reason for mitigation models is, that system security does not exclusively depend on the existence of vulnerabilities and weaknesses, instead it is mainly driven by the interaction of a human or machine attacker against the resistance of a system. By allowing to also cover the victim assets and deployed mitigation mechanisms, the model proposed in this work, allows estimating the system resistance strength too. However, the proposed model must still be enhance to capture both, passive (already covered) as well as active security measures allowing to deter, detect, report, and react against threats.

Since we are aiming towards a quantitative risk assessment, the model proposed in this work uses the established FAIR method for risk estimation. However, we propose to extend the FAIR method to be applicable on whole attack graphs, instead of single events only, which we are planning to model by an attacker evolving after each successful attack. To finally obtain a model that covers the whole system lifecycle, we are planning to introduce a time based risk prediction model to capture the evolution of attacker capabilities and the system resistance decay over time.

References

1. Caltagirone, S., Pendergast, A., Betz, C.: The diamond model of intrusion analysis. Technical report, Center for Cyber Intelligence Analysis and Threat Research Hanover MD (2013)
2. Cox, A.L.: What's wrong with risk matrices? Risk Anal. **28**(2), 497–512 (2008). https://doi.org/10.1111/j.1539-6924.2008.01030.x
3. Cox, L.A.: Some limitations of "risk = threat vulnerability consequence" for risk analysis of terrorist attacks. Risk Anal. **28**(6), 1749–1761 (2008)
4. Elmaghraby, A.S., Losavio, M.M.: Cyber security challenges in smart cities: safety, security and privacy. J. Adv. Res. **5**(4), 491–497 (2014)
5. European Commission. A European strategy on Cooperative Intelligent Transport Systems, a milestone towards cooperative, connected and automated mobility. Technical report, European Commission, November 2016
6. Freund, J.: Measuring and Managing Information Risk: A FAIR Approach. Butterworth-Heinemann, Oxford (2015)
7. Hubbard, D., Evans, D.: Problems with scoring methods and ordinal scales in risk assessment. IBM J. Res. Dev. **54**(3), 2 (2010)
8. Hubbard, D.W., Seiersen, R.: How to Measure Anything in Cybersecurity Risk. Wiley, Hoboken (2016)
9. IEC: IEC 60812: Analysis techniques for system reliability - Procedure for failure mode and effects analysis (FMEA) (2006)
10. ISO: ISO 31000 - risk management - guidelines
11. ISO: ISO 26262 Road vehicles - Functional safety (2011)
12. ISO/IEC: ISO/IEC directives, part 1
13. ISO/IEC: ISO/IEC 15408: Information Technology Security Evaluation (2005)
14. Johnson, C.W.: Why we cannot (yet) ensure the cybersecurity of safety-critical systems. In: Proceedings of 24th Safety-Critical Systems Symposium, pp. 171–182 (2016)
15. Joint Task Force Transformation Initiative: Guide for conducting risk assessments. https://doi.org/10.6028/NIST.SP.800-30r1
16. Lisova, E., Sljivo, I., Causevic, A.: Safety and security co-analyses: a systematic literature review (2018)
17. Macher, G., et al.: Integration of security in the development lifecycle of dependable automotive CPS (2017)
18. Macher, G., Höller, A., Sporer, H., Armengaud, E., Kreiner, C.: A comprehensive safety, security, and serviceability assessment method. In: Koornneef, F., van Gulijk, C. (eds.) SAFECOMP 2015. LNCS, vol. 9337, pp. 410–424. Springer, Cham (2015). https://doi.org/10.1007/978-3-319-24255-2_30

19. Macher, G., Sporer, H., Berlach, R., Armengaud, E., Kreiner, C.: SAHARA: a security-aware hazard and risk analysis method. In: Design, Automation and Test in Europe Conference and Exhibition (2015)
20. Malcolm, D.G., Roseboom, J.H., Clark, C.E., Fazar, W.: Application for a technique for research and development program evaluation (1959)
21. Microsoft Corporation: The STRIDE Threat Model (2005). http://msdn.microsoft.com/en-us/library/ee823878%28v=cs.20%29.aspx
22. Schmittner, C., Gruber, T., Puschner, P., Schoitsch, E.: Security application of failure mode and effect analysis (FMEA). In: Bondavalli, A., Di Giandomenico, F. (eds.) SAFECOMP 2014. LNCS, vol. 8666, pp. 310–325. Springer, Cham (2014). https://doi.org/10.1007/978-3-319-10506-2_21
23. Schneier, B.: Attack trees (1999). http://www.schneier.com/attacktrees.pdf
24. International Organization for Standardization (ISO), I.E.C.I.: Information technology – Security techniques – Information security risk management (2008)
25. The Open Group: Risk Analysis (O-RA), October 2013
26. The Open Group: Risk Taxonomy (O-RT) 2.0, October 2013
27. Xu, L.D., Xu, E.L., Li, L.: Industry 4.0: state of the art and future trends. Int. J. Prod. Res. 56(8), 2941–2962 (2018)

Potential Use of Safety Analysis for Risk Assessments in Smart City Sensor Network Applications

Torge Hinrichs[(⊠)] and Bettina Buth[(⊠)]

HAW Hamburg, Berliner Tor 5, 20099 Hamburg, Germany
{torge.hinrichs,buth}@haw-hamburg.de

Abstract. Smart City applications strongly rely on sensor networks for the collection of data and their subsequent analysis. In this paper we discuss whether methods from dependability engineering could be used to identify potential risk relating to safety and security of such applications. The demonstration object of this paper is a sensor network for air quality analysis and dynamic traffic control based on these data.

Keywords: Dependability · Smart Cities · Safety methods ·
Sensor networks risk assessment

1 Introduction

Sensor networks are ubiquitous. They can be used to measure the environment and help to process the data. Soon, these sensor networks could be used to automatically monitor the air quality in a city and to control the traffic flow for in- and outgoing traffic during peaks [1]. In general, a sensor network consists of several sensor nodes, which can be fixed installations or flexible, moving sensors. For example, in the application of Smart Cities it is state-of-the-art to use fixed installations on points with a high traffic throughput, but it would also be possible to use mobile, moving sensors such as those available in mobile phones or cars. These nodes can be configured in different arrangements. For example, they can use a thermometer to measure the temperature, a microphone for the noise level, a CO_2 or NO_x Sensor for measuring the air quality. Examples can be found in the open source project "Smart Citizen Project" [2]. They provide kits, which connect to a sensor network and contribute their data to the public.

The sensor nodes can be installed in different locations to serve various applications. For example, they can be attached to a traffic light by an authority to sense the current noise and air pollution. This information could be used by traffic planners to reroute the traffic through the city and reduce the pollution in the city. In addition, citizens should be able to contribute to the system by installing a sensor node on the exterior wall of their homes. Therefore, a higher resolution in an area can be archived and more precise data could be taken into consideration.

© Springer Nature Switzerland AG 2019
A. Romanovsky et al. (Eds.): SAFECOMP 2019 Workshops, LNCS 11699, pp. 117–126, 2019.
https://doi.org/10.1007/978-3-030-26250-1_9

With sensor networks it likely that some sensors fail from time to time. Failure modes of single sensor nodes typically are [3]:

- **Inaccurate measurements (Hardware):** This can be created by a broken sensor or a manipulated connection between the node and the sensor.
- **Dislocation or destruction:** Dislocating the sensor node will make the sensor measure correct values but for the wrong area. Note that a sensor node in general will not be able to determine its own location. Destruction by e.g. vandalism will cause a complete failure of the node.
- **Manipulation of sensor data (Software):** If a node is corrupted by an attacker it can act malicious and influence the behavior of the sensor network.
- **Loss of power or connection:** This is most likely to happen in a sensor network. The system is design considers that any participants can be offline or even out of power from time to time. This is especially the case for solar- or battery-operated devices.

Sensor networks currently used are privately organized for the most part. The previously described problems are no real issues due to the non-critically of the usual application. Data collections are mainly informative. Consequences might be an irritated user, who is often able to detect a significantly wrong sensor reading directly, or an area that has a low or even no coverage of sensor nodes. In general, a loss of a single node or several sensor nodes will not influence overall the functionality of the network. Note, that mobile sensors in smart phones or cars moving out of an area will not be distinguishable from a sensor dislocated or destroyed.

In this paper we would like to take this idea of using sensor networks in Smart City applications one step further. We aim at pointing out the emerging risks, when such networks are used in a more distinct way as for example as a basis traffic rerouting during rush hours or taxation of certain areas based on their particle output. The first European countries like Germany are investigating such ideas [1]. A reliable and fault-tolerant system is needed. We discuss the use of well-known safety analysis techniques as a guideline to identify potential risks introduced by using sensor networks in Smart City application e.g. automatic traffic rerouting which can be the basis for deriving mitigation strategies.

This paper has five parts. After the introduction we present related work. Followed by a discussion of potential problems caused by unreliable sensor networks. We suggest using methods typically used for safety and security risk assessment to identify the hazards for Smart City applications. We conclude with an overview of next steps.

2 Related Work

In the literature, other examples are found for making a sensor network reliable. In this section, we present some of these other projects.

Pouryazdan et al. [4] introduce a voting-based approach to assure trustworthiness in Smart City crowd-sensing applications. The system can detect outliers and ensure the trustworthiness of the data sources. They provide a detailed study with a simulation.

Sutaone et al. [5] discuss the use of a trust-based validation for mobile wireless sensor networks with a focus on outlier detection using a clustering technique to organize the sensor nodes.

To conquer dynamic changes in the network structure a centralized indexing could be used as presented by Sitnaysah [6]. The system can detect failing nodes and provide backup strategies to keep the overall system functional.

3 What Could Possibly Go Wrong

In general applications based on sensor networks are not per se safety critical. Due to the known risks of defects in individual nodes or deviation in measurements, these networks often rely on redundancy and in general do not perform critical functions. Where decisions need to be taken, calibrations of individual sensors are another way to check the reliability of values delivered [7]. This may not suffice for the envisioned use of sensor networks in Smart Cities. On the one hand the data will be used for decisions which influence the overall traffic throughput in the cities as well as local pollution values. On the other hand, the idea for the data collection is to use officially installed sensors as well as include sensors privately installed and even fluctuating sensor coverage due to the availability of data from smart phones or moving cars [8].

The question for this position paper is: what can possibly go wrong and how do we identify and possibly mitigate the risks?

First let us consider the following scenario of a problem that needs to be considered:

A sensor network must rely on the data provided by the sensor nodes in an area. Outliers can easily be detected, if there are other sources in the same area to verify the information against other sensor nodes. A typical approach would be to calculate the mean of the provided samples of all sensor nodes within an area. A node that is constantly deviating from the mean value in a significant way could be considered as unreliable but also manipulates the mean value of the area relative to the overall number of sensors in the area. In an area with a low coverage this would be significant. A different approach would be a voting that votes off the outlier and the manipulated value would not be taken into consideration. This solves the previously described problem. Both approaches rely on the fact, that the overall number of nodes is large enough and that deviation is an exception, i.e. only few of the overall set deviate at the same time. In current installations this may not be justified. In that case an attacker may take over the control of a large enough number of nodes or may provide manipulated data himself and manipulates all nodes at the same time. Consider a situation such as in a current installation in London where 2 to 3 sensors are officially installed, and an attacker installs 10 additional sensors from an open source kit that are linked into the public network. The attacker than can manipulate the data for the CO_2 level and the temperature data for his sensors. For example, cigarette smoke can be blown on them at the same time. His sensor data than easily dominates the overall value calculated from the officially and privately installed sensors. Consider that this data is used for an automatic traffic control application, the consequences can be serious:

The mean particle concentration of the area rises and in case of hot smoke the mean temperature values as well. The sensor network will detect a high concentration of particles on multiple sensors. The traffic control center will decide that the traffic in the area should be restricted and redirected through other areas. This behavior is hazardous and causes the system to work not in its intended way.

To mitigate such scenarios some key characteristics of the sensor network need to be defined: The sensor network needs to be a robust and dependable system, that can deal with manipulations on hardware and software level.

This can be archived by three steps, which are well known in the domain of safety and security engineering.

- The first step is to analyze the sensor network and create models that consider, on one hand, an abstract view of the system, on the other hand a detailed view that shows individual sensors and their characteristics.
- Secondly, the models can be used to identify possible risks by using analysis techniques common in the domain of safety and security engineering.
- As a last step, mitigation strategies can be derived from the previous analysis and overcome the shortcomings of the system.

The next section focuses on the safety methods that might be appropriate to use for the identification of risks in sensor networks. Even though a sensor network is not a safety critical system, the methods and techniques might help in this application.

4   Identifying Risks in Sensor Networks

Safety methods are used in applications with a high risk of harm or damage to humans or the environment with the aim to lower the risk of a system failure to a manageable amount, thus, making the system safe to use or work with. Such a system is called "dependable" and comprises of the following properties, when used in a safety context:

- **Functional Sustainability**
  This characteristic represents the degree to which a product or system provides functions that meet stated and implied needs when used under specified conditions.
- **Reliability**
  Degree to which a system, product or component performs specified functions under specified conditions for a specified period.
- **Availability**
  Degree to which a system, product or component is operational and accessible when required for use
- **Maintainability**
  This characteristic represents the degree of effectiveness and efficiency with which a product or system can be modified to improve it, correct it or adapt it to changes in environment and in requirements.
- **Security**
  Degree to which a product or system protects information and data so that persons or other products or systems have the degree of data access appropriate to their types and levels of authorization.

The dependability of a critical system is mandatory and regulated by general and domain specific standards and authorities. For example, in airborne application the DO-178C "Software Considerations in Airborne Systems and Equipment Certification" [9] is applicable and it's use is controlled by authorities like the Federal Aviation Administration [10] or the European Aviation Safety Agency [11]. For road vehicles ISO 26262 "Road vehicles – Functional safety" [12] is mandatory; the regulation is done by e.g. the German "Federal Ministry of Transport and Digital Infrastructure".

As described in the previous section, the above quality characteristics are key characteristics desirable for a sensor network in an automated traffic control application.

For the identification of risks two approaches must be taken into consideration.

First, analytical methods- which focus on identifying problems on the design level. Secondly, constructive methods that help to reduce the probability of a failure.

In the following sections we briefly summarize typical methods for the analytical approach as well as the constructive approach to dependability. For this paper we will focus on the applicability of Fault Tree Analysis in the example.

4.1 Analytical Approaches

These methods are mainly used to determine how a system can fail, which events contribute to the failure and how errors propagate through the system.

Typical representatives are the Failure Modes and Effects Analysis (FMEA) [13] or the Fault Tree Analysis (FTA) [14].

Failure Modes and Effects Analysis. The Failure Modes and Effects Analysis (FMEA) [13] is a structured method, that can be used to identify the impact of a failing or misbehaving component. This structured approach is based on a reliability study, that is performed by domain experts. They review each critical subsystem and their components to identify failure-modes, when they occur and the respective consequences. The results are reported e.g. in worksheets, that are collected in a database for future use. A report can focus for example on functional, design or process criteria.

Even though this method is common in safety analysis, it is not directly applicable for sensor networks. The analysis focuses on the failure propagation from a single component to neighbor components. As described in Sect. 3 the sensor network as to deal with this problem already. For this type of analysis additional information needs to be adopted. A Fault Tree Analysis might provide insight into the causes of overall system or component failure and how individual components contribute to such failures; a subsequent FMEA could be focused on identifying how local failures lead to these problems [15].

Fault Tree Analysis. The Fault Tree Analysis (FTA) is a top-down analysis which starts with a failure of the system as its root element. Each level of the tree constructed displays the possible combination of immediate causes for the failure one level above. For general fault trees the combination of basic failures consists of Boolean operators. A failure X can occur if a set of lower level failures occur at the same time (AND-Gates) or if one of a set of lower level failures occurs (OR-Gates). Each of the cause nodes can itself be analyzed as a failure if other components failures lead to its occurrence event can then again be refined by other events until a basic level event is reached, which does not depend on other causes. An important note is, that both abstract system structure as well as low-level components are taken into consideration. The Fault Tree Analysis is standardized in the IEC 61025. This method will be used later in this paper to perform an example analysis and to show how risk can be identified.

4.2 Constructive Approaches

After identifying risks in a system, countermeasures need to be taken. This can usually be archived by lowering the probability of the failure to occur. In general, an in-depth analysis can reveal shortcomings in the design, such as bottlenecks. A fix to this would be to alter the design and change it to be more fault tolerant.

In most cases, this is not enough; the system must ensure that it is capable to detect the failure of subcomponents and take mitigation action by itself on the fly.

This can be done using a "Watchdog". A watchdog senses the status of a critical component and communicates it with the system. If the critical component fails, the watchdog alerts the system and actions can be taken.

Another way of lowering the probability is to build redundant components. In aviation applications for example this is a common method to ensure the system stays operable if one component fails [16]. If a failure is detected the redundant system takes over and the systems stays intact.

4.3 Example Analysis

In order to discuss the applicability of the methods from the previous section we use the scenario presented in Sect. 3. the situation shows how an attacker can manipulate the decision-making process for the area by blowing smoke on several sensor nodes under his control. Assuming that the sensor network has a low coverage in the respective area.

Figure 1 shows a partial fault tree analysis for the sensor network not measuring the particle concentration correctly. The figure focuses mainly on hardware issues concerning the network. Software issues like a hacking attack must be taken into consideration as well, but this is not part of this initial discussion.

The root element shows the failure of the system, the NO_x readings are not correct and therefore the basis for the automatic traffic rerouting is inaccurate. This can be caused by two events. On the one hand, the sensor node is dislocated. This means the node is sensing data for an area it is not supposed to and the readings are not correct. On the other hand, the node can be in the correct area, but the sensing is not correctly. A typical NO_x sensor for smart environment application is the Nova PM Sensor Laser PM2.5 Air Quality Detection Sensor [17] or like products. These types of sensors use a fan to suck air into a measuring chamber. The general structure of the sensor is shown in Fig. 2.

The particle concentration will be detected by a laser inside the chamber. After the reading the air will be blown out by the fan through an outlet in the case. There are several things that can fail in this context. First, the intake can be blocked due to a physical issue, the fan is not able to suck air into the sensor and no correct reading is possible. The particle concentration will most likely be too low. This issue can happen to the outlet as well, but the consequences are a different. The fan can suck air into the sensor but is not able to build up enough pressure to blow the air out of the system.

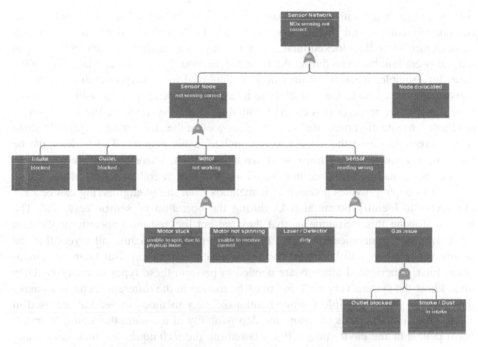

Fig. 1. Example FTA for the demonstration scenario (partial)

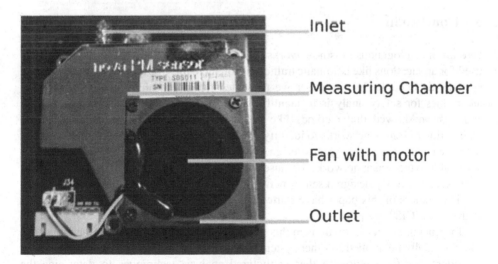

Fig. 2. Nova PM sensor laser PM2.5 air quality detection sensor

The air is trapped in the chamber and will be read repeatedly. The particle reading will most likely be higher than expected. Another possible issue is the motor, which is driving the fan. The motor/fan is mounted outside of the sensor case. So, it is possible that the fan is stuck by a physical issue. Another issue might be the cable, which is supplying the motor with power is damaged or broken and the motor is not able to receive any current and therefore not spinning. Both issues will result in incorrect measurements like the blocked intake. The so far presented issues are exceptions from normal operation, but even during the normal operation the reading can fail. This is the case, for example, when the sensor node is deployed in a dusty environment, like a construction site. Due to the fact, that the measuring is optical it is most likely that the laser diode or the receiver gets covered with dust over time and therefore has incorrect readings. The situation presented in Sect. 3 shows that the attacker must combine some of the events to cause the system to manipulate in his manner. The outlet must be blocked, and smoke or dust must be blown into the inlet. Therefore, the smoke cannot escape the measuring chamber and the sensor sees a high concentration of particles.

This example provides a sketch how methods from safety engineering can be used effectively to identify potential risks during the operation of sensor networks. The benefit of using this technique is, that they are not focused on a specific application layer, like the communication or the hardware separately, because all layers that the failure is caused by will be traced and taken into consideration. But there are limitations. First, experienced analysts are needed to perform these types of analysis. They must know the system very well and must be trained in the different scenario to make them able to detect possible failure situations. Safety methods in general are used in safety critical applications to ensure the dependability of a system that could overwise harm people or the environment. For this reason, the techniques are time consuming and base on skilled teams.

5   Conclusion

Overall, if heterogenous sensor networks organized by private and authorities should be used for applications like automatic traffic control, there must be a focus on making these systems dependable. In this paper we presented our proposal, to apply well known techniques for safety analysis to identify and analyze potential risks. In an example analysis we showed that methods like the Fault Tree Analysis can be used in the application of sensor networks to identify potential failure points. They can also help to increase confidence in the system design. Other methods such as FMEA are not directly applicable to the sensor networks, because they focus on the failure of a single component or its subsystem. By design a sensor network must deal with such failures anyway.

The authors of this paper have started an exchange with the smart city community at the WorldCIST'19 [18].

In general, the considerations in this paper are not restricted to sensor networks but can potentially be applied to other systems of systems as well. There currently are first considerations for employing these structured analysis techniques to determine the effect of security breaches to safety functions of autonomous vehicles.

5.1   Future Work

For the Smart City Sensor Network example, the next steps should focus on the identification of further risks for the application and their detailed analysis. This includes to analyze in more details whether an attack by adding multiple sensor nodes in an area and manipulating them at the same time will change the overall values of the area or the decision-making process. Secondly it needs to be identified how large the risk of manipulating the sensor data really is. For the mitigation of the problem it needs to be determined what a sound ratio between fixed sensor node installations and moving nodes might be. It is also necessary to evaluate other analysis approaches like the hazard and operability study (HAZOP), particularly to identify further risks for a dependable data base of sensor data. This approach could be used as a prototypical approach to analyze reliable sensor network applications which are prone to similar risks.

References

1. Borken-Kleefeld, J., Dallmann, T.: Remote sensing of motor vehicle exhaust emissions, February 2018. https://www.theicct.org/publications/vehicle-emission-remote-sensing. Accessed Mar 2019
2. Smart Citizen Projekt (2019). https://smartcitizen.me/. Accessed Mar 2019
3. Akyildiz, I.F., Wang, X., Wang, W.: Wireless mesh networks: a survey. Comput. Netw. **47**, 445–487 (2005)
4. Pouryazdan, M., Kantarci, B., Soyata, T., Song, H.: Anchor-assisted and vote-based trustworthiness assurance in smart city crowdsensing. IEEE Access **4**, 529–541 (2016)
5. Sutaone, M., Mukherj, P., Paranjape, S.: Trust-based cluster head validation and outlier detection technique for mobile wireless sensor networks. In: 2016 International Conference on Wireless Communications, Signal Processing and Networking (WiSPNET), Chennai, India (2016)
6. Sitanayah, L.: Robust sensor network deployment with priority based on failure centrality. In: 10th International Conference on Information Technology and Electrical Engineering (ICITEE), Kuta, Indonesia (2018)
7. Rossini, R., Ferrera, E., Conzon, D., Pastrone, C.: WSNs self-calibration approach for smart city applications leveraging incremental machine learning techniques. In: 8th IFIP International Conference on New Technologies, Mobility and Security (NTMS), Cyprus (2016)
8. Bogatinoska, D.C., Malekian, R., Trengoska, J., Nyako, W.A.: Advanced sensing and internet of things in smart cities. In: 39th International Convention on Information and Communication Technology, Electronics and Microelectronics (MIPRO), Opatija, Croatia (2016)
9. RTCA DO-178C, Software Considerations in Airborne Systems and Equipment Certification (2011)
10. Federal Aviation Administration. https://www.faa.gov/. Accessed Mar 2019
11. European Union Aviation Safety Agency: European Union Aviation Safety Agency. https://www.easa.europa.eu/. Accessed Mar 2019
12. Standardization IOf: ISO 26262:2018 Road vehicles – Functional safety, Geneva (2018)
13. International Electrotechnical Commission: Failure Mode and Effects analysis (FMEA) (IEC 56/1579/CD:2014) (2015)
14. International Electrotechnical Commission: IEC 61025:2006 Fault tree analysis (FTA) (2006)
15. Woodhouse, R.M., Lutz, R.R.: Requirements analysis using forward and backward search (1997)

16. Sklaroff, J.R.: Redundancy management technique for space shuttle computers. IBM **20**, 20–28 (1976)
17. Nova Fitness Co., Ltd.: Laser PM2.5 Sensor specification, 9 October 2015. https://cdn-reichelt.de/documents/datenblatt/X200/SDS011-DATASHEET.pdf. Accessed Mar 2019
18. Hinrichs, T., Buth, B.: Applying Safety Methods To Sensor Networks. Springer, La Toja Island (2019)

Increasing Safety of Neural Networks
in Medical Devices

Uwe Becker$^{(\boxtimes)}$ (iD)

Draegerwerk AG&CoKGaA, Moislinger Allee 53-55, 23552 Luebeck, Germany
uwe.becker@draeger.com

Abstract. Neural networks are now widely used in industry for applications such as data analysis and pattern recognition. In the medical devices domain neural networks are used to detect certain medical/decease indications. For example, a potential imminent asthma insult is detected based e.g. on breathing pattern, heart rate, and a few optional additional parameters. The patient receives a warning message and can either change his behavior and/or take some medicine in order to avoid the insult. This directly increases the patient's quality of life. Although, currently medical devices mostly use neural networks to provide some guidance information or to propose some treatment or change of settings, safety and reliability of the neural network are paramount. Internal errors or influences from the environment can cause wrong inferences. This paper will describe the experiences we made and the ways we used in order to both increase safety and reliability of a neural network in a medical device. We use a combination of online and offline tests to detect undesired behavior. Online tests are performed in regular intervals during therapy and offline tests are performed when the device is not performing therapy.

Keywords: Safety · Neural networks · CNN · DNN · Systems engineering ·
STPA · Fault tolerance · Bit error · Error detection · Online test ·
Error correction

1 Introduction

Today, neural networks are widely used in industry for tasks such as big data analysis, pattern recognition, and many other applications. In the medical devices domain for example, pattern recognition is used to detect certain medical or disease indications. A potential imminent asthma insult may be detected based on breathing pattern, heart rate, and a few optional additional parameters. The patient receives a warning message and can either change behavior and/or take some medicine in order to avoid the insult. This directly increases the patient's quality of life. In intensive care units complications e.g. signals of sepsis or other changes of a patient's health status are detected. Care givers can react accordingly in an earlier stage of the complication. Currently, medical devices mostly use neural networks to provide some guidance information or to propose some treatment or setting changes.

Despite their widely use, it is hard to determine whether neural networks function as intended. The math behind neural networks is advanced and it is very hard to predict

© Springer Nature Switzerland AG 2019
A. Romanovsky et al. (Eds.): SAFECOMP 2019 Workshops, LNCS 11699, pp. 127–136, 2019.
https://doi.org/10.1007/978-3-030-26250-1_10

classification results from outside the neural network. In addition, safety and reliability of neural networks or even neurocomputing systems is a challenging problem. Their complexity of functions and structures keeps continuously growing [1] while the feature size of the chips themselves keeps shrinking. For this reason, in most medical applications there is no closed-loop control, but a human in the loop or in a supervising position to react or take control if necessary. It is, of course, desirable to increase safety and reliability of the neural networks as much as possible to off-load or even eliminate the human supervisor. This paper shows the experiences we made in order to find errors in neural networks and to improve their safety.

In this paper we will refer to an example medical application to detect worsening of breathing and oxygen uptake in an intensive care medical setting. The example application uses a convolutional neural network (CNN) implemented in an FPGA to detect certain patterns in a set of medical parameters such as breathing frequency, tidal volume, and breathing flow and pressure. The parameters are analyzed as trend as well as on a breath-by-breath basis. Safety requirements for this application are quite high. A System Theoretic Process Analysis (STPA) in very early stages [2] of the development raises some issues that have to be mitigated. If a critical situation is not detected, the patient will not receive treatment in time and the situation will get worse until it may reach a critical or life-threatening level. User acceptance will decrease with the increase of false alarms. Applications that indicate critical situations were in fact there are none, will be de-activated and considered unreliable and annoying. False alarms may also lead to unnecessary treatment or changes thereof.

The paper is organized as follows: In the next section we show the safety issues identified and the challenges that arise therefrom. Section 3 will highlight the actual implementation and safety measures in the medical device. Section 4 describes the scalability of our approach. The paper concludes with a summary.

2   Safety Issues Using Neural Networks in Medical Devices

The medical device in this case study is an intensive care ventilator. A neural network is used to detect complications in the airway of a patient. Such complications might be pneumonia or obstruction of the upper airway caused by secretion. Care givers should react as early as possible on such complications to avoid larger impact on patient's health. The ventilator will provide information about the detected complication and will propose to change ventilation settings. Changing the setting of a ventilator means changing therapy and thus can impact patient's safety. STPA [2] results in the requirement that detection of the complication should have low error probability.

Detection of a medical complication is a pattern recognition problem. Input signals are e.g. breathing parameters such as airway pressure, gas flow and gas composition (e.g. concentration of CO_2 or other components in the exhaled gas). The classification of the neural network shall be reliable. At least during training, the neural network shall detect all relevant events and should not show false classifications. The training data set shall be large enough to cover the clinically relevant situations. Modern neural networks are able to out-perform human beings in pattern recognition. Convolutional

Neural Networks (CNN) perform exceptionally well in this task. With the appropriate training pattern, accuracy of detection has increased to 99.79% [4].

Safety and reliability are essential for medical devices. A combination of model-based systems engineering and STPA is used to find the optimal combination of design elements that fulfills all safety requirements. This means that every development step is accompanied by risk management activities. Every function a medical device provides has to be of clinical relevance and the risk associated with it has to be acceptable in comparison with its clinical benefit. In general, a medical device has to be developed such that the risk associated with its usage is as low as (reasonable) possible. A STPA for the detection of the complication results in three main hazards: (1) No treatment is performed or treatment is performed too late. (2) Wrong treatment is performed. (3) Unnecessary treatment is performed. The reasons for the hazards are: (R1) The CNN does not detect the complication. (R2) The CNN detects the wrong complication. (R3) The CNN detects a complication where there is none

All of them may have the following same root causes: (E1) Weights or other memory content is changed by external influences e.g. high-energy particles. (E2) For some reason the network detects features but the inference is not as expected (i.e. it either does not indicate a detection or it indicates a wrong event). (E3) There is an error in the training data. (E4) Deployment or architecture of the network has changed (by external disturbances or internal errors).

In the following chapter we describe which measures were taken to tackle and mitigate the causes for wrong inferences. For some of them we even implemented online tests. In addition, we performed formal verification of the CNN. Verification of neural networks may be difficult to perform. It may even be a harder task to guarantee safety of neural networks. Fortunately, there has been some progress in this regard recently. For some trained neural networks, it is possible to mathematically prove correctness. Thus, detection and classification can be proven to be correct in the error free case. For this purpose, the verification of neural networks is mapped to a reachability problem. To keep the reachability problem decidable, some constraints have to be met. It is common sense in literature that Schanuel's conjecture [3] has to be fulfilled when the inputs and outputs of the neural networks are given as real-arithmetic properties. In this case, reachability can be stated with transcendental functions that are decidable with the conjecture mentioned. Ivanov et al. [6] showed that the reachability problem is decidable for neural networks with sigmoid and hyperbolic tangent activation functions. They also showed that safety of closed-loop control systems containing such neural networks can be proven under certain conditions. One of the conditions is that the networks always start from the same starting point. A second condition is that if control has to follow a certain trajectory, this trajectory has to be piece-wise linearized. There has to be, a more or less large, tolerance band around the trajectory. For these conditions it could be shown that the neural network can control the system in such a way that it follows the given trajectory without leaving the allowed tolerance band.

The implementation of the neural network fulfills Schanuel's conjecture [3] and thus its correct operation can be mathematically proven. After the network successfully passes formal verification, the network's architecture is considered to have low error probability. Validation will give evidence whether the network successfully detects the desired patterns in recordings not used for training.

3 Implementing Neural Networks in an Intensive Care Ventilator

To achieve the desired reliability and safety of neural networks in a medical device, our approach combines running a periodic check task for online detection of errors, ECC memory, the introduction of default values to ensure correct inference despite detected errors, structured sparsity learning, and a certain distribution of the neurons over the processing elements (PEs) of the underlying hardware [10, 13, 15, 16]. In the following paragraphs we describe which measures were taken to mitigate the errors identified during STPA of the neural network.

Measures to Prevent Errors in the Training Data (E3): Training of the neural network will only be performed offline with verified datasets to increase safety and to minimize the probability of malicious learning. Experts in the field of ventilation therapy tag training data for the network. Training data are recorded from patients showing or developing the complication [18, 19]. The training data has been recorded in real-life scenarios. It has been collected over a longer period of time from different hospitals around the world and with different patient categories and population. Therefore, we are sure that the training data does not contain bias and it matches what we expect the network to see in real life. Before the system is released to the market, a clinical evaluation is done in various sites. There was no indication of any bias in the training data. The clinical evaluation also confirmed the quality of the labeling of the test data. The labels represent a concrete medical problem/complication which reduces ambiguity and ensures that different experts consistently label the data. Training data labeled by different experts can be used without any rework.

In addition, it was clear even during recording that a balanced set of training data is required. Already existing recordings could be used together with new recordings to achieve a good set of training data. This training data even includes other events and complications the system will see in real-life applications. At the end it turned out that there even is some (insignificant) more data without the complication. The training data is a very good approximation of the data the system will see during real-life operation. It contains recordings with the complication that is to be detected, recordings without any complications, and recordings with complications that can occur but shall not trigger detection. It is known that in certain clinical settings or treatments detection or prediction of the complication is very hard. This is especially true when breathing pressure is higher than usual. An extra confirmation is required to treat a patient with such a high breathing pressure. Now this confirmation also triggers switching off the detection of the complication. It is automatically re-enabled after the patient is treated with a breathing pressure in the usual range.

Measures to Lower the Probability of Errors During Executions (E2/E4): During our experiments, we found that parameter ranges should be adapted for the problem and network at hand. If variables are capable to cover a very wide range of values, then a bit-flip in one of the higher order bits can cause a very large error. This leads to an error in the output with high probability. If the value range of a variable is tailored to the problem, the error is much smaller and so is the probability of an erroneous output.

Tailoring could be done for each layer. For easy handling and for increased performance, we chose a single 32-bit fix point notation for all values. In addition, two normalization layers are implemented because such layers of a network average out large values (and thus errors) in preceding layers [6, 8]. The additional layers reduce effects of errors in weights, internal values, and external input values that are out of range for any reason.

The neural network of the design example is realized in an FPGA. The FPGA has a built-in multi-core processor and several processing elements (PEs). The PEs are optimized for neural networks and provide the necessary multiply/accumulate (MAC) functions for this purpose. Both the processor and the specialized PEs run in parallel and perform independent tasks. The distribution of neurons over the PEs of the FPGA has large effect on reliability and performance of the network. The number of specialized processing elements constrains the number of neurons that can be processed in a single step. Our primary goal is to design the network such that it directly fits into the FPGA or that it fits into the FPGA after pruning and compression [9, 15, 17, 20]. Otherwise, the inference needs multiple steps and intermediate results have to be saved. An additional distribution step could also be a source of new avoidable errors.

We, similar to Han [21], prefer the row wise distribution of neurons to the processing elements. This distribution scheme takes advantage of the sparsity of the weight matrix and the locality of the results, which is favorable for FPGA implementation. In addition, it results in a harmonized processing time for each row in the matrix of processing elements thus solving the problem of the unequal processing times. Structured sparsity learning further harmonizes processing time and avoids waste of processing power. Therefore, even though the weight matrix is already sparse, we increase sparsity by setting very small weights to zero. This both reduces memory requirements of the weight storage and increases throughput as the number of operations is lowered [11, 12, 14, 15]. Furthermore, we decouple the processing elements. As soon as all input data for a processing element are available, the computation is started. The processing times will more or less average out resulting in considerable performance gain. The reduction in storage requirement reduces the probability of a bit-flip caused by the hit of a high energy particle, because most particles will hit unused memory.

Measures to Lower the Influence of Bit-Flips (E1): The ever-shrinking feature size of modern integrated circuits lets them increasingly be vulnerable against single event upsets caused by high energy (e.g. Alpha) particles [4, 5]. A single high energy particle may not only change a single bit of the information stored but may change multiple bits of a single data or multiple bits in adjacent data. Despite that, the safety-relevant neural network is required to be robust at least against single bit errors. Therefore, we store the weight values in ECC memory and use ECC memory for internal values also. Nevertheless, situations may arise that the ECC memory may not be able to restore the original data. It may only be able to indicate the error. If correction of the wrong values is not possible on-the-fly, it shall occur within a certain error toleration period. This toleration period varies with the physiological parameter supervised or analyzed and is stated in a standard or based on experience. We signal a detected event only after some consecutive positive detection. Currently we investigate whether this threshold should be combined with the indicated confidence indicator.

It is not sufficient to just detect a wrong inference. Wrong inferences should either be avoided or (wrong) values that lead to the wrong inference should be corrected. We use a "default values matrix" for immediate error handling. This default value matrix has the same size as the weight matrix and for each entry of the weight matrix it has a default value for error handling. If a value in the weight matrix is detected to be erroneous, first, error detection is indicated. Second, the index value of the weight is fetched. With the index, the respective default value is obtained from the matrix and its value is used for computation. This ensures very small delay in error handling and correct inference results are available despite the error in the storage. We have chosen to implement 16 default values. This value is a trade-off between the amount of storage required, the number of bits required to store the index (limited by hardware), and the classification error resulting from the usage of the default value. The actual memory configuration would allow for a 5-bit default value. The application did not require finer grained default values. In case of an error, the default values resulted in the correct classification. We set the first bit of the default values to zero and keep it for future updates or enhancements of the functionality.

When developing the neural network, we set all weights below a "threshold for zeroing" to zero. Although the default values can be chosen arbitrarily, they were chosen to be equidistantly distributed in the range of 1 − (threshold for zeroing). The default values are in the middle of intervals of size (1 − threshold for zeroing)/16 i.e. at (threshold for zeroing) + (2n + 1) * (1 − threshold for zeroing)/32.

This equidistant distribution facilitates the check task and further reduces storage requirements as only the threshold and "n" has to be stored. The periodic check task checks the column checksums of the weights stored. In addition, it checks whether the values of the weights are within a defined range around the default value that is indicated in the respective bits. In the actual design, default values are stored in 9-bit ECC protected memory. If default values are applied to shared weights, they will be identical to the shared weights. For nonshared weights, they will be an approximation of the weight (the middle of the interval in which the weight happens to be). Weight and default value can either be in the same memory line or in different memory lines. We propose to place them in the part of memory after the weight matrix and use the offset of the data in the weight matrix to also address the default value if required.

Periodic Check Task (E2): Safety of medical devices is ensured by design but also by safety circuitry and safety software. Some of the measures to detect and correct errors are implemented in hardware. Other measures are implemented in software (in a part of the software called "safety software"). The safety software performs tests to ensure that the network detects all patterns it ought to detect. One core of the main processor is dedicated to all safety related tasks. This includes the tasks for the main medical function i.e. ventilation and for the secondary functions. The implementation of the safety software and thus the check tasks for the secondary function (the neural network) shall be lightweight. A check task should only have low or modest performance requirements. Lightweight implementation eases certification and formal verification (if required). A parallel neural network should be avoided. To lower resource requirements, a few (e.g. 5) seconds delay in reactions on errors can be tolerated [7].

We use two different check tasks. During startup and during stand-by a thorough check task sends test data to the CNN and checks its results. If a deviation is detected, the CNN is re-initialized. After the test, the neural network is reset to a known starting state such that it always starts from the same starting point for each patient. During normal operation a (lightweight) periodic check task is run.

It is known from the training data that when a positive inference is made, either some defined neurons are active or there are some groups or group patterns of active neurons. This knowledge can be used for online detection of the correct function of the network. We also use the detection of some input conditions and training patterns for online verification of the inference output. To keep the check task simple, only a few group patterns and training patterns are stored. In some cases, there may also be an algorithm-based detection of some situations. The check task may use these algorithms or parts of them for online verification of the correct function of the network. If the algorithm detects a complication, the CNN has to indicate the same complication with a certain minimum confidence value.

In addition, the check task permanently checks all weights in the weight matrix and the error flag of the ECC memory. Worst case detection time is the time the task needs to process the whole matrix. Errors in hidden layers only propagate with certain probability to the output. Therefore, the probability of a wrong output even for multiple bit errors further decreases. The function of the check task is given in the pseudo code below.

```
1. Test for some training data, (some) values above
   defined thresholds, or group patterns on inner lay-
   ers and check for expected output
2. Re-write weights and re-initialize network on error
3. Every x cycles perform check of weights (step 12)
4. for every layer n - Start short check
5.     Read weights of layer n
6.     Perform ECC check of the weights and indicate
       error
7.     On error go to error handling (step 13)
8.     For every 32 weights perform XOR function of 8
       weights to calculate the 4 column check words
9.     Check the 4 column check words
10.    On error go to error handling - perform step 13
       for all weights
11.End short check - next layer
12. Check every weight against its boundaries (in-
    cludes ECC check on reading the weight)
13. Re-write the weight(s)
```

Both the weights and the input values are in defined pre-known ranges. Thus, range checking on the values inside the network during operation is performed. In general, it is not required to perform this checking during each inference. Thus, the checks are realized in multiple steps, i.e. during each step only one layer of the network is checked. Therefore, a complete check for "n" layers of a network needs "n" time steps. This is a tradeoff between the time required to perform the check, the resources required to perform the check, and the time to find and to react on an error. The periodic check task checks whether certain features have been detected when the data is classified positive. Only if a certain amount of sub features has been detected, the net should come to a positive conclusion. If this requirement is not fulfilled, there is some kind of error either in the operation or in the training data set. As it is sometimes relatively complex to detect the presence of certain features, we use some heuristic. We know that if certain training patterns are detected or certain values (either input values or values in inner layers of the network) are above certain thresholds, the desired features are present. If the network classifies this as the desired event, its correct function is proven. This heuristic only gets a subset of the correct detections but provides some additional tests between the more thorough tests.

4   Scalability of the Approach

The approach scales very well and is suited for all kinds of neural networks and all kinds of different layers within such networks. Its application to a CNN is just an example. It is only required that an error in the weights and in the default values is detected. Automatic correction of the error can be dropped in favor of a simpler implementation. In this case the default values are always used on a detected error in the weights. If the check task detects an error in the default values, the defective value is overwritten. This decision against ECC can be made based on the underlying error model. Hardware restrictions may also direct in this direction.

Another tradeoff may be used regarding the number of bits in the byte containing the default value. If the default byte does not contain error correction information, all bits save a single check/parity bit may be used for the default values. This will allow for a larger number of default values and thus higher precision of the default values in favor over safety/error correction capability. Depending on the application one may decide on the intervals to run the check task. Running it more often will detect and correct errors sooner but requires more processing resources. In addition, one can place more operations in a single run of the check task. It may for instance check two layers of the neural network in each run instead of a single layer. Such decisions also depend on the processing power available. We proposed an intensive check of the values of the weights and the default values. This check of values may also be replaced by periodic overwriting weights with their stored values. This saves processing power without compromising safety. Some operations of the check task may be realized in hardware especially if an FPGA is used for implementation. We prefer the compression of neural networks and take profit from the sparsity of weights in compressed networks. We added four check words every 32 entries in the weight matrix to allow for error correction on the fly. For simpler implementations with reduced error correction capability, these check words may be reduced or even omitted.

Our approach will detect any changes of the weights of a neural network. The detection of changes of the activation functions, in the MAC units, or PEs will only partly be done online. During device startup, during standby phases, or on explicit demand of the user, a more intensive (offline) test will be performed. Some test data is fed to the network and the reaction of the neural network on this test data is checked. As input data is known, the results of the network should be the same as the stored known good answers. If mean time between failures is larger than the time between two such test runs, hardware defects will be improbable between the tests.

5 Summary

Experiences regarding the safe use of neural networks in a medical device were presented. The applied safety measures fulfill the requirements resulting from the STPA during the systems engineering phase. The implementation of the CNN combines known approaches and new approaches to increase safety of a CNN in a medical device. The known approach of using error correcting memory is combined with the new introduction of default values. In the case error correction for a memory cell is not possible, a default value is used. It is an approximation of the original value and will guarantee the correct result despite the uncorrectable error in the memory. Another new approach to increase safety is the online detection of wrong inferences. Based on the detection of certain input values or values and patterns in inner layers of the neural network, an expected inference result is generated. This expected result is compared to the actual result of the CNN. Within a certain tolerance period, either the error is corrected or if this is not possible, the confidence indicator is set to a low value.

Using the described safety measures, it was shown that safety of neural networks can be achieved and safety-critical closed-loop systems become possible. Additional benefit is taken from the sparsity of the weight matrixes of today's neural networks. Structured sparsity learning is used to ease certification because it reduces complexity during formal verification. In addition, the reduced number of weights improves performance both of the inference and the periodic check task (for error detection and correction).

A real-world design, a medical ventilator system, has been used as a design example. The approach taken is both feasible and ensures safe use of neural networks in medical systems by design. The design approach is scalable and can be adapted to the available hardware and software resources. The current implementation detects and corrects errors in the weights of neural networks. Errors in the activation functions and in the processing elements (PE) are mostly detected during offline self-test phases such as startup. Future work will include thorough on-the-fly detection of above-mentioned errors; especially those in the PEs.

References

1. Chervyakov, N.I., et al.: The architecture of a fault-tolerant modular neurocomputer based on modular number projections. Neurocomputing **272**, 96–107 (2017)
2. Becker, U.: STPA guided systems engineering. In: Gallina, B., Skavhaug, A., Schoitsch, E., Bitsch, F. (eds.) SAFECOMP 2018. LNCS, vol. 11094, pp. 164–176. Springer, Cham (2018). https://doi.org/10.1007/978-3-319-99229-7_15

3. Wilkie, A.J.: Schanuel's conjecture and the decidability of the real exponential field. In: Hart, B.T., Lachlan, A.H., Valeriote, M.A. (eds.) Algebraic Model Theory, pp. 223–230. Springer, Dordrecht (1997). https://doi.org/10.1007/978-94-015-8923-9_11

4. Sum, J., Leung, C.-s., Ho, K.: Prediction error of a fault tolerant neural network. In: King, I., Wang, J., Chan, L.-W., Wang, D. (eds.) ICONIP 2006. LNCS, vol. 4232, pp. 521–528. Springer, Heidelberg (2006). https://doi.org/10.1007/11893028_58

5. Qin, M., Sun, C., Vucinic, D.: Robustness of Neural Networks against Storage Media Errors, arXiv:1709.06173v1, September 2017

6. Invanov, R., Weimer, J., Alur, R., Pappas, G.J., Lee, I.: Verisig: verifying safety properties of hybrid systems with neural network controllers, CoRR abs/1811.01828v1 (2018)

7. Schorn, C., Guntoro, A., Ascheid, G.: Efficient on-line error detection and mitigation for deep neural network accelerators. In: Gallina, B., Skavhaug, A., Bitsch, F. (eds.) SAFECOMP 2018. LNCS, vol. 11093, pp. 205–219. Springer, Cham (2018). https://doi.org/10.1007/978-3-319-99130-6_14

8. Li, G., et al.: Understanding error propagation in Deep Learning Neural Network (DNN) accelerators and applications. In: Proceedings of the International Conference for High Performance Computing, Networking, Storage and Analysis (2017)

9. Sze, V., Chen, Y.-H., Yang, T.-J., Emer, J.: Efficient Processing of Deep Neural Networks: A Tutorial and Survey, August 2017. arXiv:1703.09039v2

10. Chen, Y., Krishna, T., Emer, J., Sze, V.: DaDianNao: a machine learning supercomputer. In: Micro (2014)

11. Han, S., Mao, H., Dally, W.J.; Deep compression: compressing deep neural networks with pruning, trained quantization and huffman coding. In: ICLR (2016)

12. Alberico, J., Judd, P., Hetherington, T., Aamodt, T., Jerger, N.E., Moshovos, A.: Cnvlutin: ineffectual-neuron-free deep neural network computing. In: ISCA (2016)

13. Reagen, B., et al.: Minerva: enabling low-power, highly-accurate deep neural network accelerators. In: ISCA 2016 (2016)

14. Han, S., Pool, J., Tran, J., Dally, W.J.: Learning both weights and connections for efficient neural networks. In: NIPS 2015 (2015)

15. Dorrance, R., Ren, F., Marković: A scalable sparse matrix-vector multiplication kernel for energy-efficient sparse-blas on FPGAs. In: ISFPGA (2014)

16. Wen, W., Wu, C., Wang, Y., Chen, Y., Li, H.: Learning structured sparsity in deep neural networks. In: 30th Conference on Neural Information Processing (NIPS 2016), Barcelona (2016)

17. Anwar, S., Hwang, K., Sung, W.: Structured pruning of deep neural networks. ACM J. Emerg. Technol. Comput. Syst. 13(3), 32 (2017)

18. Chiu, C.T., et al.: Modifying training algorithms for improved fault tolerance. In: ICNN 1994, vol. I, pp. 333–338 (1994)

19. Dutta, S., Jha, S., et al.: Learning and Verification of Feedback Control Systems using Feedforward Control Systems using Feedforward Neural Networks, Boulder (2017)

20. Anwar, S., Hwang, K., Sung, W.: Structured pruning of deep convolutional neural networks. In: Conference on Neural Information Processing (NIPS 2015)

21. Han, S.: Efficient Methods and Hardware for Deep Learning, Stanford University Dissertation, September 2017

Smart Wristband for Voting

Martin Pfatrisch[1,2](✉) [iD], Linda Grefen[1] [iD], and Hans Ehm[1]

[1] Infineon Technologies AG, Am Campeon 1-15, 85579 Neubiberg, Germany
Martin.Pfatrisch@infineon.com
[2] Group of Information and Knowledge Management,
Technische Universität Ilmenau, Ilmenau, Germany

Abstract. Nowadays sensor networks are not solely used in industrial settings anymore but are accessible to the public and thus allow for broad and diverse applications. The technical advancement of cyber-physical systems (CPS) paved the way for an easy and fast development of Internet of Things (IoT) devices. In this work, a voting wristband that uses hand gestures and the measurement of the corresponding barometric air pressure for voting has been developed. Audience response systems are often used as a way to improve participation and spark interest in a topic during a presentation. The intuitive wrist movement allows for multiple choice voting results. Textile integration of the wristband guarantees comfort and allows for an adaptable design for different events. Furthermore, an application that makes live updating of voting results and visualization thereof possible was implemented. This illustrates the endless possibilities of wearables and approaches to IoT design with sensors in times of CPS.

Keywords: Wearables · DPS310 · CPS · Sensor networks

1 Introduction

In the past, the internet changed the way people interacted with each other by making the communication from one human being to another much easier and more convenient. With the introduction of the Internet of Things (IoT), it is possible to connect anything to the internet without any human intervention. The focus of IoT is mainly on connecting objects to the internet and retrieving data form the real (physical) world. In addition to that, cyber-physical systems (CPS) try to build a connection between the physical world and the cyber world. Data from the physical world is collected by sensors, then computed, and finally used to influence ongoing processes in the physical world in real time. In CPS the task of data collection is mainly accomplished by wireless sensor networks. This concept of CPS can be applied to a large field of applications and brings several benefits for the user. Especially in the industrial context, CPS increase enterprise's efficiency, sustainability, agility, flexibility and even safety and security in the production processes [1, 2].

Not only in the industrial manufacturing context, but also in presentations, talks, or lectures CPS could improve the interaction of the speaker with the audience, which

---

M. Pfatrisch and L. Grefen—These authors contributed equally as first authors.

A. Romanovsky et al. (Eds.): SAFECOMP 2019 Workshops, LNCS 11699, pp. 137–147, 2019.
https://doi.org/10.1007/978-3-030-26250-1_11

plays an essential role for the take-home value of the audience. Audience response systems have been shown beneficial for audience participation and learning results as they encourage the audience to engage in the presentation. They also provide instant and helpful feedback to the speaker. With this, the speaker is able to estimate the existing knowledge of a specific topic among the audience and can spike interest in topics with the most response [3, 4]. Currently a number of different voting systems for audience voting sessions are available. In general, voting results can be obtained by using device-dependent voting systems that are contributed within the audience or online voting systems that require the audience to use their smartphones/tablets. However, the operation of such a device usually constitutes a distraction from the talk for the members of the audience.

Considering all the above mentioned drawbacks a more intuitive solution for an audience response system could be established. One common and therefore intuitive method for a voting process, is to ask the audience to raise their hands if they agree to a given statement. The presenter then determines the voting result by counting the show of hands. Whilst simple and effective, this method is error-prone and not applicable for large audiences.

This method can, however, be improved by the combined use of CPS and sensor networks to use the simple and intuitive hand gestures for voting processes within large audiences.

2   Related Work

The increasing amount of smart wristbands and IoT devices have enhanced the human computer interaction greatly [5]. The scope is not solely fitness or health tracking anymore but seems endless considering industry, agriculture or any conceivable field of application [6, 7].

IoT and sensor development have broadened the area of application immensely. Technical progress not only allows for more precise measurements but also for new and innovative approaches of implementations of sensors. Typical sensors (force/pressure, humidity, etc.) can be used for a variety of different applications and the use of such still holds plenty of opportunity for surprising new approaches and devices [8–10].

3   Basic Concept

In the herein presented work, a wristband for a wireless voting process is introduced. The wristband carries a printed circuit board (PCB) containing a barometric pressure sensor and a WiFi microcontroller that enables the wristband to connect to a WiFi network. For the voting process (Fig. 1), every member of the audience wears a wristband, which measures the altitude of the voter's hand. This enables the user to vote for questions by the intuitive hand gesture of raising or lowering the hand. This can also be performed in a seated position. Since the wristband is connected to a WiFi network, authorized devices in the same network can receive the sensor data. In the following, data of all wristbands can be consolidated and stored in a database to further estimate a voting result. Eligible voting categories are Yes/Neutral/No. Since all the above described processes are executed within milliseconds, the voting results can be presented in real time during the talk or presentation.

Fig. 1. Basic concept drawing of the voting process.

4   Components

4.1   Sensor

In every single voting process, the vertical position of the voter's arm has to be determined. This is done by the digital barometric air pressure sensor DPS310 (Infineon Technologies AG, Germany). The sensor's capacitive sensing principle makes it possible to measure both pressure and temperature with high accuracy. Furthermore, its low current consumption makes it suitable for battery operation. In high precision mode and considering one measurement per second it consumes only 38 µA, while in standard and low precision mode the current consumption is even less. The peak current consumption is specified as 345 µA and during standby it is only 0.5 µA. In addition to that, the DPS310 provides an operation range of 30,000–120,000 Pa [11].

A crucial factor in the application is the precision of the pressure measurement. The higher the precision of the sensed data, the higher the accuracy of the voting result. In the sensor's data sheet a precision of ±0.5 Pa, which equals 5 cm altitude, is promised in high precision mode [11].

For the communication with Infineon's DPS310, a data processing unit can be connected via SPI or I^2C [11], with the latter being the case for the Smart Wristband for Voting. During the voting process the temperature doesn't have any effect on the voting result. Therefore, the temperature measurement is neglected and only the barometric air pressure data is determined and further processed.

4.2   Microcontroller

With the selection of an appropriate sensor, the sensor's data had to be processed by a microcontroller in the next step. For this task, a WiFi module was used and connected to Infineon's DPS310 via the I^2C bus. The WiFi module is based on the low-power WiFi microcontroller ESP8266 (Espressif Systems Co., LTD., China). The WiFi antenna on the module enables the microcontroller to transmit the processed data via WiFi [12].

4.3   Power Supply

Both the data processing unit and the sensor are powered with the same power supply unit. While the microcontroller module requires a power supply with voltage in the range of 3.0–3.6 V, the barometric pressure sensor needs to be operated in the range of 1.7–3.6 V. Since the electronic circuit is used inside the wristband, the power supply also has to be portable. Due to these requirements a rechargeable Lithium Polymer battery with a voltage of 3.7 V and a capacity of 200 mAh is used to power the sensor and the microcontroller module. However, the concept of the circuitry and the PCB allows the attachment of different batteries with higher or lower capacity depending on the runtime requirements.

Since the voltage of the battery is too high for both components, a Low-Drop-Out voltage regulator is used to down-regulate and keep the voltage steady at 3.3 V [13].

Due to the voltage regulation, ripple can occur that has to be smoothed out for a reliable functioning circuit. For this task a smoothing capacitor is integrated in parallel to the load [14].

4.4   Circuitry

Due to the microcontroller's small size, programs can't be uploaded without further components. In order to connect it to a computer, an USB adapter is required and the connection between the USB adapter and the microcontroller has to be established. An external FTDI adapter can be attached to the circuit (pins RXD, TXD, and GND) and a counterpart of three female header pins on the circuit itself. These are connected to the corresponding pins of the microcontroller. In addition to that, two push buttons are integrated into the circuit. One to set the microcontroller into flash mode for uploading code and the other one for restarting the program. For a reliable operation of the circuit several resistors and capacitors of different values are integrated. Another important part of the circuitry is the JST-connector for the power supply. This connector makes it possible to detach the battery from the circuit and recharge it as soon as it is empty. Furthermore, it allows the user to attach any other battery providing voltage in the allowed range and a 2 pin JST-connector.

4.5   Prototyping

At first, wireless data transmission protocols have been reviewed and evaluated. After choosing a WiFi-based protocol to be the most suitable, the necessary hardware components for the electronic circuit have been selected. With this, a first circuit was developed using the software Autodesk Eagle (v9.1.1, Autodesk Inc., USA).

A first prototype (Fig. 2A) was wired up using a bread board with removable jumper wires and the Pressure Shield2Go (Infineon Technologies AG) was connected to a NodeMCU [15]. The basic software development for the communication between the components as well as data transmission was carried out with this prototype.

After the successful setup of the selected components, a less bulky and battery powered prototype was soldered up with the bare components (Fig. 2B).

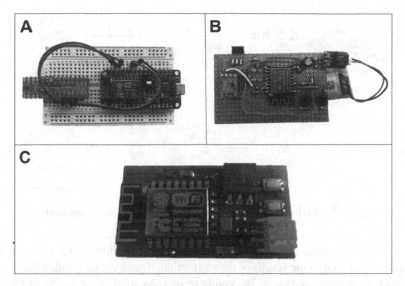

Fig. 2. Prototyping for smart wristband (**A**) Breadboard prototype with Pressure Shield2Go and NodeMCU for fast prototyping and software development. (**B**) Soldered up prototype with advanced circuitry and individual components. (**C**) The final PCB measures only 24.5 mm × 43.5 mm.

As a last step the schematic of the electronic circuit was further refined and a PCB layout was created using the software Altium Designer (v19.0.12, Altium Limited, Australia). The aim was to reduce the width of the circuit board as much as possible in order to fit into a wristband made out of flexible fabric. Finally the PCB has been produced and assembled by a PCB manufacturer (Fig. 2C).

5 Software

The ready-to-use software for the voting wristband was developed using different entities (Fig. 3). The data transmission was carried out via TCP/IP using the MQTT (message queuing telemetry transport) publish/subscribe-protocol. Further analysis was performed with a Python script that stored the data in a database and enabled the live visualization of voting results.

5.1 Data Collection and Processing

The acquisition of air pressure data was conducted by the designed PCB using the Arduino IDE (v1.8.8). The sensors' data was not filtered for the here described voting processes. The precise measurement of the DPS310 allowed the accurate detection of the altitude of the wrist with a change up to ±5 cm.

On command, when the corresponding button in the voting software was clicked, a calibration was performed to determine the air pressure value at the position of the

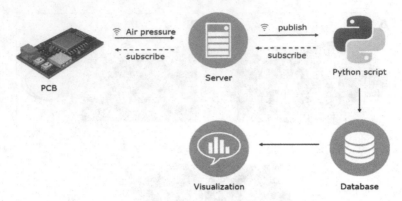

Fig. 3. General overview of the voting software and its components.

raised and lowered hand, respectively. In the next step, a minimal and maximal value was set in accordance to the results of the calibration. These values defined the range of possible wrist positions and hence the voting results. As soon as the voting process was launched and the hand was moved into the desired voting position, the barometric air pressure was measured for 5 s. With an oversampling rate of 6, an average pressure was measured during the voting process and further expressed as a percentage value.

5.2 Data Transmission

A WiFi-based network was chosen for device connectivity and data transmission. This was due to the fact that an internal WiFi-based IoT network has been established at the Infineon working site (Campeon) in Munich, Germany. The MQTT protocol was used as a message transmission system in this work. It's a publish/subscribe push protocol, that is extremely lightweight and efficient in low bandwidths and very useful for IoT devices [16]. The basic concept consists of a publisher and a subscriber and the use of general topics. A certain topic is published and subscribed to at the same time by different clients.

In case of the voting wristband, the microcontroller was a client who published a certain topic to a Raspberry Pi that constituted as a broker (server). The data is furthermore published to/subscribed by a Python script that proceeded with the analysis (Fig. 3). The MQTT push protocol provided the ability to trigger the transmission of selected messages on command. This enabled the reception of the converted voting results from the PCB.

With the use of the IoT network, it was possible to set up a Raspberry Pi as a broker once in any building and use the voting wristbands in every other building and conference room of Infineon Technologies AG in Munich.

5.3 Data Analysis and Visualization

For the final data analysis and subsequent visualization, a Python script was used. This script included the MQTT implementation, a graphical user interface (GUI, built with the PyQt5 library [17]) and the graphical plotting of the results with live updates (matplotlib library [18]). Voting results are received via the MQTT protocol and stored as the corresponding voting category for live plotting.

The application has buttons to start the voting process, the calibration, to reset the results, and to get back to the home screen (Fig. 4). The layout of the GUI allows for customization depending on the event. A countdown timer for the voting process as well as a count of calibrated wristbands has been implemented.

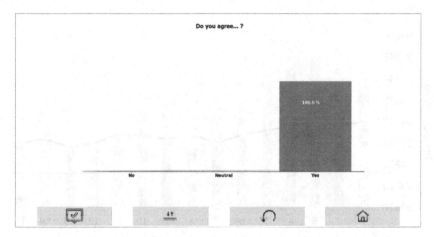

Fig. 4. Voting software user interface. The displayed questions can be adapted according to the given presentation. The first button on the left starts the voting process, whereas the second button is used for the calibration. A button to reset the results and to get back to the home screen are also implemented.

6 Evaluation

6.1 Experimental Setup

We conducted a short experiment of a voting process as a proof-of-concept. 5 rounds of calibration with subsequent voting for each category were performed with one PCB. The test person was standing in a conference room with closed windows and doors and wore the wristband on the right wrist. Evaluation of data transmission reliability, calibration performance, and voting accuracy was performed.

The wristband was initially calibrated before every voting process. This was performed by lowering the wrist to the lowest point first and staying in this position for 2 s. After that, the wrist was slowly moved upwards until the hand was completely raised. This position was also held for 2 s. The results were sent wirelessly and saved. As mentioned above, this produced the minimal and maximal value that defined the pressure range for voting.

Following the calibration, the voting process was executed. After the question was asked, the voting was possible for 10 s to assure a stable position of the wrist. To determine the voting accuracy, 5 rounds were carried out for each voting category

(Yes/Neutral/No). For testing the accuracy, the chosen answer was announced beforehand and compared to the voting result of the outcome.

6.2 Experimental Results

The conducted experiment revealed reliable voting results. Every desired voting result was successfully displayed by the voting software as well as the pressure values themselves (Fig. 5).

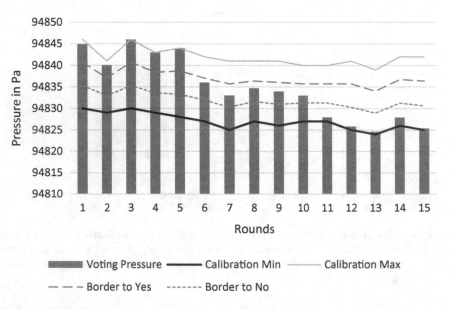

Fig. 5. Diagram showing results of the experimental evaluation. Bars representing the accurate air pressure value and consistent lines showing the values of minimal (black line) and maximal (red line) values that were obtained with the performed calibration before every voting process. Dashed lines display the range of each voting category with 'Neutral' in between 'Yes' and 'No'. (Color figure online)

Round 1–5 constituted testing rounds for the voting category 'Yes', round 6–10 tested the outcome of 'Neutral', and lastly rounds 11–15 tested the answer 'No' (Fig. 5). Minimal and maximal values that were obtained by the calibration revealed an average range of 94,827 Pa for the minimal calibration value and 94,842 Pa for the maximal calibration value. This results in an average difference of 15 Pa, which simultaneously sets the range for the voting categories to 5 Pa, respectively.

Even though the position of the wristband has not been changed significantly during the voting processes for each category, a noteworthy difference in the measured percentage was observed (Table 1). This is especially observable in the category 'Yes' with a voting result of 92% in round 2 and 100% in round 3–5 as well as the category 'No' with the percentage ranging from 2–12%.

Table 1. Detailed voting results

Round	Desired voting result	Voting result in %	Voting result
1	Yes	93	Yes
2	Yes	92	Yes
3	Yes	100	Yes
4	Yes	100	Yes
5	Yes	100	Yes
6	Neutral	60	Neutral
7	Ncutral	50	Neutral
8	Neutral	55	Neutral
9	Neutral	53	Neutral
10	Neutral	46	Neutral
11	No	7	No
12	No	5	No
13	No	4	No
14	No	12	No
15	No	2	No

The average battery time of the PCB during voting sessions was approximately 4 h, detailed tests on this, however, are still pending.

7 Conclusion

In this work, a novel application of a pressure sensor for voting procedures with an intuitive use of hand gestures and a textile wristband has been described.

The results from the conducted proof-of-concept experiment showed a reliable outcome of voting results with precise barometric air pressure measurements with an error rate of 0%. There were, however, fluctuations among the voting results within each category. Those were small enough to not influence the final outcome of the voting result, but they could affect the voting accuracy and quality overall in cases with additional weather-ascendancies.

The data transmission worked well and enabled the possibility of live updates of the voting results. This proofs the integrity of the designed PCB, its circuitry and the combination of components as well as the connection between software and hardware.

It was, however, necessary to perform a calibration before each and every voting process. This is not desirable for simple voting processes and the work on that is still in progress. The barometric pressure sensor reacts sensitively to changes of the weather or in the room, e.g. windows or doors that were opened. Furthermore, rapid movement of the wristband could result in the occurrence of negative pressure inside the sensor's vent hole and therefore cause a lower pressure value than assumed. The application of a 3D-printed solid housing could prevent this effect. Another conceivable improvement is the implementation of two additional sensors in the same room that send reference data for minimal and maximal pressure values so that no further calibration is needed.

8 Future Work

The development of the Smart Wristband for Voting is still in progress. Since a first functioning prototype of the wristband has been tested, some improvements regarding the wearing comfort are intended. At the moment a rigid PCB is used to integrate the electronic circuit into the flexible wristband. Further improvements will target the flexibility of the PCB, to improve the wearer's comfort. Approaches for this goal are the development of flexible PCBs, as well as integrating the electronic circuit directly into the wristband's fabric, which would make the use of a circuit board redundant.

Regarding the voting software there are many other ways to visualize the voting results. Currently the software runs on the Raspberry Pi (broker) itself, which can be controlled remotely by any computer in combination with a suitable software. Another solution would be the development of a web application that every authorized user has access to. Furthermore, it's also possible to develop a PowerPoint Add-In so the voting processes could be directly integrated into any presentation.

Furthermore, for voting processes outside of the Infineon working site and the IoT network, a Bluetooth setup can be developed to make the wristbands more versatile.

Acknowledgments. This work has been performed in the course of the EU-funded projects H2020/ECSEL, productive40, and iDev40 as well as Safe-DEED and the BMWi-funded project GeniusTex. The authors also would like to thank Andreas Krammer for his contribution of the concept drawing.

References

1. Kim, S., Park, S.: CPS (cyber physical system) based manufacturing system optimization. Procedia Comput. Sci. **122**, 518–524 (2017). https://doi.org/10.1016/j.procs.2017.11.401
2. Moiş, G., et al.: Communication in cyber-physical systems. In: 2015 19th International Conference on System Theory, Control and Computing (ICSTCC) (2015)
3. Salzer, R.: Smartphones as audience response systems for lectures and seminars. Anal. Bioanal. Chem. **410**, 1609–1613 (2018). https://doi.org/10.1007/s00216-017-0794-8
4. Boscardin, C., Penuel, W.: Exploring benefits of audience-response systems on learning: a review of the literature. Acad. Psychiatry **36**, 401–407 (2012). https://doi.org/10.1176/appi. ap.10080110
5. Nelson, E.C., Verhagen, T., Noordzij, M.L.: Health empowerment through activity trackers: an empirical smart wristband study. Comput. Hum. Behav. **62**, 364–374 (2016). https://doi. org/10.1016/j.chb.2016.03.065
6. Wang, N., Zhang, N., Wang, M.: Wireless sensors in agriculture and food industry—recent development and future perspective. Comput. Electron. Agric. **50**(1), 1–14 (2006). https:// doi.org/10.1016/j.compag.2005.09.003
7. Lu, Y.: Industry 4.0: a survey on technologies, applications and open research issues. J. Ind. Inf. Integr. **6**, 1–10 (2017). https://doi.org/10.1016/j.jii.2017.04.005
8. Muller, R.S.: Plenty of opportunity as well as "room at the bottom" some examples in optical MEMS. In: 2007 Fourth International Conference on Networked Sensing Systems (2007)
9. Irwin, C.B., Yen, T.Y., Meyer, R.H., Vanderheiden, G.C., Kelso, D.P., Sesto, M.E.: Use of force plate instrumentation to assess kinetic variables during touch screen use. Univ. Access Inf. Soc. **10**, 453–460 (2011)

10. Beigl, M., et al.: Typical sensors needed in ubiquitous and pervasive computing (2004)
11. Infineon Technologies AG. https://www.infineon.com/cms/de/product/sensor/barometric-pressure-sensor-for-consumer-applications/. Accessed 10 May 2019
12. Espressif Systems. https://www.espressif.com/sites/default/files/documentation/0a-esp826-6ex_datasheet_en.pdf. Accessed 10 May 2019
13. Microchip Technology. http://ww1.microchip.com/downloads/en/DeviceDoc/MCP1700-Low-Quiescent-Current-LDO-20001826E.pdf. Accessed 05 September 2019
14. Whitfield, J.: Electrical Craft Principles, p. 152. The Institution of Electrical Engineers (1995)
15. NodeMCU Documentation. https://nodemcu.readthedocs.io/en/master/. Accessed 04 May 2019
16. MQTT Documentation. http://mqtt.org/documentation. Accessed 04 May 2019
17. PyQt5 Documentation. https://www.riverbankcomputing.com/software/pyqt/intro. Accessed 04 May 2019
18. matplotlib Documentation. https://matplotlib.org/contents.html. Accessed 04 May 2019

8th International Workshop on Next Generation of System Assurance Approaches for Safety-Critical Systems (SASSUR 2019)

8th International Workshop on Next Generation of System Assurance Approaches for Safety-Critical Systems (SASSUR 2019)

Alejandra Ruiz[1], Jose Luis de la Vara[2], John Favaro[3], Fabien Belmonte[4]

[1] TECNALIA, Spain
alejandra.ruiz@tecnalia.com
[2] Universidad Castilla-La Mancha, Spain
jvara@inf.uc3m.es
[3] Intecs, Italy
john.favaro@intecs.it
[4] Alstom, France
fabien.belmonte@alstomgroup.com

SASSUR 2019 is the 8th edition of the International Workshop on Next Generation of System Assurance Approaches for Safety-Critical Systems. The SASSUR workshop is intended to explore new ideas on compositional, evolutionary, architecture-driven, multi-concern, and reuse-oriented assurance and certification of safety-critical systems. SASSUR aims at bringing together experts, researchers, and practitioners from diverse communities, such as safety and security engineering, certification processes, model-based technologies, software and hardware design, safety-critical systems, and application communities.

New system characteristics such as connectivity, autonomy, and adaptation, and recent situations such as crashes of autonomous vehicles, delays in aircraft delivery due to insufficient confidence in system safety, and unclear regulatory needs and requirements for assurance of systems with advanced features, all motivate the need for novel and cost-effective system assurance approaches. The topics of interest of the workshop include, among others, industrial challenges for safety and security assurance and certification, challenges for assuring safety and security in autonomous and adaptable systems, trends on regulations, human factors in safety and security assurance, and reusability in a safe and secure context.

The program of SASSUR 2019 consists of four high-quality papers. We have divided the papers into three categories based on their focus and the topics that they cover:

– Automotive

1. Automotive Cybersecurity standards - relation and overview, by Christoph Schmittner and Georg Macher
2. A Runtime Safety Monitoring Approach for Adaptable Autonomous Systems, by Nikita Bhardwaj Haupt and Peter Liggesmeyer

– Safety-Security Assurance

3. Structured Reasoning for Socio-Technical Factors of Safety-Security Assurance, by Nikita Johnson and Tim Kelly

– Reuse

4. The SISTER approach for Verification and Validation: a lightweight process for reusable results, by Andrea Ceccarelli, Davide Basile, Andrea Bondavalli, Lorenzo Falai, Alessandro Fantechi, Sandro Ferrari, Gianluca Mando', Nicola Nostro and Luigi Rucher

Acknowledgements. We are grateful to the SAFECOMP organization committee and collaborators for their support in arranging SASSUR. We also thank all the authors of the submitted papers for their interest in the workshop, and the steering and programme committees for their work and advice. Finally, the PDP4E project (H2020 European Project Number: 787034) and AQUAS project (H2020 ECSEL grant agreement nor 737475) to support the workshop.

Workshop Committees

Organization Committee

Alejandra Ruiz	TECNALIA, Spain
Jose Luis de la Vara	University of Castilla-La Mancha, Spain
John Favaro	Intecs, Italy
Fabien Belmonte	ALSTOM, France

Programme Committee and Reviewers

Markus Borg	RISE SICS AB, Sweden
Barbara Gallina	Mälardalen University, Sweden
Huascar Espinoza	CEA LIST, France
Ibrahim Habli	University of York, UK
Maritta Heisel	University of Duisburg-Essen, Germany
Garazi Juez	Tecnalia, Spain
Sahar Kokaly	University of Toronto, Canada
Georg Macher	Graz University of Technology, Austria
Johnny Marques	Brazilian Aeronautics Institute of Technology (ITA), Brazil
Silvia Mazzini	Intecs, Italy
Thor Myklebust	SINTEF ICT, Norway
Christoph Schmittner	AIT Austrian Institute of Technology, Austria

152   A. Ruiz et al.

Daniel Schneider   Fraunhofer Institute for Experimental Software Engineering,
                        Germany
Irfan Sljivo   Mälardalen University, Sweden
Kenji Taguchi   AIST, Japan
Stefano Tonetta   Fondazione Bruno Kessler, Italy
Marc Zeller   Siemens, Germany

Automotive Cybersecurity Standards - Relation and Overview

Christoph Schmittner[1]($\boxtimes$) and Georg Macher[2]

[1] Austrian Institute of Technology, Vienna, Austria
christoph.schmitttner@ait.ac.at
[2] Institute for Technical Informatics, Graz University of Technology, Graz, Austria
georg.macher@tugraz.at

Abstract. Today many connected and automated vehicles are available and connectivity features and information sharing is increasingly used for additional vehicle-, maintenance- and traffic safety features. This highly connected networking also increase the attractiveness of an attack on vehicles and the connected infrastructure by hackers with different motivations and thus introduces new risks for vehicle cybersecurity.

Highly aware of this fact, the automotive industry has therefore taken high efforts in designing and producing safe and secure connected and automated vehicles. Therefore the domain invested efforts in the development of industry standards to tackle automotive cybersecurity issues and protect their assets. The joint working group of the standardization organizations International Organization for Standardization (ISO) and Society of Automotive Engineers (SAE) has recently established and published a committee draft of the "ISO-SAE Approved new Work Item (AWI) 21434 Road Vehicles - Cybersecurity Engineering" standard. In addition to that SAE is also working on a set of cybersecurity guidance, ISO is addressing specific automotive cybersecurity related topics in additional standards and European Telecommunications Standards Institute (ETSI) and International Telecommunication Union (ITU) is working on security topics of connected vehicles. Further activities are national and international regulations on Automotive Cybersecurity. In the course of this document, a review of the available work and ongoing developments is given and the outline of the automotive cybersecurity framework is given. The aim of this work is to provide a position statement for discussion of available standards, methods and recommendations for automotive cybersecurity.

Keywords: ISO 21434 · ISO 26262 · Automotive · Security analysis

1   Introduction

Today electronic components make up over 50% of the total manufacturing cost of a car and contain over 100 million lines of code [2]. The automotive industry has an annual increase rate of software-implemented functions of about 30% [4]

© Springer Nature Switzerland AG 2019
A. Romanovsky et al. (Eds.): SAFECOMP 2019 Workshops, LNCS 11699, pp. 153–165, 2019.
https://doi.org/10.1007/978-3-030-26250-1_12

and these systems account for over 80% of product innovation [23]. With the nearly 112 million vehicles now connected around the world potentially at risk from some form of cyber threat, the global market for automotive cybersecurity is expected to exponentially grow to USD 759 million by 2023 [6]. Nevertheless, these embedded systems are enablers for an increasing degree of digitalization; which in turn leads to an increase of competitiveness on existing markets as well as opening the door to new markets.

Before the introduction of connectivity features and automated driving functionalities, safety engineering was at the forefront of the automotive domain's priorities. Therefore, functional safety engineering methods and processes become industry standard and critical part of the development. Today, many connected and automated vehicles are available and connectivity features and information sharing is increasingly used for additional vehicle-, maintenance- and traffic safety features. This also increased the attractiveness of an attack on vehicles by hackers with different motivations and thus introduces new risks for vehicle cybersecurity.

Consequently, new challenges regarding automotive cybersecurity emerged; these in turn require additional efforts, engineering approaches and a very specific skill-set to deal with threats, risk management, secure design, awareness, and cybersecurity measures over the whole lifecycle of the vehicle. Well aware of this fact, the automotive industry has therefore taken high efforts in designing and producing safe and secure connected and automated vehicles. As the domain geared up for the cybersecurity challenges, they can leverage experiences from many other domains, but nevertheless, must face several unique challenges. Similar to the situation which lead to the development of ISO 26262 based on International Electrotechnical Commission (IEC) 61508 a automotive cybersecurity standard can be tailored to the automotive engineering landscape (e.g. distributed development). It can collect specific guidance and can be better adapted to the domain, e.g. collect methods, threat landscape and give guidance on how to integrate cybersecurity engineering into existing engineering processes.

Automotive industry has recognized these requirements and therefore invested in the development of industry standards to tackle automotive cybersecurity issues and protect their assets. The joint working group of the standardization organizations ISO and SAE has recently established a committee draft of the "ISO-SAE AWI 21434 Road Vehicles - Cybersecurity Engineering" standard. While this standard focus on the security engineering of automotive systems there are additional standards, recommendation and guidance documents in development or already published. ISO-SAE 21434 needs to define a consistent engineering framework, considering existing work and describing the state of the art for automotive cybersecurity engineering.

From the point of view of the automotive industry, these standards need to achieve a common understanding of security by design in product development and along the entire supply chain.

In the course of this document, a review of the available documents and ongoing work is given. The aim of this work is to provide a position statement of the available documents, the presented analysis methods and recommendations given, also in context of safety-related development.

This paper is organized as follows: Sect. 2 presents related safety engineering and security engineering approaches. The review and overview of guidance, standards and regulations is given in Sect. 3. Based on this review, Sect. 4 analyses the automotive cybersecurity framework under development. Finally, Sect. 5 concludes the work.

2   Established Safety and Security Frameworks

We focus on the automotive cybersecurity landscape. Documents were identified by a survey of ongoing activities and personal involvements in standardization communities. We focused on standards, regulations and guidance with a certain detail level and clear focus on the automotive domain and therefore a potential for conflicting or overlapping guidance.

Example of a guidance we excluded, is the National Highway Traffic Safety Administration (NHTSA) cybersecurity best practices for modern vehicles [1]. While these document contains valuable guidance, we see from the level of guidance a low probability of conflict.

In addition we also excluded Intelligent Transportation System (ITS) specific guidance which is developed by ETSI and also ISO. We see here some potential for overlaps and benefits in an unified approach, but this would go beyond the scope of this work. For not yet publicly available standards we refer to presentations and existing overviews about the status like [5, 18].

Safety and security engineering are very closely related disciplines. They both focus on system-wide features and could greatly benefit from one another if adequate interactions between their processes are defined.

2.1   Safety Engineering Standards

Safety engineering is already an integral part of automotive engineering and safety standards, such as the road vehicles – functional safety norm ISO 26262 [10] and its basic norm IEC 61508 [28], are well established in the automotive industry. Safety assessment techniques, such as Failure Mode and Effects Analysis (FMEA) [26] and Fault Tree Analysis (FTA) [27], are also specified, standardized, and integrated in the automotive development process landscape.

IEC 61508 Edition 2.0 provides a first approach of integrating safety and security; security threats are to be considered during hazard analysis in the form of a security threat analysis. However, this threat analysis is not specified in more details in the standard and it is in discussion for Edition 3.0 to be more elaborated on security-aware safety topics.

ISO 26262 Edition 2.0, which was published end of 2018, includes recommendations for the interaction between safety and security. Based on a initial discussion on how to treat safety and cybersecurity in Automotive standardization it was decided to publish separate standards, but describe the interaction.

It should be remarked that his content had to be finalized before the development of ISO-SAE 21434 started. Annex E of ISO 26262 gives then additional guidance on the interaction. For the management, coordination of plans and milestones are suggested as well as field monitoring is also mentioned. During concept phase a focus is on the interaction between HARA and TARA and the coordination between countermeasures. In the development phase a focus is on consecutive analysis and the identification of potential impacts between the disciplines. The Annex is concluded with guidance on the interaction in the production phase.

2.2   Security Engineering Standards

The SAE J3061 [29] guideline is a predecessor of ISO-SAE 21434 and establishes a set of high-level guiding principles for cybersecurity by:

- defining a complete lifecycle process framework
- providing information on some common existing tools and methods
- supporting basic guiding principles on cybersecurity
- summarizing further standard development activities

SAE J3061 states that cybersecurity engineering requires an appropriate lifecycle process, which is defined analogous to the process framework described in ISO 26262. Further, no restrictions are given on whether to maintain separate processes for safety and security engineering with appropriate levels of interaction or to attempt direct integration of the two processes.

Apart from that, the guidebook recommends an initial assessment of potential threats and an estimation of risks for systems that may be considered cybersecurity relevant or are safety-related systems, to determine whether there are cybersecurity threats that can potentially lead to safety violations. A report on the application of SAE J3061 was published [22]. Due to the joint development of ISO-SAE 21434, SAE J3061 was pulled from the market and will be reworked to cover additional topics, outside the scope of ISO-SAE 21434.

While other standards, like the IEC 62443 [7] or the ISO 27000 series [8] are not directly aimed at automotive systems, they are nevertheless relevant for the production and back-end systems of the automotive domain and need to be considered for a complete framework.

In [19] we reviewed available threat analysis methods and the recommendations of the SAE J3061 guidebook regarding Threat Analysis and Risk Assessment (TARA) in context of ISO 26262 (2011) and SAE J3061. We provided an evaluation of available analysis methods together with a review of recommended threat analysis methods. Furthermore, we investigate systematic approaches to support the identification of trust boundaries and attack vectors for the safety- and cybersecurity-related aspects of complex automotive systems also in context of ISO 26262 (2011) and SAE J3061 in [20].

Aside from this, in [21] we presented a first overview about the ongoing development and status of ISO-SAE 21434. In comparison to these works we updated the overview to consider the ongoing development, reviewed the current status regarding methodological guidance, consider the complete set of available standards and give a first evaluation how to integrate cybersecurity into established automotive processes.

3 Overview on Automotive Cybersecurity

3.1 ISO-SAE 21434

ISO and SAE collaborate on the development of a cybersecurity standard for the engineering of road vehicles. The purpose of the standard to be created (ISO-SAE 21434) was to (a) define a structured process to ensure cybersecurity engineering of in-vehicle systems, (b) thus reducing the potential for a successful attack and reducing the likelihood of losses, and (c) provide clear means to react to cybersecurity threats consistently across global industry.

As mentioned, ISO-SAE 21434 is intended for application to road-vehicles and focuses on setting minimum criteria for automotive cybersecurity engineering. In the standard neither specifics to cybersecurity technologies, solutions or remediation methods are given. Nor, are there unique requirements for autonomous vehicles or road infrastructure given. A risk-oriented approach for prioritization of actions and methodical elicitation of cybersecurity measures is encouraged.

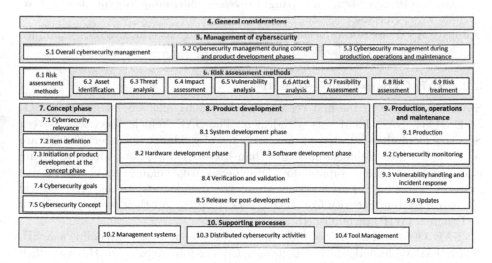

Fig. 1. Overview of the ISO-SAE 21434 chapter structure [18]

Key principle focused by the ISO-SAE 21434 [18] are cybersecurity engineering, considering all phases of the vehicle life-cycle; ranging from design and development, production, operation and maintenance to decommissioning. In this section the structure of the ISO-SAE 21434 draft, depicted in Fig. 1, is briefly described.

Section 1 defines the Scope of the norm.

Section 2 provides normative references.

Section 3 defines abbreviated terms and definitions of terms used in the document.

Section 4 is an *informative part* describing the vehicle ecosystem, organizational cybersecurity management and the related automotive lifecycle.

Section 5 includes descriptions regarding the organizational cybersecurity strategy, policy and objectives.

Section 6 defines risk management requirements, which includes a plan and method to determine the extent to which the road user is threatened by a potential circumstance or event.

Section 7 deals with the concept phase and defines cybersecurity goals, resulting from a threat analysis and risk assessment; as well as cybersecurity requirements definition to achieve the cybersecurity goals.

Section 8 specifies the implementation and verification of cybersecurity requirements specific to product development phase.

Section 9 is focusing on production, operation and maintenance phase and specifying requirements to ensure that the cybersecurity specifications are implemented in the produced item; also covering in-field cybersecurity activities.

Section 10 describes supporting processes, including organizational processes.

Annexes A - J are also *informative parts* describing several activities, examples and methods.

3.2 SAE Cybersecurity Activities

Since the content of the first version of SAE J3061 [29] was merged into ISO-SAE 21434, SAE J3061 was withdrawn. The SAE Vehicle Electrical System Security Committee started to develop a set of guidance documents which are more in depth or technical in nature than ISO-SAE 21434 and aimed at giving additional guidance or support for the cybersecurity engineering of automotive systems. Table 1 gives an overview about the five documents the SAE Vehicle Electrical System Security Committee is developing and their status, e.g. Work in Progress (WIP) or published.

SAE J3061 will be divided into three parts. The first part will define a AcSIL and a TARA Method which will classify threats into AcSIL. For threats which can cause a safety impact guidance will be included how the AcSIL can be related to the ASIL. Parts two and three will focus on security testing. Part two focus on a vendor agnostic overview on security testing methods for hardware and software which is updated in regular intervals. SAE J3061-3 will contain an overview about manufacturers of security related tools and their capabilities. In addition to an rework of SAE J3061, SAE is also working on guidance on how to implement hardware-based security in ground vehicles and on how to protect the OBDII interface.

Table 1. Overview about ongoing automotive cybersecurity related activities at SAE

Document	Description	Status
SAE J3061-1 Automotive Cybersecurity Integrity Level	Cybersecurity Classification Scheme for automotive systems. Relation between Automotive Cybersecurity Integrity Level (AcSIL) for safety related threats to Automotive Safety Integrity Level (ASIL)	WIP
SAE J3061-2 Security Testing Methods	Overview of currently available software and hardware security testing methods	WIP
SAE J3061-3 Security Testing Tools	Overview of security related tools and their capabilities	WIP
SAE J3101 Requirements for Hardware-Protected Security for Ground Vehicle Applications	Set of requirements for implementing hardware-based security in ground vehicles	WIP
SAE J3138 Guidance for Securing the Data Link Connector (DLC)	Guidance on securing the communication with devices connected to the Data Link Connector (OnBoard Diagnostics (OBD)II Port)	WIP

3.3 ITU-T SG17 Q13 (Security Aspects for Intelligent Transport System)

The ITU works on security aspects for Intelligent Transport System [13]. The focus is on Vehicle to X (V2X) communication, but also in-vehicle systems and their security is considered. Table 2 gives an overview about ongoing activities.

Table 2. Overview about ongoing automotive cybersecurity related activities at ITU

Document	Description	Status
X.1373 [17]	Secure software update capability for intelligent transportation system communication devices	Published
X.itssec-2 [15]	Security Guidelines for V2X Communication Systems	WIP
X.itssec-3 [12]	Security requirements for vehicle accessible external devices	WIP
X.itssec-4 [11]	Methodologies for intrusion detection system on in-vehicle systems	WIP
X.itssec-5 [16]	Security guidelines for vehicular edge computing	WIP
X.eivnsec [14]	Security guidelines for the Ethernet-based in-vehicle networks	WIP

X.1373 is a recommendation on secure software updates for ITS communication devices in order to prevent threats such as tampering of and malicious intrusion to communication devices on vehicles. It contains a basic model of software updates, presents a threat and risk analysis for software updates and gives the resulting security requirements and specifies a abstract data format for update software modules.

X.itssec-2 will give similar guidance for V2X communication. It will present a basic model and use cases of a V2X communication system, conduct a TARA and give security requirements.

X.itssec-3 has a similar goal like SAE J3138 and will identify security issues if external devices, with or without telecommunication interface, are connected to the OBDII Port and define suitable security requirements to protect this external interface.

X.itssec-4 aims at a complete guidance on Intrusion Detection System (IDS) in vehicular networks. The recommendation will include classification and analysis of attack types on in-vehicle networks and systems. The focus is on in-vehicle networks like Controller Area Network (CAN) or CAN with Flexible Data-Rate (CAN-FD) which cannot be supported by general IDS.

X.itssec-5 will present Vehicular Edge Computing (VEC), e.g. a dedicated computing platform for computing-intensive tasks. A set of such tasks will be presented in use cases. Based on a threat analysis and risk assessment security requirements for VEC will be presented.

X.eivnsec will contain a reference model of automotive Ethernet and a threat analysis and vulnerability assessment for the Ethernet-based in-vehicle network. Security requirements and potential use cases for Ethernet-based in-vehicle network will be defined.

3.4   ISO Activities on Automotive Cybersecurity

Outside of ISO-SAE 21434 automotive cybersecurity is also considered in additional ISO standards. Table 3 gives an overview.

Table 3. Overview about ongoing automotive cybersecurity related activities at ISO

Document	Description	Status
ISO 20078-3	Extended vehicle (ExVe) web services – Part 3: Security	Published
ISO Technical Reports (TR) 23791	ExVe web services – Result of the risk assessment on ISO 20078 series	WIP
ISO 20828 [9]	Security certificate managements	Published

For accessing vehicle data ISO developed the ExVe concept. This follows the goal of minimizing the attack surface, e.g. instead of having a interface for each service, car data is transferred to a remote and secure server from where service providers can access the data. In order to ensure fair competition between all stakeholders it is assumed that this "car data" server is operated by a neutral party [3]. In ISO TR 23791 a risk assessment for the concept of extended vehicle was conducted and the security for the extended vehicle is described in ISO 20078-3. ISO 20828 describe how to issue and manage certificates in a vehicular public key environment.

3.5 United Nations Economic Commission for Europe (UNECE) Activities on Automotive Cybersecurity

Besides standardisation, cybersecurity is increasingly also a topic for regulation. The World Forum for Harmonization of Vehicle Regulations as a working party (WP.29) of the Sustainable Transport Division of the UNECE was commissioned to work on draft regulations on cybersecurity [24] and over-the-air updates [25]. UNECE defines the rules for type approval in 62 states. Based on the two draft recommendation a first evaluation period was started, to test the applicability of the new regulation. The recommendation on cybersecurity contains a sections with regulations related to (a) requirements for approving and certifying a Original Equipment Manufacturer (OEM) Cybersecurity Management System and (b) approval of vehicle type cybersecurity. This is completed with guidance on processes and procedures and best practices (threats & mitigations). The recommendation on software update regulation consists of three parts. The Software update regulation contains requirements for approving OEM Software update Management, including process verification and audits & assessment of OEM capabilities, requirements on the process include requirements on safe and secure updates. Additional regulations are given for updates of software which can impact the vehicle type approval. All software components of a vehicle type which impact the type approval need to have a Software Identification Number (RxSWIN) assigned and an update of such a software requires a new type approval. This draft regulation is also completed by guidance on software updates processes and procedures, and advice to support national registration processes.

4   Review

We did focus in our review on cybersecurity standards directly related to automotive systems. Considering ITS systems, including on-board units and road-side stations there are also standards from ETSI for this type of systems. Based on this, one of the challenges of ISO-SAE 21434 is to define a consistent cybersecurity engineering framework. In Fig. 2 we give an overview about the presented standards for vehicular elements.

One special challenge is here the partial overlap between standards. As example the security of the OBDII interface is considered in two different groups, and while there is guidance on hardware-based security, there is also guidance on certificates, which was published in 2006 and does not consider the new work on hardware-based security. Looking at the process and engineering side, the situation is similarly complex. Figure 3 gives a overview about process interactions.

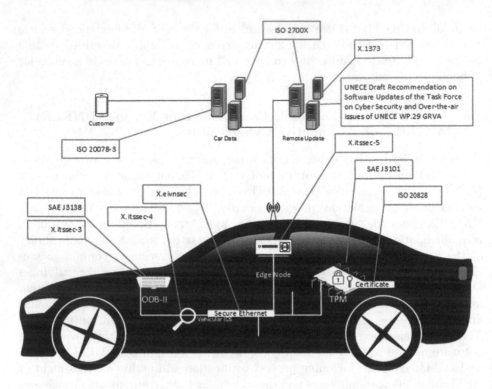

Fig. 2. Overview of the Automotive cybersecurity standards and guidance documents for technical elements

The difficult task of the ISO-SAE 21434 committee is to create a brand new cybersecurity standard for the specifics of the automotive industry, while considering existing or ongoing developments.

As an example, to engineer a secure remote update *(X.1373, UNECE Draft Recommendation on Software Updates)* for a safety critical system *(ISO 26262)* where the gateway is a secure edge node *(X.itssec-5)* which also offers extended vehicle capabilities *(ISO 20078-3)* and is updating a Electronic Control Unit (ECU) with an Trusted Platform Module (TPM) *(SAE J3101)* and certificates *(ISO 20828)* via Ethernet *(X.eivnsec)* one has eight documents with additional guidance on the cybersecurity, excluding back-end security and communication security topics. For the process there is a safety process *(ISO 26262)* and security process *(ISO/SAE 21434, UNECE WP29)* with additional guidance on security analysis and safety and security integrity levels *(SAE J3061-1)* and security testing *(SAE J3061-2/3)*.

A consistent process and security framework is one of the precondition of having a secure systems. We see currently a risk of mismatch between guidance documents, especially in distributed engineering environments where different companies could base their internal documents on different sources.

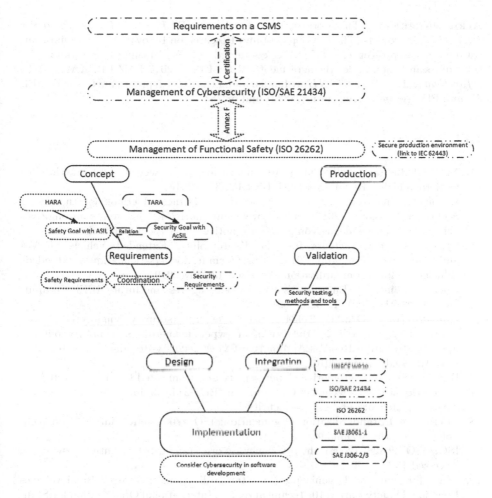

Fig. 3. Overview of the Automotive cybersecurity standards and guidance documents for the lifecycle process

5   Conclusion

While SAE J3061 was an important step forward it was also recognized that this guidebook could not fulfill a similar role like ISO 26262 for the cybersecurity engineering of road-vehicles. With "ISO-SAE 21434 Road Vehicles - Cybersecurity Engineering, the goal is to provide a basis for an entire uniform cybersecurity development process in the automotive industry. The topic cybersecurity in the automotive context is a very new one and the ambition to provide a framework that includes requirements for cybersecurity process and a common language for communicating and managing cybersecurity risk among stakeholders is aiming high. The cross-relations between standards, guidance, recommendation and regulation makes the development of a consistent standard difficult.

Acknowledgments. This work is supported by the *DRIVES*, *Afarcloud* and the *PRYSTINE* projects. The Development and Research on Innovative Vocational Educational Skills project (*DRIVES*) is co-funded by the Erasmus+ Programme of the European Union under the agreement 591988-EPP-1-2017-1-CZ-EPPKA2-SSA-B. *Afarcloud* and the *PRYSTINE* are funded under the ECSEL programm by the ECSEL JU and FFG (grant agreement nr 783221 and nr 783190).

References

1. National Highway Traffic Safety Administration: Cybersecurity best practices for modern vehicles. Report No. DOT HS **812**, 333 (2016)
2. Automotive iQ: Automotive Cyber Security - Dedicated eBook for the Cyber Security professional (2017). https://www.automotive-iq.com/events-automotive-cyber-security/downloads/complete-automotive-cyber-security-ebook
3. Comité des constructeurs français d'automobile: Extended Vehicle (ExVe) and Standardisation, May 2019. https://ccfa.fr/dossiers-thematiques/extended-vehicle-exve-and-standardisation. Accessed 13 May 2019
4. Ebert, C., Jones, C.: Embedded software: facts, figures, and future. IEEE Comput. Soc. **0018–9162**(09), 42–52 (2009)
5. Hunjan, H.: ISO/SAE 21434 automotive cybersecurity engineering, July 2018. http://2pe5rtjld2w41m0dy17n5an1-wpengine.netdna-ssl.com/wp-content/uploads/2018/07/8_Renesas_Automotive-Cyber-Security-Standardistation-v1.0.pdf. Accessed 12 May 2019
6. IHS Automotive: Automotive Cybersecurity and Connected Car Report (2016)
7. International Electrotechnical Commission: IEC 62443: Industrial communication networks - network and system security
8. International Standardization Organization: ISO 27000 series, information technology - security techniques
9. ISO: ISO 20828 (2006). https://www.iso.org/standard/41891.html?browse=tc. Accessed 13 May 2019
10. ISO - International Organization for Standardization: ISO 26262 Road vehicles Functional Safety Part 1–10. Technical report, International Organization for Standardization (2011)
11. ITU: Methodologies for intrusion detection system on in-vehicle systems, February 2019. https://www.itu.int/itu-t/workprog/wp_item.aspx?isn=14395. Accessed 12 May 2019
12. ITU: Security requirements for vehicle accessible external devices, February 2019. https://www.itu.int/itu-t/workprog/wp_item.aspx?isn=14394. Accessed 12 May 2019
13. ITU: Security aspects for Intelligent Transport System, May 2019. https://www.itu.int/en/ITU-T/studygroups/2017-2020/17/Pages/q13.aspx. Accessed 12 May 2019
14. ITU: Security guidelines for the Ethernet-based in-vehicle networks, May 2019. https://www.itu.int/itu-t/workprog/wp_item.aspx?isn=14819. Accessed 13 May 2019
15. ITU: Security guidelines for V2X communication systems, February 2019. https://www.itu.int/itu-t/workprog/wp_item.aspx?isn=13549. Accessed 12 May 2019
16. ITU: Security guidelines for vehicular edge computing, February 2019. https://www.itu.int/ITU-T/workprog/wp_item.aspx?isn=14396. Accessed 12 May 2019

17. ITU-T: Itu-t x.1373secure software update capability for intelligent transportation system communication devices (2017). https://www.itu.int/rec/T-REC-X.1373/en. Accessed 12 May 2019
18. Krzeszewski, J.T.: ISO 21434 - current status. Recording of a Presentation at the 3rd Vector Automotive Cybersecurity Symposium, April 2019. https://youtu.be/2MaG5D1kLt0?t=760. Accessed 12 May 2019
19. Macher, G., Armengaud, E., Brenner, E., Kreiner, C.: A review of threat analysis and risk assessment methods in the automotive context. In: Skavhaug, A., Guiochet, J., Bitsch, F. (eds.) SAFECOMP 2016. LNCS, vol. 9922, pp. 130–141. Springer, Cham (2016). https://doi.org/10.1007/978-3-319-45477-1_11
20. Macher, G., Messnarz, R., Armengaud, E., Riel, A., Brenner, E., Kreiner, C.: Integrated safety and security development in the automotive domain. In: SAE Technical Paper. SAE International (2017). http://papers.sae.org/2017-01-1661/
21. Schmittner, C., Griessnig, G., Ma, Z.: Status of the development of ISO/SAE 21434. In: Larrucea, X., Santamaria, I., O'Connor, R.V., Messnarz, R. (eds.) EuroSPI 2018. CCIS, vol. 896, pp. 504–513. Springer, Cham (2018). https://doi.org/10.1007/978-3-319-97925-0_43
22. Schmittner, C., Ma, Z., Reyes, C., Dillinger, O., Puschner, P.: Using SAE J3061 for automotive security requirement engineering. In: Skavhaug, A., Guiochet, J., Schoitsch, E., Bitsch, F. (eds.) SAFECOMP 2016. LNCS, vol. 9923, pp. 157–170. Springer, Cham (2016). https://doi.org/10.1007/978-3-319-45480-1_13
23. Scuro, G.: Automotive industry: innovation driven by electronics (2012). http://embedded-computing.com/articles/automotive-industry-innovation-driven-electronics/
24. Secretary of TF-CS/OTA UNECE WP29: Draft Recommendation on Cyber Security of the Task Force on Cyber Security and Over-the-air issues of UNECE WP.29 IWG ITS/AD, April 2018. https://wiki.unece.org/pages/viewpage.action?pageId=58524794. Accessed 27 Mar 2019
25. Secretary of TF-CS/OTA UNECE WP29: Draft Recommendation on Software Updates of the Task Force on Cyber Security and Over-the-air issues of UNECE WP.29 IWG ITS/AD, September 2018. https://www.unece.org/fileadmin/DAM/trans/doc/2018/wp29grva/GRVA-01-18.pdf. Accessed 27 Mar 2019
26. TC 56: IEC 60812 Analysis techniques for system reliability - Procedure for failure mode and effects analysis (FMEA). Technical report, International Organization for Standardization (2006)
27. TC 56: IEC 61025 Fault tree analysis (FTA). Technical report, International Organization for Standardization, December 2006
28. TC 65: IEC 61508 Functional safety of electrical/electronic/programmable electronic safety-related systems. Technical report, International Organization for Standardization
29. Vehicle Electrical System Security Committee: SAE J3061 Cybersecurity Guidebook for Cyber-Physical Automotive Systems. Technical report, SAE (2016)

A Runtime Safety Monitoring Approach for Adaptable Autonomous Systems

Nikita Bhardwaj Haupt$^{(\boxtimes)}$ and Peter Liggesmeyer

TU Kaiserslautern, 67663 Kaiserslautern, Germany
{haupt,liggesmeyer}@cs.uni-kl.de

Abstract. Adaptable Autonomous Systems are advanced autonomous systems which not only interact with their environment, but are aware of it and are capable of adapting their behavior and structure accordingly. Since these systems operate in an unknown, dynamic and unstructured safety-critical environment, traditional safety assurance techniques are not sufficient anymore. In order to guarantee safe behavior, possibly at all times in all possible situations, they require methodologies that can observe the system status at runtime and ensure safety accordingly. To this end, we introduce a runtime safety monitoring approach that uses a rule-based safety monitor to observe the system for safety-critical deviations. The approach behaves like a fault tolerance mechanism where, the system continuously monitors itself and activates corrective measures in the event of safety-critical failures, thereby aiding the system to sustain a safe behavior at runtime. We illustrate the presented approach by employing an example from autonomous agricultural domain and discuss the case study with initial findings.

Keywords: Runtime safety monitoring ·
Adaptable Autonomous Systems · Safety monitor · Reconfiguration

1 Introduction

Over the last few decades, software-intensive systems have experienced an evident upsurge in demand for autonomy. Entitled as autonomous systems, these systems are capable of accomplishing intricate tasks and achieving designated goals, with little or no human assistance, in highly dynamic, complex and at times entirely unknown environments. All autonomous systems interact with their environment in which they operate. Some autonomous systems are, however, advanced in a way that they not only interact with their environment, but are aware of it along with their own operational state. These systems are capable of adaptivity that is, they can learn from the environment and adapt their behavior or structure accordingly. We call such systems as Adaptable Autonomous Systems (AAS).

Adaptivity is a characteristic of autonomous systems and thus all adaptive systems are autonomous, but not all autonomous systems are adaptive. System

© Springer Nature Switzerland AG 2019
A. Romanovsky et al. (Eds.): SAFECOMP 2019 Workshops, LNCS 11699, pp. 166–177, 2019.
https://doi.org/10.1007/978-3-030-26250-1_13

adaptivity is a result of *awareness* and *automation* where, awareness further relies upon the knowledge and the monitoring capabilities of the system [1]. Based on the knowledge an AAS is provided and the information it monitors, it can be a *self-aware* system with in-depth knowledge about its own components, behaviors and states, or a *context-aware* system with detailed information about its context along with intrinsic capabilities to sense, comprehend and respond to the dynamic changes.

AAS are predominant in safety-critical application domains like healthcare, automotive, avionics and agriculture. A failure or malfunctioning of a component can cause severe damage to people or the property and at times can even lead to catastrophic consequences like death. This is why ensuring safety while adaptation at runtime becomes crucial. Conventional safety assurance techniques like fault tree analysis (FTA) and failure mode and effects analysis (FMEA) are carried out assuming that all possible system behaviors along with its operating environment are fully known at design time. Even in functional safety standard ISO 26262 [2], system verification and validation is based on the presumption that all system requirements are precisely and correctly known at design time. Moreover, in order to certify that a system is safe, it must be in correspondence with the standard. AAS, however, are complex systems that operate in dynamic and unstructured environment. Due to complexity of the system and uncertainty of the environment it is not adequate to determine all possible system behaviors at design time. Thus, in addition to traditional safety approaches, these systems necessitate runtime safety techniques that are capable of handling unpredictable operating conditions, evaluate system behavior and adapt accordingly.

At runtime, safety-critical situations may arise due to random errors in hardware components (e.g. sensors) or due to unexpected operational environment and cause an *unintended behavior* of the system that may result in a hazard, or even an accident of higher severity, if left undetected. As it is unknown at design time which error would occur in which operational situation and result in an unsafe circumstance, to avoid it and maintain safety, it is necessary to be aware about it on the first place. To this end, we employ a *safety monitor* that utilizes self-awareness property of the system. The main task of the monitor is to observe system states and its behavior and trigger restorative actions in case of any safety violations. In this way, the system is not only capable of detecting both design time and runtime defects, that occur in software/hardware due to unplanned context or runtime faults, but is also able to handle such deviations and bring system back to a safe state during operation. This approach of safety monitoring behaves like a fault tolerance mechanism where, the system continuously monitors itself and activates corrective measures on detection of safety-critical failures, thereby aiding itself in sustaining a safe behavior in all situations at all times.

In this paper, we present a detailed specification of a runtime safety monitor that monitors the system for *safety-critical deviations* using a set of predefined *safety rules*. In order to derive these rules, a systematic and thorough four-step procedure is followed. The process commences with determining all operational modes along with the potential configurations of the system and is followed by evaluating set of services associated with each configuration. A scenario-oriented hazard and risk analysis is then performed to assess the consequences of the safety-critical deviations during system operation. Finally, based on the risk associated with the deviations, safety rules representing the safety status and safety measures for the system are derived.

This paper is organized as follows: In Sect. 2, we introduce the definitions used in our approach along with an elaborated step-wise specification for the monitor. We then demonstrate a case study of the safety monitor using an example of an AAS from autonomous agriculture domain. In Sect. 3, we give an outline of the related work. We conclude our paper with discussions and future work in Sect. 4.

2   Runtime Safety Monitoring

As defined by Avizienis in [3], safety is "the absence of catastrophic consequences on the user(s) and the environment". Based on this definition, safe behavior of an AAS can be defined as the capability of the system to accomplish its tasks make decisions according to the changes in itself or the environment and at the same time ensure safety. The magnitude of safe behavior depends upon the level of autonomy, likelihood of human intervention and the environmental context. For instance, taking into consideration an autonomous vehicle as an AAS, in presence of a human driver, a system malfunction can be tolerated by switching-off the function and giving driver the complete control of the vehicle. However, in case of a fully-autonomous vehicle, in the absence of a human assistance, the vehicle must be capable of detecting and tolerating a safety-critical situation on its own. Runtime safety monitoring extends safety assurance capabilities of autonomous systems capable of adaptation in dynamic and unstructured environments. In the unknown safety-critical environment, safety monitoring aims at assisting the system to maintain a safe state at all times of operation. A safety monitor can thus be seen as a safety mechanism that monitors the system for safety-critical deviations and triggers corrective measures to avoid catastrophic consequences. Monitoring safety of AAS at runtime complements traditional safety assurance as it facilitates the system in finding design time as well as runtime defects that could potentially occur in software or hardware due to unexpected environmental conditions or runtime faults [4].

2.1   Basic Definitions

In this paper we have used terminologies like, *safety-critical deviations*, *operational modes*, *configurations* etc. As these terms already hold a certain meaning in the safety context, for a better understanding of them with respect our approach, we introduce their respective connotations below:

– A **Safety-Critical Deviation** is an unplanned behavior of a system service that can result into hazardous situations or sometimes an accident, if left undetected. It is an aftermath of malfunctioning of the component either due to physical wear&tear or unsuitable environmental conditions.

- A **Safety-Critical Service** is a service whose deviation during an operation might result in a hazardous situation. It is different from other system services whose failure would influence system attributes like performance but, not safety.
- **Safety Measure** is a system response to handle safety critical deviations. It determines what should be done to bring system back to a safe state, e.g. adaptation in form of reconfiguration.
- **Safety Status** is a condition that represents whether a system is in a safe or unsafe state. If an unsafe status is reached, its corresponding safety measure is prompted immediately.
- A **Safety Rule** is a combination of safety status and its corresponding measure that is applicable in a particular situation at runtime.
- **Safety Monitor** is a module responsible for monitoring safety status of the system with respect to a set of safety rules. In the event of a safety-critical deviation, a safety measure corresponding to a safety status is triggered.
- A **Configuration** is a state of the system that can operate with different component malfunctions and environmental conditions. An AAS consists of multiple configurations out of which only one can be activated at a time.
- **Reconfiguration** is a procedure of changing configuration of the system in order to sustain safe behavior. It is a safety measure that is generated in response to a safety status in case of a deviation.
- A **Collaboration Profile** is a particular composition of configurations of different components to perform a specific task. When a system reconfigures, the overall system switches from one collaboration profile to another.
- An **Operational Mode** represents the level of autonomy with which system is operating. It considers the components required to carry out the operation/functionality, e.g. a vehicle driving at fully-autonomous mode without any human-assistance.
- **Severity** is the consequence of a hazardous situation occurred in the system due to safety-critical deviation at runtime. A deviation can result in different severities based on the operational mode and the surrounding environment of the system.

2.2   Safety Monitor Specification

By means of a safety monitor we employ runtime monitoring to ensure safe operation of an AAS (or its components) by monitoring its potential configurations for safety-critical deviations in its services. In this way, the presented monitoring approach does not aim at fault prevention or fault removal, but at fault tolerance as it detects the safety violations in they system and prompts safety measures to avoid any unsafe situations at runtime. The behavior of the monitor is a declarative collection of safety rules, where each rule represents the safety status of the system and corresponding to it its restorative measure. To derive the safety rules and demonstrate the monitoring approach, we make use of an example of Tractor-Implement-Automation (TIA) [5] from autonomous agriculture domain.

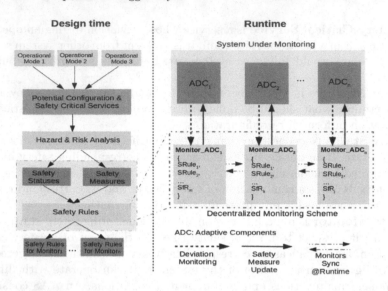

Fig. 1. Design and runtime safety monitoring procedure

In TIA, an implement is a device or a component that is attached to a tractor to perform a specific task. For instance, a harvester for harvesting the crops or a baler for baling the swath are some common implements used in agriculture industry. Figure 2 shows components of a TIA for baling purposes. There is a Tractor which is integrated with a Baler implement in order to perform baling on the field. The tractor consists of a SwathScanner that aids Baler with services required in carrying out baling. Tractor, as well as, Baler and SwathScanner are adaptive components having multiple configurations out of which only one configuration can be activated at a time. All the components and their respective configurations are pre-defined at design time. The decision which configuration must be activated depends upon the level of autonomy of the vehicle and the functionality being provided during operation. Thus, the entire *TIA-Baling* is an autonomous system that is capable of adaptation, in form of reconfiguration, at runtime.

In order to obtain the safety rules to specify the monitor for *TIA-Baling* system, we perform the step-wise procedure shown in Fig. 1: We begin with determining all operational modes of the vehicle along with their potential configurations that can be activated during operation. We then ascertain complete set of services associated with each configuration for their respective operational modes. This is followed by carrying out hazards and risk analysis to identify the potential deviations in services that could result in hazardous situations during operation. Lastly, we assign these deviations an integrity level based on the risk associated them. Followed by this, we analyze dependencies between services and their deviations for a given operational mode and environmental situation, and based on them construct safety statuses and corresponding measures to form the rules.

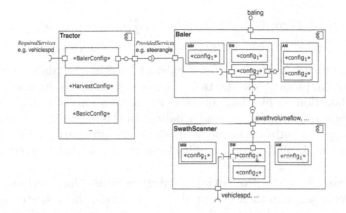

Fig. 2. Operational modes & configurations of TIA vehicle

Step I - Operational Modes and Configurations: First and foremost, we begin with determining all possible operational modes (OPM) that a vehicle is capable of and classify them into: fully-autonomous (AM), semi-autonomous (SM) and manual mode (MM). A fully-autonomous mode is where all configurations of the vehicle are capable of carrying out operations automatically i.e. without the presence of a human driver. However, in case of the other two, presence of a human driver is always required. For instance, in fully-autonomous mode a tractor is solely responsible to drive along the farm and park itself at the end of its assigned task (e.g. harvesting or seeding). Subsequently, we determine the potential configurations for each operational mode. Each mode can have multiple configurations out of which only one can be activated at a time. Normally, configurations differ from each another in terms of functionality or redundancy. In case of TIA, a Tractor (*Trac*) can have separate configurations for different implements e.g. a Baler or a Harvester, or redundant configurations in case of graceful degradation or maintenance purposes. Moreover, the *BalerConfig* of the tractor itself can have multiple configurations for different operational modes. Similarly, implements like Baler (*Bal*) and SwathScanner (*SwSc*) can have multiple configurations in different operational modes for baling specific tasks.

$$\langle Trac^{AM}_{Cf_1}, Trac^{SM}_{Cf_1}, Trac^{SM}_{Cf_2}, ...\rangle \in Bal\_Trac^{OPM_i}_{potCf_j},$$
$$\langle Bal^{AM}_{Cf_1}, Bal^{AM}_{Cf_2}, Bal^{SM}_{Cf_1}, ...\rangle \in Bal^{OPM_m}_{potCf_n} \tag{1}$$

Identification and categorization of the potential configurations based on their operational modes has a twofold advantage: On the one hand, it assists in ascertaining the possible collaborations profiles (*CollabProf*) between multiple configurations of the vehicle and its implements in different operational modes. On the other hand, it aids in an intensive hazard analysis since, the risk associated with a particular deviation, and the magnitude of the corresponding safety measures to be taken in order to ensure safety, depends upon the activated configuration and the mode in which vehicle is operating.

$$\langle Trac^{AM}_{Cf_1} :: Bal^{AM}_{Cf_1} :: SwSc^{AM}_{Cf_1} \rangle \in CollabProf_1,$$
$$\langle CollabProf_1, CollabProf_2, ... \rangle \in CollabProf_n{}^{Bal} \qquad (2)$$

In TIA, for each implement, there exist at least one collaboration profile to carry out the implement specific task. The equations above manifest an exemplary collaboration profile that consists of configurations of a *Trac*, *Bal* and a *SwSc* collaborating together to render baling. In this case, the tractor as well as the baler support multiple operational modes and configurations thus, there exist multiple potential collaboration profiles for carrying out baling specific tasks.

Step II - Services and Potential Configurations: Once we have all operational modes along with their potential configurations, the next step is to determine services associated with each of those configurations. Each configuration has a set of services that includes both required and provided services. Required services (rs) are the ones that a configuration receives from another components, whereas provided services (ps) are the services that a configuration renders for other components and their configurations.

$$\langle ReqSv, ProvSv \rangle \in safety\ critical\ services,$$
$$\langle vehspd_{rs}, frontobst_{rs}, steerang_{ps}, ... \rangle \in Trac^{AM}_{Cf_1} \qquad (3)$$

The reason behind ascertaining all services of a configuration is to filter the safety critical services from the non-safety critical ones. Typically, deviation in a required service influences the provided service thereby, causing an unplanned behavior of the entire configuration. For instance, a deviation in the speed sensor of the tractor results in an incorrect value of vehicle speed (*vehspd*). As a consequence, the tractor doesn't decelerate while steering thereby, loosing control over itself. However, it is also possible that the provided service suffers a deviation despite of no deviation(s) in the required services. Regardless of whether the deviation is at the required service or at the end of provided service, it results in an unsafe and unplanned behavior of the configuration thereby, in a hazardous situation of the entire vehicle.

Step III - Hazard and Risk Analysis: After determining the set of safety critical services, we perform hazard and risk analysis to analyze their possible deviations and their consequences. We classify these deviations based on their discrepancies attributed to time, value or provision. For instance, in case of a tractor, if the service *vehspd* must be generated within 10 ms from request time, but is generated after a delay of 2 ms, then the service suffers a deviation attributed to time. In a fully-autonomous mode, even such small time-deviation might result in a hazardous situation as the tractor is unaware of its own speed for this duration. Moreover, if the speed generated after the delay (i.e. at 12 ms) is incorrect, the safety of the vehicle, along with its implements, gets more vulnerable Table 1.

Table 1. Hazard & severity analysis of safety critical services

Services	Deviation	Operational Mode	Environmental Situation	Hazardous Situation	Potential Accident	Severity
vehspd	delayed value	fully-autonomous mode (AM)	another tractor driving ahead in the field	tractor does not decelerate and fails to brake when required	collision with the tractor or group of farmers in the field ahead	catastrophic
...	...	...	...	...	...	

A particular deviation in a service can have different severities based on the operational mode and the environmental situation during vehicle operation. For instance, an incorrect value of *vehspd* in an autonomous mode is highly critical compared to in the semi-autonomous mode when the driver is present and can take control of the vehicle almost immediately. Moreover, when another tractor is driving ahead in the field, a delay in *vehspd* can result in delayed deceleration and thus collision of the two vehicles however, in case of no additional vehicle ahead delay deviation in *vehspd* would be still critical, but would not have collision as an outcome. Therefore, while performing hazard analysis, we take the operational mode of the vehicle and its context into consideration because it aids in an in-depth analysis of the consequences of the deviations in services.

Step IV - Safety Statuses and Corresponding Measures: Subsequent to hazard identification, we estimate the risk associated with the deviations and assign them a corresponding integrity levels. Since we have an autonomous agricultural vehicle, we do the risk estimation in accordance with standard ISO 25119 [6] and consider the parameters: *Severity* of the accident caused by the deviation, the *likelihood* of the accident and the *controllability* of the situation to assign agricultural performance levels (AgPL) from 'a' to 'e' [7] for different levels of risk.

$$\langle if \; SafStatus \Rightarrow SafMeasure \rangle \in SRule \qquad (4)$$

Following the AgPL assignment, the very last step is to construct safety statuses (*SafStatus*) for the safety rule (SRule). Each status acts like a condition which when true, indicates the vehicle being in an unsafe state and thereby, triggers a corresponding countermeasure (*SafMeasure*). During the TIA case study, we observed that not all deviations, despite being in the safety critical services, result in hazardous situations. These are the deviations that are either improbable to occur or are easily controllable and thus, have a corresponding AgPl of 'a' or below (QM). We filter such deviations and consider the ones that have AgPL 'b' or higher for the safety statuses. Besides, we realized that creating safety statuses and an equivalent corrective measure for each individual service would result in a safety rule explosion. Especially, when the number of safety critical services is higher. Moreover, there exist certain associations between the some services where, a particular deviation in one along with a certain deviation in the other, in a specific operational mode, results in a hazardous situation with potentially catastrophic consequences.

To this end, a safety rule consists of a safety status that represent an unsafe state of the vehicle caused either due to individual service deviation or a deviation due to the associated services having an AgPL of 'b' or above, in a particular operational mode during a specific scenario. As a safety measure, we reconfigure the system to a configuration that brings the system back to a safe state. For each safety status, safety measure is a collection of potential configurations that the vehicle can configure to. These configurations are pre-defined at design time but, evaluated at the runtime based on the risk associated with them [8].

2.3 Case Study and Initial Results

The aforementioned specification was followed to implement a safety monitor for *TIA-Baling* system using Simulink. The safety monitor has been implemented in a decentralized manner. This means each adaptive component Tractor, Baler and SwathScanner has its own safety monitor to supervise their operational status at runtime. As a consequence, there are two potential ways to reconfigure system in case of violation of safety. On the one hand, in the event of a safety-critical deviation in the service of an adaptive component that does not influence the other components directly, the component executes reconfiguration within itself. This implies that the only monitor that detects a deviation is the monitor of the affected adaptive component itself. We define it as an *intra-component reconfiguration*, since reconfiguration occurs only inside the adaptive component that is affected by the deviation and not others. On the other hand, in case of a safety-critical deviation in the service that influences more than one adaptive components, monitors corresponding to each of these components identify this violation and trigger their components for a subsequent reconfiguration. To this end, collaboration profiles play a significant role, as which configuration of which adaptive component can be activated in the current operational mode is decided by these profiles. We define this as an *inter-component reconfiguration*, because multiple adaptive components switch configurations simultaneously to bring the system to a safe state.

We evaluated the system by running simulations in specific scenarios along with a set of safety-critical deviations. Figure 3 represents simulation outcome of a particular scenario where the TIA tractor is driving in fully-autonomous mode while executing baling operation in parallel. Meanwhile, there's an obstacle in front and the front obstacle detection sensor suffers a deviation and generates an incorrect value. Since obstacle detection is one of the safety-critical service, its deviation triggers a safety rule and requests for a reconfiguration as safety measure for the tractor and the entire TIA system. System reconfiguration is accomplished and the tractor begins to decelerate. In essence, all system and component reconfigurations are conducted in conformity with collaboration profiles of the system that are pre-defined at the design time. This implies each time there is a reconfiguration, regardless of inter/intra, system switches its collaboration profile from one to another. In the following simulated scenario, tractor reconfiguration results in an *inter-component reconfiguration* owing to the collaboration profile: $\langle Trac_{Cf_1}^{SM} :: Bal_{Cf_1}^{SM} :: SwSc_{Cf_1}^{SM} \rangle \in CollabProf_2$ that

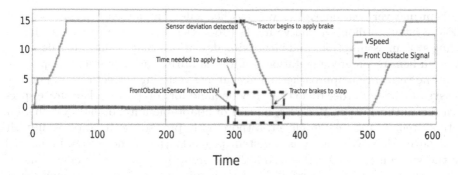

Fig. 3. Safety monitor evaluation in the event of *FrontObstacle* sensor deviation

requires, along with the tractor, all other adaptive components to switch to semi-autonomous mode. This can however be modified as deciding collaboration profiles is a design decision and must take into consideration other system properties like efficiency, performance and certainly the costs. Taking into account the overhead each reconfiguration has on system performance, an *intra-component reconfiguration* of the tractor from fully- to semi-autonomous mode, and its compatibility with fully-autonomous modes of other components, could be indeed a better alternative in this case. Therefore, in the context of our subsequent research, we intend to create collaboration profiles in view of system properties which includes most importantly performance and efficiency.

3   Related Work

Runtime safety monitoring realizes fault tolerance by bringing system to a safe state of operation in the event of safety-critical situations. Monitoring system in accordance with safety has been studied and implemented in domains like automotive [9] and robotics [10], and the term safety monitor has been coined differently in various researches as safety bag [11], diverse monitor [12], or emergency layer [13]. Though named differently, the basic idea behind safety monitoring in all researches is the same where, there exist a set of safety rules or policies that the monitor follows and triggers safety measures in order to prevent the hazardous situation from occurring. However, the methodology for safety rule specification might differ from approach to approach. In [14], monitoring rules are formally specified using hazard analysis followed by formal verification methods. In others like [15], hazard and operability analysis is used to discern hazards associated with the system thereby establishing a set of if-then-rules for the system. Adam et al. [10] uses domain specific language to specify safety-rules that the system must obey and activate corrective actions should there be any violation.

Runtime verification [16] is yet another safety monitoring technique that allows system to monitor and verify its properties at runtime. It aims at monitoring system assumptions and identifying deviations that result in unsafe situations and ensures if any adaptation resulted in infringement of safety properties. Runtime verification approaches mainly targets verifying correctness property of the system, and in order to do that they demand for complete and accurate specification of the system. However, in case of adaptable autonomous systems, for both system and the environment, a thoroughly precise specification is difficult to achieve. Moreover, safety is a system property that is not solely influenced by the system, rather by the system functioning in a particular environment. Therefore, we intend to accomplish safety monitoring by employing monitor as an additional module to the system that observes system behavior apropos of its own operational state along with the environment in which it is operating. The monitor specification is derived in a step-wise procedure that begins with detecting hazards associated with deviations in the system in a given scenario and based on the severity of their risk safety rules are derived. Safety monitor follow these rules and triggers corresponding restorative measures for the system in case of unsafe situations at runtime.

4 Summary and Future Work

We are certain that runtime safety monitoring is a promising approach for safety assurance for adaptable autonomous systems. It allows the system to monitor itself during operation and bring it back to a safe state, allowing them to maintain and ensure safe behavior in the event of safety-critical situations that might occur due to random errors in the hardware or due to unknown operational environment at runtime. In this paper, we present a safety monitor that monitors the system for safety-critical violations using a set of predefined safety rules. A tractor implement automation has been used to illustrate and evaluate the monitoring approach. We believe that for distributed autonomous system like TIA, such a safety monitor not only aids in achieving fault tolerance by prompting safety measures in form of reconfiguration, but allows it to be self-aware and adapt its behavior to sustain a safe operational state at runtime.

We are currently implementing our monitoring approach in the domain of autonomous road vehicles. When compared to agricultural autonomous vehicles, road vehicles operate in a much more complex environment and have a higher involvement of other systems and thus there exist far more unexpected and unintended safety-critical circumstances. We intend to comprehend the challenges and nuances associated with this safety monitor while operating in domains with distinct levels of safety criticality, timing and performance restrictions. As a part of our future work, we aim to refine safety rules so that not each safety-critical deviation results in a structural adaptation, but can be handled via parameter adaptation like altering the driving speed and continue operation in the currently activated configuration. This aids in controlling the reconfiguration overhead and simultaneously improve performance and efficiency of the system.

References

1. Vassev, E., Hinchey, M.: Adaptation to the unforeseen: can we trust autonomous and adaptive systems? In: 3rd International Conference on Vehicle Technology and Intelligent Transport Systems, pp. 366–372 (2017)
2. ISO - ISO 26262 Road vehicles Functional Safety Part 1–10 (2011)
3. Avizienis, A., Laprie, J.-C., Randell, B., Landwehr, C.: Basic concepts and taxonomy of dependable and secure computing. IEEE Trans. Dependable Secure Comput. **1**(1), 11–33 (2004)
4. Koopman, P.: Challenges in representing CPS safety. In: Developing Dependable and Secure Automotive Cyber-Physical Systems from Components, March 2011. http://users.ece.cmu.edu/~koopman/pubs/koopman11_cps_safety.pdf
5. Hoyningen-Huene, M., Baldinger, M.: Tractor-implement-automation and its application to a tractor-loader wagon combination. In: Machine Control & Guidance, pp. 171–185 (2010)
6. ISO 25119: Tractors and machinery for agriculture and forestry - Safety-related parts of control systems
7. Barreiro, P., et al.: Safety functional requirements for "robot fleets for highly effective agriculture and forestry management". In: 1st International Workshop on Robotics and Associated High Technologies and Equipment for Agriculture (RHEA-2011) (2011). http://www.rhea project.eu
8. Bhardwaj, N., Liggesmeyer, P.: A conceptual framework for safe reconfiguration in open system of systems. In: Proceedings of the 6th International Workshop on Software Engineering for Systems-of-Systems, SESoS 2018, pp. 17–20 (2018)
9. Watanabe, K., Kang, E., Lin, C-W., Shiraishi, S.: Runtime monitoring for safety of intelligent vehicles. In: Proceedings of the 55th Annual Design Automation Conference on - DAC 2018, pp. 1–6 (2018)
10. Adam, S., Larsen, M., Jensen, K., Schultz, U.P.: Towards rule-based dynamic safety monitoring for mobile robots. In: Brugali, D., Broenink, J.F., Kroeger, T., MacDonald, B.A. (eds.) SIMPAR 2014. LNCS (LNAI), vol. 8810, pp. 207–218. Springer, Cham (2014). https://doi.org/10.1007/978-3-319-11900-7_18
11. Klein, P.: The safety-bag expert system in the electronic railway interlocking system Elektra. Expert Syst. Appl. **3**(4), 499–506 (1991)
12. Functional Safety of Electrical/Electronic/Programmable Electronic Safety-Related Systems-Part 7: Overview of Techniques and Measures, IEC 61508, 153 (2010)
13. Haddadin, S., Suppa, M., Bodenmüller, T., Albu-Schäeffer, A., Hirzinger, G.: Towards the robotic co-worker. In: Pradalier, C., Siegwart, R., Hirzinger, G. (eds.) Robotics Research. Springer Tracts in Advanced Robotics, vol. 70, pp. 261–282. Springer, Heidelberg (2011). https://doi.org/10.1007/978-3-642-19457-3_16
14. Mason, L., Guiochet, J., Waeselynck, H., Desfosses, A., Laval, M.: Synthesis of safety rules for active monitoring: application to an airport light measurement robot. In: 2017 1st IEEE International Conference on Robotic Computing, pp. 263–270 (2017)
15. Woodman, R., Winfield, A.F., Harper, C., Fraser, M.: Building safer robots: safety driven control. Int. J. Rob. Res. **31**(13), 1603–1626 (2012)
16. Rushby, J.: Runtime certification. In: Leucker, M. (ed.) RV 2008. LNCS, vol. 5289, pp. 21–35. Springer, Heidelberg (2008). https://doi.org/10.1007/978-3-540-89247-2_2

Structured Reasoning for Socio-Technical Factors of Safety-Security Assurance

Nikita Johnson(✉) and Tim Kelly

Department of Computer Science, University of York, York, UK
{nikita.johnson,tim.kelly}@york.ac.uk

Abstract. Current research presents several approaches to safety-security technical risk analysis. Indeed, many safety standards now have the requirement that security *must* be considered. However, with greater knowledge of what makes assuring both attributes in an industrial context difficult, it becomes clear that it is not just the technical assurance that is challenging. It is the entirety of the socio-technical system that supports assurance. In this paper, the second part of the Safety-Security Assurance Framework - the Socio-Technical Model (SSAF STM) is presented as one way of reasoning about these wider issues that make co-assurance difficult.

Keywords: Safety · Security · Assurance · Socio-technical factors

1 Introduction

Assuring systems for both safety and security is of increasing concern, especially in those circumstances where a security concern has the potential to impact safety, such as the attack on Ukraine's national power grid [14], and ofcourse, Stuxnet - the attack on the Iranian Nuclear Facility [7]. There are an increasing number of these instances, which is motivating governmental and regulatory bodies, as well as organisations, to address the issue of assuring systems for both safety and security.

There have been different approaches to addressing the issue: some from a regulatory perspective have attempted to align security standards with their safety counterparts (*e.g.* aerospace: DO-326A [12] and ARP 4754A [13]; medical devices: AAMI TIR 57 [1] and ISO 14971 [3]), whilst others have attempted to create complementary standards and sets of principles (*e.g.* UK ONR Safety [9] and Security [10] Principles. In addition there exist technical analyses that integrate the attributes in different ways, such as using systems theory [15] or using additional security guidewords in the safety assessment [8].

However, the co-assurance issue persists. The reasons for this are many - a subset have been briefly discussed in [5]. The technical challenge lies in the fact that both attributes are system properties and emergent, so they cannot be coupled with particular functionality in the same way that other attributes

© Springer Nature Switzerland AG 2019
A. Romanovsky et al. (Eds.): SAFECOMP 2019 Workshops, LNCS 11699, pp. 178–184, 2019.
https://doi.org/10.1007/978-3-030-26250-1_14

might, such as reliability or availability. The gap that this loose coupling creates means that there is an heavy reliance on expert judgement to create bridges.

As a result, integrating safety and security is not only a technical issue of creating new analysis techniques and standards, but also a *socio-technical* issue which must link the domains on several levels of interaction.

1.1 Structure of the Paper

The core ideas of this paper are presented in three parts. First, the Safety-Security Assurance Framework (SSAF) and the conceptual model of an *Assurance Surface* are explored in Sect. 2. Next, Sect. 3 discusses the alignment argument and introduces the SSAF Socio-Technical Model (STM). Lastly, Sect. 4 explores some of the advantages and challenges to the SSAF STM, and concludes with a discussion about the need for co-assurance arguments.

2 The Safety-Security Assurance Framework

The Safety-Security Assurance Framework (SSAF) is an approach to attribute integration. It relies on the new paradigm of *independent co-assurance* whose main premise is keeping the attributes separate, and maintaining the expertise in each domain, but exchanging *the right information with the right people at the right time*. This is no simple task, however it reframes the problem in such a way that uncertainty, and therefore assurance, can be better managed.

2.1 SSAF Technical Risk Model (TRM)

SSAF has two distinct parts that handle different concerns. The first is the Technical Risk Model (TRM) which defines a five-step meta-process for attribute integration [4,6]. A key part of the TRM is the underlying causal meta-model which is shown in Fig. 1. The core idea of the meta-model is that different conditions can be linked to other conditions, which are possibly in a different domain. By explicitly modelling these relationships it is possible to gain a greater understanding about their interactions, thereby enabling not only aligned assurance, but a greater adaptability to change. A small case study in [6] is used to demonstrate how the impact of new vulnerabilities being added to an attack vector can be propagated (through a TRM model) to a related hazard.

This modelling of the causal relationship is very powerful, but an important thing to note is that it is over the *modelled* conditions. One of the subtle ways that security concerns undermine safety assurance is that they increase uncertainty. For safety risk analysis, assumptions are often made about the operational context and how the system functions, and analysis is performed over what is known. However, the presence of an intelligent adversary means that unknown (actual) conditions can be exploited.

It is not sufficient merely to limit impact propagation across modelled conditions; uncertainty propagation must also be limited if there is to be confidence

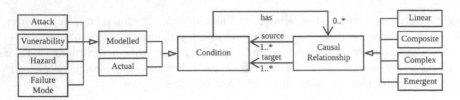

Fig. 1. SSAF TRM causal meta-model

in a single attribute argument (for example, a safety case). The creation of an integration argument is the mechanism by which this is achieved. However, the integration argument is at a higher level of abstraction than either the safety or security technical risk arguments, therefore it must consider many more factors than just the technical risk and the models that represent it. The socio-technical system that supports the development of the technical risk argument must be considered.

2.2 . The Assurance Surface

The security risk concept of an attack surface, *i.e.* the ways that a system can be compromised, was introduced by Microsoft researcher Michael Howard in 2003, and later formalised to create a Relative Attack Surface Quotient (RASQ) that explored different attack opportunities along specified dimensions [2]. This idea that risk can be explored and managed in different dimensions is a powerful one.

The *assurance surface* concept that is proposed here is analogous to the attack surface; however, instead of representing attack vectors, it represents the ways in which uncertainty can be propagated. For example, from a technical risk perspective, different methodologies have different limitations; using complementary techniques would address different concerns on the assurance surface. Much like reducing the security attack surface, it is difficult to ensure coverage of the assurance surface because of the existence of epistemic uncertainties. Figure 2 illustrates some of the layers when assuring a system:

- The first is Tier 0, the System layer which contains all the models of the system (this includes risk analysis models).
- Next, on Tier 1 is the SSAF TRM model which is a meta-model of the interactions of the conditions on the system layer.
- Tier 2 is the technical risk argument, or the assurance case that refers to artefacts on Tiers 0 and 1 to provide evidence for its claims.
- Tier 3 is the SSAF Socio-Technical Model (STM) which is a meta-model of processes, people, structure and tools that support the creation of the technical assurance argument.
- Lastly, Tier 4 is where primary and secondary confidence arguments are made, although their representation is often implicit or embedded in organisational governance policies, *etc.*

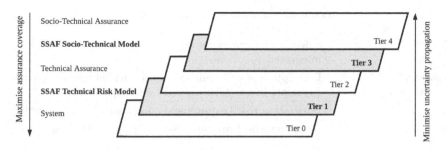

Fig. 2. Assurance layers of abstraction

To assure a system, risk and uncertainty must be managed at each of the layers. The concept is similar to Reason's risk model of accident causation [11, p. 9]. However, unlike Reason's model, SSAF has specific focus on the integration of safety and security, and explicitly modelling the interactions between the two domains. The objective of this approach is to systematically and demonstrably reduce the uncertainty propagation, maximise assurance coverage, and increase confidence at each layer for safety and security.

3   Arguing Alignment of Safety and Security

The alignment or integration argument for safety and security will have several types of claims - some related to the technical interactions of risk, but some related to the confidence in the assurance integration process itself. Table 1 demonstrates what a typical integration claim might be. To satisfy this instance, not only will evidence need to be given at the system level, but at higher levels of abstraction too; these claims are encapsulated in the confidence arguments CP1 and CP2.

3.1   SSAF Socio-Technical Model (STM)

In order to model confidence claims CP1 and CP2, SSAF has a Socio-Technical Model (partial model shown in Fig. 3). Similar to the TRM causal model, the STM model describes the relationships between assurance factors in five dimensions - conceptual, structure, process, people and technology. Many of the specific socio-technical factors are discussed in [5].

Conceptual assurance factors underpin the other four socio-technical factors. This is because they fundamentally affect each of the other dimensions. For example, how loss is conceptualised affects the types of claims that can be made or the mental models of the practitioners who will be analysing risk.

Structure and *Process* factors affect assurance activities through all the abstraction layers. For example, if there is a regulatory structure (secondary confidence) that mandates a specific assurance case structure or assurance process - IEC 61508:3 prescribes MCDC code testing, then that affects the models (primary confidence) that are produced, *i.e.* test results.

Table 1. Partial integration argument

Claim G1	Safety and Security for the {System} are sufficiently integrated
Context C1	Description of sufficient safety-security integration for the {System} in an {Operational Context}
Strategy St1	Integration risk {requirements divergence} is mitigated
Claim G2	{Requirements} are reconciled at {Level n} of the {System}
Evidence Sn1	TRM model of linked safety and security requirements, and DOORS database with both attribute requirements at {Level n}
Confidence Claim CP1 (Primary)	The appropriate method was used to combine requirements and it was performed by competent people. The reconciliation is complete and at the right level of detail. The software tools used do not discard valuable information
Confidence Claim CP2 (Secondary)	The regulatory and organisational structure supports the requirements reconciliation process. There are review structures to mitigate cognitive bias

The last two dimensions are *People* and *Technology*. Competence is one of the primary factors that affect confidence in the assurance argument. If suitably qualified and experienced people (SQEP) have not performed the analyses, then there can be little confidence in the arguments that use the analyses as evidence. In addition, the tools used such as a particular modelling environment may not be sufficient for the purposes which it is used. for example, modelling timing errors using a block diagram.

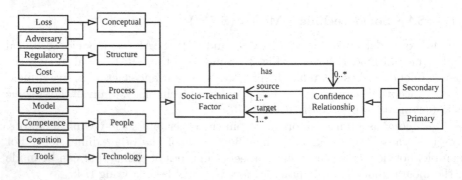

Fig. 3. SSAF Socio-Technical Model (STM) Meta-model.

By explicitly modelling the socio-technical interactions that constrain the technical interactions, it increases understanding of the overall safety-security integration issue. Through STM models it is possible to pinpoint where trade-off decisions must be made in the assurance processes and define the procedures for these trade-offs. An example is creating a model of the synchronisation process and points, and discovering that there is no procedure for handling the impact of security patches on the safety argument. The situation can be left as it is, with low confidence in the safety claims related to those patches, however a new procedure can be put in to place to deal with that specific interaction. Thus, confidence in the integration or alignment argument can be incrementally improved.

4 Discussion

The integration claims which would require STM models are numerous and, currently, not well understood. These include, but are not limited to, claims about how the assurance processes communicate with each other and when, how to reason about trade-off decisions at different layers, what a qualified integration practitioner is or if it is sufficient to train practitioners form one domain to perform the integration task. Modelling each of these interactions requires resource that could be spent on risk reduction and engineering activities that have a direct impact on the product. However, understanding these interactions is a fundamental part of making an argument for co-assurance, or in the safety-critical domain - claiming that security has been considered.

   This is complex and resource intensive task, but it is one that is not unique to SSAF. Indeed, through a combination of the STM and TRM models, it is possible to structure reasoning and analysis of these factors and potential improve effectiveness. The models are also an invaluable tool for communication, not only across domains, but also to communicate with decision makers who might not otherwise appreciate the impact of integration factors that do not fall solidly within a single domain.

5 Conclusion

The core idea presented in this paper is that of the Safety-Security Assurace Framework - Socio-Technical Model (SSAF STM). It is a meta-model that enables implicit assurance integration interactions between safety and security to be modelled at several layers of abstraction. These models can then be used provide evidence for integration claims, and to analyse and reason about the overall integration processes. This makes managing uncertainty propagation a primary goal, not only through system models (product), but through the socio-technical system of the organisation developing and operating the product.

Acknowledgements. Research and development of SSAF supported by the University of York, the Assuring Autonomy International Programme (AAIP), BAE Systems, and the UK EPSRC (Award Ref: iCASE 1515047).

References

1. Association for the Advancement of Medical Instrumentation: AAMI TIR57:2016 Principles for medical device security - Risk management. Technical report, June 2016
2. Howard, M., Pincus, J., Wing, J.M.: Measuring relative attack surfaces. In: Lee, D.T., Shieh, S.P., Tygar, J.D. (eds.) Computer Security in the 21st Century, pp. 109–137. Springer, Boston (2005). https://doi.org/10.1007/0-387-24006-3_8
3. ISO 14971:2007 Medical devices - Application of risk management to medical devices. Standard, International Organization for Standardization, Geneva, CH, September 2007
4. Johnson, N., Kelly, T.: Safety-security assurance framework (SSAF) in practice. In: 37th International Conference on Computer Safety, Reliability, & Security SAFECOMP2018 (Abstract Paper) (2018)
5. Johnson, N., Kelly, T.: An assurance framework for independent co-assurance of safety and security. In: Muniak, C. (ed.) International System Safety Society (January 2019), Presented at: the 36th International System Safety Conference (ISSC), Arizona, USA, August 2018. J. Syst. Saf
6. Johnson, N., Kelly, T.: Devil's in the detail: through-life safety and security co-assurance using SSAF. In: International Conference on Computer Safety, Reliability, and Security. Springer (2019)
7. Langner, R.: Stuxnet: dissecting a cyberwarfare weapon. IEEE Secur. Priv. **9**(3), 49–51 (2011)
8. Macher, G., Sporer, H., Berlach, R., Armengaud, E., Kreiner, C.: SAHARA: a security-aware hazard and risk analysis method. In: Proceedings of the 2015 Design, Automation & Test in Europe Conference & Exhibition, pp. 621–624. EDA Consortium (2015)
9. Safety Assessment Principles for Nuclear Facilities. Standard, Office for Nuclear Regulation, Merseyside, UK, November 2014
10. Security Assessment Principles for the Civil Nuclear Industry. Standard, Office for Nuclear Regulation, Merseyside, UK, March 2017
11. Reason, J.: Managing the Risks of Organizational Accidents. Ashgate, Farnham (1997)
12. RTCA: RTCA DO-326: Revision A Airworthiness Security Process Specification. Technical report, Washington, DC, USA, August 2014
13. SAE International: SAE ARP4754: Rev A Guidelines for Development of Civil Aircraft and Systems. Technical report, December 2010
14. U.S. Cybersecurity and Infrastructure Security Agency (CISA): Alert (IR-ALERT-H-16-056-01): Cyber-attack against Ukrainian critical infrastructure. Technical report, National Cybersecurity and Communications Integration Center (NCCIC) Industrial Control Systems, February 2016. https://ics-cert.us-cert.gov/alerts/IR-ALERT-H-16-056-01
15. Young, W., Leveson, N.G.: An integrated approach to safety and security based on systems theory. Commun. ACM **57**(2), 31–35 (2014)

The SISTER Approach for Verification and Validation: A Lightweight Process for Reusable Results

Andrea Ceccarelli[1(✉)], Davide Basile[1], Andrea Bondavalli[1],
Lorenzo Falai[2], Alessandro Fantechi[1], Sandro Ferrari[3],
Gianluca Mandò[3], Nicola Nostro[2], and Luigi Rucher[3]

[1] University of Florence, Florence, Italy
andrea.ceccarelli@unifi.it
[2] Resiltech S.R.L., Pontedera, Italy
[3] Thales S.P.A., Florence, Italy

Abstract. The research project SISTER aims to improve the safety and autonomy of light rail trains by developing and integrating novel technologies for remote sensing and object detection, safe positioning, and broadband radio communication. To prove safety of the SISTER solution, CENELEC-compliant Verification and Validation (V&V) is obviously required. In the SISTER project, we tackled the challenge of defining and applying a compact V&V methodology, able to provide convincing safety evidence on the solution, but still within the reduced resources available for the project. A relevant characteristic of the methodology is to produce V&V results that can be reused for future industrial exploitation of SISTER outcomes after project termination. This paper presents the V&V methodology that is currently applied in parallel to the progress of project activities, with preliminary results from its application.

Keywords: Design · Verification and Validation · Hazard analysis ·
Model checking · Model-Driven Engineering · Stochastic modeling ·
Railway standards

1 Introduction

Light rail trains have been increasingly promoted in our cities, as they deliver efficient and green urban mobility with reasonable resources, especially with respect to alternative solutions as undergrounds. Since light rail trains operate on the ground surface, they are integrated into a complex mobility ecosystem that includes roads, pedestrian areas, bicycle lanes among others. It is a straight consequence that safety and availability measures for light rail trains should also consider the protection of the trains from such mobility ecosystem. As a simple example, a vehicle on the line can lead to service disruption (availability issue) or even collisions (safety issue).

The research project SISTER [18] aims to equip light rail trains with novel solutions for remote sensing and object detection, safe positioning, and broadband radio communication. The ultimate objective of the project is to improve the safety and autonomy of light rail trains, through the increased capability to autonomously detect

© Springer Nature Switzerland AG 2019
A. Romanovsky et al. (Eds.): SAFECOMP 2019 Workshops, LNCS 11699, pp. 185–197, 2019.
https://doi.org/10.1007/978-3-030-26250-1_15

obstacles, accurate positioning of the train on the track, and enhanced communication with multiple endpoints.

To prove safety of SISTER architecture, Verification and Validation (V&V, [2]) according to railway standards [2–4] is required. In the SISTER project, we tackled the challenge of defining and applying a reduced V&V methodology, that does not meet all the requirements from the standards [2–4], but that provides initial indications on the quality of the solution, and that is tailored on project resources. In fact, *SISTER targets a prototype* and not a market-ready product, thus the definition of a complete safety case on a market-ready product as prescribed by standards is out-of-scope. Consequently, we devised a V&V methodology with specific requirements in mind. First, the methodology should be able to provide safety evidence of the solution, to endorse further investments on the SISTER outcomes after project termination. Second, V&V results should be easily reusable in the future industrial exploitation of SISTER results, in both short- and long-term perspectives. Third, V&V techniques should be appropriate to deal with the complex architectural problems that are faced in SISTER.

This paper presents the V&V methodology that has been applied during the SISTER project, which is now walking towards its conclusion, expected in June 2019.

2 The SISTER Project and Its V&V Challenges

The objective of the SISTER project is to improve safety and autonomy of light rail train, through the inclusion of standard-compliant, safety-critical novel solutions for (i) efficient remote communication, (ii) automatic surveillance of the track to detect obstacles, and (iii) accurate positioning. First, the project aims to develop a resilient and secure radio broadband solution to protect the communication systems from interferences and attacks. Such communication system will be based on 802.11 g technology with frequency hopping in a software-defined radio (SDR) system. Second, a highly reliable and safe remote sensing system will guarantee that the track is free from obstacles, thus allowing the train to move safely without incurring in unexpected collisions. This track surveillance system is based on a *set* of radars. Third, on-board equipment will provide accurate positioning and safe operation with minimal support from ground installations, thus reducing costs for deployment and maintenance of the infrastructure. This will be achieved through data fusion from various on-board sensors.

Since SISTER is a pre-competitive research project with the purpose of building a prototype that breaks the technological frontier in the light rail domain, we do not have the possibility to apply a complete V&V process according to the CENELEC standards [2–4] within the frame of the project. This observation leads us to devise a light V&V methodology, which can be applied during the project but can still be of use for successive product-oriented development of SISTER. For such purpose, together with the industrial partners of the project, we defined the following requirements for the SISTER V&V methodology. The authors are well-aware of the existence of several research works tailored to reduce certification cost through more efficient methodologies and tools, as for example investigated in the AMASS [22] and CECRIS [23] projects. However, for this specific work we observe that V&V is often difficult to do in research and development activities and our goal with the methodology here provided is to give a first indication and produce reusable result.

REQ1. The methodology shall comprise techniques that offer *safety evidence* i.e., it shall be able to discuss if the SISTER solution has the potential to match certification requirements according to railway standards [2–4]. In fact, while compliance to the applicable safety standards is obviously required, it isn't possible to apply the certification process in its entirety within the scope of the project. To collect safety evidence, the focus shall be placed on the architectural design, as the target is more on the architectural concepts than on the peculiarities of implementing a prototype.

REQ2. Results shall be easily reusable for future exploitation of SISTER. It is important that industrial partners will be able to easily build on the collected results. This requirement impacts not only exploitation, but also maintenance and reusability of V&V results on the long term.

REQ3. The methodology shall be appropriate to deal with the complex V&V issues of the SISTER project. Especially, this concerns data fusion, accurate positioning, and complex interaction protocols between light rail trains as a consequence of the removal of ground systems.

3   Background Notions and Relevant Works

Hazard Analysis. Regardless of the domain of interest and related standards, most of the life cycle phases are typically influenced by the outputs of the hazard analysis. *Hazard Analysis* [2] identifies hazardous events that may have a potentially serious impact on the system, on the environment and on people who interact with the system either directly or indirectly. To the best of our knowledge there are *no well-established, largely accepted tools* that allow automating the application of a hazard analysis: the activity is usually performed by hand, thus becoming a time-consuming and error-prone activity, albeit some supports exist [6, 16, 17, 21]. In SISTER we are developing a supporting tool and related methodology for hazard analysis, to (i) bind hazard analysis to system design; (ii) save manual effort for performing the analysis, and (iii) reduce the likelihood of mistakes e.g., some functions or interfaces could be inadvertently omitted.

Model Checking. *Model Checking* [11] is applied inside the SISTER project to support and complement the hazards identification and mitigation. Model checking is a technique for automatically verifying correctness properties, which is exhaustive for finite-state systems. In particular, an advantage of *Statistical* Model Checking is that it avoids the exploration of the whole state-space of a model, which is a main drawback of standard model checking techniques [20]. During the SISTER project, models have been specified in the *stochastic extension of Timed Automata* [12] formalism while formula have been specified using the Metric Interval Temporal Logic (MITL, [11]), with the Uppaal tool [12].

Model-Driven Engineering. *Model-Driven Engineering* (MDE) refers to the systematic use of models as primary artefacts throughout the engineering lifecycle [1]. In MDE, a semi-formal engineering language as Unified Modeling Language (UML) is used not only for specification and design purposes, but also to support other activities, like code formal verification, evaluation, and testing. In SISTER, the modeling of the system under analysis is realized with a specialization of Blockly [7], called Blockly4SoS [8], that has been defined for modeling System of Systems (SoS). It is extendable with custom blocks and supports code and XML generation. It facilitates the realization of the graphical representation of the functional model of the system to be analyzed, at different levels of abstraction.

Among MDE supporting techniques, we focus on *model transformations* for dependability and safety analysis. These transformations allow automatically traducing models in mathematical formalisms such that dependability analysis (and safety analysis) can be run. Among many available approaches, the CHESS tool [5] allows engineers to specify the fault behavior of individual components with a UML profile, where dependability sub-models have been previously defined; then, quantitative dependability evaluations are performed thanks to a model based on Stochastic Petri Nets that can be simulated using tools as DEEM [9]. In SISTER we will exploit the CHESS solution as it aims to produce quantitative evaluation while reducing the skills required on dependability evaluation, also in case of complex architectures.

4   The V&V Methodology Devised for SISTER

The devised V&V methodology combines aspects of qualitative and quantitative analysis. It focuses on the *requirements definition* and *design* phases: in fact, implementation and deployment are targeting prototypes in the course of the project, while the previous two phases will become closer to a market-ready solution. In the following is described how the techniques, reviewed in Sect. 3, are composed in the proposed V&V methodology, as illustrated in Fig. 1.

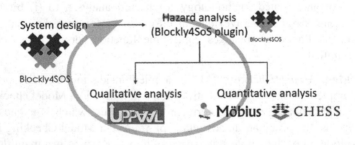

Fig. 1. Overview of the SISTER V&V methodology

First, starting from the system requirements, the SISTER architecture is designed using the tool Blockly4SoS (Sect. 4.1). Then, hazard analysis is performed using an enhancement of Blockly4SoS (Sect. 4.2). In fact, the Blockly4SoS tool was enhanced with a plugin, specifically crafted to perform hazard analysis using the same architectural model build with Blockly4SoS.

The system architecture and the results of the hazard analysis will be input to qualitative analysis, together with the operational scenarios and the refined requirements. This analysis is performed relying on Statistical Model Checking (SMC) and the Uppaal tool (Sect. 4.3). In SISTER, SMC allows modeling the use cases and operational scenarios to capture the complex interactions by modeling the behavior of the system, analyze hazards described by tailored formula and prove absence of residual hazards. Moreover, SMC allows to express in the model the intrinsic uncertainty of the autonomous positioning as well as real time delays of communications for a more accurate analysis of the system specification.

Finally (Sect. 4.4), models to quantitatively measure the safety and availability of the system are derived in an automated fashion from the architectural design of SISTER. In this way, means for both qualitative and quantitative analysis on the architecture are included in the methodology. As explained in Sect. 4.4, the input models for quantitative analysis with the CHESS tool must be in UML formalism and not in Blockly4SoS. Noteworthy, Blockly4SoS features include model transformation from Blockly4SoS to UML (and viceversa): consequently, it is possible to use the output of a Blockly4SoS model as input for the analysis with CHESS.

The methodology should be executed iteratively, as the SISTER project is firmly research-oriented and as such design specifications or technical solutions may evolve through time.

4.1   System Design

Once the requirements documents have been analyzed, the scenarios described in the requirements are further refined, together with the SISTER partners, to build *operational scenarios*. This activity, carried out jointly by consortium members, represents the starting point for both the qualitative and quantitative analysis, as well as the analysis of the system's hazards. Hence, the various analysis tasks of the SISTER system are standardized by a single specification document.

In order to support the modeling of the system under analysis, Blockly4SoS [8] is used, Blockly4SoS provides several types of blocks, as it includes all the elements that are deemed necessary to model complex Systems-of-Systems according to the glossary in [10]. For the purpose of the work planned in SISTER, we plan to use the following block types: *System-of-Systems* (SoS), *Constituent System* (CS), *interface, service*.

The *System-of-Systems* (SoS) is the whole distributed system to be modeled, composed of interacting components including sensors and actuators, and that is operated by humans. In our case, the SoS is the entire SISTER architecture. A *Constituent System* (CS) is an operating component of the SoS. A Constituent System is an autonomous subsystem of an SoS, consisting of computer systems and possibly of controlled objects and/or human role players that interact to provide a given service [10]. In the SISTER system modeled with Blockly4SoS, a CS is any of the functional blocks of the overall functional logical model. The block *interface* is used to represent any interface through which the CSs exchange information. There are two types of interfaces: RUMI (Relied Upon Message Interfaces) and RUPI (Relied Upon Physical

Interfaces). The first one is for information exchange in the cyber domain (usually, data exchanged through a network), the second one is dedicated to information exchange in the physical domain (e.g., with sensors and actuators). Each RUMI models one or more messages exchanges, represented by sequences of bits and based on a specific protocol. Each RUPI models interfaces used for one or more physical signals. Finally, the block *service* represents any function of the functional logical model.

As example, Fig. 2 shows an initial description of a *Tag Reader*, which is one of the blocks composing the overall SISTER model. The Tag Reader is an on-board component, with two functions, modeled in Fig. 2 as the following two services: (i) *acquisition of data from a TAG* (a ground component transmitting messages) by using the HF RFID technology; (ii) *transmission through a serial RS422 interface of the acquired data to the SISTER core for elaboration*. The Tag Reader interfaces with Tags located on the field, and with the SISTER core elaborator. Consequently, it has two interfaces that are modeled respectively through two different RUMIs: *TagReader_Tag* and *TagReader_Elaborator*. The RUMI *TagReader_Elaborator* contains also a *message* element, which models the information exchanged through this interface (it is the current *Position* of the train).

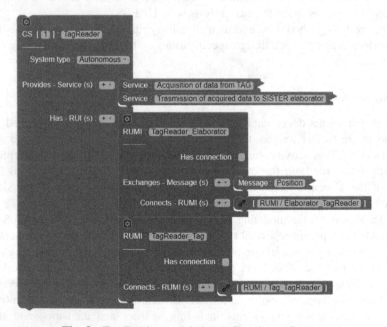

Fig. 2. Tag Reader modeled as a Constituent System.

Moreover, Blockly4SoS allows defining functional and non-functional requirements and matching them to the involved CSs. Each CS has a set of requirements associated; this allows verifying requirements traceability using the Blockly4SoS interface.

Another feature of Blockly4SoS that we exploit in SISTER is the ability to set modeling constraints, in order to avoid errors during the modeling phase of the system. These constraints can be defined by the user through JavaScript code; when one of the constraints is not satisfied by a block, that block is highlighted and an error message appears. Only once the constraint is satisfied, the block returns to the normal color. This feature is applied to enforce that architectural properties are satisfied, for example to assure that the proper message types are matched to each interface, or the proper number and type of sensors and actuators is associated to each CS.

4.2 Hazard Analysis

In the context of the SISTER project we devised a tool that offers automated support to apply a systematic approach to hazard analysis; the objective is to improve the *correctness* and *completeness* of the analysis. Through the application of model-based approaches and in particular an architectural model specified using Blockly4SoS, it is possible to automate the extraction of the relevant information for the hazard analysis, such as functions, blocks, interfaces and data flows. The approach relies on a new Blockly4SoS plugin, specifically created for SISTER. Blockly4SoS is enhanced with a plugin to perform hazard analysis, such that: (i) hazard analysis is performed operating on the architecture design, (ii) results are extracted from information placed in the architecture blocks, and (iii) checks for integrity are automatically run based on the architectural structure.

First, Blockly4SoS is employed for the realization of the functional logical model of the system. Successively, the obtained model is used for:

- a *Functional Hazard Analysis* (FHA), aiming at identifying the potential hazardous scenarios through the application of guide words on the system's functions represented through the model.
- an *Interface Hazard Analysis* (IHA), aiming at identifying the potential hazardous scenarios through the application of guide words on both internal and external system's interfaces represented through the model.

The automation of the hazard analysis is obtained exploiting the XML generated by Blockly, which is elaborated through scripting code to generate a template, pre-compiled with hazards described through guidewords selected by the safety engineer, for both the FHA and IHA. Such pre-compiled list of hazards is then visualized in Blockly4SoS, matched to the different Blockly4SoS blocks (SoS, CSs, interfaces, services), and analyzed using graphical support in Blockly4SoS.

Moreover, the detailed representation of specific hazardous scenarios represents a relevant input for the qualitative and quantitative analysis performed respectively through Statistical Model Checking and Stochastic modeling.

4.3 Qualitative Analysis (Model Checking)

The purpose of the qualitative analysis of the SISTER system is to verify that certain safety and reliability properties are met. Given the high complexity of a light rail train system, it is important to abstract away from the details that are not relevant for the purposes of the safety properties that have to be verified. If, for example, it has to be verified that the system enters a safe state in the event of a failure in communications between the train and the operations center, it is necessary to model the communication protocol between the parties (that is, their behavior), and possible delays in communications. However, it is not necessary to comprehensively model the contents of packets exchanged in messages, nor voltage or other physical parameters that come into play in wireless communications.

It is therefore useful to construct a model of the system, which specifies the aspects relevant to the new SISTER system and abstracts from non-relevant aspects. In fact, as the complexity of the model increases, the difficulty in verifying certain safety properties will increase, so that they could even become completely unverifiable for systems with millions of states.

As stated above, for the qualitative analysis phase of the SISTER project Timed automata, Metric Interval Temporal Logic and the toolbox Uppaal Statistical Model Checking are used. Thanks to the possibility of modeling mainly temporized, but also probabilistic and hybrid aspects, Uppaal has been identified as an effective tool in the modeling of the SISTER system, and in its analysis. Moreover, Metric Interval Temporal Logic allows to express real-time aspects, those that cannot be expressed through standard Linear Temporal Logic.

In particular, communications delays are modeled in a classical manner using clocks, an aspect that can be modeled primarily in Uppaal, without further encodings that would complicate the model and its analysis. Likewise, the possibility of loss of messages, a realistic scenario in the SISTER system where communications are wireless, is easily modeled using probabilistic transitions. From the probability of failure of a single wireless communication (data obtainable from the suppliers of the used devices), it is possible to calculate safety properties, such as the probability of reaching a fail-safe state in the case of prolonged communication failure. These properties are expressed using the available metric temporal logic.

This type of analysis is useful to provide further evidence of the correctness of the proposed solution, which can be of help for the certification. Moreover, a state machine formalization can be easily integrated in the life-cycle of a railway system, and in particular in the design phase, which mainly uses state-machine formalisms as UML State Machine Diagrams.

Model Checking at Work. An example of an early formalization of a SISTER component is now described. One of the innovative aspects of the SISTER system is the possibility of replacing the physical Train Detections (track circuits and axle counters), with virtual devices. Virtual devices (called *Virtual Track Circuits* - VTCs) are contiguous location ranges (track sections) within a virtual map on each train and on the ground. The detection (that is to say if a train occupies a VTC), is implemented through a geolocation function (called *LocationReferencing*) that compares the coordinates of the train with the map.

Below we call *virtual coordinates* the positioning data calculated using the algorithm to merge the data of the various sensors on board the train, while we call *real coordinates* the real position (in a given moment of time) of the train.

The SISTER system provides a mapping function of the virtual coordinates of a train (Lv) on the virtual map (M). VTCs are identified by intervals $[a, b]$ within the map. For each VTC is $[a, b]$ the start and end interval of the VTC in the map. Furthermore, Lv is the calculated virtual location (the reference position is the center of mass of the front chassis of the train). The length of the train is denoted by l, and PL denotes the *protection level* [19], and is such that $Lv - PL \leq L \leq Lv + PL$ does not hold with a very low probability (called *integrity risk*), e.g. 10^{-9}.

Then *LocationReferencing* $(Lv, PL, a, b) = true$ and the corresponding VTC is busy, otherwise in the case *LocationReferencing* $(Lv, PL, a, b) = false$ the corresponding TD is free where: *LocationReferencingVTC* $(Lv, PL, a, b) = (a - PL - l/2 \leq Lv) \wedge (Lv \leq b + PL + l/2)$.

The automaton describing a VTC has as input parameters among the others two integers a and b that identify the track section where the VTC is positioned. Its two states are *Free* and *Occupied*, which intuitively identify the occupation and release status of the VTC and each of them has an invariant to respect (the invariants identify the conditions that must always be valid when the system is in that particular state, otherwise the model is not valid). Transitions from states will be performed according to *LocationReferencingVTC* function. In the *Free* state, the invariant is:

$$forall \, (tid : int[0, nTrain - 1])!(a - PL - (l/2) < = Loc[tid]\&\&$$
$$Loc[tid] < = b + PL + (l/2)) \tag{1}$$

This invariant implements within it the *LocationReferencingVTC(Lv, PL, a, b)* function that evaluates to *true* in the case of occupation of the modeled VTC. In particular, for all the trains in the system *(forall (tid: int [0, nTrain − 1])*), the *LocationReferencingVTC* function should not evaluate to true (*!LocationReferencingVTC (Lv, PL, a, b)*). Intuitively, the VTC is in the free state if no train is occupying it.

The invariant for the *Occupied* state is:

$$exists(tid : int[0, nTrain - 1])((a - PL - (l/2) < = Loc[tid])\&\&$$
$$(Loc[tid] < = b + PL + (l/2))) \tag{2}$$

This invariant is simply the negation of the previous one: the VTC is in the occupied state if and only if there is at least one train that occupies it i.e., the *LocationReferencing* function evaluates to true.

Through the invariants it is possible to model the safety properties that the VTC model must respect. Hazards in which those safety properties are not respected are indeed an output from the hazard analysis phase. A specific analysis verifies that the invariants are always respected in any system execution, and it is of help in providing further evidence of the correctness of the system specification.

A detailed presentation of the application of Statistical Model Checking to prove these safety properties is reported in [13].

4.4   Quantitative Analysis (Stochastic Modeling)

Quantitative analysis of SISTER dependability properties, with an obvious focus on safety and typically aimed at producing a numerical failure rate [4], is based on the integration of two different techniques. First, the basis of the approach is the exploitation of MDE through the usage of the tool CHESS [5], which allows to represent and model the system architecture. Second, the results achieved with the tool CHESS are completed with an analysis of operational scenarios, that instead are represented using the formalism Stochastic Activity Networks (SAN, [14]), and that are simulated using the tool Möbius [15].

Architectural Analysis with the CHESS Tool. We model the reliability and safety properties of the SISTER architecture using the CHESS tool and an MDE approach. The starting point is the Blockly4SoS architecture. Since CHESS operates only with UML models, interoperability between Blockly4SoS and CHESS is achieved via a two-way transformation from Blockly4SoS to UML and vice-versa. This transformation is already provided by Blockly4SoS.

The resulting architectural model includes both physical (hardware, sensors, and actuators) and software parts of each component; this is a direct consequence of having the system modeled with Blockly4SoS, that requires modeling both the cyber and physical parts of cyber-physical systems.

CHESS takes as input the Blockly4SoS model to investigate failure propagations between the cyber and physical parts of a system. In fact, we use CHESS sub-models to define fault-error-failure propagation paths within the same components and through different components. Finally, CHESS sub-models allow defining the fault tolerance and error detection mechanisms that are devised for the SISTER architecture as a result of the requirements definition and hazard analysis. The main objective of this activity is to quantify the impact of faults with respect to the reliability, availability and safety of the individual components and the overall architecture. The hazard analysis in Sect. 4.2 offers the fault and the failure models that are exploited for the analysis.

Analysis of Operational Scenarios with Möbius. Möbius is a very well-known tool for modeling and quantitative analysis of dependable systems. Amongst the various modeling techniques, Möbius includes a graphical editor and an engine to represent and simulate Stochastic Activity Networks (SANs), a formalism derived from Stochastic Petri Nets that is effective in representing and analyzing operational scenarios. In fact, we model all the SISTER scenarios that will be defined during requirements analysis using the SAN and Möbius tool. Currently, SAN and Mobius are not integrated in CHESS (which instead integrates the DEEM [9] formalism, based on Stochastic Petri Nets), and consequently generation of SAN from the CHESS architecture is currently not automated. However, the integration of SAN and Mobius with CHESS is also one of our target achievements for the SISTER project.

The main objective of this activity is to quantify safety, reliability and availability for various operational scenarios, and for different values of key parameters. This is achieved with SAN models, that allow structuring the operational scenarios in multiple steps, and describing the occurrence of hazards from the hazard analysis. For each step of an operational scenario, the possible hazards that may occur are linked to the components. The operational scenarios are exercised using different parameters, to extract dependability metrics under different values of hazard likelihood, detection time, and fault coverage. In particular, two relevant aspects of the SISTER architecture that we are investigating with our SAN models and Möbius are:

- The accuracy of the positioning system that geo-localizes a train on the track, to understand what is the maximum positioning errors that can be allowed without penalizing safety or availability.
- The safety threshold to determine the occupancy of a VTC. In other words, we aim to investigate the condition under which a train safely occupies a VTC. Multiple combinations of parameters for system variables and hazards are simulated. Certain combinations may show that safety is satisfactory but there is a drop in availability, while other combinations may show that safety decreases. We aim to find the best trade-off between (acceptable) safety and availability.

4.5 Compliance to Target Requirements

Concerning REQ1 (*the methodology shall comprise techniques that offer safety evidence*), the techniques we include in our methodology are either *recommended* or *highly recommended* across several system life-cycle phases according to railway standards [2–4]. The difference between being recommended or highly recommended is based on the target Safety Integrity Level of the system. Hazard analysis is largely applied since system definition phase in the CENELEC EN 50126 [2] and it continues through design and implementation, commissioning and decommissioning phases. Formal methods, such as model checking, and stochastic model-based approaches are often applied during requirements specification, design and implementation phases, mostly for verification purposes: in fact, they are mathematically rigorous techniques that are well-perceived through different system life-cycle phases. They are marked as either Recommended or Highly Recommended in the standards, for example formal methods are Highly Recommended in [3] for software requirements specification and Recommended in [4] for system requirements specification. Concerning instead architecture design, the standards explicitly ask for model-based approaches for system and software architecture, and the Blockly4SoS formalism matches this requirement.

Concerning REQ2 (*results shall be easily reusable for future exploitation of SISTER*), Blockly4SoS is intuitive to understand, reuse and modify. It was built to model complex Systems of Systems, as it reduces the incidence of *spaghetti diagrams*. All the V&V activities we discussed are based on the architecture: if the architecture is well-understood, performing the analyses is much easier. Further, since transformation from Blockly4SoS to UML is already available as a Blockly4SoS feature [8], compatibility with tools as CHESS is not an issue. On top of this, our MDE approach is integrated with the CHESS tool for quantitative dependability evaluation, to reduce the necessity of specific skills on dependability modeling and to exploit the benefit of backannotations for iterative improvement (backannotations [5] are a feature of CHESS that enriches the initial architectural model with feedbacks from the analysis performed). Finally, model checking has been performed on a state-machine formalism (i.e., timed automata), which is easily transferrable to a UML State Machine Diagram for further exploitation in a software life-cycle.

Concerning REQ3 (*methodology shall be appropriate to deal with complex V&V issues*), Statistical Model Checking was selected as it is effective in describing complex protocols and interactions, as well as positioning uncertainty and timed aspects, and confirm the correct specification of an architecture, protocol or algorithm. Further, our quantitative analysis is able to define quantitative indications on the safety of the system, and on acceptable operating conditions.

5   Conclusions and Future Works

This work discussed the V&V methodology that we are applying in a research project, called SISTER, that aims to build a prototypal solution of an innovative light rail train with autonomy-oriented features. The V&V methodology was devised to meet specific aspects of the project, that require a trade-off between (i) time and budget limitations, (ii) technical difficulties for the assessment of the most innovative parts of the project, (iii) deliver results that can be reused for future product-oriented initiatives, (iv) achieve adequate evidence of certifiability according to railway standards for electronics equipment.

The individual assessment activities that constitute our methodology are either currently being carried forward or already completed. Despite some of such V&V activities are still ongoing, the methodology already allowed to detect small inconsistencies in the VTC specification, showing how one of the hazards was not mitigated adequately [13]. Indeed, this was possible thanks to the tight link between both hazard analysis and qualitative analysis phases in our proposed methodology.

Acknowledgement. This work has been partially supported by the Tuscany Region project POR FESR 2014–2020 SISTER - SIgnaling & Sensing Technologies in Railway application.

References

1. Bondavalli, A., Lollini, P., Majzik, I., Montecchi, L.: Modelling and model-based assessment. In: Wolter, K., Avritzer, A., Vieira, M., van Moorsel, A. (eds.) Resilience Assessment and Evaluation of Computing Systems, pp. 153–165. Springer, Heidelberg (2012). https://doi.org/10.1007/978-3-642-29032-9_7
2. CENELEC EN 50126: Railway applications - The specification and demonstration of Reliability, Availability, Maintainability and Safety (RAMS) (1999)
3. CENELEC EN 50128: Railway applications - Communication, signaling and processing systems - Software for railway control and protection systems (2011)
4. CENELEC EN 50129: Railway applications - Communication, signaling and processing systems - Safety related electronic systems for signaling (2003)
5. Cicchetti, A., et al.: CHESS: a model-driven engineering tool environment for aiding the development of complex industrial systems. In: IEEE/ACM ASE, pp. 362–365. ACM (2012)
6. Ericson, C.: Hazard Analysis Techniques for System Safety. Wiley, Hoboken (2015)

7. Google Blockly. https://developers.google.com/blockly
8. Blockly4SoS. https://blockly4sos.resiltech.com/
9. Bondavalli, A., et al.: DEEM: a tool for the dependability modeling and evaluation of multiple phased systems. In: Proceeding International Conference on Dependable Systems and Networks (DSN), pp. 231–236. IEEE (2000)
10. Ceccarelli, A., Bondavalli, A., Froemel, B., Hoeftberger, O., Kopetz, H.: Basic concepts on systems of systems. In: Bondavalli, A., Bouchenak, S., Kopetz, H. (eds.) Cyber-Physical Systems of Systems. LNCS, vol. 10099, pp. 1–39. Springer, Cham (2016). https://doi.org/10.1007/978-3-319-47590-5_1
11. Baier, C., Katoen, J.-P.: Principles of Model Checking. MIT Press, Cambridge (2008)
12. David, A., et al.: Uppaal SMC tutorial. Int. J. Softw. Tools Technol. Transfer 17(4), 397–415 (2015)
13. Basile, D., Fantechi, A., Rucher, L., Mandò, G.: Statistical model checking of hazards in an autonomous tramway positioning system. In: Collart-Dutilleul, S., Lecomte, T., Romanovsky, A. (eds.) RSSRail 2019. LNCS, vol. 11495, pp. 41–58. Springer, Cham (2019). https://doi.org/10.1007/978-3-030-18744-6_3
14. Sanders, W.H., Meyer, J.F.: Stochastic activity networks: formal definitions and concepts*. In: Brinksma, E., Hermanns, H., Katoen, J.-P. (eds.) EEF School 2000. LNCS, vol. 2090, pp. 315–343. Springer, Heidelberg (2001). https://doi.org/10.1007/3-540-44667-2_9
15. Möbius User Manual: PERFORM – Performability Engineering Research Group, University of Illinois at Urbana-Champaign, 2.0 edition
16. Hamoy, C., Hemer, D., Lindsay, P.: HazLog: tool support for hazard management. In: Proceedings of the 9th Australian Workshop on Safety Critical Systems and Software - Volume 47, pp. 77–87. Australian Computer Society, Inc. (2004)
17. Müller, M., Roth, M., Lindemann, U.: The hazard analysis profile: linking safety analysis and SysML. In: Annual IEEE Systems Conference (SysCon), pp. 1–7 (2016)
18. POR-FESR 2014–2020 SISTER - SIgnaling & Sensing Technologies in Railway application. http://www.progetto-sister.com/
19. Legrand, C., et al.: Approach for evaluating the safety of a satellite-based train localisation system through the extended integrity concept. In: ESREL 2015-European Safety and Reliability Conference (2015)
20. Basile, D., Di Giandomenico, F., Gnesi, S.: Statistical model checking of an energy-saving cyber-physical system in the railway domain. In: ACM Proceedings of the Symposium on Applied Computing, pp. 1356–1363 (2017)
21. Ceccarelli, A., et al.: Threat analysis in systems-of-systems: an emergence-oriented approach. ACM Trans. Cyber-Phys. Syst. 3(2), 18 (2018)
22. de la Vara, J.L., et al.: The AMASS approach for assurance and certification of critical systems. In: Embedded World Conference (2019)
23. Bondavalli, A., Brancati, F. (eds.): Certifications of Critical Systems-The CECRIS Experience. River Publishers, Gistrup (2017)

2nd International Workshop on Safety, securiTy, and pRivacy In automotiVe systEms (STRIVE 2019)

2nd International Workshop on Safety, securiTy, and pRivacy In automotiVe systEms (STRIVE 2019)

Gianpiero Costantino and Ilaria Matteucci

Istituto di Informatica e Telematica - CNR, Via G. Moruzzi, 1, Pisa, Italy
{gianpiero.costantino,ilaria.matteucci}@iit.cnr.it

1 Preface

The introduction of ICT systems into vehicles make them more prone to cyber-security attacks. Such attacks may impact on vehicles capability and, consequently, on the safety of drivers, passengers. The strong integration among dedicated ICT devices, the physical environment, and the networking infrastructure, leads to consider modern vehicles as Cyber-Physical Systems (CPS).

In 2013, more than 1 billion of sensors were sold to the automotive industry, doubling 2009 levels, and embedded connectivity solutions began appearing in 2014. As a consequence, serious concerns arise regarding, among others, privacy, safety, and security of automotive ecosystems, and related standards. A connected vehicle can track the overall behaviour of the driver, including information about location, driving style and additional trip parameters, such as fuel economy, and more sensitive parameters, such as the phone-book of a mobile phone, information about home location, and data related to the home-link remote control. Without complete, efficient, and robust security control systems, a concrete risk exists that such private information could be accessed by third parties, e.g., interested in pushing offers or in profiling the user. Thus, security has become a serious issue for connected vehicles.

Several studies investigated the cyber-crime through automotive networks and the risks related to losing control of autonomous vehicles. As emerged from these studies, a series of potential attacks involving intra/inter-vehicle system communications can be conceived, spanning from a "simple" traffic jam to more complex and dangerous attacks, driving a vehicle without any authorizations. Hence, the convergence of safety and security requirements is one of the main outstanding research challenges in CPS and in the automotive scenario in particular.

STRIVE aims at providing a forum for researchers and engineers in academia and industry to foster an exchange of research results, experiences, and products in the automotive domain from both a theoretical and practical perspective. Its ultimate goal is to envision new trends and ideas about aspects by designing, implementing, and evaluating innovative solutions for the CPS with a particular focus on the new generation of vehicles. In this context, the automotive domain presents several challenges in the fields of vehicular network, Internet of Things, Privacy as well as Safety and Security methods and approaches. The workshop aims at presenting the advancement on the state of art in these fields and spreading their adoption in several scenarios involving main stockholders of the automotive domain. Furthermore, STRIVE aims at promoting the discussion between industrial stakeholders, manufacturers, and academia on these research challenges targeting safety, security, and privacy aspects as well as all the different phases of the development process of IoT and automotive software and systems.

2   Workshop Program

The program of STRIVE 2019 consists of 5 high-quality papers grouped as follows:

- **Session 1: In-vehicle Security**

  - *CarINA - Car sharing with IdeNtity based Access control re-enforced by TPM* - Bogdan Groza, Lucian Popa and Pal-Stefan Murvay.
  - *Combining Safety and Security in Autonomous Cars Using Blockchain Technologies* - Lucas Davi, Denis Hatebur, Maritta Heisel and Roman Wirtz.
  - *Enhancing CAN security by means of lightweight stream-ciphers and protocols* - Aymen Boudguiga, Jerome Letailleur, Renaud Sirdey and Witold Klaudel.

- **Session 2. Security in Vehicular Network and IoT**

  - *Analysis of Security Overhead in Broadcast V2V Communications* - Paul Kearney, Mujahid Muhammad, Adel Aneiba and Andreas Kunz.
  - *You overtrust your printer* - Giampaolo Bella and Pietro Biondi.

Each paper was selected according to at least three reviews produced mainly by PC members. Selected papers come from several countries around the world.

As part of STRIVE 2019 workshop day, we are glad to present a live demo of a CANDY CREAM, a post-exploit that works on an Android In-Vehicle Infotainment (IVI) system connected to the CAN bus of a car. CANDY CREAM first exploits a misconfiguration to remotely access the Android infotainment system. Then, our exploit is injected into the Infotainment system to attack the instrument cluster of the target car. During the live DEMO, we will show CANDY CREAM in action to send crafted CAN data frames to activate the speedometer and others indicators of the instrument cluster.

3   Thanks

We would like to thank the SAFECOMP organization committee and collaborators for their precious help in handling all the issues related to the workshop. Our next thanks go to all authors of the submitted papers who manifested their interest in the workshop. With their participation the second edition of the Workshop on Safety, securiTy, and pRivacy In automotiVe systEms (STRIVE 2019) becomes a real success and an inspiration for future workshops on this new and exciting area of research. Special thanks are finally due to PC members and additional reviewers for the high quality and objective reviews they provided.

4   Workshop Co-chairs

Gianpiero Costantino   IIT-CNR, Italy
Ilaria Matteucci   IIT-CNR, Italy

5   Program Committee

Giampaolo Bella   University of Catania, Italy
Silvia Bonomi   University of Rome "La Sapienza", Italy
Jeremy Bryans   Coventry University, UK
Francesco Di Cerbo   SAP, France
Bogdan Groza   Politehnica University of Timisoara, Romania
Mathias Johanson   Alkit, Sweden
Erich Leitgeb   University of Graz, Austria
John Mace   University of Newcastle, UK
Eda Marchetti   ISTI-CNR, Italy
Francesco Mercaldo   IIT-CNR, Italy
Paolo Santi   MIT, USA
Francesco Santini   University of Perugia, Italy
Daniele Sgandurra   Royal Holloway - University of London, UK
Renaud Sirdey   CEA, France

6   Sub-reviewer

Filippo Lauria   IIT-CNR, Italy

Demo: CANDY CREAM

Gianpiero Costantino[✉] and Ilaria Matteucci

Istituto di Informatica e Telematica, Consiglio Nazionale delle Ricerche,
Via G. Moruzzi, 1, Pisa, Italy
{gianpiero.costantino,ilaria.matteucci}@iit.cnr.it

Abstract. The attack performed back to 2015 by Miller and Valasek to the Jeep Cherokee proved that modern vehicles can be hacked like traditional PCs or smart-phones. Vehicles are no longer purely mechanical devices but shelter so much digital technology that they resemble a network of computers. Electronic Control Units (ECUs), that regulate all the functionalities of a vehicles, are commonly interconnected through the Controller Area Network (CAN) communication protocol. CAN is not secure-by-design: authentication, integrity and confidentiality are not considered in the design and implementation of the protocol. This represents one of the main vulnerability of modern vehicle: getting the access (physical or remote) to CAN communication allows a possible malicious entity to inject unauthorised messages on the CAN bus. These messages may lead to unexpected and possible very dangerous behaviour of the target vehicle. Here, we describe how we implement and perform CANDY CREAM, an attack made of two parts: CANDY aiming at exploiting a misconfiguration exposed by an infotainment system based on Android operating system connected to the vehicle's CAN bus network, and CREAM, a post-exploitation script that injects customized CAN frame to alter the behaviour of the vehicle.

Keywords: Automotive · Cyber-security attack ·
Infotainment system · Android · Remote exploit

1 CANDY CREAM Attack

CANDY CREAM [1] is an attack designed to gain the control of a vehicle via its Android In-Vehicle Infotainment (IVI) System. As represented in Fig. 1, it consists of two parts: CANDY and CREAM. CANDY has two main phases: (i) Android IVI exploitation to take advantages of a possible flaw discovered through a vulnerability assessment and (ii) in-vehicle CAN bus network exploitation to pass through the Android IVI on-board, where CREAM is the post-exploitation script to inject forged CAN data frames to alter the behaviour of the vehicle.

© Springer Nature Switzerland AG 2019
A. Romanovsky et al. (Eds.): SAFECOMP 2019 Workshops, LNCS 11699, pp. 203–209, 2019.
https://doi.org/10.1007/978-3-030-26250-1_16

Fig. 1. CANDY CREAM attack flow

1.1   CANDY: Android IVI Exploitation

To obtain the control of a remote Android IVI, we covered all steps described in [2] to exploit a remote device. The target device is equipped with Android 6.0 operating system, quad-core at 1.2 GHZ and 1 Gbyte of RAM. In addition, the Android IVI sports the WI-FI and Bluetooth network interfaces and it is possible to get access to the 3 G/4 G mobile network by plugging-in a USB-dongle.

Recon. Both the attacking computer and the target device must be visible each other and so covered by the same network. This can apply when a vehicle, which hosts the Android IVI, and the attacker are relatively close, for instance, in a parking area that offers free Wi-Fi connectivity, or in a wider scenario, where the attacker and the vehicle are under the same 3 G/4 G network.

Scanning. The scanning phase is done by triggering a *vulnerability assessment* on the target device by specifying the IP of the Android IVI. The vulnerability assessment was done using both (i) Nmap [3] to network discovery and security auditing and (ii) OpenVas [4] that allows the tester to deeply analyse the found vulnerabilities and discover the related Common Vulnerabilities and Exposures (CVEs).

The first scan was run through Nmap to discover the opened ports on the target device: it highlighted a service running on port 5555. OpenVas provided more details on the vulnerable service running on port 5555. The OpenVas Network Vulnerability Test found a vulnerability with score of 7.5 points in a range from 1 to 10, meaning that the vulnerability may be exploited to access the target device. In particular, the report says: *"The script checks if the target host is running a service supporting the Android Debug Bridge (ADB) protocol without an enabled authentication."* and the impact states that *"This issue may be exploited by a remote attacker to gain access to sensitive information or modify"*.

The Android Debug Bridge (ADB) [5] is a tool developed by Google and used by developers for debugging purposes. ADB allows developers to remotely access the device. The ADB is a tool that should be used only during the configuration phase of the devices and should be stopped when not needed anymore. This action, however, is not always performed by devices vendors and it may expose devices to relevant cybersecurity risks. In fact, as reported by Beaumont in his blog [6] in June 2018, thousand of Android devices can be exploited since hardware manufactures sell their device with the adb port, i.e., 5555, opened and without any authentication mechanism.

Fig. 2. Our test-bed

Exploitation. To exploit the vulnerability found and described in the previous step, we used the adb command line client, available for the majority of operating systems, spanning from Microsoft Windows to Mac Os X. This command line tool allows a developer to connect to the device with a simple command and to interact with it by exploiting other additional commands. So, we just needed the target device IP address. Once, the connection is up, it is possible to control the Android IVI exploiting the set of commands available through the adb. For instance, entering the command adb shell, we spawn a remote shell on the device that allow us to explore the remote file-system. In addition, with the command adb push, it is possible to transfer local files to the remote device.

Elevation of Privileges. This phase is usually performed by attackers to get higher privileges on the controlled devices, e.g., obtaining *root* privileges. As it is customary, processes running on computers should never run with high privileges unless the access to important operating system files is requested, then the root access is mandatory.

In our attack, the adb command tool gave a remote control of the device with root privileges and no additional vulnerabilities were required to have more privileges on the Android IVI.

Maintaining Access and Covering their Tracks. These last two phases are out of scope of this paper. However, they should not be left uncovered when an attack is performed.

1.2 CANDY: In-Vehicle CAN Bus Network Exploitation

The second phase of the attack consists in gaining the control of the vehicle. To reproduce it in our test-bed with an Android IVI connected to the CAN bus, we leveraged a real Android IVI connected to an real instrument cluster.

Fig. 3. Speedometer activation   **Fig. 4.** Alert indicators on   **Fig. 5.** Light indicators on

The target instrument cluster is connected via USBtin [7], which is a simple USB to CAN interface able to monitor CAN bus and to transmit CAN messages, to the CAN interface of the Android IVI (Fig. 2).

ADB Connection to the Android IVI. By using the adb command line it is possible to establish a remote connection to the target Android IVI. So, to obtain access to the remote device, as attacker, we opened a new shell in our local operating system with the adb tool installed, and we inserted the command:

```
adb connect TARGET_IP
```

Then the attacker obtains a direct connection with the target devices. Now, the connection with the vehicle has been achieved and the next step is to access the CAN bus network. This is made by using the USBtin interface that physically connects the Android IVI to the CAN bus of the instrument cluster.

Environment Preparation. To execute our CREAM post-exploitation script, a python environment must be available within the Android IVI. Since, the Android IVI operating system does not host by default the python environment, we leverage again the adb command to remotely install the application to obtain the python environment running on the Android IVI. In particular, the application installed in the python environment is *qpython3*, which is available at: https://github.com/qpython-android/qpython3/releases. So, once the application is downloaded from the store, it can be installed in the Android IVI with this two simple commands:

```
adb push qpython3-app-release.apk /sdcard/
adb shell pm install /sdcard/qpython3-app-release.apk
```

The first command just copy the application from the attacker's computer to the target device. Then, the second command installs the python environment on the Android IVI. However, when reproducing the attack, we observed that through the adb shell pm install command, not all needed files to run the python environment are properly installed. This issue can be simply overtaken using this additional command:

```
adb push org.qpython.qpy3/ /data/data/
```

This command will copy the missing files from the attacker's computer to the Android IVI to achieve a complete and working python environment.

1.3   CREAM: Post-exploitation Script

CREAM script is written in python and uses the remote server to inject forged CAN data frames to the instrument cluster. CREAM is written to trigger the following unexpected actions against our instrument cluster:

1. Send valid crafted CAN data frames to activate the odometer: CREAM will inject into the CAN bus crafted data frames that will move the odometer indicator into a random positions (Fig. 3).
2. Show the alert indicators: CREAM will send a CAN frame that turns on the alert indicators, such as problem to the engine, the absence of oil, too high water temperature (Fig. 4).
3. Show the lights indicators: CREAM will send a CAN frame to active the lights indicators (Fig. 5).

To move the exploit from our local Kali computer to the victim device, we run the following command:

```
adb push CREAM.py /sdcard/
```

At this point, CREAM resides on the Android IVI but to be properly executed it must leverage the python environment installed before. So, the next step is to active the python environment by entering the following commands on the attacker's shell:

```
adb shell
cd /data/data/org.qpython.qpy3/files/bin
./qpython-root.sh
```

Last command will execute the python environment as it is shown in Fig. 6.
Reached this phase, we are ready to run CREAM by simply executing the following two commands:

```
root@t3-p2:/ # cd /data/data/org.qpython.qpy3/files/bin
root@t3-p2:/data/data/org.qpython.qpy3/files/bin # ./qpython-root.sh
Python 3.2.2 (default, Jun 18 2015, 19:03:02)
[GCC 4.9 20140827 (prerelease)] on linux-armv7l
Type "help", "copyright", "credits" or "license" for more information.
>>> []
```

Fig. 6. Python environment on the Android IVI

```
import subprocess
subprocess.call(['python','/sdcard/CREAM.py'])
```

These commands execute the exploit. Below the excerpt of the code able to activate the odometer till 40 km/h.

```
...
can = serial.Serial(port, baud, timeout=timeout)
can.write(("S2\r").encode('ascii'))
sys.stdout.write("Opening CAN channel\n"); sys.stdout.flush()
can.write(("O\r").encode('ascii'))
sys.stdout.write("Sending command to set odometer speed at ~40kmh...\n"); sys.stdout.flush()
can.write(("t0E520196\r").encode('ascii'))
sys.stdout.write("Command sent\n"); sys.stdout.flush()
...
```

2   Conclusion and Ethical Issue

We present CANDY CREAM as a real example of a possible attack that can be perpetrated on vehicles by exploiting possible existing vulnerabilities of Android IVI. In this paper, we describe how, by using open source tools and following well defined steps, we discovered a vulnerability on our target Android IVI, remotely took control of it and, consequently of the vehicle on which it has been installed.

We are conscious that the description of the attack is detailed enough to be replicated not only for research purposes but also for malicious activities. We declare that our purposes are research-oriented and we aim at pinpointing these kind of issues in order to carry on activities to overcome them.

Acknowledgments. This work has been partially supported by the GAUSS national research project (MIUR, PRIN 2015, Contract 2015KWREMX) and by H2020 EU-funded projects C3ISP (GA n700294).

References

1. Costantino, G., Matteucci, I.: CANDY CREAM - haCking infotAiNment anDroid sYstems to Command instRument clustEr via cAn data fraMe. In: Proceedings of the 17th IEEE International Conference on Embedded and Ubiquitous Computing, IEEE EUC 2019 (2019, in press)

2. Dieterle, D.W.: Basic Security Testing with Kali Linux 2. Copyright 2016 by Daniel W. Dieterle (2016)
3. NMap. https://nmap.org. Accessed 5 Mar 2019
4. OpenVas. http://www.openvas.org. Accessed 5 Mar 2019
5. adb. https://developer.android.com/studio/command-line/adb. Accessed 5 Mar 2019
6. Beaumont. https://tinyurl.com/yd7mvp2f. Accessed 5 Mar 2019
7. USBtin. https://www.fischl.de/usbtin/. Accessed 30 April 2019

CarINA - Car Sharing with IdeNtity Based Access Control Re-enforced by TPM

Bogdan Groza[✉], Lucian Popa, and Pal-Stefan Murvay

Faculty of Automatics and Computers, Politehnica University of Timisoara,
Timisoara, Romania
{bogdan.groza,lucian.popa,pal-stefan.murvay}@aut.upt.ro

Abstract. Car sharing and car access control from mobile devices is an increasingly relevant topic. While numerous proposals started to appear, practical deployments ask for simple solutions, that are easy to implement and yet secure. In this work we explore the use of TPM 2.0 functionalities along with identity-based signatures in order to derive a flexible solution for gaining access to a vehicle. While TPM 2.0 specifications do not have support for identity-based primitives we can easily bootstrap identity-based private keys for Shamir's signature scheme from regular RSA functionalities of TPM 2.0. In this way, key distribution becomes more secure as it is re-enforced by hardware and the rest of the functionalities can be carried from software implementations on mobile phones and in-vehicle controllers. We test the feasibility of the approach on modern Android devices and in-vehicle controllers as well as with a recent TPM circuit from Infineon.

1 Introduction and Motivation

Despite their simplicity and well established foundational concepts, i.e., authentication protocol, traditional car keys tell a long shameful story about insecurity, e.g., [8,18,20,22]. The use of smartphones as car keys has been proposed in numerous works. For example [3] proposes a complex platform for car access and rights delegation and uses a secure microSD smart-card to further increase the security level. Identity-based cryptography for car sharing has been also proposed in [21]. Some works go even further by proposing secure multiparty protocols [17] but these may be too computational intensive for the current infrastructure.

Our goal in this work is to deploy a simple solution that takes advantage of identity-based primitives and also of the increased security provided by the use of TPM (Trusted Platform Module) devices. Naturally, we require for the solution to be deployed on modern smartphones and in-vehicle units. The use of modern smartphones comes with many advantages since numerous functionalities can be implemented, e.g., car sharing and car localization, etc., while the flexibility of Java support opens road for numerous cryptographic primitives. In particular, identity-based cryptography has the advantage that it does not require storing

© Springer Nature Switzerland AG 2019
A. Romanovsky et al. (Eds.): SAFECOMP 2019 Workshops, LNCS 11699, pp. 210–222, 2019.
https://doi.org/10.1007/978-3-030-26250-1_17

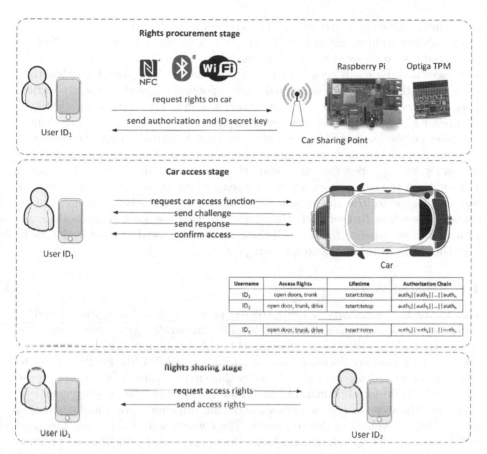

Fig. 1. CARINA: concept and scenarios

public-key certificates. Handling certificates in particular may be uneasy on in-vehicle components. In contrast, using principal identities is more easy to handle and nonetheless it offers better anonymity since users can choose pseudonyms that leave no traces inside the car. Of course, due to legal purposes, users should still need to provide proper credentials and prove their right to drive the car at a sharing center. But the privacy of the user should not be exposed inside the vehicle that is rented.

Scenarios. Figure 1 shows a graphical depiction of the scenario that we address. As stated, we opt for identity-based cryptography since it is more intu-itive, it protects user's privacy by relying on pseudonyms and avoids storing and sending digital certificates which may be a problem both because it requires bandwidth and due to storage memory constraints. In the depicted scenario, users receive their identity-based private keys from a sharing point via NFC connectivity. The sharing-point is implemented around Raspberry Pi and the TPM circuit to ensure security. The sharing-point may be in an unsupervised place and may be subject to physical access by the adversary, a reason for which the hardware security offered by TPM 2.0 is a significant advantage. NFC is suggested due to its short range which makes it harder to compromise but other interfaces may be used, even very long range such as LTE, provided that they are sufficiently secure. To make credentials spoofing unfeasible, the credentials may be encrypted and the user transaction key may be sent via an additional channel, e.g., SMS or c-mail. Whenever requesting access to the car a challenge-response protocol is run. The car stores the users identities in a table similar to Unix credential files, e.g., the passwd files, along with the expiry time and the access rights, e.g., open the car or start the engine. Not all users will be granted full rights on the car. For example, a passenger may be allowed to open the car but may not start the engine assuming that he has no driving license. Subsequently, users may further share their rights to other users over Bluetooth, again in a challenge-response fashion. All these actions will be discussed in details in a forthcoming section dedicated to our protocol.

1.1 Related Work

One of the first mentions of using trusted platform modules in the context of automotive systems comes as early as 2004 [2]. In parallel with the development of generic TPM specifications, researchers in the automotive area have proposed the use of a Hardware Security Module (HSM) with TPM-like functionalities to suit the specific requirements of the vehicular environment. Wolf et al. propose the use of a HSM for implementing an automotive digital rights management system [24]. The work in [23] describes the design, implementation and evaluation of an HSM for vehicular environments. The comparison of the three proposed HSM variants with specifications of an industry-proposed vehicular secure hardware, smart cards and TPM 1.2 devices illustrates superior features in all but the light HSM implementation.

The use of TPM functionalities were proposed for various automotive applications especially those in which the vehicle communicates with the outside environment, where existing automotive grade platforms cannot provide adequate performance for software implementations of security solutions. The usage of TPMs for implementing security in Vehicular Ad-Hoc Networks (VANETs) was proposed in [11]. The authors of [9] use a TPM as root of trust for their implementation of car-to-car communication system. Proposals for over-the-air automotive firmware updates involve public key operations which could be efficiently implemented in the vehicle with the use of a TPM or HSM. One such approach which uses an off-the-shelf TPM chip connected to the wireless vehicle unit is proposed in [16].

Another use case is the communication between the vehicle and smart devices. An example is the use of smartphones to delegate usage rights over cars in a car sharing/renting application. Symeonidis et al. [17] propose such a system in which the on-board unit responsible with the verification of usage rights is equipped with a HSM providing secure key storage and support for cryptographic operations.

2   Components

Table 1 provides a summary of the platforms that we used in our work. We discuss more details on the TPM and TriCore controllers next. Figure 2 depicts the setup of our work: an Infineon Optiga TPM connected to a Raspberry Pi.

Fig. 2. Experimental setup: the Infineon Optiga TPM connected to a Raspberry Pi

The trusted platform module (TPM) is a security standard which was defined by the Trusted Computing Group (TCG)[1] and standardized as ISO/IEC 11889:2009 for TPM 1.2 and ISO/IEC 11889:2015 for TPM 2.0. There are various properties of the TPM which makes it an ideal solution for hardware-based security operations such as secure storage of security data (e.g. cryptographic keys), keeping track of the running platform software trust state using platform configuration registers (based on integrity measurements recorded before each software application is executed), generation of symmetric keys or asymmetric key-pairs based on a unique, externally inaccessible, endorsement key and generation of random numbers using a TRNG.

For our experiments, we chose to use the OPTIGA SLB 9670XQ2.0 TPM from Infineon which is compliant to the specifications of TPM 2.0. We used the OPTIGA TPM evaluation board mounted on a Raspberry Pi 3B+ for implementing the protocol building blocks. The OPTIGA TPM datasheet, its parametrics and other technical documents are given by Infineon as public information [14]. Based on the OPTIGA TPM parametrics, we determined that it can execute, by requests over the SPI interface, the following commands: (i) generate randomness, (ii) asymmetric encryption/decryption on a given input using

---

[1] https://trustedcomputinggroup.org.

Table 1. Platforms used in our work

Platform	Core	Flash	RAM	Clock	Manufacturer
Optiga TPM	16-bit CPU	6962 B	Not specified	Not specified	Infineon
TriCore TC297	TriCore 1.6P, 32-bit CPU	8 MB	728 KB	300 MHz	Infineon
Raspberry Pi 3B+	Cortex-A53, Quad-Core, 64-bit CPU	32 GB	1 GB	1.4 GHz	Raspberry Pi Foundation
Samsung Note 8	Exynos 8895, Octa-Core, 2.3 GHz Quad + 1.7 GHz Quad	128 GB	6 GB	2.3 GHz	Samsung

a loaded key (i.e., RSA-2048 encryption), (iii) asymmetric signing/verification given the input and using a loaded key (i.e., ECDSA-256 signature), (iv) symmetric signing/verification of a given input and using a loaded key (i.e., HMAC - Hash-based Message Authentication Code), (v) computing a hash function (i.e., SHA-256) on a given input. Also, according to the TCG requirements for TPM 2.0 and the OPTIGA TPM datasheet we determined that the chip has the following storage characteristics: (i) 6962 bytes of non-volatile memory, (ii) 1420 bytes I/O buffer, (iii) 1024 bytes for command/response parameters, (iv) 768 bytes for non-volatile read/write operations, (v) can handle up to 7 objects loaded in the non-volatile memory area, (vi) can handle up to 3 objects loaded in the volatile memory area.

Given the open nature of the TPM 2.0 library specification there exist opensource libraries containing the implementation of TPM functions (e.g., https://github.com/Infineon/eltt2, https://github.com/tpm2-software). These libraries can be built and executed on embedded devices in order to send any of the presented commands and receive the requested data from a TPM device. Additionally to the communication with the real trusted platform module there is also the possibility to use a tpm2-simulator https://sourceforge.net/projects/ibmswtpm2/ on a Linux machine with the mentioned open-source libraries in order to send/receive commands. This simulator can be used for testing and development as it emulates a hardware TPM.

3   Protocol

In this section we first discuss the building blocks behind our protocol proposal, then we give precise details on the protocol.

3.1 Cryptographic Building Blocks

We rely on standardized cryptographic primitives for encrypting, i.e., AES, and message authentication codes, i.e., HMAC. In addition to these, we use Shamir's identity-based signature [15] which can be easily described in what follows:

1. Setup(k) is the key setup algorithm that generates the master secret key msk and the public key pk. The Setup algorithms, generates two random primes p, q, each having k bits in length, computes $n = pq, \phi(n) = (p-1)(q-1)$, selects random integer $e \in Z_{\phi(n)}$ s.t. $\gcd(e, \phi(n)) = 1$ and computes $d - e^{-1} \mod \phi(n)$. The master secret key is msk $= \{n, d\}$ and the public key is pk $= \{n, e, h\}$. Here h is a hash function that maps the name of a user to an element of $Z_{\phi(n)}$, i.e., $h : \{0,1\}^* \to Z_{\phi(n)}$.

2. KeyDer(msk, I) is the key derivation algorithm that uses the master secret key msk and the identity of the user I to generate his private key by computing $I^d \mod n$. The user secret key is sk $= \{I^d \mod n, n\}$ (the public key to verify the signatures of this user is the identity of the user I along with system parameters pk).

3. Sign(sk, m) is the signature algorithm that takes as input the user's secret key sk and a message m the returns the signature σ. For this, the signing algorithm selects a random $r \leftarrow Z_n$, computes $t = r^e \mod n$, the hash of t concatenated with message m denoted as $h = hash(t\|m)$, then $s = I^d r^h \mod n$. The signature is $\sigma = \{s, t\}$.

4. Ver(pk, I, m, σ) is the verification algorithm which takes as input the system parameters pk, the identity of the user I, the message m and the signature σ and returns $true$ if the signature is correct otherwise it returns $\perp$. To verify that the signature is correct the algorithm computes s^e and checks if this is equal to $It^h \mod n$ and returns $true$ if so or $\perp$ otherwise.

Identity-based primitives are not supported by the current TPM 2.0 specifications. Though, current standards such as the ISO/IEC 14888-2:2008 support identity-based signatures based on the Guillou-Quisquater scheme [12] for use in embedded devices such as smart-cards [13]. By using regular RSA support from TPM 2.0 we can however easily bootstrap identity-based keys for Shamir's scheme as we discuss in the experimental section. The reasons for choosing Shamir's scheme [15] in favour of Guillou-Quisquater scheme [12] was its simplicity and straight-forward way to derive secret keys from our TPM circuit.

3.2 Protocol Description

The proposed protocol consists of three stages: rights procurement from the car sharing center, the car access and the rights delegation sub-protocols. For brevity we do not include a rights revocation procedure. User rights have an expiry time, if rights need to be revoked sooner than that, then the car sharing entity should be able to maintain a revocation list inside each car which takes priority over the credential of the user. This should be easy to deploy if the cars

I) Rights procurement (secure channel)

1. Usr $\to$ Shr: $m_{\mathsf{Usr}} = \{\mathsf{ID}_1, \mathsf{ID}_{\mathsf{Car}}, \mathsf{ID}_{\mathsf{Shr}}, \mathit{func}^*, \mathit{time}, \mathit{ltime}\}$

2. Usr $\to$ Shr: $\mathsf{sk}(\mathsf{ID}_1), s_{\mathsf{Shr}} = \mathsf{Sig}(\mathsf{sk}(\mathsf{Shr}), m_{\mathsf{Usr}})$

3. Usr sets $<authChain>_{\mathsf{Usr}} = \{m_{\mathsf{Usr}}, s_{\mathsf{Shr}}\}$

II) Car access (insecure channel)

1. Usr $\to$ Car: $m'_{\mathsf{Usr}} = \{\mathsf{ID}_{\mathsf{Usr}}, \mathsf{ID}_{\mathsf{Car}}, \mathit{func}^*, \mathsf{rand}^{128}_{\mathsf{Usr}}\}, <authChain>_{\mathsf{Usr}}$

2. Car $\to$ Usr: $m'_{\mathsf{Car}} = \{\mathsf{rand}^{128}_{\mathsf{Car}}\}, s'_{\mathsf{Car}} = \mathsf{Sig}(\mathsf{sk}(\mathsf{Car}), m'_{\mathsf{Car}} || m'_{\mathsf{Usr}})$

3. Usr $\to$ Car: $s'_{\mathsf{Usr}} = \mathsf{Sig}(\mathsf{sk}(\mathsf{Usr}), m'_{\mathsf{Usr}} || m'_{\mathsf{Car}})$

4. Car $\to$ Usr: $s''_{\mathsf{Car}} = \mathsf{Sig}(\mathsf{sk}(\mathsf{Car}), s'_{\mathsf{Usr}})$

III) Rights sharing (insecure channel)

1. $\mathsf{Usr}_1 \to \mathsf{Usr}_2$: $m'_{\mathsf{Usr}_1} = \{\mathsf{ID}_{\mathsf{Usr}_1}, \mathsf{ID}_{\mathsf{Car}}, \mathsf{ID}_{\mathsf{Usr}_2}, \mathit{func}^*, \mathit{time}, \mathit{ltime}\},$
$s'_{\mathsf{Usr}_1} = \mathsf{Sig}(\mathsf{sk}(\mathsf{Usr}_1), m'_{\mathsf{Usr}_1})$

2. $\mathsf{Usr}_2 \to \mathsf{Usr}_1$: $m'_{\mathsf{Usr}_2} = \{\mathsf{ID}_{\mathsf{Usr}_2}, \mathsf{ID}_{\mathsf{Car}}, \mathsf{ID}_{\mathsf{Usr}_1}, \mathit{func}^*, \mathsf{rand}^{128}_{\mathsf{Usr}_2}, \mathit{time}, \mathit{ltime}\},$
$<authChain>_{\mathsf{Usr}_1}, s'_{\mathsf{Usr}_2} = \mathsf{Sig}(\mathsf{sk}(\mathsf{Usr}_2), m'_{\mathsf{Usr}_2})$

3. Usr_1 sets $<authChain>_{\mathsf{Usr}_1} = \{<m_{\mathsf{Usr}}, s_{\mathsf{Shr}}> || <authChain>_{\mathsf{Usr}_1}\}$

Fig. 3. Protocol procedures: rights procurement, car access and rights sharing

have Internet connectivity but is out of scope for this work. Protocol procedures are summarized in Fig. 3 and we discuss each step in detail next.

The *rights procurement* stage occurs over a secure channel. We assume that this happens at a registration desk or, in case it is an unsupervised selling point, we assume a secure short-range interface such as NFC. If this is unavailable, then the credentials can be encrypted and the encryption key sent by a secondary channel such as SMS or e-mail. We do not insist on this additional procedure. The user registered by $\mathsf{ID}_{\mathsf{Usr}}$ requests rights on car $\mathsf{ID}_{\mathsf{Car}}$ from sharing center $\mathsf{ID}_{\mathsf{Shr}}$. The rights are encoded in the string func^* and may consist in full rights over the car or maybe just some restricted functions, e.g., opening the trunk in case the user forgets some belongings from a previous sharing. The rights start at current time encoded in time and have a fixed lifetime ltime. The sharing center will check that current time time does not drift significantly from a real-time clock (drifts in the order of seconds should be acceptable). To grant credentials, the sharing center returns a secret identity-based key $\mathsf{sk}(\mathsf{ID}_1)$ and signs the rights of the user as $s_{\mathsf{Shr}} = \mathsf{Sig}(\mathsf{sk}(\mathsf{Shr}), m_{\mathsf{Usr}})$.

The *car access* stage occurs over an insecure channel, e.g., Bluetooth or WiFi, between the smartphone of the user and some in-vehicle controller (e.g., an embedded unit or an infotainment device). The user $\mathsf{ID}_{\mathsf{Usr}}$ requests to car $\mathsf{ID}_{\mathsf{Car}}$ a specific functionality func^*. The message contains some random value to ensure freshness $\mathsf{rand}^{128}_{\mathsf{Usr}}$ and in case this is the first time the user connects to the

```
step trans4(X, Y, SID, ACT, PkUsr, PkCar, NC, NU):=
state_car(1, X, Y, ACT, PkUsr, PkCar, NC, NU).
iknows(crypt(inv(PkUsr), pair(X, pair(Y, pair(ACT, pair(NU,NC))))))
=>
iknows(crypt(inv(PkCar),
           crypt(inv(PkUsr), pair(X, pair(Y, pair(ACT, pair(NU,NC))))))).
state_car(2, X, Y, ACT, PkUsr, PkCar, NC, NU)
```

Fig. 4. Code snippet for the last transition of the car access protocol in the AVISPA [1] IF format

car it also contains the authorization chain $<authChain>_{Usr}$. The authorization chain consists in the message containing the rights of the user and the signature of an authorized party. For users that have freshly received rights from the sharing center, the authorization chain is just $m_{Usr}, s_{Shr} = \mathsf{Sig}(\mathsf{sk}(Shr), m_{Usr})$. Other users may have acquired rights from a regular user as discussed next and will present the authorization chain resulting from the next protocol component. The car checks that the authorization chain is correct and the time intervals specified in it match the current time. The car replies by sending a random value $\mathsf{rand}_{Car}^{128}$, authenticates and links this value to the previous values by signing, i e , $s'_{Car} = \mathsf{Sig}(\mathsf{sk}(Car), m'_{Car}||m'_{Usr})$. The user confirms his identity by signing the received challenge, i.e., $\mathsf{Sig}(\mathsf{sk}(Usr), m'_{Usr}||m'_{Car})$. If the signature is correct the car executes the corresponding functionality and confirms this to the user by a new signature, i.e., $\mathsf{Sig}(\mathsf{sk}(Car), s'_{Usr})$.

The *rights delegation* stage occurs over an insecure channel, e.g., Bluetooth or WiFi, between two smartphones. First, user Usr_1 requests particular functionalities from Usr_2, this is done in identical manner as when asking functionalities from the sharing center. Then user Usr_2, if he agrees to share his rights, will reply with a message containing a signature over the rights as well as his authorization chain $<authChain>_{Usr_1}$ which proves that he indeed has access to the corresponding functionalities. Subsequently Usr_1 sets his authorization chain as $<authChain>_{Usr_1} = \{<m_{Usr}, s_{Shr}> || <authChain>_{Usr_1}\}$.

Security Analysis. Our protocol is designed for the general case of a Dolev-Yao [7] adversary that has full control of the communication channel. Since we build upon regular cryptographic blocks (which are considered to be secure) a formal verification of the protocol should be sufficient in assessing its security. For this, we use the AVISPA platform [1] and model the protocol in the IF language. As model-checker we choose CLAtse [19] which is one of the AVISPA [1] back-ends. For brevity, we modeled only the car access sub-protocol II. Figure 4 contains the code snippet in IF for the last transition of the car access sub-protocol. Signatures are modeled in AVISPA as encryption with the inverse of the public-key, i.e., $crypt(inv(PkUsr), message)$. Messages can be formed under the *pair* operator and the entire communication is mediated by the intruder knowledge by the persistent fact *iknows* (this responds to the Dolev-Yao model since the intruder is the channel). Verifying the protocol consists in defining one action for the honest user, e.g., *open car*, and another for the adversary, e.g., *start engine*, and determine whether the car will execute the intruder action. The model-checker reported the protocol to be safe. Verifying the entire protocol suite may be subject of an extended version of our work.

4   Experiments

In this section we clarify experiments on the platforms of our setup: Raspberry Pi with Optiga TPM, Android devices and in-vehicle controllers.

4.1   Deployment on Infineon TriCore

While medium to high-end car models will benefit from the performance of info-tainment unit processors which is comparable to that provided by smartphones, this is not the case for low-end models. To cover the low-cost vehicle sector we employ the Infineon AURIX TC297, an embedded platform dedicated to specific automotive functionalities such as powertrain, chassis and body.

The TC297 is equipped with three 32 bit cores optimized for signal processing each of which can operate at a top frequency of 300 MHz. A total of 729 KBytes of RAM and 8 MBytes of Flash are available on chip. Members of the AURIX family of microcontrollers can be equipped with a hardware security module (HSM) which provides a secure key storage and execution environment along with HW implemented True Random Number Generator (TRNG) and 128-bit AES. Since the chip provides no HW support for implementing RSA we based our implementation on Miracl (Multiprecision Integer and Rational Arithmetic Cryptographic Library) https://github.com/miracl/MIRACL.

We tested the computational performance of the TC297 in executing basic steps of the proposed protocol on a single core. An RSA signature is performed in 26 ms, while the verification is executed in 462 ms. The implementation requires 74 and 73 ms for executing the sign and verify steps respectively using Shamir's ID-based signature with a 2048 bit key.

4.2   TPM Simulator and the Optiga TPM on Raspberry Pi

As a first step to test the functionalities of TPM 2.0 we have installed tpm2-simulator [10], tpm2-tss [4], tpm2-abrmd [6] and tpm2-tools [5] on a 32-bit Ubuntu Linux running on a virtual machine.

To obtain a crisper image on TPM 2.0 functionalities, we first managed to send commands to the tpm2-simulator using tpm2-tools for the following operations: (i) generate random numbers up to 48 bytes (limited by max hash size), (ii) create a primary key by selecting the key type, hash method and hierarchy under which the key-pair is created, (iii) create a local object under the primary key consisting of public and sensitive part of a new key-pair, (iv) import the created object as transient in the TPM, (v) link an OpenSSL generated key-pair to a primary key in the TPM, (vi) import an OpenSSL key-pair in the

TPM, (vii) encrypt local files using the imported object, (viii) decrypt the local files using the imported object, (ix) make the transient object persistent in the TPM, (x) generate the hash digest of local files.

Once all these operations were tested, we ensured that all the TPM functionalities required by our experiments are available on the Raspberry Pi 3B+ connected to an Infineon OPTIGA TPM2.0 evaluation board. For the hardware experiments with the Raspberry Pi we have used Raspbian Stretch Lite April 2019 with Kernel version 4.14. In order to be able to identify the Optiga TPM on the Raspberry Pi we had to patch and build the Raspbian Kernel of the Raspberry Pi following the application note from [14] by adding the TPM support and also the Infineon TPM board in the device tree overlay. Afterwards we updated the kernel on the microSD card of the Raspberry Pi and managed to communicate with the TPM board after installing tpm2-tss [4], tpm2-abrmd [6] and tpm2-tools [5].

Considering the commands sent to the simulated TPM in Linux, we have benchmarked the duration of each public-key operation performed by the Raspberry Pi and the OPTIGA TPM (neglecting the transmission time to and from the TPM). The measurement results are shown in Table 2.

Table 2. Operation time for TPM commands

Command	Output	Output size [bytes]	Duration [ms]
Create a RSA-2048 primary key	primary.ctx	1036	20736
Create an RSA-2048 encryption key	key.pub, key.priv	280, 192	237
Load an RSA-2048 encryption key	object.ctx	1032	227
Perform RSA encryption	file.encrypted	256	164
Perform RSA decryption	file.decrypted	256	326

Table 3. Execution time for operations of the Shamir signature on the evaluated platforms

Operation	Platform			
	TPM	Raspberry Pi 3 B+	Samsung Note 8	Infineon TC297
Shamir IBS Gen	342 ms	n/a	n/a	n/a
Shamir IBS Sign	n/a	284 ms	5.3 ms	74 ms
Shamir IBS Ver	n/a	50 ms	3.5 ms	73 ms

Table 4. Execution time for operations of the RSA signature on the evaluated platforms

Operation	Platform			
	TPM	Raspberry Pi 3 B+	Samsung Note 8	Infineon TC297
RSA Gen	220 ms (gen) + 220 ms (load)	5.1 s	190 ms	n/a
RSA Sign	342 ms	121 ms	3.7 ms	462 ms
RSA Ver	198 ms	5.2 ms	0.3 ms	26 ms

4.3   Android Implementation

The Android implementation uses secret keys for the Shamir identity-based signature provided by the Optiga TPM module. The signing and verification functionalities are implemented using the Java BigInteger class. Currently the implementation is software based. An improvement on this (in terms of security) is to use the TPM as cryptographic co-processor. That is, while support for identity-based schemes does not exist on TPM, we can still perform modular exponentiations as regular RSA encryptions. However, the TPM implementation that we had does not allow loading large public exponents (the default is 65537). Thus, only the computations of r^e mod n and s^e mod n could be performed which are fast anyway (since e is small). We did not succeed in loading a arbitrary exponent h (which is the hash of the message) to compute r^h mod n and t^h mod n so the client/car-side implementation was entirely software based.

Tables 3 and 4 give an overview of the computational results on each of the platforms. Shamir's identity-based signature is contrasted with regular RSA signatures. The computational results are graphically summarized in Fig. 5.

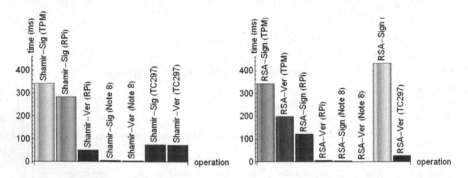

Fig. 5. Graphic summary of computational results for Shamir's signature (left) and regular RSA signature (right)

5   Conclusion

A full scale implementation of our protocol may be subject to future work. The aim of this shorter communication was to establish whether the associated building blocks, e.g., identity-based crypto, and technologies, e.g., TPM, are within reach for an automotive scenario. Clearly, high-end in-vehicle controllers such as the Infineon TriCore are ready for public-key primitives and identity-based cryptography in particular. Mobile phones and single-board computers have even greater computational power and memory resources. As proved by our easy-to-use car sharing scenario, there are clear advantages in terms of flexibility when using these cryptographic primitives. The future may bring single-board computers similar to Raspberry Pi inside cars if not delivered by the manufacturers then as a result of home projects. Aftermarket equipments are common in the automotive sector and DIY projects are also routine. Since CAN bus support exists for Raspberry Pi, turning this device into an in-vehicle body controller may not be a distant dream.

Acknowledgement. We thank the reviewers for helpful comments on our work. This work was supported by a grant of the Romanian National Authority for Scientific Research and Innovation, CNCS-UEFISCDI, project number PN-III-P1-1 1 -TE-2016-1317 (2018–2020) http://www.aut.upt.ro/~bgroza/projects/presence/.

References

1. Armando, A., et al.: The AVISPA tool for the automated validation of internet security protocols and applications. In: Etessami, K., Rajamani, S.K. (eds.) CAV 2005. LNCS, vol. 3576, pp. 281–285. Springer, Heidelberg (2005). https://doi.org/10.1007/11513988_27
2. Brandl, H.: Trusted Computing: The TCG Trusted Platform Module Specification. In: Embedded Systems. New Munich Trade Fair Centre (2004). http://opensgug.net/utilisec/embedded/Shared%20Documents/Device%20Security/VariousInputs/ShrinathInputs/Basic_Knowledge_EC2004.pdf. Accessed 3 May 2019
3. Busold, C., et al.: Smart keys for cyber-cars: secure smartphone-based NFC-enabled car immobilizer. In: Proceedings of the Third ACM Conference on Data and Application Security and Privacy, pp. 233–242. ACM (2013)
4. Developer Community: TCG TPM2 Software Stack. https://github.com/tpm2-software/tpm2-tss. Accessed 15 April 2019
5. Developer Community: The source repository for the TPM (Trusted Platform Module) 2 tools. https://github.com/tpm2-software/tpm2-tools. Accessed 15 April 2019
6. Developer Community: TPM2 Access Broker and Resource Management Daemon. https://github.com/tpm2-software/tpm2-abrmd. Accessed 15 April 2019
7. Dolev, D., Yao, A.: On the security of public key protocols. IEEE Trans. Inf. Theor. **29**(2), 198–208 (1983)
8. Francillon, A., Danev, B., Capkun, S.: Relay attacks on passive keyless entry and start systems in modern cars. In: NDSS (2011)

9. Glas, B., Sander, O., Stuckert, V., Muller-Glaser, K.D., Becker, J.: Car-to-car communication security on reconfigurable hardware. In: VTC Spring 2009-IEEE 69th Vehicular Technology Conference, pp. 1–5. IEEE (2009)
10. Goldman, K.: IBM's Software TPM 2.0. https://sourceforge.net/projects/ibmswtpm2/. Accessed 15 April 2019
11. Guette, G., Bryce, C.: Using TPMs to secure vehicular ad-hoc networks (VANETs). In: Onieva, J.A., Sauveron, D., Chaumette, S., Gollmann, D., Markantonakis, K. (eds.) WISTP 2008. LNCS, vol. 5019, pp. 106–116. Springer, Heidelberg (2008). https://doi.org/10.1007/978-3-540-79966-5_8
12. Guillou, L.C., Quisquater, J.-J.: A "Paradoxical" indentity-based signature scheme resulting from zero-knowledge. In: Goldwasser, S. (ed.) CRYPTO 1988. LNCS, vol. 403, pp. 216–231. Springer, New York (1990). https://doi.org/10.1007/0-387-34799-2_16
13. Guillou, L.C., Ugon, M., Quisquater, J.J.: Cryptographic authentication protocols for smart cards. Comput. Netw. **36**(4), 437–451 (2001)
14. Infineon: Optiga TPM SLB 9670XQ2.0. https://www.infineon.com/cms/en/product/security-smart-card-solutions/optiga-embedded-security-solutions/optiga-tpm/slb-9670xq2.0/. Accessed 22 April 2019
15. Shamir, A.: Identity-based cryptosystems and signature schemes. In: Blakley, G.R., Chaum, D. (eds.) CRYPTO 1984. LNCS, vol. 196, pp. 47–53. Springer, Heidelberg (1985). https://doi.org/10.1007/3-540-39568-7_5
16. Steger, M., et al.: An efficient and secure automotive wireless software update framework. IEEE Trans. Ind. Inf. **14**(5), 2181–2193 (2018)
17. Symeonidis, I., Aly, A., Mustafa, M.A., Mennink, B., Dhooghe, S., Preneel, B.: SeP-CAR: a secure and privacy-enhancing protocol for car access provision. In: Foley, S.N., Gollmann, D., Snekkenes, E. (eds.) ESORICS 2017. LNCS, vol. 10493, pp. 475–493. Springer, Cham (2017). https://doi.org/10.1007/978-3-319-66399-9_26
18. Tillich, S., Wójcik, M.: Security analysis of an open car immobilizer protocol stack. In: Mitchell, C.J., Tomlinson, A. (eds.) INTRUST 2012. LNCS, vol. 7711, pp. 83–94. Springer, Heidelberg (2012). https://doi.org/10.1007/978-3-642-35371-0_8
19. Turuani, M.: The CL-atse protocol analyser. In: Pfenning, F. (ed.) RTA 2006. LNCS, vol. 4098, pp. 277–286. Springer, Heidelberg (2006). https://doi.org/10.1007/11805618_21
20. Verdult, R., Garcia, F.D., Balasch, J.: Gone in 360 seconds: Hijacking with hitag2. In: Proceedings of the 21st USENIX Conference on Security Symposium, p. 37. USENIX Association (2012)
21. Wei, Z., Yanjiang, Y., Wu, Y., Weng, J., Deng, R.H.: HIBS-KSharing: hierarchical identity-based signature key sharing for automotive. IEEE Access **5**, 16314–16323 (2017)
22. Wetzels, J.: Broken keys to the kingdom: security and privacy aspects of RFID-based car keys. arXiv preprint arXiv:1405.7424 (2014)
23. Wolf, M., Gendrullis, T.: Design, implementation, and evaluation of a vehicular hardware security module. In: Kim, H. (ed.) ICISC 2011. LNCS, vol. 7259, pp. 302–318. Springer, Heidelberg (2012). https://doi.org/10.1007/978-3-642-31912-9_20
24. Wolf, M., Weimerskirch, A., Paar, C.: Automotive digital rights management systems. In: Lemke, K., Paar, C., Wolf, M. (eds.) Embedded Security in Cars, pp. 221–232. Springer, Heidelberg (2006). https://doi.org/10.1007/3-540-28428-1_13

Combining Safety and Security in Autonomous Cars Using Blockchain Technologies

Lucas Davi, Denis Hatebur, Maritta Heisel, and Roman Wirtz[✉]

University of Duisburg-Essen, Duisburg, Germany
{lucas.davi,denis.hatebur,maritta.heisel,roman.wirtz}@uni-due.de

Abstract. Modern cars increasingly deploy complex software systems consisting of millions of lines of code that may be subject to cyber attacks. An infamous example is the Jeep hack which allowed an attacker to remotely control the car engine by just exploiting a software bug in the infotainment system. The digitalization and connectivity of modern cars demands a rethinking of car safety as security breaches now affect the driver's safety. To address the new threat landscape, we develop a novel concept that simultaneously addresses both car safety and security based on the arising blockchain technology, which we mainly exploit to ensure integrity. Previous related work exploited the blockchain for the purpose of forensics, where vehicle data is stored on an externally shared ledger that is accessible by authorized third parties. However, those approaches cannot ensure integrity of information used by the vehicle's components. In contrast, we propose a blockchain-based architecture based on a shared ledger inside the car, where each ECU can act as a miner and shares its information with other ECUs. The architecture does not only improve the integrity of information for forensics. Some algorithms, e.g. the recognition of dangerous situations, are adaptive and can be improved using for example sensor data. Using our architecture, we ensure that those algorithms only take verified and correct information as input.

Keywords: Blockchain · Safety · Security · Autonomous vehicles

1 Introduction

Modern vehicles and especially next-generation autonomous cars increasingly face both security and safety challenges. On the one hand, car safety is crucial to ensure that a car functions correctly under various environmental circumstances. In particular, driving assistance systems help reducing the risk of a crash, e.g., the electronic stability program (ESP) significantly improves stability of the car, or recent automatic breaking systems reduce the risk of a collision by automatically braking the car. On the other hand, the increasing complexity and diverse features of a modern car require a vast amount of software and availability of communication channels to the Internet. This dramatically shifts the

© Springer Nature Switzerland AG 2019
A. Romanovsky et al. (Eds.): SAFECOMP 2019 Workshops, LNCS 11699, pp. 223–234, 2019.
https://doi.org/10.1007/978-3-030-26250-1_18

threat model as software running on a car is now interfacing with the Internet, thereby opening a new door to attackers. That is, similar to modern PC and mobile systems, attackers can gain access to a remote channel to hijack modern automobiles. As one infamous example, researchers have demonstrated that a software bug in the Jeep infotainment system allowed them to remotely exploit the bug to threaten the driver's safety by gaining control on car internals such as engine, wipers, and fan [1]. This new interplay between security and safety aspects demands for a hybrid framework that considers both security and safety requirements. For instance, when adding new driver assistance technologies to increase the safety of the car, we also need to make sure that the software running on a car cannot be compromised to disable safety components.

In this paper, we devise a novel approach to develop such a framework based on blockchain technologies. In general, blockchain systems are mainly deployed to ensure secure and tamper-proof records of transactions. These transactions are typically exchanges of cryptocurrency (Bitcoin) or execution of the so-called smart contracts (Ethereum). The blockchain offers decentralized storage (i.e., a distributed ledger) to guarantee integrity of the transactions and non-repudiation. Further, and probably most importantly, it removes the need for a trusted third party (e.g., a bank). On the other hand, we observe in this paper that the blockchain features properties that are either similar to or can be exploited for safety requirements. First, the security of blockchain systems relies on replicating the current state of the blockchain on each client participating in the network. This introduced redundancy is similar to m-out-of-n (MooN) systems in the safety domain which ensure the functionality of the systems as long as m out of n systems are functioning correctly. Second, blockchain systems are based on consensus or majority voting algorithms to accept a newly proposed state (in form of a new block). Again, this is similar to safety systems based on modular redundancy which perform a majority voting to produce a single output. Furthermore, recording safety-relevant transactions in a decentralized fashion enables reliable and fast verification of accidents (forensics). This is similar to a blackbox used in airplanes. In the context of automobiles, recall the recent Tesla accident where it was unclear for several weeks whether the car was driving in autopilot mode before the accident occurred [2]. By manipulating recorded data, it is possible to blame innocent stakeholders. Therefore, integrity of recorded data is of high importance.

When mapping the aforementioned considerations to modern automobiles, the decentralized blockchain storage allows to securely record the transactions occurring inside a car and from a car to its environment (e.g., other cars or the infrastructure). Transactions inside a car are (i) messages sent between the different components - typically electronic control units (ECUs) - of a car, and (ii) state information of the car. When stored on the blockchain, every component participating in the internal network is able to inspect previous states and messages to decide whether the next state represents a legitimate state change. Basic example policies are (1) to not turn off the engine while the car is in driving state, (2) to not turn off the ESP if the designated button has not been physically pressed by the driver, i.e., this ensures that compromised software does not broadcast a malicious message to turnoff the ESP, or (3) to detect abnormal state changes from the environment, e.g., sensors return mismatching results.

In fact, recent proposals leverage blockchain technologies to enable forensic investigation of autonomous cars [3,4]. However, these proposals target a higher abstraction layer, whereas we consider the layer of CAN messages to develop a framework that covers both safety and security requirements inside a car.

Deploying a blockchain framework to ensure security and safety of a modern car involves many challenges. First, there is a vast amount of messages constantly processed by the different ECUs in the car (cf. Sect. 2). Processing each of these messages in the blockchain would raise significant scalability problems due to performance reasons. Hence, the approach has to provide filter mechanisms for those messages that are relevant for the safety and security of the car. Second, there currently exists no framework that would allow us to determine whether the subsequent state is benign. As such, the next challenge to address involves new consensus algorithms that allow ECUs to make a decision on whether accepting or rejecting the next state. Finally, for the case of forensic-based validations, we need to develop a robust method to retrieve and process the current state of the blockchain. Our framework forms the basis for addressing those challenges by providing a blockchain-based architecture for an application inside cars.

The remainder of this paper is structured as follows: In Sect. 2, we introduce fundamentals on which our work is based, followed by a threat and system model in Sect. 3. We describe our blockchain-based architecture in Sect. 4 which is our main contribution. In Sect. 5, we discuss the results of an implementation of our architecture, and in Sect. 6 we discuss related work. Section 7 provides a summary of the paper and an outlook for future research directions.

2 Background

In this section, we introduce blockchains on which we built our architecture, followed by a description of a threat and system model stating assumptions on which we rely in the following.

2.1 Blockchain

Blockchain systems have become very popular over the last few years. The most famous examples of such systems are Bitcoin [5] and Ethereum [6]. The former allows anonymous transfer of cryptocurrency (Bitcoin) without requiring a trusted third party. Ethereum goes one step further than Bitcoin as it is not limited to transfer of cryptocurrency, but allows the execution of arbitrary computer programs (called smart contracts) on the blockchain. Prominent targets for smart contracts are crowdfunding, supply chain, decentralized autonomous organizations (DAOs), or micro-insurances which perform automated claim processing, thereby reducing the operating costs of insurance companies.

Abstractly speaking, the blockchain allows a secure, decentralized storage of blocks, where each block usually contains a limited number of transactions. Each block is cryptographically chained to its previous block by embedding the hash value of the previous block, thereby ensuring the integrity of the blockchain. As long as the majority of the network is not compromised by an attacker, the blockchain can prevent double-spending of coins and reversing of transactions. Blockchain systems are based on a consensus algorithm to accept a newly proposed block. The most well-known systems like Bitcoin and Ethereum deploy the so-called *proof-of-work (PoW)* consensus algorithm in which each node that participates in the so-called mining process must solve a mathematical puzzle and gets rewarded if it solves the puzzle first. Since PoW requires a lot of computational power and induces a high consumption of energy, *proof-of-stake (PoS)* algorithms have been proposed [7]. Rather than requiring every full node to solve a mathematical puzzle, PoS randomly selects miners, called validators or forgers in PoS, to mine the next block. The probability of being chosen as validator linearly increases based on the amount of owned tokens.

The most popular smart contract platform Ethereum plans a hard fork to PoS in the near future [8].

2.2   Architectural Setup

Today's car have between 20 and 250 ECUs (electronic control units) [9]. Their functionality is to realize anti-blocking systems (ABS), lane departure warning, stability control, airbag deployment, wiper control, light control, adaptive cruise control, automatic parking, and many others. These ECUs are connected with bus systems, in most cases with CAN [10] (controller area network) buses. In some cases FlexRay is used instead of CAN. FlexRay [11] inherits all properties of CAN and provides higher bandwidth and real-time. Because of bandwidth limitations, in most cars several CAN bus systems are used (see Fig. 1). One ECU can be connected to more than one bus because it works with or provides messages on different buses. It is also possible that one ECU acts as a gateway and forwards messages to a different bus. Together, they transmit (considering a car with many features) more than 10,000 messages per second. These messages are used to give state information (like vehicle speed or button status) to other ECUs. This is usually done with cyclic messages. If other ECUs have to be informed immediately about a status change, an additional message is sent. It is possible that an ECU reacts on state changes. For example, the ECU performs a certain action if the button value for "pressed" is received. To realize information redundancy for a better reliability, in some cases the action is only performed if the value has the required state for some time. In this time several messages are received. The cycle rate varies between 20 ms and in rare cases 100 ms depending on the kind of signal. With these cycle rates, more than 200 different types of messages may be sent. All ECUs connected to the bus system can read all messages but only consider information being relevant for their functionality.

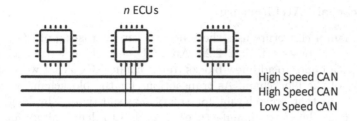

Fig. 1. Architecture overview

3 Threat and System Model

In an autonomous vehicle, information on the vehicle itself (like speed and steering angle) and its environment perceived by appropriate sensors (like lane, traffic signs and position/movement of other traffic participants) is used for improving the algorithms which control the autonomous vehicle. That information can also be used to analyze accidents. It should not be possible to tamper with this information, because false information could lead to algorithms that cause accidents. Furthermore, the analysis of incorrect data impedes discovering the true reason in case of an accident.

We target an attacker that aims to veil its own responsibility for an accident, to blackmail the OEM (original equipment manufacturer), or to kill a certain car driver. To perform such an attack, the attacker may modify information. This can be done by using an existing wireless connection to exploit a vulnerability that can be used to access the internal bus system. Information can also be changed by replacing an ECU with a modified ECU that sends forged information to other ECUs. An attacker can also modify information by accessing the internal bus system using the diagnosis connector that exists in all vehicles being built in the last 15 years. The diagnosis connector is directly connected to the internal bus. Since diagnosis connectors usually also provide electric power, a device can be connected that establishes a wireless connection with direct access to the internal bus.

We assume that the attacker does not have the capabilities to perform a 51%-attack as is typical for most blockchain-based systems based on majority voting because in our scenario the attacker has to replace more than half of the ECUs.

We also assume that the ECUs send messages with MACs (message authentication codes) to show that these messages come from a authentic device.

4 Architecture

In this section, we propose a blockchain-based architecture to combine safety and security for an application inside autonomous cars.

228 L. Davi et al.

4.1 Blockchain Architecture

Our blockchain architecture uses the infrastructure consisting of ECUs and the connecting CAN buses (cf. Sect. 2.2). An ECU can add new transactions and also works as a miner to add new blocks to the chain. ECUs that work as miners hold a copy of the blockchain. As transactions for the blockchain, we consider status messages that are relevant for safety or security, e.g. braking, steering commands etc. Therefore, manufacturers are able to define filters for types of messages that are safety or security critical. Each ECU implements those filter mechanisms to select relevant messages.

Since blockchain ensures integrity of stored data, our approach can be used as a blackbox for cars. Additionally, the blockchain consensus algorithms only allow to add validated transactions to the blockchain. With regard to safety, validated data is of high importance, e.g. for machine learning to improve algorithms for driver assistance or autonomous driving.

Currently, the performance that is needed for real-time operating on the blockchain is a big challenge. Since we use the CAN bus of a vehicle to broadcast all transactions and blocks, our architecture still allows reacting on the status messages before these are added to the blockchain.

For operating the blockchain of our architecture, the ECUs have to carry out different steps we describe in the following.

4.2 Step 1: New Status Message

As mentioned earlier, we only consider security and safety related status messages as new transactions for the blockchain. For those messages, we proceed in the following way: Each ECU holds a private key to sign its messages and a set of public keys from all other ECUs. Before broadcasting a transaction, an ECU signs the corresponding status message with its private key. Later, the signature can be verified by others using the related public key. The ECU adds the transaction to the set of transactions which are already stored in the ledger.

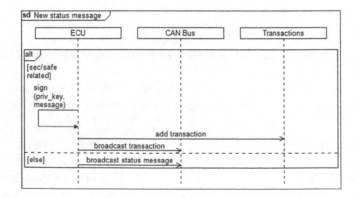

Fig. 2. New status message from ECU

Those are represented by the lifeline *Transactions*. Afterwards, the ECU broadcasts the transaction via the CAN bus on which other ECUs listen.

In case that the status message is not security or safety related, the ECU broadcasts it directly via the CAN bus.

The corresponding sequence diagram is given in Fig. 2.

4.3   Step 2: Verify Transaction

As mentioned before, other ECUs are listening on the CAN bus for new transactions. When an ECU receives a transaction, it needs to be verified prior to being accepted. The verification process consists of two steps: First, using the public key of the sender, the ECU verifies the signature of the message. In case that the verification fails, the message will not be further processed. Otherwise, the ECU checks the plausibility of the status message using reference values or specific algorithms. For example, a ECU can compare values of different sensors. If the verification succeeds, the ECU adds the transactions to the list of transactions to be added to the blockchain.

When reaching a certain threshold which is defined by a given number of transactions to be added to the blockchain, the ECU proposes a new block. It requests the last block and the list of transactions and calculates the corresponding hash for the new block. Last, the ECU adds the new block to its own copy of the blockchain and broadcasts via the CAN bus.

In case the verification fails, the ECU broadcasts an error. We show the corresponding sequence diagram in Fig. 3.

4.4   Step 3: Update Blockchain

Whenever a new block has been broadcasted, each ECU has to update its own copy of the blockchain. Before accepting a new block, the ECU has to verify the block itself and the contained transactions. For verifying a transaction, we use the procedure as described in the second step. When the transactions and the hash for the proposed block are valid, the ECU appends the proposed block to its copy of the blockchain. When a block is not valid, it is not processed further, and the ECU broadcasts an error message. We show the corresponding sequence diagram for the last step in Fig. 4.

Since each ECU now holds a redundant and validated copy of all status messages in form of transactions in the blockchain, all ECUs works on the same data set, and there is no single point of failure. The data set can be used for machine learning of algorithms, and for accident forensics. Assuming that a real-time processing of the blockchain is possible, the architecture can also be used to realize a MooN safety architecture. The blockchain validation process works with majority voting, and broadcasted error messages can be used to identify malfunctioning of equipment.

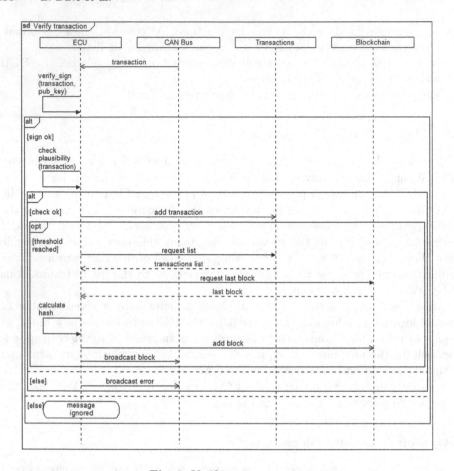

Fig. 3. Verify status message

5 Discussion

In the following, we discuss the results we obtained from our proposed architecture.

5.1 Performance and Scalability

One of the main drawbacks of using blockchains inside vehicles is the increasing need for computational power. We suggest to focus on security and safety-relevant status messages and to combine a certain number of those messages into one block. The reduced number of transactions and block will limit the required computational power and required storage capacity.

Another approach can be to use *Trusted Platform Modules (TPM)* for cryptographic operations, e.g. hash calculation and creating Message Authentication Codes (MACs) as specified in the *TPM Automotive Thin Profile* [12].

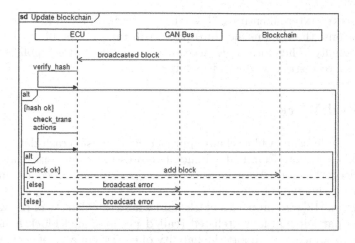

Fig. 4. Add block

For inserting a block into the blockchain, we suggest using *Proof-of-Stake*. In contrast to *Proof-of-Work*, which is for example used by Bitcoin, the required computational power is limited, because the different ECUs do not compete in proposing new blocks. Calculating a hash for a new block does not require to solve cryptographic puzzles.

Last, we suggest using our framework for future autonomous vehicles. Due to the various sensors and real-time algorithms which processes the measured values, those vehicles provide higher storage capacity and more computational power than current vehicles.

5.2   Safety and Security

Our blockchain-based framework focusses on preserving integrity for security and safety-related status messages which are broadcasted via the CAN bus in vehicles. The processes we described in Sect. 4 include plausibility checks and message signatures for those messages. Those checks ensure that only valid data is further processed by the blockchain and other ECUs. Furthermore, the history of received messages provided by the blockchain ensures that those messages cannot be manipulated by compromising a single ECU or by injecting malicious status messages. To manipulate the blockchain, it is necessary to perform a 51% attack which means that an attacker has to compromise more than half of ECUs.

5.3   Privacy

Since blockchain-based architectures store a history of messages which cannot be altered or partially deleted anymore, it raises the need for considering privacy aspects, as well. Autonomous cars process sensitive data like GPS coordinates. Since we only use blockchain for internal vehicle communication, those data is not processed to external entities. Nevertheless, in case of accidents or for maintenance reasons, the responsible third party will take a copy of the blockchain, at least partially. Therefore, it is necessary to define privacy policies for the blockchain or to restrict access to the data.

6 Related Work

Cebe et al. [3] describe a blockchain approach for forensic crash data investigation. For this, e.g. data from traffic lights, tire pressure, wiper state, and vehicle speed are used. The authors make use of an externally shared ledger which does not allow to verify the vehicle's data.

Oham et al. [13] also propose a blockchain where the identity of the validators or even the participants is whitelisted (called permissioned blockchain) in the vehicle's environment to support the liability of entities in case of accidents. The focus of the proposed architecture lies on liability attribution for entities such as car manufacturers in case of an accident.

Ugwu et al. [4] state that neither with the blockchain in [3] nor with the blockchain in [13] the proof of vehicle state is possible. In this paper, the authors suggest proving the state of the sensors in a smart vehicle by tracking the changes in the state of the smart vehicle's sensors and to record changes in the blockchain. The approach still requires a trusted authority for maintaining the externally shared ledger. Additionally, the approach requires a permanent connection to this authority in case of an accident to transmit the vehicle's state information.

Dorri et al. [14] propose a distributed blockchain-based framework to address security and privacy in interconnected smart vehicles. The authors state several use cases for their framework, e.g. car-sharing services or central payment for the power consumption of electric vehicles. Privacy-related information such as location data is still stored locally inside the vehicle and is not transferred to the public blockchain. Therefore, the benefits of the approach for accidents forensics is limited. The locally stored data can still be modified.

There is a new initiative called *Mobility Open Blockchain Initiative (MOBI)*[1] in which several well-known OEMs and suppliers take part. The aim of this group is to elaborate on blockchain-based solutions in the vehicle's environment.

To the best of our knowledge, there is no related work considering blockchain architectures inside vehicles. Our blockchain-based architecture may be considered as an extension to verify the vehicle's data for the above-mentioned works.

An alternative to using a blockchain is a realization with cryptographic methods as described in CC PPs (Common Criteria Protection Profiles) being already available for the Digital Tachograph [15] consisting of a Smart Card (Tachograph Card), the External GNSS Facility, the Motion Sensor, and the Vehicle Unit. This PP shows the potential structure for the realization of a device collecting information for insurances to collect data relevant for accident forensics. Advantages

---

[1] https://www.t-systems.com/at/de/newsroom/blog/automotive/automotive/blockchain-technologie-fuer-fahrzeuge-823460.

of using a blockchain are the synergies to safety, the redundant storage and that for a successful attack several ECUs have to be compromised.

7 Conclusion

In this paper, we proposed a blockchain-based architecture for autonomous vehicles to combine safety and security aspects. Using a blockchain ensures the integrity of security and safety-relevant status messages of electronic control units (ECUs). The recorded history of messages can be exploited for accident forensics and machine learning.

A distinguishing feature of our approach is that we store the blockchain internally and make use of the existing CAN bus infrastructure. Existing approaches only describe the usage of external blockchains which do not ensure integrity of data inside vehicles.

Furthermore, using internal storage solutions for the blockchain improves the privacy of the car owner and driver since the data will not be made available for third parties. We described a high-level algorithm in detail to perform message authentication and plausibility checks in our framework that ensures that ECUs add only valid data to the blockchain.

As future research directions, we will implement a prototype of our proposed architecture to assess its performance and therefore its scalability. The obtained results will further be used to develop a suitable consensus algorithm.

In addition, our approach complements orthogonal work on accident forensics. Making parts of our blockchain accessible to external authorized third parties will improve several use cases, e.g., insurances can benefit from the integrity of data provided by the car. Therefore, we will elaborate on combining external blockchain solutions (cf. Sect. 6) with our approach.

References

1. Miller, C., Valasek, C.: Securing self-driving cars (one company at a time), August 2018. http://illmatics.com/carhacking.html
2. Tesla: Tesla Blog - What we know about the last weeks accident. https://www.tesla.com/de_DE/blog/what-we-know-about-last-weeks-accident. Accessed 15 Jan 2019
3. Cebe, M., Erdin, E., Akkaya, K., Aksu, H., Uluagac, S.: Block4forensic: an integrated lightweight blockchain framework for forensics applications of connected vehicles. IEEE Commun. Mag. 56(10), 50–57 (2018)
4. Ugwa, M.C., Okpala, I.U., Nwakanma, C.I.: A tiered blockchain framework for vehicular forensics. IJNSA 10(5), 36 (2018)
5. Nakamoto, S.: Bitcoin: A peer-to-peer electronic cash system (2008). https://bitcoin.org/bitcoin.pdf
6. Wood, G.: Ethereum: a secure decentralised generalised transaction ledger. Ethereum Proj. Yellow Pap. 151, 1–32 (2014)

7. Kiayias, A., Russell, A., David, B., Oliynykov, R.: Ouroboros: a provably secure proof-of-stake blockchain protocol. In: Katz, J., Shacham, H. (eds.) CRYPTO 2017. LNCS, vol. 10401, pp. 357–388. Springer, Cham (2017). https://doi.org/10.1007/978-3-319-63688-7_12
8. Cavicchioli, M.: When will ethereum's proof of stake arrive? November 2018. https://cryptonomist.ch/en/2018/11/01/when-will-ethereums-proof-of-stake-arrive/
9. Ebert, C., Jones, C.: Embedded software: facts, figures, and future. Computer 42(4), 42–52 (2009)
10. International Organization for Standardization - ISO Geneva, Switzerland: Road vehicles - Controller area network (CAN) series (2015)
11. Regler, R., Schlinkheider, J., Maier, M., Prechler, R., Berger, E., Pröll, L.: Intelligent electrics/electronics architecture. ATZextra Worldwide 15(11), 246–251 (2010)
12. TCG: TCG TPM 2.0 Automotive Thin Profile (2018). https://trustedcomputing-group.org/resource/tcg-tpm-2-0-library-profile-for-automotive-thin/
13. Oham, C., Kanhere, S., Jurdak, R., Jha, S.: A blockchain based liability attribution framework for autonomous vehicles (2018)
14. Dorri, A., Steger, M., Kanhere, S.S., Jurdak, R.: Blockchain: a distributed solution to automotive security and privacy. IEEE Commun. Mag. 55(12), 119–125 (2017)
15. European Commission DG JRC: Common Criteria Protection Profile - Digital Tachograph, May 2017. https://www.commoncriteriaportal.org/search/?cx=016233930414485990345

Enhancing CAN Security by Means of Lightweight Stream-Ciphers and Protocols

Aymen Boudguiga[1,4]([✉]), Jerome Letailleur[2,4], Renaud Sirdey[1,4], and Witold Klaudel[3,4]

[1] CEA-LIST, 91191 Gif-sur-Yvettes, France
{aymen.boudguiga,renaud.sirdey}@cea.fr
[2] Prove & Run, 75017 Paris, France
jerome.letailleur@provenrun.com
[3] Renault, 78288 Guyancourt, France
witold.klaudel@renault.com
[4] IRT SystemX, 91120 Palaiseau, France
{aymen.boudguiga,jerome.letailleur,renaud.sirdey,
witold.klaudel}@irt-systemx.fr

Abstract. The Controller Area Network (CAN) is the most used standard for communication inside vehicles. CAN relies on frame broadcast to exchange data payloads between different Electronic Control Units (ECUs) which manage critical or comfort functions such as cruise control or air conditioning. CAN is distinguished by its simplicity, its real-time application compatibility and its low deployment cost. However, CAN major drawback is its lack of security support. Indeed, CAN does not provide protections against attacks such as intrusion, injection or impersonation. In this work, we propose a framework for CAN security based on Trivium and Grain, two well-known lightweight stream ciphers. We define a simple authentication and key exchange protocol for ECUs. In addition, we extend CAN with the support of confidentiality and integrity for at least critical frames.

Keywords: Controller Area Network · Confidentiality · Integrity

1 Introduction

With the advent of autonomous vehicles and intelligent transportation systems, vehicle embedded architectures will evolve to support more Advanced Driver Assistance Systems (ADAS) and wireless car-to-car and car-to-infrastructure connectivity. However, the combination of wireless connectivity and automatic driving capabilities creates new threats for vehicle and driver safety, and raises new challenges for securing car embedded network.

A vehicle internal network interconnects around a hundred Electronic Control Units (ECUs) [1]. This network is formed by various communication buses such

© Springer Nature Switzerland AG 2019
A. Romanovsky et al. (Eds.): SAFECOMP 2019 Workshops, LNCS 11699, pp. 235–250, 2019.
https://doi.org/10.1007/978-3-030-26250-1_19

as automotive Ethernet and Controller Area Network (CAN) bus [2]. Different CAN buses can be deployed inside the same vehicle to group ECUs with respect to their functionalities. For example, a vehicle may embed dedicated CAN buses for infotainment, comfort and powertrain management.

In practice, CAN buses are accessible through the On-Board Diagnostics (OBD) plug. This plug provides access to diagnostics features necessary for cars control and troubleshooting, or for new services such as the pay how you drive service provided by some insurance companies. In some cases, white hats aimed at tuning their own cars performances. For example, they modified the engine ECU configuration to increase engine power or reduce its fuel consumption. Meanwhile, black hats aimed for car theft, and attacks targeting drivers and passengers safety by attacking critical ECUs became more and more plausible.

CAN attacks have been already demonstrated in literature. In 2008, Hoppe et al. [3] performed a successful attack against the ECU that lifts windows. Meanwhile, Nilsson and Larson [4] presented a virus to eavesdrop messages over the CAN bus. In 2010, Koscher et al. [5] successfully ran attacks such as CAN sniffing, CAN spoofing and malware installing on safety related ECUs. They noticed that no security mechanisms were applied during software updates. In 2011, Checkoway et al. [6] extended the analysis to external attack surface on a modern vehicle. Their results were again alarming. Indeed, they compromised a car radio using a tampered CD. They even controlled the car telematics via a call to a car integrated cellular phone. Then, they were able to unlock car doors and inhibit anti-theft measures. In Black Hat 2015, Miller and Valasek demonstrated how they hacked a Jeep Cherokee ECUs via a remote exploit. They controlled the steering, braking, acceleration and display systems [7]. Recently, in Black Hat 2017 and 2018, the team of Keen Security Lab hacked remotely into Tesla Autopilot ECU, analyzed its CAN frames and got control of the steering system [8].

In this work, we rely on lightweight stream ciphers to provide CAN payloads confidentiality and integrity. Indeed, we investigate the possible use of Trivium [9] and Grain [10], two well-known and respected stream ciphers, for ECUs authentication, payloads encryption and message authentication codes. Note that Trivium and Grain are part of the eSTREAM hardware portfolio. That is, Trivium and Grain are naturally suited for hardware implementation in electronic boards with restricted resources. However, they are also amenable to highly software implementations.

The remainder of the paper is organized as follows. Section 2 reviews CAN main features. Section 3 describes the state of the art regarding CAN authentication, key distribution and intrusion detection. Section 4 presents our chosen attacker model and the list of considered attacks on CAN bus. Section 5 depicts in details our proposed security framework for CAN. Finally, Sect. 6 gives implementation results.

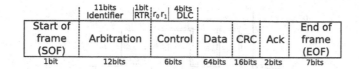

Fig. 1. CAN Data frame

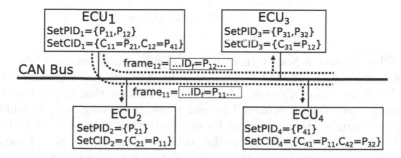

Fig. 2. CAN Data frames transmission

2   Controller Area Network

The Controller Area Network (CAN) connects Electronic Control Units (ECUs) via a broadcast bus. Each ECU is in charge of controlling actuators or sensors. ECUs communicate by exchanging CAN frames of the following types: Data, Remote, Error or Overload. Data frames exchange data between ECUs. Remote frames request the transmission of a specific Data frame. Remote frames have the same format as Data frames (Fig. 1). However, they have a *recessive* Remote Transmission Request (RTR) field and an empty payload. Error frames warn about the existence of errors on the CAN bus. Finally, Overload frames serve to delay next frames transmission.

CAN frames do not contain information about their source or destination. They do not rely on interface addressing. In practice, each ECU manages a limited set of *unique* and *distinct* frame identifiers (Fig. 1). A frame identifier (ID_f) distinguishes a unique payload information that interests a set of receivers. We call ID_f *producer* the node broadcasting Data frames having a given ID_f. Meanwhile, we refer by ID_f *consumers* to the nodes reading Data frames containing a given ID_f. The consumers of frames produced by an ECU_i form a unique set of consumers $SetConsumers_i$. Consumers can belong simultaneously to different sets of consumers associated to different producers.

We denote by $SetPID_i = \{P_{i1}, \ldots, P_{in}\}$ the set of Data frames identifiers that are produced by ECU_i. Meanwhile, we define as $SetCID_i = \{C_{i1}, \ldots, C_{in}\}$ the set of Data frames that are consumed by ECU_i. That is, C_{ik} corresponds to a frame identified with $ID_f = P_{jl}$ and produced by a distinct $ECU_{j,j \neq i}$, i.e. $C_{ik} = P_{jl}$ and $ECU_i \in SetConsumers_j$. Figure 2 depicts an example of frame transmission on the CAN bus.

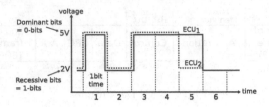

Fig. 3. CAN bitwise arbitration

CAN bits respect a Non-Return to Zero (NRZ) coding where 0-bits and 1-bits are encoded with different non-null voltage. The value of a transmitted bit is sampled at the end of a *nominal bit time* i.e. a bit time slot. In practice, CAN 0-bits are referenced as *dominant* bits and 1-bits as *recessive* bits. In addition, *bit stuffing* is applied to the start of frame, arbitration, control, data and CRC fields of a CAN frame (Fig. 1). Bit stuffing consists on inserting a complementary bit after five consecutive bits of same value. For example, we insert a 1-bit after the transmission of 5 0-bits. The only exception to bit stuffing are the Error and Overload frames which are identified by flags of 6 consecutive bits of same polarity.

CAN relies on CSMA/CA with a *bitwise arbitration* as bus access method. The bitwise arbitration concerns the value of frame identifiers. When two ECUs start the delivery of two different frames at the same time, the ECU sending the frame with the greatest ID_f value stops its transmission at the reception of a dominant bit while it is transmitting a recessive bit. In Fig. 3 example, ECU_2 stops the transmission of its frame after detecting a dominant bit transmission at time slot 5 while transmitting a recessive bit. Consequently, ECU_1 keeps the channel for itself and frame collision is avoided.

3   CAN Network Security

The CAN bus is well-suited for *real time* applications where data transmission delay is a concern. The real time constraint and the small size of Data frame payload (64-bits) make the introduction of security mechanisms in CAN specification a challenging problem. The integration of cryptographic algorithms to provide message integrity and confidentiality is complex. On the one hand, it is impossible to use *asymmetric* cryptography to provide ECUs authentication and frames integrity or confidentiality. Indeed, the output length of asymmetric signature and encryption algorithms is longer than one CAN payload i.e. 64-bits. For example, RSA signature length is at least 1024-bits while ECDSA signature length is at least 160-bits. Consequently, not only the number of CAN frames needed to send a signature increases but also data processing and transmission time raises due to signature verification time. On the other hand, the use of *symmetric* cryptography for ECUs authentication in a broadcast context has to thwart the insider attack. The use of a shared key for an authentication within a group of nodes is deprecated because any node can impersonate as the key owner and compute valid Message Authentication Codes (MACs). Sharing a symmetric key between more than two nodes does not provide non-repudiation property.

In 2008, Oguma et al. [11] proposed a polynomial key distribution scheme to share pairwise keys between all ECUs. They relied on a master ECU to authenticate other ECUs and to provide them with a session secret. The secret is used later during ECUs pairwise authentication. Oguma et al. solution provides anti-replay attacks thanks to the use of counters. It also avoids malware installation by including a proof of authenticity for each ECU ROM code. In 2009, Szilagyi and Koopman [12] proposed to pre-share pairwise keys between ECUs. Then, a frame producer concatenates in the frame payload as many MACs as receivers. For example, if the frame payload contains 32 bits of data and the number of the frame consumers is equal to 4, then the 32 remaining bits of the payload will contain 4 concatenated MACs, each 8 bits long. Each MAC is computed with the pairwise key that is shared with the corresponding consumer. Schweppe et al. [13] used symmetric keys and MACs to provide CAN frames authenticity. They used truncated MACs of 32 bits long. They were the pioneers to define a Hardware Security Module (HSM) for keys secure storage and tagging. They associated a tag to every key to indicate either it was needed for signing or for verifying a signature. As such, they thwarted the insider attack.

In 2012, Woi and Sangionvanni-Vincentelli [14] relied on pairwise keys and MACs to provide CAN frames authenticity. They sent a separate signed CAN frame to each consumer. In addition, they included a counter in the frame payload to prove its freshness. To avoid counter rollover problem, they sent only the Least Significant Bits (LSB) of the counter in the CAN frame. Meanwhile, they kept secret the counter Most Significant Bits (MSB). A frame consumer accepts frames with a counter value superior to its local one. Groza et al. [15] proposed a master/slave model to distribute keys between ECUs. Slaves must register to the master to get their symmetric keys. Once keys are received, frame producer concatenates MACs, destined to the frame consumers, in the same frame payload. In 2013, Groza and Murvay [16] used key chains and time synchronization to implement a broadcast authentication protocol. Their solution was inspired from the TESLA protocol [17].

All the aforementioned solutions rely on pairwise keys and MACs to mutually authenticate ECUs. Meanwhile, other work investigated Intrusion Detection Systems (IDS) for the CAN bus. For example, in 2010, Hoppe et al. [18] described three intrusion detection patterns for CAN networks. The first pattern evaluates the frequency of messages. The second pattern studies the possible misuse of frame identifiers. The last pattern learns the communication characteristics of each ECU. Examples of such characteristics are fingerprints of transmitted signals. This last approach requires a training phase to learn all ECUs communication characteristics. In 2011, Kleberger et al. [19] defined two intrusion detection methods: specification-based and anomaly-based. The specification-based detection evaluates deviations from CAN specification and ECUs expected behavior. It was investigated in depth by Larson et al. [20]. The latter implemented in each ECU a dedicated entity called the *detector* to spot any deviation from CAN

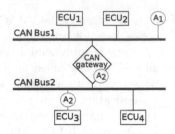

Fig. 4. Attacker position in CAN bus

specification. Meanwhile, the anomaly-based detection estimates deviations regarding the number of transmitted messages. It refers to Hoppe et al. [18] analysis of messages frequency. Hoppe et al. [21] defined also a method for an adaptive dynamic reaction to incidents in in-vehicle network via visual, acoustic or haptic notifications.

In 2016, Boudguiga et al. [22] made each legitimate ECU register periodically with other ECUs using a new authentication frame. Then, the registered ECU monitors the CAN bus to check that no Data frames are being sent on its behalf. That is, the authenticated ECU checks if received Data frames do not contain one of its own frame identifiers. In case of attack, the ECU erases the intruder frame by sending an Error frame. Then, it notifies other ECUs about the detected intrusion. The same idea was proposed later by Nurnberger and Rossow [23] for bus monitoring against spoofing attacks. In addition, they added an authentication message following each critical frame using Keccak for HMAC calculus.

In 2019, Groza et al. [24] exploited the fine-grained control of timers in CAN to design a time-covert authentication and intrusion detection system. They succeeded in embedding at most 20 bits of a truncated hash in delays, and showed an interesting detection rate of impersonation attacks. Bella et al. [25] added a 24-bit long MAC to each 40-bit of CAN payload. In addition, they encrypted with AES-128 all the CAN payloads. As such, as such they provided frames integrity and confidentiality.

4   CAN Attacker Model

In this work, we consider a Dolev and Yao attacker model [26]. That is, the attacker is able to Read, Drop and Send valid CAN frames. A Read action refers to receiving or intercepting frames. Meanwhile, a Send action refers to forging and replaying frames. A Drop action refers to frame filtering. The attacker can connect to the CAN bus at different points as presented in Fig. 4. Attackers A_1 and A_2 target all the ECUs. In practice, attacker A_1 can be a simple malware installed on a diagnostic plug connected to the OBD interface. Such plugs are provided by insurers for the *Pay How You Drive* service where driving data are used for customized insurance fees computation. Meanwhile, the attacker A_2 can be a malware installed on a CAN gateway that isolates a whole CAN bus, or it may target only one ECU as presented in Fig. 4. That is, A_2 is not only able to read and send frames on behalf of ECU_3 but she can also filter and drop frames going to or coming from ECU_3. In practice, isolating one ECU requires mastery of vehicle architecture and getting physical access to vehicle's buses.

In this work, we are interested in the following attacks on CAN bus:

- **Sensitive data spoofing:** As CAN buses are more and more exposed to external services such as the Pay How You Drive service, it is compulsory to provide the confidentiality of sensitive frames. By sensitive frames, we refer to frames containing data reflecting personal driving style or data exchanged by critical ECUs.
- **Denial of Services attack (DoS):** we distinguish two types of DoS: BUS DoS and ECU DoS. BUS DoS is a trivial attack aiming at preventing ECUs from accessing the CAN bus. The attacker has just to connect to the bus and send a sequence of dominant bits, Error frames or fake Data frames with priority identifier to monopolize the channel. Consequently, she prevents legitimate ECUs from sending frames. For autonomous vehicles in a C-ITS context, a BUS DoS attack immobilizes the vehicle. In risk analysis, we talk about an attack having an *Operational* impact [27–30]. That is, this attack affects the returned quality of service of the vehicle and so the manufacturer corporate image. In practice, BUS DoS cannot be thwarted.

  ECU DoS attack targets a unique ECU. For example, the attacker installs a malware in the Brake ECU (BCU) or floods it with wrong frames to put it out of service. This attack has a *Safety* impact. If it succeeds, the attacked vehicle will have no brakes and driver and passengers lives will be threatened. ECU DoS attacks via malwares are avoided by using secure software updates, secure boot and disabling ECU debug interfaces. In this work, we consider ECU DoS attacks via flooding with malicious frames.
- **Impersonation attack:** consists in usurping the identity of a legitimate ECU logically or physically. That is, the attacker can impersonate as an ECU by sending frames on its behalf. Or, it can replace the legitimate ECU i.e. the hardware with a fake ECU. For example, the attacker can impersonate as the decisional ECU i.e. the vehicle control unit (VCU) for autonomous vehicles. Then, it sends braking orders to BCU.
- **Isolation attack:** consists in isolating an ECU by dropping and filtering all the frames going to or coming from it. Isolation attack is only executed by A_2. It can be catastrophic when it targets vital ECUs such as BCU.

5   CAN Security Framework

Our security framework relies on a lightweight stream-cipher for ECUs authentication, key exchange, and frames payload encryption and authentication. A stream-cipher maintains an internal state which is initialized after a warm-up with a secret key and an initialization vector.

In this work, we consider two lightweight stream-ciphers: Trivium [9] and Grain-128a [10]. Table 1 depicts the size in bits of keys, initialization vectors and

242 A. Boudguiga et al.

Table 1. Stream-ciphers configuration

Stream-cipher	Trivium	Grain-128a
Key length (in bits)	80	128
IV length (in bits)	80	96
State length (in bits)	288	256
Warm-up rounds number	1152	256

internal states for Trivium and Grain-128a, respectively. In addition, Table 1 gives the number of rounds needed for Trivium and Grain-128a warm-ups. That is, the number of rounds until initializing the stream-cipher internal state.

In the sequel, we define a set of functions required for our protocol definition.

- $n \leftarrow \text{length}(v)$: returns the size in bits n of the input v. For example, this function will return the size of the key (key_A) and the initialization vector (iv_A) of the stream-cipher A.
- $r \leftarrow \text{rng}(l)$: generates a random number r of size l in bits. rng can be a software pseudo-random generator or a hardware true random generator.
- $s \leftarrow \text{warmUp}_A(k, iv)$: takes as inputs a key (k) and an initialization vector (iv) and returns the stream-cipher internal state (,) after warm-up.
- $k' \leftarrow \text{genStream}_A(s, l)$: takes as inputs the stream-cipher internal state and the desired output size in bits l and outputs k'. That is, A is clocked l-times to output l bits. In addition, this function *updates* the stream-cipher internal state at every iteration (i.e. bit computation).
- $c \leftarrow \text{encr}_A(s, m)$: takes as input the stream-cipher internal state and the message to be encrypted m and outputs a ciphertext c. Encryption consists in generating with A a stream (k') having the same length in bits as m and then XOR it with m to get c.
- $m \leftarrow \text{decr}_A(s, c)$: takes as input the stream-cipher internal state and the message to be decrypted c and outputs a plaintext m. Decryption consists in generating with A a stream (k') having the same length in bits as c and then XOR it with c to get m. Successful decryption requires a synchronization between the encrypting and decrypting entities. That is, they must share the same value of the internal state before encryption and decryption, respectively.
- $mac \leftarrow \text{computeMac}_A(s, m)$: takes as input the stream-cipher internal state and a message m and outputs a message authentication code (mac) corresponding to m. We rely on Grain-128a authentication method [10] to compute mac. Grain-128a authentication method is compatible with any stream-cipher and outputs a 32-bit long mac.

5.1 Authentication and Key Management

We rely on a dedicated ECU, called authentication control unit (ACU), for ECUs authentication and keys derivation at vehicle start-up. First, the driver authenticates to ACU with vehicle key/card using the key anti-theft protocol. The latter is secretly developed by the car manufacturer and is out-of-scope of this work. If the authentication succeeds, ACU sends a *Wake-up* signal to other ECUs. The latter are kicked-off and respond with a *Ready* signal. After noticing that ECUs woke-up, ACU starts their authentication. ACU authenticates frame producers and their consumers starting from most critical ECU to least critical ones. By critical ECUs, we refer to ECUs controlling vital functions of the vehicle such as the engine controller, the automatic braking system controller or the automatic cruise controller. As such, when a critical ECU fails to authenticate to ACU, the vehicle will not start and driver will receive an alert concerning the origin of the failure.

Keys Management. ACU shares a distinct long term symmetric key (LTK_i) with each ECU_i. Long term keys serve for ECUs authentication at vehicle start-up. Long term keys are often stored in a tamper resistant memory[1]. Once a frame producer ECU_i and its consumers $ECU_j \in SetConsumers_i$ are authenticated, the ACU provides them with a session key (SK_i) and a session initialization vector (SIV_i). The latter will serve later for frames encryption or/and authentication with the chosen stream-cipher.

One can argue that ACU is a single point of failure, and that sharing different group keys between frame a producer ECU_i and its consumers ($SetConsumers_i$) is more interesting, as we do not rely on a dedicated key management server. Imagine now that a producer ECU_i or an $ECU_j \in SetConsumers_i$ is removed from vehicle due to a technical problem and is changed by a new microcontroller. A new group key will have to be burned on ECU_i and $SetConsumers_i$ for security reasons. However, changing keys in microcontrollers that are already connected to the vehicle architecture is not practical at all, especially when keys are stored in tamper resistant memories. Consequently, we argue that having a dedicated server for key management in a vehicle embedded architecture is a the most appropriate architectural choice.

ECUs Authentication. When a vehicle is started, each ECU_i authenticates to ACU using the protocol of Fig. 5. To authenticate mutually, ECU_i and ACU engage on a challenge-response protocol where challenges are c_1 and c_2, and responses are r_1 and r_2, respectively. The exact responses are only generated with the stream-cipher A after a warm-up with the shared long term secret key LTK_i and a fresh initialization vector. We assume that each ECU_i and ACU share a secret counter ctr_i. A fresh initialization vector for the stream-cipher warm-up is computed per authentication as the XOR of ctr_i, c_1 and c_2. So, ctr_i has the same size in bits of the initialization vector of the stream-cipher.

Session Keys Establishment. At the end of the authentication, ACU and ECU_i generate simultaneously a session key $SK_i = genStream_A(s, length(key_A))$

---

[1] All new automotive microcontrollers come with a secure memory area dedicated to keys storage. Freescale McKinley, Infineon AURIX or Boundary Devices Nitrogen6X and Sabrelite are examples of such microcontrollers.

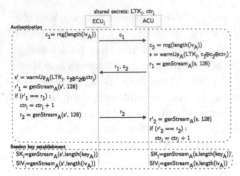

Fig. 5. Authentication of a frame producer (ECU_i)

Fig. 6. Authentication of a frame consumer ($ECU_j \in SetConsumers_i$)

and a session initialization vector $SIV_i = genStream_A(s, length(iv_A))$, where s is the updated value of the stream-cipher internal state. Then, ACU shares SK_i and SIV_i with the frame consumers of ECU_i. That is, ACU authenticates each $ECU_j \in SetConsumers_i$, then shares with it SK_i and SIV_i (as presented in Fig. 6).

When ECU_i and $ECU_j \in SetConsumers_i$ receive SK_i and SIV_i, they run $warmUp_A(SK_i, SIV_i)$ to get (S_i), the internal state associated to the current session. ECU_i and $ECU_j \in SetConsumers_i$ will use S_i to generate later key streams for encrypting and providing the integrity of CAN frames as presented in Sect. 5.2.

For every session (i.e. from a vehicle start-up until its complete stop), ACU maintains a database indexed by ECUs identifiers. It stores SK_i and SIV_i associated to a frame producer ECU_i (Table 2). The stored data are compulsory for ECUs synchronization, for example after a microcontroller reboot due to a dysfonction (detailed in Sect. 5.2).

5.2 Secure CAN Frames Exchange

In this work, we add frame security to two types of CAN frames: critical and private frames. Critical frames deliver information regarding critical functions such as braking and accelerating. Meanwhile, private frames transport driver sensitive data that reflect her driving style or her vehicle personal configuration.

Table 2. ACU database of session data

ECU		Long term data		Session specific data	
Identifier	Consumers	Long term key	Counter	Session initialization vector	Session key
...					
ECU_i	$SetConsumers_i$	LTK_i	ctr_i	SIV_i	SK_i
...					

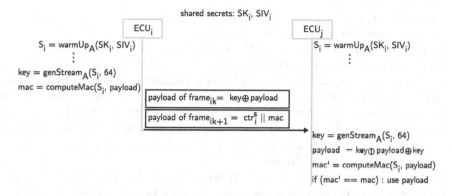

Fig. 7. CAN secure frame exchange

For every critical CAN frame, we add an integrity frame that contains a 32-bit MAC computed with the computeMAC() function. The added frame will have as identifier the original frame identifier incremented by 1. That is, if the original frame identifier value is n, its associated integrity frame identifier will be $n + 1$. As such, we ensure to frame consumers the reception of the integrity frame directly after the original frame. Consequently, they check promptly the integrity of the data they have just received.

For private CAN frames, we propose to encrypt the frame payload before adding an integrity frame. Encryption ensures the confidentiality of the payload. Meanwhile, the integrity frame ensures that the payload has not been tampered with. Figure 7 depicts an example of a private frame exchange between a frame producer ECU_i and one of its consumers ECU_j.

In addition, we introduce a 32-bit long counter ctr_i^s that we concatenate to the mac value to create the payload of the integrity frame. ctr_i^s reflects the number of bits (or bytes or 32-bit words) that have been generated since the stream-cipher warm-up with SK_i and SIV_i. It serves for $ECU_j \in SetConsumers_i$ synchronization with the producer ECU_i. Indeed, if the ECU_j local counter $ctr_{i,j}^s$ is inferior to the one provided in the integrity frame ctr_i^s, ECU_j will be clocked $\left(ctr_i^s - ctr_{i,j}^s\right)$ times to get the same internal state S_i as ECU_i.

5.3 Security Analysis

– **CAN sensitive data spoofing:** As sensitive frames are encrypted with the chosen stream-cipher, their payloads are no more accessible for attackers A_1 and A_2. The adversary has to get the session key SK_i and the session initialization vector SIV_i to compute the session internal state S_i of the stream-cipher and then to generate the necessary streams for frame decryption. However, to get SK_i and SIV_i, the adversary must break the authentication scheme, or recover the long term secret LTK_i and the counter ctr_i shared between ACU and ECU_i. Breaking the authentication scheme is equivalent to breaking the stream-cipher. Meanwhile, getting LTK_i corresponds to a successful attack against ACU or ECU$_i$, granting a privileged access to the tamper-resistant memory where the long term key is stored.

- **Impersonation attack:** As CAN critical or private frames are followed by their corresponding integrity frames which authenticate their contents, an adversary A$_1$ or A$_2$ will not be able to impersonate a legitimate ECU$_i$. Identity usurpation will work if the adversary succeeds in getting the session internal state required for streams generation to compute valid MACs. Or as discussed previously, getting the session internal state S$_i$ requires breaking the authentication protocol. Of course, A$_1$ and A$_2$ can still impersonate as producers of non-critical frames.

- **Isolation attack:** our proposed extension to the CAN protocol does not provide countermeasure to an isolation attack which is carried by attacker A$_2$ (Fig. 4). Indeed, A$_2$ controls all the data flow of its target. Consequently, she can still drop packets going to or coming from targeted ECUs without being noticed. However, she will not be able to impersonate as a critical frame producer. One way to avoid frames dropping is acknowledging the reception of frames.

- **Denial of Services attack (DoS):** our proposed CAN security framework avoids ECU DoS attacks via malicious frames. Indeed, the transceiver of a frame consumer will check the integrity of a received CAN frame before transferring its content to the application layer for treatment.

  We do not provide a countermeasure to ECU DoS with flooding. However, our solution is compliant with state of the art solutions targeting flooding. For example, our proposed ECUs authentication, key distribution and MAC computation can be directly integrated with Nurnberger and Rossow [23] or Boudguiga et al. [22] intrusion detection method where a legitimate ECU monitors a CAN bus to detect attackers sending frames on its behalf. In addition, when combined with these solutions, our framework provides security against impersonation attacks targeting non-critical frame producers.

- **Replay attacks:** our proposed security framework avoids replay attacks. Replayed frames are detected, by the frame consumer, as coming from an intruder because the frame freshness counters would be invalid.

5.4   Performance Analysis

In this section, we discuss the performance results of CAN frames encryption and their MAC computation with Trivium and Grain128a. Although initially included as part of the hardware profile of the eSTREAM portfolio, Trivium and Grain128a also allow efficient sofware implementations.

On high-end platforms, the so-called bitslicing parallelization technique can be used to boost the algorithm's performances by multiplexing either as many IV or as many keys (depending on the use-case) as there are bits in the processor registers. Table 3 provides typical performances of bitsliced implementation of Trivium on an Intel processor. Most notably, using AVX registers and instructions, the algorithm can reach 22.4 Gbits/s (when AES-128 using AES-NI ISA extensions runs at around 5.6 Gbits/s on these platforms) translating in 0.79

Table 3. Software performances of bitsliced implementations of Trivium on *one* Intel i5-5200U core 2.2 Ghz.

# slices	State size	Throughput
8	288 bytes	1 Gbit/s
64	2304 bytes	7.5 Gbit/s
256	$\approx$1 Mo	22.4 Gbit/s

cycle per keystream byte (when e.g. SOSEMANUK requires 4 to 9 cycles per keystream byte)[2]. On these kinds of platforms, Trivium is therefore a solution of choice to either achieve very high throughput (through IV-multiplexing) or serve many users or devices (through key-multiplexing). The same results apply to Grain128a.

Bitslicing can be used by ACU for managing many ECUs authentications simultaneously, at vehicle start.

In addition, Trivium and Grain128a admit fairly efficient compact 8-bit and 32-bit software implementations suitable for more constrained platforms. Indeed, let us consider the example of Trivium, since it takes 64 (bit-level) cycles for the re-injection of t_3 to have an effect on t_1 [9], up to 64 cycles can be performed in parallel leaving the possibility for byte-oriented, 32-bit-word-oriented and 64-bits-word-oriented implementations requiring only 36 bytes of memory for the internal state (slightly more for 64-bits implementations as 288 is not a multiple of 64) when AES-128 (say in CTR mode) would require 192 bytes (counter plus key schedule). The same analysis applies to Grain128a.

We present in Table 4 the performance results obtained with our custom Trivium and Grain128a 8-bit and 32-bit implementations when encrypting a CAN payload (i.e. 64 bits) and computing its corresponding MAC (32-bit MAC). We run our code on a Boundary Device Nitrogen6X and a Freescale QorIQ LS1021.

We notice from Table 4 that the 32-bit implementations of Trivium and Grain128a have an acceptable computation time when compared to OpenSSL optimized implementations of AES-128 and HMAC (i.e. optimized with threading and hardware acceleration support). That is, a single primitive (i.e. a stream-cipher) can be used for ECUs authentication, frame encryption and MAC computation while providing interesting computation times.

---

[2] Note that same SIMD instruction sets exist also for ARM architecture. They are called Scalable Vector Extension (SVE).

Table 4. Performance analysis of CAN frames encryption and authentication with stream-ciphers

Algorithm	Task	Computation time (in micro-seconds)	
		Nitrogen6X	QorIQ LS1021
Trivium-8-bit	frame encryption	16.954	19.774
Trivium-8-bit	MAC computation	22.455	25.005
Trivium-32-bit	frame encryption	3.128	2.224
Trivium-32-bit	MAC computation	6.252	5.051
Grain128a-8-bit	frame encryption	9.549	8.890
Grain128a-8-bit	MAC computation	16.690	15.507
Grain128a-32-bit	frame encryption	2.312	2.006
Grain128a-32-bit	MAC computation	5.758	5.262
AES-128-CBC	frame encryption	3.251	2.578
AES-128-CTR	frame encryption	2.948	2.449
HMAC-SHA1	MAC computation	6.483	6.305

6   Conclusion

We investigate in this paper the possible use of stream-ciphers (e.g. Trivium and Grain128a) for enhancing CAN security. We propose a simple ECUs authentication protocol and provide confidentiality and integrity for CAN critical and private frames. In addition, we demonstrate through simulations that stream-cipher performance for CAN frames encryption and authentication can be attractive when compared to classical algorithms such as AES and HMAC.

Our future work consists in proving formally the security of the proposed authentication protocol after specifying a formal attacker model. In addition, we will extend our performance analysis by the evaluation of: (1) frames encryption and authentication success/failure rates and (2) CAN throughput and transmission time when encryption and integrity are added to frames.

References

1. Robert, C.: This car runs on code. http://spectrum.ieee.org/transportation/systems/this-car-runs-on-code
2. Bosch: CAN Specification Version 2.0, September 1991
3. Hoppe, T., Kiltz, S., Dittmann, J.: Security threats to automotive CAN networks - practical examples and selected short-term countermeasures. In: Proceedings of the 27th International Conference on Computer Safety, Reliability, and Security (SAFECOMP 2008) (2008)
4. Nilsson, D.K., Larson, U.E.: Simulated attacks on CAN buses: vehicle virus. In: Proceedings of the Fifth International Conference on Communication Systems and Networks (AsiaCSN 2008) (2008)

5. Koscher, K., et al.: Experimental security analysis of a modern automobile. In: Proceedings of the 2010 IEEE Symposium on Security and Privacy (2010)
6. Checkoway, S., et al.: Comprehensive experimental analyses of automotive attack surfaces. In: Proceedings of the 20th USENIX Conference on Security
7. Schneider, D.: Jeep hacking 101
8. Tencent Keen Security Lab: Experimental security research of tesla autopilot
9. De Cannière, C., Preneel, B.: TRIVIUM. In: Robshaw, M., Billet, O. (eds.) New Stream Cipher Designs. LNCS, vol. 4986, pp. 244–266. Springer, Heidelberg (2008). https://doi.org/10.1007/978-3-540-68351-3_18
10. Ågren, M., Hell, M., Johansson, T., Meier, W.: Grain-128a: a new version of grain-128 with optional authentication. IJWMC 5, 48–59 (2011)
11. Oguma, H., Yoshioka, A., Nishikawa, M., Shigetomi, R., Otsuka, A., Imai, H.: New attestation based security architecture for in-vehicle communication. In: IEEE Global Telecommunications Conference (GLOBECOM 2008) (2008)
12. Szilagyi, C., Koopman, P.: Flexible multicast authentication for time-triggered embedded control network applications. In: 2009 IEEE/IFIP International Conference on Dependable Systems Networks (2009)
13. Schweppe, H., Roudier, Y., Weyl, B., Apvrille, L., Scheuermann, D.: Car2X communication: securing the last meter -A cost-effective approach for ensuring trust in Car2X applications using in-vehicle symmetric cryptography. In: 4th IEEE International Symposium on Wireless Vehicular Communications (WiVeC 2011) (2011)
14. Lin, C. W., Sangiovanni-Vincentelli, A.: Cyber-security for the Controller Area Network (CAN) communication protocol. In: 2012 International Conference on Cyber Security (CyberSecurity 2012) (2012)
15. Groza, B., Murvay, S., van Herrewege, A., Verbauwhede, I.: LiBrA-CAN: a lightweight broadcast authentication protocol for controller area networks. In: Pieprzyk, J., Sadeghi, A.-R., Manulis, M. (eds.) CANS 2012. LNCS, vol. 7712, pp. 185–200. Springer, Heidelberg (2012). https://doi.org/10.1007/978-3-642-35404-5_15
16. Groza, B., Murvay, S.: Efficient Protocols for secure broadcast in controller area networks. IEEE Trans. Industr. Inf. 9(4), 2034–2042 (2013)
17. Perrig, A., Canetti, R., Song, D., Tygar, J.D.: Efficient and secure source authentication for multicast. In: 2001 Network and Distributed System Security Symposium, pp. 35–46 (2001)
18. Hoppen, T., Kiltz, S., Dittmann, J.: Security threats to automotive CAN networks-Practical examples and selected short-term countermeasures. Reliab. Eng. Syst. Saf. 96(1), 11–25 (2011)
19. Kleberger, P., Olovsson, T., Jonsson, E.: Security aspects of the in-vehicle network in the connected car. In: 2011 IEEE Intelligent Vehicles Symposium, pp. 528–533, June 2011
20. Larson, U., Nilsson, D., Jonsson, E.: An approach to specification-based attack detection for in-vehicle networks. In: 2008 IEEE Intelligent Vehicles Symposium, pp. 220–225, June 2008
21. Hoppe, T., Kiltz, S., Dittmann, J.: Adaptive dynamic reaction to automotive IT security incidents using multimedia car environment. In: Fourth International Conference on Information Assurance and Security (ISA 2008) (2008)
22. Boudguiga, A., Klaudel, W., Boulanger, A., Chiron, P.: A simple intrusion detection method for controller area network. In: 2016 IEEE International Conference on Communications (ICC), pp. 1–7, May 2016

23. Nürnberger, S., Rossow, C.: – vatiCAN – Vetted, authenticated CAN bus. In: Gierlichs, B., Poschmann, A.Y. (eds.) CHES 2016. LNCS, vol. 9813, pp. 106–124. Springer, Heidelberg (2016). https://doi.org/10.1007/978-3-662-53140-2_6

24. Groza, B., Popa, L., Murvay, P.-S.: INCANTA - INtrusion detection in controller area networks with time-covert authentication. In: Hamid, B., Gallina, B., Shabtai, A., Elovici, Y., Garcia-Alfaro, J. (eds.) CSITS/ISSA -2018. LNCS, vol. 11552, pp. 94–110. Springer, Cham (2019). https://doi.org/10.1007/978-3-030-16874-2_7

25. Bella, G., Biondi, P., Costantino, G., Matteucci, I.: TOUCAN: a protocol to secure controller area network. In: Proceedings of the ACM Workshop on Automotive Cybersecurity, AutoSec 2019, pp. 3–8. ACM, New York (2019)

26. Dolev, D., Yao, A.: On the security of public key protocols. IEEE Trans. Inform. Theory **29**, 198–208 (1983)

27. ETSI TS 102 893 v1.1.1: Intelligent Transport Systems (ITS); Security; Threat, Vulnerability and Risk Analysis (TVRA). ETSI WG5 Technical report, pp. 1–29, March 2010

28. Henniger, O., Apvrille, L., Fuchs, A., Roudier, Y., Ruddle, A., Weyl, B.: Security requirements for automotive on-board networks. In: 2009 9th International Conference on Intelligent Transport Systems Telecommunications, pp. 641–646, October 2009

29. Monteuuis, J.P., Boudguiga, A., Zhang, J., Labiod, H., Servel, A., Urien, P.: Sara: Security automotive risk analysis method. In: Proceedings of the 4th ACM Workshop on Cyber-Physical System Security, CPSS 2018, pp. 3–14. ACM, New York (2018)

30. Boudguiga, A., Boulanger, A., Chiron, P., Klaudel, W., Labiod, H., Seguy, J.C.: RACE: risk analysis for cooperative engines. In: 7th International Conference on New Technologies, Mobility and Security (NTMS 2015) (2015)

Analysis of Security Overhead in Broadcast V2V Communications

Mujahid Muhammad[1][(✉)] [iD], Paul Kearney[1] [iD], Adel Aneiba[1] [iD],
and Andreas Kunz[2]

[1] Birmingham City University, Birmingham, UK
mujahid.muhammad@mail.bcu.ac.uk,
{paul.kearney,adel.aneiba}@bcu.ac.uk
[2] Lenovo, Oberursel, Germany
akunz@lenovo.com

Abstract. This paper concerns security issues for broadcast vehicle to vehicle (V2V) messages carrying vehicle status information (location, heading, speed, etc.). These are often consumed by safety-related applications that e.g. augment situational awareness, issue alerts, recommend courses of action, and even trigger autonomous action. Consequently, the messages need to be both trustworthy and timely. We explore the impact of authenticity and integrity protection mechanisms on message latency using a model based on queuing theory. In conditions of high traffic density such as found in busy city centres, even the latency requirement of 100 ms for first generation V2V applications was found to be challenging. Our main objective was to compare the performance overhead of the standard, PKC-based, message authenticity and integrity protection mechanism with that of an alternative scheme, TESLA, which uses symmetric-key cryptography combine with hash chains. This type of scheme has been dismissed in the past due to supposed high latency, but we found that in high traffic density conditions it outperformed the PKC-based scheme. without invoking congestion management measures. Perhaps the most significant observation from a security perspective is that denial of service attacks appear very easy to carry out and hard to defend against. This merits attention from the research and practitioner communities and is a topic we intend to address in the future.

Keywords: V2V · Security · Performance · Queuing theory

1 Introduction

The term Intelligent Transportation System (ITS) covers a range of advanced road transport applications. These include safety related services employing direct radio communications between vehicles (V2V) and between vehicles and roadside infrastructure (V2I), which are included in the topic of Connected Vehicles (CV) in the US and Cooperative ITS (C-ITS) in Europe.

In the US, Society of Automotive Engineers (SAE) International has defined standard J2735 [1] covering the format, structure and contents of V2V and V2I messages. Sixteen message types are listed, plus provision for regionally defined text

© Springer Nature Switzerland AG 2019
A. Romanovsky et al. (Eds.): SAFECOMP 2019 Workshops, LNCS 11699, pp. 251–263, 2019.
https://doi.org/10.1007/978-3-030-26250-1_20

messages. The main type of concern to this paper is the Basic Safety Message (BSM), which is broadcast by vehicles to provide status information (location, heading, speed, etc.) to other vehicles in the vicinity. The information is utilized by a variety of applications in receiving vehicles to (in conjunction with data from on-board sensors and other sources) to augment the driver's situational awareness, issue alerts, recommend courses of action, and potentially to trigger autonomous action. By default, BSMs are broadcast 10 times per second.

In Europe, ETSI has published two related standards:

- EN 302 637-2 [2] gives the specification of a Co-operative Awareness Basic Service including the syntax and semantics of the Cooperative Awareness Message (CAM).
- EN 302 637-3 [3] does likewise for a Decentralised Environment Notification (DEN) Basic Service and the associated DEN Message (DENM).

Like BSMs, CAMs provide vehicle status data and are broadcast periodically. The CAM transmission frequency can be varied between 1 and 10 Hz depending on conditions. In contrast DENMs are alerts that are sent when particular events occur. Broadly speaking, BSMs and CAMs are comparable, and work is going on to align the two standards. The typical latency requirement for CAMs from first-generation use cases such as Forward Collision Warning and Emergency Vehicle Warning is better than 100 ms. For next generation use cases such as Vehicle Platooning, the requirement reduces to 10 ms and for Autonomous Driving, as low as 1 ms.

Clearly, the utility of the applications built on the V2V messaging services depends critically on the timeliness and trustworthiness of the received messages. These two concerns are linked in that measures taken to protect and assure the integrity and authenticity of a message consume time and tie up resources, thereby increasing the time taken to deliver a message. The main purpose of this paper is to examine the trade-off between security and timeliness, and to compare the performance of different approaches to security. In particular, we address the question of whether utilization of a derivative of the Timed Efficient Stream Loss-tolerant Authentication (TESLA) protocol [4] is a viable alternative to the prevailing solutions based on Public-Key Cryptography (PKC). Note that this paper is only concerned with the per-message overhead of the schemes. We recognise that longer-timescale issues such as certificate distribution and revocation and/or renewal in the case of PKC and key-chain generation and distribution of initial commitments in the case of TESLA are also germane, and these will be addressed in subsequent papers.

There are two main families of network infrastructure that have been proposed to support V2V message transmission. The one that has been around longest and is arguably better-established uses WiFi technology based on the IEEE 802.11p standard running in the 5.9 GHz frequency band. Its use is specified by the Dedicated Short-Range Communication (DSRC) collection of standards in the US and by ITS-G5 within the European Cooperative ITS initiative in the EU. The second, which its proponents argue to be the better long-term bet, is known as Cellular-V2X (C-V2X) and is being defined by the 3GPP consortium as an extension to its mobile network architecture. In C-V2X, longer-range communications are sent via the cellular network, but shorter-range, low latency communications utilize the so-called PC5 interface (also known as the sidelink channel). PC5 messages are sent directly over the air and not via the cellular network. In this paper, we mainly consider C-V2X PC5 communications, but the basic issues and conclusions apply to both families.

The paper is structured as follows. After discussion related work, we outline the model based on queuing theory that we have used. We briefly describe the C-V2X PC5 mode with network managed resource allocation and derive an appropriate choice of model parameters to describe its behaviour. We then examine a traffic scenario corresponding to a busy city centre and the necessity for congestion management. The next sections compare the performance overheads of the standard, PKC based authenticity and integrity protection scheme and one based on the TESLA protocol. The main finding is that there is no clear winner: PKC prevails at low message traffic densities, and TESLA when they are high. There then follows a discussion of the implications of the study and recommendations for future work. Of particular concern is the potential for disruption of V2V messaging by denial of service attacks that are simple to carry out and difficult to defend against.

2 Related Work

Queuing theory has been used widely to model telecommunication systems including vehicular networks. The authors of [5] proposed an analytical model describing the performance of periodic broadcasts in vehicular ad hoc networks, in terms of packet collision probability and average packet delay. A comprehensive $M/M/\infty$ model of vehicular traffic dynamics over a roadway, with intermittently connected networks is presented in [6]. Also, the work of [7] describes analytical models to assess how queue length estimation at an intersection is influenced by the percentage of probe vehicles in the traffic stream. A discrete time $D/M/1$ model for analysing the performance periodic broadcast in VANETS is presented in [8]. The model shows numerical results of packet collision probability and average packet delay. In [9], the authors utilise an $M/M/m$ queuing model to evaluate the probability that a vehicle finds all channels busy, and to derive the expected waiting times.

None of these works has modelled the security overhead for broadcast messages and its effect on the system performance. In the study presented, the overheads of PKC- and TESLA-based security mechanisms have been modelled and compared in a saturated vehicular traffic condition. A further difference from previous works is that we consider LTE-V2V as the network technology used, and specifically the variant exploiting in-coverage operation where the radio resources are assigned to transmitting vehicles by the infrastructure.

3 A Simple Queuing Theory Model

The delivery of a broadcast message has three main stages. First, the message is composed and formatted ready for transmission, then it is broadcast, and finally it is received and decoded/interpreted by all the receivers in range. All three steps involve shared use of finite resource. In the first and third steps, the resource is a processor assumed to be able to process one message at a time, and in the second step it is the wireless medium. There are numerous strategies for sharing the available bandwidth among transmitters, but ultimately its message-carrying capacity is finite.

If a message arrives at a resource and finds it is busy, then it must either be added to a queue to wait its turn, or else it will be lost. Conversely, if a resource finishes processing one message and finds its queue empty, then it will be idle until the next message arrives. Increasing the average message arrival rate makes it more likely that a given message will find the resource busy, and so the average queue length and time spent in the queue will grow. However, the greater the average queue length, the less likely that the resource will be idle, so that more messages will be processed per unit time. Provided that the average message arrival rate is less than the capacity of the resource, an equilibrium will be reached such that on average, input and output rates are equal. The higher the throughput, the greater will be the queue length and the longer the time taken.

The simplest model of a queuing system is a memoryless continuous time Markov chain denoted in so-called Kendall notation as an M/M/1 model. In an M/M/1 queuing system, the is no limit on the length of the queue, the queuing discipline is 'first come first served', the distributions of message arrival intervals and of time take to process a message are both exponential, and there is a single processing resource. In such a case, the average time a message spends in the system (including time spent being processed) and the average queue length are respectively:

$$T = 1/(\mu - \lambda) \text{ and } L = \lambda T = \lambda/(\mu - \lambda)$$

where λ is the average message arrival frequency and μ is the average rate at which messages can be processed by the resource. Notice that there is a singularity when $\lambda = \mu$ indicating that the steady state equilibrium model breaks down and the values of T for $\lambda \geq \mu$ have no physical meaning. Performance targets will not typically be expressed in terms of averages, but rather as expectations regarding exceptions to the norm. It is also useful, therefore, to consider the time within which a fraction x of messages is likely to be processed:

$$T_x = -\ln(1 - x)/(\mu - \lambda) \tag{1}$$

Note that $T_{1-1/e} = T$.

As shown in Fig. 1, we model each of the three stages mentioned above as such an M/M/1 queuing system, so that the average end-to-delay is given by:

$$T_{Total} = T_S + T_T + T_R + A; \tag{2}$$

$$T_S = 1/(\mu_S - \lambda); \quad T_T = 1/(\mu_T - N\lambda); \quad T_R = 1/(\mu_R - N\lambda);$$

Where the subscripts S, T and R stand for Sender, Transmission and Receiver respectively, N is the number of vehicles within reception range and A is a constant term added for generality. λ is the rate at which messages are generated by applications in each of the N vehicles. The multiplicative factor N is applied to the message traffic

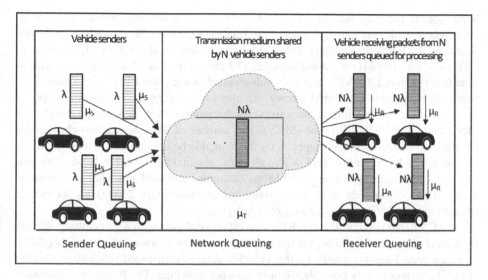

Fig. 1. End-to-end queuing delay model

flowing through the transmission medium as it is shared by all vehicles, and to that for reception because each message is received by all vehicles.

We assume that the message processing times have a component proportional to message length and a fixed component independent of length, so that:

$$\mu_i = 1/(\mathrm{l}r_i + c_i); i = \ \mathrm{S}, \mathrm{T}, \mathrm{R} \tag{3}$$

where l is the message length in bytes, r_i is the time to process one byte and c_i is the additional per-message processing time. Message authenticity and integrity measures affect both message length and the per-message processing time.

4 Network-Specific Issues

3GPP started work on Vehicle to Everything (V2X) in its Release 14 [10], utilizing the Long Term Evolution (LTE) radio and Evolved Packet Core (EPC) for message transmission for the different scenarios Vehicle to Vehicle (V2V), Vehicle to Infrastructure (V2I), Vehicle to Network (V2N) and Vehicle to Pedestrian (V2P). V2V reused the previously defined PC5 interface for mission critical subscribers (Proximity Services [11]) and made it applicable for public usage in vehicles, but in a different radio band. Currently work in 3GPP is ongoing to specify V2X for the 5G system [12].

LTE-V2V is based on the uplink Physical and Medium Access Control (MAC) layer radio network protocols of LTE. Thus, it utilizes Orthogonal Frequency Division Multiplexing at the Physical layer and Single Carrier Frequency Division Multiple Access at the MAC layer. A given LTE physical channel is divided into smaller fragments, both in time and frequency, which are referred to as frames. Every LTE frame is 10 ms wide in the time domain and its length is equal to the system bandwidth in the frequency domain. LTE-V2V supports 10 MHz and 20 MHz channels, where each channel is divided into frames, Resource Blocks (RBs), and sub-channels. An RB is the smallest unit of frequency resources that can be allocated to an LTE user. It is 180 kHz wide in frequency (12 sub-carriers of 15 kHz) and one slot in time (i.e. 0.5 ms). LTE-V2V defines a sub-channel as a group of RBs in the same sub-frame. Sub-channels are shared among vehicles for the transmission and reception of messages. The number of data bits carried by the group of RBs depends on the chosen Modulation and Coding Scheme (MCS). The number of RBs in each sub-channel for the transmission of messages depends on the available bandwidth and by configuration of the network. A typical LTE-V2V physical channel of 20 MHz bandwidth can support a maximum data rate of 50 Mbps (assuming 16QAM modulation scheme is used). This corresponds to a transmission of approximately 21,000 messages per second, given a safety message size of 300 bytes.

In PC5-based communication. RBs may either be allocated to a transmitting vehicle by a local element of radio access network infrastructure known as an eNodeB (eNB), or else selected autonomously by the vehicles using a distributed scheduling scheme [13]. The former is only possible when in network coverage. The following discussion applies to the case where RBs are allocated by an eNB.

As shown in Fig. 2, in Mode 3, a vehicle V_S with data to transmit sends a scheduling request to the eNB and receives an allocation of slots in return. Vs then begins transmission after a so-called alignment time, defined as the waiting time for decoding the received scheduling grants and processing the packets ready for transmission. Time advances in units referred to as the transmission time interval (TTI = 1 ms). The total time elapsed between V_s sending a scheduling request and being able to begin transmission is 9TTI, i.e. 9 ms. This contributes a fixed increment to the overall delay, i.e. it is part of A in Eq. (2) above. The value can, however, be reduced using a semi-persistent scheduling technique whereby the grant of a resource block remains valid for a period of time, so that a new request is not needed for every message.

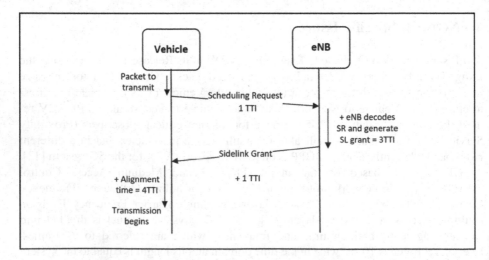

Fig. 2. Network-assisted sidelink resource allocation procedure

5 Congestion Management

We used a simulation of a busy city centre scenario following a method detailed in [14] to obtain an initial 'worst case' assumption of 400 for the number of vehicles within the awareness range of a receiver. Combining this with the default message frequency of 10 messages per second per vehicle gives $N\lambda = 4000$ messages per second, meaning that both μ_T and μ_R must be much greater than this figure to avoid the rapid rise in latency and queue length as the singularities are approached. An estimate for transmission resource capacity of 21000 messages per second was given above, yielding $N\lambda/\mu_T \approx 0.2$. However, if the receiver capacity just meets the C-V2X requirement [15] of being able to process one message in 2 ms, $N\lambda/\mu_R = 8$, which is well outside the region of validity of the queuing model.

Both the SAE and ETSI message standards provide for congestion management mechanisms For example, SAE J2945/1 [16] includes a congestion control algorithm that includes adaptive functions for calculation of Inter-Transmission Time (ITT) and transmission power for BSMs. To adjust the ITT, each vehicle keeps track of the number of other vehicles within 100 m. If this exceeds a threshold value, then the ITT is increased linearly until a maximum value is reached. This corresponds to the message transmission frequency decreasing from 10 Hz to 1.6 Hz. Similarly, the transmission power decreases from 20 dBm to 10 dBm as the 'channel busy ratio' grows from 50% to 80%, which results in fewer vehicles being within reception range. The ETSI CAM standard is less prescriptive but provides for a reduction in CAM generation frequency from the nominal 10 Hz to 1 Hz. A reduction of the message generation frequency to 1.6 Hz and of vehicles in range to 60 would result in $N\lambda/\mu_R \approx 0.2$.

6 The Overhead of Authenticity and Integrity Protection

Both the US and EU ITS schemes use PKC as described in IEEE standard 1609.2 to provide source authentication, data integrity and non-repudiation in vehicular communication. This solution involves signing a message using ECDSA (Elliptic Curve Digital Signature Algorithm), and attaching a public key certificate to each signed message to enable verification of the message at the receiving end. This process incurs a high computational cost per message for (a) signature generation by the sender and (b) verification by the receiver, although the cost is significantly reduced by use of a hardware security module (HSM) with support for ECDSA. The service rate or processing capacity of the vehicle on-board unit is reduced in consequence. There are two components to this overhead resulting respectively from:

1. The increased length of the message due to appending the signature and the certificate. This affects all three queuing systems, and
2. The per-message delay due to generation and verification of the signature by sender and receiver respectively.

Based on specification sheets of HSMs, the signature generation and verification times are estimated to be 0.125 ms and 0.5 ms. Taking 300 bytes as the basic message size, 64 bytes as the signature length and 194 bytes as the signature length, we can use (3) to estimate the per-byte processing speeds needed to meet the C-V2X requirements of $\mu_T \geq 1000$ Hz and $\mu_R \geq 500$ Hz as $r_T \approx 1.6 \times 10^{-6}$s and $r_R \approx 2.7 \times 10^{-6}$s. For simplicity we take $r_T = r_R = 1.5 \times 10^{-6}$s.

The overhead for symmetric-key cryptography (SKC) is much lower than for PKC. This is because generation and verification of a symmetric-key Message Authentication Code (MAC, not to be confused with the Medium Access Control) requires much less computation than a PKC signature, the MAC itself is shorter than a signature, and no digital signature is included. However, MACs do not provide a solution to the message integrity and authenticity requirement without a secure and efficient means of sharing symmetric keys.

Hash chain techniques potentially offer a way to combine the best of both worlds. One commonly used protocol for broadcast authentication in wireless ad hoc networks is TESLA [4]. TESLA uses an SKC MAC algorithm to protect the integrity of messages but introduces the element of asymmetry by delaying the disclosure of the secret key used. A given key may only be used by a sender to generate MACs within a well-defined time window, after which it is made public and may be used by receivers to verify the integrity of messages sent within that window. A new key is then used for the next window. A sequence of keys used by a given sender is generated such that the Nth key used is the result of applying a hash function to the N+1th key. Thus, the hash function can be used to verify a sequence of keys used by a given sender, and hence the sequence of messages it sent, provided that the first key in the sequence can reliably be attributed to that sender. The main benefits of TESLA are low computation overhead, low communication overhead, and robustness to packet loss. However, TESLA also has some shortcomings: the basic version cannot provide non-repudiation which is crucial in V2V systems; the one-way key chain has a finite length, so new chains need to be created periodically; and there is a requirement for loose synchronization between sender and receivers. All of these can be addressed, e.g. access to trusted time-stamping permits non-repudiation, and there are various options for synchronisation, which is required by cellular protocols anyway. Such measures do add complications and overheads on longer timescales that must be weighed against the infrastructure required to support the competing PKC-based approach in a comprehensive comparison. Such topics will be covered in a future paper; here we focus on the per-message overhead. As a lightweight message authentication mechanism, TESLA has been employed in several research proposals to address the security problems in V2V systems [17, 18].

In TESLA, the delayed key disclosure results in a delay before safety messages are verified. Each key is disclosed in the following safety message packet broadcast from the sending vehicle. This means that each receiver has to buffer the received messages for at least one time interval and wait for the corresponding key in the following safety message broadcast.

Comparing TESLA's performance with that of a PKC-based scheme, TESLA gains because it uses SKC (shorter messages and lighter-weight computation), but loses out because the receiving vehicle must wait a full time interval before receiving the key that enables it to verify and process a message. Clearly, the length of the time interval (Q) is crucial to whether TESLA is competitive with PKC. It must be chosen so that the vast majority of messages arrive at the receiver within the same interval in which they were sent. In order to choose an appropriate value for Q we drop the receiver term from (2) and apply the logarithmic factor from (1) with x = 0.99 to the S and T terms. This gives a conservative measure of the time taken for a message to reach the receiver that assumes 99th percentile delays at the sender and in the network and results on a choice of Q ≈ 0.012 s. This value appears as an additional contribution to A in (2) when modelling TESLA.

Figure 3 uses (2) to compare the average end-to-end delays as a function of λ for the following cases: no security (solid line), PKC security (dashed line), SKC security (dash-dot line) and TESLA (long dashes). Also shown (dotted line) is the curve corresponding to the 99th percentile sender and transmission terms for the SKC case that was used to derive a value for Q.

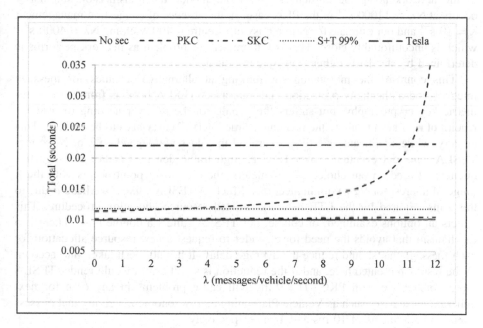

Fig. 3. Overhead from use of integrity and authenticity protection schemes

It is apparent that while the PKC overhead is small when message traffic is low, it increases rapidly when the λ/μ ratio approaches 1 for one of the queuing systems. The receiver queuing system appears to be the critical one, with a singularity at λ ≈ 12.5 for our estimated values. Notice that the TESLA curve is fairly flat whereas the PKC curve increases rapidly above λ ≈ 7 s^{-1}. The two cross around λ = 11 s^{-1}, which is close to the default rate of λ = 10 s^{-1}. Below this rate, the PKC-based mechanism is preferable, but above it incurs a severe penalty. Given the many estimates made and the simplicity of the queuing theory model, it is not wise to infer much from the exact numbers. However, it appears that a TESLA-based scheme should not be ruled out without more detailed study.

7 Discussion

It is clear from the study that V2V message latency is a serious issue for ITS, particularly for scenarios with high traffic density. For the parameter values chosen here, the main concern is with the ability of receivers to process messages sufficiently quickly. Sender performance is of much less concern as a vehicle only processes its own messages when sending, but it receives messages from all vehicles within range. Improving the receiver's per-byte processing performance helps, but when PKC is used, the time required to verify the digital signature is still large enough that the receiver delay remains the critical term. However, even if signature verification performance is considerably better than that assumed, this merely shifts the problem to one of the network being the bottleneck. With our model, the transmission singularity occurs at $N\lambda \approx 11000$ s^{-1} in the PKC case. In the absence of congestion management $\lambda = 10$ s^{-1} and our estimate for N in a busy city centre is 400, yielding $N\lambda = 4000$ s$^{-1,}$ which is uncomfortably close. This is a more serious problem as network performs is determined by standards rather than by equipment.

This confirms the motivation for looking at alternative schemes for message integrity and authenticity protection and assurance. TESLA benefits from using symmetric key cryptography, but suffers the penalty of the receiver needing to wait for receipt of new keys to allow the preceding time interval's messages to be verified. This penalty, while significant, is a fixed overhead that does not depend on λ or N, so that TESLA wins out eventually over PKC at high traffic densities and/or message frequencies. Based on our choice of parameters, the cross-over point occurs with the λ range of interest for V2V communications. Much of TESLA's fixed overhead is due to the 9 ms required by the LTE network-assisted resource allocation procedure. This affects all options examined, of course, but TESLA suffers a double dose. There is a mechanism that avoids the need for a sender to request a new resource allocation for each message that should reduce the average delay. It has not been taken into account in the results presented here, and if the reduction is significant it would render TESLA more competitive with PKC. The 9 ms will cause problems in any case for next generation use cases such as Vehicle Platooning and Autonomous Driving that possess latency requirements of 10 ms and 1 ms respectively.

Our model assumes infinite queues, which is obviously not realistic. In reality, messages would be dropped when queues reach their limit. This would alleviate the load on the receivers' resources and would reduce the latency experienced by the delivered messages at the expense of infinite latency for the dropped messages. Given the safety-relevance of many V2V applications it seems unwise to leave it to chance to decide which messages get through and which do not.

It is clear that standards organisations SAE and ETSI recognise that there is a problem as both provide mechanisms for congestion management, albeit their main concern is with the transmission resources rather than the receiving vehicles. Whether reduction of the message transmission frequency and/or transmitter power based on vehicle density is acceptable depends on the application requirements. For example, what really matters is not the message frequency or latency, but whether the receiving application has sufficiently accurate and up-to-date information. Fortunately, those scenarios in which vehicle densities are highest, such as busy city centres, are also likely to feature the lowest vehicle speeds and hence require less frequent updating of information. Intermediate density scenarios such as busy highways may offer the most challenging combination of message traffic volumes and application requirements.

The SAE and ETSI congestion management mechanisms rely on sending vehicles being co-operative—the senders must detect high vehicle density and respond by reducing transmission frequency and/or power. They can, therefore, be thwarted by senders that are non-compliant because they implement the standard badly or not at all, because they malfunction, or because they are intentionally selfish. In this last category, consider that a small minority of vehicles that continue to broadcast at high frequency and power, while the majority follow the congestion management algorithms. The selfish minority benefit from the congestion control while the lawful majority suffer the costs.

Beyond selfish behaviour there is considerable potential for malicious disruption of V2V applications. Consider a malicious agent that simply broadcasts messages at high frequency and power in order to fill up the message queues of receiving vehicles causing delays and lost messages. Conventional authenticity protection cannot help, because the cost of verifying the authenticity of messages is contributing to the vulnerability being exploited by the attacker. This type of attack is likely to become common because of the low cost and skill requirement and is extremely difficult to defend against. Until a solution is found, the deployment of safety related applications that rely on timely information from other vehicles rather than simply benefiting from it may be judged to incur too high a risk. As an example, consider vehicle platooning. If the vehicles in a convoy rely on message exchange to enable shorter inter-vehicle distances and higher convoy speeds, then a sudden denial of service could well result in a collision.

8 Conclusions

In the study presented here we have used a simple three-stage queuing theory model to explore performance issues in broadcast V2V communication. Despite its simplicity it has proved valuable in developing a qualitative understanding of performance. The model is capable of representing a variety V2V broadcast technologies. The parameter values used here were based on the LTE-V2V mode with network-allocated resource blocks. We need to extend the study to the LTE-V2V autonomous allocation mode and also to US and European wifi-based solutions, but we expect broadly-similar results.

A first observation is that in conditions of high traffic density such as found in busy city centres, even the latency requirement of 100 ms for first generation V2V applications appears challenging without invoking congestion management measures. The critical element is the queuing system representing a vehicle acting in message-reception role. This has to process messages from all vehicles within range whereas the sending queuing system only has to process outbound messages from its parent vehicle.

Our main objective was to compare the performance overhead of the standard, PKC-based, message authenticity and integrity protection mechanism with that of an alternative scheme, TESLA, which uses symmetric-key cryptography combine with hash chains. This type of scheme has been dismissed in the past due to supposed high latency, but we found that in high traffic density conditions it outperformed the PKC-based scheme. Simulation-based studies combined with benchmarking of representative equipment are needed to confirm this result and explore where the performance crossover occurs. Subject to this confirmation, the result indicates that TESLA merits deeper consideration. Subsequent papers will explore options for integration of TESLA with cellular communications standards and infrastructure. Various shortcomings of TESLA were noted in Sect. 6, and we intend as far as possible to leverage network capabilities to address them.

Perhaps the most significant observation from a security perspective arising from this study is that denial of service attacks appear very easy to carry out and hard to defend against. This merits attention from the research and practitioner communities and is a topic we intend to address in the future.

References

1. SAE International: Dedicated Short Range Communications (DSRC) Message Set Dictionary, V2X Core Technical Committee. https://doi.org/10.4271/J2735_200911
2. ETSI EN 302 637-2 V1.3.2 (2014-11), Intelligent Transport Systems (ITS); Vehicular Communications; Basic Set of Applications; Part 2: Specification of Cooperative Awareness Basic Service
3. ETSI EN 302 637-3 V1.2.2 (2014-11), Intelligent Transport Systems (ITS); Vehicular Communications; Basic Set of Applications; Part 3: Specifications of Decentralized Environmental Notification Basic Service
4. Perrig, A., Canetti, R., Tygar, J.D., Song, D.: The TESLA broadcast authentication protocol. CryptoBytes 5(2), 2–13 (2002). Summer/Fall
5. Yang, Q., Zheng, J., Shen, L.: Modeling and performance analysis of periodic broadcast in vehicular ad hoc networks. In: 2011 IEEE Global Telecommunications Conference-GLOBECOM, pp. 1–5. IEEE, 5 December 2011
6. Khabbaz, M.J., Fawaz, W.F., Assi, C.M.: A simple free-flow traffic model for vehicular intermittently connected networks. IEEE Trans. Intell. Transp. Syst. 13(3), 1312–1326 (2012)
7. Comert, G., Cetin, M.: Analytical evaluation of the error in queue length estimation at traffic signals from probe vehicle data. IEEE Trans. Intell. Transp. Syst. 12(2), 563–573 (2011)
8. Khabbaz, M.J., Fawaz, W.F., Assi, C.M.: Modeling and delay analysis of intermittently connected roadside communication networks. IEEE Trans. Veh. Technol. 61(6), 2698–2706 (2012)
9. Fowler, S., Häll, C.H., Yuan, D., Baravdish, G., Mellouk, A.: Analysis of vehicular wireless channel communication via queueing theory model. In: 2014 IEEE International Conference on Communications (ICC), pp. 1736–1741. IEEE, 10 June 2014
10. 3GPP TS 23.285, Architecture enhancements for V2X services, Release 16, V16.0.0., March 2019
11. 3GPP TS 23.303, Proximity-based services (ProSe); Stage 2, Release 15, V15.1.0., June 2018
12. 3GPP TS 23.287, Architecture enhancements for 5G System (5GS) to support Vehicle-to-Everything (V2X) services, Release 16, V0.3.0. April 2019
13. 3GPP TS 36.331, Evolved Universal Terrestrial Radio Access (E-UTRA); Radio Resource Control (RRC); Protocol specification, Release 15, V15.5.1., April 2019

14. Bazzi, A., Masini, B.M., Zanella, A.: How many vehicles in the LTE-V2V awareness range with half or full duplex radios?. In: 2017 15th International Conference on ITS Telecommunications (ITST), pp. 1–6. IEEE, 29 May 2017
15. 3GPP TS 22.186, Enhancement of 3GPP support for V2X scenarios; Stage 1, Release 16, V16.1.0., December 2018
16. SAE International: On-Board System Requirements for V2V Safety Communications, version 201603 (2016)
17. Lyu, C., Gu, D., Zeng, Y., Mohapatra, P.: PBA: prediction-based authentication for vehicle-to-vehicle communications. IEEE Trans. Dependable Secure Comput. **13**(1), 71–83 (2016)
18. Lyu, C., Gu, D., Zhang, X., Sun, S., Tang, Y.: Efficient, fast and scalable authentication for vanets. In: Wireless Communications and Networking Conference (WCNC), pp. 1768–1773. IEEE (2013)

You Overtrust Your Printer

Giampaolo Bella[1](✉) and Pietro Biondi[1,2](✉)

[1] Dipartimento di Matematica e Informatica, Università di Catania, Catania, Italy
giamp@dmi.unict.it
[2] Istituto di Informatica e Telematica - Consiglio Nazionale delle Ricerche, Pisa, Italy
pietro.biondi94@gmail.com

Abstract. Printers are common devices whose networked use is vastly unsecured, perhaps due to an enrooted assumption that their services are somewhat negligible and, as such, unworthy of protection. This article develops structured arguments and conducts technical experiments in support of a qualitative risk assessment exercise that ultimately undermines that assumption. Three attacks that can be interpreted as post-exploitation activity are found and discussed, forming what we term the Printjack family of attacks to printers. Some printers may suffer vulnerabilities that would transform them into exploitable zombies. Moreover, a large number of printers, at least on an EU basis, are found to honour unauthenticated printing requests, thus raising the risk level of an attack that sees the crooks exhaust the printing facilities of an institution. There is also a remarkable risk of data breach following an attack consisting in the malicious interception of data while in transit towards printers. Therefore, the newborn IoT era demands printers to be as secure as other devices such as laptops should be, also to facilitate compliance with the General Data Protection Regulation (EU Regulation 2016/679) and reduce the odds of its administrative fines.

1 Introduction

The era of the Internet of Things (IoT) has only just begun [1]. Electronic devices of various nature are starting to be endowed with WiFi modules that connect them to the local network. This revolution concerns both private contexts, such as peoples' houses and devices, as well as professional contexts, such as peoples' (institutional) workplaces. For example, doors, gates, power switches, heating systems, water timers, blood pressure monitors and many other devices can be connected and operated via a remotely connected computer.

However, the comfort of using such smart equipment, for example, via a smartphone while the user sits on her sofa, comes at the cost of a drastically increased risk of remote, malicious activity by some attacker. A remarkable example published these days shows an after-market, Android 6.0 car radio suffering a simple vulnerability: an unauthenticated, root-level, remote access [2]. In consequence, Costantino and Matteucci tailor a post-exploitation script that packages CAN bus traffic to vandalize the odometer of the car. Their attack

A. Romanovsky et al. (Eds.): SAFECOMP 2019 Workshops, LNCS 11699, pp. 264–274, 2019.
https://doi.org/10.1007/978-3-030-26250-1_21

assumes the attacker to have gained access to the in-vehicle network, for example through the diagnostic OBD2 port or by exploiting a vulnerability that the e-call box system of the car may have. While cars become more and more interconnected with the IoT, the researchers' assumption gets more and more realistic by the minute.

Our work concentrates on printers, devices that are still tremendously used in every context, despite a perceivable quest for a paperless revolution. We find out that a large number of printers is publicly exposed over the Internet and that, at the same time, data sent to printers is often unsecured in the sense that a printer may honour unauthenticated print jobs—remarkably, even if these are sent from a remote network thanks to the printer being visible over the Internet. Moreover, such jobs do not transfer user data confidentially, namely data will traverse the local network in the clear towards the printer.

As a consequence of the lack of authentication, printers may suffer vulnerabilities that may turn out to be exploitable even remotely; moreover, those printers may be put at stake by (local or remote) jobs that are sent repeatedly with a malicious aim. As a consequence of the lack of confidentiality, should an attacker get on any node of the local network (by exploiting a vulnerability of that node), he could intercept the print jobs sent by a legitimate user, understand and abuse them causing a data breach. If this happens in the institution where the user is employed, and the intercepted print jobs carry anyone's personal data, then EU Regulation 2016/079, the General Data Protection Regulation (GDPR) [3] states that the institution may be severely fined, as we shall see below.

Our attack resembles the mentioned one to the odometer of the car because the CAN bus also lacks authentication and confidentiality measures. In the car, the attacker leverages CAN bus traffic being in the clear to understand how the odometer would react to specific CAN frames; he can then bombard the odometer with chosen frames without any authentication hurdle. By contrast, our attack to printers appears to be more multi-faceted than that, and in fact shapes up as three different attacks, the Printjack (which stands for *printer* hi*jack*ing) family of attacks to printers.

2   Summary of the Contributions

This article evaluates some of the possible consequences of the use of raw 9100 port printing. As a start, we used a free student account on Shodan, the search engine for the IoT [4], to determine how common the bad practice of exposing public IP addresses over the Internet with a responding 9100 port is. We were surprised to find out almost three thousand occurrences in the authors' country, which we obtained by querying Shodan with:

```
port:9100 country:"IT"
```

By varying the country identifier, we continued to obtain unexpected results. Table 1 sorts European countries by their 2018 Gross Domestic Profit (GDP) [5] and reports the number of IPs with open 9100 port that are exposed over the Internet from that country, according to the data we gathered through our Shodan queries. For example, it turns out that the country with highest GDP, Germany, also exposes the highest number of devices.

Table 1. IPs with responding 9100 port per country, sorted by country's GDP

GDP	Country	IPs with responding 9100 port
1	Germany	12.891
2	Russia	9.737
3	United Kingdom	6.349
4	France	6.634
5	Italy	2.787
6	Spain	2.088
7	Turkey	835
8	Poland	1.425
9	Netherlands	4.934
10	Switzerland	624

We interpret the high numbers noted above as a widespread, publicly available, potential vulnerability. Of course, we refrained from attempting to connect to those devices for ethical reasons. It must be noted, however, that, although one can configure any service behind any port, raw printing is the default service for 9100 port, hence it is likely to be left as is. These findings give strength to the remaining contributions of this article. We define the Printjack family of attacks to printers as post-exploitation activity following the reported vulnerability:

– Printjack 1 attack: zombies for traditional DDoS (Sect. 3)
– Printjack 2 attack: paper DoS (Sect. 4)
– Printjack 3 attack: privacy infringement (Sect. 5)

We evaluate each attack using a qualitative risk assessment approach based upon the ISO/IEC 27005:2018 standard [6]. In particular, we develop structured arguments and conduct technical experiments to evaluate the *likelihood* and the *impact* of each attack with the aim of calculating the *risk level* of the attack. The calculation is based on Table 2.

To our own surprise, all Printjack attacks are found to bear risk level HIGH. Despite the inherent subjectivity of the risk assessment exercise, we are confident that it synthesises our arguments and experiments correctly as well as profitably.

This manuscript continues with a discussion of the related work (Sect. 6) and concludes by deriving lessons learned and outlining possible fixes (Sect. 7).

3   Printjack Attack 1: Zombies for Traditional DDoS

It is well known that Denial of service (DoS) perhaps is the most severe attack in the modern Internet era. The implicit loss caused by an unresponsive service can

Table 2. Evaluation of the risk level according to ISO/IEC 27005:2018

		risk impact				
		MINOR	MODERATE	MAJOR	SEVERE	CATASTROPHIC
	RARE	LOW	LOW	LOW	LOW	LOW
	UNLIKELY	LOW	LOW	MEDIUM	MEDIUM	MEDIUM
risk likelihood	POSSIBLE	LOW	MEDIUM	MEDIUM	HIGH	HIGH
	LIKELY	LOW	MEDIUM	HIGH	HIGH	EXTREME
	ALMOST CERTAIN	LOW	MEDIUM	HIGH	EXTREME	EXTREME

be enormous, and figures get continuously updated [7]. The distributed version of this attack (DDoS) sees an attacker operate a *Command and Control* server to administer a number of infected computers that are normally called *zombies* or *botnets*.

One of the implications of the IoT era is that zombies could be farmed from any interconnected device with some computational power, provided it suffers some vulnerability that would enable its remote hijacking. A recent scandal saw more than a million cameras zombied to mount a massive DDoS [8]. It is clear that the inherent performance of each zombie, which may be relatively low, is offset by the huge number of available devices.

Turning the focus back to printers, it can be noted that there exist a number of documented vulnerabilities on various printers, which can be found on the Common Vulnerabilities and Exposures (CVE) database by the MITRE [9]. These observations motivate a daunting research question: how significant is the risk that worldwide printers get exploited to mount a massive DDoS attack? We argue that risk to be high hence worthy of mitigation, and provide supporting evidence for this argument below.

3.1 Supporting Evidence

We take a stab at answering the question posed above by addressing the risk that a DDoS attack sourced from printers would take place. This can be done, in turn, by means of a qualitative risk assessment approach. There are a number of CVEs about printer vulnerabilities, precisely 179 can be found by querying the CVE database with keyword "printer" [10] and 77 by querying it with keyword "printers" [11], totalling 223 by adding up and removing intersections. In particular, we observe that a few dozens of these allow for the remote execution of arbitrary commands or code. For example, CVE-2014-3741 *"allows remote attackers to execute arbitrary commands via unspecified characters in the lpr command"* [12].

We contend that these findings, in combination with the potential for zero-day attacks, raise the attack likelihood to POSSIBLE. Similarly, the widespread reachability of the 9100 port on real printers we noted above, of nearly 50 K units only across the top ten wealthiest EU countries (Table 1), justifies a CATAS-TROPHIC attack impact. According to Table 2, the assessed likelihood and impact of the Printjack 1 attack lead to a HIGH risk level. A risk of this level must be mitigated as soon as possible.

4   Printjack Attack 2: Paper DoS

Müller et al. exhibit a proof of concept on how to mount a DoS on printers [13]. It keeps the PostScript interpreter of the printer busy forever by means of an infinite loop (based on an empty instruction and an empty exit condition). The researchers confirmed this attack on all their twenty tested printers but the HP LaserJet M2727nf, which automatically rebooted after ten minutes.

We note that raw port 9100 printing can be exploited to potentially exhaust the printing facilities of an institution. It can be done by abusing via the 9100 port any printer that becomes known through its IP address. An attacker would send repeated print jobs till the victim printer runs out of paper from all its paper trays. Looping on all institutional printers would then complete the attack. We conjecture that, in practice, a legitimate print attempt in front of a printer that processed all available paper (by printing something on each sheet and making it useless) would lead the employees to reload some paper trays. As an extreme, the institution would run out of paper should the reloads persist before the attack is found and removed.

The Printjack 2 attack is of socio-technical nature because it is rooted in people's most obvious reaction to an aborted print attempt of theirs. It would be worth conducting field studies to verify our conjecture that people would feed their printers more and more paper unless they get their printout. This is beyond our present aims; by contrast, we provide a proof of concept implementation of the technical part below.

4.1   Supporting Evidence

The technical part of the Printjack 2 attack can be easily implemented in Python as shown in Table 3. By looking at it from the inside out, we see a loop that sends each line, stored in `textlines`, of a bot ASCII file `bot.txt`, stored in `textfile`, to a printer for a thousand times. The bot could contain anything that the attacker may want to print in order to process and spoil paper sheets. The printer is identified via its IP address, and a socket connects to its 9100 port. The outermost loop ranges on the target IP addresses, which are read from file `IPs.txt`.

We run our script on our institutional LAN. More in detail, we launched it from within the network, precisely from private IP address 192.168.65.36, towards a target printer of IP address 192.168.65.59. The printer exhausted its available paper by marking each sheet with the test phrase "hacked printer!!!!". Feeding it more paper would of course continue the paper abuse because the stated one thousand threshold had not been reached yet. We had to reset the printer manually to terminate the ignominy. Our experiment can be confirmed by observing the network traffic as sniffed by Wireshark [14]. The screenshot in Fig. 1 highlights the appropriate TCP connection and the test phrase.

Reproducing the Printjack 2 attack on a large scale, by targeting remote printers, does not seem difficult although we have obviously not tried that for

Table 3. Python script for our paper DoS attack

```
import socket
f = open("IPs.txt", "r") #file containing IPs of target printers
lines = f.readlines()
for ip in lines:
        textfile = open("bot.txt", "r") #ascii file to be printed
        textlines = textfile.readlines()
        for count in range(0,1000): #number of print jobs
                s = socket.socket()
                s.connect((ip, 9100))
                for line in textlines:
                        s.send(line+"\n")
                s.close()
```

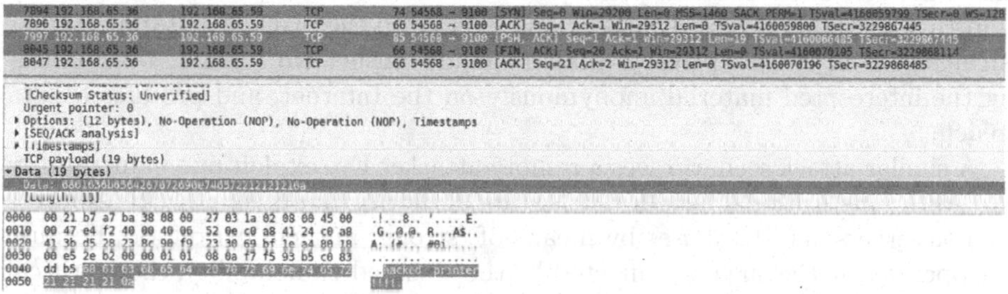

Fig. 1. The Printjack 2 attack monitored via Wireshark

ethical reasons. In a practical scenario, file IPs.txt could be built by appropriately querying Shodan. We decided to query the EU country with the highest GDP, that is, Germany. Therefore, our query was:

port:9100 country:"DE"

The results can be conveniently exported as a CSV file by paying some Shodan credits. We decided to pay one Shodan "export credit", which obtained us ten thousand entries. Our student account granted us one hundred Shodan credits for free, so it is remarkable that it was free to obtain that much information and that it would still be free to obtain (much) more. For the sake of demonstration, Table 4 shows public information, a small excerpt of the 2.3 MB file that Shodan built for us to download.

In conclusion, the public availability of remote 9100 printer ports noted above (Sect. 2), which can be practically leveraged by building tables such as Table 4, supports the claim that this attack is reproducible remotely on a large scale.

It is worth to qualitatively risk-assess also the Printjack 2 attack. Because our conjecture on the socio-technical part is yet unverified, we contend a POSSIBLE attack likelihood. However, it is evident that the attack impact is SEVERE, hence the resulting risk level is HIGH.

Table 4. An excerpt of the 10000 entry file with target IPs exported from Shodan

IP	Port
87.156.104.144	9100
79.231.20.111	9100
141.24.208.236	9100

5   Printjack Attack 3: Privacy Infringement

The treatment unfolded thus far emphasises that print jobs may be sent in the clear. Suppose that an attacker Mallory sits on the same network as some target employee Alice. This scenario is normally addressed as an *insider threat*. We note that whenever Alice sends a print job in the clear, Mallory could carry out a Man In The Middle (MITM) attack and eavesdrop the printed material, a clear infringement of Alice's privacy. Mallory could misbehave further, by publishing the intercepted material anonymously on the Internet, and produce a data breach.

A similar attack scenario sees a remote attacker Eve exploit one vulnerability into Alice's institutional network. It is state of the art to protect critical resources such as servers and databases by means of (strong) authentication. So, because Eve operates on the one node affected by the assumed vulnerability, those critical resources remain protected. By contrast, Eve could still perform the print job eavesdropping described above. Because printing is still common practice today, we cannot fully justify why data stored on a server would normally be protected and, by contrast, data sent off for printing would not.

The impact of such events would be very serious in our epoch, at least in the EU, where citizens' data protection is regulated by the GDPR. With its 99 articles, the regulation empowers people with a number of rights to be exercised over their personal data as hosted by any data controller institution. The GDPR also stresses the responsibilities of the controller, for example article 5 paragraph 2 states that *"The controller shall be responsible for, and be able to demonstrate compliance with, paragraph 1 ('accountability').",* with the mentioned paragraph 1 setting the requirement, among others, that data be *"processed in a manner that ensures appropriate security of the personal data, including protection against unauthorised or unlawful processing and against accidental loss, destruction or damage, using appropriate technical or organisational measures ('integrity and confidentiality').".* Moreover, article 83 threatens *"administrative fines up to 20 000 000 EUR, or in the case of an undertaking, up to 4 preceding financial year, whichever is higher.".*

Alice's institution has a great lot to worry about, equally because of Mallory's misconduct and because of Eve's.

5.1 Supporting Evidence

Evidence seen in Fig. 1 is valid also in the threat models embodied respectively by Mallory and Eve. In such cases, the visible traffic could be interpreted as Alice's, clearly intelligible, private data that Alice sent off for printing in a file intercepted by the attacker.

To inform a qualitative risk assessment upon the Printjack 3 attack, conducted in the following, we remark that raw port 9100 printing is massively used worldwide. For example, we observe that it is the default print method that the Common UNIX Printing System (CUPS) leverages, and that CUPS is vastly used in modern Linux distributions and Apple systems. As a demonstration, we used Ettercap [15] to interpose through sender and printer, then Wireshark to intercept the PDF file of the GDPR as from its official URL [3]. The outcome is intelligible with some decoding. The excerpt in Fig. 2 highlights in red the mentioned text of article 5 as intercepted over a print job sent from a Fedora 28 machine. It would be easy to implement a pretty-priting script.

Our print job sniffing experiments took a different course when the jobs were sent from an updated Windows 10 machine. While Müller et al. claim that Microsoft Windows printing architecture uses raw port 9100 printing by default [13], our sniffing experiments yielded no comprehensible material. Although more experiments are needed to fully scrutinise this scenario, it would seem that 9100 no longer is the default printing port on Windows, thus supporting the claim that printing is more secure from Windows machines at present than from other systems.

Nevertheless, we succeeded in intercepting the print job metadata on Windows. Figure 3 shows the metadata intercepted over port 65002, precisely fields USERNAME, USERID, HOSTID, JOBNAME as well as the printer model. Although this is less intrusive than accessing the contents of the printed file, it still counts as a data breach at least for the meaningful association of the file name to the user name. This claim rests on the socio-technical assumption that people give files meaningful names.

In light of the above experiments and collected evidence, we argue the likelihood of the Printjack 3 attack to be LIKELY and its impact to be SEVERE, hence its resulting risk level is HIGH.

6 Related Work

The most eminent piece of research in the areas of printer security and privacy is due to Müller et al. [13]. They conduct a full-breadth vulnerability assessment and penetration testing session over a range of twenty commercial printers, comparing and contrasting a number of attacks on each of them. Their work is the first to note that raw 9100 port printing may be risky.

It must be mentioned that the work by Müller et al. also led to the development of the Printer Exploitation Toolkit (PRET), which is available on GitHub [16]. However, we report that the technical parts of the Printjack family of attacks discussed above did not work using the tool against our main testbed printer, a

```
-189.179 -23.1216 Td
[(2)1(.)-1500.02[T]1[h]1[e]1( )-96.9832[c]1[o]1[n]1[t]1(
[r]1[o]1[l]1[l]1.00162[e]1[r]1( )-105.02[s]1[h]1[a]0.998278
[t]1.00162[l]1( )-97.0133[b]1[e]1.00162( )-103.976[r]1(
[e]1.00162[s]0.998278[p]1[o]1[n]1[s]1[i]1[b]1[l]-1.97819(
[e]1( )-97.9848[f]19.9857[o]1[r]39.993[,]1( )-95.9732[a]
0.998278[n]1.00162[d]1.00162( )-101.985[b]0.998278[e]
0.998278( )-97.9916[a]]TJ
185.369 0 Td
[[b]1.00162[l]0.998278[e]0.998278( )-104.011[t]1.00162(
[o]1.00162( )-90.0254[d]1.00162[e]0.998278[m]0.998278(
[o]1.00162[n]0.998278[s]1.00162[t]1.00162[r]0.998278[a]
0.998278[t]1.00162[e]0.998278( )-90.0087[c]0.998278(
[o]1.00162[m]0.998278[p]1.00162[l]0.998278[i]0.998278[a]
0.998278[n]1.00162[c]-1.98988[e]0.998278( )-90.9869[w]
0.998278[i]0.998278[t]1.00162[h]1.00162[,]1.00162(
)-103.013[p]0.998278[a]1.00162[r]0.998278[a]0.998278(
[g]1.00162[r]0.998278[a]1.00162[p]0.998278[h]-1.99656(
)-94.0218[l]1.00162( )-98.9965<28>1.00162<91>1.00162[a]]TJ
181.667 0 Td
[[c]0.998278[c]0.998278[o]1.00162[u]1.00162[n]0.998278(
[t]1.00162[a]1.00162[b]0.998278[i]-1.97652[l]0.998278(
[l]1.00162[t]1.00162[y]0.99494<92>1.00162<29>1.00162(.)
0.99494( )1.00162]TJ
```

Fig. 2. Sniffing a PDF file (containing the GDPR) as printed from Linux

```
@PJL SET STRINGCODESET=UTF8
@PJL SET USERNAME="Pietro"
@PJL SET LMULTIPAGEPRINT=OFF
@PJL COMMENT Lexmark MS620 Series XL
@PJL LJOBINFO USERID="Pietro" HOSTID="PIETRO-BIONDI"
@PJL SET LHOSTID="PIETRO-BIONDI"
@PJL SET LHOSTJOBID="2"
@PJL SET JOBNAME="myfile.pdf"
@PJL SET LCOLORMODEL=BLACK
@PJL SET RENDERMODE=GRAYSCALE
```

Fig. 3. Sniffing the metadata of a PDF file on Windows

Lexmark MS620. PRET is the newest and best developed of a small bunch of tools [17], which could not be used successfully for our purposes either.

In the same year when the research findings by Müller et al. appeared, 2017, they were sided with breaking news reporting large-scale printer hacking somewhat for fun [18], and the news was reiterated in 2018. The technical foundations behind the news remain vague, of course. Moreover, it is not obvious to what extent the research findings inspired the events outlined in the news and, vice versa, whether the news partly ignited the researchers' investigations.

7   Conclusions

There is awareness that the IoT era has only just began, and more and more devices will be connected to the Internet over time. The Printjack family of attacks demonstrates that printers are routinely *not* configured and used with security and privacy in mind. Although the IoT revolution has driven the security-and-privacy eye that we have casted at printers, it must be noted that printers started to be networked even before the inception of the IoT era, and this makes our findings all the more surprising.

In conclusion, we remark that the HIGH risk level of the Printjack 1 attack was mostly determined by its impact rather than by its likelihood. The Printjack 2 attack could be carried out both from a local attacking machine or from a remote one if the target printers are exposed over the Internet. By contrast, the Printjack 3 attack can only be mounted against a user and a printer only if the attacking machine is local to them, hence the attacker must have exploited some vulnerability over a (node of) the network.

Well beyond the technicalities of the attacks lies a clear lesson learned. Printers ought to be secured equally as other network devices such as laptops normally are. A few appropriate security measures can be envisaged. For example, if user access to a laptop is normally authenticated, then so should be user access to the web-server-based admin panel of a printer, which often allows, for example, printer reset, printer name change, access to list of printed file names, etc. Similarly, remote connection to a port of a laptop will be bound to authentication to some daemon and, likewise, sending a print job should require an extra level of authentication to the printer.

Analogous considerations apply to data normally being encrypted while in transit between computers; this leads to the idea of encrypting print jobs too. All these specifications could be implemented, for example, by enabling IPSec-only connections to printers, a feature that inexpensive printers currently offer. The reason why this feature does not seem commonly used may boil down to the traditional usability imbalance at the expenses of protection. Since appropriate technology is available to mitigate the risks of the Printjack family of attacks to printers, the biggest effort ahead of us seems to be the training of users to bear security and privacy measures also through their routine printing tasks.

Acknowledgements. We are indebted to Gianpiero Costantino and Ilaria Matteucci for arousing innumerable inspiring discussions. This work has been partially supported by the GAUSS national research project (MIUR, PRIN 2015, Contract 2015KWREMX).

References

1. Shemshadi, A., Sheng, Q.Z., Qin, Y., Sun, A., Zhang, W.E., Yao, L.: Searching for the internet of things: where it is and what it looks like. Pers. Ubiquit. Comput. **21**, 1097–1112 (2017)
2. Costantino, G., Matteucci, I.: CANDY CREAM - haCking infotAiNment anDroid sYstems to Command instRument clustEr via cAn data fraMe. In: Proceedings of the 17th IEEE International Conference on Embedded and Ubiquitous Computing EUC 2019. IEEE (2019, in press)

3. Union, E.: General Data Protection Regulation (EU Regulation 2016/679) (2016). https://eur-lex.europa.eu/legal-content/EN/TXT/PDF/?uri=OJ:L:2016: 119:FULL
4. Shodan: search engine for the Internet of Things (2019). https://www.shodan.io/
5. Wikipedia: European states by GDP. https://en.wikipedia.org/wiki/List_of_ sovereign_states_in_Europe_by_GDP_(nominal)
6. International Organization for Standardization: Information technology - Security techniques - Information security risk management (2018). https://www.iso.org/ standard/75281.html
7. Sirbu, M.: Security concerns in a 5G era: are networks ready for massive ddos attacks? (2019). https://www.scmagazineuk.com/security-concerns-5g-era-networks-ready-massive-ddos-attacks/article/1584554
8. Vice: How 1.5 Million Connected Cameras Were Hijacked to Make an Unprecedented Botnet (2016). https://www.vice.com/en_us/article/8q8dab/15-million-connected-cameras-ddos-botnet-brian-krebs
9. MITRE (2019). https://cve.mitre.org/
10. MITRE: CVE-printer (2019). https://cve.mitre.org/cgi-bin/cvekey.cgi?keyword= printer
11. MITRE: CVE-printer (2019). https://cve.mitre.org/cgi-bin/cvekey.cgi?keyword= printers
12. NIST: CVE-2014-3741 (2014). https://nvd.nist.gov/vuln/detail/CVE-2014-3741
13. Müller, J., Mladenov, V., Somorovsky, J., Schwenk, J.: SoK: exploiting network printers. In: 2017 IEEE Symposium on Security and Privacy (SP), pp. 213–230 (2017)
14. Wireshark: Wireshark project (2019). https://www.wireshark.org/
15. Ettercap: Ettercap project (2019). https://www.ettercap-project.org/
16. GitHub: Printer Exploitation Toolkit (2018). https://github.com/RUB-NDS/ PRET
17. Muller, J.: Printer Tool Wiki (2017). http://hacking-printers.net/wiki/index.php/ Main_Page
18. Vice: This Teen Hacked 150,000 Printers to Show How the Internet of Things Is Shit (2017). https://www.vice.com/en_us/article/nzqayz/this-teen-hacked-150 000-printers-to-show-how-the-internet-of-things-is-shit

2nd International Workshop on Artificial Intelligence Safety Engineering (WAISE 2019)

2nd International Workshop on Artificial Intelligence Safety Engineering (WAISE 2019)

Zakaria Chihani[1], Simos Gerasimou[2] (iD), Andreas Theodorou[3] (iD), and Guillaume Charpiat[4]

[1] CEA LIST, CEA Saclay Nano-INNOV, Point Courrier 174, 91191 Gif-sur-Yvette, France
zakaria.chihani@cea.fr
[2] Department of Computer Science, University of York, Deramore Lane, York YO10 5GH, UK
simos.gerasimou@york.ac.uk
[3] Department of Computer Science, Umeå University, Claverton Down, BA2 7AY Bath, UK
andreas.theodorou@bath.ac.uk
[4] TAU Team INRIA Saclay/LRI, Bat. 660 Université Paris Sud, 91405 Orsay Cedex, France
guillaume.charpiat@inria.fr

1 Introduction

To achieve the full potential of *Artificial Intelligence (AI)* we need to guarantee a standard level of safety and settle issues such as compliance with ethical standards and liability for accidents involving, for example, autonomous cars. Deploying AI-based systems for operation in proximity to and/or in collaboration with humans implies that current *safety engineering* and legal mechanisms need to be revisited to ensure that individuals –and their properties– are not harmed and that the desired benefits outweigh the potential unintended consequences. Researchers, engineers and policymakers from different areas of expertise will need to be engaged in this huge challenge.

The different approaches taken to *AI safety* range from pure theory (moral philosophy or ethics) to pure practice (engineering). It appears as essential to combine philosophy and theoretical science with applied science and engineering in order to create safe machines. This should become an interdisciplinary approach covering technical (engineering) aspects of how to create, test, deploy, operate, and evolve safe AI-based systems, as well as broader strategic, ethical and policy issues.

Increasing levels of AI in "smart" sensory-motor loops allow intelligent systems to perform in increasingly dynamic uncertain complex environments with increasing degrees of *autonomy*, with human being progressively ruled out from the control loop. Adaptation to the environment is being achieved by *Machine Learning (ML)* methods rather than more traditional engineering approaches, such as system modelling and programming. Recently, certain ML methods are showing promising performance and usability in real-world applications, such as deep learning, reinforcement learning, and their combination. However, the *inscrutability* or opaqueness of their statistical models for perception and decision making we build through them pose yet another challenge. Moreover, the combination of autonomy and inscrutability in these AI-based systems is particularly challenging in safety-critical applications, such as autonomous vehicles, personal care or assistive robots, and collaborative industrial robots.

The *International Workshop on Artificial Intelligence Safety Engineering (WAISE)* is dedicated to explore new ideas on AI safety, ethically aligned design, regulations, and standards for AI-based systems. WAISE aims at bringing together experts, researchers, and practitioners from diverse communities, such as AI, safety engineering, ethics, standardization, certification, robotics, cyber-physical systems, safety-critical systems, and application domain communities such as automotive, healthcare, manufacturing, agriculture, aerospace, critical infrastructures, and retail. The second edition of WAISE was held on September 10, 2019, in Turku (Finland) as part of the 38th International Conference on Computer Safety, Reliability, & Security (SAFE-COMP 2019).

2   Programme

The Programme Committee (PC) received 19 submissions, in the following categories:

- Short position papers – 7 submissions.
- Full scientific contributions – 11 submissions.
- Proposals of technical talk/sessions – 1 submission.

Each of the papers was peer-reviewed by at least three PC members, by following a single-blind reviewing process. The committee decided to accept 10 papers (3 position papers and 7 scientific papers) for oral presentation (acceptance rate 55%) and 3 for a poster presentation.

The WAISE 2019 programme was organized in three thematic sessions, with a keynote speech, and a poster session.

The thematic sessions followed a highly interactive format. They were structured into short paper pitches and a common panel slot to discuss both individual paper contributions and shared topic issues. Three specific roles were part of this format: session chairs, presenters and session discussants.

- *Session Chairs* introduced sessions and participants. The Chair moderated session and plenary discussions, took care of the time, and gave the word to speakers in the audience during discussions.
- *Presenters* gave a paper pitch in 10 minutes and then participated in the debate slot.
- *Session Discussants* prepared the discussion of individual papers and the plenary debate. The discussant gave a critical review of the session papers.

The mixture of topics has been carefully balanced, as follows:

Session 1: Machine Learning Safety and Reliability

* Improving ML Safety with Partial Specifications. Rick Salay and Krzysztof Czarnecki
* An Abstraction-Refinement Approach to Formal Verification of Tree Ensembles. John Törnblom and Simin Nadjm-Tehrani
* A Self-Certifiable Architecture for Critical Systems Powered by Probabilistic Logic Artificial Intelligence. Jacques Robin, Raul Mazo, Henrique Madeira, Raul Barbosa, Daniel Diaz and Salvador Abreu
* RL-Based Method for Benchmarking the Adversarial Resilience and Robustness of Deep Reinforcement Learning Policies. Vahid Behzadan and William Hsu

Session 2: Automated Driving

* A Safety Standard Approach for Fully Autonomous Vehicles. Philip Koopman, Uma Ferrell, Frank Fratrik and Michael Wagner
* Open Questions in Testing of Learned Computer Vision Functions for Automated Driving. Matthias Woehrle, Christoph Gladisch and Christian Heinzemann
* Adaptive Deployment of Safety Monitors for Autonomous Systems. Nico Hochgeschwender

Session 3: Uncertainty

* Uncertainty Wrappers for Data-driven Models - Increase the Transparency of AI/ML-based Models through Enrichment with Dependable Situation-aware Uncertainty Estimates. Michael Klaes and Lena Sembach
* Confidence Arguments for Evidence of Performance in Machine Learning for Highly Automated Driving Functions. Simon Burton, Lydia Gauerhof, Bibhuti Bhusan Sethy, Ibrahim Habli and Richard Hawkins
* Bayesian Uncertainty Quantification with Synthetic Data. Buu Phan, Samin Khan, Rick Salay and Krzysztof Czarnecki

The *keynote* was given by *Prof. Mario Trapp.* Mario Trapp is an apl. Professor at the Department of Computer Science of the University of Kaiserslautern and the Executive Director of the Fraunhofer Institute for Embedded Systems and Communication Technologies ESK. For many years Mario Trapp has been contributing his expertise in the development of innovative embedded systems in the context of successful partner projects, in cooperation with both leading international corporations and small and medium-sized enterprises.

The posters were the following peer-reviewed papers:

- The Moral Machine: Is It Moral? Alexandre Moreira Nascimento, Lucio Vismari, Anna Carolina Muller Queiroz, Paulo Cugnasca, Joao Camargo and Jorge Rady
- Three Reasons Why: Framing the Challenges of Assuring AI. Xinwei Fang and Nikita Johnson
- Tackling Uncertainty in Safety Assurance for Machine Learning: Continuous Argument Engineering with Attributed Tests. Yutaka Matsuno, Fuyuki Ishikawa and Susumu Tokumoto

3 Acknowledgements

We thank all those who submitted papers to WAISE 2019 and congratulate the authors whose papers were selected for inclusion into the workshop programme and proceedings. We also thank Poster presenters who kindly accepted to share their work as part of the event.

We would like to thank the Steering Committee (SC) for their support and advise to make WAISE 2019 a successful event:

- Rob Alexander, University of York, UK
- Nozha Boujemaa, DATAIA Institute & Inria, France
- Virginia Dignum, Umea University, Sweden
- Huascar Espinoza, CEA LIST, France
- Philip Koopman, Carnegie Mellon University, USA
- Stuart Russell, UC Berkeley, USA
- Raja Chatila, ISIR - Sorbonne University, France

We especially thank our distinguished PC members, for reviewing the submissions and providing useful feedback to the authors:

- Rob Alexander, University of York, UK
- Nozha Boujemaa, DATAIA Institute & Inria, France
- Virginia Dignum, Umea University, Sweden
- Huascar Espinoza, CEA LIST, France
- Philip Koopman, Carnegie Mellon University, USA
- Stuart Russell, UC Berkeley, USA
- Raja Chatila, ISIR - Sorbonne University, France
- Vincent Aravantinos, Autonomous Intelligent Driving GmbH, Germany
- Rob Ashmore, Defence Science and Technology Laboratory, UK
- Orlando Avila-García, Atos, Spain
- Alec Banks, Defence Science and Technology Laboratory, UK
- Andrew Banks, LDRA, UK
- Markus Borg, RISE SICS, Sweden
- Simon Burton, Bosch, Germany
- Jose Faria, Safe Perspective Ldt, UK
- John Favaro, INTECS, Italy

- Simon Fuerst, BMW, Germany
- Mario Gleirscher, University of York, UK
- Jérémie Guiochet, LAAS-CNRS, France
- Carlos Hernández, TU Delft, Netherlands
- José Hernández-Orallo, Universitat Politècnica de València, Spain
- Nico Hochgeschwende, DLR, Germany
- Edith Holland, Jaguar Land Rover, UK
- Bernhard Kaiser, ANSYS, Germany
- Guy Katz, Hebrew University of Jerusalem, Israel
- Philippa Konmy, Adelard, UK
- Philip Koopman, Carnegie Mellon University, USA
- Timo Latvala, Space Systems Finland, Finland
- Loizos Michael, Open University Cyprus, Cyprus
- Chokri Mraidha, CEA LIST, France
- Jonas Nilsson, Nvidia, Sweden
- Philippa Ryan, Adelard, UK
- Mehrdad Saadatmand, RISE SICS, Sweden
- Rick Salay, University of Waterloo, Canada
- Erwin Schoitsch, Austrian Institute of Technology, Austria
- Hao Shen, Fortiss, Germany
- François Terrier, CEA LIST, France
- Mario Trapp, Fraunhofer ESK, Germany
- Ilse Verdiesen, TU Delft, Netherlands
- Zakaria Chihani, CEA LIST, France
- Simos Gerasimou, University of York, UK
- Andreas Theodorou, Umeå University, Sweden
- Guillaume Charpiat, Inria, France

We thank Mario Trapp for the interesting talk. Finally, yet importantly, we thank the SAFECOMP organization for providing an excellent framework for WAISE.

Three Reasons Why: Framing the Challenges of Assuring AI

Xinwei Fang and Nikita Johnson[✉]

Department of Computer Science, University of York, York, UK
{xinwei.fang,nikita.johnson}@york.ac.uk

Abstract. Assuring the safety of systems that use Artificial Intelligence (AI), specifically Machine Learning (ML) components, is difficult because of the unique challenges that AI presents for current assurance practice. However, what is also missing is an overall understanding of this multidisciplinary problem space. In this paper, a model is given that frames the challenges into three categories which are aligned to the reasons why they occur. Armed with a common picture of where existing issues and solutions "fit-in", the aim is to help bridge cross-domain conceptual gaps and provide a clearer understanding to safety practitioners, ML experts, regulators and anyone involved in the assurance of a system with AI.

Keywords: Machine Learning · Safety · Assurance · Sensors

1 Introduction

There are several advantages of adopting systems which use machine learning (ML) components. These advantages range from improving mobility in the automotive industry to innovative uses in industrial control and hazardous zones. It seems that very few safety-critical domains remain unaffected by this trend.

Whilst the scale and rate of adoption of ML is novel, the underlying ML technologies, such as Artificial Neural Networks, are not. Nor are many of the safety assurance challenges we face when using artificial intelligence - Rushby's 1988 report expertly explores the issues arising from attempting to assure knowledge-based AI, and presents some approaches to address these [10]. Thirty years later, many of the issues remain largely unresolved; one example is our poor understanding of software metrics that should take into account, not only the software behaviour in isolation, but consider the human developer (knowledge, skills and experience), the development and operational environment, and the objective of the product [10, p. 26]. Without this understanding or theory of software development, our existing metrics applied to ML algorithms are still insufficient for safety assurance.

There have been several research advances and approaches developed to improve ML safety, such as - modelling safety assurance arguments for ML [3], characterising viewpoints for ML assurance [4], developing appropriate testing

© Springer Nature Switzerland AG 2019
A. Romanovsky et al. (Eds.): SAFECOMP 2019 Workshops, LNCS 11699, pp. 281–287, 2019.
https://doi.org/10.1007/978-3-030-26250-1_22

models and argument structures [7], creating models of how and when AI might become unsafe [11]. However, there remains no consensus on how to resolve the assurance challenge, namely - how do we *know* that a system with ML is safe. In addition, the introduction of ML components to a system not only creates new challenges, but acts as a force multiplier for the existing problems in safety assurance (such as the inheritance of context to subsystems, evidence sufficiency for claims, epistemic uncertainty introduced during design, *etc.*).

In order to assure the safety of ML we must first understand assurance and begin to build a picture of how these new and existing challenges and solutions relate to each other. To this end, this paper will briefly discuss views of assurance and current practice in Sect. 2; explore some of the specific differences between traditional systems and systems with ML components in Sect. 3; Sect. 4 explores the three core challenges that are the subject of this paper; Followed by a discussion in Sect. 5; lastly, Sect. 6 will conclude the discussion by presenting a potential way forward for assurance of ML.

2 Assurance: Current Practice

At its core, assurance is concerned with managing uncertain negative outcomes. This is reflected in the definition of assurance in safety standards across several domains. Even though there is variance in the definitions, all of the standards approach assurance from at least one of three perspectives.

2.1 Assurance as an Outcome

This is the *reasoning* why a system is safe. It can exist in the minds of those developing the system; often as an argument and mental model of how safety works for that system. It is usually a requirement that this reasoning or *justified true belief in the safety of the system* be recorded for internal audit and external evaluation by regulatory bodies. It is represented and communicated through a combination of system artefacts, risk analysis models, test reports, justification reports and safety cases, *etc.*.

2.2 Assurance as a Process

This describes the steps required to *develop* and *record* the safety reasoning for a system. Whilst the *develop* part of assurance is concerned with risk reduction activities and good engineering (sometimes called *ensurance*), the *record* part of the process is concerned with systematically documenting the activities, and argumentation for building convincing reasoning. The result of this Assurance Process is the Outcome.

2.3 Assurance as a Relationship

This is the *relationship* that exists between the person making the assurance argument and the person whom they wish to persuade. There is an intuitive understanding of this when phrases such as *"I assure you that ..."* are used in everyday speech; however the relationship is not as obvious from current assurance practice and the standards. This is because there are implicit assumptions and shared understanding, *e.g.* when utilising a standard, of who is making an argument, and to whom it is being made.

Each of these perspectives present unique challenges when ML is incorporated into a system.

3 Differences Between Traditional and New

Having explored the existing assurance approaches in the previous section, the difference between traditional (non-autonomous system) and new systems (autonomous system) is discussed in this section.

Table 1. Differences between AGV and SGV

AGV (traditional system)	SGV (now AI system)
Navigation along preplanned paths	Unplanned paths
Static map of environment	Dynamic environment modelling
Separation from humans and hazard zones	Interaction with humans
Linear *sense* function *e.g.* detect magnetic strip	Complex non-linear *sense* function *e.g.* detect "a person"
Programmed decision-making	Autonomous decision-making

Table 1 shows the differences between an Automated Guided Vehicle (AGV) and Self-Guided Vehicle (SGV). Pre-programmed AGVs have been manufactured and use for over thirty years, especially for applications where the tasks are simple and repetitive, such as moving stock in a warehouse. SGV are new systems because they allow for greater flexibility and capabilities through autonomous interaction with the environment. One of the major differences is in their *sensing* process. Both processes might have the sensing requirement not to collide with an object. However, for the added capability of interacting with humans, the SGV also needs to identify what a 'human' is.

To formulate the sensing process, let us denote S as the sensing state in real physical environment and X as the domain of sensors, and consider a sensing process as a function $\hat{S}()\colon X \to S$. Then, a data mapping from the sensor X can be formalised as $\hat{S}(X)$. In the AGV application, the sensed data $\hat{S}(X)$ is directly related to the sensing state S (the objects). For example, the output of a proximity sensor is directly related to the presence of objects. Therefore, the relationship between a sensing state and data can be represented as $\hat{S}(X) + \epsilon_s = S$, where the ϵ stands for uncertainties. We often say that data $\hat{S}(X)$ is ϵ_s accurate with respect to the sensing state S, denoted as $Q(\hat{S}(X), \epsilon_s)$. By minimising ϵ_s and analysing the cause of it, the uncertainty ϵ_s can be bounded. In that case, the requirements on data $\hat{S}(X)$ can be directly decomposed into requirements on sensor X, and evidence can be collected by testing sensor X.

However, in the SGV application, since no sensors can physically and directly sense a 'human', the sensed data $\hat{S}(X)$ is no longer directly related to the sensing state S (human). For example, a camera produces images which are RGB values. In order to identify a person from the images, a process of images is often needed. We symbolise such process as $F()$. As a result, the previous relationship can be written as $F(Q(\hat{S}(X), \epsilon_s)) + \epsilon_F = S$, where ϵ_s and ϵ_F are the accuracy for the sensing and the processing respectively. Since it is difficult for system developers to determine the $F()$, ML is the alternative that provides an approximation for $F()$. However, the $F()$ determined by ML is sensitive to many variables such as data distribution, sensor accuracy, or model parameters [2], which prevent the safety requirements propagating through them. This causes issues for safety assurance.

4 Understanding Challenges for Assuring ML

The objective of safety assurance is to bound uncertainty and build belief in the safety through various means, such as past experience, best practice and standards. Safety assurance often involves a number of tests such as code verification,

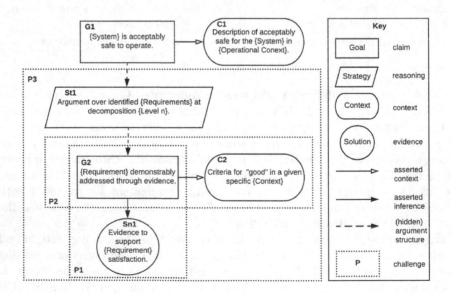

Fig. 1. Argument structure showing ML assurance challenges

timing, independence and formal tests to evaluate whether lower level requirements can be met. This is based on the assumption that the lower level safety requirements maintain the intent of higher level requirements through decomposition [6], however since requirements are not *decomposed* in the traditional sense with ML components, the assumptions that form the foundation for standards are violated. Current practice is not directly applicable [2]. In this section, three challenges related to assuring ML are identified. Figure 1 illustrates these.

4.1   Challenge 1 - Specifying Tests Without Considering Contexts (P1)

The existing safety standards require a system to undertake a number of tests (e.g. timing analysis). By passing those tests, evidence to support lower level requirements is provided. In traditional system satisfying lower level requirements leads to higher level requirements being satisfied because of the strong traceable decomposition and context inheritance. However, current standards were not designed for systems with ML, therefore it is possible for them to pass the tests, but behaviour to be unsafe[1]. For example, the issues of reward hacking in ML component is unrelated to how the software is coded [1].

4.2   Challenge 2 - Specifying Contexts Without Providing Tests (P2)

The behaviour of a ML component is difficult to bound as it is sensitive to many variables as discussed in Sect. 3. There are many works available that try to bound the behaviours of a ML component [3,4,9]. Despite being from different perspectives (e.g. argue from performance level [9], functional viewpoints [4], and insufficiency [3]), they all provide a clear context that the behaviour of their ML components can be bounded. However, the challenge then becomes how to provide evidence to support their argument as no test options were given. For example, one of a lower level goal in [3] is *'The function is robust against distributional shift in the environment'*. Since it is not clear how evidence can be collected to support this requirement, the problem is still unsolved.

4.3   Challenge 3 - Connecting to the Overall Safety Argument (P3)

The primary requirement in current work for assuring ML components are not related to the overall safety case. For example, the primary requirement in [3] is *'The residual risk associated with functional insufficiencies in the object detection function is acceptable'*. This is analogous to using reliability as a measure for safety. As a violation of these lower level requirements does not necessarily lead to unsafe behaviours, nor does meeting these requirements guarantee safety. It is therefore important to understand how the safety case for ML can be connected to the overall one, and how domain specific concerns can be traded-off to produce a safe system.

---

[1] Note that this is true for traditional systems, however there is exponentially more uncertainty for ML system behaviour.

5   Implications

The statistic that humans are the cause of 94% of road accidents [8] is often used as motivation for the adoption of autonomous vehicles; it is implied that the number of accidents would be reduced if the human driver was replaced with AI. Whilst there are *many* issues with this claim, what this data does not take in to account is all the accidents that human intervention prevented. By its nature this kind of data is difficult to model, however it is paramount that these subtle domain interactions are understood so that "good" safety criteria for ML algorithms can be established. This could be achieved through different ways through assurance process and outcome.

5.1   Change in Process and Outcome

In current assurance arguments, higher level safety requirements are decomposed into several lower level requirements with respect to properties such as hardware and software functionality. Therefore, it is proposed that decomposition of requirements through ML components should follow the same philosophy. However, the decomposition should occur with respect to domain-specific safety properties. This requires a deep understanding of the domain interactions, that must be skilfully mapped to the new operational context. For example, the *intent* of the heuristics that people use to avoid being on a designated AGV path should be incorporated into the SGV design. This presents a paradigm shift that goes well beyond the requirements specific only to the ML component, such as mitigating the effects of distributional shift.

5.2   Change in Relationship

Humans being assisted or replaced by systems that use AI necessitates a new way of thinking about trust and confidence that is different to traditional human-human assurance. The consideration of this area is outside the scope of this paper, however there has been significant advances to understand what is occurring inside the ML algorithm [5] which is likely to have a significant effect on the assurance process and outcome.

6   Conclusion

The nature of ML systems means that, whilst there is a strong consensus on many of the problems introduced, there is no unifying conceptualisation of the problem of assuring ML. This forms a barrier of communication between safety, ML developers, system engineers, *etc.*. In this paper, a new tripartite model of the challenge of assuring ML was presented to address this understanding issue. Using such a model for communication it is possible to co-ordinate inter-disciplinary work and improve both the quality and safety of the system.

Acknowledgments. Thanks to the Assuring Autonomy International Programme (AAIP) for support of this work.

References

1. Amodei, D., Olah, C., Steinhardt, J., Christiano, P., Schulman, J., Mané, D.: Concrete problems in AI safety (2016). arXiv preprint arXiv:1606.06565
2. Banks, A., Ashmore, R.: Requirements assurance in machine learning. In: Proceedings of the AAAI Workshop on Artificial Intelligence Safety 2019. pp. 14–21. Springer (2018)
3. Burton, S., Gauerhof, L., Heinzemann, C.: Making the case for safety of machine learning in highly automated driving. In: Tonetta, S., Schoitsch, E., Bitsch, F. (eds.) SAFECOMP 2017. LNCS, vol. 10489, pp. 5–16. Springer, Cham (2017). https://doi.org/10.1007/978-3-319-66284-8_1
4. Douthwaite, M., Kelly, T.: Safety-critical software and safety-critical artificial intelligence: integrating new practices and new safety concerns for AI systems. In: Proceedings of the Twenty-sixth Safety-Critical Systems Symposium (2018)
5. Gunning, D.: Explainable artificial intelligence (XAI). Defense Advanced Research Projects Agency (DARPA), nd Web (2017)
6. Hawkins, R., Habli, I., Kelly, T.: The principles of software safety assurance. In: 31st International System Safety Conference (2013)
7. Koopman, P., Kane, A., Black, J.: Credible autonomy safety argumentation. In: 27th Safety-Critical Systems Symposium, February 2019
8. NHTSA: National Motor Vehicle Crash Causation Survey: Report to Congress. Technical report. National Highway Traffic Safety Administration, July 2008
9. Picardi, C., Hawkins, R., Paterson, C., Habli, I.: A pattern for arguing the assurance of machine learning in medical diagnosis systems. In: International Conference on Computer Safety, Reliability, and Security (to appear, 2019)
10. Rushby, J.: Quality measures and assurance for AI (artificial intelligence) software (1988)
11. Yampolskiy, R.: Taxonomy of pathways to dangerous AI (2015). arXiv preprint arXiv:1511.03246

Improving ML Safety with Partial Specifications

Rick Salay$^{(\boxtimes)}$ and Krzysztof Czarnecki

University of Waterloo, Waterloo, Canada
{rsalay,kczarnec}@gsd.uwaterloo.ca

Abstract. Advanced autonomy features of vehicles are typically difficult or impossible to specify precisely and this has led to the rise of machine learning (ML) from examples as an alternative implementation approach to traditional programming. Developing software without specifications sacrifices the ability to effectively verify the software yet this is a key component of safety assurance. In this paper, we suggest that while complete specifications may not be possible, partial specifications typically are and these could be used with ML to strengthen safety assurance. We review the types of partial specifications that are applicable for these problems and discuss the places in the ML development workflow that they could be used to improve the safety of ML-based components.

Keywords: Safety · Machine learning · Specification

1 Introduction

The use of machine learning (ML) is on the rise in many sectors of software development. In particular, Advanced Driver Assistance Systems (ADAS) and Automated Driving Systems (ADS) are two areas where ML plays a significant role [13,27]. In automotive development, safety is a critical objective, and the emergence of standards such as ISO 26262 [10] has helped focus industry practices to address safety in a systematic and consistent way. Unfortunately, these standards were not designed to accommodate technologies such as ML or the type of functionality that is provided by an ADS and this has created a tension between the need to innovate and the need to improve safety.

Safety standards such as ISO 26262 do not focus on explicitly measuring and reducing error rates of software. Instead, they define the development rigor needed to reduce the error rate to an acceptable level by recommending specific development methods. In previous work [23], we have shown that up to three quarters of the verification and half the testing methods recommended by ISO 26262 rely on a software specification being available. There is an assumption in ISO 26262, which follows the standard V model for software development, that the safety requirements of a component are completely specified and each refinement can be verified with respect to its specification [27]. This assumption

© Springer Nature Switzerland AG 2019
A. Romanovsky et al. (Eds.): SAFECOMP 2019 Workshops, LNCS 11699, pp. 288–300, 2019.
https://doi.org/10.1007/978-3-030-26250-1_23

is also made in other safety-critical domains such as aerospace [1]. This is important in order to trace the behaviour of the implementation to its design, safety requirements and ultimately, to the hazards that are mitigated. Yet for ML-based software, a key obstacle to realizing the appropriate level of rigor needed for safety critical software is the lack of specifications.

Spanfelner et al. [27] point out that many kinds of advanced automated driving functionality require perception of the environment, and this functionality may not be completely specifiable. For example, what is the specification for recognizing a pedestrian? Since a vehicle must move around in a human world, advanced functionality must involve perception of human categories (e.g., pedestrians). There is evidence that such categories can only partially be specified using rules (e.g., necessary and sufficient conditions) and also need examples [21]. This has been long understood in the field of cognitive linguistics [15].

The fact that functionality like perception is difficult to specify has motivated the use of ML-based approaches for implementing software components by training from examples instead of programming from a specification. However, a training set is not an adequate substitute for a specification. The training set is necessarily incomplete and there is no guarantee that it is even representative of the space of possible inputs [28]. In contrast, a characteristic of a specification that makes it valuable for safety assurance is that it says something about a (potentially infinite) set of input/output cases. Thus, with a training set, it is not clear how to create assurance that the corresponding hazards are always mitigated. Furthermore, the training process cannot be considered to be equivalent to a verification process since the trained model will be "correct by construction" with respect to the training set, up to the limits of the model and the learning algorithm.

One response to the inadequacy of safety standards is the recent release of the standard ISO/PAS 21448 [11]. This moves toward addressing ML (specifically, in Annex G) and the corresponding limitations of functions ML is used to implement. However, the focus is heavily on testing and only lightly on verification; thus, the specification issue remains.

We propose to reduce the safety assurance gap of developing ML components purely through training by instead considering a hybrid approach – even when a complete specification is not available, a *partial specification* may still be and this should be used to augment the training dataset. We first introduced the idea of a partial specification in the context of analyzing the applicability of ISO 26262 to ML-based components [23,24]. In this paper, we explore this topic in detail for the case of supervised learning (we leave addressing other types of ML for future work). Our contributions are as follows:

- we give requirements for specification languages and identify types of specification that are well-suited to ML-based components
- we identify approaches for incorporating partial specifications into the ML development process and give examples for this from the literature
- we analyze the approaches from the perspective of impact on safety

Note that although we are motivated by and take examples from the perception task in automated driving, our contributions apply more broadly to the use of supervised learning based ML components in any context.

The remainder of the paper is structured as follows. In Sect. 2 we outline what we mean by partial specification and identify different types of specification appropriate for ML. In Sect. 3 we identify the places in the ML development process where a partial specification can be used. Finally, in Sect. 4 we discuss decision criteria for the usage of a partial specification and draw conclusions.

2   Partial Specifications

Given a function of $F : \mathcal{I} \rightarrow \mathcal{O}$, supervised ML is a method of learning a model ω_F implementing F using a finite training set of input/output pairs $(I, O)_{i=1..N}$ with $(I, O) \in \mathcal{I} \times \mathcal{O}$. A specification defines properties that ω_F must satisfy in order to be acceptable. Safety requirements are a subset of a specification that focus on the safety-relevant aspects of ω_F. These include both functional requirements that define what the I/O behaviour of ω_F must be and non-functional requirements that define how ω_F should carry out this behaviour. Non-functional safety relevant requirements typically *can* be completely specified and include metrics on the degree of correctness (i.e, how close ω_F is to F), performance (e.g., inference time, memory usage, etc.), robustness, etc. For example, classifier correctness metrics include recall, precision, area under the receiver operating curve, etc. In contrast, functional requirements specify properties that characterize F and that all input/output pairs of ω_F must satisfy. These typically *cannot* be completely specified as discussed in Sect. 1. Thus, in this section we focus on partial specifications of functional requirements.

2.1   Requirements on Specification Languages for ML

Before discussing the types of specifications suitable for ML, we consider some requirements on specification languages motivated by safety.

A key requirement of a specification is *interpretability*. Semantically, a functional property of F defines a set of allowable or prohibited input/output pairs. Interpretability requires that the limits of such a set should be graspable by a human from an examination/analysis of the specification allowing them to have a high degree of confidence that this accurately characterizes F. One reason why partial specifications are important to use with ML is that complex types of ML (e.g. DNNs) are not interpretable – it is not easy to understand what a neural network does by examining the neural connections. Lack of interpretability is an obstacle to safety [23]. If specifications are interpretable and there are ways to ensure the model satisfies the specification, then this provides a path to safety through verification.

Another important characteristic of a specification is that it is an *abstraction*. As discussed in Sect. 1, a specification abstracts information about an arbitrarily large and potentially infinite set of input/output pairs rather than a finite set as represented by a training set. Abstraction is also important for helping humans understand such sets [3] and thus supports interpretability.

Another requirement we expect of specifications is to be *formal* so that the semantics are unambiguous and precise. This also makes it possible to reason about the specification, possibly in an automated way.

The specification language should allow specifications to accommodate *uncertainty*. The focus of ML-based components is on uncertain domains that are difficult to specify and for which there are many exceptions. Furthermore, the environment in which components like perception operate contain uncertainty [4]. For example, camera images are subject to sensor noise and interfering factors such as occlusion, weather and lighting variation.

Finally, the specification language should be *appropriate* for the input domain. For example, assume the specification language is first order logic (FOL) and we give a specification for pedestrians such as $\texttt{Ped1}(I) \equiv \texttt{Object}(I) \land \exists l, l', t, a, a', h \in \mathcal{I} \cdot \texttt{Leg}(l) \land \texttt{Leg}(l') \land \texttt{Torso}(t) \land \texttt{Arm}(a) \land \texttt{Arm}(a') \land \texttt{Head}(h) \land \texttt{Connected}(l, l', t, a, a') \land l \neq l' \land a \neq a'$. Although this symbolic expression can be used to express a characteristic of (some) pedestrians, it suffers from a symbol grounding problem [8] – it attempts to specify an unspecifiable concept "Pedestrian" in terms of other unspecifiable concepts "Leg", "Torso", "Arm" and "Head". Thus, to check whether some particular input pixel array I_{29} satisfies $\texttt{Ped1}$ we need definitions for the other concepts, but since they are unspecifiable, no complete definition exists.

One way to address the problem is use a specification language that is better suited to the input domain. In this case, and in many perception functions, the input I is a low level sensor representation such as a pixel array which is sub-symbolic and not suited to a symbolic specification language like FOL. However, a kinematic wire-frame representation of a body can capture both the human intuition of the sufficient condition as well as be used as a way to actually check for satisfaction by a pixel array. The Deformable Part Model approach has been successfully used this way for pedestrian detection [34]. In fact, a Deformable Part Model is still partially trained from examples given a seed model, but it can still be considered to be a specification language because of the interpretability of the representation.

2.2 Types of Specification

We consider the types of properties that could play a role in a partial specification.

Pre and Post Conditions. There are many styles of software specification (See [16] for an overview) but one well-suited to specifying functions is contract based specification [19]. Here a specification gives pre and post conditions on the function. Let $S = \langle pre_S, post_S \rangle$ be such a specification of function $F : \mathcal{I} \to \mathcal{O}$ where pre_S and $post_S$ are conditions expressed in a formal specification language.

The specification says that for all inputs $I \in \mathcal{I}$ if I satisfies pre_S then $\langle I, F(I) \rangle$ satisfies $post_S$. More formally:

$$\forall I \in \mathcal{I} \cdot I \models pre_S \Rightarrow \langle I, F(I) \rangle \models post_S \tag{1}$$

A partial specification admits *at least* one output value for every legal input I, whereas a complete specification admits *exactly one* output value for each legal input. Thus, a complete specification defines the I/O behaviour of F exactly, whereas a partial specification can allow for some uncertainty about the output of the function for some inputs.

In the special case where the function is a classifier, we can define a pre/post specification using necessary and sufficient conditions. Consider binary classifiers (i.e., having type $\mathcal{I} \rightarrow \{\text{yes}, \text{no}\}$). For example, the function `Pedestrian :` `PixelArray` $\rightarrow \{\text{yes}, \text{no}\}$ is one that classifies a camera image according to whether a pedestrian is present. For arbitrary binary classifier $F : I \rightarrow \{\text{yes}, \text{no}\}$, a *sufficient condition* C_{suf} for input I to be in the class (i.e., $F(I) = \text{yes}$) is one such that $I \models C_{suf} \Rightarrow F(I) = \text{yes}$. A *necessary condition* C_{nec} is one such that $I \not\models C_{nec} \Rightarrow F(I) = \text{no}$.

For example, a sufficient condition for `Pedestrian` may be `Ped1(I)` $\equiv$ "I is an object that has two legs, two arms a torso and a head appropriately connected and is in a standing posture." Any object in an image that satisfies `Ped1` is (with high likelyhood) a pedestrian. However, it is not a necessary condition because there are pedestrians that do not fit this description—e.g., a person sitting in a wheelchair, missing an arm, with their head occluded by another object, etc. Thus, a sufficient condition can identify inputs that are definitely in the class. A necessary condition is `Ped2` $\equiv$ "is an object that is less than 8 feet tall". Thus, an object 8 feet or taller is (with high likelyhood) not a pedestrian. This is not a sufficient condition because being less than 8 feet tall does not mean the object is a pedestrian. A necessary condition can identify inputs that are definitely not in the class.

Note that in these examples we actually weakened the conditions by adding the qualifier "with high likelyhood". These were needed because, as discussed in Sect. 1 concepts like human defined concepts such as pedestrian are difficult to characterize using logical conditions [15]. One reason for this is that it is often easy to find (possibly rare) exceptions to any condition. For example, a person on stilts might still be considered a pedestrian even though they violate necessary condition `Ped2`. Thus, partial specifications expressed in terms of such properties typically require consideration for the likelyhood of exceptions. This is discussed further below.

Equivariants and Invariants. A common and useful way to define a constraint on a function is to specify its invariants – i.e., the ways the input can change without affecting the output. For example, a common requirement for the classification of objects (e.g. a pedestrian) in an image is that the classification should be invariant to translation. That is, if something is classified as a pedestrian then it must still be classified as a pedestrian even if it is moved to a different position in the image. An equivariant is more general than an invariant

– it states that a particular kind of change in the input should result in a particular corresponding change in the output. For example, an object detector that extracts the bounding box of a pedestrian in an image is equivariant to rotation since a rotation of the input image results in the same rotation of the bounding box at the output.

We can define these formally. Given function $F : \mathcal{I} \to \mathcal{O}$, an *equivariant* of F is a pair of bijective functions $\langle g : \mathcal{I} \to \mathcal{I}, g' : \mathcal{O} \to \mathcal{O} \rangle$ such that $\forall I \in \mathcal{I} \cdot F(g(I)) = g'(F(I))$. An equivariant where g' is the identity function is called an *invariant* and denoted by a single function $g : \mathcal{I} \to \mathcal{I}$. Thus, $\forall I \in \mathcal{I} \cdot F(g(I)) = F(I)$.

In the above pedestrian classifier example, the function moveRight $: \mathcal{I} \to \mathcal{I}$ that moves the content of an input image one pixel to the right is an invariant of the pedestrian classifier. The pair of functions $\langle$Clockwise90 $: \mathcal{I} \to \mathcal{I}$, Clockwise90$' : \mathcal{O} \to \mathcal{O} \rangle$ that rotate images 90° clockwise is an equivariant of the object detector.

Pure invariants and equivariants as defined above preserve information because they are defined in terms of bijective functions. However, in perception problems, it is common to have "near" invariance to lossy transformations. For example, consider invariance to the presence of snow. A pedestrian should still be classified as such even if there is some snow on the pedestrian or it is snowing around them. Yet, adding snow to a pedestrian image is lossy because it occludes part of the pedestrian. Furthermore, we expect that there is a limit to how much snow we can add before it would be reasonable to change the classification (or at least reduce confidence in it)—e.g., a snowman is not a pedestrian. In this case, we will say that the classification as pedestrian is *quasi*-invariant to the presence of snow. Similar quasi-invariants can be defined relative to other factors such as lighting level, season, clutter, image noise, etc.

Other Kinds of Specification. A general way to view a partial specification is as prior knowledge about F that must be integrated into ω_F. Prior knowledge about a function can come in many forms. In the discussions above we focused on classical logic-based input/output properties of F. Other possibilities include the following:

– Probabilistic constraints: e.g., the height of pedestrians may be known to fit a particular probability distribution. Although this knowledge cannot be used to constrain particular input/output pairs, it can be used to identify when a large set of input/output pairs (e.g., the training data set, the observed input/output pairs during operation, etc.) deviates from expectations.
– Hierarchical constraints: Specifications of concepts can be partially ordered into hierarchies with more abstract concepts at higher levels to handle uncertainty. E.g., Even if class "Pedestrian" is difficult to specify, it is a specialization of the class "Dynamic Object" which may be specifiable. Thus, when we have uncertainty about whether an input can be classified as a pedestrian, it can still be *under*-classified as a dynamic object.

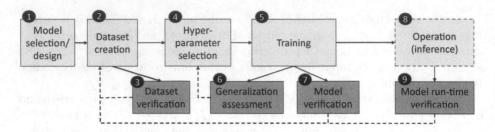

Fig. 1. The ML development process for supervised learning. Verification related activities shown in red (Color figure online).

- Non-monotonic logic constraints: Specifications using non-monotonic logic (e.g., default logic [20]) could help handle exceptions gracefully. E.g., a pedestrian usually has two legs (default) but sometimes has one or no legs (exceptions).
- Pattern-based constraints: e.g., using kinematic wire-frame representations of a body for specifying pedestrians with a Deformable Part Model [34]. Pattern languages such as these must be formally defined.
- Contextual constraints: e.g., a pedestrian must be within x meters of the road, cannot be in a store window (because then they may be a mannequin), etc. In general, these constraints require that the input/output pair first be embedded into a broader "situational" representation that includes context information.

3   Using Partial Specifications with ML

In this section, we identify the potential ways that a partial specification can be used with ML and point to examples of relevant research. A recent survey by von Rueden et al. [22] covers papers that integrate prior knowledge into the ML, but does not focus on safety. Figure 1 shows the ML development process for supervised learning. We have separated out and identified the verification-related steps in red.

Assume that we are training a model ω_F to represent function F. First, model selection and design (1) considers what type of model is appropriately expressive given the complexity of F. Then a dataset is created (2) consisting of correctly labeled (3) input/output examples of F. Most model types have hyper-parameters that must be selected (4) and then model training (5) can proceed using a subset of dataset as a training set. A trained model is then checked against a validation subset of the dataset to ensure that the model is generalizing well (6) and, if not, new hyper-parameters are explored. If the generalization is adequate, the performance of the model is assessed on a testing subset of the dataset (7) If this is adequate, the model can be put into operation to do inference (8) and this may be further monitored to identify problems (9) triggering modifications to the model. Partial specifications can play a role in many of these steps and we detail this below.

3.1   Model Selection

Given a partial specification, it may be possible to select a model type that incorporates part of the specification intrinsically in its architecture. For example, if the function classifies shapes in an image and the specification says that the classification must be invariant to translations of the shape within the image, then Convolutional Neural Networks (CNNs) are a good choice because they exhibit translational invariance. Research is active on defining models that incorporate various equivariants. For example, Worrall et al. [32] describe rotation-invariant CNNs; Cohen and Welling [2] describe an approach for generalizing CNNs to be equivariant to arbitrary sets of discrete symmetries of the input domain; and Hinton et al. [9] define a network architecture that achieves equivariance across all viewpoints of an object.

A different approach is to design the model to be biased toward a particular prior distribution. For example, the object detection architecture AVOD [14] produces bounding boxes on occurrences of pedestrians, cyclists and cars in a scene by regressing them from predefined boxes (called anchors) that cover the scene. The anchors incorporate knowledge about the three classes by being predefined with the typical aspect ratio for instances of each class. For example, pedestrian anchors are much taller than wide and car anchors are wider than tall.

3.2   Dataset Creation and Verification

The partial specification can help to define better quality datasets for training, testing and validation. Specifications can provide guidance to the data collection process by identifying important dimensions of variation and boundary conditions. When a dataset is collected and labeled, the specification can be used to confirm the correctness of the dataset since all the samples must satisfy the specification.

The specification can also be used to directly augment the dataset through the synthetic generation of data. For example data can be synthesized that satisfies sufficient conditions (positive examples) and that violate necessary conditions (negative examples). Constrained sampling has been proposed as a way to generate examples satisfying constraints [18]. Invariants and equivariants can be used to generate new samples from existing ones. For example, Generative Adversarial Networks (GANs) have been used to implement transformations that can convert a scene into another one with different attributes such as adding snow, rain, etc. [17]. If this is used to implement a snow quasi-invariant addSnow : $\mathcal{I} \rightarrow \mathcal{I}$ that adds snow to an input image, then the "with snow" examples can be generated from the manually curated examples. Research on data augmentation is active. Recent papers by Perez and Wang [30] and Wong et al. [31] compare the effectiveness of different data augmentation approaches.

3.3 Training

Ideally, the partial specification should be incorporated into training to constrain the learning algorithm and ensure that the trained model satisfies the partial specification "by construction". Some research into such an integration of symbolic knowledge into training exists but is in its infancy. For example, Xu et al. [33] show how to incorporate such knowledge as a constraint directly in the loss function used during learning, whereas Vedaldi et al. [29] incorporate equivariants into the training process of an SVM.

3.4 Model Verification

Partial specifications can be used in many ways in the verification process. Some traditional testing uses of specifications from software engineering are applicable to ML and include deriving test cases for software unit testing, generation and analysis of equivalence classes and boundary values. Metamorphic testing can make use of invariants and equivariants (e.g., [6]).

More specialized methods are being developed for formal verification of ML using specifications. Falsification for ML is the process of efficiently finding inputs that produce the wrong output (e.g., [5]). Formal verification requires the ability to prove that the partial specification logically follows from the content of a trained model. Some early proposals on doing formal verification of ML models can be found in [25]. Static analysis involves property checking of the ML model. Work in this direction includes an SMT solver by Katz et al. [12] and the use of abstract interpretation [7] for checking properties of DNNs.

3.5 Operation and Run-Time Verification

Partial specifications can be used as part of fault-tolerance architectures to prevents ML faults (e.g., misclassifications) from potentially causing hazardous events. We consider three architectural patterns.

The first is a use of partial specifications to do run-time verification – if the output from the ML component violates a property in the specification, then there is an error. Such checks can either be done in-line or by an external monitor. A fail-safe architecture can be obtained by using a high integrity error checking monitor that disables the functionality on error and transitions the system to a safe state [13].

Another architectural configuration is to "gate" the ML component by putting it in series after a programmed implementation of the partial specification. For example, for pedestrian detection, the image can first be checked to determine if it satisfies sufficient conditions (e.g., Ped1) or violates necessary conditions (e.g., Ped2) and if so, it is immediately classified. Only cases that cannot be handled are passed on to the ML classifier. In addition, the ML classifier could be trained only on inputs that cannot be classified by the partial specification.

Table 1. Summary of different methods for incorporating partial specifications into the steps of the ML development process shown in Fig. 1. The Usage Mode is *Integrate* if the partial specification is incorporated into the component design and construction or *Verify* if it is used as a check after construction. Assurance Strength is *Guarantee* if the method guarantees that the component satisfies the specification either by integration or verification, *Influence* if the component is influenced toward satisfying the specification during construction or *Evidence* if evidence is produced that the component satisfies the specification after construction. A Guarantee provides stronger assurance than either Influence or Evidence.

Step	Method	Specification type	Usage mode	Assurance strength
1	Intrinsic to the model	(Equi/In)variant	Integrate	Guarantee
1	Bias the model	Any	Integrate	Influence
2	Guidance to data collection	Any	Integrate	Influence
2	Dataset augmentation	Any	Integrate	Influence
3	Check dataset	Any	Integrate	Influence
5	Add to loss function	Any	Integrate	Influence
7	Deriving test cases	Any	Verify	Evidence
7	Metamorphic testing	(Equi/In)variant	Verify	Evidence
7	Falsification	Logic-based	Verify	Guarantee
7	Proof	Logic-based	Verify	Guarantee
7	Property checking	Logic-based	Verify	Guarantee
8	Gated architecture	Any	Integrate	Guarantee
8	Simplex architecture	Any	Integrate	Guarantee
9	Run-time verification	Any	Verify	Evidence

Finally, the Simplex architecture [26] was originally proposed to provide safe control systems but can be adapted for classification. This can be used when there is a conservative, but verifiably safe, version of the classifier in addition to the ML-based classifier. The ML classifier is used as the primary classifier. If the result of the primary classifier has low confidence (e.g., low predictive entropy), then the conservative but verifiably safe classifier is used as a fall-back. The safe classifier is conservative in the sense that it over-approximates the safe classification decision (low precision) and the necessary condition part of a partial specification could be used for this purpose. For example, if missing a pedestrian is a safety hazard then when the ML classifier has low confidence, any object less than 8 feet tall (i.e., using Ped2) can be classified as a pedestrian.

4   Discussion and Conclusion

In this paper, we have put forth the idea that safety assurance gap of ML perceptual components due to lack of specifications can be ameliorated by using partial specifications. We discussed requirements for specification languages, identified suitable types of specifications and identified multiple methods for using partial specifications in the ML development process.

Table 1 summarizes these methods and categorizes them according to specification type, usage mode and assurance strength. Most methods are applicable to any specification type but the verification related methods are biased toward logic-based specifications. This points to a gap in the research. We observed in Sect. 2 that many properties that could be given as specifications for perception functions typically have a probabilistic aspect; however, methods for checking probabilistic properties are atypical for traditional software verification.

A key observation impacting safety is that the different methods vary in assurance strength. Furthermore, there are broadly two modes of using a partial specification. Either the specification can be integrated into the behaviour of the component or it can be used to verify the component. Although satisfaction of the specification can be guaranteed by either mode, if verification cannot show satisfaction then the construction phase must be re-entered to address this. Thus the guarantee by the integration mode potentially requires less development effort. Both modes also have weaker assurance counterparts that do not provide guarantees but increase the likelihood that the specification is satisfied. While not ideal, this type of partial assurance can be combined and coupled with other sources of evidence (e.g., system level testing results) to make a stronger safety argument.

Acknowledgements. We would like to thank Mark Costin for insightful comments that have contributed to this work.

References

1. Bhattacharyya, S., Cofer, D., Musliner, D., Mueller, J., Engstrom, E.: Certification considerations for adaptive systems. In: 2015 International Conference on Unmanned Aircraft Systems (ICUAS), pp. 270–279. IEEE (2015)
2. Cohen, T., Welling, M.: Group equivariant convolutional networks. In: International Conference on Machine Learning, pp. 2990–2999 (2016)
3. Cooke, D., Gates, A., Demirörs, E., Demirörs, O., Tanik, M.M., Krämer, B.: Languages for the specification of software. J. Syst. Softw. **32**(3), 269–308 (1996)
4. Czarnecki, K., Salay, R.: Towards a framework to manage perceptual uncertainty for safe automated driving. In: Gallina, B., Skavhaug, A., Schoitsch, E., Bitsch, F. (eds.) SAFECOMP 2018. LNCS, vol. 11094, pp. 439–445. Springer, Cham (2018). https://doi.org/10.1007/978-3-319-99229-7_37
5. Dreossi, T., Donzé, A., Seshia, S.A.: Compositional falsification of cyber-physical systems with machine learning components. In: Barrett, C., Davies, M., Kahsai, T. (eds.) NFM 2017. LNCS, vol. 10227, pp. 357–372. Springer, Cham (2017). https://doi.org/10.1007/978-3-319-57288-8_26
6. Dwarakanath, A., et al.: Identifying implementation bugs in machine learning based image classifiers using metamorphic testing. In: Proceedings of the 27th ACM SIGSOFT International Symposium on Software Testing and Analysis, pp. 118–128. ACM (2018)

7. Gehr, T., Mirman, M., Drachsler-Cohen, D., Tsankov, P., Chaudhuri, S., Vechev, M.: Ai2: safety and robustness certification of neural networks with abstract interpretation. In: 2018 IEEE Symposium on Security and Privacy (SP), pp. 3–18. IEEE (2018)
8. Harnad, S.: The symbol grounding problem. Physica D **42**(1–3), 335–346 (1990)
9. Hinton, G.E., Sabour, S., Frosst, N.: Matrix capsules with EM routing. In: 6th International Conference on Learning Representations, ICLR 2018, Vancouver, BC, Canada. Conference Track Proceedings, 30 April–3 May 2018. https://openreview.net/forum?id=HJWLfGWRb
10. International Organization for Standardization: ISO 26262: Road Vehicles - Functional Safety, 2nd edition (2018)
11. International Organization for Standardization: ISO/AWI PAS 21448: Road Vehicles - Safety of the Intended Functionality, 1st Edition (2019)
12. Katz, G., Barrett, C., Dill, D.L., Julian, K., Kochenderfer, M.J.: Reluplex: an efficient SMT solver for verifying deep neural networks. In: Majumdar, R., Kunčak, V. (eds.) CAV 2017. LNCS, vol. 10426, pp. 97–117. Springer, Cham (2017). https://doi.org/10.1007/978-3-319-63387-9_5
13. Koopman, P., Wagner, M.: Challenges in autonomous vehicle testing and validation. SAE Int. J. Transp. Saf. **4**(1), 15–24 (2016)
14. Ku, J., Mozifian, M., Lee, J., Harakeh, A., Waslander, S.L.: Joint 3D proposal generation and object detection from view aggregation. In: 2018 IEEE/RSJ IROS, pp. 1–8. IEEE (2018)
15. Lakoff, G.: Women, Fire, and Dangerous Things: What Categories Reveal About the Mind. University of Chicago press, Chicago (1987)
16. Lamsweerde, A.V.: Formal specification: a roadmap. In: Proceedings of the Conference on the Future of Software Engineering, pp. 147–159. ACM (2000)
17. Liu, M.Y., Breuel, T., Kautz, J.: Unsupervised image-to-image translation networks. In: Advances in Neural Information Processing Systems, pp. 700–708 (2017)
18. Meel, K.S., et al.: Constrained sampling and counting: universal hashing meets SAT solving. In: Workshops at the Thirtieth AAAI Conference on Artificial Intelligence (2016)
19. Meyer, B.: Applying 'design by contract'. Computer **25**(10), 40–51 (1992)
20. Reiter, R.: A logic for default reasoning. Artif. Intell. **13**(1–2), 81–132 (1980)
21. Rouder, J.N., Ratcliff, R.: Comparing exemplar and rule-based theories of categorization. Curr. Dir. Psychol. Sci. **15**(1), 9–13 (2006)
22. von Rueden, L., Mayer, S., Garcke, J., Bauckhage, C., Schuecker, J.: Informed machine learning-towards a taxonomy of explicit integration of knowledge into machine learning. arXiv preprint arXiv:1903.12394 (2019)
23. Salay, R., Czarnecki, K.: Using machine learning safely in automotive software: An assessment and adaption of software process requirements in ISO 26262. arXiv preprint arXiv:1808.01614 (2018)
24. Salay, R., Queiroz, R., Czarnecki, K.: An Analysis of ISO 26262: Machine Learning and Safety in Automotive Software. SAE Technical Paper (2018)
25. Seshia, S.A., Sadigh, D., Sastry, S.S.: Towards verified artificial intelligence. arXiv preprint arXiv:1606.08514 (2016)
26. Sha, L.: Using simplicity to control complexity. IEEE Softw. **4**, 20–28 (2001)
27. Spanfelner, B., Richter, D., Ebel, S., Wilhelm, U., Branz, W., Patz, C.: Challenges in applying the ISO 26262 for driver assistance systems. Tagung Fahrerassistenz, München **15**(16), 2012 (2012)
28. Varshney, K.R.: Engineering safety in machine learning. arXiv preprint arXiv:1601.04126 (2016)

29. Vedaldi, A., Blaschko, M., Zisserman, A.: Learning equivariant structured output SVM regressors. In: Proceedings of 2011 International Conference on Computer Vision, pp. 959–966. IEEE (2011)
30. Wang, J., Perez, L.: The effectiveness of data augmentation in image classification using deep learning. In: Convolutional Neural Networks Vision Recognition (2017)
31. Wong, S.C., Gatt, A., Stamatescu, V., McDonnell, M.D.: Understanding data augmentation for classification: when to warp? In: 2016 International Conference on Digital Image Computing: Techniques and Applications (DICTA), pp. 1–6. IEEE (2016)
32. Worrall, D.E., Garbin, S.J., Turmukhambetov, D., Brostow, G.J.: Harmonic networks: deep translation and rotation equivariance. In: Proceedings of the IEEE Conference on Computer Vision and Pattern Recognition, pp. 5028–5037 (2017)
33. Xu, J., Zhang, Z., Friedman, T., Liang, Y., Broeck, G.V.D.: A semantic loss function for deep learning with symbolic knowledge. arXiv preprint arXiv:1711.11157 (2017)
34. Yan, J., Zhang, X., Lei, Z., Liao, S., Li, S.Z.: Robust multi-resolution pedestrian detection in traffic scenes. In: 2013 IEEE Conference on Computer Vision and Pattern Recognition (CVPR), pp. 3033–3040. IEEE (2013)

An Abstraction-Refinement Approach to Formal Verification of Tree Ensembles

John Törnblom(✉) and Simin Nadjm-Tehrani

Department of Computer and Information Science, Linköping University,
Linköping, Sweden
{john.tornblom,simin.nadjm-tehrani}@liu.se

Abstract. Recent advances in machine learning are now being considered for integration in safety-critical systems such as vehicles, medical equipment and critical infrastructure. However, organizations in these domains are currently unable to provide convincing arguments that systems integrating machine learning technologies are safe to operate in their intended environments.

In this paper, we present a formal verification method for tree ensembles that leverage an abstraction-refinement approach to counteract combinatorial explosion. We implemented the method as an extension to a tool named VoTE, and demonstrate its applicability by verifying the robustness against perturbations in random forests and gradient boosting machines in two case studies. Our abstraction-refinement based extension to VoTE improves the performance by several orders of magnitude, scaling to tree ensembles with up to 50 trees with depth 10, trained on high-dimensional data.

Keywords: Formal verification · Decision trees · Tree ensembles

1 Introduction

Machine learning technologies have enabled great progress in many domains in recent years, e.g. computer vision, anomaly detection, and automatic control. Manufactures of safety-critical systems such as vehicles, medical equipment and critical infrastructure are now considering integrating these advances in their products. However, safety-critical systems are often subject to strict regulations, and as such, require convincing arguments that the systems are safe to operate in their intended environments. Current industry standards often rely on software testing and human experts capable of identifying circumstance under which the software should (not) be tested. Unfortunately, these methods are often unsuitable when machine learning technologies have been used to develop software artifacts subject to verification.

Complementing software testing that relies on human experts who comprehend the internal structure of the software under test, formal verification techniques offer additional evidence for correctness. Most research is so far focused

© Springer Nature Switzerland AG 2019
A. Romanovsky et al. (Eds.): SAFECOMP 2019 Workshops, LNCS 11699, pp. 301–313, 2019.
https://doi.org/10.1007/978-3-030-26250-1_24

on formally verifying neural networks (see e.g. the survey by Liu et al. [9]), but there are other learning models that may be more appropriate when verifiability is important e.g. random forests [1], and gradient boosting machines [6].

Recent work by Törnblom and Nadjm-Tehrani [13] demonstrates that formal verification of tree ensembles trained on low-dimensional data is practical. However, the proposed method struggles with combinatorial explosion when tree ensembles are trained on high-dimensional data. In this paper, we address these shortcomings by extending that work with an abstraction-refinement approach that counteracts combinatorial explosion, and thus enables formal verification of tree ensembles trained on high-dimensional data. The contributions of this paper are as follows.

- A formal abstraction-refinement based verification method tailored specifically for tree-based ensembles.
- A realization[1] of the method, implemented as an extension to the toolsuite VoTE [13].
- Application of the method in two case-studies from current literature.

The rest of this paper is structured as follows. Section 2 presents a background on tree-based ensembles and the toolsuite VoTE which our implementation is based upon. Section 3 presents our abstraction-refinement technique, and how we realized it in VoTE. Section 4 presents applications of the method on two case studies; a collision detection problem, and a digit recognition problem. Section 5 discusses related works on verification of tree-based ensembles. Finally, Sect. 6 concludes the paper and summarizes the lessons learned.

2   Background

In this section, we present the required background on tree-based ensembles and the toolsuite VoTE. We also provide a definition of the classifier robustness property which we will verify in case studies in Sect. 4.

2.1   Decision Trees

In machine learning, decision trees are used as predictive models to capture statistical properties of a system of interest.

Definition 1 (Decision Tree). *A decision tree implements a prediction function* $t : X^n \to \mathbb{R}^m$ *that maps disjoint sets of points* $X_i \subset X^n$ *to a single output point* $\bar{y}_i \in \mathbb{R}^m$, *i.e.*

$$
t(\bar{x}) = \begin{cases} (y_{1,1}, \ldots, y_{1,m}) & \bar{x} \in X_1 \\ \quad\vdots \\ (y_{k,1}, \ldots, y_{k,m}) & \bar{x} \in X_k, \end{cases} \tag{1}
$$

---

[1] Published at https://github.com/john-tornblom/VoTE/releases/tag/v0.2.1.

where k is the number of disjoint sets and $X^n = \bigcup_{i=1}^{k} X_i$.

The n-dimensional input domain X^n includes elements $\bar{x}$ as tuples in which each element x_i captures some feature of the system of interest as an input variable. Each internal node in the tree is associated with a decision function that separates points in the input space from each other, and the leaves define output values. The tree structure is evaluated in a top-down manner, where decision functions determine which path to take towards the leaves. When a leaf is hit, the output $\bar{y} \in \mathbb{R}^m$ associated with the leaf is emitted.

In general, decision functions are defined by non-linear combinations of several input variables at each internal node. In this paper, we only consider binary trees with linear decision functions with one input variable, which Irsoy et al. call univariate hard decision trees [7]. Although it has been demonstrated that non-linear [7] and multivariate decision trees [14] can be useful, state-of-the-art implementations of tree-based ensembles typically use univariate hard decision trees, e.g. scikit-learn [10] and CatBoost [11].

2.2   Random Forests

Decision trees are known to suffer from a phenomenon called overfitting. Models suffering from this phenomenon can be fitted so tightly to their training data that their performance on unseen data is reduced the more you train them. To counteract this issue with decision trees, Breiman [1] proposes random forests.

Definition 2 (Random Forest). A random forest $f : X^n \to \mathbb{R}^m$ is an ensemble of B decision trees that produces outputs by averaging the values emitted by each individual tree, i.e.

$$f(\bar{x}) = \frac{1}{B} \sum_{b=1}^{B} t_b(\bar{x}), \tag{2}$$

where t_b is the b-th tree in the ensemble.

To reduce correlation between trees, each tree is trained on a random subset of the training data, using potentially overlapping random subsets of the input variables.

2.3   Gradient Boosting Machines

Similarly, Freidman [6] introduces a machine learning model called gradient boosting machine that uses several decision trees to implement a prediction function. Unlike random forests, these trees are trained in a sequential manner. Each consecutive tree compensates for errors made by previous trees by estimating the gradient of errors (using gradient decent, hence the name). In a learning context, this is conceptually very different from random forests, but during prediction, these two models have many things in common.

Definition 3 (Gradient Boosting Machine). *A gradient boosting machine* $f : X^n \rightarrow \mathbb{R}^m$ *is an ensemble of B additive decision trees, i.e.*

$$f(\bar{x}) = \sum_{b=1}^{B} t_b(\bar{x}), \tag{3}$$

where t_b is the b-th tree in the ensemble.

2.4   Classifiers

Decision trees and tree ensembles may be used as classifiers. A classifier is a function that categorizes samples from an input domain into one or more classes and assigns each sample a label unique to its class. In this paper, we only consider functions that map each point from an input domain to exactly one class.

Definition 4 (Classifier). *Let $f(\bar{x}) = (y_1, \ldots, y_m)$ represent a model trained to predict the probability y_i associated with a class i within disjoint regions in the input domain, where m is the number of classes. A classifier $f_c(\bar{x})$ may then be defined as*

$$f_c(\bar{x}) = \operatorname*{argmax}_i y_i. \tag{4}$$

A random forest typically infers probabilities by capturing the number of times a particular class has been observed within some hyperrectangle in the input domain of a tree during training. Training a gradient boosting machine to predict class membership probabilities is somewhat different, and depends on the characteristics of the used learning algorithm, often involving post-processing the sum of all trees. For example, when training multiclass classifiers in Cat-Boost [11], individual trees emit values from a logarithmic domain that are summed up, and finally transformed and normalized into probabilities using the softmax function, i.e.

$$\mathrm{softmax}(y_1, \ldots, y_m) = \frac{(e^{y_1}, \ldots, e^{y_m})}{\sum\limits_{i=1}^{m} y_i}. \tag{5}$$

2.5   Classifier Robustness

Bruneau et al. [2] describe robustness as the ability of a system of interest to withstand a given level of stress without suffering degradation or loss of function. In the context of machine learning, such a description includes a classifier's ability to maintain decisiveness in its predictions despite noisy or adversarial input. Formally, such an equivalence relationship between input and output may be defined as follows.

Definition 5 (Robustness against Perturbations). *Let $f_c : X^n \to L$ be the classifier subject to verification, $X_l \subset X^n$ a set of samples with label $l \in L$ where robustness against perturbations is desirable, $\epsilon \in \mathbb{R}_{\geq 0}$ a robustness margin, and $\Delta = \{\delta \in \mathbb{R} : -\epsilon < \delta < \epsilon\}$ perturbations. We denote by $\bar{\delta}$ a tuple of perturbations, i.e. an n-tuple of elements drawn from Δ. The classifier is robust against perturbations with respect to X_l and Δ iff*

$$\forall \bar{x} \in X_l, \ \forall \bar{\delta} \in \Delta^n, f_c(\bar{x}) = f_c(\bar{x} + \bar{\delta}) = l. \tag{6}$$

Note that this definition does not capture all possible input perturbations. Depending on the application, other equivalence relationships such as axial rotations may also be of interest, but are out of scope for this paper.

2.6 Verifier of Tree Ensembles

VoTE (Verifier of Tree Ensembles) [13] is a toolsuite for formally verifying that tree ensembles comply with requirements. The toolsuite implements two techniques, one approximate but conservative technique that bounds the output of a tree ensemble, and one precise and exhaustive technique that computes and enumerates equivalence classes in a tree ensemble, i.e. sets of points in the input domain that yield the same output tuple. The approximate technique has been used to verify e.g. that probabilities computed in a classifier are in the range $[0, 1]$, and the precise technique can be used to verify robustness.

As shown in Fig. 1, the toolsuite consists of two components, VoTE Core and VoTE Property Checker. VoTE Core is instantiated from the ensemble subject to verification, $f : X^n \to \mathbb{R}^m$. It takes as input a hyperrectangle defining X^n, and emits all equivalence classes in f, i.e. sets of points in the input space that yield the same output. These equivalence classes are then checked for compliance against a property $\mathbb{P}$ by a VoTE Property Checker.

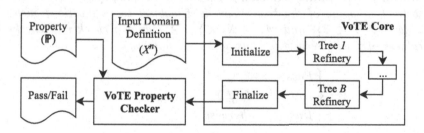

Fig. 1. The design of VoTE.

3 Abstractions and Refinements

In this section, we present our abstraction-refinement based verification approach that combines the two verification techniques mentioned in Sect. 2.6. The basic idea is to abstract multiple input-output mappings of a system subject to verification using the approximate technique, and then iteratively refine them using the precise technique.

3.1 Terminology

Requirements on systems considered in this paper may be expressed in terms of input-output mappings, expressions which we call *mapping specifications*.

Definition 6 (Mapping Specification). *Let X^n be the n-dimensional input domain of a system subject to specification, and $\mathbb{R}^m$ its m-dimensional output range. A mapping specification $\mathbb{P}$ is a set of pairs $(\bar{x}, \bar{y})$ where $\bar{x} \in X^n$ and $\bar{y} \in \mathbb{R}^m$, that specifies the expected input-output mappings of the system. More specifically, we expect that any implementation of the system maps $\bar{x}$ to $\bar{y}$.*

Verification of software with respect to a mapping specification may be carried out by means of exhaustive testing if the specification has a small enough cardinality. For large specifications, abstraction techniques may be used. Generally, an abstraction is a description that omits information that is irrelevant to the problem at hand. For example, classifier requirements are often only concerned with the most probable class in a prediction, in which case numerical probabilities and the order of less probable classes are irrelevant. To capture several input-output mappings with a single data structure, we use *abstract mappings*.

Definition 7 (Abstract Mapping). *An abstract mapping of a function $f : X^n \rightarrow \mathbb{R}^m$ is a pair of sets (X_i, Y_a) where $X_i \subseteq X^n$ denotes a precise input region, and $Y_a \subseteq \mathbb{R}^m$ is a conservative approximation of the output of f with respect to X_i, i.e. $Y_a \supseteq \{f(\bar{x}) : \bar{x} \in X_i\}$.*

Our goal is to systematically construct abstract mappings from an implementation of a system and then reason about the implementation's compliance with a mapping specification using a *mapping checker*.

Definition 8 (Mapping Checker). *Let $\mathbb{P}$ be a mapping specification, (X_i, Y_a) an abstract mapping of the tree ensemble f subject to verification, such that $X_i \subseteq \{\bar{x} : (\bar{x}, \bar{y}) \in \mathbb{P}\}$, and $M_a = X_i \times Y_a$. A mapping checker C checks the correctness of f with respect to $\mathbb{P}$ using M_a as follows:*

$$C(M_a) = \begin{cases} Pass & M_a \subseteq \mathbb{P} \\ Fail & M_a \not\subseteq \mathbb{P} \wedge Y_a \cap \{\bar{y} : (\bar{x}, \bar{y}) \in \mathbb{P}\} = \emptyset \\ Unsure & otherwise. \end{cases} \qquad (7)$$

A mapping checker is unsure whenever an abstract mapping used together with the function provides an output set which is neither compliant with $\mathbb{P}$, nor falls completely outside $\mathbb{P}$. In that case, we call an abstraction *inconclusive* whenever the checker returns "Unsure". The abstract mapping must then be refined (as described in Sect. 3.2) to determine compliance with the mapping specification.

Example 1 (Robustness Checker). Let $f : X^n \rightarrow \mathbb{R}^m$ be a tree ensemble trained to predict probabilities associated with a classifier that shall assign the label l to samples in a set X_l, and M_a an abstract mapping of f according to Definition 8. A mapping checker for this verification problem may then be implemented as

$$C(M_a) = \begin{cases} \text{Pass} & \{l\} = L_a \\ \text{Fail} & l \notin L_a \\ \text{Unsure} & \text{otherwise,} \end{cases} \tag{8}$$

where $L_a = \{\operatorname{argmax} \bar{y} : (\bar{x}, \bar{y}) \in M_a\}$.

3.2   Abstraction-Refinement Loop

Our formal verification approach may be described as an iterative process as illustrated by Fig. 2. Starting with an initialization step, an initial input region capturing the entire input domain is created. Next follows an abstraction step that, given an input region X_i, produces an output approximation Y_a from a set of trees T, thus forming an abstract mapping (X_i, Y_a). Next, the abstract mapping is evaluated by a mapping checker. If the abstract mapping is conclusive, the process is terminated and the final outcome is reported, i.e. "Pass" or "Fail".

If the abstract mapping is inconclusive, a refinement step removes an arbitrary tree t from T. The input region X_i is then split into k disjoint subsets $X_{i_1}, \ldots, X_{i_k}$ according to the decision functions in t, where k is the number of leaves in t. The succeeding iteration then produces abstract mappings from these subsets, i.e. $(X_{i_1}, Y_{a_1}), \ldots, (X_{i_k}, Y_{a_k})$, which again are evaluated by the mapping checker. When $T = \emptyset$, the abstraction-refinement loop is identical to the precise technique mentioned in Sect. 2.6, and all abstract mappings capture exactly one output tuple each (thus conclusive).

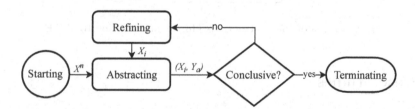

Fig. 2. Flowchart of our abstraction-refinement loop.

3.3   Implementation

We realize the abstraction-refinement loop in the toolsuite VoTE by extending its previous pipeline architecture with alternating abstraction and refining components, as illustrated by Fig. 3.

The first processing element in the pipeline constructs and initializes a hyperrectangle that captures the entire input domain. The final processing element executes a post-processing algorithm that is specific to a particular model. In the case of a random forest for example, the post-processing algorithm divides the sum of all tree outputs with the number of trees in the random forest.

In between, there is an alternating sequence of abstraction and refinery elements. An abstraction element takes as input a hyperrectangle capturing X_i, and computes a hyperrectangle Y_a (using the approximate technique mentioned in Sect. 2.6) that captures all values from all possible path combinations in a set of trees. The first abstraction element in the pipeline contains $B - 1$ trees, while the succeeding one contains $B - 2$ trees, and so on. If the abstraction (X_i, Y_a) is conclusive, no further refinement is necessary, and the outcome from the mapping checker is reported. If the abstraction is inconclusive, X_i is split into smaller input hyperrectangles by the succeeding refinery, and each new input hyperrectangle is transmitted to the succeeding abstraction element.

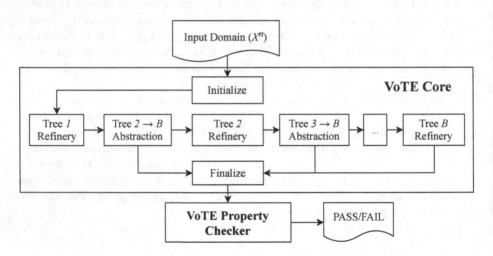

Fig. 3. Design of the abstraction-refinement extension to VoTE.

4   Case Studies

In this section, we evaluate our abstraction-refinement approach by verifying the robustness property in two case studies. Each case study defines a training set and a test set, and we used scikit-learn [10] to train random forests, and CatBoost [11] to train gradient boosting machines. Experiments were conducted on a machine with an Intel Core i5 2500K CPU and 16 GB RAM. We also used a GeForce GTX 1050 GPU to speed up training of gradient boosting machines. For both case studies, we compare the outcome of the evaluation with an earlier method [13] as a baseline (VoTE without the abstraction-refinement loop).

4.1   Vehicle Collision Detection

In this case study, we verified tree ensembles trained to detect collisions between two moving vehicles traveling along curved trajectories. We used the same dataset used in an earlier study [13], which contains 30,000 training samples and 3,000 test samples generated by a simulation tool from Ehlers [4]. All samples are given in normalized form (position, speed, and direction are in the range $[0, 1]$, and rotation speed in the range $[-1, 1]$).

To keep comparability with the baseline, we defined input regions surrounding each sample in the test set with the robustness margin $\epsilon = 0.05$, which amounts to a 5% change since the data is normalized. Table 1 lists random forests (RF) and gradient boosting machines (GB) included in the experiment with their maximum tree depth d, number of trees B, accuracy on the test set (Accuracy), the percentage of samples from the test set where there were no misclassifications within the robustness region (Robustness), the elapsed time during verification (Time), and the elapsed time when using the baseline (Baseline).

Table 1. Performance impact of our abstraction-refinement approach in the vehicle collision detection case study.

Parameters		Accuracy (%)		Robustness (%)		Time (s)		Baseline (s)	
d	B	GB	RF	GB	RF	GB	RF	GB	RF
5	20	93.4	85.8	44.5	**65.6**	1	1	1	2
5	25	93.8	85.7	40.4	65.5	1	1	3	4
10	20	95.5	90.4	34.4	48.9	1	1	23	56
10	25	95.6	90.0	34.0	50.3	1	1	64	285
15	20	95.6	93.0	34.0	34.1	2	1	213	271
15	25	**96.0**	92.9	34.0	35.1	5	2	576	1637

When the tree depth was increased, accuracy increased, but robustness decreased. This suggests that the models were over-fitted with noiseless examples during training, and thus adding noisy examples to the training set may improve robustness. Compared to the baseline setup, our approach is several orders of magnitude faster.

4.2   Digit Recognition

The MNIST dataset [8] is a collection of hand-written digits commonly used to evaluate machine learning algorithms. The dataset contains 70,000 gray scale images with a resolution of 28×28 pixels at 8bpp. Each image is encoded as a tuple of 784 pixels, and the dataset was randomized and split into two subsets; a 85% training set, and a 15% test set.

We defined input regions surrounding each sample in the test set with the robustness margin $\epsilon = 1$, which amounts to a 0.5% lightning change per pixel in a 8bpp gray-scaled image. Due to scalability issues with the baseline setup, earlier work [13] had reduced the complexity of the high-dimensional problem by only considering all possible perturbations within a sliding window of 5×5 pixels. We apply the same complexity reduction technique in this case study to obtain comparable results.

Table 2 lists random forests (RF) and gradient boosting machines (GB) included in the experiment with their maximum tree depth d, number of trees B, accuracy of the test set (Accuracy), the percentage of samples from the test set where there were no misclassifications within the robustness region (Robustness), the elapsed time during verification (Time), and the elapsed time in our baseline setup (Baseline).

Table 2. Performance impact of our abstraction-refinement approach in the digit recognition case study where perturbations across a sliding window were considered.

Parameters		Accuracy (%)		Robustness (%)		Time (s)		Baseline (s)	
d	B	GB	RF	GB	RF	GB	RF	GB	RF
5	25	92.5	84.5	48.2	43.0	58	46	66	236
5	50	94.2	86.1	60.2	50.2	90	91	122	21041
5	75	94.4	85.9	60.8	54.7	127	137	191	-
10	25	94.7	94.2	66.0	74.8	63	55	107	1118
10	50	95.7	94.7	71.0	80.8	105	88	287	-
10	75	**95.9**	94.6	75.1	**82.2**	183	141	689	-

Our abstraction-refinement approach was particularly effective on random forests, demonstrating a speedup by several orders of magnitude. The baseline setup was unable to compute the robustness of large random forests within a reasonable amount of time, so we aborted long-running experiments after 7 hours (denoted by "-" entries in the table). With gradient boosting machines, the abstraction-refinement approach was consistently faster than the baseline setup, demonstrating speedup factors between 1.4–4.9 that increased with the size of the tree ensembles.

To explore the limitations of our approach, we reran the experiments without the baseline setup, and considered perturbations across the entire input domain (instead of sliding windows of 5×5 pixels). Table 3 lists the results in the same format as before.

We note that the robustness of the learned system with respect to the larger set of possible perturbations is much lower (between 8–31%), which is somewhat expected. What is positive in the context is the fact that performing such analyses is at all possible considering the large search space (2^{784} possible perturbations).

Table 3. Accuracy, robustness, and elapsed verification time when using the abstraction-refinement approach in the digit recognition case study and considering perturbations across the entire input domain.

Parameters		Accuracy (%)		Robustness (%)		Time (s)	
d	B	GB	RF	GB	RF	GB	RF
5	25	92.5	84.5	8.5	13.6	70	7
5	50	94.2	86.1	12.1	14.2	316	851
5	75	94.4	85.9	9.7	-	13239	
10	25	94.7	94.2	16.1	25.7	293	12
10	50	95.7	94.7	16.0	**31.4**	23292	7636
10	75	**95.9**	94.6	-	-	-	-

During these experiments, we noticed that some images are harder to verify than others. In one of the more time consuming experiments, a single image accounted for 34% of the elapsed time. This suggests that evaluations of methods that verify robustness against perturbations need a significant amount of test samples to reveal the expected performance when collecting evidence for industrial-sized safety arguments.

5   Related Works

As mentioned earlier, this work is related to the work by Törnblom and Nadjm-Tehrani [13]. Specifically, in this paper we extend the tool VoTE with an abstraction-refinement scheme, and we use results from that paper as baselines in our evaluations.

Chen et al. [3] study the problem of training tree-based ensembles that are robust against adversarial attacks, and propose a technique to address the issue. They evaluate their technique by quantifying robustness against perturbations by means of testing, and demonstrate that their technique significantly improves robustness. In this paper, we take a formal approach that aims for a conclusive outcome compared to informal testing.

Recently, several researchers have pursued a formal approach to the verification of gradient boosting machines. Einziger et al. [5] verify the robustness of gradient boosting machines using an SMT solver. Similarly, Sato et al. [12] leverage an SMT solver, but address a regression problem in their case study, namely gradient boosting machines trained to predict continuous outputs. Due to significant differences in benchmarks and implementations of tree ensembles, we leave a systematic comparison between these three approaches for future works.

6   Conclusions and Future Works

Recent advances in machine learning are now being considered for integration in safety-critical systems. However, there is currently a lack of verification methods which yield convincing arguments that such systems are safe enough to operate.

In this paper, we presented an abstraction-refinement based approach to formal verification of tree-based machine learning models. We combined two verification techniques from related works [13], a conservative and fast approximation technique, and a precise and exhaustive technique. We realized the abstraction-refinement approach as an extension to the earlier toolsuite VoTE, and evaluated its performance impact on two case studies; a collision detection problem, and a digit recognition problem. Compared to previous work, our approach demonstrated speedups by several orders of magnitude.

In case studies addressed by this paper, we verified the robustness property using incomplete specifications. For example, the dataset in our digit recognition case study only contains 70,000 images, while the actual number of images that resemble a digit is enormous. The lack of complete formal specifications in applications where machine learning is useful is still an open research question, an issue we intend to address in future works.

As mentioned before, earlier work by Einziger et al. [5] and current work by Sato et al. [12] suggests that SMT solvers can verify gradient boosting machines. However, there are significant differences between test benches and implementations of tree ensembles used in their case studies, thus making a direct comparison difficult. Consequently, there is a need for plug-n-play benchmarks that can point towards fruitful future lines of research. Other potential lines of research based on this paper include a more strict formalization to enable formulating the decision procedure with soundness and completeness proofs, and a systematic analysis of abstraction and refinement criteria, e.g. the order in which to choose trees in the refinement steps.

Acknowledgements. This work was partially supported by the Wallenberg AI, Autonomous Systems and Software Program (WASP) funded by the Knut and Alice Wallenberg Foundation.

References

1. Breiman, L.: Random forests. Mach. Learn. **45**(1), 5–32 (2001)
2. Bruneau, M., et al.: A framework to quantitatively assess and enhance the seismic resilience of communities. Earthq. Spectra **19**(4), 733–752 (2003)
3. Chen, H., Zhang, H., Boning, D., Hsieh, C.J.: Adversarial defense for tree-based models. In: Safe Machine Learning workshop at ICLR (2019)
4. Ehlers, R.: Formal verification of piece-wise linear feed-forward neural networks. In: D'Souza, D., Narayan Kumar, K. (eds.) ATVA 2017. LNCS, vol. 10482, pp. 269–286. Springer, Cham (2017). https://doi.org/10.1007/978-3-319-68167-2_19
5. Einziger, G., Goldstein, M., Sa'ar, Y., Segall, I.: Verifying robustness of gradient boosted models. In: AAAI Conference on Artificial Intelligence (2019)

6. Friedman, J.H.: Greedy function approximation: a gradient boosting machine. Ann. Stat. **29**, 1189–1232 (2001)
7. Irsoy, O., Yildiz, O.T., Alpaydin, E.: Soft decision trees. In: International Conference on Pattern Recognition (ICPR). IEEE (2012)
8. LeCun, Y., Bottou, L., Bengio, Y., Haffner, P.: Gradient-based learning applied to document recognition. Proc. IEEE **86**(11), 2278–2324 (1998)
9. Liu, C., Arnon, T., Lazarus, C., Barrett, C., Kochenderfer, M.J.: Algorithms for verifying deep neural networks. arXiv preprint arXiv:1903.06758 (2019)
10. Pedregosa, F., et al.: Scikit-learn: machine learning in Python. J. Mach. Learn. Res. **12**, 2825–2830 (2011)
11. Prokhorenkova, L., Gusev, G., Vorobev, A., Dorogush, A.V., Gulin, A.: Catboost: unbiased boosting with categorical features. In: Advances in Neural Information Processing Systems (NIPS) (2018)
12. Sato, N., Kuruma, H., Nakagawa, Y., Ogawa, H.: Formal verification of decision-tree ensemble model and detection of its violating-input-value ranges. arXiv preprint arXiv:1904.11753 (2019)
13. Törnblom, J., Nadjm-Tehrani, S.: Formal verification of input-output mappings of tree ensembles. arXiv preprint arXiv:1905.04194 (2019)
14. Wang, F., Wang, Q., Nie, F., Yu, W., Wang, R.: Efficient tree classifiers for large scale datasets. Neurocomputing **284**, 70–79 (2018)

RL-Based Method for Benchmarking the Adversarial Resilience and Robustness of Deep Reinforcement Learning Policies

Vahid Behzadan[✉] and William Hsu

Kansas State University, Manhattan, USA
{behzadan,bhsu}@ksu.edu

Abstract. This paper investigates the resilience and robustness of Deep Reinforcement Learning (DRL) policies to adversarial perturbations in the state space. We first present an approach for the disentanglement of vulnerabilities caused by representation learning of DRL agents from those that stem from the sensitivity of the DRL policies to distributional shifts in state transitions. Building on this approach, we propose two RL-based techniques for quantitative benchmarking of adversarial resilience and robustness in DRL policies against perturbations of state transitions. We demonstrate the feasibility of our proposals through experimental evaluation of resilience and robustness in DQN, A2C, and PPO2 policies trained in the Cartpole environment.

Keywords: Deep Reinforcement Learning · Adversarial attack ·
Policy generalization · Resilience · Robustness · Benchmarking

1 Introduction

Since the reports by Behzadan and Munir [1] and Huang et al. [5], the primary emphasis of the state of the art in DRL security [2] has been on the vulnerability of policies to state-space perturbations. In particular, the manipulation of the policy via adversarial examples [4] has remained the main focus of current literature on this issue. However, this bias towards adversarial example attacks gives rise to a critical shortcoming: the analyses of such attacks fail to disentangle the vulnerability caused by the learned representation and that which is due to the sensitivity of the DRL dynamics to distributional shifts in state transitions. Also, the performance of defenses proposed for adversarial example attacks are inherently limited to the considered attack mechanisms. As the most successful technique for mitigation of adversarial examples, adversarial training is known to enhance the robustness of machine learning models to the type of attack used for generating the training adversarial examples, while leaving the model vulnerable to other types of attacks [8]. Furthermore, the current literature fails to provide solutions and approaches which can be used in practice to evaluate and improve the robustness and resilience of DRL policies to attacks that exploit

© Springer Nature Switzerland AG 2019
A. Romanovsky et al. (Eds.): SAFECOMP 2019 Workshops, LNCS 11699, pp. 314–325, 2019.
https://doi.org/10.1007/978-3-030-26250-1_25

the sensitivity to state transitions. Also, there remains a need for quantitative approaches to measure and benchmark the resilience and robustness of DRL policies in a reusable and generalizable manner.

In response to these shortcomings, this paper aims to address the problem of quantifying and benchmarking the robustness and resilience of a DRL agent to adversarial perturbations of state transitions at test-time, in a manner that is independent of the attack type. This improves the generalization of current techniques that analyze the model against specific adversarial example attacks. Accordingly, the main contributions of this paper are as follows:

1. We present formulations of the resilience and robustness problems that enable the disentanglement of limitation in representation learning from sensitivity of policies to state transition dynamics.
2. We propose two RL-based techniques and corresponding metrics for the measurement and benchmarking of resilience and robustness of DRL policies to perturbations of state transitions,
3. We demonstrate the feasibility of our proposal through experimental evaluation of their performance on DQN, A2C, and PPO2 agents trained in the Cartpole environment.

The remainder of this paper is organized as follows: Sect. 2 defines and formulates the problems of adversarial resilience and robustness in DRL. Our proposed methods for benchmarking the test-time resilience and robustness of DRL policies are presented in Sects. 3 and 4. Section 5 provides the details of experimental setup for evaluating the performance of our proposals, with the corresponding results presented in Sect. 6. The paper concludes in Sect. 7 with a summary of findings and remarks on future directions of research.

2   Problem Formulation

We consider the generic problem of RL in the settings of a Markov Decision Process (MDP), described by the tuple $MDP := < \mathbb{S}, \mathbb{A}, \mathbb{R}, \mathbb{P} >$, where $\mathbb{S}$ is the set of reachable states in the process, $\mathbb{A}$ is the set of available actions, $\mathbb{R}$ is the mapping of transitions to the immediate reward, and $\mathbb{P}$ represents the transition probabilities (i.e., state dynamics), which are initially unknown to RL agents. At any given time-step t, the MDP is at a state $s_t \in \mathbb{S}$. The RL agent's choice of action at time t, $a_t \in \mathbb{A}$ causes a transition from s_t to a state s_{t+1} according to the transition probability $P(s_{t+1}|s_t, a_t)$. The agent receives a reward $r_{t+1} = R(s_t, a_t, s_{t+1})$ for choosing the action a_t at state s_t. Interactions of the agent with MDP are determined by the policy π. When such interactions are deterministic, the policy $\pi : S \rightarrow \mathbb{A}$ is a mapping between the states and their corresponding actions. A stochastic policy $\pi(s)$ represents the probability distribution of implementing any action $a \in \mathbb{A}$ at state s. The goal of RL is to learn a policy that maximizes the expected discounted return $E[R_t]$, where $R_t = \sum_{k=0}^{\infty} \gamma^k r_{t+k}$; with r_t denoting the instantaneous reward received at time t, and γ is a discount factor $\gamma \in [0, 1]$.

To facilitate the formal statement of adversarial resilience and robustness, we first introduce the following definitions:

- *Adversarial Regret* at time T is the difference between return obtained by the nominal (unperturbed) agent at time T and the return obtained by the perturbed agent at time T. Formally: $\hat{R}_{adv}(T) = R_{nominal}(T) - R_{perturbed}(T)$. The time T may represent either the terminal time step of an episode, or the time-horizon of interest in the analysis.
- *Adversarial Budget* is defined by one or more of the following parameters: the maximum number of features that can be perturbed in the observations ($O_{max} \in [0, \infty]$), the maximum number of observations that can be perturbed ($N_{max} \in [0, \infty]$), and the probability of perturbing each observation ($P(perturb) \in [0, 1]$).

Building on these two concepts, we define the problems of adversarial resilience and robustness as follows:

1. *Test-Time Resilience:* The minimum number of state perturbations required to incur the maximum reduction to the total return at time T (denoted by $\hat{R}_{adv}(T)$) for an agent driven by a policy $\pi(s)$ in an environment with transition dynamics $\mathbb{P}$.
2. *Test-Time Robustness:* The maximum adversarial regret $\hat{R}_{adv}(T) = \epsilon_{max}$ achievable via a maximum of δ_{max} state perturbations for an agent driven by a policy $\pi(s)$ in an environment with transition dynamics $\mathbb{P}$.

The following sections provide the details of our proposed solutions to each of the aforementioned problem settings.

3   Benchmarking of Test-Time Resilience

This problem can be modeled as that of finding an optimal adversarial policy $\pi_{adv}(s)$ that minimizes the cost incurred to the adversary C_{adv} in order to impose the maximum adversarial regret $\hat{R}_{adv}(T)$, the worst-case value of which is the highest cumulative reward achieved by the target policy R_{max}. Our proposed approach is through the formulation of this problem in the settings of reinforcement learning. The state space in the corresponding MDP is the set of states in the target MDP, augmented with the action of the target in that state, i.e., $S' = \{\forall s \in \mathbb{S} : (s, \pi(s))\}$. For the purpose of measuring a lower bound for the resilience, we consider the worst-case white-box adversary, which is able to impose targeted state perturbations with a 100% success rate, to induce any action within the permissible action-set of the target $\mathbb{A}$ which has the lowest Q-value at any state s according to the target's optimal state-action value function Q^*. In this case, the set of permissible adversarial actions at any state s is given by:

$$A_{adv}(s) = \{\text{No Action}\} \cup \mathbb{A} \setminus \pi^*(s) \tag{1}$$

where $\mathbb{A}$ is the action set of the targeted agent, and $\pi : S \rightarrow A$ is the policy of the targeted agent. In the proposed approach, the adversarial reward value is determined via the procedure detailed in Algorithm 1:

Algorithm 1. Reward Assignment of RL Agent for Measuring Adversarial Resilience

---

Require: Target policy π^*, Perturbation cost function $c_{adv}(.,.)$, Maximum achievable score R_{max}, Optimal state-action value function $Q^*(.,.)$, Current adversarial policy π^{adv}, Current state s_t, Current count of adversarial actions $AdvCount$, Current score R_t

Set ToPerturb $\leftarrow \pi^{adv}(s_t)$
if ToPerturb is False then
    $a_t \leftarrow \pi^*(s_t)$
    $Reward \leftarrow 0$
else
    $a_t' \leftarrow \arg\min_a Q^*(s_t, a)$
    $Reward \leftarrow -c_{adv}(s_t, a_t')$
end if
if either s_t or s_t' is terminal then
    $Reward+ = (R_{max} - R_t)$
end if

---

where $c(s_t, a_t')$ is the cost of imposing the state perturbation which induces the adversarial action a_t' at state s_t. It is noteworthy that if the value of $c(s_t, a_t')$ is invariant with respect to a_t', the adversarial action set reduces to:

$$A_{adv}(s) = \{\text{No Action, } \textit{Induce} \arg\min_a Q(s, a)\} \tag{2}$$

To obtain the test-time resilience of policy π^* to state perturbations, we propose the following procedure:

1. If the state-action value function of the target Q^* is not available (i.e., black-box testing), approximate Q^* via policy imitation [6].
2. Train the adversarial agent against the target following π in its training environment, report the optimal adversarial return $R^*_{perturbed}$ and the maximum adversarial regret $R^*_{adv}(T)$.
3. Apply the adversarial policy against the target in N episodes, record total cost C_{adv} for each episode,
4. Report the average of C_{adv} over N episodes as the mean test-time resilience of π in the given environment.

This procedure introduces three metrics for the quantification of test-time resilience: the optimal adversarial return $R^*_{perturbed}$ achieved in the training process of the adversarial policy, the maximum adversarial regret $R^*_{adv}(T)$ achieved during training, and the mean per-episode of the total cost C_{adv}. These metrics provide the means to benchmark and compare the test-time resilience of different policies trained to optimize the agent's performance in a given environment.

For the purpose of measuring resilience, we consider convergence to be reached if the average adversarial regret over 200 episodes remains constant. This definition relaxes the instabilities that may arise due to the configuration and architecture of the DRL training process. It is noteworthy that depending on the training algorithm and design parameters, this procedure is not guaranteed to converge to global optima. However, by reporting the number of iterations and configuration of random number generators with a constant seed, the reported results present a reproducible loose lower bound on the adversarial resilience of the target. Also, the trained adversarial policy can be use to test other policies for comparison of such lower bounds under the same adversarial strategy.

4   Benchmarking of Test-Time Robustness

For this problem, we propose a modified version of the procedure developed for benchmarking the test-time resilience. Accordingly, the reward function is adjusted to account for the lack of a target ϵ, as well as the addition of an adversarial budget constraint δ_{max}. The reward measurement of this process is outlined in Algorithm 2:

Algorithm 2. Reward Assignment of RL Agent for Measuring Adversarial Robustness

---

Require: Maximum perturbation budget δ_{max}, Perturbation cost function $c_{adv}(.,.)$, Maximum achievable score R_{max}, Optimal state-action value function $Q^*(.,.)$, Current adversarial policy π^{adv}, Current state s, Current count of adversarial actions $AdvCount$, Current score R_t
    Set AdversarialAction $\leftarrow \pi^{adv}(s)$
    if AdversarialAction is NoAction **then**
        $Reward \leftarrow 0$
    else if $AdvCount \geq \delta_{max}$ **then**
        $Reward \leftarrow -c_{adv}(s, AdversarialAction) \times \delta_{max}$
        $AdvCount+ = 1$
    else
        $Reward \leftarrow -c_a dv(s, AdversarialAction)$
        $AdvCount+ = 1$
    end if
    if s is terminal **then**
        $Reward+ = 1.0 * (R_{max} - R_t)$
        $AdvCount \leftarrow 0$
    end if

The proposed procedure for measuring the test-time robustness of a given DRL policy to adversarial state perturbations is as follows:

1. If the state-action value function of the target Q^* is not available (i.e., black-box testing settings), approximate Q^* from the policy using imitation learning (e.g., [6]),
2. Train the adversarial agent against the target policy π^* in its training environment, report the maximum adversarial regret $R^*_{adv}(T)$ for time T achieved at adversarial optimality,
3. Apply the adversarial policy against the target for N episodes, record the adversarial regret at the end of each episode $R_{adv}(T)$,
4. Report the average of $R_{adv}(T)$ over N episodes as the mean per-episode test-time robustness of π^* in the given environment.

5   Experiment Setup

Environment and Target Policies: To demonstrate the performance of the proposed procedures for benchmarking the test-time robustness and resilience in DRL policies, we present the analysis of the aforementioned measurements for policies trained in the CartPole environment in OpenAI Gym [3]. The considered policies are chosen to represent the commonly-adopted state of the art method from each class of DRL algorithms. From value-iteration approaches, we consider DQN with prioritized replay. From the class of policy gradient approaches, we consider PPO2. As for actor-critic methods, we investigate the A2C method. Table 1 presents the specifications of the CartPole environment, and Tables 2, 3 and 4 provide the parameter settings of each target policy.

Table 1. Specifications of the CartPole environment

Observation Space	Cart Position $[-4.8, +4.8]$
	Cart Velocity $[-\inf, +\inf]$
	Pole Angle $[-24°, +24°]$
	Pole Velocity at Tip $[-\inf, +\inf]$
Action Space	0: Push cart to the left
	1: Push cart to the right
Reward	+1 for every step taken
Termination	Pole Angle is more than $12°$
	Cart Position is more than 2.4
	Episode length is greater than 500

Adversarial Agent: In these experiments, the adversarial agent is a DQN agent with the hyperparameters provided in Table 5. We consider a homogeneous perturbation cost function for all state perturbations, that is, $\forall s, a' : c_{adv}(s, a') = c_{adv}$. For both the resilience and robustness measurements, we set $c_{adv} = 1$ (i.e., each perturbation incurs a cost of 1 to the adversary). The training process is terminated when the adversarial regret is maximized and the 100-episode average of the number of adversarial perturbations is quasi-stable for 200 episodes.

Table 2. Parameters of DQN policy

No. Timesteps	10^5
γ	0.99
Learning Rate	10^{-3}
Replay Buffer Size	50000
First Learning Step	1000
Target Network Update Freq.	500
Prioritized Replay	True
Exploration	Parameter-Space Noise
Exploration Fraction	0.1
Final Exploration Prob.	0.02
Max. Total Reward	500

Table 3. Parameters of A2C policy

No. Timesteps	5×10^5
γ	0.99
Learning Rate	7×10^{-4}
Entropy Coefficient	0.0
Value Function Coefficient	0.25
Max. Total Reward	500

Table 4. Parameters of A2C policy

No. Environments	8
No. Timesteps	10^6
No. Runs per Environment per Update	2048
No. Minibatches per update	32
Bias-Variance Trade-Off Factor	0.95
No. Surrogate Epochs	10
γ	0.99
Learning Rate	3×10^{-4}
Entropy Coefficient	0.0
Value Function Coefficient	0.5
Max. Total Reward	500

Table 5. Parameters of DQN policy

Max. Timesteps	10^5
γ	0.99
Learning Rate	10^{-3}
Replay Buffer Size	50000
First Learning Step	1000
Target Network Update Freq.	500
Experience Selection	Prioritized Replay
Exploration	Parameter-Space Noise
Exploration Fraction	0.1
Final Exploration Prob.	0.02

6 Results

6.1 Resilience Benchmarks

We consider the white-box settings in the training of adversarial agents for resilience measurement. For the DQN target, the optimal state-action value function Q^* of the target is directly utilized. As for the A2C and PPO2 targets, the state-action value function is calculated from the internally-available state value estimations $V^*(s)$ according to the following transformation:

$$Q^*(s_t, a) = r(s_t, a) + \gamma V^*(s_{t+1}) \tag{3}$$

where s_{t+1} is the state resulting from a transition out of state s_t by implementing action a.

Training Results: The training progress plots of adversarial DQN policy on the three target policies are presented in Figs. 1, 2 and 3. It can be seen that all three policies converge to the same optima. However, for the adversary targeting the DQN policies, the convergence is achieved at a higher number of training steps.

It is noteworthy that for all three policies, the mean-per-100 episodes of the minimum number of perturbations at convergence is almost similar (as reported in Table 6), with A2C having the largest value of 7.69 perturbations, PPO2 at a value of 7.49 perturbations, and DQN having the lowest value of 7.13. Also, the test-time performance of these trained policies indicate similar results, with DQN requiring 6.95 perturbations to incur an adversarial regret of 491.15, PPO2 requiring 7.72 perturbations for an adversarial regret of 490.47, and A2C requiring 8.71 perturbations for an adversarial regret of 488.16. Accordingly, we can interpret these results as follows: the DQN policy has the lowest adversarial resilience among the three, followed by the PPO2 policy. Within the context of this comparison, the A2C policy is found to be the most resilient to state-space perturbation attacks.

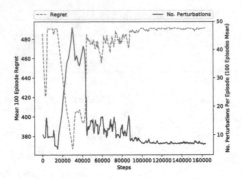

Fig. 1. Adversarial training progress for resilience benchmarking of the DQN policy

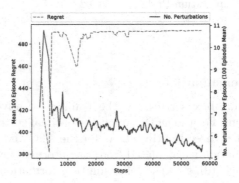

Fig. 2. Adversarial training progress for resilience benchmarking of the A2C policy

Table 6. Comparison of test-time and training-time resilience measurements for DQN, A2C, and PPO2 policies

Target policy	Max. regret	Avg. regret (Training)	Avg. no. perturbations (Training)	Avg. regret	Avg. no. perturbations
DQN	492	491.24	7.13	491.15	6.95
A2C	492	491.44	7.69	488.16	8.71
PPO2	492	491.72	7.49	490.47	7.72

6.2 Test-Time Step-Perturbation Distribution

To investigate the state-transition vulnerability of each policy, we also study the frequency of perturbing states at each time step of an episode for the three adversarial policies. The results, presented in Figs. 4, 5 and 6, illustrate that in all three policies, the initial time steps have been the subject of most perturbations. This result is noteworthy, as it contradicts the assumption of Lin et al. [7] that the most effective adversarial perturbations are those that are mounted towards the terminal state of the environment.

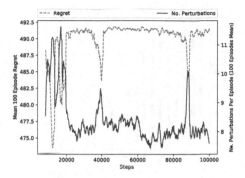

Fig. 3. Adversarial training progress for resilience benchmarking of the PPO2 policy

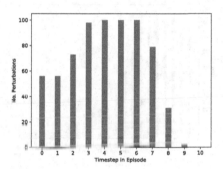

Fig. 4. Perturbation count per episodic time step in 100 runs targeting DQN policy

6.3   Robustness Benchmarks

To demonstrate the performance of our proposed technique for benchmarking the robustness of DRL policies, we provide the training-time results for two cases of $\delta_{max} = 10$ and $\delta_{max} = 5$ for DQN, A2C, and PPO2 Policies. As illustrated in Fig. 7a–c, all three adversarial policies converge with similar minimum perturbation counts as those obtained in resilience analysis. This is expected, as the resilience analysis established that the minimum number of actions required for maximum regret is 7.5, which is less than the available budget of $\delta_{max} = 10$ As for the case of $\delta_{max} = 5$, Fig. 8a–c demonstrate significant differences between the three policies. In Fig. 8a, it can be seen that at 5 actions, the convergence occurs with an adversarial regret of 462.5, while for A2C, the best 5-action indication of convergence occurs at an adversarial regret of 224. As for PPO2, this value is at 268.2. These results indicate a similar ranking of the robustness in these policies, with DQN being the least-robust to maximum of 5 perturbations, and the A2C prevailing as the most robust policy to maximum of 5 perturbations.

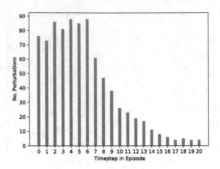

Fig. 5. Perturbation count per episodic time step in 100 runs targeting A2C policy

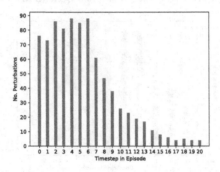

Fig. 6. Perturbation count per episodic time step in 100 runs targeting PPO policy

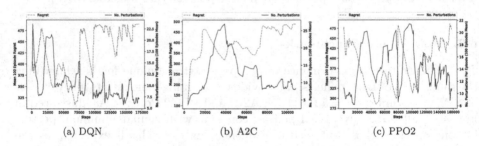

Fig. 7. Adversarial training progress for robustness benchmarking, $\delta_{max} = 10$

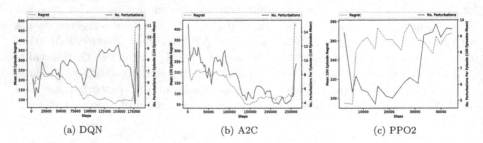

Fig. 8. Adversarial training progress for robustness benchmarking, $\delta_{max} = 5$

7   Conclusion

We presented two RL-based techniques for benchmarking the resilience and robustness of DRL policies to adversarial perturbations of state transition dynamics. Experimental evaluation of our proposals demonstrates the feasibility of these techniques for quantitative analysis of policies with regards to their sensitivity to state transition dynamics. A promising venue of further exploration is to study and extend the proposed methodologies for evaluation of generalization in DRL policies.

References

1. Behzadan, V., Munir, A.: Vulnerability of deep reinforcement learning to policy induction attacks. In: Perner, P. (ed.) MLDM 2017. LNCS (LNAI), vol. 10358, pp. 262–275. Springer, Cham (2017). https://doi.org/10.1007/978-3-319-62416-7_19
2. Behzadan, V., Munir, A.: The faults in our pi stars: security issues and open challenges in deep reinforcement learning. arXiv preprint arXiv:1810.10369 (2018)
3. Brockman, G., et al.: Openai gym. arXiv preprint arXiv:1606.01540 (2016)
4. Goodfellow, I.J., Shlens, J., Szegedy, C.: Explaining and harnessing adversarial examples (2014). arXiv preprint arXiv:1412.6572 (2014)
5. Huang, S., Papernot, N., Goodfellow, I., Duan, Y., Abbeel, P.: Adversarial attacks on neural network policies. arXiv preprint arXiv:1702.02284 (2017)
6. Hussein, A., Gaber, M.M., Elyan, E., Jayne, C.: Imitation learning: a survey of learning methods. ACM Comput. Surv. (CSUR) 50(2), 21 (2017)
7. Lin, Y.C., Hong, Z.W., Liao, Y.H., Shih, M.L., Liu, M.Y., Sun, M.: Tactics of adversarial attack on deep reinforcement learning agents. arXiv preprint arXiv:1703.06748 (2017)
8. Tramèr, F., Kurakin, A., Papernot, N., Goodfellow, I., Boneh, D., McDaniel, P.: Ensemble adversarial training: Attacks and defenses. arXiv preprint arXiv:1705.07204 (2017)

A Safety Standard Approach for Fully Autonomous Vehicles

Philip Koopman[1,2(✉)] ⓘ, Uma Ferrell[3], Frank Fratrik[1],
and Michael Wagner[1]

[1] Edge Case Research, Pittsburgh, PA 15201, USA
koopman@cmu.edu, {ffratrik,mwagner}@ecr.ai
[2] Carnegie Mellon University, Pittsburgh, PA 15213, USA
[3] The MITRE Corporation, McLean, VA 22102, USA
uferrell@mitre.org

Abstract. Assuring the safety of self-driving cars and other fully autonomous vehicles presents significant challenges to traditional software safety standards both in terms of content and approach. We propose a safety standard approach for fully autonomous vehicles based on setting scope requirements for an overarching safety case. A viable approach requires feedback paths to ensure that both the safety case and the standard itself co-evolve with the technology and accumulated experience. An external assessment process must be part of this approach to ensure lessons learned are captured, as well as to ensure transparency. This approach forms the underlying basis for the UL 4600 initial draft standard.

Keywords: Self-driving cars · Autonomous vehicles · Safety standard · UL 4600

1 Introduction

Self-driving cars are (eventually) coming, and could have a profound impact on transportation [13]. On-road testing is underway in a number of locations across the world, and announcements regularly proclaim that cars will be able to operate without a human driver "soon" (or perhaps later [13]). Overall, safety looms as a significant concern.

Standards that address computer-based system safety for conventional vehicles have existed for decades [3, 9], with ISO 26262:2018 [4] being a recent incarnation. A more recent standard addresses Advanced Driver Assistance System (ADAS) Safety Of The Intended Function (SOTIF) [5].

These existing standards are essential, but do not achieve comprehensive coverage of how to ensure that deployed fleets of Highly Autonomous Vehicles (HAVs) will operate safely. While safety standards from other domains such as aviation and military systems can provide additional insight, designers in those domains also struggle with issues unique to building safe autonomous systems. Additionally, HAV technology can benefit from an agile, iterative approach to ensuring and regulating safety [14].

© Springer Nature Switzerland AG 2019
A. Romanovsky et al. (Eds.): SAFECOMP 2019 Workshops, LNCS 11699, pp. 326–332, 2019.
https://doi.org/10.1007/978-3-030-26250-1_26

This position paper seeks to outline a number of issues that must be addressed in a comprehensive HAV safety standard. The strategy described is the basis of the draft "UL 4600 Standard for Safety for the Evaluation of Autonomous Products" [16] that is intended to cover HAVs and eventually other related domains.

2 Current Standards

2.1 ISO 26262

Traditionally, automotive designers have based their overall safety strategy on a principle that a human driver is ultimately responsible for safety. This has resulted in, among other things, a focus in ISO 26262 [4] on functional safety.

Broadly speaking, functional safety ensures the system has a capability to mitigate failure risk sufficiently for identified hazards. The amount of mitigation required depends upon the severity of a potential loss event, operational exposure to hazards, and human driver controllability of the system when failure occurs. These factors combine into an Automotive Safety Integrity Level (ASIL) per a predetermined risk table. The assigned ASIL for a function determines which technical and process mitigations must be applied, including specified design and analysis tasks that must be performed. ISO 26262 is consistent with safety standards such as IEC 61508 [2] on items such as:

- Specifies a V-based process reference model
- Addresses software, hardware, and system aspects using integrity levels
- Includes lifecycle topics such as production, operation, support, and tools
- Specifies approach to safety incorporating hazards, safety goals, and ASILs
- Specifies analysis, design, and verification techniques based on ASIL

In summary, the emphasis on ISO 26262 is on avoiding design faults (e.g., via software quality requirements) and mitigating the effect of equipment faults during operation (e.g., via failsafes).

2.2 ISO/PAS 21448 (SOTIF)

More recently, the automotive industry has created a safety standard for driver assistance functions that could fail to operate properly even if no equipment fault is present. The ISO/PAS 21448 "Safety of the Intended Functionality" (SOTIF) standard [5] addresses those issues. It primarily considers mitigating risks due to unexpected operating conditions (the intended function might not always work in these due to limitations of sensors and algorithms) and gaps in requirements (lack of complete description about what the intended function actually is). Highlights of this standard include covering:

- Insufficient situational awareness
- Foreseeable misuse and human-machine interaction issues
- Issues arising from operational environment (weather, infrastructure, etc.)

- An emphasis on identifying and filling requirement gaps (removing "unknowns")
- In practice, an emphasis on enumerating operational scenarios (e.g., [10])

In summary, ISO 21448 extends the scope of ISO 26262 to cover ADAS functionality. Both explicitly permit extending scope further. But as a pair they are not architected to cover the full extent of HAV safety. (A pending, not-yet-public revision of ISO 21448 aims go further).

2.3 Other Safety Standards

There are numerous other safety standards from other domains including: IEC 61508 [2] for chemical process control; CENELEC EN 50128 [1] for rail systems; MIL-STD-882E [15] for military systems; and SAE ARP 4754A [11] as well as SAE ARP 4761 [12] for aviation. While these provide additional safety perspective, none covers the full range of HAV issues. Mainly this is due to assumptions of human operator availability (e.g., aircraft pilots), complete requirements identification, and/or significantly simplified operational environment compared to HAVs (e.g., protected rail right of way). While these standards provide valuable insight and principles, more is needed to provide thorough guidance for HAVs.

3 Constraints on Acceptable Standards

The need to have an HAV safety standard is urgent. Companies regularly promise to deploy HAVs to production without "safety drivers." While we could wait for the usual decade(s) of field experience for designs to converge before writing a safety standard, it is highly desirable to have a standard sooner rather than later.

Despite the excellent foundation provided by current standards, significant challenges await any would-be standard authors for HAVs. These include both the type and immaturity of the technology being used. However, they also include some profound implications of removing the human driver from the vehicle safety equation.

3.1 Novel Technology

HAVs as currently envisioned use technology that is inherently incompatible with legacy safety standards approaches. A standard must address at least [6]:

- Use of Machine Learning (ML) technology. A significant advantage of using ML is using a training-based approach to resolve intractable design situations. However, that same lack of requirements impedes traceability and ability to do design reviews.
- Use of unpredictable algorithms. Randomized algorithms and other so-called Artificial Intelligence (AI) techniques tend to behave in an unpredictable way, generally characterized as being non-deterministic. This complicates creating repeatable tests.

Traditional safety standards employ update cycles of perhaps 5 to 10 years, but HAV technology is evolving much more rapidly. Premature standards could inhibit innovation. Additionally, a traditional consensus-based standard approach is difficult when developers are still figuring out how to make the technology work acceptably well. Any standard will need an unprecedented level of flexibility to be viable.

3.2 No Human Driver

The contents of any standard will have to address fundamental changes in system-level fault management. Controllability evaporates with an HAV, because there is no human driver to exercise control. Therefore, autonomy itself must manage vehicle failures.

An additional issue with the removal of the human driver is that a large number of other operational and lifecycle activities beyond the actual driving must also be covered. This includes safely interacting with humans such as potentially unruly passengers and emergency personnel. Moreover, autonomy might need to mitigate risk due to operational faults (e.g., passenger evacuation in a car fire) and handle lifecycle faults.

4 A Safety Case Approach

We believe that the difficult constraints of creating a safety standard for HAVs can be met with an approach that combines: use of a safety case for the overarching structure, specifying breadth of safety case scope, incorporating lessons learned, updating for a changing environment, and using a multi-layered feedback approach that includes independent assessment. This approach accounts for not only managing the risk presented by unknowns, but also the evolving technology and changing operational environment.

4.1 Safety Cases with Specified Scope

Safety case approaches have been used previously (e.g., [4, 8]). We believe that rather than being just a part of the safety package, the safety case should be the primary overarching structure containing essentially everything. This approach permits keeping items such as tools to be used and engineering processes to be followed flexible. By the same token, this means that the safety case must not only present fully substantiated arguments that appropriate and necessary processes and practices have been used, but also that the selection choices are in fact sufficient to ensure safety.

As long as the other elements of our approach are followed, in principle the standard need not specify any particular tool or process step approach. Rather, it can require that certain high-level claims and argumentation be present. As an example, the standard can require that all hazards and associated risks be identified, but not what techniques must be used to accomplish that. To avoid unnecessary effort and expense, credit can be taken for conformance to ISO 26262, ISO 21448, and other relevant standards to the degree conformance is credible and actually applies to HAV safety.

A potential concern is the creation of a safety case that is lacking in depth or evidence. The draft standard requires a certain level of depth by enumerating required sub-claims and safety case coverage. (As an example, hazards associated with the supply chain must be identified). At a high level, we have identified the following topics that must be specifically addressed for HAVs beyond the level of detail in other standards:

- Definition of Operational Design Domain (e.g., weather, scenarios [7])
- Machine learning faults (e.g. training data gaps, brittleness)
- External operational faults (e.g., other vehicles violating traffic rules)
- Faulty behavior by non-driver humans (e.g., pedestrians, lifecycle participants)
- Non-deterministic, variable system behavior (e.g., test planning, acceptance criteria)
- High residual unknowns (e.g., requirements gaps and post-deployment surprises)
- Lack of human oversight (e.g., operational fault handling, passenger handling)
- System-level safety metrics (e.g., use of leading and lagging metrics)
- Transitioning the system to degraded modes and minimum risk conditions

4.2 Ongoing Risk Assessment

Considering the novelty, complexity, and consequences involved with HAV deployment, challenges are expected in creating a bulletproof initial safety case. Rather than adopting a fiction that mere conformance to a standard at deployment results in flawless risk mitigation, instead it is important to continually evaluate and improve the residual risk present in the system. Identifying latent and emergent risks is essential to enable identifying, implementing, and verifying additional mitigation measures.

By the same token, it is important to address known safety issues before exposing testers and the public to undue safety risk. Developers should strive for a culture of responsible safety risk identification and ownership rather than simply checking boxes. This includes taking ownership of development mistakes as well as gaps in design, test, and the safety case itself. Honest self-assessment and iteration over the system development and deployment lifecycle is vitally important to mature the safety case.

We also believe that independent assessment is essential. This is especially true in light of the high-stakes, high pressure environment of HAV development. Beyond providing essential checks and balances on system safety, independent assessment can provide a way to share lessons learned without revealing proprietary design details.

4.3 Feedback and Lessons Learned

Rather than treat the rapid evolution of HAV technology as an obstacle, we intend to embrace it. Neither waiting until the dust settles (which might not ever really happen) nor prematurely freezing the standard seem viable. Instead, we plan to evolve the standard in tandem with the technology. Here is how we believe it can work (Fig. 1):

- Seed the initial standard with required essential practices and anti-patterns that have proven value (e.g., identifying hazards, avoiding known unsafe design patterns) based on stakeholder inputs.
- Require essential elements of the safety case (e.g., pick and adapt any reasonable hazard analysis approach from your favorite safety standard).
- Include a list of safety case acceptable patterns and excluded anti-patterns.

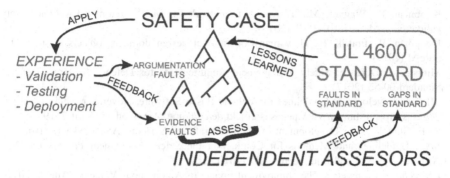

Fig. 1. The standard informs safety case construction. Field experience provides feedback.

- Require plausible argumentation that residual risk and "unknowns" will be tracked.
- Require feedback paths based on root cause analysis of incidents and loss events during both development and deployment to identify weak spots in the process:
  - Gaps in enumerated lists in the safety case (e.g., a new hazard)
  - Gaps in safety case evidence (e.g., an "impossible" failure occurs in the field)
  - Flaws in argumentation and assumptions (e.g., real world assumption violations)
  - Gaps in patterns, anti-patterns, and required elements in the safety standard itself
  - Adoption of new practices that have proven to provide value into the standard

5 Conclusions

We believe that a goal-based safety case approach with pre-seeded feedback paths is a practical way to create a safety standard for HAVs. This can encourage the use of accepted safety practices at first, yet still evolve and mature along with the industry. A potential outcome is an agile alternative to inflexible regulations for ensuring safety.

Disclaimer. We are subject matter experts working with UL to create an initial draft version of UL 4600 using this approach. The final standard may differ.

Acknowledgements. The authors wish to thank the UL 4600 drafting team participants from UL and Edge Case Research for their support and thoughtful comments.

References

1. CENELEC: Railway applications - Communication, signaling and processing systems - Software for railway control and protection systems, EN 50128:2011
2. IEC: Functional safety of electrical/electronic/programmable electronic safety-related systems, IEC 61508:2010
3. ISO: Road Vehicles – Functional Safety ISO 26262:2011
4. ISO: Road Vehicles – Functional Safety ISO 26262:2018
5. ISO: Road Vehicles – Safety of the Intended Function ISO/PAS 21448:2019

6. Koopman, P., Wagner, M.: Toward a framework for highly automated vehicle safety validation. SAE 2018-01-1071 (2018)
7. Koopman, P., Fratrik, F.: How many operational design domains, objects, and events? SafeAI (2019)
8. Ministry of Defence: Safety Management Requirements for Defence Systems. Defence Standard 00-56 (2017)
9. MISRA: Development Guidelines for Vehicle Based Software, November 1994
10. Pegasus Project. https://www.pegasusprojekt.de/en/home. Accessed 21 April 2019
11. SAE: Guidelines for Development of Civil Aircraft and Systems, ARP4754A (2010)
12. SAE: Guidelines and Methods for Conducting the Safety Assessment Process on Civil Airborne Systems and Equipment, ARP4761 (2012)
13. US Dept. of Commerce: The employment impact of Autonomous Vehicles, August 2017
14. US Dept. of Commerce, 7 June 2019. https://www.commerce.gov/issues/regulatory-reform
15. US DoD: Standard Practice: System Safety, MIL-STD-882E, 11 May 2012
16. Yoshida, J.: UL Takes Autonomy Standards Plunge, EE Times, 16 April 2019

Open Questions in Testing of Learned Computer Vision Functions for Automated Driving

Matthias Woehrle, Christoph Gladisch[✉], and Christian Heinzemann

Robert Bosch GmbH, Corporate Research,
Robert-Bosch-Campus 1, 71272 Renningen, Germany
{Matthias.Woehrle,Christoph.Gladisch,Christian.Heinzemann}@de.bosch.com

Abstract. Vision is an important sensing modality in automated driving. Deep learning-based approaches have gained popularity for different computer vision (CV) tasks such as semantic segmentation and object detection. However, the black-box nature of deep neural nets (DNN) is a challenge for practical software verification. With this paper, we want to initiate a discussion in the academic community about research questions w.r.t. software testing of DNNs for safety-critical CV tasks To this end, we provide an overview of related work from various domains, including software testing, machine learning and computer vision and derive a set of open research questions to start discussion between the fields.

1 Introduction

Deep learning-based approaches have achieved impressive performance results on a wide range of benchmarks in various domains such as computer vision [40]. As industrial application of deep neural networks (DNNs) increases, there is an increased need for verification and validation (V&V). This paper focuses on practical verification and concretely on testing of computer vision (CV) software. The Software under Test is a CV task, such as object detection and semantic segmentation, embedded in an automotive camera.[1] For simplicity, we focus on stateless CV functions that evaluate each image individually. Our concrete application domain is autonomous driving (AD), so the software may be safety-relevant.

We focus on *falsification of the software* during development, *i.e.* identifying defects in the software early in the development cycle, rather than validation-specific topics such as distributional shifts or global performance characteristics. Our verification context is testing of DNNs that extract information from individual images, *e.g.* objects and their bounding boxes or annotate pixel-wise semantic labels, as shown in Fig. 1. This is challenging as the input space for

---

[1] Many verification techniques are up to now only applied to image classification. While this simpler CV task is not relevant for our application, the corresponding methods are good starting points for further study.

© Springer Nature Switzerland AG 2019
A. Romanovsky et al. (Eds.): SAFECOMP 2019 Workshops, LNCS 11699, pp. 333–345, 2019.
https://doi.org/10.1007/978-3-030-26250-1_27

a typical CV function is vast, *e.g.* for a Cityscapes [8] image approximately $10^{5681751}$ inputs would be theoretically possible. While the subspace of relevant images is many orders of magnitudes lower than this astronomical number, there is no natural constraint or generative model available from which we can sample tests incl. ground truth as we could from a test input model such as a formal grammar [3].[2] For test specification, we additionally need to consider checking of the CV function output. Getting ground truth labels via manual labeling is a labor- and time-consuming and expensive task [10,19], *e.g.* for the Cityscapes semantic segmentation task it required on average more than 1.5 hours for the 5000 images [8].

The open and real-world context of AD and the high-dimen-sional and unstructured input space of computer vision exacerbate the oracle problem of software testing [3] leaving us with the question: *How do we create good (relevant and meaningful) test data efficiently for a CV function interpreting images of driving scenes in the physical world? How do we verify relevant properties of the corresponding DNNs?*

We are interested in the question how one can ensure that a DNN works correctly based on a finite test set (*cf.* [40])? Previous work has surveyed the general topics of testing of machine learning (ML) software considering both implementation and conceptual issues [5]. Additionally, Borg *et al.* [4] review V&V challenges for ML in the automotive industry. However, due to our specific application domain and CV task, our verification context differs considerably. The contribution of this paper is a discussion of approaches that may contribute to obtaining a good test set for DNNs and CV functions in the automated driving context.

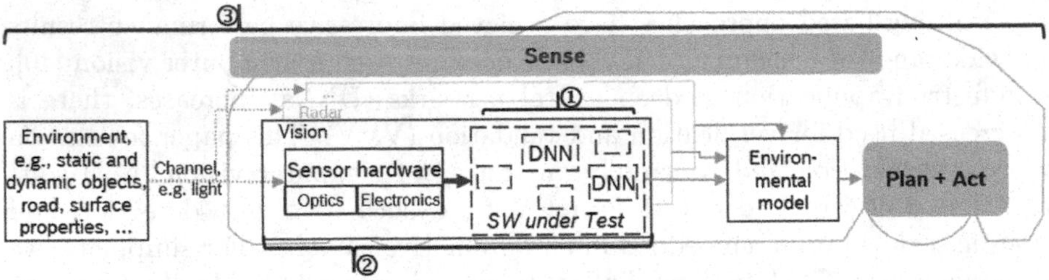

Fig. 1. Overview of the V&V task detailing on the Software (SW) under test and its system embedding with 3 exemplary test setups.

Note that in an industrial development process, testing is performed throughout various development stages in complementary ways to provide an overall argument that the system implementation is correct. To this end, various (*i*) test methods and (*ii*) test setups are used. First, different test methods are used to address various test concerns such as checking for implementation errors, security aspects, data pre-processing issues, labeling errors, leakage, quantization

[2] We discuss first steps in this direction in the context of synthetic data in Sec. 2.3.

issues, timing and consistency constraints, robustness guarantees and satisfaction of requirement specifications. Second, as examples for different test setups, Fig. 1 depicts three examples using curly braces. The smallest brace (1) concerns isolated testing of CV functions that we focus on in the following, where test images are directly processed by the SW under Test (a DNN). As we can see in the figure, we can also enlarge the test setup, *e.g.* (2) include the sensor hardware in our test setup (either in a real hardware-in-the-loop setup or using a model thereof) or (3) perform end-to-end testing [33]. Note that for (3), we perform closed-loop testing as the loop is closed through the vehicle interacting with the real world.

In the following, we discuss selected approaches from software testing, machine learning and computer vision and present several open exemplary research questions to initiate a discussion. Due to space limitations, further topics such as model explainability and interpretability, debugging of ML models, software, system and ML safety, AD V&V, modeling and simulation, (automatic) labeling, data science, data cleaning and exploratory data analysis are omitted. Section 2 presents three approaches for generating test inputs. First, we consider sampling around test images (Sect. 2.1). The most prominent approach in this category is generating (minimal) adversarial examples. Second, we consider analysis approaches that characterize relevant and important factors to be considered for a good test set (Sect. 2.2). Third, we consider testing based on synthetic test data (Sect. 2.3).

For test evaluation (Sect. 3), we discuss ground truth as well as relevant properties and metrics. Here, we need to differentiate the general approach of testing guided by a particular test concern such as checking for average case behavior (*e.g.* IoU on a test set [8]), exceptional behavior (*e.g.* uncertainty assessment in edge cases), and specifications in particular use cases (*e.g.* detection of relevant, far-away objects). Note that recent academic work has focused on comparing average case behavior based on cost metrics - mainly to evaluating competing designs - while verification and testing is typically concerned with (worst-case) behavior w.r.t. specific properties.

2   Test Input Generation

2.1   Sampling Around Labeled Test Images

One input model used for testing DNNs is to sample around labeled example images. Sampling is performed by considering some distance metric around a reference image, *i.e.* only on the input and independent of the CV task.

Adversarial Data Generation. Adversarial examples for image classification is a main research topic, where the input model is sampled around a given image under the assumption that the label stays the same as long as the distance of the new sample is below a selected threshold. A typical norm in the context of (minimal) adversarial examples are L_p norms, *e.g.* L_∞ used in [35,38]. Such a metric integrates well into current deep learning frameworks and thus can be used to generate tests efficiently. However, for autonomous driving and other notions of robustness, other distance metrics may be more relevant, *e.g.* based on noise characteristics of the imager. An impressive in-depth overview of algorithms for verifying neural networks for image classification w.r.t. adversarial robustness is [23]. The authors detail on several algorithms, classify them into an intuitive framework, and detail on soundness and completeness of the approaches. However, these techniques cannot be directly applied to CV tasks for automated driving, *e.g.* due to (*i*) scalability constraints and (*ii*) their focus on image classification. In a generalization for verification of non-linear properties, it is noted that defining a relevant input set is a hard task and a concrete first step is to consider sampling sets around test examples (using *e.g.* an L_p norm) and perform "weaker verification" [29]. Apart from formal worst-case analyses of minimal, additive adversarial perturbations, there are various notions of robustness [10], *e.g.* datasets considering robustness to corruption and common perturbations [16] as well as computer vision hazards [41].

Concolic Testing and "Exhaustiveness". Concolic test generation, *e.g.* [32], is a white-box software test generation technique which extends symbolic execution of source code using concrete test executions to remedy that source code may not be available or too complex for symbolic execution. Concolic testing allows generating an exhaustive test suite based on a coverage criterion, such as branch coverage. There is first work to apply concolic testing to deep learning functions [36], which is based on input coverage on the adversarial input model described above. The major concern for any method trying to completely sample the input space is that only a subspace of the vast input space is actually functionally relevant and this space is very difficult to characterize. Cheng *et al.* [7] argue for learning (parts of) an input space representation alongside the function. However, this would be a discriminative model not a generative one.[3] Apart from generating test inputs, we also need to provide corresponding oracles for new test inputs. Apart from top-1 label invariance within a threshold described above it is unclear what such an oracle would look like for concolic testing.

Data Augmentation. Data augmentation for CV functions leverages a large variety of transformations on images like rotations and flips. While its main purpose is multiplication of training data, these transformations can also be leveraged as a basis for testing. Data augmentation may either be integrated into machine learning frameworks or used with dedicated libraries [18]. In these libraries, transformation of inputs is coupled with corresponding transformation of ground truth, e.g. of a segmentation map. Some data augmentation techniques may be even amenable to a formal analysis such as the support of rotations in DeepPoly [35]. Augmentation techniques are obviously only an approximation, since transformations in the real world are much more complex than the transformation in the image space, *e.g.* considering illumination. Additionally, realistic parameterization of image augmentations including thresholds and equivalence

---

[3] With the discriminative model we could only dismiss generated irrelevant test inputs, while with a generative model, we could directly generate relevant tests.

classes is a major concern for verification. As an example, we might not use horizontal flipping as this is outside the Operational Design Domain (*cf.* Sect. 2.2) of the function, but may use vertical flipping to represent left- and right hand traffic. Based on this, we can identify a difference in augmentation for training versus verification. In training, on-line augmentation with random transformations is used to sample the input space sparsely for a large training set. Verification may rather focus on a small set of important test images where augmentation is performed densely, *e.g.* to better characterize robustness.

Summary. All the discussed methods sample around individual test images and indiscriminately modify images independently of concrete image content. However, image-specific modifications can also be considered for testing: Shetty *et al.* [34] consider image specific object removals and Yuille *et al.* check the effect of occluders on object detection [40]. Some of the discussed methods aspire exhaustive sampling and formal verification, however all results are local around individual test samples.

Exemplary Research Questions. (*i*) What notions of robustness and corresponding test images should be included in a good test set? (*ii*) Which kind of coverage criterion could be used to argue exhaustiveness of a test set? (*iii*) What data augmentations should be used on images in a good test set?

2.2   Domain and Data Analysis

Domain and data analysis creates and leverages additional information of the relevant context. This includes an analysis of relevant inputs, *e.g.* analyze distributions in pixel space, and an analysis of the outputs, *e.g.* analyze the distribution of ground truth labels. Most importantly for the following discussion is an identification of nuisance factors [40,44] and robustness criteria that are not explicitly available in image and label space. In the context of automotive and autonomous driving applications, such factors include environmental conditions (*e.g.* rain, dusk) as well as state of the ego-system (*e.g.* view change due to braking maneuver) and other actors in the environment (*e.g.* cyclists and pedestrians).

Hazard Analysis. CV-Hazop [42] is a hazard analysis approach for computer vision. 1470 hazards are currently available for CV-Hazop [1]. A concrete task in our application domain of interest is presented in context of the WildDash dataset [41]. It shows that the extensive list of hazards that are relevant for generic CV tasks can be broken down to a small number of 9 hazard clusters for a concrete segmentation task. Based on CV-Hazop, Zendel *et al.* discuss different aspects of analyzing image data and in particular negative test cases [41]. For negative test cases, we expect the algorithm to fail, yet with expected behavior, *e.g.* signaling high uncertainty. Negative test cases additionally provide a means to check that the limits of algorithms as well as the fidelity of the test environment are well-defined. A similar analysis has been performed by Zhang *et al.* [44] for stereo video focusing on specularity, texturelessness, transparency and disparity jumps. The work also describes mapping of hazards to testing via synthetic data (*cf.* Sect. 2.3). Their analysis shows that algorithms that perform better on average are not necessarily better in handling specified hazards. The Data Safety Guidance [31] describes an approach for data used in safety-related systems and provides concrete guidance such as properties of data that should be considered in the analysis of a data-driven system as well as concrete guide words for a data-focused Hazop analysis similar to CV-Hazop.

Operational Design Domain (ODD). An automated driving system operates in a defined Operational Design Domain [21]. As an example, adverse weather conditions such as heavy rain or snowstorms may be explicitly excluded. The analysis of the ODD is thus very related to the hazard analysis discussed above, as a reduction in ODD may explicitly result in a reduction of relevant hazards. Similarly, an Object and Event Detection and Response (OEDR) describes the proper handling of external situations that the automated vehicle encounters, including perception [21]. The description of ODD and OEDR necessitates an analysis for relevant factors that include similar considerations as described above for CV-Hazop such as weather, glare and sensor noise [21]. However, there are differences between an ODD/OEDR analysis and a CV-Hazop analysis: CV-Hazop is a generic analysis for any CV function, while an ODD/OEDR analysis is focused on a specific AD system implementation. On the one side, due to the generic nature of CV-Hazop, many impact factors need to be considered that may not be relevant for a specific application and the system context the application is embedded in. The result is that we may considerably reduce the number of hazards for a given implementation, because hazards may not apply to the system by design (*cf.* WildDash [41] mentioned above). On the other side, a vision function analyzed based on CV-Hazop may still be directly usable even when the scope in ODD or OEDR are extended.

Top-Down/Bottom-Up. Abstract top-down analysis methods should be complemented with bottom-up data analysis, *e.g.* in an iterative approach: This may include error analysis from machine learning, exploratory data analysis, *e.g.* for confounding factors, coverage considerations, *e.g.* label distribution [8], and novelty detection for interesting tests. As one example, Cordts *et al.* [8] investigate why performance on Cityscapes changes over the seasons and their analysis concluded that this most likely depends on "softer lighting conditions in the frequently cloudy fall". Many issues such as corrupted images or labels, imbalances [8], variations, label noise [11] and preprocessing or data quality issues can only be detected by inspecting the data. While approaches such as data inspections, mis-prediction and outliers analysis are vital, they are rather discussed in practical discussions, *e.g.* [20].

Summary. All discussed analyses support testing by identifying test concerns, hazards, nuisance factors, novel aspects, environmental and operational conditions that should be considered in a test set. For an abstract domain analysis, we need to consider a concretization from abstract domain to tests either with a mapping to a dataset [41] or by generating data synthetically [40,44] as further described below.

Exemplary Research Questions. (*i*) What would be a basic check list of nuisance factors and other hazards that should be considered for a good test set? (*ii*) How do we integrate knowledge from the analysis of the ODD and OEDR into designing a good test set? (*iii*) How to concertize abstract tests into concrete images?

2.3 Synthetic Data

Several works discuss simulation, i.e. 3D rendered graphics, as a key enabler for large-scale testing in the domain of AD [12,22]. Borg *et al.* [4] discuss that a promising approach to ML safety engineering is to simulate test cases. There are several benefits of simulation including (*i*) flexibility and control of the visual effects and the scene content, (*ii*) massive automatic generation of inputs, (*iii*) inherent availability of precise and unambiguous ground truth and (*iv*) early availability in the development cycle.

Synthetic Data Approaches. One specific question for simulation is the required fidelity such that results transfer to the real world [22]. Previous work has mostly focused on comparing average performance. In particular, several authors have reported similar performance between simulations and related datasets [2,24,28,44]. Note that there are several different approaches as to whether (*i*) images are created from learned models (using GANs, *e.g.* Deep-Road [43]), (*ii*) created from a 3D World simulation (*e.g.* for pedestrian detection [28]), (*iii*) augmented with sensor effects such as chromatic aberration and blur [6] and other style transfer, (*iv*) perturbed for robustness testing [27], (*v*) augmented with additional relevant agents and objects (*e.g.* for urban driving scenes [2]) or (*vi*) using probabilistic scene grammars combined with learning an adaption of generated scenes for dataset and task-specific synthetic content generation [19]. The focus of these methods is typically on training and showing a benefit of leveraging synthetic data. Considerations for testing may be different: instead of improving average-case behavior over a realistic distribution, we may rather be interested in improving the least worst-case behavior [10]. Additionally, depending on the type of property, tests may be interested in addressing the content gap and/or the appearance gap of a simulation [19].

Evaluation of Synthetic Data. Note that simulation with a sufficient fidelity has significant cost in creation, maintenance, validation and execution. However, a benefit of simulation is that testing can be scaled economically [40]. Obviously, we can only synthesize what we have already considered and so the focus is on discovering critical interaction of known effects, rather than *unknown unknowns*. A concrete simulation used as a test environment in the context of safety-critical systems needs to consider whether results from simulation transfer to real executions and do not create "false alarms". This concerns many testing tools and has recently been discussed in the context of static analysis results by Meyer [25] from which we reuse the nomenclature. Although from a verification perspective false alarms are not harmful, "false alarms kill an analyzer" [25] w.r.t. user acceptance. Missed violations may be catastrophic and thus need to be specifically considered when using simulation in a safety-related process step. We refer to Meyer [25] for a discussion on the relation of soundness and completeness considerations for verification tools. Note that in the context of testing with synthetic data, we can neither remove all missed violations nor all false alarms and thus need to consider the relative performance. Zhang *et al.* [44] compare evaluation w.r.t. specific hazards (described above) and verify the results on synthetic data with selected, corresponding test data from standard benchmarks, *e.g.* [13]. We refer to Koopman *et al.* [22] for a discussion on residual risk with respect to simulation and its fidelity. These are general simulation concerns, *i.e.* how to accurately represent the real world. One particular difference in the vision domain is that we cannot rely on human evaluation of realism, since two images that may look the same for a human can have a significant difference in algorithmic evaluation in testing [14].

Summary. In general using synthetic data, *e.g.* via simulation, is a commonly-used technique in testing automotive embedded systems. A discussion in the context of simulation models for hardware-in-the-loop systems can be found in [17]. While their focus is on classical automotive systems such as motor control or vehicle stability control, the discussion of model affordances (What sort of functionality should the model provide?) and fidelity (What fidelity does the test need to decide whether a specification is satisfied in the actual system?) is valuable for any simulation-based testing. For the concrete question of fidelity of images and relevant image KPIs in the automotive domain, we also may refer to the *IEEE–SA P2020* working group on automotive imaging standards [15].

Exemplary Research Questions. (*i*) Which affordances should a simulation provide to support building a good test set with domain coverage? (*ii*) How can we leverage synthetic data to economically scale a good test set?

3   Test Evaluation

Labels. Deep learning in computer vision mostly relies on supervised learning, *i.e.* ground truth labels are provided for training. Predictions are compared to ground truth labels based on task-dependent cost metrics such as intersection-over-union (IoU). If synthetic data is used, ground truth labels can be generated automatically. Getting ground truth is a common task for learning, validation and verification and often one of the most expensive and time-consuming tasks [10,19] and a key bottleneck [30]. As an example, fine segmentation maps for Cityscapes required more than 1.5 hours on average [8]. We refer to literature from computer vision [24,40] and benchmarks for autonomous driving [8,13] and machine learning [9,19] for data collection and labeling. There are similarities between manual labeling and manual software testing as both rely on a specification subject to interpretation by humans [10]. One difference is that for V&V we typically want to use high-quality ground truth, while training may also rely on weak signals based on automatic labeling [30]. However, we can compare automatic labeling efforts such as Snorkel [30] with partial specifications in software testing [3] that allow us to automatically test for certain properties.

Properties. While a single cost/loss metric is required for the machine learning problem, a tester is less constrained in the form and number of evaluation functions to apply between ground truth and prediction. Evaluation in machine learning relies on average performance over a dataset, where rare mis-predictions may not have a visible impact. In contrast, the focus of verification is typically on individual tests that each feature a clear pass or fail condition and thus their predictions can be evaluated individually using several complementary criteria. Ground truth is the reference, a point-wise specification, with predictions assumed to be (approximately) equivalent. Ground truth in combination with image augmentation frameworks as described above, can also be used to describe local invariance and equivariance properties: (*i*) *Local invariance*: Small changes on the input do not cause a change on the output. An example is the setup for minimal adversarial examples in image classification as described above, where around images the top-1 classification shall remain the same. (*ii*) *Equivariance*: A change on the input, causes an equivalent change on the output. An example in the context of image augmentation for semantic segmentation is the translation and rotation of a segmentation mask alongside its input image.

Seshia *et al.* [33] survey the landscape of formal specifications for DNNs. The paper mentions that a complete end-to-end perspective may be appealing, since system level constraints, requirements and rules are more intuitive and easier to specify on a system level. Moreover, breaking down constraints and requirements across the functional chain is a challenging task. However, for practical verification a decomposition is necessary.

Metrics. Frtunikj *et al.* [12] discuss a refinement of performance metrics to application-specific quantities depending on safety requirements: This may include the consideration of the environment such as weather and the context of the ego vehicle, *e.g.* in the form of distance- and speed-based mAP (mean average precision). Metrics with more structure are intuitively appealing, since speed and distance are relevant parameters in following stages of the AD functional chain, *e.g.* for computing threat metrics of a planner. The context-dependent performance metrics discussed in [12] are obviously linked to a domain analysis such as CV-Hazop [1]. However, detailed metrics also necessitate availability of the corresponding information for relevant object classes, which is often times not available in standard datasets.

Derived Specifications. There has been work on differential and metamorphic testing of machine learning functions, both so-called derived specifications [3]. First, differential testing or the more general variant of n-version testing is a derived test oracle [3] where the results of n versions of the same function are compared with each other. Here we rely on a comparison of functions that observably differ in their implementations. This can be either based on different implementation approaches or on evolutions of a single implementation, *e.g.* for regression testing. DeepXplore [26] uses differential testing for different applications including a simple example from the AD domain. Note that the use of redundant paths in safety-critical applications, whether through different sensing modalities or redundant implementations, supports a use of differential testing and can help to identify inconsistencies, but not common weak spots. Second, metamorphic testing uses metamorphic relations that check the relative change between different executions of the same SW under test. Note that a metamorphic relation may describe a local (epsilon) invariance property and as such currently formulated adversarial robustness properties are instances of metamorphic relations. Local invariance is also mainly used in previous work on metamorphic testing for classical supervised learning algorithms (classification) on structured data [39]. DeepTest [37] uses the test setup and input generation as DeepXplore, however checking whether a projected driving vector remains invariant within some ϵ bound based on a metamorphic relation. A recent work called Deep-Road [43] uses GANs to apply transformations on the input image, e.g. with respect to weather conditions, and checks that the output, in this case driving behavior, stays invariant within some ϵ bound.

Domain Considerations. As in any test setup, if a test execution fails, the error may be due to the implementation or due to the test. For reference-based tests, the actual reference, *i.e.* in our case ground-truth label, may be at fault. There are several sources of errors and label noise [11] including errors of automatic pre-labeling, errors in the labeling specification and errors in labeling [8,10]. Concrete challenges in labeling are domain-specific. As an example, in AD a fine-grained classification may not be necessary (*cf.* 30 classes in Cityscapes [8]), yet there may be subtle interpretations required, e.g. of drivable space on road boundaries. Additionally, in a development environment with separated responsibilities, coordination of labeling specification, the concrete labeling process and quality control of labeling results are important for the high-quality labeling.

Summary. Ground truth is required for verification. For detailed evaluation further task-specific labeling and metadata may be required, especially considering domain-specific evaluation metrics that necessitate details about the environment. However there is an imbalance between the high importance, effort and cost of labeling data in practice versus its prevalence in published works.

Exemplary Research Questions. (*i*) How do we obtain ground truth for diverse test data in a cost-effective manner? (*ii*) What are relevant, task- and domain-specific evaluation metrics? (*iii*) How can we use specifications and formal methods to reap a larger benefit from ground truth data to effectively multiply our test set?

4   Conclusion

We discussed approaches and open research questions for testing of learned CV functions in the particular context of autonomous driving. To this end, we presented existing research from different fields such as software testing, machine learning and computer vision and posed several relevant research questions to provide a basis for a discussion between the individual fields. However, due to space limitations we omitted further topics such as model explainability and interpretability, software, system and ML safety, AD V&V, modeling and simulation, (automatic) labeling, data science and exploratory data analysis.

References

1. AIT Austrian Institute of Technology GmbH: CV-HAZOP VITRO. https://vitro-testing.com/cv-hazop/. Accessed 28 Mar 2019
2. Alhaija, H.A., Mustikovela, S.K., Mescheder, L.M., Geiger, A., Rother, C.: Augmented reality meets computer vision: efficient data generation for urban driving scenes. J. Comput. Vis. **126**(9), 961–972 (2018)
3. Barr, E.T., Harman, M., McMinn, P., Shahbaz, M., Yoo, S.: The oracle problem in software testing: a survey. IEEE Trans. Software Eng. **41**(5), 507–525 (2015)
4. Borg, M., et al.: Safely entering the deep: a review of verification and validation for machine learning and a challenge elicitation in the automotive industry. arXiv preprint arXiv:1812.05389 (2018)
5. Braiek, H.B., Khomh, F.: On testing machine learning programs. CoRR arXiv:abs/1812.02257 (2018)
6. Carlson, A., Skinner, K.A., Vasudevan, R., Johnson-Roberson, M.: Sensor transfer: learning optimal sensor effect image augmentation for sim-to-real domain adaptation. IEEE Robot. Autom. Lett. **4**(3), 2431–2438 (2019)
7. Cheng, C.H., Huang, C.H., Brunner, T., Hashemi, V.: Towards safety verification of direct perception neural networks. arXiv preprint arXiv:1904.04706 (2019)
8. Cordts, M., et al.: The cityscapes dataset for semantic urban scene understanding. In: CVPR 2016 (2016)
9. Deng, J., Dong, W., Socher, R., Li, L., Li, K., Li, F.: Imagenet: a large-scale hierarchical image database. In: IEEE CVPR 2009, pp. 248–255 (2009)
10. Franke, U.: 30 years fighting for robustness, June 2018. http://www.robustvision.net. Talk at Robust Vision Challenge (2018)
11. Frénay, B., Kabán, A.: A comprehensive introduction to label noise. In: ESANN 2014 (2014)
12. Frtunikj, J., Fuerst, S.: Engineering safe machine learning for automated driving systems. In: 27th Safety-Critical Systems Symposium (2019)
13. Geiger, A., Lenz, P., Urtasun, R.: Are we ready for autonomous driving? The KITTI vision benchmark suite. In: IEEE CVPR 2012, pp. 3354–3361 (2012)
14. Goodfellow, I.J., Shlens, J., Szegedy, C.: Explaining and harnessing adversarial examples. In: ICLR (2015)
15. Group, W.A.I.Q.W.: Standard for automotive system image quality. In: IEEE P2020, IEEE (2019)
16. Hendrycks, D., Dietterich, T.: Benchmarking neural network robustness to common corruptions and perturbations. arXiv preprint arXiv:1903.12261 (2019)
17. Hutter, A.: Einsatz von Simulationsmodellen beim Test elektronischer Steuergeräte. In: Sax, E. (ed.) Automatisiertes Testen Eingebetteter Systeme in der Automobilindustrie. Hanser (2008)
18. Jung, A.: Image augmentation for machine learning experiments (2019). https://github.com/aleju/imgaug. Accessed 9 Apr 2019

19. Kar, A., et al.: Meta-Sim: Learning to Generate Synthetic Datasets. arXiv e-prints arXiv:1904.11621, April 2019

20. Karpathy, A.: A recipe for training neural networks, April 2019. http://karpathy. github.io/2019/04/25/recipe/. blog Accessed 2019 Apr 30

21. Koopman, P., Fratrik, F.: How many operational design domains, objects, and events? In: Workshop on AI Safety @ AAAI 2019 (2019)

22. Koopman, P., Wagner, M.: Toward a framework for highly automated vehicle safety validation. Technical report, SAE Technical Paper (2018)

23. Liu, C., Arnon, T., Lazarus, C., Barrett, C., Kochenderfer, M.J.: Algorithms for verifying deep neural networks. CoRR arXiv:abs/1903.06758 (2019)

24. Mayer, N., et al.: What makes good synthetic training data for learning disparity and optical flow estimation? Int. J. Comput. Vis. **126**(9), 942–960 (2018)

25. Meyer, B.: Soundness and completeness: with precision, April 2019. https:// bertrandmeyer.com/2019/04/21/soundness-completeness-precision. blog Accessed 02 May 2019

26. Pei, K., Cao, Y., Yang, J., Jana, S.: DeepXplore: automated whitebox testing of deep learning systems. In: Proceedings of SOSP 2017, pp. 1–18 (2017)

27. Pezzementi, Z., et al.: Putting image manipulations in context: robustness testing for safe perception. In: 2018 IEEE International Symposium on Safety, Security, and Rescue Robotics (SSRR), pp. 1–8 (2018)

28. Poibrenski, A., Sprenger, J., Muller, C.: Toward a methodology for training with synthetic data on the example of pedestrian detection in a frame-by-frame semantic segmentation task. In: SEFAIAS@ICSE 2018, pp. 31–34 (2018)

29. Qin, C., et al.: Verification of non-linear specifications for neural networks. CoRR arXiv:abs/1902.09592 (2019)

30. Ré, C.: Software 2.0 and snorkel: beyond hand-labeled data. In: Proceedings of 24th ACM KDD 2018, 19–23 August 2018, p. 2876 (2018)

31. SCSC: Data safety guidance. SCSC Version 3.1, The Safety-Critical Systems Club, York, Great Britain (2019)

32. Sen, K., Marinov, D., Agha, G.: CUTE: a concolic unit testing engine for c. In: ACM SIGSOFT Software Engineering Notes, vol. 30, pp. 263–272. ACM (2005)

33. Seshia, S.A., et al.: Formal specification for deep neural networks. In: Lahiri, S.K., Wang, C. (eds.) ATVA 2018. LNCS, vol. 11138, pp. 20–34. Springer, Cham (2018). https://doi.org/10.1007/978-3-030-01090-4_2

34. Shetty, R., Schiele, B., Fritz, M.: Not using the car to see the sidewalk: quantifying and controlling the effects of context in classification and segmentation. CoRR arXiv:abs/1812.06707 (2018)

35. Singh, G., Gehr, T., Püschel, M., Vechev, M.T.: An abstract domain for certifying neural networks. PACMPL **3**(POPL), 41:1–41:30 (2019)

36. Sun, Y., Wu, M., Ruan, W., Huang, X., Kwiatkowska, M., Kroening, D.: Concolic testing for deep neural networks. In: Proceedings of ASE 2018, pp. 109–119 (2018)

37. Tian, Y., Pei, K., Jana, S., Ray, B.: DeepTest: automated testing of deep-neural-network-driven autonomous cars. In: arXiv:1708.08559 (2017)

38. Wong, E., Schmidt, F.R., Metzen, J.H., Kolter, J.Z.: Scaling provable adversarial defenses. In: NeurIPS 2018, pp. 8410–8419 (2018)

39. Xie, X., Ho, J.W.K., Murphy, C., Kaiser, G.E., Xu, B., Chen, T.Y.: Testing and validating machine learning classifiers by metamorphic testing. J. Syst. Softw. **84**(4), 544–558 (2011)

40. Yuille, A.L., Liu, C.: Deep nets: What have they ever done for vision? arXiv preprint arXiv:1805.04025 (2018)

41. Zendel, O., Honauer, K., Murschitz, M., Steininger, D., Domínguez, G.F.: Wild-Dash - creating hazard-aware benchmarks. In: Ferrari, V., Hebert, M., Sminchisescu, C., Weiss, Y. (eds.) ECCV 2018. LNCS, vol. 11210, pp. 407–421. Springer, Cham (2018). https://doi.org/10.1007/978-3-030-01231-1_25
42. Zendel, O., Murschitz, M., Humenberger, M., Herzner, W.: CV-HAZOP: introducing test data validation for computer vision. In: ICCV 2015, pp. 2066–2074 (2015)
43. Zhang, M., Zhang, Y., Zhang, L., Liu, C., Khurshid, S.: DeepRoad: GAN-based metamorphic testing and input validation framework for autonomous driving systems. In: ASE 2018, pp. 132–142 (2018)
44. Zhang, Y., Qiu, W., Chen, Q., Hu, X., Yuille, A.L.: UnrealStereo: controlling hazardous factors to analyze stereo vision. In: Proceedings of 3DV 2018, pp. 228–237 (2018)

Adaptive Deployment of Safety Monitors for Autonomous Systems

Nico Hochgeschwender[✉]

German Aerospace Center (DLR),
Simulation and Software Technology, Cologne, Germany
`nico.hochgeschwender@dlr.de`

Abstract. This article discusses the problem of deploying safety-critical software for an autonomous system, namely a collaborative robot operating in domestic environments. We present a deployment infrastructure to enhance both humans and robots in carrying out their deployment activities. We develop means to enable humans to explicitly specify the requirements of the software to be deployed, along with the resources of the robot platform on which the software will be executed. In addition, we propose an architecture which enables robots to autonomously re-deploy their software at run-time in order to account for changing requirements imposed by their task, platform and environment. We show how the architecture enables a collaborative robot to autonomously re-deploy *safety monitors* for detecting in-hand slippage often occuring in human-robot handover tasks. By doing so, the robot autonomously maintains a certain safety level as the functioning of the monitor depends on both selecting and deploying the correct monitoring strategy for the situation at hand.

Keywords: Runtime AI safety monitoring ·
Model-based engineering approaches to AI safety

1 Introduction

Autonomous systems such as collaborative robots (see Fig. 1) are expected to carry out many different tasks in challenging environments not only over a long period of time, but also in a trustworthy manner. To do so, robots are equipped with a wide variety of software components ranging from solving functional problems such as planning, perception and control to safety-critical components required for execution monitoring, diagnosis and fault detection and isolation [14]. To achieve a certain level of autonomy robots are required to autonomously plan and execute actions and at the same time to cope with varying requirements for the software. Many of those variations are difficult to predict as they are induced by changing tasks, goals and environmental features. It is important to emphasize that the changing requirements are not only influencing core functional components, but also safety-critical modules such as *functional safety* features which aim to control hazards such that risks are mitigated.

© Springer Nature Switzerland AG 2019
A. Romanovsky et al. (Eds.): SAFECOMP 2019 Workshops, LNCS 11699, pp. 346–357, 2019.
https://doi.org/10.1007/978-3-030-26250-1_28

Therefore, deployment in robotics can be considered as an ongoing activity as different software components both functional and safety-critical are likely to be re-deployed at run-time in order to fulfill varying requirements. As we aim for truly autonomous systems robots themselves should be endowed with means to deploy their software. By doing so, the need for human intervention is reduced which paves the way for long-running robot applications.

Even though, in robotics deployment information is already available in terms of architectural and platform models [4,12] and configuration files [3,15] we identified in [6] that the majority of deployment approaches tend to be inflexible as they do not cover use cases where there is a need to respond to runtime changes. To this end, we generalized and described in [6] a *reference architecture* for deploying component-based robot software. In this article we instantiate this architecture (see Sect. 4) for a collaborative robot appli-

Fig. 1. The collaborative Care-O-bot 3 robot in a domestic environment.

cation (see Sect. 2) and thereby validate its applicability. We show how the architecture and corresponding deployment algorithms enable a collaborative robot to autonomously re-deploy safety monitoring strategies. By re-deploying the monitors we can assure that in-hand slippage is detected even in the presence of varying requirements induced, for example, by the robots task.

2   Motivating Example

We consider collaborative robots as those shown in Fig. 1 to exemplify our work on deploying safety monitors. Collaborative robots are becoming more and more widespread not only in industrial and factory-like applications [16], but also in domestic scenarios. While traditionally in industrial scenarios robots are separated from human workers by fences collaborative robots share their workspace with humans. In those workspaces collaborative robots are expected to carry out a wide variety of tasks simultaneously or even in cooperation with humans. The close interaction with humans requires to adequately address safety concerns over the complete life-cycle of a robotic application. By conforming to standards such as ISO TS 15066 [10] and ISO 12011 [9] the collaborative workspace and type of tasks are specified which enables safety engineers to perform risk assessment. In the context of this work we consider the Care-O-bot 3 (see Fig. 1) as a collaborative robot capable of preparing, transporting and handing over coffee mugs to inhabitants of an apartment. For this application the risk assessment identified a unacceptable risk, namely that the robot could scald a person by dropping a mug with hot coffee while handing it over to a user. Thus, the risk assessment recommends to implement risk reduction techniques, namely safety monitoring which is described in the following section.

2.1   Safety Monitor for Detecting In-Hand Slippage

To safely execute manipulation tasks (e.g. object picking, placing and human-robot handover) collaborative robots need to be equipped with means to detect slippage. That is, whether an object is moving within the robot's grasp. To detect in-hand slippage on the Care-O-bot 3 service robot (see Fig. 1), Sanchez *et al.* [1] proposed three different types of slip detectors based on tactile (exteroceptive) and force (proprioceptive) measurements and as a fusion of these (see Fig. 2). The force slip detector assumes a slip occurs whenever a force is exerted in the right direction (e.g. downwards with respect to the grasp frame). The tactile slip detector estimates the tangential force on the sensor caused by a sliding pressure (e.g. a grasped object slipping). The combined slip detector fuses both slip signals from the tactile slip detector and the force slip detector in a rule-based manner where experimentally obtained threshold values for the tactile and force slip detector are compared with each other.

From a safety perspective the three slip detectors represent an active safety feature, namely a *safety monitor* which aims to preserve safety by checking safety-relevant information and possibly altering the robots behavior. Safety monitors are well-developed techniques in robotics which generally aim to prevent an autonomous robot of performing unsafe actions [14]. In our scenario, an unsafe

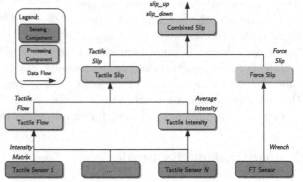

Fig. 2. The high-level functional architecture of the force, tactile and combined slip detector.

action could be dropping a coffee mug while handing it over to a user. The slip detector can be used to prevent dropping the mug by detecting slippage and by exerting a higher force on the grasped mug. However, the performance of each slip detector varies considerably depending on the action, for example, the tactile slip detector outputs a slip whenever grasping an object. Contrary, the force slip detector achieves perfect accuracy for detecting actual slips, however its performance is poor when no slippage occurs, for example, when the robot base is moving. Thus, the evaluation of the approach carried out on the Care-O-bot 3 platform [1], highly suggests that the actions and motions performed by the robot during grasping should be taken into account for improved safety performance. Therefore, it is necessary to adapt the safety monitor to the current robot's actions at run time.

2.2   Deployment Requirements of the Safety Monitor

To this end, it is not only crucial to select the correct monitoring strategy for the task at hand, but also to deploy the safety monitor on the best matching platform. That is, a platform which fulfills the deployment requirements of the selected safety monitor. In the context of this work the Care-O-bot 3 robot is a distributed system with several computational platforms, thus several deployment options. For the described slip detectors we can formulate the following deployment requirements:

R1: The force slip detector should be deployed on a platform to which the force sensor is connected.

R2: The tactile slip detector should be deployed on a platform to which all tactile sensors are connected.

R3: The combined slip detector should be deployed on a platform with at least 250MB working memory.

Those requirements are based on experimentally obtained timing results of different deployment options.

3   Specifying Safety Monitors

We employ the textual, Ruby-based domain-specific languages RPSL (Robot Perception Specification Language) and DepSL (Deployment Specification Language) [8] to model architectural and deployment concerns of safety monitors (see Fig. 3). With RPSL one can model multi-stage slip detectors as those introduced in Sect. 2 as directed acyclic graphs composed of sensor components (e.g. force sensors) and processing components. In RPSL those graphs are called *perception graphs* and represent an executable and deployable unit. DepSL is used to attach platform requirements to each each safety monitor (cf. Sect. 2.2). To this end, DepSL supports the following requirement types proposed by the OMG deployment specification [13]:

Quantity. This requirement allows to express a certain number of required elements. For example, a certain number of tactile sensors connected to a platform (cf. **R2**).

Capacity. This requirement allows to express a certain capacity of a platform resource which can be consumed by one or more perception graphs. For example, the size (capacity) of working memory (cf. **R3**).

Minimum. This requirement allows to express an acceptable lower bound of a platform property. For example, maximum latency of a networking connection.

Maximum. This requirement allows to express an acceptable upper bound of a platform property. For example, the maximum latency of a networking connection.

```
1   rpsl.perception_graph do
2      name "force_slip_detector"
3      connect "force_sensor", "out_port",
4              "slip_detection", "in_port"
5      ...
6   end
7
8   depsl.deployment_specification do
9      name "force_slip_detector"
10     add_constraint :attribute, :platform_has, "force_sensor"
11     ...
12  end
```

Fig. 3. An excerpt of the RPSL domain model of the force-based slip detector. DepSL is employed to specify deployment constraints for the force_slip_detector perception graph, namely that the platform where the graph will be eventually deployed has a force sensor attached to it.

Attribute. This requirement allows to express the existence of certain platform properties. For example, a certain hardware version of a sensor or a specific operating system installed on the platform (cf. **R1**).

Selection. This requirement allows to express a set of elements where one or more should be available on the platform. For example, different sensors of the same modality, but from different manufacturers.

Those requirements are used by the deployment architecture (see Sect. 4) to identify suitable platforms for each safety monitor.

4 Deploying Safety Monitors

The deployment architecture depicted as a component-based diagram in Fig. 4 conforms to the reference architecture specified in [6]. The basic idea of the architecture is to separate the concern of *what* should be deployed from the *where* it should be deployed. In the following sections we focus on the latter. Note, as the deployment architecture has been developed in the context of RPSL and as the safety monitors are specified with RPSL we will use the term *perception graph* interchangeably with the term *safety monitor*.

4.1 Context Monitoring

One or more context monitoring components are composed in the deployment architecture in order to provide the contextual information needed to select (see Sect. 4.3) and deploy (see Sect. 4.4) safety monitors. To this end, context monitors collect – hence requiring additional interfaces (see Fig. 4) – and interpret all the measurements required to infer the current state of robots' environment, platform (e.g. sensors, actuators and computational elements) and tasks and skills. Context monitors make this information accessible to other components by inserting them in the repository (see Sect. 4.2). In the context of the case study the main objective of the context monitor is to retrieve the current action performed by the Care-O-bot 3. To this end, three different actions are detectable by the context monitor. First, whether the fingers of the gripper are closed to hold an object (cf. **grasp**). Second, whether the robot's base moves while holding an object (cf. **move_base**). Third, whether

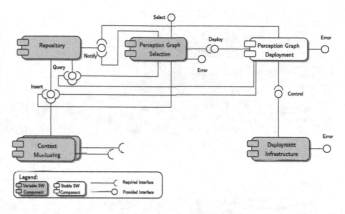

Fig. 4. The architecture for deploying the safety monitors depicted as a UML-like component diagram.

the fingers of the gripper are open to hand-over an object (cf. **release**).

4.2 Repository

The repository plays a central role in the deployment architecture as it contains all the knowledge required for carrying out the deployment activities. Broadly speaking, the knowledge can be classified in design time and run time knowledge. Examples of the former are domain models expressing knowledge about the safety monitors (see Sect. 2) and the robot platform, and examples for the latter are information about the current memory usage or the availability of sensors required, for example, by the safety monitors. The repository component provides three interfaces, namely **Insert**, **Query** and **Notify**. The **Query** interface is used to retrieve information about design and run time knowledge. The **Insert** interface is used to create and update information in the repository, and the **Notify** interface is employed to inform other components about those changes in the repository. In the context of the case study both the **RPSL** and **DepSL** (see Fig. 3) were employed to create domain models representing the knowledge relevant for deploying the safety monitors. Those domain models represent not only the three different slip detectors, but also their associated deployment descriptions and the computational hardware of the Care-O-bot 3 robot. It is important to note that the repository in the context of this case study is realized as a graph database [7]. Thus, both **RPSL** and **DepSL** domain models have been translated to a labeled property graph representation. As demonstrated in [7] this representation paves the way to execute semantic queries to retrieve implicitly defined information required to infer on which platform, for example, the safety monitor should be deployed. As shown in Fig. 5a–d excerpts of the graph expressing the case study are depicted.

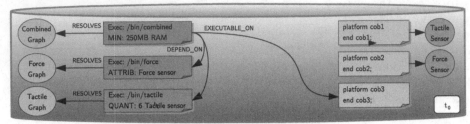

(a) An excerpt of the repository at time t_0.

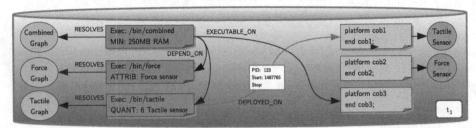

(b) An excerpt of the repository at time t_1.

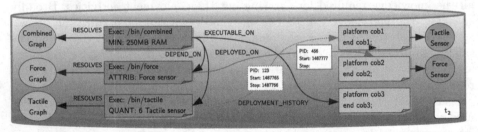

(c) An excerpt of the repository at time t_2.

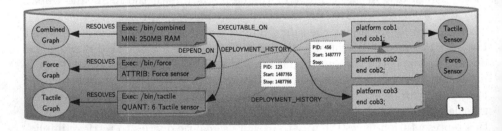

(d) An excerpt of the repository at time t_3.

Fig. 5. Snapshots of the graph-based repository during the case study. Note, the snapshots are an excerpt of the complete graph database and focus on how the links between the deployment description (and their corresponding requirements) and the available platforms are established during the case study.

4.3   Selection of Safety Monitors

The perception graph selection component (see Fig. 4) is in charge of selecting one or more perception graphs suitable for the task at hand. To this end,
activation is either triggered – in a reactive manner – by changes of context conditions using the `Notify` interface or by higher-level components via the `Select`
interface provided by the component. In order to select a safety monitor which is
appropriate for the current action context a simple, yet powerful rule-based approach is applied. During design time a set of of decision rules have been devised.
Here, the action context is part of the rule condition and the selection of a
safety monitor is part of the rule body. The rules are based on the experiments
described in [1].

Algorithm 1. Finding a platform satisfying the deployment requirements.

```
 1: function Deploy.perceptionGraphs(G)      ▷ G is the set of graphs to be deployed.
 2:     for each gᵢ ∈ G do
 3:         dᵢ ← Query.getDeploymentInformation(gᵢ)
 4:         if dᵢ ≠ ∅ then
 5:             if Query.hasFixedDeployment(dᵢ) then
 6:                 p ← Query.getFixedPlatform(dᵢ)
 7:                 if Control.start(gᵢ, p) then
 8:                     return success
 9:                 else
10:                     Error.deploymentFailed(gᵢ, p)
11:                     return error
12:             else
13:                 C ← Query.getConstraints(dᵢ)      ▷ C, the deployment constraints.
14:                 P ← checkValidity(C)                    ▷ P, the acceptable platforms.
15:                 if P ≠ ∅ then
16:                     if not Query.isDeployed(gᵢ, P) then
17:                         if Control.start(gᵢ, pₖ ∈ P) then
18:                             return success
19:                         else
20:                             Error.deploymentFailed(gᵢ, pₖ ∈ P)
21:                             return error
22:                     else
23:                         Error.noAcceptablePlatforms(gᵢ)
24:                         return error
25:         else
26:             Error.deploymentInformationMissing(gᵢ)
27:             return error
```

4.4   Adaptive Deployment of Safety Monitors

The perception graph deployment component (see Fig. 4), or just deployer, is
responsible for deploying one or more perception graphs. To do so, the deployer
provides a `Deploy` interface which is used by the selector to inform the deployer

which perception graphs have to be deployed. After receiving such a request, Algorithm 1 is used to find those platforms which meet the deployment requirements for the given graphs. In case no platform is suitable, for example, if no platform satisfies the memory requirements, an error is reported via the Error interface. The implementation of the Error interface depends significantly on *(a)* how the reference architecture is realized in an application context, and *(b)* how the overall error management is implemented (see e.g. Garcia *et al.* [5] for a survey). The deployment algorithms shown in Algorithms 1 and 2 are explained in the following paragraphs by making use of the case study described in Sect. 2. We assume that at time t_0 the robot is located in the kitchen and has a mug in its hand. At this point in time the repository (see Sect. 4.2) is composed of nodes and edges as shown in Fig. 5a. Subsequently, a user requests the robot to deliver the mug to the living room. At time t_1 the robot starts moving it's base, hence the context monitor (see Sect. 4.1) detects the move_base action context and updates the repository. Based on the context update, the selector (see Sect. 4.3) component requests the tactile slip detector to be deployed. Thus, the selector calls the perceptionGraphs() method of the Deploy interface provided by the deployer.

As shown in Algorithm 1 for each selected perception graph g_i corresponding deployment information d_i is retrieved. That is, the node which resolves the perception graph is retrieved. In case no deployment information for g_i is available an error is reported. Subsequently it is checked whether or not a fixed deployment is given. That is, it is checked whether d_i has an edge to a platform which is labeled :EXECUTABLE_ON. As shown in Fig. 5a no fixed deployment for the tactile slip detector is provided. Thus, all the deployment requirements of d_i are retrieved in order to find an acceptable platform meeting the requirements. The checkValidity() method takes the requirements and returns those platforms P satisfying them. In the context of this example, checkValidity() checks which platform provides nine tactile sensors as those are required for the tactile slip detector. Basically two situations can occur, namely no platform is meeting the requirements or one or more platforms meet the requirements. In the former case an error is reported and for the latter case it is checked whether or not g_i is already deployed on one of the acceptable platforms. If g_i is not yet deployed on one of the acceptable platforms the deployer calls the start() method of the Control interface provided by the infrastructure component[1] in order to request the execution of g_i on $p_k \in P$. Having successfully deployed g_i on p_k the infrastructure component creates an edge labeled :DEPLOYED_ON from the tactile deployment node to the platform node (see Fig. 5b).

At time t_2 the robot reaches the living room and hands-over the mug to the user. The robot opens the fingers of the gripper to release the mug. Thus, the context monitor detects the release action. Subsequently, the selector chooses an appropriate slip detector for the observed context, namely the force slip detector. The selector requests the deployer to stop the current slip detector and to

---

[1] The infrastructure component abstracts the concrete runtime environment, e.g. a robot software framework.

deploy the force slip detector. Depending on the implementation of the perception graphs it would be also possible to simply send a pause signal to the slip detector.

As shown in Fig. 5c once the tactile slip detector is stopped, the edge from the deployment to the platform node is updated, namely the label is changed from :DEPLOYED_ON to :DEPLOYMENT_HISTORY. Like at time t_1 deployment requirements are checked and the force slip detector is deployed on the platform to which the force sensor is connected. At time t_3 the force sensor breaks and no force signal is provided anymore. The context monitor detects this failure and updates the corresponding platform model, namely the edge from the platform node to the sensor/device node is removed (see Fig. 5d). The repository notifies the deployer about those changes. Subsequently, the deployer executes the checkDeployment() method shown in Algorithm 2. The main objective of Algorithm 2 is to ensure that deployments remain valid in the presence of platform changes. To this end, each active deployment on the updated platform p_i is checked whether or not the requirements are met (cf. Algorithm 1). Three situations can occur, namely *(a)* no platform meets the requirements, *(b)* p_i meets the requirements, or *(c)* other platforms than p_i meet the requirements. In the context of the case study no platform satisfies the requirements, thus, the force slip detector is stopped.

Algorithm 2. Checking whether or not deployments are valid.

```
 1: function checkDeployment(p_i)
 2:     D ← Query.getActiveDeployments(p_i)        ▷ D, the active deployments on p_i.
 3:     for each d_i ∈ D do
 4:         g_i ← Query.getPerceptionGraph(d_i)            ▷ g_i, the perception graph.
 5:         C ← Query.getConstraints(d_i)               ▷ C, deployment constraints.
 6:         P ← checkValidity(C)                        ▷ P, the acceptable platforms.
 7:         if P = ∅ then
 8:             Error.noAcceptablePlatforms(g_i)
 9:             if Control.stop(g_i, p_i) then
10:                 return success
11:             else
12:                 Error.stoppingFailed(g_i, p_i)
13:                 return error
14:         if p_i ∈ P then
15:             return success
16:         if not P = ∅ and p_i ∉ P then
17:             if Control.start(g_i, p_k ∈ P) then
18:                 return success
19:             else
20:                 Error.deploymentFailed(g_i, p_k ∈ P)
21:                 return error
```

---

5   Related Work and Discussion

Software deployment for autonomous systems and robotics in particular is usually achieved by some kind of deployment infrastructure provided by the underlying robot software framework. For example, the `roslaunch` deployment tool of the popular ROS [15] framework takes a XML-based description of the ROS architecture as an input and initiates the deployment according to it. To this end, components in ROS also known as nodes are started, stopped, parameters are set and so forth. Another notable deployment approach in robotics is proposed by Ando *et al.* [2]. Here – in the context of the OpenRTM robot software framework – deployment is considered as a part of component and system lifecycle management. The approach mainly deals with implementation-level details, for example, how manager services interact and how components are instantiated. Like in ROS, the OpenRTM deployment infrastructure relies on dedicated deployment files expressing crucial deployment information such as the location of an executable and so forth. Although these approaches help to automate the deployment task they are limited as they are not capable of expressing and resolving deployment requirements as presented in this paper. The deployment architecture proposed in this paper is inspired by the MAPE-K [11] reference architecture for self-adaptive software systems as it contains similar building blocks as those proposed in MAPE-K such as monitoring, knowledge storage, analysis and so forth. However, the introduced deployment architecture is more fine-grained as, for example, a stepwise deployment is supported. Here, the selector (see Sect. 4.3) deals with what should be deployed and the deployer (see Sect. 4.4) deals with how and where it should be deployed. It is important to note that currently, all deployment requirements are treated equally by Algorithm 1 as no preferences, weights or the like are given. Thus, if a platform is not meeting all the requirements it is not in the set of acceptable platforms P (cf. Algorithm 1). In addition, the current implementation ensures that the deployment requirements are not modified at run time. However, supporting dynamic, modifiable requirements could be feasible in even more dynamic situations such as in the context of cloud-robotics where resources are requested on demand.

6   Concluding Remarks

This article presented an approach for deploying safety monitors at run-time even in the presence of varying requirements. The presented work has been developed and integrated on a real robotic system which demonstrates its applicability to re-deploy safety monitors at run-time.

References

1. Sanchez, J., Schneider, S., Hochgeschwender, N., Kraetzschmar, G.K., Plöger, P.G.: Context-based adaptation of in-hand slip detection for service robots. IFAC-PapersOnLine **49**(15), 266–271 (2016)

2. Ando, N., Suehiro, T., Kotoku, T.: A software platform for component based RT-system development: OpenRTM-Aist. In: Carpin, S., Noda, I., Pagello, E., Reggiani, M., von Stryk, O. (eds.) SIMPAR 2008. LNCS (LNAI), vol. 5325, pp. 87–98. Springer, Heidelberg (2008). https://doi.org/10.1007/978-3-540-89076-8_12
3. Bruyninckx, H., Soetens, P., Koninckx, B.: The real-time motion control core of the OROCOS project. In: Proceedings of the IEEE International Conference on Robotics and Automation (2003)
4. Dhouib, S., Kchir, S., Stinckwich, S., Ziadi, T., Ziane, M.: RobotML, a domain-specific language to design, simulate and deploy robotic applications. In: Noda, I., Ando, N., Brugali, D., Kuffner, J.J. (eds.) SIMPAR 2012. LNCS (LNAI), vol. 7628, pp. 149 160. Springer, Heidelberg (2012). https://doi.org/10.1007/978-3-642-34327-8_16
5. Garcia, A.F., Rubira, C.M., Romanovsky, A., Xu, J.: A comparative study of exception handling mechanisms for building dependable object-oriented software. J. Syst. Softw. **59**(2), 197–222 (2001)
6. Hochgeschwender, N., Biggs, G., Voos, H.: A reference architecture for deploying component-based robot software and comparison with existing tools. In: 2018 Second IEEE International Conference on Robotic Computing (IRC), pp. 121–128, Jan 2018
7. Hochgeschwender, N., Schneider, S., Voos, H., Bruyninckx, H., Kraetzschmar, G.K.: Graph-based software knowledge: storage and semantic querying of domain models for run-time adaptation. In: 2016 IEEE International Conference on Simulation, Modeling, and Programming for Autonomous Robots (SIMPAR), pp. 83–90 (2016)
8. Hochgeschwender, N.: Model-based specification, deployment and adaptation of robot perception systems. Ph.D. thesis, University of Luxembourg, Luxembourg (2017)
9. Safety of machinery - General principles for design - Risk assessment and risk reduction. Standard, International Organization for Standardization, Geneva, CH (2010)
10. Robots and robotic devices - Collaborative robots. Technical specification, International Organization for Standardization, Geneva, CH (2016)
11. Kephart, J.O., Chess, D.M.: The vision of autonomic computing. Computer **36**(1), 41–50 (2003)
12. Nordmann, A., Hochgeschwender, N., Wigand, D., Wrede, S.: A survey on domain-specific modeling and languages in robotics. J. Softw. Eng. Rob. **7**(1), 75–99 (2016)
13. Object Management Group: Deployment and configuration of component-based distributed applications specification (2004). http://www.omg.org/spec/DEPL/4.0/. Accessed 05 May 2019
14. Pettersson, O.: Execution monitoring in robotics: a survey. Robot. Auton. Syst. **53**(2), 73–88 (2005)
15. Quigley, M., et al.: ROS: an open-source robot operating system (2009)
16. Villani, V., Pini, F., Leali, F., Secchi, C.: Survey on human-robot collaboration in industrial settings: safety, intuitive interfaces and applications. Mechatronics **55**, 248–266 (2018)

Uncertainty Wrappers for Data-Driven Models

Increase the Transparency of AI/ML-Based Models Through Enrichment with Dependable Situation-Aware Uncertainty Estimates

Michael Kläs[(⊠)] and Lena Sembach

Fraunhofer Institute for Experimental Software Engineering IESE,
Fraunhofer Platz 1, 67663 Kaiserslautern, Germany
{michael.klaes,lena.sembach}@iese.fraunhofer.de

Abstract. In contrast to established safety-critical software components, we can neither prove nor assume that the outcomes of components containing models based on artificial intelligence (AI) or machine learning (ML) will be correct in any situation. Thus, uncertainty is an inherent part of decision-making when using the outcomes of data-driven models created by AI/ML algorithms. In order to deal with this – especially in the context of safety-related systems – we need to make uncertainty transparent via dependable statistical statements. This paper introduces both a conceptual model and the related mathematical foundation of an uncertainty wrapper solution for data-driven models. The wrapper enriches existing data-driven models such as provided by ML or other AI techniques with case-individual and sound uncertainty estimates. The task of traffic sign recognition is used to illustrate the approach, which considers uncertainty not only in terms of model fit but also in terms of data quality and scope compliance.

Keywords: Artificial intelligence · Machine learning · Dependability · Safety engineering · Data quality · Operational design domain · Model validation

1 Motivation

More and more software-intensive systems contain components that make use of data-driven models (DDMs) [1, 2], such as those provided by the application of AI and ML. In particular, autonomous systems need to process various kinds of sensor input to recognize and interpret their context and collaborate with other agents. Unlike traditionally engineered components, which are developed by software engineers who define their functional behavior by writing code or models, the behavior of data-driven components (DDCs) is determined by algorithms based on a sample of training data.

The functional behavior expected from DDCs can therefore only be specified and tested on a selection of example cases, and we cannot assure that DDCs will behave as intended in all cases. As a consequence, the outcome of DDCs is afflicted with uncertainty, which has to be appropriately understood and managed during design time and runtime to provide a dependable system.

© Springer Nature Switzerland AG 2019
A. Romanovsky et al. (Eds.): SAFECOMP 2019 Workshops, LNCS 11699, pp. 358–364, 2019.
https://doi.org/10.1007/978-3-030-26250-1_29

Previous work [3] proposes separating the sources of uncertainty in DDCs into three major classes, distinguishing between uncertainty caused by limitations in terms of model fit, data quality, and scope compliance. Whereas *model fit* focuses on the inherent uncertainty in a DDM, *data quality* covers the additional uncertainty caused by its application to input data obtained in suboptimal conditions. *Scope compliance* finally covers the phenomenon that a model might be applied in situations outside the scope for which it was intended (i.e., for which it was trained and tested).

Building upon this classification, we derive and illustrate a mathematical model for capturing information about the different sources of uncertainty and combining it into situation-aware and statistically sound uncertainty statements (Sect. 3). First, Sect. 2 motivates this work, positioning it in the context of existing work. The paper concludes with possible applications and provides an outlook on future work (Sect. 4).

2 Related Work

Uncertainty estimates are usually expressed by probabilities for categorical outcomes and by probability distributions or prediction intervals in combination with a confidence level for numerical outcomes [4]. In the literature, different approaches can be identified for obtaining such estimates [5].

In the domain of computation and simulation models, uncertain model inputs are commonly addressed by forward uncertainty propagation [6]. Founded on the propagation of error theory, related techniques consider probability distributions instead of concrete values as model inputs to express inherent uncertainty and propagate them through the model. In the context of DDMs, however, it appears difficult to express uncertainty in unstructured data such as images using a probability distribution. Moreover, computation time requirements complicate reasonable applications at runtime.

In the context of AI/ML, some common techniques used to train models implicitly include a kind of uncertainty information (e.g., decision trees [7] also provide probability values for each class, besides their categorical outcomes). For other techniques, revisions have been proposed to provide uncertainty estimates (e.g., for some (deep) neural networks [8–10], hybrid models [11], and analogy-based techniques [12]). Moreover, some meta-techniques are available that can be applied on top of existing modeling techniques [13, 14] to obtain uncertainty estimates.

A limitation observed for many existing techniques that include means for providing uncertainty estimates is that these estimates are computed on training data. In consequence, they may suffer from overfitting, leading to overconfidence when applied to yet unseen data during application. A further drawback of integrating the calculation of uncertainty estimates directly into a DDM is that the provision of realistic uncertainty estimates and the provision of accurate outcomes do not necessarily require the same inputs and features. For example, the meta-information that an image has low quality does not help to recognize an object in this image, but may indicate that there is a higher degree of uncertainty in the outcome of the applied object recognition model. Finally, existing approaches largely ignore the fact that a DDM might also be applied outside the target application scope for which it was trained and tested.

3 Uncertainty Wrapper Approach

In this chapter, we derive and illustrate a mathematical model that allows encapsulating an existing DDM in a DDC via an uncertainty wrapper, which extends the outcome of the DDC (o^m) by a situation-aware uncertainty estimate ($\hat{u}^\alpha$) considering a requested degree of confidence (α). Such a DDC can be, e.g., a traffic sign recognition component that decides in a given situation (*case*) based on the provided input (*in*), e.g. an image, whether the detected sign is or is not a 'Stop Sign' (Fig. 1). To provide situation-aware uncertainty estimates, the wrapper addresses model fit, data quality, and scope compliance related uncertainty [3] using the outcome of the DDC, a quality impact model, and a scope compliance model to process the respective parts of the uncertainty estimate.

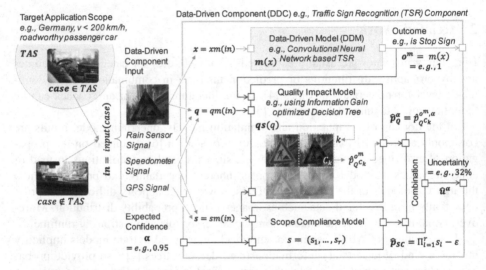

Fig. 1. Overview of important concepts and the data flow when providing uncertainty estimates

In the following, we will limit our considerations to binary outcomes (i.e., $o^m \in \{0, 1\}$) for the sake of simplicity. However, an extension to DDCs with an arbitrary number of categories as possible outcomes is straightforward (cf. one hot encoding).

In the following, we will first introduce the fundamental mathematics needed to probabilistically describe uncertainty for our setting; next, we will separate uncertainty into a quality-related (p_Q) and a scope-compliance-related (p_{SC}) part. Then we will propose estimators for both parts and finally combine them into an overall statement on case-specific uncertainty ($\hat{u}^\alpha$).

Uncertainty. We define a *case* as a specific situation in which the DDC should provide an outcome; for example, passing with a specific car at a certain point in time at a specific location, which leads to an **input in** to the DDC. This input can include, for example, the image with the detected traffic sign, which needs to be identified, but also other sensor signals provided, e.g., by the GPS, rain sensor, and speedometer. *in*, which can be assumed as a tensor of a predefined structure, is the result of applying a measurement function *input* to the case, i.e., $in = input(case)$.

To provide an outcome, parts of *in* are preprocessed and provided to the DDM with the ***model function m*** generating the outcome, i.e., $o^m = m(x)$ with $x = xm(in)$. In our example, x could be a tensor representing the normalized RGB channels of all pixels of the camera image. Let us now assume that we have some realizations (x_1, o_1), $(x_2, o_2), \ldots$ of random variables (X, O) where o_i is the true label, i.e., the real outcome of a case. o_i is known for training and test cases but not for cases in the application phase, and o_i^m is the outcome by applying m on x_i. Accordingly, the random variable O models the true label associated with X and $O^m = m(X)$ the predicted ones.

Let us further assume that the realizations (x_i, o_i) are captured under common conditions $S = \{s_1, \ldots s_N\}$, under which the DDM is intended to be applied later on. This defines the ***target application scope TAS*** of the model. The *TAS*, which is also called operational design domain in the context of autonomous driving, could be traveling on German public roads with a roadworthy passenger car and a max. speed of 200 km/h. For reasons of completeness, we further define *UAS* as a superset of *TAS* containing all possible cases, i.e., under intended as well as unintended conditions. *UAS* is highly abstract since it contains, put simply, "the whole universe".

Now we can define ***uncertainty*** as the probability that DDM outcomes are wrong:

$$u((X, O)) = p(m(X) \neq O) = 1 - p(m(X) = O) \tag{1}$$

Separating Quality (p_Q) and Scope Compliance (p_{SC}). When dealing with uncertainty during the application, we cannot simply assume that the case for which we make an estimate is part of the target application scope *TAS*. Thus, we apply the law of total probability to separate $cases \in UAS$ into cases that are in *TAS* and cases that are not[1]:

$$p(m(X) = O) = p(case \notin TAS)\, p(m(X) = O \,|case \notin TAS)$$
$$+ \underbrace{p(case \in TAS}_{=:\, p_{SC}}\ \underbrace{p(m(X) = O \,|case \in TAS)}_{=:\, p_Q} \geq p_{SC}\, p_Q \tag{2}$$

As we want to derive a case-specific estimate of uncertainty in our approach and as *TAS* might be highly imbalanced (e.g., more '0's than '1's in the case of 'stop signs'), uncertainty estimates should distinguish between cases where $o^m = 0$ and where $o^m = 1$. We also indicate this in Fig. 1 with an arrow from the outcome to the quality impact model. Hence, the considerations below are limited to those cases for which the model predicts a stop sign ($o^m = 1$); the consideration for $o^m = 0$ is analogous. Thus X now denotes more specifically the conditional random variable $X|m(X) = 1$.

---

[1] Since we cannot obtain representative samples for all *caseTAS*, we make a worst-case approximation by assuming $p(m(X) = O|caseTAS) = 0$, i.e., outcomes are never correct.

Scope Compliance (p_{SC}). We assume that for each case some scope-related information is available. Without loss of generality, we assume that the first r characteristics of S are measurable and can be checked on in via the function sm, i.e., $s = sm(in) = (1_{s_1}, 1_{s_2}, \ldots, 1_{s_r})(in)$ and that 1_{s_l} is the indicator function for some characteristic s_l, $s_l \in S, 1 \leq l \leq r$; e.g., $s_1 = \{pos_{GPS} \in Germany\}$ and $s_2 = \{v_{speedometer} \leq 200km/h\}$. Next, we define the estimator $\hat{p}_{SC}^s = \prod_{l=1}^r s_l$. Because some characteristics of TAS are not checked, $\hat{p}_{sc}^s$ systematically overestimates p_{SC} and may be extended by a correction term ε (which, however, needs to be defined based on expert opinion).

Quality Impact (p_Q). Besides an estimated general true-positive rate for TAS, quality-related knowledge for the specific input in can be taken into account for the assessment of uncertainty of a single case. Information about quality-related factors (e.g., rain intensity and car velocity) is computed by qm, i.e., $q = qm(in)$. Next, q is used by a function qs to return the index k of a **cluster C_k** of all cases $caseTAS$ with comparable quality challenges and $o^m = 1$. Thus, we refine p_Q by

$$p_{Q^{c_k}}^{o^m=1} := p(m(X) = O|case \in TAS, qs(qm(input(case))) = k) \tag{3}$$

Assuming TS is a test dataset that is appropriately (randomly) sampled from TAS, i.e., each case in TAS has the same probability of being part of TS, we can construct an estimator for $p_{Q^{c_k}}$ based on the test data belonging to cluster c_k. For estimating $p_{Q^{c_k}}^{o^m=1}$, the reuse of DDM training data should be avoided due to the risk of overfitting.

$$\hat{p}_{Q^{c_k}}^{o^m=1} = \frac{1}{|C_k|} \sum_{case \in C_k} 1_{\{case:o=1\}}(case) \tag{4}$$

with $C_k = \{case \in TS : o^m = 1 \wedge qs(qm(input(case))) = k\}$

The statistical uncertainty of the estimator has not been considered yet and is denoted by the expected **confidence** α of the uncertainty wrapper. For this, we construct the Bernoulli-distributed random variable $Y := 1_{\{m(X)=O|X\in TAS\}}$ and compute the lower bound $\hat{p}_{Q^{c_k}}^{\alpha}$ of a single-sided confidence interval for the given confidence level (e.g. $\alpha = 0.95$). An example formula for the lower bound can be derived by the Wilson interval:

$$\hat{p}_{Q^{c_k}}^{o^m=1,\alpha} = \frac{1}{1+z_{1-\alpha}^2} (\hat{p}_{Q^{c_k}}^{o^m=1} + \frac{z_{1-\alpha}^2}{2} - z_{1-\alpha}\sqrt{\hat{p}_{Q^{c_k}}^{o^m=1}\left(1 - \hat{p}_{Q^{c_k}}^{o^m=1}\right) + \frac{z_{1-\alpha}^2}{4}}), \tag{5}$$

where $z_v = \Phi^{-1}(v)$ with Φ^{-1} being the quantile function of the standard normal distribution and $v \in (0,1)$. A comparison of alternative confidence intervals for the Bernoulli parameter is provided by Brown et al. [15] and the R-package 'binom' [16].

Case-Specific Uncertainty ($\hat{u}^\alpha$). Let $case_a$ be a case of actual application, i.e., not part of the training or the test dataset; hence, the "real" outcome o_a is not available. With in_a being the respective input to the DDC and α the requested confidence, we get a case-specific estimator for the uncertainty

$$\hat{u}^{\alpha}(case_a) \leq 1 - (\hat{p}_{SC}^{s_a} - \varepsilon)\hat{p}_{Q^{c_{qs(qa)}}}^{m(x_a),\alpha} \tag{6}$$

with $s_a = sm(in_a), x_a = xm(in_a), q_a = qm(in_a)$, and $\varepsilon \in [0, \hat{p}_{SC}^{s_a}]$.

Note that the effect of α is limited to the quality-related part of uncertainty because the estimator for scope compliance cannot be statistically derived from a test dataset TS.

4   Conclusion and Outlook

The proposed uncertainty wrapper approach considers not only uncertainty caused by model fit (general misclassifications) but also case-specific uncertainty introduced by the quality of the input data and uncertainty caused by the fact that the component might be applied in situations that were not intended when it was built and tested. In summary, this can provide a more realistic picture of uncertainty in a specific situation. The uncertainty estimate can therefore help to make better-informed decisions and initiate countermeasures if uncertainty exceeds accepted thresholds, e.g., slow down the car if the DDC is not sufficiently certain that there is no stop sign.

In the next step, we plan to instantiate the approach in a concrete case study.

Acknowledgments. Parts of this work is being funded by the German Ministry of Education and Research (BMBF) under grant number 01IS16043H.

References

1. Solomatine, D., Ostfeld, A.: Data-driven modelling: some past experiences and new approaches. J. Hydroinform. **10**(2), 3–22 (2008)
2. Solomatine, D., See, L., Abrahart, R.: Data-driven modelling: concepts, approaches and experiences. In: Abrahart, R.J., See, L.M., Solomatine, D.P. (eds.) Practical Hydroinformatics, pp. 17–30. Springer, Heidelberg (2009). https://doi.org/10.1007/978-3-540-79881-1_2
3. Kläs, M., Vollmer, A.M.: Uncertainty in machine learning applications – a practice-driven classification of uncertainty. In: First International Workshop on Artificial Intelligence Safety Engineering (WAISE 2018) (2018)
4. Armstrong, J.S.: The Forecasting Dictionary. In: Principles of Forecasting: A Handbook for Researchers and Practitioners, Springer Science & Business Media (2001)
5. Kläs, M.: Towards identifying and managing sources of uncertainty in AI and machine learning models - an overview. arXiv preprint arXiv:1811.11669 (2018)
6. Lee, S., Chen, W.: A comparative study of uncertainty propagation methods for black-box-type problems. Struct. Multidiscip. Optim. **37**, 239 (2009)
7. Safavian, S., Landgrebe, D.: A survey of decision tree classifier methodology. IEEE Trans. Syst. Man Cybern. B Cybern. **21**(3), 660–674 (1991)
8. Khosravi, A., Nahavandi, S., Creighton, D., Atiya, A.: Comprehensive review of neural network-based prediction intervals and new advances. IEEE Trans. Neural Networks **22**(9), 1341–1356 (2011)
9. Gal, Y.: Uncertainty in Deep Learning, University of Cambridge (2016)
10. McAllister, R., et al.: Concrete problems for autonomous vehicle safety: advantages of Bayesian deep learning, In: International Joint Conferences on Artificial Intelligence (2017)

11. Kläs, M., Trendowicz, A., Wickenkamp, A., Münch, J., Kikuchi, N., Ishigai, Y.: The use of simulation techniques for hybrid software cost estimation and risk analysis. Adv. Comput. **74**, 115–174 (2008)

12. Angelis, L., Stamelos, I.: A simulation tool for efficient analogy based cost estimation. Empir. Softw. Eng. **5**(1), 35–68 (2000)

13. Shrestha, D., Solomatine, D.: Machine learning approaches for estimation of prediction interval for the model output. Neural Netw. **19**(2), 225–235 (2006)

14. Solomatine, D., Shrestha, D.: A novel method to estimate model uncertainty using machine learning techniques. Water Resour. Res. **45**(12), W00B11 (2009)

15. Brown, L., Cai, T., DasGupta, A.: Interval Estimation for a Binomial Proportion. Stat. Sci. **16**(2), 101–133 (2001)

16. Dorai-Raj, S.: Cran R packages: 'binom', February 2015. https://cran.r-project.org/web/packages/binom/binom.pdf. Accessed May 2019

Confidence Arguments for Evidence of Performance in Machine Learning for Highly Automated Driving Functions

Simon Burton[1,3], Lydia Gauerhof[2(✉)], Bibhuti Bhusan Sethy[2], Ibrahim Habli[3], and Richard Hawkins[3]

[1] Systems Engineering Vehicle, Robert Bosch GmbH,
Schwieberdinger Str. 76, 71636 Ludwigsburg, Germany
Simon.Burton@de.bosch.com
[2] Corporate Research, Robert Bosch GmbH,
Robert-Bosch-Campus 1, 71272 Renningen, Germany
{Lydia.Gauerhof,BibhutiBhusan.Sethy}@de.bosch.com
[3] Assuring Autonomy International Programme, The University of York, York, UK
{Ibrahim.Habli,Richard.Hawkins}@york.ac.uk

Abstract. Due to their ability to efficiently process unstructured and highly dimensional input data, machine learning algorithms are being applied to perception tasks for highly automated driving functions. The consequences of failures and insufficiencies in such algorithms are severe and a convincing assurance case that the algorithms meet certain safety requirements is therefore required. However, the task of demonstrating the performance of such algorithms is non-trivial, and as yet, no consensus has formed regarding an appropriate set of verification measures. This paper provides a framework for reasoning about the contribution of performance evidence to the assurance case for machine learning in an automated driving context and applies the evaluation criteria to a pedestrian recognition case study.

Keywords: Highly automated driving · Machine learning · Safety Assurance

1 Introduction

Highly Automated Driving (HAD) has the potential to radically decrease the number of road accidents as well as introducing significant convenience and ecological benefits. At the same time, HAD functions are themselves safety-critical and must therefore be demonstrated to meet strict safety criteria before their release for use on public roads. Existing safety standards such as ISO 26262 [3] define prerequisites that must be fulfilled to minimise the risk of hazards caused by random hardware and systematic failures in the electrical/electronic systems. Due to the complexity of the systems and inherent uncertainty in the operating environment, HAD systems also require an increased focus on demonstrating

© Springer Nature Switzerland AG 2019
A. Romanovsky et al. (Eds.): SAFECOMP 2019 Workshops, LNCS 11699, pp. 365–377, 2019.
https://doi.org/10.1007/978-3-030-26250-1_30

that hazards are not caused by inherent restrictions in the sensors, actuators or decision logic. ISO PAS 21448 [1] addresses the "Safety of the Intended Functionality" by considering such effects. However, this standard is currently focused on Level 1 to 2 [4] driver assistance systems rather than Level 3 to 5 HAD systems which include higher levels of autonomy and for which machine learning is seen as a key enabling technology.

Machine learning algorithms and in particular Deep Neural Networks (DNNs) [15] are being applied to the task of providing an accurate perception for highly automated driving functions. One of the challenges caused by applying machine learning methods to these tasks is that a precise specification of the required behaviour is often not possible. Indeed, it is the very fact that the machine learning functions are able to infer the target function without a detailed specification, based on the presented training data that makes them so appealing. The lack of a precise specification combined with the unpredictable and opaque nature of the algorithms introduce high degrees of uncertainty into the safety assurance process.

This paper is organised as follows: A generic safety case pattern for arguing the performance of machine learning models previously proposed by the authors is summarised in Sect. 2. This is then used to derive a model for reasoning about the contribution of evidence to this assurance case pattern in Sect. 3 and used to formulate a corresponding confidence argument approach. In Sect. 4, the confidence argument approach is then applied to techniques that have been developed for verifying DNN-based perception functions for highly automated driving. Feature map sensitivity analysis is also used to provide counter-evidence for the confidence argument. The paper closes with a discussion of the need for a more rigorous approach to developing and proposing performance evaluation methods within a safety context and proposes future work in this area.

2   Safety Case Patterns for Machine Learning

In order to support the claim that the Machine Learning Model (MLM) meets its performance requirements, it is important to understand the causes of such insufficiencies. As interest in machine learning safety has grown, a number of authors [6, 25, 26] have investigated different causes of performance limitations in machine learning functions. Some examples applicable to HAD are described below:

– **Distributional shift:** Critical or ambiguous situations, within which the system must react in a predictably safe manner, may occur rarely or may be so dangerous that they are not well represented in the training data. It must be argued that the training data contains an appropriate distribution of all classes of critical situations and object classes or that the selected training leads to an appropriate level of generalisation. In addition, the system should continue to perform safely even if the operational environment differs from the training environment over time [6].

- **Robustness deficits of the trained function:** An adversarial perturbation [16,19,20] is an input sample that is similar (at least to the human eye) to other samples but that leads to a completely different categorisation with a high confidence value. It has been shown that such examples can be automatically generated and used to "trick" the network. The challenge, therefore, is to ensure that the machine learning algorithms focus on those properties of the inputs relevant to the target function without becoming distracted by irrelevant features. In other words, act within the same hierarchical dimensions as the target function [18].
- **Differences between the training and execution platforms:** When using machine learning to represent a function that is embedded as part of a wider system, the input to the neural network will have typically been processed by a number of elements already [25], such as lenses, image filters and buffering mechanisms. These elements may vary between the training and target execution environments leading to the trained function becoming dependent on hidden features of the training environment not relevant in the target system.

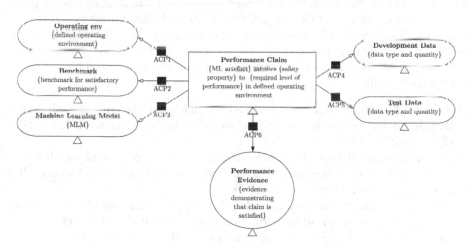

Fig. 1. Safety case pattern for machine learning model

Previous work by the authors as well as others have introduced concepts of applying assurance case structures to arguing the performance of an MLM within a safety-critical context [8,17,22]. Figure 1 describes a generic assurance case pattern for arguing the safety properties of a machine learning function (derived from the description in [23] using GSN [2]). This assurance case pattern is centered on discharging the claim that the MLM fulfills its safety properties (defined by benchmarks) to a required level of performance in a defined operation environment.

A contract-based approach to specifying safety properties of the MLM was proposed in [8], by which the MLM is specified as a component within its system context and defined by a set of assumptions on its operating environments under which certain safety guarantees (for example formulated as benchmark performance requirements) must hold. These performance requirements could include definitions of accuracy and failure rates to be achieved by the function. This allows for the assurance case for the MLM to focus on the safety-relevant properties of the trained function whilst the validity of the assumptions and appropriateness of the guarantees are discharged as part of a system level assurance activity.

In contrast to classical software-based approaches, existing safety standards do not define a set of accepted methods for evaluating the performance of machine learning in a safety critical context. Therefore during assessment and homologation, any proposed assurance case will inevitably lead to questions regarding the strength of argument presented and the relevance of the presented supporting evidence. Assurance Claim Points (ACPs) [12], indicated by the black squares in the pattern, are used to represent points in the argument where further assurance is required through the provision of a more detailed confidence argument. The confidence in the assurance case is therefore achieved by supporting the claims within the following ACPs. ACP1 and ACP2 must be supported by arguments that consider the overall system context [11], whilst ACPs 3...6 are specific to the machine learning function. These confidence arguments can be then used to aid the certification process, especially where accepted best practice has yet to be defined.

- **ACP1:** Argument that the assumptions made on the operational design domain as well as on the interfaces to other technical components within the system are valid.
- **ACP2:** Argument that the benchmark performance requirements allocated to the guarantees of the safety contract for the MLM are sufficient to fulfill the overall system safety requirements.
- **ACP3:** Argument that the adopted training process and the choice of model and hyperparameters lead to a function that fulfills its requirements.
- **ACP4:** Argument that the training data are sufficient to lead to a MLM that fulfills its performance requirements.
- **ACP5:** Argument that the test data that is used is sufficient to support the performance claim.
- **ACP6:** Argument that the performance evidence generated from the test data is sufficient to support the performance claim.

3   Confidence Arguments for Performance Evidence

In this Section we develop the concept of performance evidence confidence. This confidence argument will then support the claim that the provided evidence sufficiently supports the performance claim. In order to derive the set of conditions to be discharged by the confidence arguments we introduce a number of definitions, which will be defined in the set of equations below. These definitions are used here to illustrate the relationships between elements of the assurance case in order to stimulate a discussion regarding under what conditions these relationships hold true and as such the authors do not intend the definitions to necessarily form a mathematically complete model. In general, the performance claim can be formulated as a simple equivalence between the specified behaviour of the system and actual behaviour.

$$\forall i \subset \mathbb{I}.M(i) = T(i) \tag{1}$$

Where i is a sample from the actual input domain $\mathbb{I}$, M represents the trained model and T the specification (or ground truth) for a given input. In other words, for all possible inputs of the input domain, the implementation provides the same result as the specification. The application of the design-by-contract approach allows us to formulate a more restrictive form of equivalence that constrains the input space that fulfills the set of assumptions and limits the properties of interest to those formulated in the guarantees. This can be formulated as follows:

$$\forall i \in \mathbb{I}.A(i) \Rightarrow G(i, M(i)) \tag{2}$$

In other words, for all possible inputs in the domain that fulfill the set of explicitly specified assumptions A, the implementation provides a result that meets the safety guarantees G for the given inputs.

Equation 2 can now also be used to define the concept of *Contract Performance* by defining the conditional probability of a safety contract being fulfilled over the set of inputs that fulfill its assumptions A. The assurance case claim that the machine learning function fulfills its guarantees G with a conditional probability (ρ) can therefore be defined as follows:

$$\forall i \in \mathbb{I}.\rho(G(i, M(i))|A(i)) > ContractPerformance \tag{3}$$

The confidence argument that a given evidence leads to an adequate assessment of the actual performance of the machine learning function can therefore be couched in terms of the relationship between the measurement provided by the evidence and the actual contract performance as described in Eq. 3. In order to perform this comparison, it is necessary to define a measurement value threshold (*MeasurementTarget*) provided by the evidence E that, if reached, is postulated to imply that the *ContractPerformance* target is met. This allows for the following definition of *EvidenceContribution* to the safety case performance claim:

$$\forall i \in \mathbb{I}, \exists S \subseteq \mathbb{I}, \forall j \in S.$$
$$(A(j) \wedge (E(S) > MeasurementTarget)) \Rightarrow \tag{4}$$
$$\rho(G(i, M(i))|A(i)) > ContractPerformance$$

Where E is a function that takes as input a set of samples (S) from the input domain that meet the defined set of assumptions and returns a quantifiable measure that can be compared against a target value. In its simplest form, E

could represent simply tests on selected inputs and return the proportion of tests that passed. The testing problem could thus be formulated as finding some minimum subset S of the input domain to use as test data such that whenever the test results pass a pre-defined target, then the performance over the entire valid input space meets the contract performance.

E could also represent a more indirect measure that is used to infer the performance of the machine learning function such as the robustness towards adversarial perturbations. The definition of *EvidenceContribution* can also be extended to combine a number of different evidences which must all fulfill their measurement targets in order to imply that the *ContractPerformance* is met, thus allowing for combining of a mixture of techniques and measurements into E and *MeasurementTarget*.

The definition of *EvidenceContribution* allows us to identify several claims that need to be made as part of the confidence arguments ACP5 and ACP6 as described in Sect. 2. ACP5 can be strengthened by providing evidence to support the claims:

- The sample set used to provide performance evidence is capable of detecting faults in the machine learning function that would lead to a violation of performance requirements.
- The sample set is representative of the input domain and the application of the performance evaluation on this sample set leads to a representative indication of the measurement target for the entire domain.

ACP6 can be strengthened by providing evidence to support the claims:

- There is a demonstrable correlation between the *MeasurementTarget* and the *ContractPerformance*.
- The measurements based on the sample set can be extrapolated to provide an indication of the expected performance for the entire input domain even in the case of root unknown causes of insufficiencies (in ISO PAS 21448 defined as unknown triggering events).

4   Case Study

In this Section we apply the assurance case structure described above to the pedestrian recognition case study introduced in [10] and demonstrate how arguments regarding typical performance evaluation techniques can be strengthened or refuted. The performance requirements of the function used for the case study can be summarised as follows:

- Pedestrians of width X pixels and height Y pixels are classified.
- Pedestrians are detected if C% of the person is occluded.
- There are less than FP% of false positive classifications per frame.
- There are less than FN% of false negative classifications per frame.
- Vertical deviation from the ground truth is less than V pixels.
- Horizontal deviation from the ground truth is less than H pixels.

Image example from CityPersons includ-   Lower part of predictions are masked. The
ing the ground truth as green bounding   woman is predicted correctly, while the
boxes [27]   road sign is a false positive.

Fig. 2. Image example from CityPersons [27] with ground truth and partly masked

For the purpose of our case study we focus on the requirement that pedestrians should be detected even if certain portions of the person are occluded. This is based on the assumption that in the operating environment pedestrians may be partially occluded by objects such as street furniture or baby strollers. A typical approach to collecting performance evidence for such requirements would be to ensure that the test data contained examples of occluded and non occluded persons. This would lead to the following instantiation of Eq. 4 to describe the relationship between the testing approach and the performance claim:

$$\forall i \in \mathbb{I}, \exists Testset \subseteq \mathbb{I}, \forall j \in Testset.$$
$$(A_{occlusion}(j) \wedge TestsPassed(Testset) > TestBenchmark) \Rightarrow \qquad (5)$$
$$\rho(G(i, M(i))|A_{occlusion}(i)) > ContractPerformance$$

Where $A_{occlusion}$ describes assumptions on the input data including that pedestrians may be occluded and $TestsPassed$ is the evidence function that returns the proportion of tests passed based on the sample set $Testset$ which also includes occluded persons. The Guarantee function G here represents the combination of performance requirements described above where $ContractPerformance$ defines the required level of conditional probability that the performance requirements are met in the field (overall target failure rate). $TestBenchmark$ represents a target proportion of the tests that should pass as part of the release process for the Machine Learning function. In reality, a set of assumptions and evidence measures would be combined to evaluate the performance requirements, not just relying on assumptions regarding occluded persons. In order to evaluate the confidence arguments related to "Adequacy of the sample set to discover faults" and "Representativeness of the sample set", we applied an experimental approach to investigate the correlation between occlusion of parts of the pedestrian and activations within the DNN. In [9] a visualization technique was introduced that gives insight into intermediate feature layers of a DNN. This method demonstrates which input pattern of the image causes the activation of a particular feature map. In our experiment, we use the same diagnostic method to trace the feature map activities back to the input pixel space

[9]. For this purpose, we trained a Squeeznet [14] on CityPersons [27]. We then evaluated the resulting activation map not only manually, but also statistically.

Table 1. Sensitivity analysis of feature maps for unmasked images and masked lower part of pedestrians. Chosen layers are mainly activated for lower part of pedestrians.

Layer name	Output channel no.	Activation for human lower part, unmasked Image	Activation for human lower part masked Image
fire5/expand3x3	108	80.68%	25.0%
maxpool5	236	84.81%	25.0%
fire6/squeeze1x1	5	81.62%	14.67%
fire6/expand3x3	72	84.63%	5.0%
fire6/concat	264	84.63%	25.0%
fire7/expand3x3	74	80.29%	19.67%
fire7/concat	266	80.29%	17.67%
fire8/concat	20	85.3%	18.33%
fire8/concat	165	80.52%	21.67%
fire9/squeeze1x1	49	80.95%	20.5%

For our experiment, we apply the diagnostic method to search for the feature maps which are activated by the lower part of the body by investigating the activation map [9]. After identifying the relevant feature maps, we verify this dependency through statistical evaluation. We mask the lower 50% of all detected pedestrians from the CityPersons data set, as shown in Fig. 2, and compare the activations against unmasked images. If the feature map is activated, the mean pixel value of the lower part of the bounding box in the activation map $ActiveMap_{lowBB}$ is higher than the mean pixel value of the total activation map $ActiveMap_{total}$. Equation 6 describes the activation of the feature map:

$$\frac{\sum_{p=1}^{\#ActiveMap_{lowBB}} ActiveMap_{lowBB}[p]}{\#ActiveMap_{lowBB}} > \frac{\sum_{d=1}^{\#ActiveMap_{total}} ActiveMap_{total}[d]}{\#ActiveMap_{total}} \quad (6)$$

The sensitivity analysis in Table 1 is conducted on the Munich test data set of CityPersons [27] with 383 images. The layers are mainly activated, when the lower part of the detected pedestrian is visible (third column). However, they are less activated, when the lower part is masked (forth column in Table 1). This analysis confirms the activation of the feature map is particularly sensitive to the visibility of the lower part of body. Consequently, we provide evidence that the relevant feature map for detecting the lower body is not activated, when the lower body is masked. Evaluation only on the prediction would not reveal what caused each prediction. This leads us to reassess the potential of the test data sets at detecting faults related to occlusion of different body parts. Furthermore, this sensitivity analysis can be now extended to other feature maps to find additional weaknesses in the DNN and identify suitable counter-measures. These could include the retraining of particular layers or of the whole DNN.

Table 2. Summary of confidence claims for test data sets

Confidence argument	Description
Adequacy to discover faults	Test data sets can give an overall evaluation of performance. However, they do not necessarily reveal specific systematic performance issues (such as undue focus on lower body when detecting pedestrians). In addition, this technique is not well suited to uncover robustness issues of the trained function
Measurement relevance	Faults discovered when applying the test data set directly indicate weaknesses in the trained model with respect to realistic input data. However, issues regarding differences between the target environment and environment used to collect training and test data must also be addressed
Sample set is representative	The test data set is likely to contain similar biases caused by scalable oversight, distributional shift to that of the training data. In addition, the sample set may be representative of the distribution of features in the input domain, however this may not guarantee the detection of critical rarely occurring corner cases
Extrapolation of results	The performance targets that can be argued are limited with respect to the size and distribution of the data set and are not focused towards particular causes of insufficiencies

5   Evaluation of Performance Evidence Approaches

Based on the confidence argument structure described in Sect. 3, we can now assess performance evaluation techniques regarding their contribution to the performance claim that a particular MLM fulfills its performance criteria. Table 2 summarises an evaluation of confidence case elements for testing based on test data sets including some insights provided by the case study described above. This analysis highlights several of the weaknesses associated with test data driven verification of machine learning functions and demonstrates the need for strong supporting evidence in the confidence argument to ensure that issues such as fault coverage and sample set representativeness are addressed.

A key weakness associated with such techniques is their apparent inability to detect robustness deficits that may not be related to feature dimensions directly relevant to the properties of the operating environment of interest.

Table 3. Summary of confidence claims for analysing robustness against adversarial perturbations [13]

Confidence argument	Description
Adequacy to discover faults	The analysis focuses on faults caused by adversarial perturbations that exploit robustness deficits in the trained function. A fault model is defined in the form of perturbations against which the trained function shall be robust and the region within the input space in which the perturbations are deemed relevant
Measurement relevance	The technique relies on a number of assumptions to allow for a tractable analysis. These include the relevance of features within (hidden) layers of the network and the size of the regions to be analysed (amount of perturbation). The correlation between the parameters of the analysis and their relevance to the overall performance in relation to the actual *ContractPerformance* is unclear
Sample set is representative	The technique performs an exhaustive search of particular regions of the neural network. The analysis is sound for a given bounded input space region. However the analysis is only performed for specific images. Therefore the results will depend greatly on the selection of the images as a starting point for the analysis
Extrapolation of results	Due to the uncertainty regarding the relevance of the performance measurement and the representativeness of the sample set, a method for extrapolating the results of the performance evaluation across the entire input domain was unclear and is likely to rely on a number of specific assumptions and constraints

Next, we assess confidence arguments for techniques that analyse the robustness of a trained function against adversarial perturbations, and in particular those that make use of introspection techniques. In Table 3 we investigate the concept outlined in [13]. In this approach, the robustness of the trained network is verified by demonstrating that regions within the input space exhibit a similarity within the activation network such that misclassifications in the case of adversarial inputs cannot occur, where the adversarial inputs may be deliberately manipulated or due to other effects such as sensor noise.

6   Summary and Future Work

This paper has shown that existing approaches to evaluating the performance of machine learning in the context of safety-related automated driving functions provide evidence of only limited value for a safety assurance case. This is admittedly a non-trivial task and as yet no industry consensus or standards exist regarding which combination of techniques should be applied for the performance evaluation of such functions. An approach was provided for constructing confidence arguments for performance evaluation techniques which could be used in future work to demonstrate their contribution to the assurance case and the conditions under which the contributions are valid. The approach was used to evaluate a pedestrian recognition function and sensitivity analysis of feature maps was used to highlight weaknesses in the trained function and also to reflect on the contribution of typical performance evaluation techniques.

The evaluations described in Sect. 5 highlight the fact that each individual performance evaluation technique is limited according to a certain set of constraints and assumptions. By better understanding these, for example through the use of techniques such as sensitivity analysis of feature maps (as described in our experiment), introspection methods [5,21], fault injection [24], mutation testing [7], a combination of evidence may be found that provides a convincing argument that the performance requirements are met. Explicitly evaluating the machine learning approach and its performance evaluation measure against the set of claims defined in the assurance claim points leads to a greater level of confidence that the performance requirements have been met. This in turn can provide additional support for safety assessment and certification activities, especially in the absence of accepted best practice and standards.

Future work will focus on deepening the understanding of insufficiencies in the MLMs by performing sensitivity analysis for a wider range of features whilst providing stronger confidence arguments for any proposed evidence to support the performance claim. The authors also propose the use of confidence arguments in future standardisation efforts in order to better motivate the contribution of particular evaluation techniques, or to provide a framework by which the use of any particular combination of techniques can be justified for a particular system context.

References

1. ISO/PRF PAS 21448: Road vehicles - safety of the intended functionality. Technical report, International Standards Organisation (ISO), Geneva (2011)
2. Goal structuring notation community standard version 2. Technical report, Assurance Case Working Group (ACWG) (2018). https://scsc.uk/r141B:1?t=1. Accessed 04 June 2019
3. ISO 26262: Road vehicles - functional safety, second edition. Technical report, International Standards Organisation (ISO), Geneva (2018)
4. SAE J3016: Surface vehicle recommended practice, (r) taxonomy and definitions for terms related to driving automation systems for on-road motor vehicles. Technical report. SAE International, Geneva (2018)
5. Alsallakh, B., Jourabloo, A., Ye, M., Liu, X., Ren, L.: Do convolutional neural networks learn class hierarchy? CoRR arXiv:1710.06501 (2017)
6. Amodei, D., Olah, C., Steinhardt, J., Christiano, P., Schulman, J., Mané, D.: Concrete problems in ai safety. arXiv preprint arXiv:1606.06565 (2016)
7. Baker, R., Habli, I.: An empirical evaluation of mutation testing for improving the test quality of safety-critical software. IEEE Trans. Software Eng. 39(6), 787–805 (2012)

8. Burton, S., Gauerhof, L., Heinzemann, C.: Making the case for safety of machine learning in highly automated driving. In: Tonetta, S., Schoitsch, E., Bitsch, F. (eds.) SAFECOMP 2017. LNCS, vol. 10489, pp. 5–16. Springer, Cham (2017). https://doi.org/10.1007/978-3-319-66284-8_1

9. Chollet, F.: Deep Learning with Python. Manning Publications Co., Greenwich, CT, USA, 1st edn. (2017), chapter: 5.4.1. Visualizing intermediate activations

10. Gauerhof, L., Munk, P., Burton, S.: Structuring validation targets of a machine learning function applied to automated driving. In: Gallina, B., Skavhaug, A., Bitsch, F. (eds.) SAFECOMP 2018. LNCS, vol. 11093, pp. 45–58. Springer, Cham (2018). https://doi.org/10.1007/978-3-319-99130-6_4

11. Hawkins, R., Habli, I., Kelly, T.: The principles of software safety assurance. In: 31st International System Safety Conference (2013)

12. Hawkins, R., Kelly, T., Knight, J., Graydon, P.: A new approach to creating clear safety arguments. In: Dale, C., Anderson, T. (eds.) Advances in Systems Safety. Springer, London (2011). https://doi.org/10.1007/978-0-85729-133-2_1

13. Huang, X., Kwiatkowska, M., Wang, S., Wu, M.: Safety verification of deep neural networks. In: Majumdar, R., Kunčak, V. (eds.) CAV 2017. LNCS, vol. 10426, pp. 3–29. Springer, Cham (2017). https://doi.org/10.1007/978-3-319-63387-9_1

14. Iandola, F.N., Han, S., Moskewicz, M.W., Ashraf, K., Dally, W.J., Keutzer, K.: SqueezeNet: AlexNet-level accuracy with 50x fewer parameters and <0.5MB model size. arXiv e-prints arXiv:1602.07360, February 2016

15. Krizhevsky, A., Sutskever, I., Hinton, G.E.: Imagenet classification with deep convolutional neural networks. In: Advances in Neural Information Processing Systems, pp. 1097–1105 (2012)

16. Kurakin, A., Goodfellow, I., Bengio, S.: Adversarial examples in the physical world. arXiv preprint arXiv:1607.02533 (2016)

17. Kurd, Z., Kelly, T.: Establishing safety criteria for artificial neural networks. In: Palade, V., Howlett, R.J., Jain, L. (eds.) KES 2003. LNCS (LNAI), vol. 2773, pp. 163–169. Springer, Heidelberg (2003). https://doi.org/10.1007/978-3-540-45224-9_24

18. Lin, H.W., Tegmark, M., Rolnick, D.: Why does deep and cheap learning work so well? J. Stat. Phys. **168**(6), 1223–1247 (2017)

19. Metzen, J.H., Genewein, T., Fischer, V., Bischoff, B.: On detecting adversarial perturbations. arXiv preprint arXiv:1702.04267 (2017)

20. Nguyen, A., Yosinski, J., Clune, J.: Deep neural networks are easily fooled: High confidence predictions for unrecognizable images. In: Proceedings of the IEEE Conference on Computer Vision and Pattern Recognition, pp. 427–436 (2015)

21. Nguyen, A.M., Yosinski, J., Clune, J.: Multifaceted feature visualization: Uncovering the different types of features learned by each neuron in deep neural networks. CoRR arXiv:1602.03616 (2016)

22. Picardi, C., Habli, I.: Perspectives on assurance case development for retinal disease diagnosis using deep learning. In: Riaño, D., Wilk, S., ten Teije, A. (eds.) Artificial Intelligence in Medicine AIME 2019. LNCS, p. 11526. Springer, Cham (2019). https://doi.org/10.1007/978-3-030-21642-9_46

23. Picardi, C., Hawkins, R., Paterson, C., Habli, I.: A pattern for arguing the assurance of machine learning in medical diagnosis systems. In: International Conference on Computer Safety, Reliability, and Security. Springer (2019)

24. Schorn, C., Guntoro, A., Ascheid, G.: Efficient on-line error detection and mitigation for deep neural network accelerators. In: Gallina, B., Skavhaug, A., Bitsch, F. (eds.) SAFECOMP 2018. LNCS, vol. 11093, pp. 205–219. Springer, Cham (2018). https://doi.org/10.1007/978-3-319-99130-6_14
25. Sculley, D., et al.: Hidden technical debt in machine learning systems. In: Advances in Neural Information Processing Systems, pp. 2503–2511 (2015)
26. Varshney, K.R.: Engineering safety in machine learning. In: 2016 Information Theory and Applications Workshop (ITA), pp. 1–5. IEEE (2016)
27. Zhang, S., Benenson, R., Schiele, B.: CityPersons: a diverse dataset for pedestrian detection. arXiv e-prints arXiv:1702.05693, February 2017

Bayesian Uncertainty Quantification with Synthetic Data

Buu Phan$^{(\boxtimes)}$, Samin Khan, Rick Salay, and Krzysztof Czarnecki

University of Waterloo, Waterloo, Canada
{btphan,sa24khan}@uwaterloo.ca, {rsalay,kczarnec}@gsd.uwaterloo.ca

Abstract. Image semantic segmentation systems based on deep learning are prone to making erroneous predictions for images affected by uncertainty influence factors such as occlusions or inclement weather. Bayesian deep learning applies the Bayesian framework to deep models and allows estimating so-called epistemic and aleatoric uncertainties as part of the prediction. Such estimates can indicate the likelihood of prediction errors due to the influence factors. However, because of lack of data, the effectiveness of Bayesian uncertainty estimation when segmenting images with varying levels of influence factors has not yet been systematically studied. In this paper, we propose using a synthetic dataset to address this gap. We conduct two sets of experiments to investigate the influence of distance, occlusion, clouds, rain, and puddles on the estimated uncertainty in the segmentation of road scenes. The experiments confirm the expected correlation between the influence factors, the estimated uncertainty, and accuracy. Contrary to expectation, we also find that the estimated aleatoric uncertainty from Bayesian deep models can be reduced with more training data. We hope that these findings will help improve methods for assuring machine-learning-based systems.

Keywords: Semantic segmentation · Uncertainty · Influence factors

1 Introduction

Deep neural network (DNN) models, although having achieved many state-of-the-art results on a variety of tasks in computer vision [1,10,17], are not perfect as their performance much depends on the input images. Since errors in prediction due to the input characteristics are inevitable, several uncertainty metrics have been proposed as failure indicators for potentially faulty predictions [6,8,9]. Before deploying these metrics as failure indicators into safety-critical applications such as autonomous driving (AD) and medical diagnosis, their behaviour should be studied extensively under different scenarios in order to improve safety assurance.

Bayesian neural networks (BNN) is a class of deep learning models that is able to provide a more reliable uncertainty estimates than traditional DNN models. Also, these models can quantify two different types of uncertainty in supervised

© Springer Nature Switzerland AG 2019
A. Romanovsky et al. (Eds.): SAFECOMP 2019 Workshops, LNCS 11699, pp. 378–390, 2019.
https://doi.org/10.1007/978-3-030-26250-1_31

learning problems, namely aleatoric and epistemic uncertainty. Aleatoric uncertainty represents the irreducible source of errors in the data (e.g., noise), and thus cannot be reduced by providing more data. In contrast, epistemic uncertainty represents the model's "lack of knowledge" about the problem and can be reduced with more training data (more details in Sect. 3.2). Inputs with high aleatoric uncertainty can be thought as inherently ambiguous, whereas inputs with high epistemic uncertainty can be viewed as "unexpected", i.e., far from the training dataset.

With recent concerns about AI safety in AD, researchers have applied BNN models to several vision tasks in AD, such as image segmentation [11,12] and object detection [15], and reported that the obtained uncertainty estimates are more reliable. However, the experiments in these works do not investigate the effects of uncertainty influence factors [4], which are factors influencing the perceptual uncertainty, on the uncertainty estimates. A possible reason could be the lack of datasets with real-world images with varying influence factors and the associated factor labels. Yet understanding how the uncertainty estimates behave under these factors is needed for assuring the system performance.

In this paper, we propose using synthetic data to investigate and study the effects of selected factors on BNN's uncertainty in the task of image semantic segmentation. In particular, we consider scene-specific factors: depth, occlusion, clouds, rain, and puddles. These factors can lead to ambiguous inputs, e.g., due to reduced information about the underlying objects in the scene because of their far distance or high occlusion level, but also unexpected inputs because of changed appearance, e.g., due to rain or puddles, if not trained for. We perform two sets of experiments, with the following results:

1. We study and quantify the uncertainty estimates of a state-of-the-art BNN under different levels of occlusion and depth for vehicles. As expected, we find a correlation between the influence factors, the estimated uncertainty, and accuracy, which is desirable for a failure indicator. Contrary to expectation, we find that the estimated aleatoric uncertainty from a BNN *can* change with more training data.
2. We explore and report on the behavior of BNN's uncertainty estimates under different weather effects. We find that cloud level has much more significant impact on the uncertainty estimates than rain and puddles—which correlates with the higher negative impact of clouds on the network performance than that of rain or puddles, as previously reported for the same dataset and network [13].

The paper is structured as follows. Section 2 briefly describes the ProcSy dataset, which we use in this research. Section 3 explains the concept of BNN, aleatoric uncertainty, and epistemic uncertainty, and how to extract these uncertainties from BNN models. Section 3.4 describes the semantic segmentation network used in the experiments. Section 4 presents two experiments using ProcSy to study the effects of influence factor variations on the uncertainty estimates. Finally, we conclude the paper and suggest future research directions in Sect. 5.

2   The ProcSy Dataset

This section briefly describes the ProcSy synthetic dataset, which we have developed in previous work [13], and use for our experiments. Being synthetically generated, ProcSy holds several benefits for studying uncertainty estimation. Section 2.1 explains these benefits in detail. Section 2.2 summarizes the content of the ProcSy dataset.

2.1   Why Synthetic Data?

In the context of autonomous driving, factors such as depth, amount of occlusion, and weather effects can produce ambiguous and unexpected inputs to the model. Studying effects of these factors with a real-world dataset is difficult, although this is desirable. Current segmentation datasets with weather effects such as Raincouver [18] have a limited quantity of data to work with. Raincouver, for instance, is meant to be used as an addendum to an existing dataset such as Cityscapes rather than by itself, as it only contains 326 finely annotated images.

Berkeley Deep Drive [19] is a more recent dataset that shows more promise in the quantity of data availability (5683 finely annotated images). However, this dataset suffers from labeling inconsistency issues. These factors make real-world segmentation datasets impractical for model uncertainty analysis. Using these datasets to supplement a high-quality segmentation dataset such as Cityscapes [3] (which has no weather effects) is also problematic, since there is a qualitative difference in the datasets.

It is also very often the case that data acquired in the real world is not repeatable under different conditions. For instance, a scene captured in ideal conditions may not be reproducible during a day with heavy rain, because a car that was originally parked in the scene is no longer there. This sort of logistical issues can prove to be very expensive to overcome in generating a real-world dataset. It is also not an easy task to annotate effects such as amount of occlusion in a real-world dataset. On the other hand, synthetic data rendered by recent computer graphics technology can provide various influence factor effects with minimal labour cost. Due to these reasons, in this paper, we use our ProcSy synthetic dataset to analyze the effect of influence factors on the uncertainty estimates of a model.

2.2   Dataset Summary

Our ProcSy dataset is comprised of road scenes captured from a virtual render of a $3 \, km^2$ map region of urban Canada. From this environment, 11,000 scene frames were curated to contain no visible artifacts such as clipping of the camera through vehicles and pedestrians. These curated frames were then split into 8000 training frames, 2000 validation frames, and 1000 test frames.

For each frame of the ProcSy dataset, along with the base RGB image, we have generated corresponding ground truth annotation labels, depth map data, and occlusion maps of the different vehicle types present in the scene.

We generate weather variations in the categories of rain, puddle, and cloud coverage. For each of these factors, we consider five different intensity levels. These are 0%, 25%, 50%, 75%, and 100%. Figure 1 shows an example frame with different intensity levels for each of the three weather factors. For our training set of 8000 images, we first consider three equal subsets for the weather categories. Within each subset, we further divide into intensity levels and render RGB images reflecting variations in these subsets. This allows us to carry out experiments without having to generate every permutation of influence factor variations.

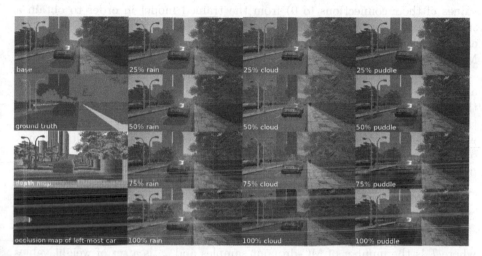

Fig. 1. Weather variations visualizing intensity level differences in the three weather categories — rain, cloud, and puddle; ground truth, depth map, and occlusion map for one vehicle type are also shown along with the base RGB image

3 Uncertainty Estimation with Bayesian Neural Networks

In this section, we describe the concept of a BNN, two types of uncertainty (aleatoric and epistemic), and how to extract measures of these types of uncertainty from a BNN's predictions. We focus on the case of classification since we are interested in uncertainty estimates of the image segmentation task.

3.1 Bayesian Neural Networks with MC-Dropout

With BNN models, instead of getting a single prediction from a learned set of weight values, we obtain the prediction by taking into account the outputs of multiple models, whose weight values are derived under the Bayesian framework. In regions with a large amount of data, the predictions of these models are consistent with each other; on the other hand, in regions that lack data, this consistency does not tend to hold. Since deep models contain a large number of weights, applying the Bayesian framework to a deep model is computationally intractable, therefore, in order to obtain different sets of weight values, we need to use Bayesian approximation techniques.

One approach to obtain an approximated BNN model from an existing DNN architecture is by inserting dropout layers and training the new model with dropout training [8]. At test time, for a given input, we perform multiple forward predictions in the network while keeping the dropout layers active. In other words, we remove a percentage of randomly-selected units (i.e., set the weight values of their connections to 0) from the trained model in order to obtain a sample prediction for the given input; then we repeat this process T times and calculate the average prediction. This technique at test time is referred to as Monte-Carlo (MC) dropout.

Specifically in classification, we are given the input data $\mathbf{X} = \{\mathbf{x}_1, \mathbf{x}_2, ..., \mathbf{x}_N\}$ and the associated labels $\mathbf{Y} = \{\mathbf{y}_1, \mathbf{y}_2, ..., \mathbf{y}_N\}$, where each $\mathbf{y}_j$ belong to one of the K classes $[1, 2, ..., K]$. We use $p(\hat{\mathbf{y}} = k|\hat{\mathbf{x}}, \omega_i)$ to denote the probability that the label $\hat{\mathbf{y}}$ of the test input $\hat{\mathbf{x}}$ is the kth class, which is given by a model (trained with dropout on $\mathbf{X}, \mathbf{Y}$) with a set of sampled weight values ω_i as its softmax output. Then, we wish to capture the mean probability $p(\hat{\mathbf{y}} = k|\hat{\mathbf{x}})$ for a test point $\hat{\mathbf{x}}$, which can be calculated as:

$$p(\hat{\mathbf{y}} = k|\hat{\mathbf{x}}) = \frac{1}{T} \sum_{i=1}^{T} p(\hat{\mathbf{y}} = \mathbf{k}|\hat{\mathbf{x}}, \omega_i) \tag{1}$$

where T is the number of MC-dropout samples and ω_i is a set of weight values for each MC-dropout sample. We note that calculating the probability for every class will give us a categorical distribution over classes for the input $\hat{\mathbf{x}}$.

3.2   Types of Uncertainty

Aleatoric uncertainty represents the irreducible noise in the data and cannot be reduced even when we gather more data [12]. For example, in the binary classification problem where we have a large amount of data, the data that lie within the intersection region of the two class distributions will have higher aleatoric uncertainty than the data in either distribution but outside the intersection. Epistemic uncertainty captures the model's lack of knowledge due to the limitation in the training data (such as bias, scarcity, novelty, etc.) [7]. It can be reduced by gathering more training data. Bayesian modelling allows us to quantify both types of uncertainty. Although approaches exist for estimating aleatoric uncertainty with non-Bayesian approaches [12], they cannot be used to estimate epistemic uncertainty. Furthermore, non-Bayesian models tend to perform poorly and give overconfident predictions in regions that lack data [7]. Bayesian approaches to neural networks, on the other hand, allow us to capture the epistemic uncertainty [12] and, thus, BNN models tend to give predictions with high uncertainty in low-density regions.

3.3   Uncertainty Estimation

There are three metrics that we will use in the experiments, namely: predictive entropy $\mathbb{H}(\hat{\mathbf{y}}|\hat{\mathbf{x}})$ (captures total uncertainty), mutual information $\mathbb{MI}(\hat{\mathbf{y}}|\hat{\mathbf{x}})$ (captures epistemic uncertainty), and aleatoric entropy $\mathbb{AE}(\hat{\mathbf{y}}|\hat{\mathbf{x}})$ (captures aleatoric uncertainty). These uncertainty estimates can be calculated as follows [5,16].

Predictive Entropy captures the total amount of uncertainty (epistemic and aleatoric) and is equal to the sum of mutual information and aleatoric entropy. It is calculated as an entropy of the mean categorical distribution:

$$\mathbb{H}(\hat{\mathbf{y}}|\hat{\mathbf{x}}) = \mathbb{MI}(\hat{\mathbf{y}}|\hat{\mathbf{x}}) + \mathbb{AE}(\hat{\mathbf{y}}|\hat{\mathbf{x}})$$
$$= -\sum_{k} p(\hat{\mathbf{y}} = k|\hat{\mathbf{x}}) \log p(\hat{\mathbf{y}} = k|\hat{\mathbf{x}}) \qquad (2)$$

Aleatoric Entropy captures the aleatoric uncertainty and is calculated by averaging the entropy of each sampled categorical distribution.

$$\mathbb{AE}(\hat{\mathbf{y}}|\hat{\mathbf{x}}) = -\frac{1}{T} \sum_{k,i} p(\hat{\mathbf{y}} = k|\hat{\mathbf{x}}, \omega_i) \log p(\hat{\mathbf{y}} = k|\hat{\mathbf{x}}, \omega_i) \qquad (3)$$

Mutual Information captures the epistemic uncertainty and is calculated as:

$$\mathbb{MI}(\hat{\mathbf{y}}|\hat{\mathbf{x}}) = \mathbb{H}(\hat{\mathbf{y}}|\hat{\mathbf{x}}) - \mathbb{AE}(\hat{\mathbf{y}}|\hat{\mathbf{x}}) \qquad (4)$$

3.4   Bayesian Neural Networks for Image Segmentation

Semantic segmentation is a task that assigns a class label to each pixel of an image. For autonomous driving, the image segmentation system enables the vehicle to perceive the visual state of the world. Since deep convolutional architectures consider this task as classifying each pixel independently using the same network [14], the BNN approach can be applied to this family of architectures to estimate the uncertainty per pixel.

For the experiments in this paper, we use Deeplab v3+ [2], one of the state-of-the-art models for segmentation, with ResNet 50 backbone architecture [10]. We inserted dropout layers with rate of 0.5 at four blocks in the middle of the backbone (specifically, at the end of the 8th till 11th block). The basis for this setup is based on the studies by Kendall et al. [11] and Mukhoti et al. [16], from which they empirically determined that inserting dropout layers in the middle flow yields a better predictive performance than for other positions in a network. Figure 2 shows examples of the three uncertainty types estimated by a BNN.

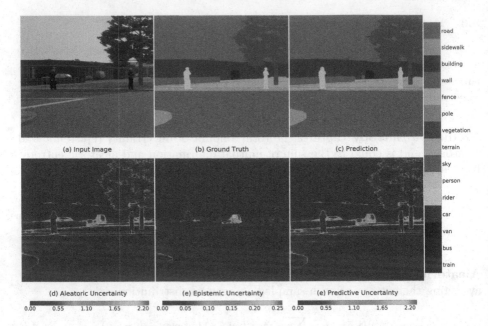

Fig. 2. Illustration for different types of uncertainty estimates in semantic segmentation. (a), (b), (c) show the input image, ground truth and prediction, respectively. (d), (e), (f) show the estimated aleatoric, epistemic and predictive uncertainty from our model. It can be visually observed that the aleatoric uncertainty is high at the class boundary (e.g., the tree). On the other hand, the epistemic uncertainty estimates are high only at several specific regions, such as the cluster in the middle of (e). This model is trained with 3000 clean images (model A in Sect. 4).

4   Experiments with Synthetic Data

In this section, we perform two experiments with two sets of influence factors. The first experiment involves the amount of depth and occlusion as factors, whereas the second experiment involves different weather effects, specifically: clouds, rain, and puddles. The reason why we treat them separately is that occluded and distant objects occur in the training set, whereas the latter factors do not.

We train two Bayesian Deeplab v3+ models: model A with 3000 clean images and model B with 8000 clean images. We note that the set of 3000 clean images is a subset of the set of 8000 images. Model A and model B are trained with 75, 000 and 180, 000 iterations, respectively, with a batch size of 16 and crop size of 512×512.

4.1   Occlusion and Depth

In this experiment, we study how different variations of occlusions and depth factors affect the uncertainty estimates. We test and measure the uncertainty estimates (aleatoric, epistemic, and predictive) of model A and B using a test set consisting of 270 clean images containing a total of 1,200 vehicles. The amount of occlusion for each vehicle is determined by calculating the fraction of the number of occluded pixels over the total number of the vehicle's pixels. We then assign this occlusion level to each visible pixel of the vehicle. For each model, we partition the pixels into subsets based on amount of occlusion and distance (each discretized into five intervals of 20%). Then we calculate the mean accuracy and uncertainty estimates for the model predictions of the pixels in each subset. Finally, we use cubic spline interpolation to obtain a contour plot. The results are shown in Fig. 3.

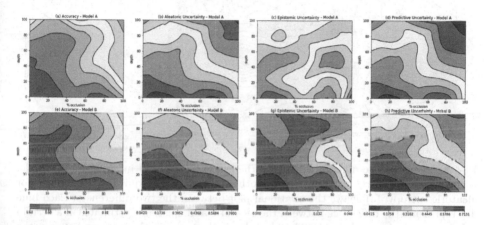

Fig. 3. The two rows show the accuracy, aleatoric, epistemic and predictive uncertainty estimates according to level of depth and occlusion of model A and B, respectively. Each color bar reflects the metric values of the plots in the corresponding column.

According to the definition of aleatoric and epistemic uncertainty, we expect that model B's epistemic uncertainty estimates should be lower than model A's, whereas the aleatoric estimates of the two models should stay similar. Based on the results in Fig. 3, we make the following observations:

1. Model B has higher accuracy and lower epistemic uncertainty than model A in general. This fits with expectations since model B is trained with more data than model A.
2. The predictive uncertainty can be observed to be correlated well with the accuracy, which is a desirable characteristic for a failure indicator. The Pearson correlation coefficient between predictive uncertainty and accuracy for model A is -0.89 and for model B is -0.90.
3. For both models A and B, the aleatoric estimates increase for objects that are more occluded and further away from the camera as expected. The same behavior can also be observed for the predictive uncertainty estimates.

4. There is a difference between the aleatoric estimates of the two models, which is surprising. Specifically, the difference between aleatoric estimates seems to increase with the epistemic difference. To validate this observation, we plot in Fig. 4 the difference between those two uncertainty estimates according to the amount of occlusion and depth, then we calculate the Pearson correlation coefficient of these quantities. The results reflect this observation as the Pearson coefficient, which values is 0.579, implies that there is a relation between the two quantities.

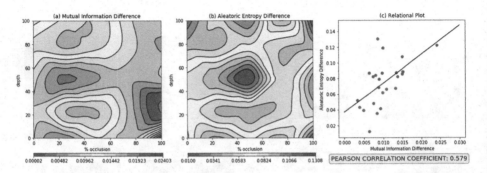

Fig. 4. (a) shows the difference between the estimated mutual information for model B and A according to occlusion and depth. (b) shows the equivalent difference for aleatoric entropy. (c) shows the relational plot between the two differences. Each blue dot represents the difference between the aleatoric and epistemic estimates in a certain subset of occlusion and depth. The black line, which shows the relation between the two variables, is fitted by using linear regression. (Color figure online)

We hypothesize that the reason why we observe the aleatoric uncertainty estimate changing when more training data is provided is that the estimate is only reliable where we have sufficient data. For regions with a sufficient amount of data, the decision boundary of model A and B are similar to each other. Thus, adding more data would not likely change the estimated aleatoric uncertainty (unless the data we already have is biased). On the other hand, the decision boundaries in regions that lack data tend to be inconsistent making the aleatoric estimate unreliable.

Finally, we note that for model B, high aleatoric estimates still occur for regions that have relatively low epistemic uncertainty, such as the middle top region in Fig. 3f, g where the objects are occluded around 50% and far away from the camera. This suggests that depth and occlusion are sources of aleatoric uncertainty in the image segmentation task.

To ensure perceptual performance in safety-critical application, developers must make sure that the training data satisfies the scenario coverage condition properly [4]. This experiment and analysis suggests that we can use the measure of epistemic uncertainty to determine the optimal amount of data to collect for occlusion and depth factors. Specifically, we should collect enough data to make the epistemic uncertainty map blue. We leave the further exploration and validation of this idea for future work.

4.2   Weather

In this experiment, we study how the uncertainty estimates vary with respect to different intensity levels of weather effects, namely: clouds, rain, and puddles. We expect that as we increase the effect's intensity, the BNN model should have worse performance and output higher uncertainty estimates. This is because high intensity effects will introduce more artifacts that would cause misclassification in the model, thus the uncertainty estimate should increase to indicate this.

For each model and effect, we calculate the mIoU (mean Intersection over Union) and the mean aleatoric, epistemic, and predictive uncertainty estimates per pixel at every intensity level. Each effect's intensity level contains 150 images. The reason why we compare the performance of model A and B is that we want to observe how the uncertainty estimates change when we train with more in-distribution data. The results are shown in Fig. 5.

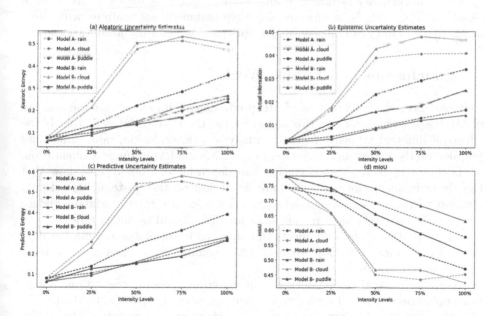

Fig. 5. (a–d) show the estimated aleatoric, epistemic, and predictive uncertainties and mIoU values for different variations of weather, factors respectively. The x-axes represent different intensity levels.

In terms of mIoU (Fig. 5d), we see that model B, which is trained with more in-distribution data, has better performance than model A when there is no factor involved. Further, model B's mIoU is higher than model A's for different

intensity levels of rain and puddles. However, surprisingly for cloudiness, there
is a sharp degradation in terms of mIoU for model B. Critically, at the 100%
cloud intensity level, model A outperforms model B (although with just a small
margin). We find that in 100% cloud conditions, the two models fail to predict
the following classes: pole, traffic lights, sky, bicycle, car and truck.

In terms of uncertainty, the three types of uncertainty estimates, in general,
increase with the intensity levels for every factor. This behavior meets our expectation for the uncertainty and it applies to both model A and B. We notice that
for clouds, there is a small decrease for the 50% to 100% levels, which requires
further investigation.

We also make two following observations. First, for model B, we see that
the epistemic uncertainty corresponds to the mIoU better than the other two
uncertainties. Specifically, at every intensity level for each effect, the ascending
order for epistemic estimates are rain, puddle and cloud, which corresponds to
the descending of that order in mIoU. For model A, on the other hand, all the
uncertainties reflect the mIoU well. Second, there is an inconsistency in terms of
the difference between model A and B's uncertainty estimates for all the factors.
For example, at 100% intensity level for rain and puddle, model B has lower
epistemic uncertainty estimates than model A, yet it is higher in the case of
cloudy images. This is unexpected since we assumed that training with more
in-distribution data can only make the epistemic uncertainty lower or intact.

5   Conclusions and Future Work

Reliable uncertainty estimation of ML predictions is important for the safe use
of ML-based components. In this paper, we use the ProcSy dataset to study the
effects of different influence factors, namely: depth, occlusion, rain, clouds and
puddles, on the uncertainty estimates of the BNN model for image segmentation.

In the experiments with occlusion and depth factors, our results show that
the aleatoric uncertainty estimates are dependent on the epistemic uncertainty
estimates. When given enough data, the epistemic uncertainty estimates reduce
but the aleatoric estimates remain high for distant and occluded objects. Furthermore, we find that cloud affects the uncertainty estimates and mIoU values
of the BNN more profoundly than rain and puddle, even when we have more
in-distribution training data.

As we have mentioned in Sect. 4a, the experiment results suggest one potential application that requires further investigation: the possibility to use the
epistemic uncertainty estimates to find an optimal amount of data for the occlusion and depth factors. Furthermore, it would be beneficial to extend this work to
understanding the risk potential of these factors. Finally, while this paper studies
how the influence factors affect the Bayesian uncertainties, future work should
address how we can use this synthetic framework to evaluate the reliability of
any uncertainty estimation method.

References

1. Chen, L.-C., Zhu, Y., Papandreou, G., Schroff, F., Adam, H.: Encoder-decoder with atrous separable convolution for semantic image segmentation. In: Ferrari, V., Hebert, M., Sminchisescu, C., Weiss, Y. (eds.) ECCV 2018. LNCS, vol. 11211, pp. 833–851. Springer, Cham (2018). https://doi.org/10.1007/978-3-030-01234-2_49
2. Chen, L.C., Zhu, Y., Papandreou, G., Schroff, F., Adam, H.: Encoder-decoder with atrous separable convolution for semantic image segmentation. In: Proceedings of the European Conference on Computer Vision (ECCV), pp. 801–818 (2018)
3. Cordts, M., et al.: The cityscapes dataset for semantic urban scene understanding. In: Proceedings of the IEEE Conference on Computer Vision and Pattern Recognition, pp. 3213–3223 (2016)
4. Czarnecki, K., Salay, R.: Towards a framework to manage perceptual uncertainty for safe automated driving. In: Gallina, B., Skavhaug, A., Schoitsch, E., Bitsch, F. (eds.) SAFECOMP 2018. LNCS, vol. 11094, pp. 439–445. Springer, Cham (2018). https://doi.org/10.1007/978-3-319-99229-7_37
5. Depeweg, S., Hernandez-Lobato, J., Doshi-Velez, F., Udluft, S.: Decomposition of uncertainty in bayesian deep learning for efficient and risk-sensitive learning. In: 35th International Conference on Machine Learning, ICML 2018, vol. 3, pp. 1920–1934 (2018)
6. DeVries, T., Taylor, G.W.: Learning confidence for out-of-distribution detection in neural networks. arXiv preprint arXiv.1802.04865 (2018)
7. Gal, Y.: Uncertainty in deep learning (2016)
8. Gal, Y., Ghahramani, Z.: Dropout as a Bayesian approximation: representing model uncertainty in deep learning. In: International Conference on Machine Learning, pp. 1050–1059 (2016)
9. Guo, C., Pleiss, G., Sun, Y., Weinberger, K.Q.: On calibration of modern neural networks. In: Proceedings of the 34th International Conference on Machine Learning, vol. 70, pp. 1321–1330. JMLR. org (2017)
10. He, K., Zhang, X., Ren, S., Sun, J.: Deep residual learning for image recognition. In: Proceedings of the IEEE Conference on Computer Vision and Pattern Recognition, pp. 770–778 (2016)
11. Kendall, A., Badrinarayanan, V., Cipolla, R.: Bayesian segnet: Model uncertainty in deep convolutional encoder-decoder architectures for scene understanding. arXiv preprint arXiv:1511.02680 (2015)
12. Kendall, A., Gal, Y.: What uncertainties do we need in Bayesian deep learning for computer vision? In: Advances in Neural Information Processing Systems, pp. 5574–5584 (2017)
13. Khan, S., Phan, B., Salay, R., Czarnecki, K.: Procsy: Procedural synthetic dataset generation towards influence factor studies of semantic segmentation networks. In: Proceedings of the IEEE Conference on Computer Vision and Pattern Recognition Workshops (to appear, 2019)
14. Long, J., Shelhamer, E., Darrell, T.: Fully convolutional networks for semantic segmentation. In: Proceedings of the IEEE Conference on Computer Vision and Pattern Recognition, pp. 3431–3440 (2015)
15. Miller, D., Nicholson, L., Dayoub, F., Sünderhauf, N.: Dropout sampling for robust object detection in open-set conditions. In: 2018 IEEE International Conference on Robotics and Automation (ICRA), pp. 1–7. IEEE (2018)
16. Mukhoti, J., Gal, Y.: Evaluating Bayesian deep learning methods for semantic segmentation. arXiv preprint arXiv:1811.12709 (2018)

17. Ren, S., He, K., Girshick, R., Sun, J.: Faster r-CNN: towards real-time object detection with region proposal networks. In: Advances in Neural Information Processing Systems, pp. 91–99 (2015)
18. Tung, F., Chen, J., Meng, L., Little, J.J.: The raincouver scene parsing benchmark for self-driving in adverse weather and at night. IEEE Rob. Autom. Lett. **2**(4), 2188–2193 (2017)
19. Yu, F., et al.: BDD100K: a diverse driving video database with scalable annotation tooling. CoRR arXiv:1805.04687 (2018)

A Self-certifiable Architecture for Critical Systems Powered by Probabilistic Logic Artificial Intelligence

Jacques Robin[1(✉)], Raul Mazo[1], Henrique Madeira[2], Raul Barbosa[2],
Daniel Diaz[1], and Salvador Abreu[1,3]

[1] Centre de Recherche en Informatique,
Université Panthéon-Sorbonne, Paris, France
{jacques.robin,raul.mazo,daniel.diaz}@univ-paris1.fr
[2] Departamento de Engenharia Informatica,
Universidade de Coimbra, Coimbra, Portugal
{henrique,rbarbosa}@dei.uc.pt
[3] Departamento de Informática, Universidade de Evora, Evora, Portugal
spa@uevora.pt

Abstract. We present a versatile architecture for AI-powered self-adaptive self-certifiable critical systems. It aims at supporting semi-automated low-cost re-certification for self-adaptive systems after each adaptation of their behavior to a persistent change in their operational environment throughout their lifecycle.

Keywords: AI certification · Autonomic architecture · Argumentation · Rule-based constraint solving · Probabilistic logic machine learning

1 Introduction

Critical systems must be certified as dependable before being legally allowed to be deployed. Today, certification consists in a dialog between two dependability experts: the expert from an engineering institution seeking certification for a new system (*i.e. the engineer*) and the expert from an independent accredited certification body (*i.e. the auditor*). It is completed when the engineer presents evidence-based arguments convincing the auditor that the system conforms to the industry dependability standard. Both the standard and the conformance arguments are formulated in natural language [1]. These arguments are of two kinds: (1) arguments, such as safety cases, that the engineered system satisfies its critical dependability requirements up to the probability threshold prescribed by the standard and (2) arguments that the process followed to engineer the system conformed to the engineering process prescribed by the standard. Today, the requirements and implementation of a critical system do not change post-deployment. Its certification is thus only questioned after repeated catastrophic failures (*e.g.* the Boeing 737 MAX).

Introducing AI in critical systems to make them autonomous and self-adaptive to new contexts disrupts this assumption. The design space of possible self-adaptations may be open and thus no longer certifiable once and for all before deployment.

© Springer Nature Switzerland AG 2019
A. Romanovsky et al. (Eds.): SAFECOMP 2019 Workshops, LNCS 11699, pp. 391–397, 2019.
https://doi.org/10.1007/978-3-030-26250-1_32

This should be the case of critical systems using on-line machine learning for lifelong self-adaptation such as autonomous cars adapting to evolving smart road infra-structures, traffic safety regulations and cybersecurity threats. Even when the self-adaptation design space can be closed, it may still be too large and sparse to be both exhaustively and cost-effectively verified and certified before deployment. The alternative is to incrementally re-certify it following each major adaptation. This makes reducing the cost overhead of certification, through automation, an absolutely crucial issue.

In this paper, we propose a generic architecture addressing this issue. Its key idea is that a sufficiently versatile AI inference engine can be reused for a wide range of both (a) the application-specific reasoning tasks needed by a dependably autonomous critical system and (b) the application-*independent meta*-reasoning tasks needed to make such system additionally autonomic [2] in the sense of being self-adaptive, self-explainable, self-verifiable, self-argumentative and consequently largely self-certifiable. In the next section, we explain why a probabilistic constraint solving rule engine can provide the needed versatility. Then in Sect. 3, we describe the various autonomous and autonomic reasoning tasks needed to make a critical system both self-adaptive and self-certifiable. Finally in Sect. 4, we discuss the main limitations of our proposed architecture and engine and outline approaches to overcome them.

2 Probabilistic Logic Constraint Solving Rules

We propose to leverage in synergy the versatility of (a) constraint solving [3] and (b) probabilistic rule-based reasoning [4] to parsimoniously support both autonomous reasoning and autonomic meta-reasoning. Among the various formalisms proposed for probabilistic rule-based constraint solving, we choose to present *CHRiSM (CHance Rules in Statistical Modeling)* [5] in this paper, because it is conceptually simple, very expressive and has been shown to support the kind of legal argumentative reasoning [6] that is central to our certification automation proposal.

A CHRiSM solver is composed of a task-independent CHRiSM engine and a task-specific CHRiSM rule base. The engine solves a *Constraint Solving Problem (CSP)* [3] by applying the rules that gradually transform an initial constraint store representing the CSP into a final constraint store representing its solution.

The store is of logical form $\forall i, L_i \wedge_i c_j(L_j)$ where the L_i are variable sets from a given mathematical domain and the c_j are so-called *constraints, i.e.* relations that restrict the possible values that the L_i can simultaneously take in their domain.

A CHRiSM rule base is a logical conjunction of two kinds of logical rules:

- Constraint *simplification* rules: $\forall i,j,k,l,m,L_m\ p::(\wedge_i g_i \Rightarrow (\wedge_j h_j \Leftrightarrow \vee_k (q_k:\wedge_l b_k^l)))$
- Constraint *propagation* rules: $\forall i,j,k,l,m,L_m\ p::(\wedge_i g_i \Rightarrow (\wedge_j h_j \Rightarrow \vee_k (q_k:\wedge_l b_k^l)))$

where the g_i, h_j, b_k^l are *logical constraints* (respectively called the *guards, heads* and *bodies* of the rule) that may match those in the store, the L_m are logical variables in g_i, h_j, or b_k^l, while p and the q_k are *arithmetic probability expressions* in [0,1]. These expressions may contain *random* variables R_n in addition to some *logical* variables also appearing the g_i or h_j, the latter allowing these expressions to depend on the result of rule guard evaluation and rule head matching. For each rule, $\sum q_k = 1$ and for each rule set sharing structurally matching g_i and h_j, $\sum p = 1$.

When the current store entails $\wedge_i\, g_i$ and contains $\wedge_j\, h_j$ (modulo logical variable pattern matching) of such rule set, then one rule from the set is fired with probability p. If it is a simplification (*resp.* propagation) rule then $\wedge_l\, b_k^l$ substitutes $\wedge_j\, h_j$ in the store with probability q_k, since, with that probability, it is logically equivalent to $\wedge_j\, h_j$ (*resp.* is *added* to the store with probability q_k since it is logically implied by $\wedge_j\, h_j$).

A CHRiSM engine can perform three kinds of inferences:

- *solve(S_i,S_f)* to compute the *most probable* solution S_f for CSP S_i; if S_i is exactly constrained, S_f has the form $\wedge_n\, L_n = v_n$, assigning a single value to each variable; if S_i is overconstrainted S_f is *false*;
- *prob(S_i ⇔ S_f, P)* to compute the probability P of S_f being a solution for CSP S_i;
- *learn(E,R,D)* to machine learn, given a set E of example pairs (S_i,S_f) where S_i is a CSP and S_f one of its solutions, the probability distribution D of the random variables R_i in the probability expressions of a CHRiSM rule base R using the *Expectation-Maximization* algorithm [7] initialized with the uniform distribution.

Any propositional or relational Bayes net can be represented by a semantically equivalent CHRiSM rule base [5]. For example, the classic alarm triggering Bayes net can be represented by the CHRiSM rule base:

$go \rightarrow P_b::burglary(yes) \vee (1\text{-}P_b)..burglary(no)$
$go \Rightarrow P_e::earthquake(yes) \vee (1\text{-}P_e)::earthquake(no)$
$burglary(B) \wedge earthquake(E) \Rightarrow P_a(B,E)::alarm(yes) \vee (1\text{-}P_a(B,E))::alarm(no)$
$P_j(A)::(alarm(A) \Rightarrow johncalls)$
$P_m(A)::(alarm(A) \Rightarrow marycalls)$

where P_b, P_e, P_a, P_j and P_m are probabilities expressions. Given this rule base, the query *prob({go} ⇔ {go, burglary(no), earthquake(yes), alarm(yes), marycalls}, P)* instantiates variable P with value $(1\text{-}P_b)*P_e*P_a(no,yes)*P_m(yes)$

A CHRiSM rule base without probability expressions is a *CHR$^\vee$* (*Constraint Handling Rules with disjunctive bodies*) rule base [3]. With CHR$^\vee$ bodies being equiprobable, they are tried in writing order and backtracking is triggered when the current choice combination leads to a *false* store. CHR$^\vee$ subsumes the three main classes of rule-based formalisms: *term rewrite rules* (corresponding to CHR simplification rules), *production and business rules* (corresponding to CHR propagation rules) and *Constraint Logic Programming (CLP) rules* (which rule sets sharing the same head are equivalent to a single-head guardless CHR$^\vee$ simplification rule [3]). In addition, CHR$^\vee$ and CLP solvers have been successfully used to implement AI reasoning paradigms as diverse as ontological reasoning with description logics and frame logic, default reasoning, abduction, belief update, belief revision, natural language processing and optimization in addition to deductive constraint solving for which the approach was initially designed[1]. Therefore, AI components providing a critical system with any

---

[1] Since lack of space prevents us to insert all the relevant references in the bibliography of this short paper, see https://dtai.cs.kuleuven.be/CHR/biblio.shtml for a more complete one.

such reasoning capability can be uniformly implemented with the conceptual parsimony and built-in explainabilty of only applying the two kinds of rules shown above with their straightforward probabilistic or logical semantic readings.

3   An Architecture Supporting Self-certification

Our proposed architecture for a *Self-Adaptive Self-Certifiable AI-Powered Critical System* is shown in Fig. 1 as a component diagram in the *Unified Modeling Language (UML)* standard (www.omg.org/spec/UML/2.5.1/). It composes:

- A *Configurable Application Component* assembly (first left on 2nd row in Fig. 1) implementing the application, with *Deep Learned AI* components (second left of 2nd row) for fine-grained perception and actuator control and *Symbolic AI* components (first left of 3rd row) for explainable high-level cognition;
- A set of abstract *Probabilistic Rule-Based Constraint Solver* components (center of 3rd row) each one composed of a distinct project-specific CHRiSM *Rule Base* but all reusing the same project and industry independent CHRiSM *Rule Engine* component, which itself contains a *Rule Learner* (center of 2nd row) component to machine learn CHRiSM rules from examples of CSP with their solutions (CSPS);
- An industry-specific but project-independent *Standard Process Model* (right of 5th row) of the process to follow to engineer the critical system in order to certify it;
- An industry-independent *Process Enactment Trace Generator* component (right of 7th row) recording the interactions of all stakeholders with the tools used in the project to generate the *Process Effectively Enacted* (right of 6th row) during it;
- The set of *Context-Aware Critical Requirements* (left of 6th row) of the system;
- A *Context Monitor* component (left of bottom row) that maintains a runtime *Context Model* (just above it) [8] that includes flags for transient or persistent errors.
- A natural language certification *Document Generator* (right of next to bottom row).

The abstract *Probabilistic Rule-Based Constraint Solver* components specialize into (a) system-specific symbolic AI components and (b) four meta-solvers, each providing a different system and industry independent autonomic capability to the system. The first of these meta-solvers is the *Critical Requirement Verification Meta-Solver* (center left of 6th row). Taking as input constraints (a) the *Context-Aware Critical Requirements* of the system (b) the current *Configurable Application Component* assembly and (c) the current *Context Model,* it verifies whether (b) still satisfies (a) in the context of (c), yielding as output the *Critical Requirement CSPS* (center left of 5th row). When this output is *false,* this triggers the second meta-solver, the *Configuration Meta-Solver* (left of 4th row) to infer a new *Configurable Application Component* assembly that satisfies the *Context-Aware Critical Requirements* in the new context. If the context change signals a fault, such automated reconfiguration can provide one form of fault-tolerance. Previous work [8] showed how rule-based constraint solving can automate context-aware requirement verification and reconfiguration.

The third meta-solver is the *Process Conformance Verification Meta-Solver* (center right of 5th row). Taking as input constraints (a) the *Process Effectively Enacted,* and (b) the *Standard Process Model,* it verifies whether (a) conforms to (b). Previous

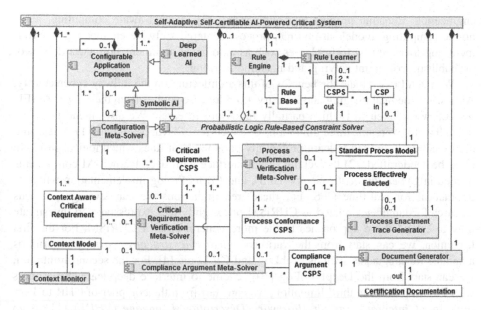

Fig. 1. Our proposed self-certifiable architecture for AI powered critical systems

research [9] showed rule-based constraint solving can automate such verification. The last meta-solver is the *Compliance Argumentation Meta-Solver* (center of bottom row). Taking as input constraints the results of the first and third meta-solver, *the Critical Requirement CSPS* and *the Process Conformance CSPS* respectively, it outputs a *Compliance Argument* (right of bottom row) combining the evidence provided by both. Previous work [6] used a CHRiSM solver to build a legal argument likely to be accepted by a judge. The key idea for this last meta-solver is the similarity between this task and that of building a compliance argument likely to be accepted by a certification auditor. This last meta-solver can also be given as additional input a counter-argument to refute provided by the certification auditor. The *Document Generator* translates the logico-probabilistic *Compliance Argument* into a natural language *Certification Documentation*.

4   Discussion and Conclusion

In this paper, we proposed an architecture model for AI-powered critical systems allowing them to self-adapt and semi-automatically generate a certification documentation update after each adaption throughout its lifecycle. This approach reflects our position that introducing self-adaptation in critical systems will require abandoning the current one-shot certification process concluded at the development stage of systems engineering and switch to an iterative certification process spanning the whole lifecycle. This will make lowering the cost of certification through certification documentation automation a crucial issue. Our architecture addresses this issue by integrating in a unique, new synergy, architectural principles from component-based engineering, dynamic product line engineering [8], context-aware computing, autonomic computing, models-at-runtime, process-centered software engineering environment, together with AI technologies such as automated argumentation and rule-based, probabilistic constraint solving and machine learning.

We intend to evaluate the benefits of this architecture on the railway cybersecurity, AI-assisted medical imaging and industry 4.0 pilot case studies from the H2020 AI4EU project (www.ai4eu.eu/) which partially funds our research. We also intend to investigate how to overcome three limitations of the current CHRiSM engine: (1) its learning ability currently limited to learn probability parameters of rules which logical structure must be handcrafted, (2) its lacking of an interface with deep-learned AI components needed in *Cyber-Physical Systems (CPS)*, and (3) its Prolog implementation which is unpractical for real-time CPS. For these tree limitations we can leverage previous research for languages related to CHRiSM but slightly less expressive and investigate how to extend those approaches to the more general case of CHRiSM. For the first limitation, we can start from the various *logical rule structure learning* algorithms available for languages such as ProbLog and CP-Logic [4]. For the second limitation, we can start from the DeepProbLog [10] scheme to interface deep-learned reasoners with ProbLog. For the third limitation, we can start from the compiler of CHR to *Very high speed integrated circuit Hardware Description Language (VHDL)* [11] from which a fast, parallel hardware implementation can then be generated. An alternative is compiling CHRiSM to native code. An implementation of our architecture with these three CHRiSM extensions would provide a parsimoniously versatile automation framework to engineer the self-adaptive, self-certifying, machine learned, neuro-logico-probabilistic, hardware implemented, real-time AI needed by the incoming next generation of autonomous, dependability-critical CPS.

References

1. Boulanger, J.: Safety Management for Software-Based Equipment. Wiley, Hoboken (2013)
2. Lalanda, P., McCann, J., Diaconescu, A.: Autonomic Computing: Principles, Design and Implementation. Springer, London (2013). https://doi.org/10.1007/978-1-4471-5007-7
3. Frühwirth, T.: Constraint Handling Rules. Cambridge University Press, Cambridge (2009)
4. Riguzzi, F.: Foundations of Probabilistic Logic Programming: Languages, Semantics, Inference and Learning, Rivers Publishers 2018
5. Sneyers, J., Wannes, M., Vennekens, J.: CHRiSM: chance rules induce statistical models. In: Proceedings of the 6th International Workshop on Constraint Handling Rules, Pasadena, CA, USA (2009)
6. Sneyers, J., De Schreye, D., Frühwirth, T.: Probabilistic legal reasoning in CHRiSM. Theor. Pract. Log. Prog. 13(4–5), 769–781 (2013)
7. Sneyers, J., Meert, W., Vennekens, J., Kameya, Y., Sato, T.: CHR(PRISM)-based probabilistic logic learning. Theor. Pract. Log. Prog. 10, 433–447 (2010)
8. Muñoz, J., Tamura, G., Raicu, I., Mazo, R., Salinesi, C.: REFAS: a PLE approach for simulation of self-adaptive systems requirements. In: Proceedings of the 19th International Software Product Line Conference (SPLC 2015), Nashville, TN, USA (2015)

9. Almeida da Silva, M., Mougenot, A., Blanc, X., Bendraou, R.: Towards automated inconsistency handling in design models. In: 22nd International Conference on Advanced Information Systems Engineering, Hammamet, Tunisia (2010)
10. Manhave, R., Dumancic, S., Kimmig, A., Demeester, T., De Raedt, L.: DeepProbLog: deep neural probabilistic programming. In: Proceedings of the 32nd Conference on Neural Information Processing (NeurIPS), Montreal, Canada (2018)
11. Triossi, A., Orlando, S., Raffaetá, A., Frühwirth, T.: Compiling CHR to parallel hardware. In: Proceedings of the 14th International ACM SIGPLAN Symposium on Principles and Practice of Declarative Programming, Leuven, Belgium (2012)

Tackling Uncertainty in Safety Assurance for Machine Learning: Continuous Argument Engineering with Attributed Tests

Yutaka Matsuno[1(✉)], Fuyuki Ishikawa[2], and Susumu Tokumoto[3]

[1] College of Science and Technology, Nihon University, Tokyo, Japan
matsuno.yutaka@nihon-u.ac.jp
[2] National Institute of Informatics, Tokyo, Japan
f-ishikawa@nii.ac.jp
[3] Fujitsu Laboratories Ltd., Kawasaki, Japan
tokumoto.susumu@fujitsu.com

Abstract. There are unique kinds of uncertainty in implementations constructed by machine learning from training data. This uncertainty affects the strategy and activities for safety assurance. In this paper, we investigate this point in terms of continuous argument engineering with a granular performance evaluation over the expected operational domain. We employ an attribute testing method for evaluating an implemented model in terms of explicit (partial) specification. We then show experimental results that demonstrate how safety arguments are affected by the uncertainty of machine learning. As an example, we show the weakness of a model, which cannot be predicted beforehand. We show our tool for continuous argument engineering to track the latest state of assurance.

1 Introduction

Arguments or assurance cases [1] will play a significant role in assuring the dependability of emerging ML-based systems. On one side, arguments describe goals and how top-level abstract goals are decomposed into concrete goals that are objectively measurable. On the other side, arguments describe how the satisfaction of the goals is supported by evidence. Arguments can serve as the foundation for analysis, discussion, and tracing done by development teams as well as third parties.

However, uncertainty in ML imposes fundamental obstacles against the use of arguments. It is more difficult or even impossible to be confident of completeness in arguments. Development teams may still claim completeness to account for their products in the best way currently known. Nevertheless, it will be increasingly more significant not to stop at releasing arguments (and products) but to continuously resolve uncertainty and react to expected or unexpected changes. The development process also has such an incremental nature as the trial-and-error style is required for uncertainty. We believe arguments can play an essential

© Springer Nature Switzerland AG 2019
A. Romanovsky et al. (Eds.): SAFECOMP 2019 Workshops, LNCS 11699, pp. 398–404, 2019.
https://doi.org/10.1007/978-3-030-26250-1_33

role in such incremental and continuous activities in addition to the currently typical role in one-shot assurance before release. There has already been work on *continuous argument engineering* to support the use of arguments under the uncertainty of ML-based systems [5]. Extended notations and patterns were provided to explicitly represent risks and the demand for continuous updates due to uncertainty. However, the work was not feature a tool implementation or experimental demonstration.

In this paper, we investigate tool support for continuous argument engineering with simple but concrete experimentation. The specific focus of our experimentation is a granular performance evaluation over the expected operational domain.

In the remainder of this paper, we discuss related work in Sect. 2. In Sect. 3, we present a prototype web-based tool for continuous argument engineering while presenting the principles of continuous argument engineering for machine learning briefly. In Sect. 4, we discuss a case study before we give concluding remarks in Sect. 5.

2   Related Work

In [4], arguments were constructed to cover the different roles of testing methods for ML based systems. However, continuous activities were not considered in the case of the existence of uncertainty.

In [2,3], the use of arguments was discussed for ML-based autonomous driving systems. Dependability goals and evidence are systematically provided to tackle risks specific to ML-based systems, such as the imperfectness of obtained functions. Typical goals and evidence were discussed to state that the risks of imperfection are mitigated. Although there is demand for runtime monitoring results, specific methods or tools were not provided for continuous activities.

One representative example from [2] is shown below.

Goal: Pedestrian classes are sufficiently accurately described Evidence: Functional specification of several validation data sub-sets shall include all variants of classes that can be derived from the environment.

Intuitively, this requires a very difficult task among an infinite number of possibilities in the real world. If we try to decompose this very abstract goal, we encounter the uncertainty of decomposition completeness. We may be worried about the sufficiency of the evidence as we cannot be sure about "all variants of pedestrian classes" (uncertainty of contributed evidence).

3   Tool for Continuous Argument Engineering

We implemented a prototype web-based GSN editor that supports the extensions described in [5]. In addition, the editor allows for linking a GSN model to monitoring values in Python code. This tool is an extension of [7], and it can be used freely via the Internet by using a conventional web browser from [6].

We implemented a pattern instantiation function for open goals, CD subgoals, and fragile goals (please refer to our previous paper [5]). Also, the soft contribution of machine learning evidence can be indicated by dotted links from the supporting goal. The pattern instantiation function is implemented by labeling goal and evidence nodes.

The continuous argument tool has a function for monitoring the parameters of ML-based systems, such as accuracy, loss, and epoch number for learning implemented in Python, which is the most widely used programming language for machine learning. In the screen of the tool, the parameters selected for the ML-based system are continuously updated while the system is working. Such parameters are attached to ML-based evidence and contexts for open and fragile goals.

4   Case Study

We used CIFAR10, one of the most popular data sets for image recognition, to classify objects into 10 classes such as cars and horses. Although the task is simple and does not directly link to practical applications, it is sufficient for demonstrating the nature of black-box ML implementation.

We constructed two versions of classifier models for CIFAR10 by using an example algorithm from the Keras library, which uses a CNN (Convolutional Neural Network) with a custom Capsule layer[1]. We obtained the two versions in the following way with 50,000 pieces of training data.

- Model 1: 17 training epochs, which is training until the performance (accuracy) gets saturated-accuracy of 79.62%
- Model 2: 30 training epochs, with data augmentation (additional training data created from the existing data) - accuracy of 81.03%

Thus, Model 2 can be considered as an improved version of Model 1.

Suppose we want to argue the dependability of a recognition model we developed and now focus on one aspect of the dependability analysis: *does the model have sufficient performance (accuracy) for images of "various expected situations?"* Then, we try to capture properties or classes that denote images in "different situations." Here, we consider simple tests to state that *images of various colors are tested well.* We divided the test data into 12 classes by using the primary color of each image, which was approximately captured by calculating the sum of the Hue value for each pixel[2].

---

[1] https://github.com/keras-team/keras/blob/master/examples/cifar10_cnn_capsule. py, Ver. f2b261b on Oct 15, 2018.

[2] The Hue value, in the HSV color model, can represent human perception of a color with a single value (differently from the RGB color model).

4.1   Scenario

Suppose we developed Model 1 and ran tests by dividing the provided test data (10,000 pieces) into classes of different colors. The result is shown on the left of Fig. 1. The vertical axis (0–9) represents the classification class ID (such as "car" and "horse"). The horizontal axis (0–11) represents the color class ID (such as "red" and "blue," though the color classes are made on the basis of hue values, not the human recognition of color names). Each grid represents the accuracy for a certain combination of classification target and color (e.g., "red car").

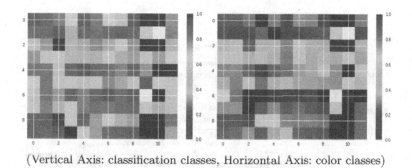

(Vertical Axis: classification classes, Horizontal Axis: color classes)

Fig. 1. Test results for different colors with two versions of models (Color figure online)

There are some weak points on the left of Fig. 1, such as (color, classification) = (8, 2), (10, 3). Thus, countermeasures for mitigating the risks of these weak points should be investigated. There are multiple possibilities of what countermeasures are feasible, and they can be selected as follows.

1. Show that the weak points are practically not significant, e.g., check that past operational data include no or little data that belong to the weak points.
2. Mitigate the risks with an additional mechanism at the system level, e.g., adding a message to the user to indicate that the confidence is low when the corresponding input data arrive at runtime.
3. Update the implementation to increase the accuracy for these points, e.g., by collecting additional training data.

Suppose later we updated the implementation of the model and obtained Model 2, which achieves higher accuracy. The result of the same tests based on the primary color of images is shown on the right of Fig. 1. We can see that the weak points have been changed from Model 1 (the left). For example, there are points that have good accuracy in Model 1 but are bad in Model 2, such as (color, classification) = (9, 2), (9, 8), (10, 2), (10, 6). This result demonstrates the uncertainty in ML-based implementations; we could not logically predict such a result or explain why this result occurred.

4.2   Arguments

Now let us capture the presented scenario from the viewpoint of arguments. Figure 2 shows the GSN argument structure for the case study drawn by using our tool.

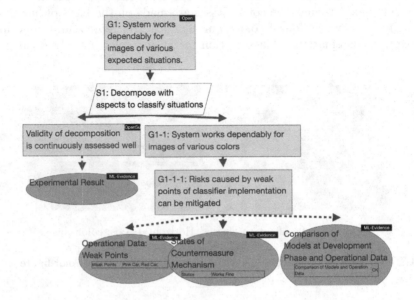

Fig. 2. GSN argument structure for case study

The rationale of the tests was the following goal.

Goal G1: Show that the system works dependably for images of various expected situations

We then considered one sub-goal.

Goal G1-1: Show that the system works dependably for images of various colors
Strategy S1 (to decompose G1): decompose on the basis of aspects to classify situations

Obviously, this sub-goal is only one of a large number of possibilities for how to interpret "expected situations" in G1. For example, we may want to be careful about what is in the background (buildings, forests, etc.). Thus, G1 is recognized as an *open goal*.

In addition, sub-goals of G1 may be decided in experiments. The results of color-based tests happened to show significant differences in terms of performance for different colors. However, it is possible that human-selected classes may not show differences in performance. Thus, experimental results may be attached as evidence to support the validity of decomposition.

It is also notable that some of the color classes may have had few pieces of data after we divided the test dataset. In such cases, we should be aware of the risks on the basis of the fact that the pieces of evidence are not that strong, i.e., *soft contributions*.

> Goal G1-1 was then decomposed in a typical way, and one of its sub-goals was focused on.
> Goal G1-1-1: Mitigate the risks caused by the weak points of the classifier implementation.

If we choose to have a granular argument model, we may decompose this goal by enumerating the weak points, e.g., "for red car." In this case, the validity of the decomposition is supported by the test result (as in Fig. 1). When we update a model implementation or test data set, then the validity is lost, and we need to rerun the tests and rewrite the arguments by updating the sub-goals, e.g., now "blue car" is a weak point. Another aspect of decomposing goal G1-1-1 is how to mitigate the risks. We listed three countermeasures in Sect. 4.1. Assuring that these countermeasures work is done by continuously monitoring as shown in Fig. 2.

5   Concluding Remarks

In this paper, we investigated the impact of uncertainty in ML for safety arguments with a prototype tool implementation. We employed an attribute testing method for evaluating an implemented model in terms of explicit (partial) specification. We then showed experimental results that demonstrate how safety arguments are affected by the uncertainty of machine learning.

References

1. Bishop, P., Bloomfield, R.: A methodology for safety case development. In: Safety-Critical Systems Symposium (SSS 98) (1998)
2. Gauerhof, L., Munk, P., Burton, S.: Structuring validation targets of a machine learning function applied to automated driving. In: Gallina, B., Skavhaug, A., Bitsch, F. (eds.) SAFECOMP 2018. LNCS, vol. 11093, pp. 45–58. Springer, Cham (2018). https://doi.org/10.1007/978-3-319-99130-6_4
3. Burton, S., Gauerhof, L., Heinzemann, C.: Making the case for safety of machine learning in highly automated driving. In: Tonetta, S., Schoitsch, E., Bitsch, F. (eds.) SAFECOMP 2017. LNCS, vol. 10489, pp. 5–16. Springer, Cham (2017). https://doi.org/10.1007/978-3-319-66284-8_1
4. Ishikawa, F.: Concepts in quality assessment for machine learning - from test data to arguments. In: The 37th International Conference on Conceptual Modeling (ER 2018), October 2018

5. Ishikawa, F., Matsuno, Y.: Continuous argument engineering: tackling uncertainty in machine learning based systems. In: The 6th International Workshop on Assurance Cases for Software-intensive Systems (ASSURE 2018), pp. 14–21, September 2018
6. Matsuno, Y.: D-Case Communicator Web Page. http://mlab.ce.cst.nihon-u.ac.jp/project/dcomm/
7. Matsuno, Y.: D-case communicator: a web based GSN editor for multiple stakeholders. In: Tonetta, S., Schoitsch, E., Bitsch, F. (eds.) SAFECOMP 2017. LNCS, vol. 10489, pp. 64–69. Springer, Cham (2017). https://doi.org/10.1007/978-3-319-66284-8_6

The Moral Machine: Is It Moral?

A. M. Nascimento[1,2(✉)], L. F. Vismari[1(✉)] 🆔, A. C. M. Queiroz[3,4],
P. S. Cugnasca[1], J. B. Camargo Jr.[1], and J. R. de Almeida Jr.[1]

[1] School of Engineering, University of São Paulo (USP), São Paulo, SP, Brazil
alexandremoreiranascimento@alum.mit.edu,
{lucio.vismari, cugnasca}@usp.br
[2] Center for Design Research (CDR), Mechanical Engineering,
Stanford University, Stanford, CA, USA
[3] School of Psychology, University of São Paulo (USP), São Paulo, SP, Brazil
[4] Virtual Human Interaction Lab (VHIL), Stanford University,
Stanford, CA, USA

Abstract. Many recent studies have been proposing, discussing and investigating moral decisions in scenarios of imminent accident involving Autonomous Vehicles (AV). Those studies investigate people's expectations about the best decisions the AVs should make when some life needs to be sacrificed to save other ones. A recent research found those preferences have strong ties to the respondents' cultural traits. The present position paper questions the importance and the real value of those discussions. It also argues about their morality. Finally, an approach based on risk-oriented decision making is discussed as an alternative way to tackle those situations framed as "moral dilemmas" under the light of safety engineering.

Keywords: Autonomous vehicles · Safety · Risk · Moral machine ·
Artificial Intelligence

1 Introduction

AVs promise a paradigm shift in many topics related to transportation. Smart cities empowered with sophisticated communication infrastructure can better orchestrate the autonomous car traffic towards its optimization, reducing traffic jams and improving transportation efficiency. The elderly, people with disabilities and without driving licenses will be able to access individual transportation. However, one of the highest AV appeals is related to the road and vehicle safety improvements due the promise of accidents reduction by eliminating the need for a human driver. In fact, 94% of accidents have human error as one of potentially many contributing factors [1].

One topic on AVs has been getting prominent attention from scientific community, automakers practitioners and broad media – moral decisions AVs will need to make when facing an accident circumstance. In fact, in November 2018, Nature published the paper "The Moral Machine experiment" [2]. From the social sciences perspective, it revealed interesting and relevant aspects about the moral decisions people made in an online experimental platform designed to explore the moral dilemmas faced by autonomous vehicles (AV). The study reported global moral preferences and their

A. Romanovsky et al. (Eds.): SAFECOMP 2019 Workshops, LNCS 11699, pp. 405–410, 2019.
https://doi.org/10.1007/978-3-030-26250-1_34

individual variations based on respondents' demographics. It also reported cross-cultural ethical variation and correlations with deep cultural traits. Other studies also investigated and discussed moral decisions.

However, many aspects of those discussions can affect their validity and its applicability on AVs. This position paper takes a step back and presents a discussion about the underlying assumptions and other aspects of those studies. It raises an alert to help the scientific and practitioner community to avoid getting trapped in them. And, it points out an alternative direction under the light of the risk-oriented (safety engineering) decision-making approach.

2   Issues of Moral Machine Discussions

Those studies tackling AV moral decisions have many questionable premises. "The Moral Machine experiment" [2] has an experimental design based on a webpage where the scenarios are static pictures presented to the subjects and they provide answers over the web. There is no control or standardization of the environment of the respondents. No control on the information and activities they were performing before replying those questions. Also, no control or restriction to normalize the device used – desktop, laptop or mobile – what affect the size of the picture and details. In addition, there are annotations indicating more information than a driver would have available in an actual driving scenario.

Also, the experimental design used in "The Moral Machine experiment" favored logical decisions to be done under a utilitarian framework. In fact, a decision making about what should be the outcome of an AV accident using a static 2D picture on a webpage triggers a specific arousal level. This is potentially different than the one that would be triggered if the experiment used a more immersive environment, such as Virtual Reality, for example. Although this is not validated yet, it is a reasonable assumption. Therefore, if the moral decisions can be influenced by the media and the way the respondents experiment them, which is their real validity?

Although those discussions could be philosophically and academically interesting to some fields, they might enhance unrealistic expectations about the AVs capabilities. This observation is not new. More than 30 years ago, it was observed there was a gap between exaggerated claims about Artificial Intelligence (AI) and the work still unfulfilled [3]. AV is an AI application, and many of the present claims about AI capabilities seems to be ahead of what can be supported by their findings and the current state of development [4]. As pointed out by Noel Sharkey, emeritus professor of AI and Robotics at the University of Sheffield: "*the wrong idea of what robotics can do and where AI is at the moment is very, very dangerous*" [4]. In fact, although there are claims such as "1 million fully autonomous Tesla taxis by 2020"[1], the reality is Google has officially reported 272 failures and 13 near misses for its self-driving car [5]. Undesirable behavior of Uber AV [6] and Tesla[2] autopilot [7] resulted in loss of life.

---

[1] https://www.engadget.com/2019/04/22/tesla-elon-musk-self-driving-robo-taxi/.

[2] Tesla is not an AV. Its Autopilot feature makes it a semi-autonomous car.

However, even if the AVs had the capabilities required to perform such moral decisions and execute them in real-time during an accident, there is an important question to ask ourselves: Is it moral to discuss who must be sacrificed? Even unintentionally, this discussion hides a very important and sensitive aspect: by making this life and death decision, there is an arbitrary attribution of distinct values to the life of those involved in the accident. In other words, there is a decision about whose life worth more. Is it moral? It seems something contrary to what the society has been fighting against for many decades. It seems somehow, we are giving the power to machines to "play God".

In fact, in a scenario where those moral decision discussion guides the AV industry and influences lawmakers and society opinion, there would be a deep transformation in our society. Maybe the next step would be to leverage on the people's background information to adjust the value attributed to the ones involved in the accident. For example, if one of the involved is convicted of a crime, maybe it would influence the moral decision and that would be the sacrificed person. Does it make sense?

Also, if the way to go is to encode rules into AVs to save some type of people rather than other, then the society should expect them to become rules supported by laws. Thus, it is reasonable to imagine the next step would be to analyze people's behavior when they are driving a car to understand if they followed those rules in the accidents. Specially during the long time where AVs will coexist with regular vehicles or semi-autonomous vehicles. Does it make sense? People would need to learn all the scenarios and be tested by the exams to get the driver license.

But, then, the word 'accident' would make no sense anymore. People would not be a victim of an accident anymore. They would be victim of "Trolley problem" [8] decision, based on an established and socially accepted "moral framework". Therefore, the insurance industry would be affected, since there would be very low random effect. For example, the risk profile of the people that could be more often victim of those decisions would affect their life and health insurance premium.

Ultimately, "The Moral Machine experiment" [2] study found distinct moral preferences tied to demographic and cultural traits of the respondents. People from distinct regions have different opinions about what would be a morally acceptable decision. As a result, would car makers adapt the moral framework the "life value hierarchy" or "local socially acceptable rules in accidents" for each specific market? Interesting would be the users need of downloading and updating new rules when they are crossing the border by car to a region where another "moral decisions" are acceptable.

3 The Risk-Oriented, Decision-Making Approach and Moral Machine Useless in AV Development

In a risk-oriented approach, risks should be kept at acceptable levels as a way to justify a system as safe [9]. Risk is defined by the '*combination of the probability of occurrence of harm and the severity of that harm*' [9, 10]. As can be inferred from it, risk is managed by two dimensions: the likelihood of a harm happens and the severity of a harm (i.e. extent of physical injury or damage to the health of persons [10]). When an accident (i.e. "*An unintended event, or sequence of events, that causes harm*" [11]) is inevitable – e.g. there is no way to avoid a collision (the main premise for the Moral Machine experiments), reducing the severity of harm (losses) produced by an accident is the only possible way to influence positively the outcome of the situation.

A risk is considered tolerable if it is judged acceptable in a given context based on the current values of society and according to valid societal moral concepts [10]. In this way, the risk related to the same likelihood of occurrence and extent of physical injury or damage to the health of persons may be acceptable in a social context and unacceptable for another. Thus, from the social sciences perspective, the 'Moral Machine' experiment is pertinent within a conceptual discussion, based on normative definitions, on risk and safety. With it, one can obtain a good qualitative inference about the tolerance of its respondents - morally and culturally diversified - to certain scenarios of losses resulting from a vehicles accident.

However, the experiment results are not applicable to AVs. A fundamental premise in the Moral Machine experiment can be neither valid nor applicable to real systems: the AV must be able, in hard-real time, to (i) to assess a situation in a broad way, identifying all the possibilities of trajectories conflicts - as well as the types of agents involved in them (people by gender, age group, ethnicity, professional activities; animals by specimen; and so on) in the short and medium term; (ii) to decide, with a high degree of certainty, that it is not possible to avoid an accident; (iii) to choose, among all possible options, what action should be taken to lead the accident severity be acceptable (considering all agents involved and the moral concepts and social values of the context); and, above all, (iv) to execute the chosen physical action (trajectory) as planned.

Moreover, an accident is considered as the result of the system's inability to behave as designed (concerning real-world, engineered systems) due to faults manifestation [9]. In this way, we significantly reduce the space of real-world states where the premise of the Moral Machine experiment would apply. In a better hypothesis, it would be applicable in case of degradation of performance of the AV braking system (loss of longitudinal movement control), but not of its capacity of perception, decision making and lateral movement control. Any other malfunctioning behaviors would limit AV ability in performing the 4 listed demanded actions previously mentioned.

However, even if an AV is fully operational and able to perform the 4 actions, few scenarios could justify the reduction of harm severity oriented by the type of agent to be involved in an accident. One of the cases would be the trajectory of a high-speed AV being abruptly obstructed in a dense and diversely occupied space. But, as a safety principle, the AV speed should not be high in a heavily occupied scenario and with the possibility of abrupt trajectory obstructions. This would create a potentially unsafe situation (high probability of collision and high severity of damage). If the speed is lower, there could be a time enough to stop the AV, reducing the chance of a collision or, in the worst case, would produce a collision with less severity. On the other hand, even if the risk of this scenario were acceptable for the given context, higher the AV speed and more abrupt AV is obstructed, lower is the maneuverability of AV. Consequently, the possibilities of trajectories to be applied (and the types of 'targets' to be achieved) in the risk management process are smaller.

Given that the 'safety' definition is related to the acceptability of risks, which is related to concept of morality (and context-dependent), it can be concluded that the discussion raised by the Moral Machine experiment is a relevant theoretical exercise for the conceptual discussion of aspects of socially acceptable decisions in an accident. However, in practical terms, it has very little applicability in the development of AVs because it will cover a very small portion of all the potential scenarios. Thus, if considered, it will contribute with very small share of the accidents produced by the AVs, with insignificant impact on the risk perception of those involved and, consequently, the safety of the AVs. In addition, if the AV makes the decision about who will be harmed, it will not be an accident anymore. This changes the accountability attributed to an AV even if there was no option of not causing harm to anyone. In fact, to justify with a high degree of certainty that it was not possible to avoid an accident will be challenging. Finally, those situations would only occur in cases where other systems have failed within the probability of an acceptable level of risk. Therefore, the adoption of the Moral Machine framework, regarding to AVs development, is untenable!

4   Concluding Remarks and Ongoing Work

When an accident is about to happen, a risk-oriented approach seems to make more sense than a rule-based decision-making approach under a moral dilemma framework based on an assessment of the life value of the potential victims. From the Safety Engineering standpoint, the AV must make the decision to reduce the life and property damage, where, of course, the life is the priority. In our opinion, AV must make the decisions to find the best outcome possible, without doing an assessment of the life value of each actor because any human life has the same value. Thus, the goal is to minimize the number of loss of life. Thus, those types of moral dilemmas, including Moral Machine experiment results, have no importance or real value on the AVs context.

More than discussing low relevant topics to the safety deployment of the AVs – and, consequently, to the advances of AI-based safety critical systems – we need to deal with core-relevant technical topics. For example, the level of automation of the AVs and the power of their Machine Perception (MP) and Machine Control (MC) will constraint how powerful realtime risk evaluation and decision making can be. If the sophistication level of the MP and MC is low, what is the reality today, expecting "super-hero" outcomes from an AV in an accident is not realistic, either under a risk-oriented approach or under a moral decision framework. However, when the level of sophistication will be high enough to enable AV to make the sophisticated moral decisions and actions in real-time discussed by many studies, then it makes sense to expect a risk-oriented decision making approach.

Thus, when facing a potential accident, the AV must quickly assess the situation and generate a decision-oriented risk map, such as a decision tree, assigning probabilities and expected values for each possible path. Also, it must update the decision-oriented risk map in real-time, based on quick changes from the other actors involved in the accident. That is, if the AV can detect the young gentleman, crossing the street from the left sidewalk, detected something is wrong, stopped, and established continuous eye-contact to the AV, there is a higher chance he will try to escape from the AV if it decides to head itself to his direction. Therefore, the risk must be updated. Then, crossing the street from the right sidewalk, previously empty, there is a young lady now. The risk-map assessment must be updated. In this hypothetical scenario, the AV must decide to head towards the right or the left side, since the brakes are damaged and heading straight would hit a couple on the crosswalk. It is not the role of the AV to detect the faces of the couple and find out they are convicted of murders and wanted by the police. The AV will try to save as many humans as possible, avoid hurting someone as much as possible, or at least minimize the hurt severity, and, secondly, reduce the property damages.

Also, sophisticated AVs will be able to test these hypotheses to get more accurate information to update the risk map. In the previously described scenario, the AV might decide to honk the horn, check how the actors involved in the situation react, update the risk map, and make the decision. Maybe, the couple crossing the street will run and make the decision easy. In the case the couple do not react as expected, or alternatively, the AV could quickly head towards the young gentlemen on the left side to test his reaction. Supposing he freezes, the AV quickly reacts and heads towards the lady on the right side and honk the horn aggressively. Maybe she will react to return to the sidewalk to protect herself, making the decision easier.

References

1. Singh, S.: Critical reasons for crashes investigated in the National Motor Vehicle Crash Causation Survey, Washington, DC (2015). https://crashstats.nhtsa.dot.gov/Api/Public/ViewPublication/812115
2. Awad, E., et al.: The moral machine experiment. Nature 563(7729), 59–64 (2018). https://doi.org/10.1038/s41586-018-0637-6
3. King, W.R.: Editor's comment: decision support systems, artificial intelligence, and expert systems. MIS Q. 8(3), iv–v (1984). http://www.jstor.org/stable/248661
4. Delcker, J.: Europe divided over robot 'personhood', POLITICO. Politico SPRL, April 2018. https://www.politico.eu/article/europe-divided-over-robot-ai-artificial-intelligence-personhood/
5. Harris, M.: Google reports self-driving car mistakes: 272 failures and 13 near misses. The Guardian. Guardian News and Media, January 2016. https://www.theguardian.com/technology/2016/jan/12/google-self-driving-cars-mistakes-data-reports
6. Wakabayashi, D.: Self-Driving Uber Car Kills Pedestrian in Arizona, Where Robots Roam, The New York Times, March 2018. https://www.nytimes.com/2018/03/19/technology/uber-driverless-fatality.html
7. BBC, Tesla in fatal California crash was on Autopilot, BBC News, 31st Mar 2018. https://www.bbc.com/news/world-us-canada-43604440
8. Thomson, J.J.: The Trolley Problem. Yale LJ. HeinOnline 94, 1395 (1985). https://doi.org/10.2307/796133
9. ISO/IEC, ISO/IEC Guide 51: Safety aspects – Guidelines for their inclusion in standards (2014)
10. ISO, ISO 26262-1:2018, Road vehicles — Functional safety — Part 1: Vocabulary (2018)
11. MoD, Safety Management Requirements for Defence Systems – Requirements, UK, p. 44 (2017)

Correction to: Combining GSN and STPA for Safety Arguments

Celso Hirata (ID) and Simin Nadjm-Tehrani (ID)

Correction to:
Chapter "Combining GSN and STPA for Safety Arguments"
in: A. Romanovsky et al. (Eds.): *Computer Safety,*
Reliability, and Security, **LNCS 11699,**
https://doi.org/10.1007/978-3-030-26250-1_1

In the originally published version of this chapter there was an error in figure 2. This has been corrected.

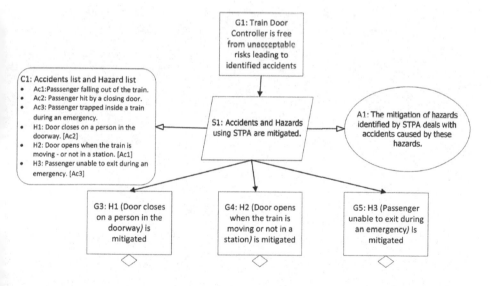

The updated version of this chapter can be found at
https://doi.org/10.1007/978-3-030-26250-1_1

Author Index